THE POLITICAL THOUGHT OF
KING ALFRED THE GREAT

This book is a comprehensive study of political thought at the court of King Alfred the Great (871–99). It explains the extraordinary burst of royal learned activity focused on inventive translations from Latin into Old English attributed to Alfred's own authorship. A full exploration of context establishes these texts as part of a single discourse which placed Alfred himself at the heart of all rightful power and authority. A major theme is the relevance of Frankish and other European experiences, as sources of expertise and shared concerns, and for important contrasts with Alfredian thought and behaviour. Part I assesses Alfred's rule against West Saxon structures, showing the centrality of the royal household in the operation of power. Part II offers an intimate analysis of the royal texts, developing far-reaching implications for Alfredian kingship, communication and court culture. Comparative in approach, the book places Alfred's reign at the forefront of wider European trends in aristocratic life.

DAVID PRATT is Fellow and Director of Studies in History, Downing College, Cambridge.

Cambridge Studies in Medieval Life and Thought
Fourth Series

General Editor:

ROSAMOND MCKITTERICK
Professor of Medieval History, University of Cambridge, and Fellow of Sidney Sussex College

Advisory Editors:
CHRISTINE CARPENTER
Professor of Medieval English History, University of Cambridge, and Fellow of New Hall

JONATHAN SHEPARD

The series Cambridge Studies in Medieval Life and Thought was inaugurated by G. G. Coulton in 1921; Professor Rosamond McKitterick now acts as General Editor of the Fourth Series, with Professor Christine Carpenter and Dr Jonathan Shepard as Advisory Editors. The series brings together outstanding work by medieval scholars over a wide range of human endeavour extending from political economy to the history of ideas.

For a list of titles in the series, see end of book.

THE POLITICAL THOUGHT OF KING ALFRED THE GREAT

DAVID PRATT

CAMBRIDGE
UNIVERSITY PRESS

CAMBRIDGE UNIVERSITY PRESS

Cambridge, New York, Melbourne, Madrid, Cape Town, Singapore, São Paulo

Cambridge University Press
The Edinburgh Building, Cambridge CB2 8RU, UK

Published in the United States of America by Cambridge University Press, New York

www.cambridge.org
Information on this title: www.cambridge.org/9780521803502

© David Pratt 2007

First published 2007

Printed in the United Kingdom at the University Press, Cambridge

A catalogue record for this publication is available from the British Library

ISBN 978-0-521-80350-2   hardback

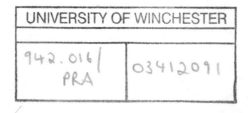

CONTENTS

v

Contents

Contents

ACKNOWLEDGEMENTS

My research interest in King Alfred actually extends back to a dissertation written in the final year of my undergraduate degree. This book is a revised and extended version of my subsequent doctoral thesis, submitted in 1999. I have incurred many debts of gratitude on the long road to this completed volume. The first is due to Rosamond McKitterick, who as my supervisor and latterly as editor has been an unfailing source of wisdom and support. I must also express my profound thanks to Simon Keynes, whose stimulating advice has encouraged my research at every stage of its progress. My PhD examiners, Nicholas Brooks and Janet Nelson, offered guidance and criticism which proved invaluable in the transition to publication. Quite widely disseminated to Alfredian scholars and others, my thesis received further helpful comments from Janet Bately, Christine Carpenter, Malcolm Godden, David Luscombe, Bruce O'Brien, Carolin Schreiber and Patrick Wormald. For advice on metalwork, I am very grateful to Leslie Webster; other important assistance was supplied by Sean Miller and Petrus Tax. Simon Whitmore, Clare Orchard and the staff at Cambridge University Press have been tireless in their efficiency. Thanks for financial support are due to the managers of the Robert Owen Bishop Scholarship at Christ's College, Cambridge; to the British Academy, an award from whom supported my doctoral research; and to Emmanuel College, Cambridge, where I spent three fruitful years as a Research Fellow. Since 2001 I have been employed by the Master and Fellows of Downing College, in whose company it has been a privilege to live, teach and research. Especial thanks are due to my colleagues Paul Millett and Richard Smith, and to the cohorts of undergraduate historians who may recognize themes pursued in College teaching. I owe many lasting debts to friends who have enriched my life in Cambridge over the past decade. Of these, Christina Pössel, Carl Watkins

Acknowledgements

and Mike Woodrow all directly aided my passage to completion. Finally, I record the deep and continuous debt that I owe to my parents and family, who have borne the effects of this project with great patience; it is to them, collectively, that this book is dedicated.

ABBREVIATIONS

AB	*Annales de Saint-Bertin*, ed. F. Grat, *et al.* (Paris, 1964)
AC	*Annales Cambriae*, ed. J. Williams, ab Ithel (London, 1860)
Af	Laws of Alfred, ed. F. Liebermann, *Die Gesetze der Angelsachsen*, 3 vols. (Halle, 1903–16) I, 16–88
AGu	Alfred-Guthrum treaty, ed. Liebermann, *Gesetze* I, 126–9
ASC	*Anglo-Saxon Chronicle* (manuscript A unless otherwise stated), cited from the edition of C. Plummer, *Two of the Saxon Chronicles Parallel*, 2 vols. (Oxford, 1892–9), but according to the corrected chronology in *The Anglo-Saxon Chronicle: a Revised Translation*, trans. D. Whitelock, with D. C. Douglas and S. I. Tucker (London, 1961)
ASE	*Anglo-Saxon England*
ASPR	The Anglo-Saxon Poetic Records, ed. G. P. Krapp and E. van K. Dobbie, 6 vols. (New York, 1931–42)
ASSAH	*Anglo-Saxon Studies in Archaeology and History*
BAR	British Archaelogical Reports
BCS (with number of document)	W. de G. Birch, *Cartularium Saxonicum*, 3 vols. (London, 1885–93)
Bo	*King Alfred's Old English Version of Boethius: De Consolatione Philosophiae*, ed. W. J. Sedgefield (Oxford, 1900)
C&S	*Councils and Synods with other Documents relating to the English Church I*, ed. D. Whitelock, M. Brett and C. N. L. Brooke, 2 vols. (Oxford, 1981)
CCCM	Corpus Christianorum, Continuatio Mediaevalis
CCSL	Corpus Christianorum, Series Latina
Cons. phil.	*Anicii Manlii Severini Boethii Philosophiae Consolatio*, ed. L. Bieler, CCSL 94, 2nd edn (Turnhout, 1984)

CP	*King Alfred's West Saxon Version of Gregory's Pastoral Care*, EETS, os 45 and 50 (London, 1871), cited from manuscripts Ci and Cii, where text is available
CSEL	Corpus Scriptorum Ecclesiasticorum Latinorum
DIL	Jonas of Orléans, *De institutione laicali*, PL 106: 121–278
DIR	*Jonas d'Orléans: Le Métier de Roi (De institutione regia)*, ed. A. Dubreucq, SC 407 (Paris, 1995)
EcHR	*Economic History Review*
EEMF	Early English Manuscripts in Facsimile
EETS	Early English Text Society
–, os	–, original series
–, ss	–, supplementary series
EHD	*English Historical Documents, c. 500–1042*, ed. D. Whitelock, English Historical Documents I, 2nd edn (London, 1979)
EHR	*English Historical Review*
EME	*Early Medieval Europe*
GD	*Bischof Wærferths von Worcester Übersetzung der Dialoge Gregors des Grossen*, ed. H. Hecht, 2 vols. (Leipzig, 1900–7)
Gneuss, *Handlist*	H. Gneuss, *Handlist of Anglo-Saxon Manuscripts: a List of Manuscripts and Manuscript Fragments Written or Owned in England up to 1100* (Tempe, AZ, 2001)
Golden Age	*The Golden Age of Anglo-Saxon Art 966–1066*, ed. J. Backhouse, D. H. Turner and L. Webster (London, 1984)
GR	William of Malmesbury, *Gesta Regum Anglorum*, ed. R. A. B. Mynors, R. M. Thomson and M. Winterbottom, 2 vols. (Oxford, 1998–9)
HE	Bede, *Historia ecclesiastica gentis Anglorum*, ed. C. Plummer, *Venerabilis Baedae Opera Historica*, 2 vols. (Oxford, 1896)
JEH	*Journal of Ecclesiastical History*
JTS	*Journal of Theological Studies*
K&L, *Alfred*	S. Keynes and M. Lapidge, *Alfred the Great: Asser's Life of King Alfred and other Contemporary Sources* (Harmondsworth, 1983)
Ker, *Catalogue*	N. R. Ker, *Catalogue of Manuscripts Containing Anglo-Saxon*, Reissue with Supplement (Oxford, 1990)
Lapidge, *ALL* I	M. Lapidge, *Anglo-Latin Literature 600–899* (London, 1996)

Lapidge, ALL II	M. Lapidge, *Anglo-Latin Literature 900–1066* (London, 1993)
Liebermann, Gesetze	F. Liebermann, *Die Gesetze der Angelsachsen*, 3 vols. (Halle, 1903–16)
Making of England	*The Making of England: Anglo-Saxon Art and Culture AD 600–900*, ed. L. Webster and J. Backhouse (London, 1991)
MGH	*Monumenta Germaniae Historica*
–, Capit.	*Capitularia. Legum Sectio* II, *Capitularia Regum Francorum*, ed. A. Boretius and V. Krause, 2 vols. (Hanover, 1883–97)
–, Conc.	*Concilia. Legum Sectio* III, *Concilia* II.i–ii, ed. A. Werminghoff (Hanover, 1906–8), III–IV, ed. W. Hartmann (Hanover, 1984–98)
–, Epist.	*Epistolae* III–VIII (= *Epistolae Merovingici et Karolini Aevi* I–VI) (Hanover, 1892–1939)
–, Leges nat. germ.	*Leges Nationum Germanicarum*, ed. K. Zeumer, K. A. Eckhardt, *et al.*, 6 vols. (Hanover, 1892–1969)
–, Poet.	*Poetae Latini Aevi Carolini*, ed. E. Dümmler, L. Traube, P. von Winterfeld and K. Strecker, 4 vols. (Hanover, 1881–99)
–, SS	*Scriptores* in folio, 38 vols. (Hanover, 1871–)
NCMH II	R. McKitterick (ed.), *The New Cambridge Medieval History II c.700–c.900* (Cambridge, 1995)
NCMH III	T. Reuter (ed.), *The New Cambridge Medieval History III c.900–c.1024* (Cambridge, 1999)
OE Bede	*The Old English Version of Bede's Ecclesiastical History of the English People*, ed. T. Miller, EETS, os 95–6 and 110–11 (London, 1890–8)
Or	*The Old English Orosius*, ed. J. M. Bately, EETS, ss 6 (London, New York and Toronto, 1980)
P&P	*Past and Present*
PBA	*Proceedings of the British Academy*
PL	*Patriologiae Cursus Completus. Series (Latina) Prima*, ed. J.-P. Migne, 221 vols. (Paris, 1844–64)
Ps.	*Le Psautier romain et les autres anciens psautiers latins*, ed. R. Weber, Collectanea Biblica Latina 10 (Vatican, 1953), for the Roman text; *Biblia Sacra Iuxta Vulgatam Versionem*, ed. R. Weber, *et al.*, 4th edn (Stuttgart, 1994), for variants from the Gallican Psalter
Ps(P)	*King Alfred's Old English Prose Translation of the First Fifty Psalms*, ed. P. P. O'Neill (Cambridge, MA, 2001)

RC	Sedulius Scottus, *Liber de rectoribus christianis*, ed. S. Hellmann, *Sedulius Scottus*, Quellen und Untersuchungen zur lateinischen Philologie des Mittelalters 1(1) (Munich, 1906)
Reg. past.	*Grégoire le Grand: Règle Pastorale*, ed. F. Rommel, with B. Judic and C. Morel, SC 381–2 (Paris, 1992)
S (with number of document)	P. H. Sawyer, *Anglo-Saxon Charters: an Annotated List and Bibliography* (London, 1968), cited according to the revised version by S. Kelly, available in electronic form
SC	Sources chrétiennes
SEHD	*Select English Historical Documents of the Ninth and Tenth Centuries*, ed. F. E. Harmer (Cambridge, 1914)
Settimane	*Settimane di studio del Centro italiano di studi sull'alto medioevo* (Spoleto)
Solil	*King Alfred's Version of St Augustine's Soliloquies*, ed. T. A. Carnicelli (Cambridge, MA, 1969)
Soliloquia	Augustine, *Soliloquiorum libri duo*, ed. W. Hörmann, CSEL 89 (Vienna, 1986), 3–98
TRHS	*Transactions of the Royal Historical Society*
VA	*Asser's Life of King Alfred, together with the Annals of St Neots, erroneously ascribed to Asser*, ed. W. H. Stevenson, new imp. (Oxford, 1959), with corrections noted by K&L, *Alfred*
Wormald, *MEL* I	P. Wormald, *The Making of English Law: King Alfred to the Twelfth Century. I: Legislation and its Limits* (Oxford, 1999)

NOTE ON CITATIONS

References to Anglo-Saxon law-codes follow the edition and numbering system of Liebermann, *Gesetze* I; apart from Alfred's laws, they are identified by the ruler's name in full. The Vulgate is cited from *Biblia Sacra Iuxta Vulgatam Versionem*, ed. R. Weber *et al.*, 4th edn (Stuttgart, 1994), with the exception of the Psalms, where I follow the text and numbering system of the Roman Psalter. In supplying modern English translations, I have prioritized sensitivity to original vocabulary and syntax. Most translations are my own: for Alfredian sources, I have borrowed where possible, and with adjustment, from K&L, *Alfred*, while renderings of the Vulgate are modelled on the Douai-Rheims version. In the dating of manuscripts, I have followed the convention of supplying two superscript numbers where appropriate, to enable flexible specification by either quarter- or half-century.

Chapter 1

INTRODUCTION

Is there anything left to say about King Alfred? In part, the question is misconstrued: every age has reinterpreted his ninth-century memory. In his own lifetime Alfred's rule was celebrated in vernacular history and Latin biography; selectively revered in the later Anglo-Saxon period, his reign was partly eclipsed by the reputations of Æthelstan and Edgar.[1] Only in the later middle ages was Alfred singled out as a possible founder of 'English' political and administrative unity. The momentous account of Alfred's viking warfare, and successful extension of West Saxon rule, combined with a natural tendency to schematize jurisdictional uniformity. It was on this basis that Alfred was first styled 'the Great': for Matthew Paris his reign had been pivotal in replacing a former 'Heptarchy' of seven kingdoms with rule over the whole of England. Only in the sixteenth century did this vision accord with political needs for a formative Alfredian past. In the learned recovery of several Alfredian texts, Elizabethan antiquaries found deeper origins for a united English church. Under Stuart and Hanoverian rule, those origins extended to English 'liberties', conveniently undermining the alternative schema of a 'Norman Yoke'. By the early eighteenth century, such interpretations reached their climax in Alfred's status as acknowledged 'founder of the English constitution'. The 'Whig' view in turn laid the basis for Victorian rituals of popular commemoration, enshrining Alfred as a symbol of ancient freedom and nationhood.[2]

Modern reassessment has frequently wrestled with the baggage of retrospection. Beyond later myth lies the reality of an abundant collection of contemporary sources, many variously associated with Alfred

---

[1] S. Keynes, 'The Cult of King Alfred the Great', *ASE* 28 (1999), 225–356; B. Yorke, 'Alfredism: the Use and Abuse of Alfred's Reputation in Later Centuries', in *Alfred the Great: Papers from the Eleventh-Centenary Conferences*, ed. T. Reuter (Aldershot, 2003), pp. 361–80.

[2] P. Readman, 'The Place of the Past in English Culture, c.1890–1914', *P&P* 186 (February 2005), 147–99.

and his patronage. These include the principal narrative accounts in the
Anglo-Saxon Chronicle and the Latin *Life of King Alfred* by the king's
Welsh assistant Asser; and, above all, a corpus of five vernacular texts
attributed to Alfred's own authorship. As translations, often of con-
siderable freedom, the latter rendered a distinctive selection of learned
Latin sources: the *Regula pastoralis* of Pope Gregory the Great; the
Consolatio philosophiae of the early sixth-century Roman aristocrat,
Boethius; the *Soliloquia* of St Augustine; the first fifty Psalms; and Mosaic
law in the introduction to Alfred's law-book. 'We hold that Alfred was a
great and glorious king in part because he tells us he was', wrote Michael
Wallace-Hadrill in his seminal paper of 1949.[3] What explained these
interests were Alfred's debts to the legacy of Charlemagne, which he
now suspected 'in almost every direction: military, liturgical, educational, literary, artistic'. Faced by viking invasion, Alfred had 'turned for
help to the experts on kingship, Charlemagne's descendants': that
assistance had shaped his success.

Similar thinking reached its full potential in 1971 in the challenge of
R. H. C. Davis, 'Alfred the Great: Propaganda and Truth'.[4] Observing
that 'almost all the sources [for Alfred's reign] may have originated with
either Alfred himself or his immediate entourage', Davis argued that 'we
must somehow liberate ourselves from the Alfredian sources to see
Alfred as he really was'. Actually then depending on these sources, Davis
proceeded to isolate logistical difficulties faced by Alfred in defending his
kingdom from attack. What mattered to Alfred had been the exceptional
burdens placed on his subjects in the course of his military reforms,
especially the building of fortifications. This had relied on the wider
nobility, but the king 'could not be sure of their strict obedience ...
unless he could indoctrinate them with loyalty to himself and enthusiasm
for his cause'.[5] This was why in Davis' view the sources were so problematic, as 'propaganda' designed for this immediate purpose. For him
the *Anglo-Saxon Chronicle* had been the prime literary instrument, but by
implication, the same applied to all Alfredian image-making.

In the event, Davis had a mixed reception, his case partly circular in
equating learned self-record with concerted deception.[6] In the *Chronicle*,
where Davis saw exaggeration of Alfred's difficulties in the 870s, there

[3] J. M. Wallace-Hadrill, 'The Franks and the English in the Ninth Century: Some Common
Historical Interests', *History* 35 (1950), 202–18, at 216–17, cf. 215 and 218; amended to 'rightly
implies this' in his *Early Medieval History* (Oxford, 1975), pp. 201–16, at 213.
[4] *History* 56 (1971), 169–82, at 169 and 177–82.   [5] *Ibid.*, p. 182.
[6] D. Whitelock, 'The Importance of the Battle of Edington', in her *From Bede to Alfred: Studies in
Early Anglo-Saxon Literature and History* (London, 1980), no. 13; S. Keynes, 'A Tale of Two Kings:
Alfred the Great and Æthelred the Unready', *TRHS* 5th series 36 (1986), 195–217, at 196–201.

were stronger signs that even the severity of his predicament may have been partly obscured.[7] Yet in other ways his argument laid the basis for all modern enquiry; together with that of Wallace-Hadrill, his piece posed questions central to the understanding of Alfred's kingship. Their respective answers, too, have returned in new guises, the Carolingian dimension weighing as strongly on many aspects of Alfredian activity, while the *Chronicle* has re-emerged as a statement of unity. But what was the role of royal learning? How much can the king's own texts reveal about the character of his rule? As Janet Nelson observes, these trans-lations were no mere exercise but displayed political thinking, consistent utterances on the source, distribution and uses of legitimate power.[8] As such they are unusual in any early medieval context, and especially so in their attribution to a king; more typical were consciously ecclesiastical acts of rhetoric. Several factors explain the limits that remain in historical engagement.

A first is the striking fragmentation of Alfredian scholarship, necessarily involving many disciplines. The texts have largely remained the province of philology and literary criticism, clarifying the extent of Alfred's œuvre and the nature of Latin source-material.[9] There is growing awareness of their sophistication as instances of translation; individual texts have been closely studied for signs of philosophical or translatory consistency.[10] In the meantime, political historians have concentrated on the 'real' business of government, represented by charters, coins and law-code.[11] In combination, the record has yielded some control to the reading of Alfredian history. The impression is of occasional distortion, more often surpassed by merely selective or wishful disclosure, combined in Asser's case with no shortage of symbolic depiction.[12] It is the latter source

---

[7] *Ibid.*, pp. 198–200.

[8] J. L. Nelson, 'The Political Ideas of Alfred of Wessex', in her *Rulers and Ruling Families in Early Medieval Europe: Alfred, Charles the Bald and Others* (Aldershot, 1999), no. 4.

[9] See esp. work cited below on authorship and the Boethius, pp. 116–17 and 271–2.

[10] Esp. K. Otten, *König Alfreds Boethius*, Studien zur englischen Philologie n.f. 3 (Tübingen, 1964); M. McC. Gatch, 'King Alfred's Version of Augustine's Soliloquia: Some Suggestions on its Rationale and Unity', in *Studies in Earlier Old English Prose*, ed. P. E. Szarmach (Albany, NY, 1986), pp. 17–46; J. C. Frakes, *The Fate of Fortune in the Early Middle Ages* (Leiden, New York, Copenhagen and Cologne, 1988); M. Godden, *The Translations of Alfred and his Circle, and the Misappropriation of the Past*, H. M. Chadwick Memorial Lecture 14 (Cambridge, 2004); N. G. Discenza, *The King's English: Strategies of Translation in the Old English Boethius* (Albany, NY, 2005).

[11] E.g. M. Blackburn and D. N. Dumville (eds.), *Kings, Currency and Alliances: History and Coinage of Southern England in the Ninth Century* (Woodbridge, 1998); D. Hill and A. R. Rumble (eds.), *The Defence of Wessex: the Burghal Hidage and Anglo-Saxon Fortifications* (Manchester, 1996).

[12] S. Keynes, 'King Alfred and the Mercians', in *Kings, Currency and Alliances*, ed. Blackburn and Dumville, pp. 1–45, at 12–19 and 40–5; S. Foot, 'Remembering, Forgetting and Inventing: Attitudes to the Past in England at the End of the First Viking Age', *TRHS* 6th series 9 (1999), 185–200; A. Scharer, 'The Writing of History at King Alfred's Court', *EME* 5 (1996), 177–206;

which has dominated debates over royal presentation; where Alfred's texts are considered directly, historians have struggled to describe the role they might usefully have performed. Failing to appear 'practical', Alfred's law-book was judged 'ideological' by Patrick Wormald; Nelson has hesitantly reinvoked 'propaganda'.[13] In Richard Abels' biography, Alfred's writings are treated separately, preceding the 'practice of kingship'.[14] Yet it is precisely this relationship which is at issue in the interrogation of Alfred's learned kingship. These texts have much to reveal about royal practice: this much was agreed by all participants in a lively debate over Alfredian 'economic planning'.[15]

A second factor is the framework of 'Carolingian reception'. Historians have long been alive to the significance of sustained contact between the West Saxon and Carolingian dynasties, exploring points of similarity between their respective means of rule.[16] The modern trend has been to maximize claims for positive Carolingian influence, taking a lead from the modelling of Asser's *Life* on Einhard's of Charlemagne; in law-making such contact has been plausibly documented.[17] The question is how far Alfredian kingship can be understood as straightforwardly implementing a Frankish programme. Carolingian rule was not monolithic: modern reassessment has highlighted regional variations, most marked between East and West Francia, in methods, shared culture and aristocratic structures.[18] Alfred's career has frequently been illumined by Carolingian

---

A. Scharer, *Herrschaft und Repräsentation: Studien zur Hofkultur König Alfreds des Großen* (Vienna, 2000); A. Sheppard, *Families of the King: Writing Identity in the Anglo-Saxon Chronicle* (Toronto, 2004), pp. 3–70.

[13] P. Wormald, '*Lex Scripta* and *Verbum Regis*: Legislation and Germanic Kingship from Euric to Cnut', in his *Legal Culture in the Early Medieval West: Law as Text, Image and Experience* (London, 1999), pp. 1–43, at 11, 13, 15 and 25; J. L. Nelson, 'Power and Authority at the Court of Alfred', in *Essays on Anglo-Saxon and Related Themes in memory of Lynne Grundy*, ed. J. Roberts and J. Nelson (London, 2000), pp. 311–37, at 332–3.

[14] R. P. Abels, *Alfred the Great* (Harlow, 1998), pp. 219–57, cf. 258–84.

[15] R. Balzaretti, J. L. Nelson and J. Maddicott, 'Debate: Trade, Industry and the Wealth of King Alfred', *P&P* 135 (1992), 142–88; responding to Maddicott's 'Trade, Industry and the Wealth of King Alfred', *P&P* 123 (1989), 3–51.

[16] W. Stubbs, *The Constitutional History of England*, 3 vols., 5th edn (Oxford, 1891–8) I, 223–7, cf. 104–6, 112–16, 165–6 and 197–202; H. M. Cam, *Local Government in Francia and England* (London, 1912).

[17] J. Campbell, 'Observations on English Government from the Tenth to the Twelfth Century', in his *Essays in Anglo-Saxon History* (London, 1986), pp. 155–70, esp. 162; P. Wormald, '*Engla Lond*: the Making of an Allegiance', in his *Legal Culture*, pp. 333–55, at 366–7.

[18] T. Reuter, 'Plunder and Tribute in the Carolingian Empire', *TRHS* 5th series 35 (1985), 75–94, at 92–4; T. Reuter, *Germany in the Early Middle Ages c. 800–1056* (London, 1991); cf. J. L. Nelson, *Charles the Bald* (Harlow, 1992); J. L. Nelson, 'Kingship and Empire in the Carolingian World', in *Carolingian Culture: Emulation and Innovation* (Cambridge, 1994), ed. R. McKitterick, pp. 52–87, at 73–80; E. J. Goldberg, '"More Devoted to the Equipment of Battle than the Splendor of Banquets": Frontier Kingship, Martial Ritual, and Early Knighthood at the Court of Louis the German', *Viator* 30 (1999), 41–78.

comparison: often revealing are suggestive differences in West Saxon experience.[19] Where Wallace-Hadrill saw in Alfred's writings how far 'the Church had influenced the western concept of kingship', Nelson observes the unusual secularity of royal imagery and thought.[20] Every statement must be judged in this context: the detection of 'influence' can be but the first step to an understanding of Alfredian theorizing and rhetoric. Often overlooked is the backdrop of existing West Saxon practices and assumptions.[21] Their recovery is vital, as the context for royal thought and action; with Alfred and his scholarly helpers, they hold the key to his rule.

Third, and most problematic, are the challenges of understanding Anglo-Saxon political structures and royal power. Behind Alfred's kingship lay a complex nexus of relationships, expectations and obligations creating effective parameters of action. Successfully negotiated, they offered considerable means of logistical and administrative control. The power involved has been well observed by its most enthusiastic proponent, James Campbell, rescuing the order and sophistication of Anglo-Saxon structures.[22] Royal resources extended to systems of taxation and military assessment, organized by territorial subdivision; the latter established a strong relationship between centre and locality. Upon these basic instruments, Campbell detects extensive innovation in the later Anglo-Saxon period, perhaps beginning under Alfred; the case has been taken further by Wormald.[23] Though their perspective is at times extreme, the general argument has considerable weight in identifying an important contrast with the fragmentation of rule in tenth-century West Francia.[24] The question is how such divergence might be explained: the answers of both relate uncomfortably to the construct of an 'Anglo-Saxon' or 'English state'. The usefulness of the latter term has long been debated by medievalists, with differing implications: as Rees Davies pertinently suggested, its application carries several problematic assumptions.[25] Notions of legitimate force have limits for structures

---

[19] J. L. Nelson, '"A King Across the Sea"': Alfred in Continental Perspective', in her *Ruling Families*, no. 1, pp. 49–52 and 62–7; Nelson, 'Political Ideas', pp. 126–7, 131, 144 and 147; D. Pratt, 'The Illnesses of King Alfred the Great', *ASE* 30 (2001), 39–90, esp. 40–55.

[20] J. M. Wallace-Hadrill, *Early Germanic Kingship in England and on the Continent* (Oxford, 1971), p. 141, cf. 141–51; Nelson, 'Political Ideas', pp. 147–8.

[21] Cf. esp. Keynes, 'Mercians', pp. 2–6.

[22] Esp. J. Campbell, 'The Late Anglo-Saxon State: a Maximum View', in his *The Anglo-Saxon State* (London, 2000), pp. 1–30.

[23] *Ibid.*, pp. 16–17; Wormald, 'Engla Lond', pp. 366–7 and 376–7.

[24] Further contextualized also by T. Reuter, 'The Making of England and Germany 850–1050: Points of Comparison and Difference', in *Medieval Europeans*, ed. A. P. Smyth (Basingstoke, 1998), pp. 53–70.

[25] S. Reynolds, 'The Historiography of the Medieval State', in *Companion to Historiography*, ed. M. Bentley (London and New York, 1997), pp. 117–38; R. Davies, 'The Medieval State: the

actively harnessing lordship and communal self-help.[26] Nor can one straightforwardly prioritize the 'public': as formalized behaviour its early medieval forms cannot safely be detached from the social and institutional forces that underpinned it.[27] Complex political and social relationships are effectively reified, relegating certain regions to 'state-lessness'. Yet it was precisely through such relationships that power was mediated and deployed.

There are real dangers of an almost circular process of conceptual recovery. A cultural dimension is acknowledged, but primarily detected in 'state-like' features of subjecthood and 'national' identity.[28] Wormald's account assumes the essential replication of Carolingian structures, yet his vision is restricted to the phenomenon of oath-taking, here finding evidence for 'allegiance'.[29] It is only on this basis that he can then claim a decisive role for 'English' ethnic identity, as if the only remaining variable.[30] In wider elite communication many practices of power are effectively sidestepped, neglecting questions of its distribution against an environmentally and socially determined resource-base. The point is important because Wormald's position has gained wider currency as an 'explanation' of English political and cultural distinctiveness, seen to reside in a unique sense of 'Englishness' promoted in antiquity by King Alfred.[31] This has in turn informed non-specialist exploration of 'state-building', influentially exporting the construct to pre- and post-colonial Africa.[32] One might only wish for some engagement with the extensive trans-European historiography of ethnic identity, which has done much to problematize the phenomenon as a feature of the post-Roman world, raising questions of its force and evidential recovery.[33]

Tyranny of a Concept?', *Journal of Historical Sociology* 16 (2003), 280–300; cf. the very qualified use of M. Innes, *State and Society in the Early Middle Ages: the Middle Rhine Valley, 400–1000* (Cambridge, 2000), p. 12, note 12, cf. pp. 6, 141–2 and 251–63.

[26] Cf. below, pp. 232–41.

[27] Innes, *State and Society*, esp. pp. 253–4, 255–9 and 261–2; S. MacLean, *Kingship and Politics in the Late Ninth Century: Charles the Fat and the End of the Carolingian Empire* (Cambridge, 2003), pp. 13–17.

[28] See esp. J. Campbell, 'Stubbs and the English State', in his *Anglo-Saxon State*, pp. 247–68, 255–6 and 261–7, effectively inviting this questioning. Cf. the more restricted critique of S. Foot, 'The Historiography of the Anglo-Saxon "Nation-State"', in *Power and the Nation in European History*, ed. L. Scales and O. Zimmer (Cambridge, 2005), pp. 125–42.

[29] Wormald, '*Engla Lond*', pp. 362–71.

[30] *Ibid.*, pp. 371–8.

[31] E.g. H. M. Thomas, *The English and the Normans* (Oxford, 2003), pp. 20–31; P. Wormald, 'Sir Geoffrey Elton's *English*: a View from the Early Middle Ages', *TRHS* 6th series 7 (1997), 318–25.

[32] A. Hastings, *The Construction of Nationhood: Ethnicity, Religion and Nationalism* (Cambridge, 1997), pp. 39–43, cf. 148–66.

[33] The literature is vast: see esp. W. Pohl, 'Conceptions of Ethnicity in Early Medieval Studies', in *Debating the Middle Ages: Issues and Readings*, ed. L. K. Little and B. H. Rosenwein (Oxford, 1998), pp. 15–25; G. Halsall, 'Review Article: Movers and Shakers: the Barbarians and the Fall of

Both are pressing for widely stratified societies primarily revealed in written sources of elite consumption and record.[34] Yet the observation is otiose against the selective teleology of statehood, the more so for accounts so insistently represented as a form of modern self-knowledge.[35] Anglo-Saxon history has often been studied for insight into later periods. As these examples demonstrate, it is here essential to abandon any quest for origins, whether of post-Conquest England or indeed our own. The only alternative is to approach Anglo-Saxon political structures on entirely their own terms, informed among other evidence by the ways in which power was understood by contemporaries.

It is towards such an understanding that this book is directed, through the evidence of Alfred's writings. Its overall aim is to reintegrate Alfred's learned kingship as a part of royal practice. This has necessitated a reconsideration and close analysis of the relationship between royal behaviour and the operation of political power. If the 'public' is to be integrated, one may proceed with the assumption that any activity might potentially be relevant to its practice. On this basis, the study seeks to recover the force and status of Alfred's texts in relation to contemporary structures of kingship and political authority. In so doing, it aims to place these textual utterances in the broader context of ninth-century thought and behaviour, with particular reference to the role of Alfred's Frankish and other scholarly helpers. Informed by this positioning both of texts and kingship, the book further seeks to assess the impact of royal writings in relation to other forces acting on contemporaries. In this complex interface one may hope to recover some of the effects of Alfred's learning as a tool of kingship; this in turn informs assessment of its longer-term legacy.

Learned kingship, royal authorship, inventive translation: each poses challenges of interpretation. Central to my approach is the minimum observation of an historical connectedness which must be embraced in any explanation. One might well focus on any one of these phenomena, yet to do so risks the neglect of this fundamental interrelationship. This is especially the case with translation, open to many forms of critical enquiry.[36] More pertinent is what irreducibly linked all three: the action

---

Rome', *EME* 8 (1999), 131–45; P. J. Geary, *The Myth of Nations: the Medieval Origins of Europe* (Princeton, NJ, 2002); J. Hines (ed.), *The Anglo-Saxons from the Migration Period to the Eighth Century: an Ethnographic Perspective* (Woodbridge, 1997).

[34] Cf. esp. A. D. Smith, *The Ethnic Origins of Nations* (Oxford, 1986), often neglected here.

[35] Wormald, '*Engla Lond*', pp. 361–2 and 380–1; Campbell, 'Anglo-Saxon State', pp. 26–7; Campbell, 'Stubbs', pp. 258–62 and 267–8.

[36] Cf. J. Beer (ed.), *Translation Theory and Practice in the Middle Ages* (Kalamazoo, MI, 1997); K. Davis, 'The Performance of Translation Theory in King Alfred's National Literary Program', in *Manuscript, Narrative, Lexicon: Essays in honour of Whitney F. Bolton*, ed. R. Boenig and

of language. The pairing has been a central object of modern philosophical concern, in the understanding that speech is a form of action, whose meaning is necessarily public in any successful act of communication.[37] One effect has been the general shift towards discourse, yet another has been to heighten understanding of the properties of texts, as speech–acts minimally constituted by their particular relationship to discourse. It is this which Quentin Skinner has usefully termed 'illocutionary force': a text's action in, for example, attacking or ridiculing a particular line of argument.[38] Both realizations have proved profitable in intellectual history: they immediately assist in prioritizing the recovery of discursive context, while clarifying the status of translation as a very particular type of text.[39] Yet it should be observed that there can be no end to this convenient hermeneutic. What did it mean to attack or to ridicule? Without addressing this problem, Skinner has upheld the recoverability of 'social meaning' in non–linguistic actions, through illocutionary redescription.[40] Sooner or later, there can be no escape from more totalizing engagement with the semantics of social behaviour, of the sort so influentially advocated by Clifford Geertz.[41] Skinner's thinking lends support to a broader project of social and cultural recovery.[42]

In pursuing its implications for King Alfred, I have drawn on further conceptual resources.[43] Speech–acts can be more or less mighty: one must confront their very complex interaction with power. Again, the question is fundamentally social: a text's action will relate most

---

K. Davis (Lewisburg, PA, 2000), pp. 149–70; R. Stanton, *The Culture of Translation in Anglo-Saxon England* (Cambridge, 2002); Discenza, *King's English*.

[37] Q. Skinner, 'Motives, Intentions and Interpretation', pp. 97–8, and 'Interpretation and the Understanding of Speech Acts', p. 120, both in his *Visions of Politics*, 3 vols. (Cambridge, 2002) I, 90–102 and 103–27.

[38] *Ibid.* ('intentions' are here detached from 'the author', as conventionally understood); J. G. A. Pocock, 'Introduction: the State of the Art', in his *Virtue, Commerce and History* (Cambridge, 1985), pp. 1–34; K. Thomas, 'Politics: Looking for Liberty', *New York Review of Books* (26 May 2005), pp. 47–53.

[39] Below, pp. 169–70.

[40] Q. Skinner, '"Social Meaning" and the Explanation of Social Action', in his *Visions of Politics* I, 128–44.

[41] C. Geertz, 'Thick Description: Toward an Interpretive Theory of Culture', in his *The Interpretation of Cultures: Selected Essays* (London, 1973), pp. 3–30, esp. 12–13 and 27–30.

[42] L. Hunt (ed.), *The New Cultural History* (Berkeley and Los Angeles, CA, 1989); cf. R. E. Sullivan, 'Introduction: Factors Shaping Carolingian Studies', in *'The Gentle Voices of Teachers': Aspects of Learning in the Carolingian Age*, ed. R. E. Sullivan (Columbus, OH, 1995), pp. 1–50, with material cited at p. 46, note 24; T. Reuter, 'Nobles and Others: the Social and Cultural Expression of Power Relations in the Middle Ages', in *Nobles and Nobility in Medieval Europe*, ed. A. J. Duggan (Woodbridge, 2000), pp. 85–98.

[43] Here I am most grateful to Nicholas Brooks and Janet Nelson for their comments on my original thesis.

consequentially to the contexts in which it is received. In considering such force, my approach is complemented by the insights of Michel Foucault into the power of language, its capacity to order and reinforce the organizing structures of social groups, through institutionalized speech and modes of thought.[44] In his attention to the cognitive dimensions of language, Foucault rightly pursued inwards the impossibility of truly 'private' meaning, the relationality of all mental acts to available discourses. One need not accept Foucault's own view of the middle ages, nor the uncritical application of his methodological apparatus.[45] Yet in probing the social basis of intellectual interaction he raised very pertinent historical questions about the political uses of knowledge, its relationship to wider social organization and collective psychology.[46] Foucault's notion of discourse is here necessary to explore the potential power of privileged language. Yet speech itself cannot be isolated from wider aspects of social practice. Here I have found useful Pierre Bourdieu's attention to the communicational basis of social distinction, its necessary reliance on shared practices and norms.[47] Primarily concerned with modern capitalist societies, Bourdieu himself has sought to isolate the 'cultural' as a field of inverted economic priorities; one should not be surprised to find different structures in the early middle ages.[48] In treating 'culture' more broadly, as the shared structures of communication and behaviour, my approach seeks to integrate the economic and political into questions of production and control.

To these general methods I have added an institutional focus, in the social and spatial operation of King Alfred's court.[49] Early medieval

[44] M. Foucault, *The Order of Things: an Archaeology of the Human Sciences* (New York, 1970); G. Danaher, T. Schirato and J. Webb, *Understanding Foucault* (St Leonards, 2000); L. H. Martin, H. Gutman and P. H. Hutton (ed.), *Technologies of the Self* (Amherst, MA, 1998).

[45] Cf. esp. J. Weeks, 'Foucault for Historians', *History Workshop Journal* 14 (1982), 106–19; M. Philp, 'Michel Foucault', in *The Return of Grand Theory in the Human Sciences*, ed. Q. Skinner (Cambridge, 1985), pp. 67–81.

[46] M. Foucault, *Discipline and Punish: the Birth of the Prison*, trans. A. Sheridan (London, 1991), pp. 135–292; M. Foucault, 'The Right of Death and Power over Life', and 'The Politics of Health in the Eighteenth Century', in *The Foucault Reader*, ed. P. Rabinow (Harmondsworth, 1991), pp. 258–72 and 273–89.

[47] P. Bourdieu, *The Field of Cultural Production*, ed. R. Johnson (Cambridge, 1993); W. Pohl, with H. Reimitz (eds.), *Strategies of Distinction: the Construction of Ethnic Communities, 300–800* (Leiden, 1998); C. Pössel, 'Symbolic Communication and the Negotiation of Power at Carolingian Regnal Assemblies, 814–840' (unpubl. PhD dissertation, Cambridge University, 2003), pp. 33–49 (publication forthcoming).

[48] Cf. the different, though in part complementary, use of Bourdieu by N. G. Discenza, 'Symbolic Capital and the Ruler in the Translation Program of Alfred the Great', *Exemplaria* 23 (2001), 433–67; Discenza, *King's English*.

[49] Cf. D. Pratt, 'Persuasion and Invention at the Court of King Alfred the Great', in *Court Culture in the Early Middle Ages: the Proceedings of the First Alcuin Conference*, ed. C. Cubitt (Turnhout, 2002), pp. 189–221.

courts and court culture have become an increasing focus for scholarly enquiry: here one may learn much from the overarching insights of Norbert Elias, also on the rise in this literature.[50] Elias's own writings sought ultimately to explain modernity, locating its origins in a transformation of behaviour cultivated 'from above' by medieval and early modern courts.[51] As such, he was also concerned with 'state-building', yet in a way which resolved 'state-like' functions into their constituent social processes. His theory was far more than a modelling of court-based cultural patronage; it extended critically to the power at stake in centralized interaction.[52] This was fundamentally material, in the control and distribution of local political authority, administering nascent monopolies over violence and taxation.[53] In the right conditions, such power had a tendency to accumulate over a larger territory, monopolizing the functions of neighbouring agencies.[54] One precondition was economic, in the binding effects of towns and use of money; another was a net shortage of redistributable land.[55] The greater the monopoly, the greater the interdependence of administering interests; the effects were strongest when participating groups were finely balanced, heightening dependence on the coordinating power.[56] These delicate interests explained the centrality of court behaviour, its tendency to develop elaborate forms of interaction centred on the ruler.[57] As the latter held advantages of coordinating agency, socialized contact became ever more potent, controlling entirely rational competition among nobles for status and power. In behavioural rules were common features of self-control and symbolic gesture, potentially transmissible to

---

[50] C. S. Jaeger, *The Origins of Courtliness: Civilizing Trends and the Formation of Courtly Ideals 939–1210* (Philadelphia, PA, 1985), cf. E. J. Goldberg, 'Creating a Medieval Kingdom: Carolingian Kingship, Court Culture, and Aristocratic Society under Louis of East Francia (840–76)' (unpubl. PhD dissertation, University of Virginia, 1998), now published in revised form as *Struggle for Empire: Kingship and Conflict under Louis the German, 817–76* (Ithaca, NY, 2006); S. Airlie, 'The Palace of Memory: the Carolingian Court as Political Centre', in *Courts and Regions in Medieval Europe*, ed. S. R. Jones, R. Marks and A. J. Minnis (York, 2000), pp. 1–20; M. de Jong and F. Theuws (eds.), *Topographies of Power in the Early Middle Ages* (Leiden, 2001); Cubitt (ed.), *Court Culture*.

[51] N. Elias, *The Civilizing Process*, trans. E. Jephcott, rev. edn (Oxford, 1994 [1939]); N. Elias, *The Court Society*, trans. E. Jephcott (Oxford, 1983 [1969]); cf. P. Burke, *The Fabrication of Louis XIV* (New Haven, CT, 1992).

[52] My assessment is more positive than that of C. Cubitt, 'Introduction', and M. Innes, ' "A Place of Discipline": Carolingian Courts and Aristocratic Youth', p. 76, both in *Court Culture*, ed. Cubitt, pp. 1–15 and 59–76; cf. J. L. Nelson, 'Was Charlemagne's Court a Courtly Society?', pp. 39–57 in the same volume.

[53] Elias, *Civilizing Process*, pp. 257–362; S. Mennell, *Norbert Elias: an Introduction*, 2nd edn (Oxford, 1992), pp. 61–93.

[54] Elias, *Civilizing Process*, pp. 268–77.   [55] *Ibid.*, pp. 206–14 and 220–30.

[56] *Ibid.*, pp. 312–44, esp. 317–23.   [57] *Ibid.*, pp. 340–4; Elias, *Court Society*, pp. 78–145.

other social contexts; these mechanisms were the underpinning of a wider 'court society'.[58]

For Elias, these processes did not intensify until the early modern period, though he recognized the much longer history of courtly interaction. In many ways his handling of the middle ages reflected the limits of his material, downplaying Carolingian structures, while too firmly generalizing from Capetian success. Frankish power can no longer be seen as essentially centrifugal, only offset by depleting the royal fisc.[59] Yet it would be quite wrong to dismiss his model on grounds of chronology. His case for the entirely modern character of depersonalized power deserves respect from medievalists, throwing earlier structures into relief.[60] More directly, his modelling of court power has many pertinent correspondences. Similarly dissatisfied with modern assumptions, Matthew Innes has located Carolingian political power in critical points of contact between centre and locality, socially negotiated through the manipulation of personal relationships.[61] Though in themselves relatively limited, enough power and resources were at stake to sustain kingship as more than a zero-sum game.[62] Elias's thinking suggests ways of tracking this game in all its complexity, heightening awareness of variables, while integrating the difficult area of collective perception. His general picture relates particularly well to the later Carolingian kingdoms of East and West Francia, aiding the juxtaposition of their respective courts.[63] If used sensitively, his model is open-ended, leaving room for any number of non-courtly arenas, with varying powers and limits of monopoly, and any configuration of aristocratic interests.[64] Rather than impressive 'states' and puny 'statelessness', the approach invites a quasi-Aristotelian vista of early medieval royal households, widely varying in their degree of social power and relationship to local authority.[65]

That vista is structural, not the 'proving' of Elias nor the tracing of 'civilization'. Violence in particular may be better viewed as an available

---

[58] Elias, *Civilizing Process*, pp. 363–447; Elias, *Court Society*, pp. 40–77 and 146–213.

[59] Elias, *Civilizing Process*, pp. 195–202.   [60] *Ibid.*, p. 276, cf. 272–4 and 312–13.

[61] Innes, *State and Society*, pp. 261–2, cf. 253–4.

[62] *Ibid.*, p. 259; cf. also MacLean, *Charles the Fat*, pp. 19–22, 75–80 and 120–2.

[63] J. L. Nelson, 'Charles le Chauve et les utilisations du savoir', in her *Ruling Families*, no. 7 (cf. below, pp. 133–4 and 150); Goldberg, 'Frontier Kingship'; Goldberg, *Empire*, esp. pp. 165–230.

[64] Elias, *Civilizing Process*, pp. 261–7, for regional variation; cf. J. L. Nelson, 'Kingship and Royal Government', in *NCMH* II, 383–430, esp. 408–22.

[65] Esp. evident further west: W. Davies, *An Early Welsh Microcosm: Studies in the Llandaff Charters* (London, 1978); W. Davies, 'Celtic Kingships in the Early Middle Ages', in *Kings and Kingship in Medieval Europe*, ed. A. J. Duggan (London, 1993), pp. 101–24; T. M. Charles-Edwards, *Early Christian Ireland* (Cambridge, 2000).

form of power, subject to varying sources of regulation and control.[66] What this thinking highlights is the relative role of court-based contact, the degree to which this was underpinned by quantifiable aristocratic interests. The question necessarily combines prosopographical enquiry with holistic attention to the effects of centrally experienced language and gesture. It makes no sense to separate these latter components: as much is demonstrated by the general character of ninth-century political discourse, frequently drawing force from aspects of interpersonal relationship.[67] Though 'public' in function, this language was commonly 'royal', combining earthly lordship with divinely imagined notions of worldly service.[68] Both had room for an idealized royal household, not always relating precisely to contemporary practice.[69] Such discourse had its own complexity, in relation to both God and the world, shaping the meaning of speech and witnessed action.[70] Texts took their place within these deeper structures, deployed by actors necessarily defined by their relationship to royal rule. Only here can one hope to recover the force of contemporary rhetoric, and its varying uses at the hands of ecclesiastics, learned laity or wise kings. To employ writing was itself a gesture, never far from these socialized relationships, while capable of complex deployment through self-description.

Texts in turn had the capacity to frame action; gestures related in often complex ways to linguistic norms. The relationship could be directly textual, richly exploited in inauguration rituals and other royal liturgy.[71] Beyond these regularized or status-changing procedures, early medievalists have increasingly acknowledged a wider role for ritualized or symbolic acts in elite communication.[72] This has been taken furthest

[66] G. Halsall (ed.), *Violence and Society in the Early Medieval West* (Woodbridge, 1998); P. Wormald, 'Giving God and King their Due: Conflict and its Regulation in the Early English State', in his *Legal Culture*, pp. 333–57, at 335–42 (with above qualifications); Innes, *State and Society*, pp. 129–36.
[67] J. Fried, 'Der karolingische Herrschaftsverband im 9 Jhdt. zwischen "Kirche" und "Königshaus"', *Historische Zeitschrift* 235 (1982), 1–43; Nelson, 'Kingship and Empire', pp. 64–9; Innes, *State and Society*, pp. 262–3.
[68] See further below, pp. 58–78 and 130–78.
[69] Airlie, 'Palace of Memory', esp. pp. 4–8; J. L. Nelson, 'Aachen as a Place of Power', in *Topographies*, ed. de Jong and Theuws, pp. 217–41, at 226–32, for Hincmar's *De ordine palatii*, discussed further below, pp. 42–3.
[70] For the social power of religious practice, cf. E. Durkheim, *The Elementary Forms of Religious Life*, ed. and trans. K. Fields (New York, 1995 [1912]); C. Geertz, 'Religion as a Cultural System', in his *Interpretation of Cultures*, pp. 87–125.
[71] J. L. Nelson, *Politics and Ritual in Early Medieval Europe* (London, 1986); E. H. Kantorowicz, *Laudes Regiae* (Berkeley and Los Angeles, CA, 1958).
[72] K. Leyser, 'Ritual, Ceremony and Gesture: Ottonian Germany', in his *Communications and Power in Medieval Europe: the Carolingian and Ottonian Centuries*, ed. T. Reuter (London, 1994), pp. 189–213; J.-C. Schmitt, 'The Rationale of Gestures in the West: Third to Thirteenth Centuries', in *A Cultural History of Gesture*, ed. J. Bremmer and H. Roodenburg (Cambridge, 1991), pp. 59–70; G. Koziol, *Begging Pardon and Favour: Ritual and Political Order in Early Medieval France* (Ithaca, NY,

for Ottonian and Salian Germany, informing an entire approach focused on representational behaviour: meaningful acts seemingly effective in regulating contact between ruler and nobility.[73] Within gestures of 'friendship' and pious humility are discerned unwritten 'rules' of king-ship, sufficient in themselves to uphold the 'game'. The resulting work has often been illuminating, though it can leave the impression of largely stage-managed public encounters, uncertainly related to material interests.[74] There are a few parallels with Geertz's 'theatre state' of Bali: neglecting power, his account found ritual as self-driven spectacle.[75] Here one may learn from Erving Goffman's profound picture of soci-ality, observing the necessary theatre of all human behaviour, merely transferred in any context of familiarity or privacy.[76] The effect is to uphold the centrality of language in all arenas, including those 'behind-the-scenes'; in Alfred's case, the latter is at least partially recoverable from its evidential imprint. Rather than ritualized social action, one must envisage interactive performance by elite actors, delicately played out against the backdrop of discourse, gestural conventions and material power.

These elements were common to all regions: most commentators have seen the use of gesture as an effective substitute for institutional means of rule.[77] 'Ritualized' Germany is contrasted with 'governed' West Francia, differentiated by the use of writing and deeper adminis-trative machinery.[78] The direct opposition is becoming unsustainable in the general reassessment of Carolingian rule. Rather than instructional instruments, capitularies are better viewed as exhortatory acts of rhetoric; familiarity and gesture have emerged as important tools of communication, both at court and in the politics of assemblies.[79] Across Europe, one is dealing with different configurations of political dis-course and social interaction, with the uses of literacy highly pertinent to

---

1992); F. Theuws and J. L. Nelson (eds.), *Rituals of Power from Late Antiquity to the Early Middle Ages* (Leiden, 2000).

[73] G. Althoff, *Family, Friends and Followers*, trans. C. Carroll (Cambridge, 2004); G. Althoff, *Spielregeln der Politik im Mittelalter* (Darmstadt, 1997); G. Althoff, *Otto III*, trans. P. G. Jestice (Pennsylvania, PA, 2003).

[74] Useful discussion by T. Reuter, 'Pre-Gregorian Mentalities', *JEH* 45 (1994), 465–74; S. Hamilton, 'Review Article: Early Medieval Rulers and their Modern Biographers', *EME* 9 (2000), 247–60; Pössel, 'Symbolic Communication', pp. 16–33.

[75] C. Geertz, *Negara: the Theatre State in Nineteenth-Century Bali* (Princeton, NJ, 1980); cf. M. Bloch, *Ritual, History and Power* (London, 1989), pp. 208–10.

[76] E. Goffman, *The Presentation of Self in Everyday Life* (Edinburgh, 1956).

[77] Leyser, 'Ritual, Ceremony', pp. 192–6; Althoff, *Otto III*, pp. 16–26.

[78] *Ibid.*, cf. J. L. Nelson, 'The Lord's Anointed and the People's Choice: Carolingian Royal Ritual', in her *The Frankish World, 750–900* (London, 1996), pp. 99–131, at 128–31.

[79] Innes, *State and Society*, pp. 253–4; Nelson, 'Aachen', pp. 232–7; Nelson, 'Courtly Society?'; Pössel, 'Symbolic Communication', pp. 56–248.

the character of aristocratic performance. All were necessarily reliant on encoded elite behaviour: Elias again assists by questioning the extent of its relationship to activity at the political centre. In many ways, Alfred's court offers a richly documented case-study, casting light on the alternative configurations of neighbouring kingdoms.

My study is divided into two parts. In the first I consider the operation of West Saxon royal power, viewing Alfred's reign against the deeper backdrop of ninth-century West Saxon rule. My survey works upwards, beginning with the economic resource-base of the West Saxon political order, before turning to the role of its principal aristocratic participants, first secular, then ecclesiastical. In each case, local activities are assessed in relation to power in the royal household; this provides the context for an exploration of court communication before King Alfred's reign, relating political discourse to the wider scope of available cultural forms. Part I ends by assessing the impact of viking activity on this political community, situating Alfredian developments against earlier aspects of West Saxon military and logistical response. To this context Part II adds the force of Alfredian political discourse, recovered within broader features of communicational innovation. Royal writings are assessed against the more general uses of vernacular prose translation, isolating their participation in a single discourse of power. Alfredian innovation is explored in relation to its material dimensions; each of Alfred's texts is then analysed in turn, tracing the impact of this discourse on royal translation, taking full account of the status of Latin source-texts, the possible role of interpretative material and likely character of Alfred's available expertise. In each case, the analysis is preliminary to reintegrating the text with its immediate context, as part of the practice of Alfredian kingship. In conclusion, I identify the uniting features of Alfred's distinctive practice, the central contribution of royal learning and the implications of both for the understanding of ninth- and tenth-century political, cultural and economic change.

PART I

The West Saxon Political Order

Chapter 2

RESOURCES AND EXTRACTION

The rise of Wessex in the first half of the ninth century was accompanied by grassroots economic change. Political expansion had been the achievement of Alfred's grandfather, Ecgberht (802–39), and father, Æthelwulf (839–58), tightening the hold of dynastic kingship; this order had itself contributed to a more intensive exploitation of expanding resources, commercial as well as agrarian. Both areas were sources of royal income: in the previous century, land and warfare had been increasingly supplemented by new forms of regularized payment, through the taxation of markets and exchange. In fiscal and monetary regulation, these structures presuppose aspects of central control; Balzaretti's reluctance to attribute any form of economic management to early medieval rulers seems inordinately destructive.[1] For Wessex, his case can be countered by many of the effects of expansion, tapping the wealth of south-eastern trade; these extended to systems of military assessment, exercised more broadly in urban defence.

WEST SAXON RESOURCES AND ROYAL POWER

Though sometimes overstated, a strong case remains for royal promotion of markets from the earliest phases of Anglo-Saxon urban development.[2] Merchants received legal protection: the control of trade enabled substantial extraction, both in bullion and in kind, through payment of tolls and issuing of coinage. The latter involved a potentially

---

[1] 'Debate: Trade, Industry', pp. 142–50.
[2] P. H. Sawyer, 'Kings and Merchants', in *Early Medieval Kingship*, ed. P. H. Sawyer and I. N. Wood (Leeds, 1977), pp. 139–58; R. Hodges, *The Anglo-Saxon Achievement* (London, 1989), still useful despite criticisms, pushed furthest in M. Anderton (ed.), *Anglo-Saxon Trading Centres: Beyond the Emporia* (Glasgow, 1999); cf. J. R. Maddicott, 'Prosperity and Power in the Age of Bede and Beowulf', *PBA* 117 (2002), 49–72; C. Dyer, *Making a Living in the Middle Ages: the People of Britain 850–1520* (London, 2002), pp. 43–70.

lucrative partnership between kings and moneyers, who were mercan-
tile third parties rather than royal officials. The estimation of coinage-
volume is fraught with difficulty, but from the second quarter of the
eighth century coins circulating in southern England should be measured at least in millions, and possibly tens of millions in later phases.[3] By
placing charges on minting, and latterly by insisting on the reminting of
all foreign coins, kings derived a considerable profit from the circulation
of currency, even after moneyers had taken their cut. This strengthened
royal interests in coastal trading-centres or 'wics', where minting and
commerce were mainly located. In Wessex, this potential seems first to
have been exploited under King Ine (688–726), whose suggested role in
the laying-out of *Hamwic* (Southampton) would expand his pivotal
position in early West Saxon kingship.

Minting nevertheless remained almost exclusively confined to the
south-east, where a concentration of 'wics' was sustained by Continental
trade. The unparalleled wealth of this region was the main cause of its
political significance, initially subject to Mercian ambitions. Under Offa
(757–96) and Cenwulf (796–821) Mercian authority was established over
the principal mints of Canterbury, Rochester and Ipswich, in addition
to the existing Mercian emporium of *Lundenwic*. Another target was the
network of Kentish royal monasteries, also participant in trade,
exacerbating tensions with the see of Canterbury which were never
satisfactorily resolved.[4] Kentish hostility, coupled with Mercian dynastic
conflict, enabled Ecgberht to launch an extraordinarily successful West
Saxon offensive, achieving a decisive shift in the balance of power.[5] In
825 Ecgberht received the submission of Kent, Surrey, the South Saxons
and the East Saxons; while in 829, according to the *Chronicle*, 'King
Ecgberht conquered the kingdom of the Mercians, and everything south
of the Humber; and he was the eighth king who was *brytenwalda*'.[6]
Probably meaning 'wide-ruler', the term bears little relation to his long-
term legacy. With Mercian independence restored in the following year,
horizons were restricted to the newly acquired south-east.

West Saxon policy proved characteristically more subtle.[7] An agreement was soon reached with the see of Canterbury at Kingston in 838;
local Kentish nobles were rewarded for their support with land and

[3] D. M. Metcalf, 'The Prosperity of North-Western Europe in the Eighth and Ninth Centuries',
cf. P. Grierson, 'The Volume of Anglo-Saxon Coinage', both in *EcHR* 2nd series 20 (1967),
344–57 and 153–60.
[4] N. P. Brooks, *The Early History of the Church of Canterbury* (Leicester, 1984), pp. 129–54 and 175–206.
[5] S. Keynes, 'The Control of Kent in the Ninth Century', *EME* 2 (1993), 111–31; S. Keynes,
'England, 700–900', in *NCMH* II, 18–42.
[6] See below, pp. 110–11.   [7] Keynes, 'Kent', esp. pp. 120–31.

offices. The south-eastern regions continued to be treated as a separate kingdom, commonly forming an appanage for successive royal sons and younger brothers, with varying degrees of autonomy. Ecgberht and his successors remained simply 'king of the West Saxons and of Kent' in charters drafted by Kentish scribes. Such rule maximized the potential of their new-found prize. By the Kingston agreement the West Saxon dynasty acquired temporal lordship of the Kentish royal monasteries, gaining access to commercial interests on a scale denied to Mercian rulers.[8] Royal resources were further boosted by flows of income from the mints of Canterbury and Rochester, now striking West Saxon regal coinage for the first time.[9] This was a dynasty fully aware of their new sources of wealth, actively exploiting large-scale currency management.

How far were such concerns shared by the wider nobility? The fundamental basis of aristocratic power remained land. It was through gifts of land that resources were effectively shared between the king and his nobles; collective demand fuelled expansionist warfare, for any new grants had to come from existing royal possessions. Ninth-century royal landholding cannot be calculated with any precision, but from the spread of estates in Alfred's will it is clear that his dynasty could draw upon extensive landed resources, stretching from the West Saxon heartlands to territory more recently acquired to the east and west.[10] The voluminous body of surviving charters in the name of West Saxon kings for the period *c.* 830–*c.* 870 reveals a steady flow of land grants up to Alfred's accession, if perhaps no further. An instructive contrast has been drawn with the comparative parsimony of Mercian kings, whose charters include an unusual preponderance of grants obtained for payment, often conferring only a lease or immunities, as if land itself were in short supply.[11] Perhaps in response, the second half of the ninth century witnessed a renewal of Mercian attacks westwards against the Welsh, but opportunities were now curtailed by the growing power of Gwynedd.[12] Whereas Mercian ambitions ended in failure, gradual West Saxon absorption of the kingdom of Cornwall may have contributed significantly to royal landholding, easing pressures elsewhere.

Of necessity, land-management remained dominant among aristocratic priorities. Everyday logistics varied significantly according to the

[8] Brooks, *Canterbury*, pp. 197–203.
[9] P. Grierson and M. Blackburn, *Medieval European Coinage I. The Early Middle Ages* (Cambridge, 1986), pp. 303–16.
[10] S 1507 (*SEHD*, no. 11; trans. in K&L, *Alfred*, pp. 173–8).
[11] P. Wormald, 'The Ninth Century', in *The Anglo-Saxons*, ed. J. Campbell (Oxford, 1982), pp. 132–57, at 138–9.
[12] See below, pp. 107–11.

tenure enjoyed by the landholder. Most prized was bookland, conveyed by royal charter; first introduced in the seventh century for ecclesiastical purposes, this tenure contrasted with land conveyed orally, known as folkland. Bookland was soon exploited by the secular nobility, initially via 'bogus' monasteries, and then from the late eighth century through charters in the name of lay beneficiaries. Bookland's defining advantage was the conferral of ownership in perpetuity, with freedom of alienation, sometimes expressed as lordship over land (*dominium* or *hlafordscipe*).[13] This flexibility was a major attraction, enabling estates to be leased, gifted or sold; another was the tendency for estates to acquire exemptions from certain royal dues, otherwise incumbent on all folkland. Most commonly specified were a range of legal rights and fines, together with the obligation to provide occasional hospitality to the king and his officials, sometimes expressed as a food-rent or tax (*feorm*). All were effectively transferred to the landholder, drawing inhabitants under greater control. The extension of bookland to secular nobles laid the basis for seigneurial lordship.[14] Progressive fragmentation of holdings forced landlords to exploit their estates more intensively; one outcome was the emergence of seigneurial units which would be known after 1066 as 'manors'. Peasant obligations included labour-services on lordly demesne, typically focused on a central residence; open-field systems also may have accompanied nucleation.

The ninth century was formative in this long-term process, a role especially evident in its social effects. In the law-books of Wihtred and Ine, the standard adjective of nobility was *gesiðcund*, with origins in the notion of personal service, especially royal. By the Mercian translation of Bede, in the later ninth century, *gesið* had become a mark of status, chiefly connoting land-ownership and power over dependants.[15] Lower in the social scale, the defining characteristic of the *ceorl* or 'commoner' remained his personal freedom, denied to the substantial class of slaves beneath him. Yet this legal status mattered less, as many *ceorlas* became tied to estate-centres by obligations of labour.[16] Men and their families are explicitly transferred with land in two Worcester charters of the 880s.[17]

[13] A. Williams in *The Blackwell Encyclopaedia of Anglo-Saxon England*, ed. M. Lapidge *et al.* (Oxford, 1999), pp. 277–8, with references.
[14] R. Faith, *The English Peasantry and the Growth of Lordship* (Leicester, 1997), pp. 153–77; D. A. E. Pelteret, *Slavery in Early Mediaeval England* (Woodbridge, 1995), pp. 4–37 and 241–59; B. Yorke, *Wessex in the Early Middle Ages* (Leicester, 1995), pp. 240–90; Dyer, *Making a Living*, pp. 13–42.
[15] H. R. Loyn, 'Gesiths and Thegns in Anglo-Saxon England from the Seventh to Tenth Century', *EHR* 70 (1955), 529–49, esp. 535–40.
[16] Wormald, 'Ninth Century', p. 142.
[17] S 217 (BCS 547) and S 1415 (BCS 559), cf. S 1285 (BCS 599; *SEHD*, no. 17); Pelteret, *Slavery*, pp. 167–70; Faith, *Lordship*, pp. 171–3.

A remarkable passage in the translation of Orosius assumes that *ceorlas* were somehow unfree through subservience to 'lords'.[18] Social relationships were no longer so clearly personal, but increasingly dependent on relationships to land. The position of *ceorlas* may well have been most constrained in the heartlands of Alfred's kingdom. The extent of manorialism was regionalized; by Domesday at least, levels of peasant freedom seem to have been lower in Wessex than elsewhere.

Even in estate-management landlords were in no way isolated from monetary transactions, or urban exchange.[19] Specialized goods were needed for aristocratic consumption, while urban populations needed food and raw materials, sustaining a growing market for rural produce. Rich charter evidence for ninth-century Canterbury reveals a buoyant market for urban property, with local nobles willing to pay up to ten times the rural price for burgage-plots linked to fields located outside the town.[20] The flexibility of income in cash and bullion is here substantiated. Any exemption from royal tolls was treasured as a valuable gift; the best evidence pertains to ecclesiastical interests. The substantial corpus of eighth-century toll-charters nevertheless reveals the wider importance of *Lundenwic* as a place of aristocratic exchange; high-status goods were acquired by the sale of specialist regional produce, transported by ship.[21] One such exemption was confirmed in the mid-ninth century, while in 857 the bishop of Worcester secured the right to use weights and measures 'freely' on an estate in London, without the normal payment for Mercian royal authorization.[22] The collection of royal dues was farmed out as a further commercial privilege. The office of king's reeve could relate either to a 'wic' or royal vill; in either case king's thegns found ample opportunities for profit. The will of the Kentish reeve Abba is laden with payments in bullion and coin.[23] Certain moneyers can be identified in written sources; they too could hold the rank of king's thegn.[24]

At the rural end of the supply chain, much depended on the geographical distribution of estates, and on the size of each aristocratic

---

[18] *Or* IV.3, p. 87. See Pelteret, *Slavery*, pp. 54–6.

[19] C. Dyer, 'Recent Developments in Early Medieval Urban History and Archaeology in England', in *Urban Historical Geography: Recent Progress in Britain and Germany*, ed. D. Denecke and S. Shaw (Cambridge, 1988), pp. 69–80; S. R. H. Jones, 'Transaction Costs, Institutional Change, and the Emergence of a Market Economy in Later Anglo-Saxon England', *EcHR* 2nd series 46 (1993), 658–78; C. Scull, 'Urban Centres in Pre-Viking England?', in *The Anglo-Saxons*, ed. Hines, pp. 269–310.

[20] Brooks, *Canterbury*, pp. 26–30.

[21] S. Kelly, 'Trading Privileges from Eighth-Century England', *EME* 1 (1992), 3–28, esp. 13–16.

[22] S 88 (BCS 152; *Rochester*, ed. Campbell, no. 2); S 208 (BCS 492).

[23] S 1482 (*SEHD*, no. 2).

[24] Lord Stewartby, 'Moneyers in the Written Records', in *Kings, Currency and Alliances*, ed. Blackburn and Dumville, pp. 151–3.

household.[25] Even for royal vills and ecclesiastical houses, food-renders might prove insufficiently flexible to be consumed directly. The commutation of renders into customary payments offered an alternative source of income, doubtless attractive to the reeves of far-flung royal and ecclesiastical holdings, but also perhaps to smaller households on tighter budgets. Farming memoranda from the tenth century onwards reveal peasants owing rent (*gafol*) or other dues partly in pennies, partly in kind.[26] One, famously relating to Hurstbourne in Hampshire, occurs in a charter dated 900: though the context commands respect, such details might well have been vulnerable to later updating and improvement.[27] In the absence of comparable earlier sources, assessment rests on the indirect evidence of coin distribution. The map of single-finds from the ninth century shows concentrations at *Hamwic*, Ipswich and *Lundenwic*, in a pattern radiating from the south-east with decreasing intensity.[28] Levels of monetization would have varied greatly according to regional and local circumstances; coinage remained virtually unknown in Wales, much of the west midlands and the south-west beyond Exeter. Yet the overall pattern shows a plentiful scatter of single-finds across the open countryside of southern and eastern England, including Wessex. Certain unexpectedly 'productive' sites point strongly to the activity of rural fairs.[29] This is highly suggestive of peasant demand for coin, at least under certain favourable conditions, and thus of aristocratic demand, through the extraction of monetary payments. Even as labour-services increased, some landlords might well have drawn a significant cash income from their estates, creating new opportunities for those peasants concerned, as well as obligations.

MILITARY SERVICE AND THE COMMON BURDENS

West Saxon expansion had been achieved militarily, but such warfare was probably not straightforwardly profitable. The south-east was

---

[25] Faith, *Lordship*, pp. 153–77; cf. Carolingian parallels in Nelson, *Charles the Bald*, pp. 22–8.

[26] Faith, *Lordship*, pp. 56–88 and 105–6, with references.

[27] S 359 (BCS 594; *Charters*, ed. Robertson, no. 110), a cartulary copy of s. xii, recording the large figure of forty pence per hide; cf. H. P. R. Finberg's case for authenticity ('The Churls of Hurstbourne', in his *Lucerna* (London, 1964), pp. 131–43).

[28] D. M. Metcalf, 'The Monetary Economy of Ninth-Century England South of the Humber: a Topographical Analysis', in *Kings, Currency and Alliances*, ed. Blackburn and Dumville, pp. 167–97, esp. 167–74.

[29] *Ibid.*, pp. 169 and 180; M. Blackburn, '"Productive" Sites and the Pattern of Coin Loss in England, 600–1180', in *Markets in Early Medieval Europe: Trading and 'Productive' Sites, 650–850*, ed. T. Pestell and K. Ulmschneider (Macclesfield, 2003), pp. 20–36; K. Ulmschneider, 'Settlement, Economy and the "Productive" Site: Middle Anglo-Saxon Lincolnshire A.D. 650–780', *Medieval Archaeology* 44 (2000), 53–72, at 62, note 20, for sites within Wessex.

absorbed as a going concern, while income from coinage will have taken time to realize. Military service was a cost in labour and equipment; even in conquest, Ecgberht faced heightened needs of viking defence. All costs were borne by the economy at large, transmitted by mechanisms of strong logistical effect. Beyond army-service lay the related obligations of bridge-building and fortress-work, as burdens collectively falling on the 'entire people', known from their reservation in certain Anglo-Saxon charters. Though many aspects of the system were long established, fulfilment could not be taken for granted. Requiring co-operation both from lords and their men, these structures related to many other forces acting on local agrarian communities.

From an early stage in Anglo-Saxon England, military service was an obligation assigned to land.[30] Assessed by the hide, its role complemented many other dues of tribute and food-render, from which bookland was frequently exempted. Yet unlike these other services, the common burdens described 'necessary' duties, explicitly reserved in statements of immunity, and expected from all types of land, whether bookland or folkland. As such, they are unlikely to have represented an entirely new imposition, from which bookland had hitherto been exempt.[31] There is no reason to suppose that military service had not always been due from ecclesiastical landholding. Explicit reservation in charters was encouraged by the fuller recording of immunities, not included in the earliest diplomatic. Yet the record seems also to reflect pressures of regular performance. Bridge-building and military service are first reserved in a Mercian context, at the council of Gumley in 749, supplemented by fortress-work from the 790s: the references correlate with the construction of Offa's dyke and other known fortifications.[32]

Bridges and border duty corresponded to the Roman public services (*munera sordida*) of the Theodosian Code; in fortress-work the common burdens expanded such collective duty.[33] The same pattern would emerge for Wessex in the context of viking defence. Only in the reign of Æthelbald (855–60) did charters regularly add fortress-work to the other two burdens, reserved from the 840s.[34] The timing coincides with other signs of urban renewal. A poem of uncertain date commemorates the construction of a new bridge at Winchester by bishop Swithhun,

---

[30] N. P. Brooks, 'The Development of Military Obligations in Eighth- and Ninth-Century England', in his *Communities and Warfare 700–1400* (London, 2000), pp. 32–47.

[31] *Ibid.*, pp. 33–9; cf. R. P. Abels, *Lordship and Military Obligation in Anglo-Saxon England* (Berkeley and Los Angeles, CA, 1988), pp. 43–57.

[32] Brooks, 'Military Obligations', pp. 33 and 39–43.

[33] *Ibid.*, p. 41, notes 45 and 46; Nelson, 'Political Ideas', pp. 128–9.

[34] Brooks, 'Military Obligations', p. 44.

completed in 859; its location, outside the east gate, suggests burgeoning use of this civic entrance.[35] Similar processes are suggested for London: as early as 857, the estate acquired by the bishop of Worcester lay close to the city's west gate, implying commerce proximate to the Roman walls.[36] The estate's former owner, Ceolmund, was probably Æthelwulf's Kentish reeve of the same name. London's political status became increasingly ambiguous in the 850s: development might well have involved West Saxon as well as Mercian interests.[37] Collectively, the evidence points to a mid-century 'take-off' in West Saxon burh-work, perhaps focused on defensive repair; uncertain in scale, such efforts laid the basis for Alfred's wider burghal network.

These were very significant costs on labour and capital. The composition of early armies has been much debated, but clearly combined noble with *ceorlisc* personnel.[38] Contrary to some accounts, all land was publicly liable: there is no reason to suppose any regular exemption for lordly demesne.[39] In practice, military service, beyond that of the king's thegnly supporters, probably fell on a disparate range of commended men. Asser mentions *bellatores* in Alfred's pay and personal service; aristocratic households probably included similar 'fighting-men', available for land or other advancement.[40] Later evidence suggests the importance of rent-paying and other types of 'free' peasantry, capable of accepting their lord's defence.[41] Though their labour services would be less onerous, they too were frequently tied to a central lordly estate.[42] Demand was compounded by bridge-building and fortress-work, assessed more intensively, but with fewer specialist requirements. Pressures would already have been great on freer tenants: pressed for labour, many landholders might well have turned to their own dependent *ceorlas*.

Securely extracted, these were formidable mechanisms of collective action, directed at shire level by royal office-holders. As such, the common burdens were distinctive, and seen to be so, on a European stage. Unusually, they attracted direct West Frankish comment: English burh-work supplied an acknowledged precedent for West Frankish fortifications of the later 860s. By the Edict of Pîtres of 864, Charles the Bald required all unable to perform military service to supply labour *inter alia*

---

[35] M. Biddle, 'The Study of Winchester: Archaeology and History in a British Town, 1961–1983', *PBA* 69 (1983), 93–135, at 120–2.

[36] D. Keene, 'Alfred and London', in *Alfred*, ed. Reuter, pp. 235–49, at 239–41; cf. *ASC* s.a. 851, referring to *Lundenburh*.

[37] Keynes, 'Mercians', pp. 8–9.   [38] *Ine* 51.

[39] Cf. Faith, *Lordship*, pp. 48–55 and 268–9, over-reliant on restricted Domesday and geld-based evidence.

[40] *VA* 100, lines 1–6.   [41] Abels, *Lordship*, pp. 143–54; Faith, *Lordship*, pp. 94–9.

[42] *Ibid.*, pp. 107–14.

for the construction of *civitates*, 'according to the custom of antiquity and of other peoples'.[43] The formula implied a distinction between Theodosian bridges and watch-duty, already supported by Frankish legislation, and the building of 'new cities', only customary overseas.[44] The Edict may well be the work of Charles's key supporter, Hincmar of Rheims; in 858 or 859, the archbishop had drawn a further contrast relating to military service from church lands.[45] According to Hincmar, English bishoprics and monasteries were less extensively endowed than their Frankish counterparts; this explained an arrangement by which military service was not rendered from bishoprics, but its costs (*stipendia militiae*) supplied 'from public resources' (*ex roga publica*). This Hincmar contrasted with wealthier Frankish bishoprics, supporting service directly from their income. To a conventional fourfold division of episcopal expenditure, between bishop, clergy, poor and church-buildings, Frankish custom had effectively added a fifth, for 'fighting-men'. Hincmar's point was the special defensive role of Frankish ecclesiastical landholding.[46]

The comparison was not merely rhetorical: though ostensibly prompted by a passage in Pope Gregory's *Libellus responsionum*, Hincmar's claims reflected genuine differences in contemporary military assessment.[47] Frankish church land had long been exploited for lay purposes, the most common involving forms of precarial grant, compensated by rent.[48] The practice intensified under Carolingian ecclesiastical reform, where such grants were formally accepted as an expedient measure, only justified by military necessity.[49] At stake was rather the extent and nature of the church's contribution, repeatedly clarified in Carolingian legislation, and a subject of intense episcopal concern.[50] Typical arrangements

[43] MGH Capit. II, no. 273, c. 27, pp. 321–2.
[44] J. L. Nelson, 'The Franks and the English in the Ninth Century Reconsidered', in her *Ruling Families*, no. 6, pp. 146–9.
[45] Hincmar, *De ecclesiis et capellis*, ed. Stratmann, pp. 119–20; J. L. Nelson, 'The Church's Military Service in the Ninth Century: a Contemporary Comparative View?', in her *Ritual*, pp. 117–32.
[46] Cf. synod of Ver (844): MGH Conc. III, no. 7, c. 12, pp. 42–3; the same division recurs in RC 19, pp. 84–7, cf. N. Staubach, *Rex Christianus: Hofkultur und Herrschaftspropaganda im Reich Karls des Kahlen – Teil II: Grundlegung der 'religion royale'*, Pictura et Poesis II/2 (Cologne, Weimar and Vienna, 1993), 266–8.
[47] *Pace* Nelson, 'Church's Military Service', pp. 118–21 and 127–8; cf. her later questioning of this position in '"King Across the Sea"', pp. 66–7, note 105. The same Gregorian text was similarly used by Hincmar's successor, Fulk (cf. below, pp. 51–2 and 223–8).
[48] G. Constable, '*Nona et decima*: an Aspect of Carolingian Economy', *Speculum* 35 (1960), 224–50; J. M. Wallace-Hadrill, *The Frankish Church* (Oxford, 1983), pp. 134–42 and 265–71; J. L. Nelson, 'Charles the Bald and the Church in Town and Countryside', in her *Ritual*, pp. 75–90; S. Reynolds, *Fiefs and Vassals* (Oxford, 1994), pp. 75–105.
[49] MGH Capit. I, no. 11, p. 28; Constable, '*Nona et decima*', pp. 224–31; Nelson, 'Church in Town and Countryside', pp. 77–9.
[50] E. Ewig in *The Church in the Age of Feudalism*, Handbook of Church History 3, ed. H. Judin and J. Dolan, trans. A. Briggs (New York and London, 1969), 97–125.

involved the recognition of lands held in benefice by royal or ecclesiastical vassals; some may have been quite minor tenants, additionally supported by payment.[51] As Hincmar was implying, all consumed the church's resources; in practice, land was more central, through the variety of threats posed to ecclesiastical title. Appropriation featured prominently among ninth-century complaints of abuse; at the margins, rulers responded with acts of selective restitution.[52] Yet, as Hincmar also recognized, the contribution was a reality of Frankish ecclesiastical wealth. The church itself had been the principal beneficiary of Carolingian military expansion; according to Herlihy's estimate, between 751 and 825 its landholding had grown from about ten to about thirty per cent of all territory in cultivation.[53] Exploited most intensively in the west, these measures supplied an important component in Frankish royal armies; they go a long way to explaining the political power of Carolingian bishops.

Both theory and practice upheld the distinctiveness of Frankish church land. Its service involved forms of 'gift' unique to such property.[54] There was indeed a contrast with English burdens, required from all land by fiscal mechanisms. Bookland retained these 'common' services: even at Gumley, churches owed what was due from all. The landholding in question was in any case more modest. Canterbury's archiepiscopal endowment has been estimated at approximately 700 hides at the end of the eighth century, placing it on a par with that of St Germain-des-Prés, at best a monastery of upper middle rank.[55] Bookland had nothing which could be lost through 'secularization'; the more appropriate comparison may be with land held on lease. Seemingly used for a variety of purposes, Anglo-Saxon leasing remained an ad hoc strategy, lacking formalized framework or explicit military concession.[56] In the ninth century, bookland was no longer restricted to ecclesiastical endowment, its ambiguity accentuated by many other aspects of Southumbrian change.[57] Central was the role of bishops, seemingly more

---

[51] Nelson, 'Church's Military Service', pp. 123–7; *casati* ('housed ones') may well have had 'houses' (Reynolds, *Fiefs*, p. 100, cf. MGH Capit. I, no. 20, c. 13).

[52] Nelson, 'Church's Military Service', pp. 77–8; C. J. Carroll, 'The Archbishops and Church Provinces of Mainz and Cologne during the Carolingian Period, 751–911' (unpubl. PhD dissertation, Cambridge University, 1998), pp. 244–67, for East Frankish comparison.

[53] D. Herlihy, 'Church Property on the European Continent, 701–1200', *Speculum* 36 (1961), pp. 81–105; cf. Innes, *State and Society*, pp. 41–50.

[54] Cf. Hincmar, *Quaterniones* (first part of *Pro ecclesiae libertatum defensione*) PL 125: 1050–1, contrasting the church's more recent 'beneficia' and 'annua dona' with support once rendered 'de publico'.

[55] Brooks, *Canterbury*, p. 107; Wallace-Hadrill, *Frankish Church*, p. 353.   [56] Below, pp. 99–102.

[57] Below, pp. 44–62.

militarized, but under different conditions. At Gumley, ecclesiastics had secured personal exemption from labour services; the contrast is striking with West Saxon bishops in the *Chronicle*, several of whom met their deaths in battle, yet the forces in question remained those of shire and king.[58] Rather than of landholding, the more likely variable were changes in the personal service of bishops, as fuller agents of West Saxon rule.

The differences were not only material but communicational. Hincmar's own remarks occurred in a text written for Charles the Bald at royal request. For ecclesiastics, the contribution was an aspect of self-definition; for Frankish rulers, it was the due support of a protected church. These roles were frequently central to the operation of kingship, in arenas prominently including monasteries and episcopal residences; just as crucially, they relied on a shared discourse, of rule exalted through ecclesiastical defence.[59] It was this field, above all, which generated active political theorizing in the Carolingian world, in 'Mirrors for Princes' and other instructional literature, dominated by acts of ecclesiastical advice.[60] Most fully developed in the west, the genre owed much to claims of property.[61] Some, under Louis the Pious, proposed radical reform; more common, especially later in the century, were more limited goals of 'justice' towards the church and its land, urged with considerable subtlety.[62] The contrast is deep with the very different uses of Alfredian political rhetoric; constituted socially in West Saxon arenas, its form was also shaped by the essential homogeneity of duties attached to land. Interests in bookland were now shared by secular and spiritual landholders; the common burdens were similarly due from all. In any hands, this was support for more unitary legal discourse; under Alfred, these conditions were central to rhetorical success.

[58] *ASC* s.a. 825, 845 and 871, cf. 836.
[59] Nelson, 'Church in Town and Countryside', pp. 77–89; Wallace-Hadrill, *Frankish Church*, pp. 231–41, 253–7, 266–8 and 277–8; S. Coupland, 'The Rod of God's Wrath or the People of God's Wrath? The Carolingian Theology of the Viking Invasions', *JEH* 42 (1991), 535–54; Staubach, *Rex Christianus*, esp. pp. 158–68.
[60] See esp. H. H. Anton, *Fürstenspiegel und Herrscherethos in der Karolingerzeit*, Bonner Historische Forschungen 32 (Bonn, 1968), 198–245 and 261–355; cf. below, pp. 60–2, 145–8 and 159–63.
[61] Cf. *ibid.*, pp. 229–36, 331–44 and 349–55; Staubach, *Rex Christianus*, pp. 158–68.
[62] Ewig in *The Church in the Age of Feudalism*, ed. Judin and Dolan, pp. 107–25, for Wala of Corbie's 'little book' of 829; *DIR* 1–4, pp. 176–202; Hincmar, *De ordine palatii*, ed. Gross and Schieffer, cc. 3 and 5, pp. 44–50 and 68–72; *RC* 11, 14 and 19, pp. 50–3, 62–5 and 84–7.

Chapter 3

ROYAL LORDSHIP AND SECULAR
OFFICE-HOLDING

The strength of the West Saxon polity is conventionally interpreted from the perspective of its most obvious beneficiaries, the house of Ecgberht; the success of this dynasty is the more remarkable given Ecgberht's obscure origins. Although several eighth-century kings enjoyed stable reigns, the West Saxon polity had remained regularly disrupted by brief but violent periods of strife over the throne. Ecgberht seems to have begun his career as another minor member of the West Saxon royal house, initially more concerned to pursue a claim to the kingship of Kent, than to try his luck in Wessex itself. Even according to the West Saxons' own genealogical material, when Ecgberht finally gained the throne in 802, he had been the first West Saxon king in his lineage for at least seven generations. Yet by the time this material was compiled the only viable athelings were Ecgberht's descendants; genealogy could be recorded in justificatory celebration, rather than self-defence.

This dynastic achievement shifts the focus onto other beneficiaries, the West Saxon secular nobility, whose support was the more powerful for its investment in a single family. Naturally this owed much to the efforts of Ecgberht himself, and the new rewards secured in the south-east. Both Ecgberht and Æthelwulf seem to have built very effectively on pre-existing structures of West Saxon royal power. Despite earlier dynastic instability, the eighth century also witnessed the emergence of a strongly consolidated form of kingship which enabled West Saxon kings to exert an unparalleled level of regional and local control, through the efficient delegation of royal authority. It was this system which underpinned the bonds between the West Saxon nobility and its new dynasty in the ninth century; its extension facilitated comparable bonds in the south-east after 825.

The West Saxon order was sustained fundamentally by the king's thegns (*cyninges ðegnas*). The word *ðegn* implied obligations of personal service to a higher lord.[1] In vernacular heroic poetry, *ðegnas* are most often the members of a lord's retinue, rewarded in his mead-hall; it is also primarily in this context that kings are encountered exercising lordship, as lord (*hlaford*) of their retainers.[2] Kings are also accorded the lordship of their entire people, but this universal bond is distinguished in *Beowulf* by the discrete use of two further terms, *frea* and *dryhten*.[3] In Bede's Northumbria, king's thegns (*milites* or *ministri regis*) seem to have been young, landless nobles, who served continuously in the king's retinue. When a thegn of this sort was rewarded with land, he seems to have lost these obligations of attendance, normally residing on his own estate, and acquiring the new status of 'companion' (*comes*, probably translating *gesið*). In early Wessex, in contrast, king's thegns were nobles of high status, normally holding estates of their own, who nevertheless remained regular members of the royal household.[4] The regular inclusion of a body of king's thegns in West Saxon charter witness-lists from the 830s onwards suggests some significant enhancement in their status. By definition, this was a position of personal service, sealed at the time of appointment by a formal oath of loyalty, each swearing 'to be faithful and true, and to love all that [his lord] loves, and hate all that he hates'.[5] A king's thegn did not bear any specific form of authority, but enjoyed the benefits of the king's personal protection (*mundbyrd* or *borg*), for which he might be expected to serve the king in any number of capacities. This sense of service as a recognized office is suitably captured by the substantive noun, *ðegnung*, most naturally translated as *ministerium*.[6]

In the more detailed accounts of Alfredian warfare, king's thegns may be observed at the forefront of defence against the vikings, forming an essential component of local and royal forces, sometimes leading military followers of their own.[7] Yet as vital agents of royal power, thegns could serve the king in further capacities. The office of king's reeve seems generally to have been entrusted to king's thegns, specifically attached

---

[1] H. M. Chadwick, *Studies in Anglo-Saxon Institutions* (Cambridge, 1905), pp. 76–102 and 308–54; Loyn, 'Gesiths and Thegns'; Nelson, 'Political Ideas', pp. 150–4; Abels, *Lordship*, pp. 17–18.

[2] *Beowulf* 719, 1081, 1309, 1419, 1644 and 1673, cf. 408, 1574 and 1871; 2642, 2935, 3142 and 3179.

[3] *Ibid.* 271, 359, 1484, 1680, 1831, 2402, 2560, 2576, 2901 and 2991; Chadwick, *Studies*, pp. 302–3.

[4] *Ine* 45; *ASC* s.a. 757. Cf. Chadwick, *Studies*, pp. 333–54, regarding the contrast as terminological (p. 349); Loyn, 'Gesiths and Thegns', pp. 540–9; Abels, *Alfred*, pp. 37–8, 40–1 and 264–6.

[5] *Swerian*, ed. Liebermann, *Gesetze* I, 396–7.   [6] See esp. *VA* 100, line 6.

[7] *ASC* s.a. 871, 893, 895 and 896; *VA* 42 and 54.

either to a 'wic' or to a particular royal vill.[8] King's reeves bore delegated royal authority, in that their diverse activities all involved intervention on the king's behalf: in the commercial sphere, for example, in
the regulation of transactions and the collection of royal dues. The same
was expected in the legal sphere, in local peace-keeping and dispute
settlement. Yet it was the royal household which offered duties of the
highest status, often of a mundane or ceremonial character in service to
the king. Alfred's own mother, Osburh, had been the daughter of Oslac,
Æthelwulf's 'famous butler' (*pincerna*); a charter of 892 reveals the duties
of three of Alfred's highest thegns. Deormod *cellerarius* bore responsibility
of some kind for the royal table, probably as the king's *discðegn*. Ælfric
thesaurarius, elsewhere identified as Alfred's 'rail-thegn' (*hræglðegn*), would
have guarded the king's treasures in his broader capacity as keeper of the
king's wardrobe; Sigewulf *pincerna* was evidently another royal butler
(OE *byrle*) or cup-bearer.[9] A further distinguished position was held by the
cynges horsðegn, twice mentioned in the *Chronicle* for 896.

Specially selected thegns, of the highest favour and loyalty, were
entrusted with regional responsibilities over an individual shire (*scir*), as
ealdormen. With the literal meaning 'chief man', the vernacular *ealdor-*
monn denoted an individual with authority. The word could sometimes be
employed very generally, yet in many political contexts it described an
individual who was not a king, with authority subordinate to a higher
power.[10] In Wessex, significantly, an ealdorman's subordinate position
was itself tightly defined, as authority delegated from the king. *Scir* could
also mean 'charge' or 'office'; a West Saxon ealdorman exercised his
authority strictly at the king's pleasure. His position was explicitly that of
cyninges ealdorman; according to a law of Ine, he was liable to forfeit his *scir*
through an act of negligence, 'unless the king wishes to pardon him'.[11]
'Ealdorman' was a common term for leading nobles in Mercia and
Northumbria as well as Wessex, yet political conditions differed. Only in
the Northumbrian evidence does the role of the West Saxon ealdorman
find any clear parallel; the standard Latin equivalent of 'ealdorman' in both
kingdoms was initially *prefectus*, bearing strong overtones of delegation.[12]

---

[8] A. Williams, *Kingship and Government in Pre-Conquest England, c.500–1066* (Basingstoke, 1999),
pp. 51–2 and 74–5.

[9] *VA* 2; S 348 (ed. Whitelock, 'Some Charters', pp. 78–9; trans. in K&L, *Alfred*, pp. 179–81).

[10] K&L, *Alfred*, p. 302 (note 2); H. R. Loyn, 'The Term *Ealdorman* in the Translations Prepared at
the Time of King Alfred', *EHR* 68 (1953), 513–25.

[11] *Ine* 36–36.1; cf. *Ine* 50 and *Af* 38–38.2; S. Keynes, 'Mercians', pp. 4–6; S. Keynes, 'Mercia and
Wessex in the Ninth Century', in *Mercia: an Anglo-Saxon Kingdom in Europe*, ed. M. Brown and
C. Farr (London, 2001), pp. 310–28.

[12] A. T. Thacker, 'Some Terms for Noblemen in Anglo-Saxon England, c. 650–900', *ASSAH* 2
(1981), 201–36, at 210–13.

The West Saxon shift from *prefectus* to *dux* in the 830s may reflect the heightened importance of ealdormen as military leaders, heading shire contingents into battle.[13] The territorial division of the shire seems to have distinguished Wessex fundamentally from practices in other early king-doms.[14] The shire system was firmly established by the end of the eighth century; it is tempting on many grounds to trace its ultimate origins to the reign of Ine.[15]

From their first emergence in the eighth century, West Saxon eal-dormen seem to have operated at shire level in ways which com-plemented the role fulfilled locally by the king's reeves.[16] Military responsibilities should not distract from more usual, everyday practices, implied most fully by Alfred's law-book. The impression is again of regular intervention on the king's behalf, in a wide range of spheres. In peace-keeping, both reeves and ealdormen were expected to play an active role in the pursuit of thieves and other offenders, while ealdor-men were accorded a further place in the regulation of homicidal feuds.[17] In more formal dispute settlement, reeves and ealdormen pre-sided over the summoning of local courts or 'meetings' (*gemot*), thus sustaining a nascent royal monopoly over the operation of justice (*riht*).[18] The question of 'private' justice remains controversial, but although the right to collect certain fines was clearly conceded to landlords in many charter immunities, it is unlikely that the ability to exclude royal officials was also conceded by these terms.[19] Whereas the king's reeve presided over the local popular meeting (*folcgemot*), the direct ancestor of the hundred court, an ealdorman could preside over a meeting (*gemot*) of his own, conceivably drawn from his shire as a whole.[20] There is just enough evidence for meetings at shire level to provide at least some precedent for the later shire court, first explicitly mentioned in Edgar's laws of the early 960s.[21] The duty of extracting royal fines and

[13] *ASC* s.a. 800, 825, 840, 845 and 851; S. Keynes, *An Atlas of Attestations in Anglo-Saxon Charters, c. 670–1066* (Cambridge, 2002), table XXII; cf. Thacker, 'Some Terms', pp. 205–7 and 222–3.

[14] Keynes, 'Mercians', p. 5 (note 16); cf. Campbell, 'Anglo-Saxon State', p. 16.

[15] N. P. Brooks, 'The Administrative Background to the Burghal Hidage', in *Defence*, ed. Hill and Rumble, pp. 128–50, at 133–4.

[16] D. Whitelock in *EHD*, pp. 61–5; H. R. Loyn, *The Governance of Anglo-Saxon England, 500–1087* (London, 1984), pp. 47–50, 69–70 and 73–7; Abels, *Alfred*, pp. 270–7. Cf. Williams, *Kingship*, pp. 52–6.

[17] *Ine* 73; *Af* 36–36.1; *Af* 42–42.7.   [18] Cf. Elias, *Civilizing Process*, pp. 257–61 and 268–77.

[19] See esp. *Ine* 50, with P. Wormald, 'Lordship and Justice in the Early English Kingdom: Oswaldslow Revisited', in his *Legal Culture*, pp. 313–32.

[20] *Af* 22 and 34; *VA* 106, lines 1–6. *Af* 38; *VA* 106, lines 1–6; cf. *Ine* 8.

[21] *Pace* P. Wormald in *The Blackwell Encyclopaedia*, ed. Lapidge, pp. 126–7. S. Keynes, 'The Fonthill Letter', in *Words, Texts and Manuscripts: Studies presented to Helmut Gneuss*, ed. M. Korhammer with K. Reichl and H. Sauer (Cambridge, 1992), pp. 53–97, at 80 and 84–5; III *Æthelstan*, with S. Keynes, 'Royal Government and the Written Word in Late Anglo-Saxon England', in *The*

imprisoning offenders seems largely to have been fulfilled by reeves, but one of Alfred's laws describes a royal fine collected by ealdormen, in terms implying some entitlement to personal profit.[22] An ealdorman was also entitled to *feorm*, and perhaps to specific estates attached to his office;[23] both would have aided mobility, in constant perambulation of his *scir*.

It has long been recognized that many West Saxon ealdormen might be detected in charters at an earlier stage, as *ministri*, yet the implications of this career route remain largely unexplored.[24] There is every sign that this was the *only* route to the office of ealdorman in normal circumstances. The *Chronicle*'s list of 'the best king's thegns' who had died before 896 includes three ealdormen; one, Beorhtwulf of Essex, cannot be detected as a *minister* in earlier charters. As in the case of royal reeves, West Saxon ealdormen *were*, and indeed *remained*, king's thegns; their office represented an additional responsibility, dependent upon prior obligations of loyalty and service. The charter record is more than consistent with this conclusion. Of the forty-five ninth-century ealdormen whose known careers end before Alfred's accession, some twelve may be plausibly identified as *ministri* of the same name in earlier charters.[25] This statistic is more impressive than it sounds, as thegnly attestations are only regularly recorded from the 830s. The Alfredian data is firmer: of twenty-six individuals known to have served as ealdormen in Alfred's reign, as many as thirteen may be plausibly identified as king's thegns in earlier charters.[26]

It is tempting to interpret these patterns as the raising of 'new men' from relative obscurity, but although certain individuals benefited significantly from royal favour, a different picture emerges from the evidence of aristocratic names, generally the only available indicator of possible familial relationships. It is striking that many leading-names recur regularly among the wider body of ninth-century king's thegns and ealdormen, whereas successive ealdormen of the same shire rarely share the same leading-name.[27] The most likely model, borne out by the few relationships that are more securely documented, is of a tightly knit body of regional aristocratic families, distinguished by their consistent

---

Uses of Literacy in Early Medieval Europe, ed. R. McKitterick (Cambridge, 1990), pp. 226–57, at 238–41.

[22] *Af* 37–37.2, with Whitelock in *EHD*, pp. 63–4.

[23] Chadwick, *Studies*, p. 171; F. M. Stenton, *Anglo-Saxon England*, 3rd edn (Oxford, 1971), p. 486; S 340 (BCS 520).

[24] Chadwick, *Studies*, pp. 295–6. Cf. Loyn, *Governance*, pp. 47–8; Abels, *Alfred*, pp. 270–2.

[25] The figures proceed from an analysis of Keynes, *Atlas*, table XXI.

[26] Cf. Abels, *Alfred*, p. 271, suggesting figures of twenty-five and fifteen respectively.

[27] Keynes, *Atlas*, table XXII.

service to the house of Ecgberht, competing among themselves for the attractive opportunities of regional delegation.[28] King Æthelwulf's Kentish *cellerarius*, Æthelmod, succeeded his own brother Ealhhere as ealdorman in 853.[29] Ælfred, ealdorman of Surrey, included provisions in his will for his son, Æthelwald, probably an ealdorman of Kent in the 880s, and for a kinsman, Sigewulf, probably to be identified as King Alfred's *pincerna*, who became an ealdorman of Kent in the late 890s.[30] A Wiltshire thegn Cenwold stipulated that a bequest to his son was to be strictly conditional on his future service to the king as ealdorman (in this case rendered as *comes*). In the event, the estate ultimately passed to Ordlaf, ealdorman of Wiltshire in the 890s, himself the grandson of another ealdorman, Eanwulf.[31]

These few, tantalizing examples help to explain what was perhaps the single most important feature of the West Saxon order in the ninth century: its enduring and unprecedented stability. It is the possibility of dynastic intrigue and rebellion which has generally received greater attention: significant tensions can indeed be detected at several points during the ninth century, yet their character, always narrowly focused on Ecgberht's dynasty, seems only to underline the stabilizing effects of this hegemony.[32] Every family that mattered had its share of king's thegns; quite understandably, they were only willing to jeopardize these positions in extreme circumstances, effectively restraining the rivalries that inevitably arose within the royal house. Shifts of loyalty could only be achieved en masse, as in 856, when Æthelwulf was forced to relinquish Wessex to his eldest son Æthelbald.[33] Dangers of 'internal strife' (*clades intestina*) seem vividly refracted in the story of Cynewulf and Cyneheard in the *Chronicle*'s annal for 757, encapsulated by the trauma of Cynewulf's surviving thegns, obliged to slay their own traitorous kinsmen.[34] Disloyalty was always costly: its heavy price in the ninth century is evident from the case of ealdorman Wulfhere, reportedly punished by forfeiture for deserting 'both his lord King Alfred and his country, in spite of the oath that he had earlier sworn to the king and

[28] For one possible family, with the leading-name 'Os', see J. L. Nelson, 'Reconstructing a Royal Family: Reflections on Alfred, from Asser, chapter 2', in her *Ruling Families*, no. 3, pp. 54–61.
[29] See Brooks, *Canterbury*, pp. 148–9.
[30] S 1508 (*SEHD*, no. 10), with Keynes, *Atlas*, table XXII.
[31] S 368 (BCS 600), with Keynes, 'Fonthill Letter', p. 57 (note 25); cf. Abels, *Lordship*, p. 44.
[32] Cf. J. L. Nelson, '"King Across the Sea"'; Nelson, 'Reconstructing a Royal Family', in her *Ruling Families*, no. 3; P. Stafford, 'Charles the Bald, Judith and England', in *Charles the Bald: Court and Kingdom*, ed. M. T. Gibson and J. L. Nelson, 2nd edn (Aldershot, 1990), pp. 139–53.
[33] *VA* 12.
[34] S. D. White, 'Kinship and Lordship in Early Medieval England: the Story of Sigeberht, Cynewulf and Cyneheard', *Viator* 20 (1989), 1–18, cf. H. Kleinschmidt, 'The Old English Annal for 757 and West Saxon Dynastic Strife', *Journal of Medieval History* 22 (1996), 209–24.

all his leading men'.[35] The incident is conventionally cited as illustrating Alfredian innovation, but the oath in question may well have been that already incumbent on office-holders, as thegns of the king.[36] Indeed, apart from the events of 856, Wulfhere supplies the only specific example of aristocratic rebellion during Alfred's lifetime. Rather than regular discord, his unusual fate points to the prevailing effectiveness of royal lordship, fully established before Alfred's accession.

THE ROYAL HOUSEHOLD

The role of king's thegns supported a special position for the West Saxon royal household, as the concentrated and continuous locus of power over the kingdom. The itineraries of ninth-century kings reveal a household in regular perambulation between favoured royal vills (*tunas*) and other centres, with a marked preference for locations within the core shires of Hampshire, Wiltshire, Dorset and Somerset.[37] The central focus at such sites would have been a large, wooden-framed open hall, sometimes described as a *palatium*; more temporary accommodation was also available in the form of tents.[38] None of these centres possessed the pre-eminence of such Frankish palaces as Aachen or Ingelheim; the West Saxon pattern of restricted itinerancy would outlive tenth-century expansion.[39] Although aided by the availability of food-renders and hunting resources, such practices were sustained more deeply by the priority of ready access to the king, so far as this was compatible with a near-continuous presence in the West Saxon heartlands. The location of the royal retinue or household (*hired*) was entirely dependent on the location of the king: whether at a royal vill (*tun*) as the 'king's home' (*cyninges ham*), at a royal assembly (his *gemot*), or at the head of an army (his *fyrd*). A passage of expansion in Alfred's translation of Augustine captures the magnetic pull of the king's presence, describing the wide variety of journeys undertaken by those seeking the royal household, whether long or short, smooth or difficult, and the widely varying degrees of honour (*ar*) and familiarity (*eaðnes*) accorded to such men upon their arrival.[40] This accords closely with the orderly administration of the royal household (*regalis familiaritas*) described by Asser. Alfred's

---

[35] S 362 (BCS 595; trans. in *EHD*, no. 100); Nelson, '"King Across the Sea"', pp. 53–6.

[36] Cf. esp. Wormald, 'Ninth Century', p. 155; below, pp. 239–40.

[37] D. Hill, *An Atlas of Anglo-Saxon England* (Oxford, 1981), pp. 83–4.

[38] *VA* 104, lines 19–20.

[39] Hill, *Atlas*, pp. 87–91; J. Campbell, 'The United Kingdom of England: the Anglo-Saxon Achievement', in his *Anglo-Saxon State*, pp. 31–53, at 47–9.

[40] *Solil* p. 77, line 5, to p. 78, line 7 (trans. in K&L, *Alfred*, pp. 143–4). Cf. *Soliloquia* I.xiii.23, p. 35, lines 3–14.

thegns are reported to have been divided into three cohorts, each spending one month in every three at the royal court (*curtus regius*), the other two 'at home' (*domum*).[41] Only the king's thegns would have possessed the necessary estates of their own, thus underlining their distinction from other royal dependants, such as the fighting-men (*bellatores*) who constituted the king's personal military retinue, who were probably landless.[42] The higher honour accorded to king's thegns reflected their ability to serve even at a distance, from their own landed estates. Neither *gesiðcund monn* nor *ðegn* appears in Alfred's own laws, suggesting some fluidity of terminology at a time when *ðegn* was rapidly supplanting *gesið* as a term of status as well as function.[43] *Ðegn* is universally preferred in Alfred's own translations; royal use of *geferscipe* or 'fellowship' as the standard collective noun strengthens the case for strong group identity.[44]

The rotation of thegns cannot be charted in detail, but the system described by Asser is consistent with the general pattern of ninth-century charter attestations, whose unusual intermittency has long been recognized.[45] One may focus on the household's operation within Wessex, though similar practices extended to the eastern regions, where it was primarily attended by thegns based in Kent.[46] It is frustratingly difficult in most cases to distinguish charters which may have emanated from an organized assembly or military expedition from those perhaps issued as part of the daily business of the royal household. So far as assemblies can be identified at all, they seem most likely to have occurred irregularly, with higher levels of attendance which were still far from comprehensive.[47] Rarer still were 'bipartite' assemblies, drawing on the king's men in the south-east as well as Wessex.[48] The West Saxon charters of Æthelwulf include the names of nearly forty king's thegns, but in no fewer than three charters, apparently providing everyday snapshots of attendance, there are in each case eight thegns as witnesses.[49] Under Æthelwulf's elder sons, some forty thegns may be identifiable as West Saxon, but the number of thegns actually in attendance ranges between five and fourteen in what seem to be normal

---

[41] *VA* 100, lines 7–22.
[42] *VA* 100, lines 1–6, cf. 53 and 55. Nelson, 'Church's Military Service', pp. 119–20; Nelson, ' "King Across the Sea" ', p. 67; cf. Nelson, 'Political Ideas', pp. 150–2, for questionable reading of *faselli* as thegns (cf. S 369).
[43] Loyn, 'Gesiths and Thegns', pp. 540–9; cf. Chadwick, *Studies*, pp. 87–102.
[44] *Bo* XXXVII, p. 111, line 15 and XXXVIII, p. 116, line 21; cf. XVII, p. 40, lines 19–23.
[45] Chadwick, *Studies*, pp. 311–15.   [46] Keynes, 'Kent', pp. 120–31.
[47] Abels, *Alfred*, pp. 261–3.   [48] Keynes, 'Kent', pp. 128–30.
[49] Figures calculated from Keynes, *Atlas*, table XXI. S 298, cf. S 1438 and S 290, both overlooked by Chadwick (*Studies*, pp. 314–15).

conditions.[50] At least thirty West Saxon thegns emerge from Alfred's charters, but the usual number of thegnly witnesses is again only seven or eight.[51]

The extent to which thegnly attendance was affected by geographical location requires further investigation; if ealdormen may serve as a guide, it seems that some journeys to the royal household were indeed lengthy and difficult.[52] Yet it is unclear whether ealdormen spent as much as a third of their time away from their shires. The relatively common attestation of as many as five or six West Saxon ealdormen suggests that different arrangements may initially have applied in their case. Yet this full complement is rarely found in Alfred's charters, where between one and three ealdormen are usually in attendance, the culmination of a trend first evident in the middle of the century.[53] The overall impression is of a political community well equipped to operate without the direct contact of regular assemblies, and increasingly forced to do so under the pressures of viking attack. Consensus was sustained fundamentally through the regular rotation of personnel in the royal household. It was perhaps often on this (indirect) basis that Alfred could claim to have acted on the advice and witness of 'all' his councillors or 'wise men' (*witan*).[54]

All these conditions placed a premium on the attractive capacity of the royal household, as the immediate locus of royal power. This was ensured above all by the presence of the king himself, which enabled the household to function as a continuous stage for the operation and renewal of royal lordship. 'Some men are in the chamber (*bur*), some in the hall (*heall*), some on the threshing-floor (*oden*), some in prison (*carcern*)': Alfred's translation emphasizes the hierarchical degrees of familiarity available at the 'king's home', before insisting nevertheless that 'all of them live through the one lord's favour (*ar*), just as as all men live under the one sun and by its light see everything that they see'.[55] The king's actions acquired meaning through the composition of those permitted to observe them; the regular feature of the king's chamber

---

[50] Keynes, *Atlas*, table XXIII(b). S 333 (BCS 510; *Sherborne*, ed. O'Donovan, no. 6) records two special occasions attended by unusually large numbers of thegns.

[51] Calculated from Keynes, *Atlas*, table XXI (S 345 and S 350 not considered because their lists include an uncertain number of south-eastern thegns). See esp. S 1275, S 352, S 348, S 356 and S 355.

[52] Keynes, *Atlas*, table XXII.

[53] Only three Alfredian charters are witnessed by more than three ealdormen: S 1275 and S 343, cf. S 345 (BCS 550), recording the household 'in expeditione' at Epsom, Surrey. Cf. Abels, *Alfred*, p. 263.

[54] *Af* Int.49.9–10; Alfred's will, in *SEHD*, no. 11, pp. 15–16 (trans. in K&L, *Alfred*, pp. 174–8).

[55] *Solil* p. 77, line 18, to p. 78, line 2 (trans. in K&L, *Alfred*, p. 144).

(*bur*) at royal vills created a hidden sphere of the highest intimacy, to which access was restricted.[56] In recounting the course of a dispute over land at Fonthill, Wiltshire, begun in the latter part of Alfred's reign, Ordlaf, ealdorman of Wiltshire, described how the relevant parties had approached while Alfred was washing his hands in his *bur* at the royal vill of Wardour.[57] Conversely, royal actions outside the chamber exhibited a further level of theatricality, doubly heightened in the case of mundane or intimate behaviour, thus consciously exposed. The king played his role primarily as lord of his household, entertaining thegns and dependants with the produce of his table in communal feasting, and with hunting expeditions along favoured royal trails. Participation in such mundane activities provided invaluable opportunities to gain the king's particular favour, and to bend his ear on matters of concern.

The vertical bonds of royal lordship were largely complemented, not weakened, by the horizontal implications of the king's friendship (*freondscipe*). Both relied fundamentally upon reciprocal expressions of love within the royal household: *familiaris dilectio*, as Asser puts it.[58] To be acknowledged as the king's friend was an honour which enhanced all obligations of service, while also yielding the prospect of additional favours.[59] Although friendship in general is a prominent concept in Alfred's translations, the term *deorling* is employed more specifically to denote those exalted by close friendship to a king or powerful man.[60] These *deorlingas* or 'dear ones' were presumably the king's most trusted advisers, whose ability to speak freely could protect the king from many potential difficulties, thus creating further, more precarious, opportunities for advancement.[61] It is important to delineate the practical benefits of royal favour, part of what is sometimes termed *Königsnähe* ('closeness to the king'). The absolute value of loyalty gave the king considerable discretion in the distribution of land and offices. The possibility of marriage into the male royal line offered a further, more exclusive reward, seemingly enjoyed to the full by the family of Æthelwulf's wife, Osburh, and

---

[56] Cf. King Cynewulf's *bur* at 'Merantun' (*ASC* s.a. 757); S. Keynes, *The Diplomas of King Æthelred 'the Unready' 978–1016* (Cambridge, 1980), p. 159, for the title *burðegn*, equivalent to Alfred's *hræglðegn*, indicating formal responsibility for the royal chamber. Cf. *VA* 104, lines 13–26, for 'windows, walls, wall-panels and partitions', all prone to cracks.

[57] Keynes, 'Fonthill Letter', pp. 73–5 (with note 91).

[58] *VA* 76, line 40.

[59] J. Barrow, 'Friends and Friendship in Anglo-Saxon Charters', and G. Althoff, 'Friendship and Political Order', both in *Friends and Friendship in Medieval Europe*, ed. J. Haseldine (Stroud, 1999), pp. 106–23 and 91–105.

[60] *Solil* p. 94, lines 2–6, and p. 96, line 23, to p. 97, line 2. *Bo* XXVII, p. 62, line 14; XXVIII, p. 64, line 28; XXIX, p. 65, line 4, and p. 67, line 15; XXXIX, p. 133, line 12.

[61] *VA* 91: 'nobilissimos sibique dilectissimos suos ministros' ('his thegns most noble and dear to him', preferable to K&L, *Alfred*, pp. 101–2).

latterly by that of Æthelred's queen, Wulfthryth, perhaps the sister of ealdorman Wulfhere.[62] Yet it was another aristocratic concern, the settlement of disputes, which arguably offered the greatest benefits of personal access. The king's role as final arbiter created powerful obligations to accept his judgement, whenever justice could not be obtained 'at home'. This was openly described in ealdorman Ordlaf's letter: Alfred's judgement after washing his hands gave much benefit of the doubt to an acknowledged thief, Helmstan, Ordlaf's own godson.[63]

GIFTS AND GIFT-GIVING

The ambiguity of royal favour was further expressed through the giving of gifts.[64] Land was fundamental: much secular landholding would have been held as folkland. Some at least of these estates represented forms of gift, held 'on loan' from the king as lord; though its precise terms have been much debated, such tenure was in some sense precarious, directly bound to faithful service.[65] Bookland conversely offered perpetual tenure; its advantages benefited both the recipient and his prospective heirs. Yet the 'booking' of land could mask a variety of transactions. By no means the majority need have involved an estate previously in royal hands; many will have concerned land already held on other terms.[66] In some cases 'booking' could be secured through payment, occasionally recorded in the charters of West Saxon kings, supplementing royal income.[67] The sheer scope and complexity of aristocratic land management shows the power at stake in its courtly negotiation, united by loanland and bookland as monopolistic royal gifts. The 'booking' of land was a deeply symbolic act, in which the written charter functioned as the title-deeds to the land in question, conducted in the presence of recorded aristocratic witnesses who may have played some active role in the ceremony.[68] As a form of document conventionally written in Latin,

---

[62] Nelson, 'Reconstructing a Royal Family', esp. p. 58.

[63] *II Æthelstan* 3, *III Edgar* 2 and *II Cnut* 17; Keynes, 'Fonthill Letter', pp. 66–7 and 73–4.

[64] M. Mauss, *The Gift: the Form and Reason for Exchange in Archaic Societies*, trans. W. D. Halls (London, 1990 [1925]); cf. Sawyer, 'Kings and Merchants', p. 141; A. J. Bijsterveld, 'The Medieval Gift as Agent of Social Bonding and Political Power: a Comparative Approach', in *Medieval Transformations: Texts, Power, and Gifts in Context*, ed. E. Cohen and M. de Jong (Leiden, 2001), pp. 123–56.

[65] Keynes, *Diplomas*, pp. 31–3, cf. E. John, *Land Tenure in Early England* (Leicester, 1960), pp. 51–3.

[66] Keynes, *Diplomas*, pp. 32–3; cf. esp. S 328 (BCS 496; *Charters*, ed. Robertson; trans. in *EHD*, no. 93).

[67] S 282, S 287, S 296, S 297, S 327, S 330, S 332, S 337, S 344 (all lying outside Wessex, in the eastern regions); J. Campbell, 'The Sale of Land and the Economics of Power in Early England: Problems and Possibilities', in his *Anglo-Saxon State*, pp. 227–45.

[68] S. Kelly, 'Anglo-Saxon Lay Society and the Written Word', in *Literacy*, ed. McKitterick, pp. 36–62, at 44.

the charter provided an additional subtext to the donation, necessarily mysterious to most secular witnesses even if it were translated orally for their benefit. A typical dispositive formula justified the king's gift of land to a thegn 'on account of his humble obedience, and because he has always been my faithful *minister* in all matters'.[69]

Perhaps in response to new conditions of warfare, the sudden sparsity of land grants after *c.* 870 threw greater emphasis onto other forms of gift, in another sphere of royal performance. Two gold finger-rings associated with the West Saxon dynasty in the mid-ninth century, respectively inscribed with the names of King Æthelwulf and of his daughter Æthelswith, as queen of the Mercians, seem more likely to represent royal gifts than personal possessions.[70] Rings are well-attested as gifts of lordship in vernacular poetry, typically directed towards secular recipients. Asser's stylized account of Alfred's redistribution of annual revenues may be mediated through papal or biblical models, yet probably also reflects a heightened concern for ordered largesse.[71] It is less clear that Alfred was any wealthier than his predecessors.[72] No less than one half of royal income was reserved for 'secular affairs', with one third of this assigned to the king's most important servants: his fighting-men, and the entire body of king's thegns. It is unlikely that such payments would have consisted entirely of coin (or indeed of bullion). Alfred's known gifts suggest other possibilities: a sword worth 100 mancuses bequeathed to ealdorman Æthelred, 'an extremely valuable silk cloak' given to Asser,[73] and the diverse output of royal craftsmen. Significantly, there is no evidence for counter-gifts (if land transactions are excluded). As a tool of power, the king's gifts created obligations which could only be redeemed through continuous service and loyalty.

Only foreigners were in a position to give gifts to the West Saxon king, often in instances of complex exchange which served to establish or affirm relationships necessarily open to negotiation. This is most clearly evident in the extensive contacts which the West Saxon dynasty sustained with important neighbours on the European mainland, encouraged by viking pressure. High-level contacts between Wessex and the Carolingian world had been initiated much earlier, during Ecgberht's exile in Francia (probably *c.* 789–92), where his presence had

---

[69] S 316 (BCS 467), dated 855 (for ? 853).

[70] C. Haith in *Golden Age*, nos. 9 and 10; L. Webster in *Making of England*, nos. 243 and 244.

[71] *VA* 99–102; Alfred's will, in *SEHD*, no. 11, p. 18, lines 16–20, implying regular apportionment at Easter; Nelson, '"King Across the Sea"', p. 51, note 36.

[72] *Pace* Maddicott, 'Trade, Industry', esp. pp. 4–6; cf. Nelson, 'Debate: Trade, Industry', esp. pp. 151–4 and 161–2.

[73] Alfred's will, in *SEHD*, no. 11, p. 18, lines 15–16; *VA* 81.

probably related primarily to the power of Offa, then supreme in Kent.[74] Only in the 830s did these contacts intensify, by which time Ecgberht and Æthelwulf could receive greater respect from their Carolingian counterparts, as founders of another ascendant dynasty, parallel to their own. Æthelwulf's marriage of 856 to Judith, daughter of the West Frankish ruler Charles the Bald, has been plausibly interpreted as sealing a formal alliance against viking activity, heightened on either side of the Channel.[75] Yet, in addition to co-ordinating intelligence and tactics, Æthelwulf and his successors acquired further advantages from their Continental contacts in the sphere of behaviour and display, no less potent for being essentially non-military. In general terms, in tending to establish monopolistic control over goods and practices which were more or less novel to the West Saxon nobility, Æthelwulf and his successors effectively established a monopoly also over what Bourdieu has usefully termed 'cultural capital': namely, 'a form of knowledge ... which equips the social agent with empathy towards, appreciation for or competence in deciphering cultural relations and cultural artefacts'.[76] Novel experiences only available at the royal household tapped the power at stake in courtly interaction, creating additional opportunities for horizontal bonding and the expression of royal favour.

One early example is the distinctive aesthetic qualities of the two royal rings, virtually unprecedented in an Anglo-Saxon context as items of secular metalwork adorned with Christian iconography, rather than abstract decoration. Although executed in the 'Trewhiddle style' of native metalwork, both schemes are themselves unprecedented in an earlier Anglo-Saxon context, but find striking parallels in art associated with the Carolingian dynasty.[77] To receive gifts of this sort from the West Saxon dynasty was to acquire exclusive access to forms of learned display, carefully adapted to existing aristocratic tastes. The ability of West Saxon rulers to deal on these terms with such prestigious figures as successive Carolingian rulers and popes can only have enhanced the desirability of their imported 'capital'. Another example is the evidence that first emerges in Æthelwulf's reign for a body of priests attached to the royal household, providing religious services of a militant character, tailor-made for warfare against pagan enemies. Parallels with Carolingian

---

[74] S. Keynes, 'The Kingdom of the Mercians in the Eighth Century', in *Æthelbald and Offa: Two Eighth-Century Mercian Kings*, ed. D. H. Hill and M. Worthington (Oxford, 2005), pp. 1–26.

[75] Wallace-Hadrill, 'Franks and the English', in his *Early Medieval History*, p. 209; Stafford, 'Charles the Bald, Judith', pp. 142–4 and 152; Nelson, 'Franks and the English', pp. 141–8; J. Story, *Carolingian Connections: Anglo-Saxon England and Carolingian Francia, c.750–870* (Aldershot, 2003), pp. 213–55.

[76] R. Johnson in Bourdieu, *Cultural Production*, ed. Johnson, p. 7.   [77] Below, pp. 65–6.

court practices suggest direct influence; it is probably no coincidence that one of Æthelwulf's priests should have been Frankish (to judge from the reported duties of his Frankish secretary Felix), even if other known priests before Alfred's reign seem most likely to have been West Saxons.[78] The efficiency of exchange is frequently striking. Alfred would acquire the versatile Grimbald of St-Bertin through the domestic gift of English guard-dogs.[79]

Both Grimbald and John the Old Saxon recall the earlier role of Felix, yet it is important to acknowledge the ingredients which made Alfredian 'capital' novel and distinctive. First, in a significant broadening of horizons beyond the Carolingian world, Alfredian cultural exchanges were consciously cosmopolitan, drawing on sources as diverse as Elias, patriarch of Jerusalem, who sent the king medicines; and the Norwegian merchant Ottar, who gave tusks of walrus-ivory, probably in return for protection.[80] At the same time, political developments facilitated the acquisition of personnel from new sources closer to home: not only from Wales and Mercia, but also Ireland and Brittany.[81] Intercourse of this sort established a further monopoly over distant news and information, from the limits of the known world. It also ensured the unique effectiveness of Alfredian 'capital', enabling an extraordinary range of influences to be combined in new and original ways, more appropriate to local conditions. The other departure was more fundamental. The highest form of 'capital' became knowledge itself, now subject to an extreme extension of control: direct appropriation of production by the person of the king. The dissemination of knowledge represented a further extension of West Saxon productive efficiency; its tangible media relied on the added value of learned expertise.

Æthelwulf and his sons were uniquely placed to exploit such 'cultural capital', in marked contrast to their nearest Insular neighbours. Simon Keynes has argued for the very different nature of Mercian political relationships, far less dynastically stable and operating in ways which hindered any accumulation of power in the Mercian royal household. Only occasionally are thegns encountered in Mercian witness-lists, never more than four together; rather than royal office-holders, Mercian

---

[78] *VA* 37–8; S. Keynes, 'The West Saxon Charters of King Æthelwulf and his Sons', *EHR* 109 (1994), 1109–49, at 1131–7 and 1146–7, esp. 1132 (note 1). Cf. D. A. Bullough and A. L. H. Corrêa, 'Texts, Chant, and the Chapel of Louis the Pious', in *Charlemagne's Heir*, ed. P. Godman and R. Collins (Oxford, 1990), pp. 489–508.

[79] Letter of Fulk, archbishop of Rheims, to King Alfred, in *C&S*, no. 4, p. 10; trans. in K&L, *Alfred*, pp. 184–5.

[80] Pratt, 'Illnesses', pp. 67–73. Or I.1, pp. 14–15; C. E. Fell in *Two Voyagers at the Court of King Alfred*, ed. N. Lund (York, 1984), pp. 58–61.

[81] *VA* 76; K&L, *Alfred*, p. 258 (note 157).

ealdormen seem more likely to have been 'the hereditary or chosen leaders of different peoples within the extended Mercian world'.[82] The primary theatre of power was supplied by comprehensive royal assemblies, where Mercian kings typically acted 'with the permission and witness of [all] the magnates (*optimates*) of the Mercian people'.[83] Further west, Asser's wonder at the grandeur of Alfred's household must be read against his experiences in the company of southern Welsh rulers, whose charters are generally witnessed only by local aristocrats, drawn from a narrow geographical radius.[84]

What distinguished the West Saxon household was the comprehensive range of privileges at the king's effective disposal; in this respect the West Saxon order more closely resembled the forms of patrimonial rule also familiar from the Carolingian world. In each case, the royal household supported a 'court society', driven by aristocratic competition for local power, expressed as delegated royal offices (Carolingian *honores*).[85] The parallel helps to explain why Carolingian ideas and models were immediately relevant to West Saxon concerns. Yet West Saxon practices remained essentially endogenous; it is their distinctiveness which best accounts for the relative strength of West Saxon royal power. Above all, with the possible exception of the East Frankish kingdom, the territories ruled by Carolingian rulers were simply too geographically diffuse to allow a comparable level of personal contact with their entire aristocracies.[86] Hincmar's idealized picture highlights different conditions of 'familiarity', in the twofold division of rule between the 'king's palace' and general assemblies (*placita*).[87] While the former supported a substantial and continuous aristocratic community, it was the latter which upheld the 'condition of the entire realm' (*totius regni status*).[88] Palace *ministeriales*, including the chamberlain (*camerarius*) and count of the palace (*comes palatii*), are portrayed as effectively constrained by the will of general assemblies, while capable of interim action on matters ideally reserved for collective decision.[89] Though Hincmar was evoking

---

[82] Keynes, 'Mercia and Wessex', esp. pp. 320–3; Keynes, 'Mercians', pp. 4–6; Keynes, 'Kingdom of the Mercians', esp. pp. 18–21.

[83] S 197 (BCS 454); cf. S 193, S 198, S 210, S 212 and S 214.

[84] Davies, *An Early Welsh Microcosm*, pp. 111–20; W. Davies, 'Land and Power in Early Medieval Wales', *P&P* 81 (November 1978), 3–23, at 13–15.

[85] See material cited above, pp. 10–11, esp. Innes, *State and Society*, pp. 195–222, documenting mechanisms of royal appointment; cf. Goldberg, *Empire*, pp. 10–11, 221–2 and 268–9.

[86] Nelson, 'Kingship and Royal Government', pp. 406–8; cf. Goldberg, *Empire*, pp. 186–200 and 206–30.

[87] *De ordine palatii*, cc. 4–5 and 5–7, pp. 56–96. Nelson, 'Aachen', pp. 226–32, for the seemingly composite nature of the text, written by Hincmar in 882, incorporating earlier material by Adalard of Corbie (*c.* 781 or 810–14).

[88] *De ordine palatii*, cc. 3–4, pp. 54–6; c. 6, p. 82.   [89] *Ibid.*, c. 6, pp. 88–90.

earlier conditions, these aspects may well have been familiar from contemporary rule: they harmonize suggestively with the power of later West Frankish assemblies, as occasions of ritualized mutual undertaking between the king and his faithful men, preceding judgements sealed by the will of all.[90]

Closely related are other differences in gift and exchange. Certainly, Carolingian courts were arenas of royal distribution: beyond the sharing of plunder, best attested under Charlemagne, lay more regularized support for *ministeriales* and other servants.[91] Hincmar describes gifts administered annually by queen and chamberlain; Notker pictured Louis the Pious giving Easter gifts of weaponry and clothing.[92] Such practices may well have related closely to gifts of land and *honores*, delicately negotiated in the same environment.[93] Yet royal gift-giving was here qualified by mechanisms in the opposite direction, from *fideles* to ruler, also in evidence at the political centre. Rendered in military equipment or in kind, Carolingian 'annual gifts' were an important form of internal taxation, matched in the east by tribute payments from external *gentes*.[94] Some of this counter-flow was probably represented at assemblies: according to Hincmar, wide attendance was necessary for all to present gifts, which the king received publicly while senior councillors were withdrawn.[95] Crucially, it was this latter direction which was more consistently exploited for books and texts, regularly presented to Carolingian rulers as part of ecclesiastical interplay.[96] When 'royal' books were given, all the best attested examples again concern favoured churches; there may have been no need, nor incentive, for comparable secular gift-giving.[97] By a variety of means, in contrast, West Saxon rulers had effectively monopolized 'generosity'. The full force of Carolingian largesse was reserved for more restricted purposes, the courtly cultivation of reforming rule.

[90] J. L. Nelson, 'Legislation and Consensus in the Reign of Charles the Bald', in her *Ritual*, pp. 91–116 (cf. *De ordine palatii*, c. 6, p. 82, specifying two assemblies per year); this seems excessively revised in J. L. Nelson, 'Alfred's Carolingian Contemporaries', in *Alfred*, ed. Reuter, pp. 293–310, at 308.

[91] For the former, cf. Reuter, 'Plunder and Tribute', pp. 75–81.

[92] *De ordine palatii*, c. 5, pp. 72–4, cf. 80–2; Notker the Stammerer, *Gesta Karoli Magni Imperatoris*, ed. Haefele, II.21, pp. 91–2, cf. I.29, pp. 39–40.

[93] Innes, *State and Society*, pp. 195–222; Nelson, *Charles the Bald*, pp. 42–3, 56–7, 177–9, 185 and 211–15, cf. 71.

[94] Reuter, 'Plunder and Tribute', pp. 85–6; Goldberg, *Empire*, pp. 195–6 and 203–6.

[95] *De ordine palatii*, c. 5, p. 82; c. 7, p. 92.

[96] See esp. R. McKitterick, 'Charles the Bald (823–77) and his Library: the Patronage of Learning', in her *The Frankish Kings and Culture in the Early Middle Ages* (Aldershot, 1995), no. 5; Goldberg, *Empire*, pp. 166, 173, 184–5 and 192, for books given to Louis the German.

[97] McKitterick, 'Charles the Bald and his Library'; R. McKitterick, 'Royal Patronage of Culture in the Frankish Kingdoms under the Carolingians: Motives and Consequences', in her *Frankish Kings*, no. 7; cf. contrasts drawn by Nelson, 'Carolingian Contemporaries', pp. 306–10.

Chapter 4

ROYAL LORDSHIP AND ECCLESIASTICAL OFFICE-HOLDING

Any consideration of ecclesiastical power in early Anglo-Saxon England must proceed from its dependence on royal support and protection. From the earliest phases of conversion, Christianity had relied on the aura of royal authorization. The endowment of religious houses sometimes drew on royal lands, and always relied upon royal approval. Such transfers of land were only possible because their recipients were also largely members of royal and aristocratic kindreds. Ecclesiastical structures offered many opportunities for the local extension of power, not only through informal networks of patronage, but also the more general task of establishing regularized Christian practices. Yet such priorities were compromised in England by the limited extent of early kingdoms, within the wider English church.[1] South of the Humber, the attendance of bishops at annual synods, summoned by the archbishop of Canterbury, sustained an episcopal agenda beyond the needs of any single ruler. Successive Mercian rulers attended merely as the most powerful among interested secular parties.[2] Synods retained a range of effective monopolies, providing an established forum for the election and consecration of bishops.[3]

A further monopoly was retained over the settlement of disputes involving bookland.[4] Royal co-operation was probably vital, yet the position of Mercian rulers was inevitably conditioned by their ambitions in the south-east. Southumbrian bishops held a strong negotiating position, which they proceeded to defend in terms which radically

[1] Nelson, '"King Across the Sea"', pp. 61–7; J. Campbell, 'Placing King Alfred', in *Alfred*, ed. Reuter, pp. 3–23, at 6–12; J. Blair, *The Church in Anglo-Saxon Society* (Oxford, 2005), pp. 121–34 and 291–341, for telling perspectives on Southumbria.

[2] C. Cubitt, *Anglo-Saxon Church Councils c.650–c.850* (Leicester, 1995), pp. 49–59 and 205–34; S. Keynes, *The Councils of Clofesho*, Brixworth Lecture 1993, University of Leicester Vaughan Paper 38 (Leicester, 1994), pp. 21–2.

[3] Cubitt, *Councils*, pp. 25 and 65.   [4] *Ibid.*, pp. 65–74.

asserted their autonomy. Just as kings presided over secular matters, so bishops were entitled to preside in all matters pertaining to God; kings were admonished to obey their bishops 'with great humility', and to respect their immunity from the judgement of secular men.[5] It was perhaps inevitable that Mercian rulers should have sought so determinedly to undermine the position of Canterbury, initially through Offa's establishment of a separate metropolitan at Lichfield, and latterly through Cenwulf's scheme to transfer Canterbury's rights to London.[6] In the event, the London scheme failed; on their conquest of 825, the West Saxons encountered a metropolitan recently restored to pre-eminence, actively concerned to promote episcopal unity. Yet within a generation, aspirations would be transformed; the synodal tradition was all but abandoned, and bishops turned to the West Saxon royal household as an alternative source of security.

A NEW ACCOMMODATION: ROYAL MONASTERIES AND THE COUNCIL OF KINGSTON (838)

In all early kingdoms, dynastic ecclesiatical interests were invested most directly in 'royal' monasteries. Individual houses were often established under the lordship of a particular noble family, successive members of which would then be appointed as abbot or abbess.[7] Monasteries of this kind under royal lordship soon developed into a flexible resource.[8] The prolonged dispute that arose over the lordship of Kentish royal monasteries encapsulates many differences between Mercian and West Saxon approaches to the Southumbrian episcopate. Although lay lordship was generally accepted as a fact of life, Bede and other reformers had portrayed such monasteries as essentially 'bogus', their incumbents condemned for behaviour more appropriate to secular relatives.[9] Though misleading as a crude description, these criticisms carry weight as an index of the openness of monasticism to lay encroachment, whether in property, dress or behaviour. Reformers typically advocated episcopal

---

[5] *Capitulare* of the papal legates (786), c. 11, in MGH Epist. IV, no. 3, pp. 19–29, at 23. Cf. synod of Chelsea (816), c. 6, in *Councils*, ed. Haddan and Stubbs III, 581; S 22 (BCS 91), with Brooks, *Canterbury*, p. 194.

[6] Brooks, *Canterbury*, pp. 111–27.

[7] P. Wormald, 'Bede, *Beowulf* and the Conversion of the Anglo-Saxon Aristocracy', in *Bede and Anglo-Saxon England*, ed. R. T. Farrell, BAR, British series 46 (Oxford, 1978), 32–95, esp. 49–58; P. Sims-Williams, *Religion and Literature in Western England 600–800* (Cambridge, 1990), pp. 115–43; Blair, *Church*, pp. 100–17.

[8] Brooks, *Canterbury*, pp. 175–206; Sims-Williams, *Religion*, pp. 144–76; Cubitt, *Councils*, pp. 223–34.

[9] Bede's letter to Ecgberht (734), in *Venerablis Baedae Opera Historica*, ed. Plummer I, 405–23; Whitelock in *EHD*, pp. 84–6; Wormald, 'Bede, *Beowulf*', esp. pp. 49–58; Cubitt, *Councils*, pp. 99–124.

control as the only means of eradicating secularity; in the case of Worcester and Canterbury there is evidence for sustained efforts to extend episcopal lordship over diocesan monasteries from the mid-eighth century.[10] One factor was probably the need to incorporate monasteries more fully in the basic provision of preaching and teaching.[11] Lay lordship itself remained largely unchallenged before the later eighth century; only amid Mercian efforts to secure control of Kent did the issue become a cause worth fighting.

In many ways this was the finest hour of the Southumbrian episcopate, defending their position with every available weapon.[12] Cenwulf's case had been bolstered by various papal privileges; archbishop Æthelheard responded by securing a mandate from Pope Leo III (795–816), declaring lay lordship to be inconsistent with the 'holy canons', endorsed by synod in 803.[13] Under the vigorous leadership of archbishop Wulfred, resistance crystallized into a series of detailed demands at the synod of Chelsea in 816, frequently appealing to canonical authority.[14] Each bishop was now authorized to be wholly responsible for the maintenance of regular life in all houses within his diocese. Wulfred's subsequent suspension from office for at least four years (c. 817–21), on papal authority at Cenwulf's behest, paradoxically reveals the underlying weakness of Mercian power in Kent.[15]

The contrast is striking with the accommodation newly reached between the West Saxon dynasty and Canterbury at Kingston in 838. In return for the restoration of various Kentish estates, archbishop Ceolnoth (833–70) agreed that Ecgberht and his heirs should always receive Canterbury's 'defence and protection', while a compromise was reached over lay lordship, largely to royal benefit.[16] Agreement was probably not restricted to Kent, and may well have applied to all dioceses under West Saxon rule.[17] Ecgberht and Æthelwulf had been

---

[10] C. Dyer, *Lords and Peasants in a Changing Society: the Estates of the Bishopric of Worcester, 680–1540* (Cambridge, 1980), pp. 9–16; Sims-Williams, *Religion*, pp. 144–76, esp. 168–76; Brooks, *Canterbury*, pp. 175–206.

[11] A. Thacker, 'Bede's Ideal of Reform', in *Ideal and Reality in Frankish and Anglo-Saxon Society*, ed. P. Wormald, with D. Bullough and R. Collins (Oxford, 1983), pp. 130–53; cf. A. Thacker, 'Monks, Preaching and Pastoral Care in Early Anglo-Saxon England', and C. Cubitt, 'Pastoral Care and Conciliar Canons: the Provisions of the 747 Council of *Clofesho*', both in *Pastoral Care before the Parish*, ed. J. Blair and R. Sharpe (Leicester, 1992), pp. 137–70 (at 164–6), and 193–211.

[12] Brooks, *Canterbury*, pp. 175–206; Cubitt, *Councils*, pp. 191–234.   [13] BCS 312.

[14] *Councils*, ed. Haddan and Stubbs III, 579–85.

[15] Campbell, 'Placing King Alfred', p. 9, with Brooks, *Canterbury*, pp. 134–5 and 181; D. P. Kirby, *The Earliest English Kings* (London, 1991), pp. 186–7.

[16] S 1438 (BCS 421 and 422).

[17] Brooks, *Canterbury*, pp. 197–203, whose interpretation of S 1438 stands, though S 281 (BCS 423) seems more likely to be a later forgery (Keynes, 'West Saxon Charters', p. 1114, note 3).

chosen to exercise 'lordship and protection' over all 'free monasteries', yet these communities had also now freely chosen their bishops as 'spiritual lords'. Both Æthelwulf and the bishops would now ensure the maintenance of regular life in these monasteries, that they might be granted liberty of election after his death. The Southumbrian episcopate had been obliged to abandon their radical stance in favour of West Saxon lordship, benevolent yet all-embracing. Its operation continued under Alfred; his assignment of one quarter of all revenue to monastic houses probably refers to their exemption from *feorm*.[18] To judge from Alfred's law-book, the notion of a 'free community' (*freo hired*) probably encompassed other houses, from which *feorm* was still expected.[19] Yet it is also assumed that monks and priests will own property, under a lord responsible for their conduct.[20] In practice the Kingston agreement fell far short of eliminating lay interests. Any liberty of election probably conferred only the freedom to choose another lord, ecclesiastical or lay.[21] Alfred had no difficulty in rewarding Asser with several houses; his dynasty's lordship remained unchallenged over a substantial monastic network.

The Kingston agreement is virtually unprecedented, as a dispute settlement involving bookland emanating from a royal assembly, rather than a synod.[22] The only earlier example is also West Saxon, from the mid-eighth century.[23] Under the Mercian supremacy, synodal jurisdiction may well have been shaped by the common siting of synods, in the region just north of the Thames, perhaps connected with London.[24] Locations within Mercian territory would help to explain why West Saxon rulers had rarely joined their Mercian counterparts in attending synods.[25] Less contentious West Saxon disputes could already have been settled at royal assemblies within Wessex. The Kingston council may well have involved an effective extension of established West Saxon procedures. This need not have seemed problematic to Canterbury, as long as her interests remained secure. Just six years later, a long-running dispute was settled in Canterbury's favour at a royal assembly in Æthelwulf's presence.[26] The dispute was heard by a synod when it had first arisen, in 810. The main factor neutralizing synodal unity was

---

[18] *VA* 102; *Af* 2, with D. Whitelock in *C&S*, p. 23, note 1.
[19] *Af* 2; cf. Liebermann, *Gesetze* I, 49.   [20] *Af* 8, 20 and 21; Brooks, *Canterbury*, p. 203.
[21] See Alfred's will, in *SEHD*, no. 11, p. 19, lines 24–7 (trans. in K&L, *Alfred*, p. 178; cf. p. 326 (note 105)).
[22] Campbell, 'Placing King Alfred', pp. 9–10; cf. Scharer, *Herrschaft*, p. 26.
[23] S 1256 (BCS 186; *Shaftesbury*, ed. Kelly, no. 1b; trans. in *EHD*, no. 55); P. Wormald, 'A Handlist of Anglo-Saxon Lawsuits', in his *Legal Culture*, pp. 253–87, at 265.
[24] Cubitt, *Councils*, pp. 27–32 and 299; cf. Keynes, *Clofesho*, pp. 14–17.
[25] Cubitt, *Councils*, pp. 29–31, cf. 236–7.   [26] S 1439 (BCS 445).

probably the collapse of Mercian ambitions in the south-east, preceding the escalation of viking activity in the 850s.[27]

Certainly, there is every reason to suppose that the absence of recorded synods after 845 reflects a genuine termination of practice, preceded by a marked decline.[28] All the forces sustaining synods were critically weakened. Canterbury held far fewer interests under Mercian control; these were now sufficiently protected by occasional archiepiscopal attendance at Mercian royal assemblies.[29] Nor, conversely, were there Mercian interests in Kent; such regression may explain Mercian royal absence from the last known synods. The absence of the two West Saxon bishops in 845 seems equally telling. In Mercia also bookland disputes were now considered at royal assemblies, the first example from 840.[30] On this basis alone, the alternative hypothesis is unlikely, that synods continued, without leaving surviving records.[31] Any remaining incentives to attend synods may be presumed to have been finally extinguished in the 850s, as the viking threat grew more immediate, stretching priorities in other directions.

THE SOUTHUMBRIAN EPISCOPATE AND THE STATE OF ECCLESIASTICAL DISCIPLINE

One must assume that in general bishops adhered at some level to the ideal practices expounded most fully by synods at *Clofesho* in 747 and before the papal legates in 786. In language heavily influenced by the writings of Pope Gregory the Great, the ideal bishop was here presented as a shepherd (*pastor*), ultimately responsible for the salvation of all, both as his flock (*grex*) and as the people of God (*populus Dei*).[32] Each bishop was expected to instruct his flock directly, through preaching and example, while also monitoring the pastoral care provided more locally by 'priests', perhaps chiefly the ordained members of religious communities.[33] All these responsibilities required the bishop's constant perambulation of his diocese, facilitated by episcopal estates and further rights and renders, potentially due from all monasteries in a diocese.[34] In the eyes of reformers, bishops were entitled to these resources solely to fulfil what was seen as a particularly exalted form of ecclesiastical office

[27] Cubitt, *Councils*, pp. 235–6.
[28] S 1194 (BCS 448). Cubitt, *Councils*, pp. 235–40; Keynes, *Clofesho*, pp. 11–13 and 50–1.
[29] Keynes, 'Kent', pp. 127–8; cf. Brooks, *Canterbury*, p. 147.   [30] S 192 (BCS 430).
[31] Cf. Cubitt, *Councils*, pp. 238–40; Keynes, *Clofesho*, pp. 50–1.
[32] Synod of *Clofesho*, c. 1; *capitulare* of the papal legates, c. 3.
[33] Synod of *Clofesho*, cc. 1 and 3, cf. 5, 6 and 25; *capitulare*, c. 3, cf. 1 and 6.
[34] Brooks, *Canterbury*, esp. pp. 139, 157–60 and 188–90; Sims-Williams, *Religion*, pp. 134–9.

(*officium*), commonly expressed in terms of service, both to God and his people, and explicitly located within the universal church.[35]

Yet such aspirations are difficult to reconcile with the state of Latinity among contemporary ecclesiastics. Alfred's own remarks about the decline of learning before his reign must be read in the context of his justificatory rhetoric; it is perhaps only to be expected that the king should have maximized the scale of crisis, thus claiming a comprehensive collapse even in 'pragmatic' literacy, necessary for the production of everyday documents.[36] The picture has received support from the desperate state of draftsmanship exhibited by single-sheet charters from the third quarter of the ninth century, but the surviving corpus is dominated by the work of Kentish scribes.[37] Keynes has redressed the balance by appealing to texts preserved in later cartulary copies; significantly higher standards might well have been maintained among West Saxon and Mercian scribes, in regions less vulnerable to viking disruption.[38]

Yet it is significant enough that Alfred could adopt such rhetoric at all, in a letter conveyed to bishops.[39] Especially pertinent are the surviving texts of episcopal professions, declarations of obedience to the archbishop of Canterbury and his see, recorded in writing. With one exception, it remains an open question whether professions were actually composed by bishops, rather than by archiepiscopal agents at Canterbury.[40] In most cases these texts draw on established formulae: many examples from the first third of the century exhibit considerable variation and originality, yet thereafter texts become shorter and formulaic, as if pretensions could no longer be sustained. Although most contain few outright errors, two examples 'reveal that their authors were unable even to manipulate stock formulas within a correct grammatical framework'.[41] No less suggestive is the exiguous evidence for production of Latin books and 'literary' texts in the mid-ninth century. As Michael Lapidge has stressed, the problem lies in the period *c.* 835–*c.* 885, which has left only three datable manuscripts from either side of the Humber, and indeed only two texts of any kind which might support contemporary 'literary'

---

[35] Synod of *Clofesho*, Prœmium and cc. 1 and 2; *capitulare* of the papal legates, cc. 1 and 14.

[36] For this useful concept cf. P. Wormald, 'The Uses of Literacy in Anglo-Saxon England and its Neighbours', *TRHS* 5th series (1977), 95–114; Keynes, 'Royal Government', pp. 226–30 and 248–57; *CP*, p. 2, lines 12–18.

[37] Brooks, *Canterbury*, pp. 167–74.

[38] S. Keynes, 'The Power of the Written Word: Alfredian England 871–99', in *Alfred*, ed. Reuter, pp. 175–97.

[39] For difficulties faced by ninth-century ecclesiastical communities, cf. Blair, *Church*, pp. 121–34; below, pp. 99–102 and 209–13.

[40] Brooks, *Canterbury*, pp. 164–7.

[41] M. Lapidge, 'Latin Learning in Ninth-Century England', in his *ALL* I, 409–54, at 434.

composition.[42] Allowances must be made for the loss or destruction of books through viking disruption, but although these processes do seem to have favoured the survival of de luxe manuscripts at the expense of schoolbooks, it is difficult to see how this could have induced any consistent discrimination against codices of recent production.[43]

The possibility arises that this decline might have been redressed by early use of the vernacular. Almost any such claim would be controversial, in the absence of manuscript evidence from the earlier ninth century. Several scholars have sought to date a range of Mercian prose texts to this period, which would have important implications for Alfredian activity.[44] Yet in an authoritative survey, Janet Bately has undermined the linguistic arguments in question, leaving just two items, the *Old English Martyrology* and Old English Bede, as the only texts demonstrably composed before the early tenth century which also lack any compelling associations with Alfred himself.[45] Even here his programme would provide at least a plausible context for either text. Much depends, with uncomfortable circularity, on one's willingness to countenance non-Alfredian contexts for 'literary' translation. Whatever the case, such material is insufficient against Lapidge's general thesis; his proposed turning-point in the mid-830s tallies with wider Southumbrian change. The overall impression is of a fundamental collapse of episcopal cohesion, doubtless exacerbated by viking pressure, which rapidly undermined learned expertise in all regions south of the Humber, even if 'pragmatic' literacy of a kind survived. What one must imagine is a major breach, in a learned tradition which extended back to the school of Theodore and Hadrian in the late seventh century, and indeed beyond.

The emerging picture receives further support from the recurring criticisms that these conditions roused among Continental correspondents writing to English recipients, initially in papal letters.[46] Criticisms

---

[42] Lapidge, *ibid.*, pp. 416–17 and 433, corrective to J. Morrish, 'King Alfred's Letter as a Source on Learning in England', in *Studies*, ed. Szarmach, pp. 87–108; J. Morrish, 'Dated and Datable Manuscripts Copied in England during the Ninth Century: a Preliminary List', *Mediaeval Studies* 50 (1988), 512–38. Cf. also H. Gneuss, 'King Alfred and the History of Anglo-Saxon Libraries', in *Modes of Interpretation in Old English: Essays in honour of Stanley B. Greenfield*, ed. P. Rugg Brown, G. R. Crompton and F. C. Robinson (Toronto, 1986), pp. 29–49; unpublished paper by D. N. Dumville, 'Manuscripts and Literate Culture in Ninth-Century England'.

[43] Lapidge, 'Latin Learning', pp. 410–17 and 425–32; R. Gameson, 'Alfred the Great and the Destruction and Production of Christian Books', *Scriptorium* 49 (1995), 180–210, at 185–93.

[44] Esp. R. Vleeskruyer, *The Life of St Chad: an Old English Homily* (Amsterdam, 1953), pp. 38–71.

[45] J. M. Bately, 'Old English Prose before and during the Reign of Alfred', *ASE* 17 (1988), 93–138, at 98–118, esp. 98 and 103–4.

[46] Whitelock in *EHD*, pp. 77–8; Nelson, ' "King Across the Sea" ', pp. 45–6 and 61–2; letters of Pope John VIII to Burgred, king of the Mercians (873×874), and to Æthelred, archbishop of Canterbury (877×878), in *C&S*, nos. 1 and 3; trans. in *EHD*, nos. 220 and 222.

focused heavily on the laxity of sexual practices, always a point of English vulnerability. The most obvious guide to native law was Pope Gregory's *Libellus responsionum*, whose provisions on marriage had been limited to encourage conversion.[47] Ninth-century letters continued an established tradition of external criticism, yet amid intensive contact between England and Rome, popes were also curiously well placed to monitor practices close at hand.[48] Particularly pressing may have been royal sexual conduct; English kings had long been reluctant to abandon the dynastic flexibility afforded by irregular unions. There is every sign of continued tolerance, not least in ninth-century Wessex, where such flexibility may well have been enhanced by the unusually low status accorded to consorts, as king's wife rather than queen.[49] Yet issues of sin also crystallized broader questions of English ecclesiastical discipline. In 851 Pope Leo IV addressed archbishop Ceolnoth and Berhtwulf, king of the Mercians; although the letter survives in summary form, its criticisms evidently identified general failure in canonical enforcement.[50] The holding of synods was a fundamental requirement of canon law; papal language may well have been pertinent.[51]

Such factors certainly informed another observer of English affairs, Fulk, archbishop of Rheims, when commending his 'faithful son' Grimbald to Alfred's service in about 886. Fulk's letter hinges on what seems to be his own frank critique of English practices, within a stylized legalistic account of English ecclesiastical history.[52] Pope Gregory's founding tolerance emerges as symbolic, of laxity in all aspects of canon law. Certainly, according to Fulk, for a period after conversion the English had engaged in ecclesiastical law-making, through their participation in synods and wider councils of the church; yet in recent times, the 'holy canons' had come to be neglected, both in transmission and observance. It was for this reason that Grimbald's expertise was now desperately needed by an enlightened king. Fulk's grand narrative was suffused with prevailing West Frankish attitudes towards canon law and ecclesiastical administration, championed by his predecessor Hincmar.[53] Yet there remained every incentive to reflect certain realities of contemporary English conditions. Fulk's subsequent alarm at the 'incestuous

---

[47] *HE* I.27, pp. 50–2; cf. *OE Bede*, pp. 68–72, where the section is relocated between Books III and IV, plausibly interpreted by Whitelock as a belated inclusion, prompted by these criticisms ('The Old English Bede', in her *Bede to Alfred*, no. 8, p. 70).

[48] Letter of Pope John VIII to Æthelred, archbishop of Canterbury, and Wulfhere, archbishop of York (873×876), on clerical dress (*C&S*, no. 2; trans. in *EHD*, no. 221).

[49] P. Stafford, 'The King's Wife in Wessex 800–1066', *P&P* 91 (May 1981), 3–27.

[50] *MGH Epist.* V, no. 14, p. 592.

[51] Cubitt, *Councils*, p. 24; synod of Hertford (672 or 673), c. 7, in *HE* IV.5.

[52] *C&S*, no. 4, at pp. 8–10; trans. in K&L, *Alfred*, pp. 182–6, at 183–4.   [53] Below, pp. 223–8.

heats of lasciviousness' acquires symbolic force against the broader collapse that he had detected in English canonical observance.[54]

As with secular office-holding, episcopal behaviour was also shaped by the attractive capacity of the West Saxon royal household. Mercian differences are reinforced by the attestation of bishops, suggesting synods and royal assemblies as the main arenas of contact with Mercian rule.[55] The pattern contrasts with that of the two West Saxon bishops, of Winchester and Sherborne.[56] As ever, it is often difficult to isolate precise circumstances of charter issue; episcopal attestations nevertheless show a striking correlation with the pattern shown by ealdormen, of increasing intermittency. One common combination is that of five or six ealdormen, with both West Saxon bishops; this high level of attendance can only be detected once in the final twenty years of Alfred's reign, correlating with defensive conditions.[57] Yet in other charters, between one and three ealdormen are found in the company of a single bishop. Although the combination is prevalent in later Alfredian charters, it can be observed much earlier, from the 840s, as soon as the record becomes fuller.[58] In several instances there is no discernible connection between the bishop in question and the land transaction being witnessed. Either or both West Saxon bishops are also regularly encountered with kings in Kentish charters, rarely as an obviously interested party.[59] In other words, the West Saxon bishops seem to have spent significant periods away from their diocesan duties, residing with the king, just as ealdormen rotated between the household and their shires.

Other southern bishops are rarely mentioned in charters issued within Wessex, but they too seem to have enjoyed comparable contact, on the many occasions when the household ventured further afield. Only occasionally does the opportunity seem to have arisen for wider episcopal contact, at an apparently new form of 'special' royal assembly, usually associated with London or its environs, whose ecclesiastical participants generally included most if not all bishops under West Saxon rule.[60] More

---

[54] Letters of Fulk to King Alfred, and to Plegmund, archbishop of Canterbury (both *c.* 890), in *C&S*, nos. 5 and 6; trans. in *EHD*, nos. 224 and 225.

[55] Keynes, *Atlas*, tables VIII, XIII and XIV.   [56] *Ibid.*, table XIX.

[57] See esp. S 1438, S 290, S 304 (and other 'Second Decimation' charters), S 340, S 1275 (witnesses at Wilton) and S 352; cf. S 345 (BCS 550).

[58] See S 348, S 354 and S 356; cf. S 298, S 301, S 1274 and S 335.

[59] Keynes, *Atlas*, table XIX; Keynes, 'Kent', p. 126.

[60] Keynes, 'Kent', pp. 128–30. Cf. esp. S 346 (BCS 561), dated 889; S 1628 (BCS 577), dated 898; Cubitt, *Councils*, pp. 238–9.

usual in the south-east were 'local' assemblies, effectively enabling one or more bishops to deal directly with the king in the presence of his household, attended by a substantial body of West Saxon nobles.[61] Similar arrangements seem to have extended, in the latter part of Alfred's reign, to the bishops of western Mercia.[62]

The royal household sustained tighter bonds between bishops and successive kings, in relationships increasingly expressed in terms equally applicable to secular nobility. The Kingston agreement was explicitly contingent on the perpetual friendship (*amicitia*) of Ceolnoth and his successors for the West Saxon dynasty, and suffused with reciprocal expectations of benevolence and love. The language of friendship could equally seal more everyday transactions between bishop and king.[63] These obligations seem largely to have been reinforced by the pervasive implications of royal lordship. The terminology itself was not unusual. Many episcopal professions are couched 'in terms that must have been deliberately reminiscent of secular oaths of loyalty'; Mercian kings also exerted lordship in some form over bishops.[64] The unusual character of the royal household distinguished West Saxon lordship from that offered to bishops by their archbishop, or by other neighbouring rulers. A bishop's presence at the 'king's home' placed him in receipt of the king's comprehensive love, and thus established his position within the hierarchy of royal intimacy. It was on this basis that Alfred could address his bishops 'lovingly' (*luflice*) as well as 'amicably' (*freondlice*), in a formula probably used widely in vernacular royal letters.[65] In regularly attending the household, bishops enjoyed the same opportunities to bond with the king that were also extended to secular nobles, especially in the mundane pursuits of hunting and feasting.[66] Nor were they denied the honour of receiving royal gifts. To Wulfsige, bishop of Sherborne, Alfred was not only his 'ring-giver', but 'the greatest treasure-giver of all kings'.[67]

For bishops, the increasing value of *Königsnähe* lay less in the hope of new land grants, much reduced in the ninth century, than royal beneficence with respect to existing holdings. The extension of charters to secular recipients, with defensive conditions, exposed ecclesiastical land to unprecedented pressures; while it was now royal assemblies which

---

[61] Keynes, 'Kent', pp. 124–30. [62] Keynes, 'Mercians', pp. 20–1 and 27–9.

[63] S 339 (BCS 518; *Rochester*, ed. Campbell, no. 26), dated 868; S 223 (BCS 579; *SEHD*, no. 13; trans. in *EHD*, no. 99).

[64] Brooks, *Canterbury*, p. 165; cf. S 1257 (BCS 241; trans. in *EHD*, no. 77).

[65] *CP*, p. 2, line 1; F. E. Harmer, *Anglo-Saxon Writs* (Manchester, 1952), pp. 11, 16–17 and 21.

[66] S 352 (BCS 549) and S 1287 (BCS 617; *Charters*, ed. Robertson, no. 15), for episcopal hunting rights.

[67] D. Yerkes, 'The Full Text of the Metrical Preface to Wærferth's Old English Translation of Gregory's *Dialogues*', *Speculum* 55 (1979), 505–13, at 513; trans. in K&L, *Alfred*, pp. 187–8.

offered final resolution to contentious disputes.[68] There was no longer any question of episcopal immunity from secular judgement; assemblies relied on the presidency of the king, however significantly bishops might contribute to proceedings. A law of Alfred declares episcopal witness as a necessity in preventing the wrongful disposal of bookland outside the holder's kindred.[69] There are only two surviving Alfredian records of ecclesiastical disputes, both from Worcester, preserved by virtue of their support for episcopal claims to land. Yet both disputes were seemingly settled in Alfred's presence; one hinged on a judgement specifically attributed to ealdorman Æthelred and his Mercian councillors.[70]

The secularity of these bonds extended beyond the royal household, to sustain a range of episcopal activities 'at home'. In the course of the ninth century, bishops under West Saxon rule may be observed to have fulfilled a largely unprecedented role as royal agents; its sheer extent is sufficient to suggest a causal relationship with the deterioration of ecclesiastical discipline. Under viking attack, it is perhaps unsurprising that royal service should have superseded pastoral discipline. It is quite unprecedented to encounter West Saxon bishops in the *Chronicle* regularly at the head of local and royal armies; the contexts tend to suggest military leadership, rather than the passive provision of prayer.[71] Off the battlefield, bishops augmented their service in further activities no less vital to defensive warfare. In the case of fortress-work, episcopal co-operation would prove indispensable to the construction of burghal defences.[72] In local peace-keeping, episcopal involvement was taken for granted in such fundamental procedures as oath-taking and the provision of surety.[73] The intensity of service helps to explain the remarkable inclusion of two bishops among 'the best king's thegns' in the *Chronicle's* list of 896. This is precisely what Alfred's bishops had become, rendering assistance in many ways indistinguishable from secular counterparts.

ROYAL PRIESTS IN THE ROYAL HOUSEHOLD

Yet such activities did not eclipse other, more exclusive forms of bonding; ample opportunities were cultivated in the sphere of personal royal devotion. Religious observance was a further drama principally staged within the West Saxon household. The needs of royal devotion

---

[68] Above, pp. 20, 26 and 47–8; Campbell, 'Placing King Alfred', pp. 9–10; Blair, *Church*, pp. 129–31; cf. A. G. Kennedy, 'Disputes about *bocland*: the Forum for their Adjudication', *ASE* 14 (1995), 175–95; Wormald, 'God and King', pp. 342–52.

[69] *Af* 41.

[70] S 1441 (BCS 574; *SEHD*, no. 14) and S 1442 (BCS 575), with Keynes, 'Mercians', pp. 28–9, notes 129 and 130.

[71] Cf. above, pp. 26–7.   [72] Below, pp. 96–105 and 209–13.   [73] *Ine* 13; *Af* 1.2, 3 and 41.

were supplied on an intensive basis from at least the mid-ninth century by the emergence of a small body of priests in some way attached to the royal household. It is entirely characteristic of West Saxon rule that such arrangements find no continuous parallel in the evidence for other Anglo-Saxon kingdoms.[74] The nature of devotion commands attention, given its unusual capacity to extract the king, however temporarily, from the prevailing secularity of everyday behaviour.

The relationship with priests exemplified the intensity of royal lordship; bonding extended to further activities centred on the written word. Competent Latin literacy may well have grown rare from the mid-ninth century; there are signs that priests were especially valued for such competence, through which they were able to serve the king in technical capacities, as scribes and draftsmen for charters and royal correspondence.[75] Letters in Latin were essential for satisfactory foreign communication, which helps to explain the value of Æthelwulf's Frankish secretary, Felix.[76] Priests would also have produced many humbler documents in the vernacular, for internal West Saxon communication. In addition to vernacular wills, legal texts, dispute settlements and miscellaneous memoranda, all attested from the ninth century, there are strong grounds for assuming some royal dependence on vernacular letters.[77] The significance of Alfred's salutational formula has been noted; no less striking is his appeal to the authority of a 'lord's letter and his seal' (*hlafordes ærendgewrit and hys insegel*), terms which described the format of later royal writs.[78]

All these activities stood in contrast to religious duties, sustaining forms of 'capital' invested quite narrowly in the communication of instructions and judgements. The honour accorded to royal priests must be assessed in this context, as the only ecclesiastics fulfilling regular service at the 'king's home'. To judge from Asser's own testimony, each priest would have been formally accepted as a *familiaris* (perhaps translating *deorling*), securing a high degree of royal intimacy through his literate expertise.[79] Royal priests exhibit a similar pattern of intermittent attestation, strengthening the suspicion that they may have been seconded to the king from religious communities, though the origins of

---

[74] Keynes, 'West Saxon Charters', pp. 1131–7 and 1146–7; Keynes, 'Mercia and Wessex', p. 322.

[75] Keynes, 'West Saxon Charters', pp. 1131–4 and 1147; cf. Keynes, *Diplomas*, pp. 134–53 and 'Royal Government', pp. 230–48 and 255–7.

[76] Letters of Lupus, abbot of Ferrières, to King Æthelwulf, and to Felix (both 852), in *Epistolae*, ed. Marshall, pp. 21–3; trans. in *EHD*, nos. 217 and 218.

[77] Kelly, 'Lay Society', pp. 46–57; Keynes, 'Royal Government', esp. pp. 244–5.

[78] *Solil* p. 62, lines 22–7 (trans. in K&L, *Alfred*, p. 141); Harmer, *Writs*, pp. 3, 10–13 and 24–5.

[79] *VA* 79, esp. lines 8–14 and 44–52; cf. esp. cc. 13–15, 74 and 87–9.

ninth-century incumbents remain at best obscure, especially those who may have been West Saxon.[80]

Ultimately at stake were rewards of higher ecclesiastical office. Episcopal appointments had long been subject to a degree of royal influence, exerted in a less formal way than power over abbatial appointment. Although bishops were technically subject to election, apparently conducted at synods before the mid-ninth century, in practice there were strong incentives for episcopal communities to favour candidates amenable to royal interests.[81] Unusual details are revealed in the profession of Helmstan, bishop of Winchester, of 838 × 839: an initial election involved not only the Winchester community, but Æthelwulf himself, his bishops and magnates, and 'all the people of the West Saxons', followed by his formal consecration at London by archbishop Ceolnoth.[82] Yet royal power depended less on procedure than the nature of favoured candidates themselves. In general in early Anglo-Saxon England, in cases where future bishops can be securely identified, successful candidates are most often found within the episcopal community, or among abbots, particularly those of dependent houses.[83] Within Wessex, in contrast, an attractive alternative was increasingly supplied by the election of royal priests; by this mechanism they acquired still greater value, in supplying future bishops whose loyalty had been enhanced through extended service in the household. The power of royal lordship is encapsulated by the priest Heahmund, whose observable service extended from the early 850s to the early 860s, before his election as bishop of Sherborne in 867; he was subsequently killed at the battle of *Meretun* in 871.[84] Another example may be Ealhheard, prominent as an abbot in the 860s; such status lends additional significance to his possible identification among Alfred's 'best thegns' in the early 890s, holding the office of bishop at Dorchester.[85]

Seen in this context, Alfred's 'summoning' of helpers in the 880s emerges as a logical intensification of these existing practices, however radical its effects. In Asser's eyes the principal service required by his lord was instruction in wisdom, supplied by 'luminaries' and 'teachers', of a kind apparently denied to Alfred during his youth.[86] It is difficult not to

---

[80] Keynes, *Atlas*, table XX; Keynes, 'West Saxon Charters', pp. 1132–4, cf. 1146–7, for apparent 'Winchester' connections in the early tenth century.

[81] Brooks, *Canterbury*, pp. 111–54, for archiepiscopal elections.

[82] *Canterbury Professions*, ed. Richter, no. 18, p. 16; cf. earlier reference to royal involvement in no. 5 (p. 5), relating to Sherborne (793 × 801).

[83] Sims-Williams, *Religion*, pp. 172–3, for Mercian examples; cf. Tunberht, bishop of Winchester in the 870s, perhaps previously abbot of the episcopal community (Keynes, *Atlas*, table XX).

[84] Keynes, 'West Saxon Charters, pp. 1132–4.

[85] Keynes, *Atlas*, tables XIX and XX. Ealhheard acceded 869 × 888; cf. K&L, *Alfred*, p. 289 (note 31).

[86] *VA* 76–9, cf. 24–5.

regard their role as collectively central to Alfredian 'capital', although each recruitment must also be seen against the contemporaneous expansion of West Saxon power. Yet the presence of all related to the role of priests: of the six teachers mentioned before Asser's own enlistment, the Mercians Æthelstan and Werwulf were both explicitly 'priests and chaplains', while Alfred himself accorded the title 'mass-priest' to Grimbald and John in his Prose Preface.[87] Of the other two there acknowledged, the Mercian Plegmund spent a significant period in royal service before his appointment as archbishop of Canterbury in 890. Asser initially agreed to grant one half of his service to Alfred, dividing his time between Wales and Wessex.[88] The only exception is Wærferth, bishop of Worcester: his absence from Alfred's list strengthens the suspicion that his teaching contribution was also slight.[89]

Service in the household was further combined with abbatial office; all teachers were reportedly showered with *honores* and *potestates* within Wessex.[90] In addition to Asser's own houses, it was probably the same John, 'of Old Saxon origin', who was the first abbot of Alfred's foundation at Athelney.[91] Later tradition asserts that Alfred installed Grimbald in a newly founded *monasteriolum* at Winchester.[92] The advancement of teachers to vacant sees marks a strong extension of patterns, towards an effective monopolization of the episcopal office. In addition to Plegmund's elevation, Asser received the see of Sherborne at some point in the 890s. At least two further priests were among the next generation of bishops, appointed *c.* 909, the Mercian Æthelstan to Ramsbury, and Frithestan to Winchester.[93] It is thus unsurprising that Grimbald's master, Fulk, should have presented his enlistment in terms suggesting the hope at least of episcopal promotion.[94] Fulk's letter remains controversial: the precise circumstances of Grimbald's arrival are less important than the later tradition that he subsequently declined the see of Canterbury, vacant after 888, paving the way for Plegmund.[95] Grimbald and John were in fact

---

[87] *VA* 77, line 13; *CP*, p. 6, lines 20–2.   [88] K&L, *Alfred*, p. 259 (note 165); *VA* 79, lines 44–52.

[89] M. Godden, 'Wærferth and King Alfred: the Fate of the Old English *Dialogues*', in *Alfred the Wise: Studies in honour of Janet Bately*, ed. J. Roberts and J. L. Nelson, with M. Godden (Cambridge, 1997), pp. 35–51, at 48.

[90] *VA* 77, lines 15–16; c. 78, line 13; and c. 79, line 19.

[91] *VA* 94, line 2, notwithstanding the caution of J. Bately, 'Grimbald of St Bertin's', *Medium Ævum* 35 (1966), 1–10, at 2.

[92] S. Keynes, *The Liber Vitae of the New Minster and Hyde Abbey Winchester*, EEMF 26 (Copenhagen, 1996), 16.

[93] D. N. Dumville, 'King Alfred and the Tenth-Century Reform of the English Church', in his *Wessex and England from Alfred to Edgar* (Woodbridge, 1992), pp. 185–205, at 192, note 31; Keynes, 'West Saxon Charters', pp. 1146–7.

[94] Letter of Fulk to King Alfred, in *C&S*, no. 4 (trans. in K&L, *Alfred*, pp. 184–5).

[95] Brooks, *Canterbury*, pp. 152–3.

the only teachers from whom episcopal office was somehow withheld. The retention of both Continental helpers within Wessex suggests the unusually indispensable nature of their service in Alfred's household.

Why was Fulk so critical of English observance? His remarks provide an important context for Grimbald's royal service. Often seen straightforwardly as a 'Carolingian' conduit, his role acquires piquancy amid many striking differences in Frankish ecclesiastical conditions. What was shared was precisely such service, the bonding of ruler with ecclesiastical personnel. Regularly appointed as former court chaplains, Frankish bishops performed comparable activities as royal agents, among the ruler's faithful men; the role fell within overarching structures of Frankish ecclesiastical reform.[96] Carolingian success offers the extreme counter-example of an order built on ecclesiastical unity. At elite level, Charlemagne's dynasty claimed rule over a single *gens*, 'the people of the Franks'; with it came opportunities to exploit the structures of a single Frankish *ecclesia*. One aspect was material, in the massive expansion of Frankish authority from the mid-eighth century onwards, extending the church to newly conquered regions while tripling its internal landholding. From the outset, this wealth fulfilled secular purposes of equivalent scale: both benefices and annual gifts supplied special contributions to Frankish defence.[97]

A further aspect was structural, in the logistics of ecclesiastical unity, directly sustained by the holding of synods and wider ecclesiastical councils, the latter often under royal presidency.[98] Under Charlemagne and Louis the Pious both had been arenas of reform. Matters were complicated after 840 by the politics of division; royal and provincial boundaries did not always coincide, but such problems were marginal. In general sufficient congruity was maintained that the vast majority of bishops under West Frankish rule could attend provincial and multi-provincial synods in the west, while similar arrangements prevailed with respect to the East Frankish kingdom.[99] The latter case is significant

---

[96] R. McKitterick, *The Frankish Church and the Carolingian Reforms 789–895* (London, 1977); G. Brown, 'Introduction: the Carolingian Renaissance', in *Carolingian Culture*, ed. McKitterick, pp. 1–51; R. E. Sullivan, 'The Context of Cultural Activity in the Carolingian Age', in *'The Gentle Voices of Teachers'*, ed. Sullivan, pp. 51–105.

[97] Cf. above, pp. 25–7.

[98] Wallace-Hadrill, *Frankish Church*, pp. 258–78; W. Hartmann, *Die Synoden der Karolingerzeit im Frankenreich und in Italien* (Paderborn, 1989).

[99] *Ibid.*, pp. 2–7, cf. 197–221, 245–73, 299–312, 331–42 and 359–72.

given regional differences within the Carolingian world: though held more infrequently, synods contributed much to East Frankish unity under Louis the German.[100] The situation was not so different in Lotharingia, as long as the kingdom survived.[101]

Unity was also consciously textual, in the shared agenda of royally authorized reform. Despite many goals in common with earlier English processes, the programme exceeded all European precedents in the scale of ambition, intensively sustained under royal and episcopal supervision. Since Pippin's anointing in 751, this dynasty had been bound to the Franks as a 'people of God'.[102] Reforming aims derived from an extreme articulation of such status, expounded for the first time in the *Admonitio generalis* of 789, demanding full restoration of the Franks to divine law, under Charlemagne as a new Josiah.[103] All activities were united by 'correction' (*correctio*): initially, of knowledge, in the form of Latin texts collectively endorsed as conveying the 'model of living rightly' (*norma recte vivendi*), and on this basis of Frankish society in its entirety, each *ordo* according to its function.[104] In book production above all Frankish contrasts are extreme, with the duplication of 'norms' on an unprecedented scale across every field of Christian life: from secular law and historical writing to sermons and homiletic material central to preaching and teaching.[105] The church itself was defined by regulating texts, in the *Dionysio-Hadriana* collection of canon law and 'Gregorian' Sacramentary: even the Bible received revision and a degree of standardization.

'Correction' extended to rulership. For Alcuin, Charlemagne had been leader and teacher of his subject flock; under Louis, rule found new expression as an office of divine service (*ministerium*).[106] Royal duties matched others now articulated for all faithful men. Initially delineated by Louis himself, such 'ministry' was soon the concern of reforming ecclesiastics. As an exemplary model for conduct, rulership began with the royal person; its fulfilment demanded exceptional self-control, applying

---

[100] Goldberg, *Empire*, pp. 175–6 and 217–20, cf. 158–63, 282–3 and 296–9; cf. S. Airlie, 'True Teachers and Pious Kings: Salzburg, Louis the German, and Christian Order', in *Belief and Culture in the Middle Ages: Studies presented to Henry Mayr-Harting*, ed. R. Gameson and H. Leyser (Oxford, 2001), pp. 89–105.

[101] H. H. Anton, 'Synoden, Teilreichsepiskopat und die Herausbildung Lotharingiens', in *Herrschaft, Kirche, Kultur: Beiträge zur Geschichte des Mittelalters*, ed. G. Jenal and S. Haarländer (Stuttgart, 1993), pp. 83–124.

[102] Nelson, 'Kingship and Empire', pp. 54–6.   [103] McKitterick, *Frankish Church*, p. 2.

[104] Brown, 'Carolingian Renaissance', pp. 17–25; J. Fleckenstein, *Die Bildungsreform Karls des Grossen als Verwicklung die norma rectitudinis* (Bigge-Ruhr, 1953).

[105] McKitterick, *Frankish Church*, pp. 81–205; Gameson, 'Destruction', p. 183.

[106] Anton, *Fürstenspiegel*, pp. 172–9 and 190–231, cf. 108–23; O. Guillot, 'Une ordinatio méconnue: le Capitulaire de 823–825', in *Charlemagne's Heir*, ed. Godman and Collins (Oxford, 1990), pp. 455–86.

equally to the ruler's body and his household.[107] Such expectations combined with increasing 'isolation' of the royal *ministerium*, towards duties owed specifically to the church and priesthood.[108] In the west, above all, rule lay open to sustained admonition and 'correction', much of it from bishops. Synodal acta appealed for the return of church lands, among other perceived abuses.[109] With one exception – the *Via regia* of Smaragdus, abbot of St-Mihiel – all the most sophisticated 'Mirror for Princes' texts were either written or commissioned by bishops; these too urged the benefits of 'justice' and ecclesiastical defence.[110] Under Charles the Bald, these appeals gained force from renewed experiment in anointing by Frankish bishops. Parallels with the episcopal profession encouraged the inclusion of a preliminary announcement or promise, declaring the king's commitment to the preservation of *leges et statuta*, in procedures increasingly monopolized by episcopal consecrators.[111]

None of this was antithetical to kingship, nor to the power of individual rulers. These patterns once led Walter Ullmann to suppose a radical subordination of royal power within an advancing episcopal hierocracy; yet as Nelson has shown, they must be seen against the church's urgent need for protection, greatest in landholding.[112] Anointing effected a symbolic 'strengthening' of the royal *ministerium*, reinforcing duties equally relevant to secular nobility, in the preservation of law.[113] The formulation echoed practices of mutual undertaking between Charles and his faithful men, sometimes expressed by oath, in which the upholding of the *honor regis* was explicitly predicated on the king's ability to preserve 'for each their due law'.[114] What anointing added was a new jurisdictional dimension to episcopal rhetoric, in the precise mediatory role which could now be assigned to bishops over an anointed king's fulfilment of his duties.[115] While this might well have suggested an episcopal power of deposition, in practice Hincmar drew back from such a claim, preferring the more viable hope that a king might be restored to proper rule through confession and repentance.[116]

---

[107] See esp. council of Paris (829), Book II, c. 1 (MGH Conc. II.ii, no. 50, pp. 649–51); *DIR* 3, pp. 184–96; *RC* 2 and 5, pp. 25–7 and 34–6.

[108] Guillot, 'Une ordinatio méconnue', p. 484, note 131.

[109] Wallace-Hadrill, *Frankish Church*, pp. 268–78.

[110] J. M. Wallace-Hadrill, 'The Via Regia of the Carolingian Age', in *Trends in Medieval Political Thought*, ed. B. Smalley (Oxford, 1965), pp. 22–41; cf. above, p. 27.

[111] J. L. Nelson, 'Kingship, Law and Liturgy in the Political Thought of Hincmar of Rheims', in her *Ritual*, pp. 133–71, at 149–55.

[112] W. Ullmann, *The Carolingian Renaissance and the Idea of Kingship* (London, 1969), pp. 111–34; Nelson, 'Lord's Anointed', esp. pp. 116–17, cf. Wallace-Hadrill, *Frankish Church*, pp. 250 and 271–2.

[113] Nelson, 'Lord's Anointed', pp. 117–19.   [114] Nelson, 'Kingship, Law', pp. 146–55.

[115] *Ibid.*, pp. 169–71, cf. 137.   [116] *Ibid.*, pp. 163–6.

Within these parameters, the case remains for power-broking by an admonitory episcopate, more delicately balanced within factionalism and dynastic dispute. The crises of Louis the Pious' reign had stemmed from tensions within as well as without his church; bishops became the conduit for wider criticisms.[117] The context was squarely 'ministerial', in an episcopal duty of judgement in respect of sin. Already in 829 roots were identified in the imperial household; conspiracy soon crystallized round the more dangerous claim of adultery between Louis' empress, Judith, and his newly elevated chamberlain, Bernard.[118] The charge resurfaced among crimes for which Louis would be held responsible in 833, in a ritual of public penance involving several reforming bishops. The emperor had already forfeited his office through repeated negligence; his new status was deemed to disqualify him permanently from secular authority.[119] Canonically debatable, the case proved no hindrance to Louis' subsequent return; though in many ways exceptional, his example held some resonance amid later inter-regional rivalry between his competing heirs.[120]

In 858, West Francia faced invasion from Louis the German, on a pretext of restoring the 'holy church'. Hincmar and his bishops deftly sidestepped the invitation, while criticizing his fulfilment of 'ministry'; Charles the Bald was partly rescued by their subsequent loyalty.[121] Meanwhile, in the middle kingdom Lothar II risked separation from his queen, Theutberga, on a charge of incest. Initially successful, his position was soon undermined by attacks on his own conduct, in failing to restrain lust for his concubine, Waldrada.[122] For Hincmar, Lothar had lost both title and office in the eyes of God; his sins were firmly a matter for priests, as 'thrones of God, on which God himself sits and through whom he determines judgements'.[123] Such status contrasted with Charles's own presentation on the same stage, as exemplary penitent and willing recipient of priestly correction.[124] Under international pressure, Lothar was forced to reinstate his queen, albeit temporarily, while his

---

[117] Ewig in *The Church in the Age of Feudalism*, ed. Judin and Dolan, pp. 118–25.

[118] *Relatio episcoporum* (829), in MGH Capit. II, no. 196, cc. 21–34, 55, 59 and 60; M. de Jong, 'Power and Humility in Carolingian Society: the Public Penance of Louis the Pious', *EME* 1 (1992), 29–52; J. M. H. Smith, 'Gender and Ideology in the Early Middle Ages', in *Gender and Christian Religion*, ed. R. N. Swanson (Woodbridge, 1998), pp. 51–73, at 69.

[119] *Relatio episcoporum* (833), in MGH Capit. II, no. 197, pp. 53 and 55.

[120] Nelson, 'Kingship, Law', p. 136, note 2, for Hincmar's gloss on 833 in *De divortio*, Resp. to Inter. VI (PL 125: 757B), cf. Charles's protested fears in 859 (pp. 165–6).

[121] MGH Conc. III, no. 41, esp. cc. 1, 4 and 5; Nelson, *Charles the Bald*, pp. 186–91, cf. Nelson, 'Lord's Anointed', p. 117.

[122] S. Airlie, 'Private Bodies and the Body Politic in the Divorce Case of Lothar II', *P&P* 161 (November 1998), 3–38, esp. 25–35.

[123] *De divortio*, Resp. to Inter. VI (PL 125: 758A).   [124] Staubach, *Rex Christianus*, pp. 173–86.

son by Waldrada escaped recognition. As Stuart Airlie observes, language here 'moulded political realities': its effects hastened the downfall of Lotharingia after Lothar's death in 869.[125] Charles in turn would use his 'ministry' to seal episcopal support within Lothar's former kingdom, intensively expressed in learned texts and de luxe manuscripts.[126] Though tempered by East Frankish partition, his gains remained considerable. In 875, against the odds, he secured imperial elevation; as Nikolaus Staubach has suggested, popes too may have been favourable to Charles's claims in conduct and rule.[127]

Such was the scope of Frankish episcopal power, at least in part discursive, within the fluid terms of 'ministerial' rule. Beyond landholding and royal service lay a distinctive role for rhetoric, flexibly deployed within a range of gestures, themselves united by the agenda of wider reform. Whether in praise, counsel or chastisement, theorizing held the capacity to shape as well as to describe legitimate behaviour and action. The contrast is suggestive with Southumbrian bishops, lacking both forum and need for collective ecclesiastical discourse. West Saxon rule offered an extreme homogeneity of political and tenurial relationships; episcopal power worked solely within these structures of service and lordship. Neither discourse nor interests were conducive to distinctive acts of rhetoric; these conditions were central to the very different character of later Alfredian communication.

[125] Airlie, 'Private Bodies', p. 35, cf. 31.
[126] Staubach, *Rex Christianus*, esp. pp. 181–93 and 223–34.
[127] *Ibid.*, pp. 335–43; a project opposed by Hincmar (Nelson, *Charles the Bald*, pp. 234–44).

Chapter 5

THE ARTICULATION OF POWER UNDER KING ALFRED'S PREDECESSORS

The articulation of power under Alfred's predecessors is a subject of potentially the utmost importance, as the context for all Alfredian developments, yet it is also problematic, given the paucity of earlier surviving sources. Evidential problems are pressing in view of the learned, textual, character of Alfredian 'capital', heavily invested in the philosophical exploration of kingship and authority. Directly pertinent is the extent of earlier reliance on the written word, but one must also be alive to other media, and the respective roles of speech, gesture and ritual. Though frustrating, the partial nature of access can be mitigated in several ways: through Continental comparison, and by evaluating and juxtaposing different types of source material.

COLLECTIVE OFFICE-HOLDING: WEST SAXON ROYAL DEVOTION

The best attested form of 'cultural capital' under Alfred's predecessors was devotional; the royal household was not the only focus, but its practices held unique significance. Ecclesiastical communities had long provided aristocratic kindreds with local sources of sacrality; patterns of gift-giving sustained strong traditions of lay piety. What distinguished 'royal' activity was the centrality of the king; in his presence, devotional activity was transformed into a potent medium for royal communication. This is an area in which Carolingian influence may have been especially strong; its meaning and significance must be considered in West Saxon context.

Alfred's own piety bears many hallmarks of contemporary Carolingian practice.[1] Though his practice was extreme, many aspects find earlier West Saxon parallels. His daily prayer and attendance at divine services bears comparison with his brother Æthelred's behaviour at Ashdown,

---

[1] Pratt, 'Illnesses', pp. 40–9.

refusing to fight before finishing Mass; evidence for royal priests first emerges under Æthelwulf.[2] In alms-giving, Alfred's 'kindness and generosity' may indeed have been 'immense and incomparable', but also evoked the memory of his father's largesse; such connections can only have been strengthened by Alfred's regular gifts to Rome, seemingly begun in 883.[3] There are grounds for regarding all such piety as in part symbolic of Æthelwulf's Carolingian alliance, within wider European posturing.[4] Æthelwulf may have had Frankish precedents in mind when dispatching the young Alfred to Rome in 853; his own journey of 855 supplied an appropriate context for his marriage to Judith, boldly departing from earlier practices of royal retirement.[5]

Yet West Saxon devotion had its own character: Æthelred's piety suggests practices at once more intimate, and more overtly militant, than procedures within the chapels of Carolingian palaces. Other glimpses reinforce the impression of prayers toward military ends. The mechanism invoked was not unusual, reliant on viking attack as a sign of divine disfavour.[6] A common formula in ninth-century charters granted rights 'as long as the Christian faith should last in Britain'; in Wessex the message was relentless. In the late 830s an English king, probably Ecgberht or Æthelwulf, sent the text of an apocalyptic vision to the court of Louis the Pious, warning against the sins of a Christian people.[7] In 852 Lupus of Ferrières wrote to Æthelwulf requesting a pious donation of roofing-lead, appealing to strength recently conferred 'against the foes of Christ', presumably at *Aclea* in 851.[8] Alfredian continuity is shown by alms given on behalf of forces besieging London in 883, 'and there, by the grace of God, their prayers were well answered after that promise'.[9] There may be a significant contrast with West Frankish experiences under Charles the Bald, where royal piety was more heavily invested in bonding rituals with ecclesiastical participants, principally located away from the court, in churches and monasteries.[10] The more promising comparison is with East Francia where ecclesiastical and logistical conditions created

---

[2] *VA* 76, lines 12–16, and cc. 37–8.

[3] *VA* 76, lines 16–26; cf. c. 16; *ASC* s.a. 883 (MSS BCDEF); Keynes, 'Mercians', pp. 22–3.

[4] Keynes, 'Anglo-Saxon Entries in the "Liber Vitae" of Brescia', in *Alfred the Wise*, ed. Roberts and Nelson, pp. 99–119; Nelson, 'Franks and the English', pp. 143–6; Scharer, *Herrschaft*, pp. 11–18.

[5] C. Stancliffe, 'Kings who Opted Out', in *Ideal and Reality*, ed. Wormald, pp. 154–76, at 171–2.

[6] S. Keynes, 'The Vikings in England, c. 790–1016', in *The Oxford Illustrated History of the Vikings*, ed. P. Sawyer (Oxford, 1997), pp. 48–82, at 48–9 and 60–2; N. P. Brooks, 'England in the Ninth Century: the Crucible of Defeat', in his *Communities and Warfare*, pp. 48–68, at 58–60; S. Foot, 'The Making of *Angelcynn*: English Identity before the Norman Conquest', *TRHS* 6th series 6 (1996), 25–49, at 37–8, with note 54.

[7] *AB* s.a. 839; Keynes, 'Anglo-Saxon Entries', p. 113, note 58.

[8] *Epistolae*, ed. Marshall, pp. 21–2; trans. in EHD, no. 217.   [9] *ASC* s.a. 883 (MSS BCDEF).

[10] Nelson, 'Lord's Anointed', esp. pp. 124–7, cf. 120–4; Nelson, ' "King Across the Sea" ', p. 67.

more opportunities for intimate contact between the king and secular aristocracy; the greater intensity of warfare along the eastern frontier encouraged a strongly martial edge.[11] Louis the German was unusual in his ability to extend royal devotion into wider rituals of secular aristocratic unity; his distinctive posturing, focused on the True Cross and Davidic warrior kingship, supplies the closest contemporary parallel.

The inclusive character of West Saxon devotion receives further support from the two royal rings.[12] Highly unusual in their Christian iconography, they seem to represent the emergence of a distinctive 'court' style of West Saxon metalwork, consistently characterized by techniques of spiritual representation.[13] The Æthelwulf ring depicts a pair of peacocks at the Fountain of Life (cf. Apocalypse XXI. 6), strongly associated with Christian immortality. The iconography is not otherwise found in Anglo-Saxon art, but frequently appears in Carolingian gospel-books; parallels are especially close in two products of Charlemagne's court school, the Godescalc Evangelistary and the St-Médard Gospels.[14] The Æthelswith ring depicts the Lamb of God, associated with redemption and peace. Otherwise attested only in later manuscripts and metalwork, the image held special significance in Carolingian art, probably once prominent on an interior mosaic in the palace chapel at Aachen. Again, the scheme finds closest parallels in art of royal patronage, in the St-Médard Gospels and Codex Aureus of Charles the Bald.[15]

The value of such gifts probably lay in an ability to facilitate, as well as to symbolize, wider participation in devotional concerns. In each case, the iconography is capable of multiple interpretations, and perhaps deliberately so, but the schemes correlate suggestively with the growing royal need for divine support. The Lamb of God bore strong symbolic potential, while the Carolingian derivation of both schemes was probably itself significant amid Æthelwulf's cross-Channel alliance. Ring-giving would have complemented directly militant royal gifts. Another 'Trewhiddle' artifact often cited is the sword found at Abingdon, whose upper guard has been interpreted as bearing the four Evangelist symbols.[16] One identification remains problematic, but such a scheme would have compelling implications on a weapon used in viking warfare. Though the style is often thought mature, a late ninth-century date cannot be ruled out, nor indeed some specific association with the West Saxon dynasty.

---

[11] Goldberg, 'Frontier Kingship'; Goldberg, *Empire*, pp. 39–47, 129–32 and 186–206.
[12] C. Haith in *Golden Age*, nos. 9 and 10; L. Webster in *Making of England*, nos. 243 and 244.
[13] *Ibid.*, p. 268; cf. above, p. 40.
[14] L. Webster, '*Ædificia nova*: Treasures of Alfred's Reign', in *Alfred*, ed. Reuter, pp. 79–103, at 91–3.
[15] *Ibid.*, p. 91. [16] C. Haith in *Golden Age*, no. 14; Webster, '*Ædificia nova*', pp. 89–90.

The repertoire is again distinctive. In the case of East Francia, the two rings seem lavish, in gold, when compared with the 'Spartan' royal image attributed to Louis the German, as one 'for whom the instruments of war were the greatest treasures', cherishing 'the hardness of iron more than glitter of gold'.[17] Borne out in his humble dress of armour with woollen clothing, Louis' image represented a conscious challenge to the elaborate ceremonial and luxurious display of the West Frankish court under Charles the Bald.[18] The West Saxon household struck a potent balance in combining swords with other, purely demonstrative, accoutrements, such as rings. The picture relates closely to Elias's model, in the correlation of symbolic expression with the more monetized nature of its West Saxon resource base, when compared with the very limited circulation of coinage east of the Rhine.[19]

Royal devotion gained potency from a further act of piety. Æthelwulf's so-called 'Second' Decimation of 854 has proved difficult to interpret precisely, often receiving cursory treatment. Certainly, a major donation occurred at this time; claims for an earlier 'First' Decimation are restricted to charters of dubious authority, lacking an attested context.[20] According to the *Chronicle*, 'King Æthelwulf "booked" the tenth part of his land throughout all his kingdom to the praise of God and his own eternal salvation'. Asser offers alternative details, with Æthelwulf freeing 'the tenth part of his whole kingdom from every royal service and tribute, and ... he made it over on the cross of Christ to the Triune God, for the redemption of his soul and those of his predecessors'.[21] There are charters associated with the same donation; Keynes has advanced strong grounds for accepting the basic form that they share, without necessarily accepting each purported transaction.[22] Each claims to have been written at the royal vill at Wilton, on Easter Sunday (22 April) 854, recording the outcome of 'wholesome counsel' (*consilium salubre*) between the king, bishops, ealdormen and other councillors. This Æthelwulf had brought to fruition in resolving to give 'the tenth part of lands throughout our kingdom not only to the holy churches but also to our thegns established in the same kingdom, to have in perpetual freedom, that such a donation

---

[17] Regino of Prüm, *Chronicon*, ed. Kurze, s.a. 876, p. 110. Cf. Notker the Stammerer, *Gesta Karoli Magni Imperatoris*, ed. Haefele, I.34, II.17 and II.18, pp. 46–7 and 87–9, cf. 83–4.

[18] Goldberg, 'Frontier Kingship', pp. 73–8; Goldberg, *Empire*, pp. 186–97.

[19] Goldberg, 'Frontier Kingship', pp. 76–7; Goldberg, *Empire*, pp. 194–5 and 204–6.

[20] Keynes, 'West Saxon Charters', pp. 1115–16 and 1119–23; cf. the unwarranted scepticism of A. P. Smyth, *King Alfred the Great* (Oxford, 1995), pp. 376–8, 382–3 and 403–6.

[21] *VA* 11, lines 1–5.

[22] S 302, S 303, S 304, S 305, S 307 and S 308 (H. P. R. Finberg, *The Early Charters of Wessex* (Leicester, 1964), pp. 209–13); Keynes, 'West Saxon Charters', pp. 1120–2.

might remain fixed and unchangeable, freed from all royal service and the burden of all secular servitude'.

As an act assessed at the tenth, the decimation may conceivably relate to Carolingian practices; the question requires further investigation, but the nature of land tenure means that its implications can only be understood in local context.[23] One suggestion is that the tenth may have applied straightforwardly to all royal land (as opposed to the king's personal property), in which case the decimation would have amounted to a significant transfer indeed, although lay grants might have included land formerly held on loan.[24] Yet this may rely too heavily on Asser's words; other possibilities are raised by an authentic charter of 855, showing the decimation in operation in Kent.[25] The land in question was initially granted to the Kentish thegn Dunn, who subsequently gave it to Rochester, subject to the life-interest of his wife. The West Saxon 'Decimation' text confirms that immediate beneficiaries could include thegns, who would then have had the opportunity at least to convey the land to an ecclesiastical community of their choice.

The crucial question is whether all grants took this form, in which case the decimation may have applied to all land capable of being 'booked', namely, to all folkland, by definition only in lay hands;[26] or whether the decimation may have applied more widely, covering all land subject to secular burdens.[27] Two effects can be inferred which would have resulted in either case. First, the decimation seems likely to have contributed significantly to the process by which bookland was widened into a tenure of secular convenience. The thegn Dunn initially retained his land for the lifetime of his wife; his final bequest to an ecclesiastical community need not have been typical. Second, the decimation can only have involved a significant reduction in secular burdens on affected land. The conversion of folkland into bookland, assumed under all interpretations, usually attracted the concession of certain exemptions from royal dues. General freedom from secular burdens is explicitly conceded in the West Saxon 'Decimation' text; the only difficulty lies in gauging the precise extent of the reduction being conceded.

---

[23] *Ibid.*, p. 1120, note 3. Cf. now J. L. Nelson, 'Rights and Rituals', *TRHS* 6th series 14 (2004), 1–24, at 14–24, for largely complementary observations; other work is imminently expected from Susan Kelly.

[24] The interpretation favoured by Finberg, *Wessex*, pp. 191–2, cf. J. M. Kemble, *The Saxons in England*, 2 vols. (London, 1849) II, 480–90.

[25] S 315 (BCS 486; *Rochester*, ed. Campbell, no. 23; trans. in *EHD*, no. 89).

[26] Preferred by Stevenson (*VA*, pp. 186–91); here against Nelson, 'Rights', pp. 15–16, envisaging grants *de novo* of Æthelwulf's personal property (her '[my]' lacks manuscript support, cf. S 315; also above, pp. 38–9). Cf. Whitelock in *EHD*, p. 525.

[27] Floated by Finberg for the supposed 'First' Decimation of 844 (*Wessex*, pp. 187–90).

The act was explicitly presented as a measure 'for the prosperity of the kingdom and the welfare (*salute*) of the people committed to me by almighty God'; this has conventionally been seen in the context of Æthelwulf's journey to Rome.[28] One can quite imagine the logic of generosity in anticipation of his future absence, yet the decimation's significance must also be judged against its likely effects, within heightened contemporary efforts towards defensive mobilization, shown by experimental use of the reservation clause in West Saxon charters of the 840s.[29] The decimation occupies a pivotal position, immediately preceding the additional reservation of fortress-work, regularly present from 858.[30] The 'Decimation' text lacks explicit reservation, but Æthelwulf is unlikely to have conceded such duties when their fulfilment was otherwise becoming more regularly stipulated.[31] A limited reduction in secular burdens would have been the more generous amid heightened extraction for defensive purposes. The decimation is best interpreted as a strategic 'tax cut', designed to encourage co-operation in defensive measures through a partial remission of royal dues. As noted, the reservation of fortress-work correlates suggestively with evidence for urban renewal; the decimation was a further instrument by which this was achieved.[32]

Royal gift received collective response: the text continues with the wishes of Ealhstan, bishop of Sherborne, and Swithhun, bishop of Winchester, 'with all those serving God, that every Saturday each community of monks and nuns would sing fifty psalms, and every priest would sing two masses, one for King Æthelwulf and the other for bishops and ealdormen (*pro episcopis et ducibus*): for the living king, "Deus qui justificas impium"; for bishops and ealdormen, "Praetende Domine"'.[33] The masses occur in both Gelasian and Gregorian liturgical traditions, with inevitable textual variations.[34] The measures are seen to strengthen Æthelwulf's gift, 'for as long as the Christian faith and religion shall remain constant among the people of the English', now represented as a collective means of honouring Christ, the Virgin Mary and all saints, in veneration of Easter, 'that almighty God may deign to be favourable (*propitiari*) to us and to our descendants'. Collective hopes of divine

---

[28] Abels, *Alfred*, pp. 68–70; Nelson, 'Rights', p. 17; cf. Stevenson (*VA*, p. 191) and Keynes, 'West Saxon Charters', p. 1120, note 4.

[29] Above, pp. 23–4.   [30] Brooks, 'Military Obligations', p. 44.

[31] Finberg, *Wessex*, pp. 204–5.   [32] Above, pp. 23–4.   [33] Finberg, *Wessex*, pp. 210–11.

[34] A point missed by Nelson, 'Rights', pp. 16–17, claiming specific Frankish derivation. 'Old Gelasian Sacramentary' (*Liber sacramentorum Romanae aecclesiae*, ed. Mohlberg *et al.*, pp. 247–8); 'Eighth-century Gelasian Sacramentary' (*Liber sacramentorum Gellonensis*, ed. Dumas and Deshusses, CCSL 159 and 159A, 241–2 and 256–7); 'Gregorian Sacramentary' (*Sacramentaire grégorien*, ed. Deshusses I, 431–4 and II, 132–4 and 143–4).

favour acquired deeper symbolic significance, not merely of unity against pagan enemies, but of some specific commitment towards the burdens of defence.

There was nothing unusual in divine placation: striking is the delicate coincidence of prayer and administrative benefit. Such thinking differed from ecclesiastical responses, exemplified by Alcuin, where the range of sins punished by the vikings was so comprehensive as to urge more general ecclesiastical reform.[35] The more appropriate comparison is with West Frankish royal devotion, in a kingdom similarly mustered in viking defence. As Nelson has observed, Frankish ecclesiastical attitudes were markedly more militant; this reflected further differences in the ecclesiastical provision of military service.[36] Divine aid in battle was regularly promised in West Frankish 'Mirror for Princes' texts, yet such statements were primarily concerned with the church alone.[37] For Frankish ecclesiastics, the church's contribution was uniquely twofold, supplying not only 'fleshly soldiers' (*carnales milites*), but also 'spiritual soldiers' (*spiritales milites*) whose greater value lay precisely in propitiatory prayer.[38] In Æthelwulf's kingdom, in contrast, the defensive contribution in question was consciously universal.

Prayer also enshrined political authority; the masses commemorated ecclesiastical gratitude extending beyond Æthelwulf to all other members of the West Saxon order. These details are the earliest evidence for an emerging West Saxon discourse of power, characterized by several key assumptions. The first was an equality of status between bishops and ealdorman, far from universal in pre-viking England and presumably encouraged by their respective roles as royal agents. The fundamental transformation would have operated on bishops, through the disintegration of ecclesiastical structures, and their increasing incorporation within royal lordship.[39] This had the effect of placing bishops in a position comparable to ealdormen, as holders of office whose conduct was equally regulated by prior bonds of lordship. Parallels can only have been encouraged by the territorial basis of both offices, and the increasing military and legal activities of bishops, together with shared patterns of royal attendance.[40]

[35] Letters of Alcuin on the attack on Lindisfarne (793): MGH Epist. II, nos. 16, 19 (trans. in *EHD*, nos. 193 and 194) and 20.
[36] Nelson, '"King Across the Sea"', pp. 62–7; cf. Coupland, 'God's Wrath', pp. 547–53.
[37] *RC* 14–16, pp. 62–77; Hincmar, *De regis persona et regio ministerio*, cc. 10–15, esp. 10, PL 125: 841–4.
[38] *RC* 19, p. 87; Hincmar, *De regis persona*, c. 10, PL 125: 842A; Staubach, *Rex Christianus*, pp. 158–68, esp. 166–7; Nelson, 'Charles the Bald and the Church', pp. 79–80, with note 25.
[39] Above, pp. 44–58.   [40] Above, pp. 30–2, 36 and 48–54.

A second feature was the conception of authority in universal terms, as divine service, united by fundamental answerability to God. The mass prescribed 'for bishops and ealdormen' is transmitted in two versions, one explicitly concerned with those in positions of authority, with each prayer offered to God on behalf of 'your faithful men, all bishops, abbots, canons, monks, or kings and governors (*gubernatores*)'.[41] In both, opening prayers take the form of general petitions; the remaining texts are more focused, soliciting aid in removing the sins of the faithful, strengthening them against temptations. The overall effect was to suggest a strong causal connection between the favourability of the entire West Saxon order, and the moral conduct of bishops and ealdormen, perhaps extending to all in worldly authority. As royal councillors all thegns were 'wise men' (*witan*); the term may well reflect comparable responsibilities of learned or informed judgement.[42] Such discourse captured the fundamental ambiguity of episcopal office, semi-detached at best from its former ecclesiastical framework, yet conferring authority far from explicitly royal. The picture harmonizes closely with Asser's perspective, listing the king's 'bishops and ealdormen, and his thegns most noble and dear to him, and reeves as well (in all of whom, after the Lord and the king, the power of the entire kingdom is seen to be invested, as is appropriate)'.[43] The same had applied a generation earlier, with an entire aristocracy sharing in the exercise of a universalized worldly authority, ultimately from God.

A final feature was the scope for implicit comparison between royal and aristocratic conduct. The tone of prayers 'for bishops and ealdormen' was shared by the mass 'for the living king', soliciting aid even more intensively against dangers of sin.[44] The king's role is consistently that of a divine servant (*famulus*), with heightened need of God's mercy and protection to preserve his faithful service, free from all temptations, while cleansed and forgiven of all sins. Considered as a liturgical whole, the effect of these provisions was to sustain a further activity consciously shared between the king and his nobles, in the concerns of office-holding itself, as authority ultimately subject to divine regulation. Potent in its own right, such discourse offers a precious context for all later royal statement.[45]

---

[41] *Sacramentaire grégorien*, ed. Deshusses I, 433–4; for the other version, see *Liber sacramentorum Romanae aecclesiae*, ed. Mohlberg et al., pp. 247–8; *Liber sacramentorum Gellonensis*, ed. Dumas and Deshusses, pp. 256–7; *Sacramentaire grégorien*, ed. Deshusses II, 143–4.

[42] For pre-Alfredian usage, see esp. *Ine* Preface and S 337 (BCS 1210; *Church of St Paul*, ed. Gibbs, no. 2), dated 867; cf. above, pp. 34–6.

[43] *VA* 91, lines 36–45 (cf. K&L, *Alfred*, pp. 101–2).

[44] *Liber sacramentorum Gellonensis*, ed. Dumas and Deshusses, pp. 241–2; *Sacramentaire grégorien*, ed. Deshusses I, 431–2 and II, 143–4.

[45] Cf. below, pp. 130–78.

The image of kingship as exemplary was common in Carolingian thought; the function of West Saxon kingship bears comparison with royal policy initiated some thirty years earlier under Louis the Pious, enshrined in the *Admonitio ad omnes regni ordines*, datable to the period 823–5.[46] Part of wider efforts to maintain imperial unity through ecclesiastical reform, the capitulary reflected Pauline conceptions of community as *corpus Christi*.[47] Louis began by reaffirming the responsibilities of his predecessors, for the honour of the church and the stability of the realm, but he had followed their example 'in our own way'.[48] For 'although the whole of this ministry seems to rest in our person', royal reasoning explained, 'it is known to have been divided into parts by divine authority and human ordering in such a way that each of you in his own place and in his own order has a part of our ministry; whence it is clear that I must be the admonisher of all of you, and all of you must be our helpers'.[49]

As Nelson observes, 'Louis' programme was summed up as the securing of *communis utilitas*', language redolent of the Roman state.[50] In the admonitions that follow, bishops and counts (*comites*) were explicitly equated as those with the greatest share in the royal *ministerium*. Episcopal 'ministry' lay principally in pastoral duties and the proper monitoring of monks and priests.[51] Comital 'ministry' was summarized as the upholding of 'peace and justice' and the honour of the church; expectations included just judgement, the protection of orphans, widows and paupers, and the restraining of theft and robbery.[52] Further admonitions urged reciprocal co-operation and monitoring of fulfilment.[53] These ideals were widely disseminated, prominently preserved in the capitulary collection of Ansegisus. Key chapters were regularly cited in the legislation of Charles the Bald, supplying the dominant discourse of office-holding throughout the later Carolingian world, with deepest impact in West Francia.[54]

How far this agenda might have exercised direct influence is an open question, but Louis' programme may well have been known in Æthelwulf's household. The judicial and peace-keeping functions of the

---

[46] MGH Capit. I, no. 150, pp. 303–7, but cited from Ansegisus, *Capitularium Collectio*, II.1–24, ed. G. Schmitz, MGH Capit. nova series I (Hanover, 1996), pp. 521–41. Guillot, 'Une ordinatio méconnue'; cf. esp. T. Zotz, 'In Amt und Würden. Zur Eigenart "offizieller" Positionen im früheren Mittelalter', *Tel Aviver Jahrbuch für deutsche Geschichte* 22 (1993), 1–23, at 15–16.

[47] Ephesians IV. 7–16 and I Corinthians XII. 4–27; Guillot, 'Une ordinatio méconnue', pp. 467–9; Fried, 'Der karolingische Herrschaftsverband', pp. 18–26.

[48] Ansegisus, *Capitularium Collectio*, II.1–2.

[49] *Ibid.*, II.3.   [50] *Ibid.*, II.13; Nelson, 'Kingship and Royal Government', p. 426.

[51] Ansegisus, *Capitularium Collectio*, II.4 and 5.   [52] *Ibid.*, II.6.   [53] *Ibid.*, II.10 and 12.

[54] Guillot, 'Une ordinatio méconnue', pp. 485–6; cf. Edict of Pîtres (864), cc. 1, 4, 10, 35 and 36 (MGH Capit. II, no. 273, pp. 312–13, 315 and 327). Carroll, 'Archbishops and Church Provinces', pp. 101–3 and 108–9, for East Frankish reception of Ansegisus; the framework was not incompatible with royal friendship (cf. Althoff, *Otto III*, pp. 16–22).

Carolingian count, exercised territorially over a *comitatus*, offered clear parallels with the role of ealdormen. Yet the shire-system lay more tightly under royal control: there were other differences of scale and number.[55] *Duces et comites* were repeatedly grouped by Frankish writers as 'those who ought to rule the people of God after the king'.[56] Reminiscent of Louis' *Admonitio*, such terms anticipate Asser's perspective. Yet much room remains for independent West Saxon development. For example, there is no way of detecting explicitly 'ministerial' language before Alfred's reign, though its presence is not unlikely. There is also a very major differentiating factor in the weakness of ecclesiastical structures. In theory at least, Louis' programme was one step towards the incorporation of kingship into a single Frankish church. Prominent in Wessex was the incorporation of bishops into a royal agenda, largely unencumbered by 'ecclesiology' or ecclesiastical reform.

ROYAL OFFICE-HOLDING: THE FIRST ENGLISH CORONATION ORDER

Further aspects of royal devotion are evident in the inauguration ritual undertaken by West Saxon kings. The status of this ritual demands separate treatment, as a form of communication deployed only rarely, in the elevation of a king. The ritualized nature of inauguration provided opportunities for collective participation, by their nature unusual. The exalted context determined the expression as normative rather than descriptive, offering a unique window onto the ideals and expectations of the political community in its entirety. Modern access to pre-Alfredian ritual is almost entirely dependent on a single source, the First English Coronation *Ordo*. The earliest such rite to survive from the early medieval west, it embodies a ritual in use from the accession of Æthelwulf, and quite possibly earlier. Although the text is preserved in later manuscripts, Nelson has identified features pointing to an earlier, English, origin; West Saxon usage depends in the first instance on its impact on Hincmar's *Ordo* for Judith's anointing in 856.[57]

Royal anointing in England has conventionally been approached from a Frankish perspective; what should be stressed are the differences

---

[55] K.-F. Werner, '*Missus-marchio-comes*. Entre l'administration centrale et l'administration locale de l' empire carolingien', in *Histoire comparée de l'administration IVe–XVIIIe siècles*, ed. W. Paravicini and K.-F. Werner, Beihefte der Francia 9 (Munich, 1980), pp. 191–239; Innes, *State and Society*, pp. 118–39.

[56] Council of Paris (829), c. 3 (MGH Conc. II, p. 654); *DIR* 5, p. 208; Hincmar, *Ad episcopos regni*, c. 14 (PL 125: 1015D); Fried, 'Der karolingische Herrschaftsverband', p. 37.

[57] J. L. Nelson, 'The Earliest Surviving Royal *Ordo*: Some Liturgical and Historical Aspects', in her *Ritual*, pp. 341–60, at 343–53; cf. D. Pratt, *English Coronation Ordines in the Ninth and Early Tenth Centuries*, ASNC Guides, Texts and Studies (forthcoming).

in biblical experiment. Frankish royal anointing, first attested as occurring in 751, was consciously expressive of gentile unity.[58] Pippin's anointing asserted a collective identity for the Frankish people, as a new Israel, under the new-found status of his dynasty. Behind such symmetry lay the assertiveness of Pippin's episcopal consecrators, in an emerging context of reform. Soissons had hosted a seminal episcopal council; Frankish identity was further expressed by a reissuing of *Lex Salica*, with a new prologue couched in biblical terms.[59] Another factor was papal involvement: for nearly a century, the only attested anointings are those by successive popes, generally applied to royal sons in the lifetime of their father.[60] Such rituals reinforced the special relationship between the Carolingian dynasty and the papacy, enhancing the status of their chosen people. The re-emergence of anointing by bishops under Charles the Bald is striking: again, the context was an expression of consensus, in the distinctive package of interrelationships which had stabilized West Francia from the early 840s.[61] At its heart lay royal functions in preserving and maintaining law, in explicit appeal to the memory of 'ministerial' rulership initiated under Louis.[62] Under Hincmar's draftsmanship, royal anointing further dramatized these expectations in key moments of transition.

How comparable were West Saxon experiences? In the period up to *c.* 825 the Southumbrian church came closest to reform along Frankish lines; the emergence of early evidence for anointing is unlikely to be coincidental. Striking are many references to the *populus Dei* or *populus Christianus*; the same terms denoted Frankish 'chosen' status.[63] Yet reforms were limited, lacking strong alliance between any single dynasty and wider episcopal power. The dynastic instability of early kingship sat differently with Old Testament models, generally stressing heredity. Offa's anxiety was symptomatic, seeking the symbolic anointing of his son; in the event, Ecgfrith outlived his father only by months, succeeded by Cenwulf, at best a distant kinsman.[64] Such ambitions were further complicated by Canterbury's location, outside the three largest kingdoms, and ecclesiastical pre-eminence.[65] The only ninth-century charter

---

[58] J. L. Nelson, 'Inauguration Rituals', in her *Ritual*, pp. 283–307, at 290–2; Nelson, 'Lord's Anointed', pp. 108–10.

[59] *Ibid.*, p. 109.   [60] *Ibid.*, pp. 110–11 and 114–15.

[61] *Ibid.*, pp. 116–19.   [62] Nelson, 'Kingship, Law', pp. 146–9.

[63] Wallace-Hadrill, *Early Germanic Kingship*, pp. 97, 107–8 and 115–18; synod of *Clofesho* (747), c. 1; *capitulare* of the papal legates (786), c. 14.

[64] Cf. D. N. Dumville, 'The Ætheling: a Study in Anglo-Saxon Constitutional History', *ASE* 8 (1979), 1–33, at 14–21 and 25–30.

[65] Cf. J. L. Nelson, 'National Synods, Kingship as Office, and Royal Anointing: an Early Medieval Syndrome', in her *Ritual*, pp. 239–57.

associated with a coronation records a grant by the Mercian king Ceolwulf, seemingly made on the same day as his consecration by Wulfred in 822.[66] The occasion was straightforwardly 'royal': the attendance of four Mercian bishops was normal for a Mercian royal assembly. The site of donation was *Bydictun*, probably within Mercia; the other known location for coronations was also a royal vill, Kingston in Surrey, attested from the accession of Edward the Elder. This compares with episcopal and archiepiscopal churches, generally favoured for Frankish anointings.

The mechanism of divine support was similarly restricted to kingdoms. The early emergence of some notion of 'English' ethnicity, and the likely role of Bede in propagating this identity, have become dominant themes after contributions by Wormald.[67] Yet as he himself argued, Bede's depiction of the English as if they were a single people, 'chosen' by God, makes most sense in the light of his purposes in constructing 'ecclesiastical' history, dominated by a need to explain the trajectory of an English church.[68] Bede's vision should not distract from the many constructions that could be placed on the English and their past, as a multiplicity of 'peoples', all potentially capable of assertion through the lens of history.[69] *Populus Dei* could be used ambigiously: the First *Ordo* is nonetheless specific on the new king's duties towards 'the Christian people subject to him'.[70] Symptomatic of English conditions, the existence of multiple *populi Christiani* has received insufficient weight in much cross-Channel comparison.[71] The new Israel being fostered was primarily political, applying equally to the Mercians or to the 'bipartite' kingdom under West Saxon rule.

The West Saxon order from the mid-ninth century offered significantly different conditions; central was the new accommodation reached with Canterbury.[72] Kingston's relevance as the location for later coronations has been noted; its adoption cannot be dated precisely. Æthelwulf might conceivably have been anointed there in 838, but

---

[66] S 186 (BCS 370; trans. in *EHD*, no. 83).

[67] P. Wormald, 'Bede, the *Bretwaldas* and the Origins of the *gens Anglorum*', in *Ideal and Reality*, ed. Wormald, pp. 99–129; P. Wormald, 'Anglo-Saxon Society and its Literature', in *The Cambridge Companion to Old English Literature*, ed. M. Godden and M. Lapidge (Cambridge, 1991), pp. 1–22; cf. also Foot, '*Angelcynn*', pp. 38–45.

[68] *HE* I.22; P. Wormald, 'The Venerable Bede and the "Church of the English"', in *The English Religious Tradition and the Genius of Anglicanism*, ed. G. Rowell (Oxford, 1992), pp. 13–32, at 17–24.

[69] Surveyed in S. Bassett (ed.), *The Origins of Anglo-Saxon Kingdoms* (Leicester, 1989).

[70] Wickham Legg, *Coronation Records*, p. 9 ('Rectitudo regis est').

[71] Cf. Wallace-Hadrill, *Early Germanic Kingship*, pp. 117–18; sceptical assessment of Frankish unity by Wormald, 'Anglo-Saxon Society', p. 15, and Wormald, 'Venerable Bede', p. 19.

[72] Above, pp. 44–8.

Alfred's legacy offers a context at least as plausible.[73] Whatever the case, its role underlines the pertinence of the new relationship. Indeed, it is quite possible that the very practice of anointing was a further consequence of West Saxon access to the south-east. For that matter, there is no proof that Mercian kings continued to be anointed in this period. Archbishop Ceolnoth's occasional attendance at Mercian assemblies should be registered, but the exclusive West Saxon relationship with Canterbury might well have extended to anointing.

The First *Ordo* acquires force in this context. Its precise origins remain uncertain, nor need the *Ordo* reflect West Saxon practice alone, given earlier evidence for Mercian (and Northumbrian) anointings.[74] Yet it enjoyed stable deployment: there are grounds for suspecting the *Ordo*'s regular use certainly as far as Alfred's accession. The next secure development is the compilation and adoption of the Second English *Ordo*, in which elements of the First *Ordo* were combined with material related to contemporary Frankish *ordines*.[75] The Second *Ordo* can strictly be dated no more closely than *c.* 880 × *c.* 925: plausible arguments have been advanced for composition during or after Alfred's reign, but in either case, its role was expressive of his political legacy.[76] The enduring stability of the First *Ordo*, respected in revision, suggests strong congruity with West Saxon power. It is therefore significant that the First *Ordo* should exhibit many features which set it apart from the mainstream tradition of Carolingian *ordines*. As Nelson has shown, the First *Ordo* is distinguished by affinities with texts either of direct Insular origin, or known Insular reception and transmission.[77] Striking are those with Insular 'Mirrors for Princes', such as Pseudo-Cyprian, the Irish *Collectio Canonum* (including extracts from the *Proverbia Grecorum*), and the letters of Boniface, Cathwulf and Alcuin.[78]

Of many distinctive procedures, most encompassing is the extreme degree of biblical re-enactment, in a genre necessarily dependent on Old Testament precedent. Among all anointed biblical leaders, the fundamental model was that of Solomon: the entire ritual was understood in Solomonic terms.[79] As in Solomon's anointing at Gibeon, oil was

---

[73] Wormald, 'Ninth Century', p. 140; cf. Keynes, 'Mercians', pp. 36–7; Scharer, *Herrschaft*, pp. 26–7; Story, *Carolingian Connections*, pp. 222–3.

[74] Nelson, 'Earliest Surviving Royal *Ordo*', pp. 352–3 and 360.

[75] J. L. Nelson, 'The Second English *Ordo*', in her *Ritual*, pp. 361–74; *Ordines Coronationis Franciae*, ed. Jackson I, 168–200.

[76] Both by Nelson: 'Second English *Ordo*', pp. 365–7, cf. her revised view in 'The First Use of the Second Anglo-Saxon *Ordo*' (forthcoming). The question is considered further in Pratt, *English Coronation Ordines*.

[77] Nelson, 'Earliest Surviving Royal *Ordo*', pp. 343–53.   [78] *Ibid.*, pp. 350–1 and 359.

[79] *Ibid.*, p. 355.

poured from a horn over the king's head by a presiding bishop, presumably the archbishop of Canterbury.[80] Anointing was a collective act involving 'all the bishops', accompanied by the antiphon 'Zadok the priest' (III Kings I. 45), and Psalm XX, 'The king shall rejoice'. Solomonic precedent was further invoked in the acclamation 'Vivat rex' and procedures for enthronement.[81] As Nelson notes, although Solomon was cited in Carolingian *ordines*, under Hincmar Old Testament symbolism was diluted by parallels with baptism and episcopal consecration.[82] This was an identifiably West Saxon form of Solomonic posturing, of significance specific to West Saxon rule.

In particular, the First *Ordo* involved a symbolic 'strengthening' of the royal office, of a form and character appropriate to West Saxon conditions. As Nelson notes, striking is the king's exercising of qualities with respect 'to his people in general rather than to the Church and its ministers', and the special position of royal judgement.[83] In later Carolingian *ordines* the function of justice was stressed by means of a formal announcement or promise by the ruler, in preliminary procedures otherwise dominated by episcopal pronouncement. In the First *Ordo*, the only comparable procedure occurs in the final section, after the king's enthronement; these took the form of 'three precepts' which the new king was 'to enjoin (*precipere*) on the Christian people subject to him', not an undertaking by king alone. In the first place, 'the church of God and the whole Christian people' were to 'preserve true peace at all times'; the king himself was to 'forbid all thefts and injustices among all orders', and to 'enjoin equity and mercy in all judgements, that the clement and merciful God may therefore grant us his mercy'.[84] Similar principles had been active at Kingston: all participants had sought to preserve 'the peace and unanimity of the churches of God and of the whole Christian people subject to their secular authority through the grace of almighty God, by the bond of very firm love'.[85]

The same precepts had force within dispute settlement, in the shift from synods to royal assemblies, which presumably had further implications for local assemblies under reeves and ealdormen.[86] Developments

---

[80] Wickham Legg, *Coronation Records*, p. 5, cf. III Kings I. 38–45; Nelson, 'Earliest Surviving Royal *Ordo*', p. 355.

[81] Wickham Legg, *Coronation Records*, p. 7, cf. III Kings I. 39 and I Chronicles XXIX. 22–4; Nelson, 'Earliest Surviving Royal *Ordo*', pp. 358–9.

[82] *Ibid.*, p. 355.   [83] *Ibid.*, p. 351.

[84] 'In primis ut ecclesia dei et omnis populus christianus veram pacem servent in omni tempore ... Aliud est ut rapacitates et omnes iniquitates omnibus gradibus interdicat ... Tertium est ut in omnibus iudiciis aequitatem et misericordiam praecipiat ut per hoc nobis indulgeat misericordiam suam clemens et misericors deus': *ibid.*, p. 358.

[85] S 1438 (BCS 421); Scharer, *Herrschaft*, pp. 26–7.   [86] Cf. above, pp. 31–2.

of this kind are first explicit in Alfredian evidence, but best regarded as a further consequence of widening use of bookland.[87] The combination of precepts assumes special significance given these heightened opportunities for personal procedural judgement. Earlier in the ritual royal responsibilities again concerned the entire people committed to the king's charge. At one point they are likened to a 'flock' (*grex*), for whom the king is exemplary, but this is the closest the *Ordo* comes to potentially pastoral duties.[88] His position is typically that of a 'servant' (*famulus*) to God, but there is no mention of a royal *ministerium*. More pressing was the need for a series of virtues, most notably justice, equity, mercy and the Solomonic virtue of wisdom (*sapientia*); all had biblical assocations with law-giving and judgement.

All were to be exercised inclusively. The word *ecclesia* appears rarely: its use conveys little sense of any special conditions in the relationship between king and bishops, or ecclesiastics in general.[89] In the Kingston agreement and 'Decimation' text, *ecclesiae* were conspicuously plural.[90] More pertinent was the physical existence of a multitude of churches, each dealing autonomously with the king and other interested secular parties. There was neither need nor opportunity for West Saxon rulers to locate their kingship within the universal church, nor for bishops to exercise any special function in the preserving of royal justice. In a further Solomonic echo, 'ealdormen' (*principes*) actively participated in enthronement.[91] Even the ritual's heart was not monopolized by bishops: in the first investiture after anointing, 'ealdormen' are again ascribed a role, with 'all bishops', in transmitting the sceptre. As Nelson notes, 'this is the only extant *Ordo* to prescribe the active participation of laymen within the liturgical rite proper – in striking contrast with the West Frankish *Ordines* tradition from Hincmar onwards'.[92] The act reinforced a key feature of West Saxon rule, in the comparability implied between bishops and ealdormen. A further unusual feature was the absence of crowning, in favour of a helmet (*galea*); on this basis Nelson identifies this short sceptre (*sceptrum*) as the central item of regalia. 'With Old Testament and specifically Davidic connotations, signifying law as equity', the sceptre encapsulated justice as shared 'royal' concern.[93]

---

[87] Cf. above, pp. 31 and 37–8.   [88] Wickham Legg, *Coronation Records*, p. 5 ('In diebus').

[89] *Ibid.*, pp. 4 ('Deus qui populis tuis'), 5 ('Deus electorum fortitudo') and 9 (first precept).

[90] 'Pax et unianimitas ecclesiarum Dei': S 1438 (BCS 421). 'Ut decimam partem terrarum per regnum nostrum non solum sanctis ecclesiis darem, verum etiam et ministris nostris': Finberg, *Wessex*, p. 210.

[91] Nelson, 'Earliest Surviving Royal *Ordo*', pp. 358–9, with note 90.

[92] *Ibid.*, p. 356.   [93] *Ibid.*

These qualities were reinforced by the hope of divine favour, also Solomonic, involving peace and prosperity.[94] Both had legal resonances in local peace-keeping: one request is limited to the king's nobles (*proceres*), but in general the hope was similarly comprehensive.[95] The king was 'to bring peace to the people subject to him in the simplicity of dove', and 'to obtain a peaceful kingdom' through Solomonic mildness (*cum mansuetudine*).[96] The Kingston agreement had explicitly preserved 'peace and unanimity' among 'the whole Christian people'. No less suggestive are associations with prosperity, frequently through images of natural abundance familiar from Insular 'Mirrors for Princes'.[97] Both helmet and staff were accompanied by blessings invoked under the patriarchs.[98] 'From the dew of heaven and the fatness of the earth, an abundance of corn and wine' (Genesis XXVII. 28): the aspirations were not far from contemporary estate-management.

For all the language of peace there was also much room for war. On several occasions the king was envisaged defending his people from the assaults of enemies through divine mercy and protection.[99] In one recension the ritual is set within the Mass, which may not be a later feature; settings prescribed include a reading from Leviticus XXVI. 6–9: 'You shall pursue your enemies, and they shall fall before you, and five of yours shall pursue a hundred others, and a hundred of you ten thousand, and your enemies shall fall by the sword. I will look on you, and make you increase, and you shall be multiplied, and I will establish my covenant with you'.[100] The flexibility of divine favour, combining victory with peace, matched the iconographic range of West Saxon metalwork. There were also harmonies with Æthelwulf's decimation. In this respect, as many others, the Solomonic dimensions of West Saxon kingship were well suited indeed to the viking age.

THE USES OF LITERACY?

So far this investigation has focused on non-literate modes of communication, at least in their execution; the picture is completed by the

---

[94] The general theme is addressed by P. Kershaw, *Peaceful Like Solomon: the Image and Practice of the Peacemaking King in the Early Medieval West* (Oxford, forthcoming).

[95] Wickham Legg, *Coronation Records*, p. 6 ('Benedic domine hunc presulem').

[96] *Ibid.*, pp. 5 ('Deus electorum fortitudo') and 6 ('Benedic domine hunc presulem').

[97] Nelson, 'Earliest Surviving Royal *Ordo*', p. 351.

[98] Wickham Legg, *Coronation Records*, p. 7 ('Omnipotens deus det tibi' and 'Benedic domine fortitudinem principis').

[99] *Ibid.*, pp. 4 ('Te invocamus'), 6 ('Benedic domine hunc presulem'), 7 ('Benedic domine fortitudinem principis') and 8 ('Deus perpetuitatis auctor').

[100] Wickham Legg, *Coronation Records*, p. 4.

role of the written word. Alfredian developments make lay experiences especially pertinent, but evidential problems are innumerable. Alfredian material supplies a context for lay education unmatched in earlier evidence. The challenge lies in assessing pre-existing practices, which cannot be reconstructed with the same precision.

Closely connected is the problem of oral communication: methodological difficulties abound in approaching the perceptions of largely illiterate groups through surviving records. Yet there can be no straightforward equation between orality and silence, nor literacy and written record. Such binary oppositions have long seemed unsustainable for societies where the potential of writing may have been widely appreciated, despite a 'restriction' of literate skills.[101] For Anglo-Saxon England, interaction between oral and written has long been recognized, but its implications have remained more controversial. In 1976, Patrick Wormald advanced a relatively sceptical view of lay literacy in Anglo-Saxon England which has remained influential among wider audiences, despite more recent specialist criticisms.[102] Wormald's case was shaped by his concern to avoid what he termed the 'Fallacy of the Anticipated Audience': that in assessing texts apparently directed towards lay audiences, allowance must be made for oral recitation rather than reading at first hand.[103] Largely on this basis, by adopting such demanding standards in the search for lay literacy, Wormald claimed a priority of *verbum* over *scriptum* throughout the Anglo-Saxon period, questioning Alfredian developments as a possible watershed.

Wormald's logic was irrefutable, but the burden placed upon it is questionable in the light of more recent approaches, not least that of Brian Stock on later medieval developments.[104] For Stock, this ability of the written word to reach a wider audience was the most important feature of its power.[105] Personal literate skills mattered less when the minimum requirement was merely a single literate reader. Stock's

---

[101] McKitterick (ed.), *Literacy*; K. O'Brien O'Keeffe, *Visible Song: Transitional Literacy in Old English Verse* (Cambridge, 1990); N. Howe, 'The Cultural Construction of Reading in Anglo-Saxon England', in *The Ethnography of Reading*, ed. J. Boyarin (Berkeley and Los Angeles, CA, 1992), pp. 58–79; M. Innes, 'Memory, Orality and Literacy in an Early Medieval Society', *P&P* 158 (February 1998), 3–36; A. Orchard, 'Oral Tradition', in *Reading Old English Texts*, ed. K. O'Brien O'Keeffe (Cambridge, 1997), pp. 101–23.

[102] Wormald, 'Literacy'; M. Clanchy, *From Memory to Written Record: England 1066–1307*, 2nd edn (London, 1993), esp. pp. 1–2 and 28–32. Cf. Kelly, 'Lay Society', and Keynes, 'Royal Government'.

[103] Wormald, 'Literacy', p. 96.

[104] B. Stock, *The Implications of Literacy: Written Language and Models of Interpretation in the Eleventh and Twelfth Centuries* (Princeton, NJ, 1983); B. Stock, *Listening for the Text: On the Uses of the Past* (Baltimore, MD, 1990).

[105] *Implications of Literacy*, pp. 3–87; *Listening for the Text*, pp. 1–49.

position rested on the distinctive potency of written texts, their capacity to transform thought and behaviour: to 'promise, if ... not always [to] deliver, a new technology of the mind'.[106] As such, it occupies appropriate middle ground on 'the consequences of literacy', between universal effects and theories placing greater weight on context.[107] It was on this basis that Stock developed his notion of a 'textual community', applicable to any group sharing common understanding of authoritative texts. Widening reception of the written word laid the basis for a 'textually oriented society', with momentous implications for all aspects of communication. Stock himself has argued for the eleventh and twelfth centuries as the period when this process gained greatest momentum.[108] In fact, 'as early as the ninth century', his approach urges re-evaluation of lay access to textual culture, and the agents or agencies by which this was secured.

The problematic relationship between oral and written is encapsulated by vernacular poetry.[109] Verse was a mode of expression among most aristocracies; Old English is distinguished by the size of its surviving corpus, and the wide variety of genres and material, offering potential insight into many aspects of contemporary life. Yet much poetry has proved difficult to contextualize; the vast bulk of the corpus is transmitted only in a few, late, manuscripts, in contexts generally less than revealing of origin and transmission. There have been innumerable attempts to date texts more closely on linguistic or historical grounds, but consensus has frequently failed to emerge, leaving most examples to float restlessly within a broader period between the seventh and tenth centuries.[110]

What remains clear is the existence of varying attitudes towards vernacular poetry, with significant implications for its preservation. Among reforming voices, a distinction was drawn between 'frivolous

---

[106] *Implications of Literacy*, p. 10.
[107] J. Goody and I. Watt, 'The Consequences of Literacy', in *Literacy in Traditional Societies*, ed. J. Goody (Cambridge, 1968), pp. 27–68; B. Street, *Literacy in Theory and Practice* (Cambridge, 1984); B. Street, *Social Literacies: Critical Approaches to Literacy in Development, Ethnography and Education* (London, 1995).
[108] Stock, *Listening for the Text*, esp. pp. 19–20.
[109] D. Whitelock, 'Anglo-Saxon Poetry and the Historian', in her *Bede to Alfred*, no. 3; Wormald, 'Bede, *Beowulf*'; D. G. Scragg, 'The Nature of Old English Verse', in *Cambridge Companion*, ed. Godden and Lapidge, pp. 55–70; P. W. Conner, 'Religious Poetry', and F. C. Robinson, 'Secular Poetry', both in *A Companion to Anglo-Saxon Literature*, ed. P. Pulsiano and E. Treharne (Oxford, 2001), pp. 251–67 and 281–95.
[110] C. Chase (ed.), *The Dating of Beowulf* (Toronto, 1981); R. M. Liuzza, 'On the Dating of *Beowulf*', in *Beowulf: Basic Readings*, ed. P. S. Baker (New York, 1995), pp. 281–302; R. E. Bjork and A. Obermeier, 'Date, Provenance, Author, Audiences', in *A Beowulf Handbook*, ed. R. E. Bjork and J. D. Niles (Exeter, 1997), pp. 13–34.

and profane verses', referring to 'heroic' poetry, and those on religious themes, which might be tolerated for didactic reasons.[111] The view is articulated, significantly, in an Alfredian context in a story told of Aldhelm. Preserved by William of Malmesbury, the account is plausibly identified as material drawn from Alfred's *Handbook*; it purports to have arisen from a poem attributed to Aldhelm, still recited in Alfred's day, and the need to explain 'why so great a man had composed these things which might be considered frivolous'.[112] Aldhelm had performed as poet for pastoral purposes, 'by inserting words of scripture gently into vernacular stories (*ludicra*)': 'if he had proposed to do this severely and with excommunication, he would have achieved absolutely nothing'. As Wormald observes, such attitudes inspire little confidence in the representative nature of the surviving corpus, in which 'religious' poetry outweighs heroic verse by almost ten to one.[113]

The metrical form of verse, dependent on alliteration, suggests pre-literate origins; Bede's early account of a poet in action describes poetry being composed and recited from memory.[114] No less suggestive are contexts envisaged in *Beowulf*, with sections describing recitation by a poet or *scop*, on one occasion a noble of the king's household.[115] Yet oral features of delivery were probably not relics of 'primary orality', unadulterated by the written word. There have been many attempts to detect oral composition in surviving verse, principally through stock phrases or formulae, but this 'oral-formulaic' approach has generally proved unconvincing: the same formulae recur in poems which demonstrably translate Latin sources.[116] Revisionism has been strengthened by appreciation of the learned character of verse, certainly extending to *Beowulf* as well as 'religious' examples.[117] There are strong grounds for regarding the eighth and ninth centuries as a formative period in the transformation of verse into a recorded, literate medium. The dangers of equating *Beowulf* with contemporary practice are here acute.

---

[111] Wormald, 'Bede, *Beowulf*', pp. 42–9.

[112] William of Malmesbury, *De Gestis Pontificum Anglorum*, ed. Hamilton, pp. 332–3; D. Whitelock, 'William of Malmesbury on the Works of King Alfred', in her *Bede to Alfred*, no. 7, pp. 78–93, at 90–1; M. Lapidge, '*Beowulf*, Aldhelm, the *Liber Monstrorum* and Wessex', in his *ALL* I, 271–312, at 277–8. See P. G. Remley, 'Aldhelm as Old English Poet: *Exodus*, Asser and the *Dicta Alfredi*', in *Latin Learning and English Lore: Studies in Anglo-Saxon Literature for Michael Lapidge*, ed. K. O'Brien O'Keeffe and A. Orchard, 2 vols. (Toronto, 2005) I, 90–108 (my reading of this passage differs slightly). Cf. D. Pratt, 'King Alfred's *Handbook*' (forthcoming); below, pp. 127 and 141.

[113] Wormald, 'Bede, *Beowulf*', pp. 47–8.   [114] *HE* IV.24.

[115] *Beowulf* 86–98, 496–8, 864–915 and 1063–1159.

[116] Orchard, 'Oral Tradition', pp. 103–10.

[117] P. Clemoes, *Interactions of Thought and Language in Old English Poetry* (Cambridge, 1995); M. Lapidge, 'Aldhelm's Latin Poetry and Old English Verse', in his *ALL* I, 247–69; cf. A. Orchard, *The Poetic Art of Aldhelm* (Cambridge, 1994), pp. 45–54 and 119–25.

SOURCES OF TEXTUAL CULTURE (I) ECCLESIASTICAL COMMUNITIES

Ecclesiastical communities require close attention given their contact with the secular world. Striking is the very limited evidence for literate skills among pre-Alfredian laymen, in this context or any other.[118] Certainly, there are occasional instances of laymen who could read, and an ecclesiastical education must always have remained a possibility. In the late seventh century, Northumbrian nobles reportedly sent their sons to be taught by bishop Wilfrid; similar arrangements are described for the church of York in the mid-eighth century.[119] Bede depicts a Mercian nobleman in the act of reading, albeit within a vision.[120] Yet there are grounds for regarding such cases as unusual.[121] Bede also describes two kings as *doctissimus* in contexts suggesting full Latin literacy, but both received their education abroad, in Francia and Ireland.[122] English experiences bear comparison with the fuller evidence for these neighbouring regions. There was no Anglo-Saxon equivalent to the body of 'professional' learned men (*filid*) in Ireland.[123] The English evidence also seems slight against the much stronger case for literate skills among the Frankish nobility, reliant on rich evidence for book ownership and numerous examples of literate education.[124] In all likelihood literacy in early Anglo-Saxon England was more tightly 'restricted'.

English conditions may well have limited the extension of ecclesiastical learning to practices of lay devotion. Both Theodore and Bede had advocated monastic disciplines for the laity, in penance and intensive prayer, but there is very limited evidence for penitential composition or use in pre-viking England, striking when compared with Ireland and Francia.[125] Lay devotion, especially aristocratic, was well served by less extreme practices, principally the veneration of saints, alms-giving and the liturgical commemoration of the departed.[126] In each case, the expiation of sins was achieved vicariously, through the giving of gifts. Yet the written word remained important, regularly

---

[118] Wormald, 'Literacy', p. 105.
[119] Stephanus, *Vita Wilfridi*, ed. Colgrave, c. 21, p. 44; *Vita Alcuini*, ed. Arndt, c. 4, p. 186.
[120] *HE* V.13.   [121] Wormald, 'Literacy', p. 105.   [122] *HE* III.18 and IV.26.
[123] Wormald, 'Literacy', pp. 101–4; cf. D. Ó Corráin, 'Nationality and Kingship in pre-Norman Ireland', in *Nationality and the Pursuit of National Independence*, ed. T. W. Moody (Belfast, 1978), pp. 1–35, at 12–19.
[124] R. McKitterick, *The Carolingians and the Written Word* (Cambridge, 1989), pp. 211–27; P. Riché, *Écoles et enseignement dans le Haut Moyen Age: fin du Ve siècle – milieu du XIe siècle*, 2nd edn (Paris, 1989), pp. 287–313.
[125] Bede's letter to Ecgberht, c. 15; Thacker, 'Monks, Preaching', pp. 152–64; A. J. Frantzen, *The Literature of Penance in Anglo-Saxon England* (New Brunswick, NJ, 1983), pp. 61–93 and 122–8.
[126] Thacker, 'Monks, Preaching', pp. 160–70; Keynes, *The Liber Vitae of the New Minster*, pp. 49–65; Keynes, 'Anglo-Saxon Entries'.

experienced in forms associated with devotional gift-giving, encapsulated by the charter or 'landbook' (*landboc*).[127] The earliest charters were produced by ecclesiastical scriptoria, contributing to the resilience of the charter form, as a document wholly or predominantly in Latin by which all gifts were pious acts, ultimately directed towards God and protected by ecclesiastical sanction. A common formula presented the gift as among 'those things salubriously defined according to the decrees of canons and the statutes of synods', which 'though the word alone should suffice as evidence, nevertheless, because of the uncertain condition of future times, ought to be strengthened by the most firm record of writing'.[128] Lay involvement was implicit in the act of witnessing, sometimes involving additional rituals, such as the symbolic transfer of a sod of earth, or the placing of the charter on an altar or gospel-book.[129]

The role of bookland must be set alongside the wider mediation of textual culture, generally through pastoral provision. One mode would have been liturgical, via attendance at Mass and other rituals, such as baptism. Both Bede and the synod of *Clofesho* had recommended translation of the Apostles' Creed and the Lord's Prayer: the concern in each case was for priestly understanding, suggesting the continued importance of Latin texts.[130] Another channel would have been the duty of preaching, regarded by Bede as a form of performance. One may wonder how far such communication relied on writing: vernacular poetry may well have been significant. Aldhelm's portrayed interest was explicitly pastoral, involving an audience of common people returning home after attending Mass. His interception of this audience 'on a bridge which joined the town to the fields' was justified as a means of leading the people to salvation.[131]

A further factor was linguistic. English experiences were heavily shaped by the sharp divide between the spoken language, Old English, and Latin, which had to be learnt from scratch.[132] This contrasted with the linguistic situation in the Frankish world, where late Latin had been

---

[127] Kelly, 'Lay Society', esp. pp. 39–57.
[128] P. Wormald, *Bede and the Conversion of England: the Charter Evidence*, Jarrow Lecture 1984 (Jarrow, 1985), pp. 9–11; S 327 (BCS 502; *Rochester*, ed. Campbell, no. 24).
[129] Kelly, 'Lay Society', p. 44.
[130] Bede's letter to Ecgberht, cc. 5 and 6; synod of *Clofesho*, c. 10, cf. 27; Thacker, 'Monks, Preaching', pp. 162–3; A. Crépin, 'Bede and the Vernacular', in *Famulus Christi*, ed. G. Bonner (London, 1976), pp. 170–92.
[131] Cf. above, p. 81, note 112.
[132] Wormald, 'Literacy', pp. 99–104; Kelly, 'Lay Society', pp. 38–9 and 57–9; G. H. Brown, 'Latin Writing and the Old English Vernacular', *Schriftlichkeit im frühen Mittelalter*, ed. U. Schaefer, ScriptOralia 53 (Tübingen, 1993), 36–57; G. H. Brown, 'The Dynamics of Literacy in Anglo-Saxon England', *Bulletin of the John Rylands University Library of Manchester* 77.1 (1995), 109–42.

inherited as the spoken language of the Frankish aristocracy, followed by a slow transition to Romance in western regions.[133] There is an important contrast with much greater toleration of the vernacular in Irish learning, partially attributable to the expertise of the *filid*. Old English was not entirely neglected: one should especially note the swiftness with which the vernacular was committed to writing in law-codes of the seventh century, and the early appropriation of poetry for religious purposes. Yet in general ecclesiastical instruction was concerned with Latin literacy alone. Bede was typical in favouring techniques of 'total immersion'.[134] Pupils would have begun with liturgical texts, including the divine Office and the psalter, before proceeding to Christian Latin poetry, and finally scripture itself, accompanied by texts of patristic authority.[135] The position of Old English was at best marginal, often literally so. Limited toleration was conceded via glosses for difficult Latin words, generally attributed to the influence of Theodore and of Irish attitudes.[136] Yet continuous use was only countenanced in extreme need. Bede presented his translations as a last resort, necessitated by a profusion of unlearned priests.[137] Two further renderings were attributed to Bede at the time of his death, the beginning of St John's Gospel and part of a text by Isidore, but none has survived: their impact is uncertain.[138] Nor did the measures of *Clofesho* effect a wider reorientation of learning.[139]

The first signs of a watershed appear in the ninth century. Especially suggestive is the earliest extensive example of continuous glossing, in the Vespasian Psalter, an early eighth-century manuscript which probably received its vernacular glosses in the early or mid-ninth century.[140] This compares with more extensive use of Old English in written documents and evidence for the written circulation of vernacular poetry.[141] Yet

---

[133] McKitterick, *Written Word*, pp. 7–22; M. Banniard, 'Language and Communication in Carolingian Europe', in *NCMH* II, 695–708.

[134] Brown, 'Dynamics of Literacy', pp. 113–18.

[135] See esp. M. Lapidge, 'Anglo-Latin Literature', in his *ALL* I, 1–35, at 1–4.

[136] Brown, 'Dynamics of Literacy', pp. 116–17 and 119; M. Lapidge, 'The School of Theodore and Hadrian', and 'Old English Glossography: the Latin Context', both in his *ALL* I, 141–68 and 169–81.

[137] Bede's letter to Ecgberht, cc. 5 and 6.

[138] Cuthbert's letter on the death of Bede, in *Venerablis Baedae Opera Historica*, ed. Plummer I, clx–clxiv.

[139] Synod of *Clofesho*, c. 10, cf. 27.

[140] London, British Library, Cotton Vespasian A. i (St Augustine's, Canterbury, *c.* 725). The gloss is now understood to be the copy of an existing text, possibly of early ninth-century composition: M. Gretsch, 'The Junius Psalter Gloss: its Historical and Cultural Context', *ASE* 29 (2000), 85–121, at 88–91 and 105, note 78, cf. M. Lapidge, 'The Archetype of Beowulf', *ASE* 29 (2000), 5–41, at 41, note 108.

[141] Below, pp. 89–91.

there may be dangers in postulating lost works of pre-Alfredian prose. Alfred claimed to recall 'very few men ... who could understand their divine services in English' at the time of his accession: the problem was continued reliance on Latin texts, amid falling standards in Latin literacy.[142] One may cite only the *Old English Martyrology* and Old English Bede, as possible, if problematic, candidates for earlier 'literary' prose.[143] The crucial question concerns lay experiences. At local level, this can only be approached indirectly, through charters and other documents affording an impression of dynamic change.[144] The record shows a marked expansion in the quality and quantity of surviving documentation. Striking is the much greater reliance on the vernacular, in new forms of document such as wills, leases, and other agreements concerning benefactions and liturgical commemoration.[145] There is also the emergence of the chirograph, authorizing multiple copies of important documents for the retention of interested parties.[146] Charters remained in Latin, but incorporated a boundary clause as a new vernacular element.[147] Widening use of bookland placed lay aristocrats in more regular contact with the written word. As Kelly notes, the increasing use of English points to functional advantages of the written vernacular, capable of being read aloud.[148]

The most detailed evidence survives from the archives of Canterbury and Worcester; change within Wessex is suggested by the large number of lay beneficiaries among ninth-century charters. Dubious claims to land could be successfully bolstered through appropriate written evidence.[149] Aristocratic families amassed sizable archives to safeguard their estates and privileges. The will of a Mercian nobleman, Æthelric, included provision of Westbury for the lifetime of his mother, Ceolburh, with reversion to the see of Worcester.[150] To demonstrate his freedom of bequest, Æthelric was required to attend a synod at *Clofesho* 'with the books of the estate (*cum libris et ruris*) ... which previously my kinsmen delivered and granted to me' for formal inspection. Æthelric twice

[142] *CP*, p. 2, lines 12–18. Cf. Gameson, 'Destruction', pp. 185 and 198.

[143] Above, p. 50.

[144] Kelly, 'Lay Society', pp. 46–57; work cited below by K. Lowe.

[145] *Ibid.*, pp. 46–51; K. Lowe, 'The Nature and Effect of the Anglo-Saxon Vernacular Will', *Journal of Legal History* 19 (1998), 23–61.

[146] K. Lowe, 'Lay Literacy in Anglo-Saxon England and the Development of the Chirograph', in *Anglo-Saxon Manuscripts and their Heritage*, ed. P. Pulsiano and E. M. Treharne (Aldershot, 1998), pp. 161–204, at 162–7.

[147] K. Lowe, 'The Development of the Anglo-Saxon Boundary Clause', *Nomina* 21 (1998), 63–100.

[148] Kelly, 'Lay Society', pp. 56–7.   [149] *Ibid.*, pp. 45–6.

[150] S 1187 (BCS 313 and 314; trans. in *EHD*, no. 81); P. Wormald, 'Charters, Law and the Settlement of Disputes in Anglo-Saxon England', in his *Legal Culture*, pp. 289–311, at 292–8; Sims-Williams, *Religion*, pp. 174–6.

entrusted charters to noble friends, first for the duration of a pilgrimage to Rome, and latterly as a means of guaranteeing his will. When the reversion was later disputed, matters again hinged on possession of the 'books' (*libri*): as Wormald notes, 'the smell of ink hovers over the whole story'.[151]

Documentation was as paramount after synodal decline. The family of two Kentish ealdormen, Ealhhere and his brother Æthelmod, maintained close ties with Canterbury over a forty-year period to the eve of Alfred's accession.[152] Many of their documents have survived as originals, drawn up by scribes from the Christ Church community.[153] Further Canterbury documents record the generosity of a later ealdorman, Ælfred, whose region of responsibility was probably Surrey. Ælfred's will, datable no more closely than 878 × 889, instructs that 'those persons to whom I am most anxious to grant my property and bookland, namely my wife Werburg and the child of us both, be made known in writing to King Alfred and all his councillors and advisers, and likewise to my kinsmen and intimate friends'.[154] His example shows gift-giving extending to books themselves. A sumptuous mid-eighth-century gospel-book bears a vernacular inscription recording the book's recovery by Ælfred and Werburg through a payment of pure gold, after it had reached the hands of a viking army.[155] The gospels were subsequently given to Christ Church, on condition that they were read each month for Ælfred and his family, 'for the eternal remedy of their souls'. The inscription is undated, but viking activity in Kent in the 850s and 860s supplies the most likely context. Quite apart from viking forbearance, these exchanges are suggestive of English lay attitudes towards the use of books, here conducted by ecclesiastical proxy.

SOURCES OF TEXTUAL CULTURE (2) THE WEST SAXON ROYAL HOUSEHOLD

Such conditions were the context for developments in the royal household, focused on the role of royal priests. Keynes has argued persuasively for such expertise as the 'central agency' responsible for the vast majority of West Saxon royal charters.[156] In Kent and in Mercia, there is good evidence that charters continued to be produced by local

---

[151] S 1433 (BCS 379, trans. in *EHD*, no. 84); Wormald, 'Charters, Law', p. 298.
[152] Brooks, *Canterbury*, pp. 147–9.   [153] *Ibid.*, pp. 169–73.
[154] S 1508 (BCS 558; *SEHD*, no. 10; trans. in *EHD*, no. 97); Brooks, *Canterbury*, pp. 151–2.
[155] S 1204a (*SEHD*, no. 9; trans. in *EHD*, no. 98); Brooks, *Canterbury*, pp. 201–2; M. Brown in *Making of England*, no. 154.
[156] Keynes, 'West Saxon Charters', pp. 1131–49.

ecclesiastical scriptoria.[157] The widening use of bookland was common to all regions: greater centralization may also be attributable to the unusual scale and character of the West Saxon royal household.

Royal priests sustained a potent monopoly over the production of royal documents. In addition to charters, this included correspondence and other forms of document, in many cases known from occasional glimpses. Royal wills, for example, could require extensive duplication. As an 'updated' version, King Alfred's will reveals concern to ensure the destruction of all earlier copies, widely distributed; similar dissemination might be suspected for Æthelwulf's will, which does not survive.[158] Alfred's gift of the monasteries of Congresbury and Banwell was accompanied by what Asser describes as two 'letters' (*epistulae*), listing their contents; the value of list-making is demonstrated by the Burghal Hidage.[159] Again, record-keeping can be detected significantly earlier: a duplicate copy of the Kingston agreement was kept by Ecgberht and Æthelwulf 'with their hereditary documents' (*cum hereditatis eorum scripturis*), while an original charter of 846 may well have passed through the royal archives.[160]

Comparison can be drawn with the use of writing in Carolingian rule. Again, there is an important difference in the impact of ecclesiastical reform. The greater quantity and diversity of surviving documentation attests to the general success of Carolingian educational initiatives.[161] In western regions, these measures were aided by linguistic conditions sustaining a narrow, if widening, gap between spoken language and written Latin.[162] Curiously, they may offer the closer parallel: English use of the vernacular removed an important barrier to lay access. This compares with more limited evidence for vernacular documentation in East Francia, probably attributable to the high value of ecclesiastical Latinity.[163] Comparative material is invaluable as an indication of what might have been possible. From Asser's two *epistulae*, one might infer the production of estate-surveys of some kind, paralleled in Carolingian polyptychs and later English examples.[164] The Burghal Hidage compares

---

[157] P. Chaplais, 'The Origin and Authenticity of the Royal Anglo-Saxon Diploma', *Journal of the Society of Archivists* 3.2 (1965), 48–61, at 58–9; Brooks, *Canterbury*, pp. 168 and 327–30; Keynes, 'West Saxon Charters', p. 1109, note 1.

[158] S 1507 (BCS 553; *SEHD*, no. 11; trans. in *EHD*, no. 96; K&L, *Alfred*, pp. 172–8); *VA* 16.

[159] *VA* 81, lines 19–24.

[160] S 1438 (BCS 421) and S 298 (BCS 451; trans. in *EHD*, no. 88), with Keynes, 'West Saxon Charters', pp. 1112–14 and 1117–18; cf. S 354 (BCS 556).

[161] J. L. Nelson, 'Literacy in Carolingian Government', in her *Frankish World*, pp. 1–36; McKitterick, *Written Word*, pp. 25–37, 60–75 and 98–115.

[162] Nelson, 'Literacy', pp. 6 and 9–10; McKitterick, *Written Word*, pp. 7–22.

[163] Nelson, 'Literacy', pp. 9–10.   [164] Campbell, 'Placing King Alfred', p. 5.

with fuller evidence for Carolingian list-making, as well as the suggestive arrangements of Æthelwulf's decimation.[165] There are again Carolingian parallels, and later English evidence, for written instructions in the regulation of coinage.[166]

Open to more precise assessment may be the role of written law. Evidence for earlier West Saxon written law is restricted to the code of Ine, only known from its inclusion in Alfred's law-book. Yet this appendix probably preserves a received text of some antiquity.[167] Some of the laws in Ine's name may be later eighth-century accretions, yet as Wormald suggests, it is unlikely 'that all would have been ascribed to Ine by Alfred's time if issued by any significantly later successor'.[168] An Alfredian compilation is unlikely to have omitted laws of Ecgberht or Æthelwulf, had any been available. At least one early collection of laws was available, but the solitary survival of Ine is matched by the fortuitous preservation of all the early Kentish laws in a single, late manuscript.[169] It is difficult to muster a case for wide dissemination prior to Alfred's own laws. All this suggests an important contrast with the intensive law-giving of many Carolingian rulers, represented by the corpus of capitularies.[170] Again, the closer parallel may be with East Francia, where capitulary material was largely restricted to texts issued with other rulers before the late ninth century.[171]

Questions remain of the household's role in formal teaching. There is abundant evidence for lay education in the households of Carolingian rulers; it was partly on this basis that the court could be described as a *schola*, 'a place of discipline', where young nobles could acquire the skills necessary for aristocratic life.[172] Alfred's own *schola* must be approached in this light; its novelty cannot be assumed given the presence of royal priests. The main evidence is Alfredian retrospection. By the early 890s, royal rhetoric was invoking a devastating analysis of recent developments. Asser attributed shortcomings in Alfred's own education to the 'shameful negligence of his parents and those involved in his upbringing (*nutritores*)'.[173] The language of 'nourishing' was used pervasively in

---

[165] Nelson, 'Literacy', pp. 14–24.

[166] Edict of Pîtres (864) (MGH Capit. II, no. 273); Nelson, *Charles the Bald*, pp. 33–4 and 207–9; M. Blackburn, 'Mints, Burhs, and the Grately Code, cap. 14.2', in *Defence*, ed. Hill and Rumble, pp. 160–75.

[167] P. Wormald, '"Inter Cetera Bona Genti Suae": Law-Making and Peace-Keeping in the Earliest English Kingdoms', in his *Legal Culture*, pp. 179–99, at 188–92; Wormald, *MEL* I, 268–9 and 277–81.

[168] Wormald, '"Inter Cetera Bona"', p. 191. [169] Wormald, *MEL* I, 244–53.

[170] Nelson, 'Literacy', pp. 21–36.

[171] Goldberg, *Empire*, pp. 18 and 210; cf. MacLean, *Charles the Fat*, p. 20.

[172] Riché, *Écoles*, pp. 294–7; Innes, '"Place of Discipline"'. Cf. below, pp. 124–6.

[173] *CP* p. 2, lines 12–18; *VA* 22, lines 10–12, cf. c. 75, lines 21–6.

Frankish contexts to describe commendation and bonding between young nobles and adult aristocratic masters.[174] Alfred's own upbringing offers evidence for earlier practices.

Asser's handling of Alfred's early education is problematic, but its apparent inconsistencies may reflect the difficulty of recovering contemporary nuances; it cannot be dismissed out of hand.[175] Alfred remained *illiteratus* until his twelfth year or even later; it was in this context, of an inability to read, that blame was accorded to Alfred's parents. Even before this time he had received instruction orally, largely in the form of vernacular poetry.[176] Frequently arousing scepticism, the story of competitive recitation between Alfred and his brothers may reveal much about Alfredian perceptions, if not approached entirely literally. After this, Alfred learnt the services of the divine Office, 'certain psalms and many prayers', probably all primarily or entirely in Latin.[177] The problems posed by Alfred's twelfth year are far from insurmountable: Asser later reports that the king 'had not yet begun to read (*legere*) anything', but this clearly relates to the complex processes of 'literary' translation.[178] The adolescent Alfred's skills had been principally directed to the written vernacular, with some limited extension to simple Latin texts.

How typical was Alfred? The problems of his illnesses have been discussed elsewhere: what needs to be stressed is the fundamental turning-point in Alfred's acquisition of literacy in his twelfth year, coinciding with the onset of his first illness, *ficus*, best interpreted as 'piles, haemorrhoids'.[179] There is no need for any putative period of monastic exile. According to Asser, 'Alfred was always brought up in the royal court (*regio curto*) to the point of inseparability'; the claim is corroborated by charter evidence from the early 860s.[180] Alfred had been driven to more intensive study by the impact of persistent illness; his earlier education was probably not unusual, and may well reflect some wider form of 'court' instruction.[181] Especially striking is the

---

[174] Innes, ' "Place of Discipline" ', pp. 61–6; D. Ganz, 'The Preface to Einhard's "Vita Karoli"', in *Einhard: Studien zu Leben und Werk*, ed. H. Schefers (Darmstadt, 1997), pp. 299–310, at 302.

[175] K&L, *Alfred*, p. 239 (note 36); Kelly, 'Lay Society', pp. 59–60. Cf. Smyth, *Alfred*, pp. 171–98 and 217–24.

[176] *VA* 22, lines 10–15, cf. c. 23.   [177] *VA* 24, lines 1–6.

[178] *VA* 77, lines 25–6; cf. c. 87, lines 1–3.   [179] Pratt, 'Illnesses', pp. 58–64.

[180] *VA* 22, lines 3–4; Pratt, 'Illnesses', pp. 51–2; cf. J.L. Nelson, 'Monks, Secular Men and Masculinity, *c.* 900', in *Masculinity in Medieval Europe*, ed. D.M. Hadley (Harlow, 1999), pp. 121–42, at 135–8.

[181] Cf. P.A. Booth, 'King Alfred versus Beowulf: the Re-education of the Anglo-Saxon Aristocracy', *Bulletin of the John Rylands University Library of Manchester* 79.3 (Autumn 1997), 41–66, from which my interpretation differs on various points of emphasis and detail.

combination of book-use with memorization and recitation. The impression is of sustained access to texts of various kinds, secured by ecclesiastical proxy. There are intriguing possibilities of lay familiarity with simple Latin, not conventionally assumed to have been common in any Anglo-Saxon context. A further implication is the role assigned to vernacular poetry; there is every sign that its recitation was a common lay pursuit. The situation bears close comparison with the better-documented example of the East Frankish royal household under Louis the German. Eric Goldberg has advanced a strong case for associating much ninth-century Germanic verse with this court environment.[182]

The young Alfred's recitation had relied on a written text. A few fragments of vernacular poetry survive from the eighth century, but Asser's account is the earliest datable evidence for a consolidated book of English verse.[183] Another early reference is similarly suggestive. According to Bede, Cædmon's poetry had transformed his monastic *doctores* into *auditores*; the ninth-century Mercian translator added that 'even his teachers wrote down the words from his lips and learnt them'.[184] The West Saxon household has long been suspected as a context for the collection or composition of vernacular poetic texts. It is therefore frustrating that pre-Alfredian 'court' poetry cannot be explored with precision. The main comparanda available are later prose texts. Most attention has focused on 'religious' poetry, and themes and genres related to Alfredian concerns. The translation of Boethius has prompted comparison with 'elegaic' poems such as *The Wanderer* and *The Seafarer*, and with other forms of 'wisdom' poetry on associated themes.[185] Yet in most cases the evidence is insufficient to demonstrate dependence in either direction. Also cited are works associated with the poet Cynewulf, often tentatively assigned to the early ninth century, including *Elene*, *Juliana*, *Christ II*, *Guthlac B* and *Andreas*. Again, the evidence is equivocal and Cynewulf's date disputed.[186] Barbara Raw has highlighted two ninth-century Old Saxon poems certainly known in later Anglo-Saxon England, *Genesis* and the *Heliand*. Both may have been imported at an early stage, but again not certainly before Alfred's reign.[187]

---

[182] Goldberg, *Empire*, pp. 36–7, 179–85 and 301–3; J. K. Bostock, *A Handbook on Old High German Literature*, rev. K. C. King and D. R. McLintock (Oxford, 1976), esp. pp. 118–212; C. Edwards, 'German Vernacular Literature: a Survey', in *Carolingian Culture*, ed. McKitterick, pp. 141–70.

[183] See esp. Whitelock, 'Anglo-Saxon Poetry', pp. 79–80.

[184] *Ibid.*, p. 80; *OE Bede*, p. 346, cf. *HE* IV.24, p. 260. [185] See below, p. 297, cf. pp. 302 and 304.

[186] P. Clemoes, 'King Alfred's Debt to Vernacular Poetry: the Evidence of *ellen* and *cræft*', in *Words, Texts and Manuscripts*, ed. Korhammer, pp. 213–38; Clemoes, *Interactions*, pp. 46–55, 112–16 and 363–408; J. Roberts in *The Blackwell Encyclopaedia*, ed. Lapidge, pp. 133–5.

[187] B. Raw, 'The Probable Derivation of most of the Illustrations in Junius II from an Illustrated Old Saxon *Genesis*', *ASE* 5 (1976), 133–48.

Nor is there reason to regard heroic poetry as necessarily alien to this royal environment.[188] The story of Cynewulf and Cyneheard has often been suggested to depend on a secular poem; the suggestion remains plausible, if incapable of satisfactory demonstration.[189] More decisive is the story from Alfred's *Handbook*: the verse attributed to Aldhelm was potentially 'frivolous', consisting of vernacular stories (*ludicra*).[190] Both terms were attached to heroic poetry by critical voices; at least one such poem seems very likely to have been known in ninth-century Wessex.[191] There are important arguments for identifying *Beowulf* as early and of West Saxon origin or transmission, though the case is inevitably disputed.[192] These possibilities are tantalizing, because the problems they raise are so open-ended. The Aldhelm story may suggest unease with the genre; one may wonder how far attitudes differed a generation earlier.

A query is therefore more constructive than a conclusion. The problematic relationship has been noted between poetic depiction and contemporary practice; discrepancies may well have been particularly marked for audiences in the West Saxon royal household. One might point to the small-scale nature of the (Scandinavian) kingship in *Beowulf*, highlighted by the absence of 'reeves' or 'ealdormen' as intermediate office-holders. No less striking is the role of tribute-taking from non-monetary resources, rather than in coin or units of account; and dependence on gifts of treasure and martial equipment, supplemented only by oral gifts of land. There was no room in *Beowulf* for written charters, or more complex exemption from royal or 'common' dues. All these features are more or less familiar as projected properties of 'heroic kingship' or the 'heroic age', after Chadwick's pioneering study. The problems associated with such terminology are many and various; a fundamental challenge remains in utilizing the rich potential of 'heroic' material in ways sensitive to the operation of contemporary Anglo-Saxon kingship.[193] In another context, Wormald tentatively identified the 'Age of Offa' as 'the end of England's heroic age'; the West Saxon

---

[188] Cf. Booth, 'Alfred versus *Beowulf*', esp. pp. 54–5.

[189] Kleinschmidt, 'Annal for 757', pp. 209–13.

[190] William of Malmesbury, *De Gestis Pontificum Anglorum*, ed. Hamilton, pp. 332–3; Whitelock, 'William of Malmesbury', pp. 90–1.

[191] Wormald, 'Bede, *Beowulf*', pp. 42–5 and 49–52, with Lapidge, '*Beowulf*, Aldhelm', pp. 277–8; cf. Remley, 'Aldhelm', pp. 91 and 103 (note 10).

[192] Lapidge, '*Beowulf*, Aldhelm', esp. pp. 304–11; Lapidge, 'Archetype'; cf. the more extreme case of D. R. Howlett, *British Books in Biblical Style* (Dublin, 1997), pp. 504–40.

[193] See esp. Clemoes, *Interactions*, pp. 13–14 and 55–67; cf. Wormald, 'Bede, *Beowulf* ', pp. 34–9 and 63–8.

royal household may have operated in ways even more distant from the Danish mead-hall Heorot.[194] Quite how such distinctions might have been received remains hidden from view. Alfredian prose offers almost the only available clues.

---

[194] P. Wormald, 'The Age of Offa and Alcuin', in *The Anglo-Saxons*, ed. Campbell, pp. 101–28, at 128.

Chapter 6

THE IMPACT OF THE VIKINGS

From as early as Ecgberht's time, the West Saxon order had faced viking defence; such pressures were central to Alfredian security. Viking activity was a dynamic political stimulus. Culturally, these Danish invaders need not have differed greatly from their opponents, yet their activities posed new challenges to native kingdoms.[1] Amorphous social organization combined with extreme mobility by land and sea to exploit weaknesses in local defence. Both war-bands and armies regularly divided resistance through convenient alliance; opportunism continued in a flexibility of strategic methods, all involving material extraction. Dominated by the redistribution of moveable wealth, viking needs tapped plunder, ransoming and tribute.[2] Initially pursued by piecemeal raiding, from mid-century such income found exploitation by larger armies, borne by substantial fleets of well over 100 ships; corroborated by independent annals, such figures support armies numbering thousands rather than hundreds.[3] Viking extraction was probably critical in elevating the goal of outright conquest, seemingly pursued with consistency by the 'Great Army' from 865. Whatever the case, its successes were swift and comprehensive, Northumbria falling in 867 and East Anglia in 869; by 877 eastern Mercia also lay under viking control. Raiding poachers had turned legitimate gamekeepers: nowhere in Europe was this transformation more effective or extreme.[4]

Only the West Saxon kingdom proved capable of surviving this campaign, narrowly reversing a partial submission to viking rule in 878.

---

[1] Brooks, 'Crucible of Defeat'; Keynes, 'Vikings in England', pp. 48–69; J. L. Nelson, 'The Frankish Empire', in *The Oxford Illustrated History*, ed. Sawyer, pp. 19–47, esp. 35–42.

[2] N. Lund, 'Allies of God or Man? The Viking Expansion in European Perspective', *Viator* 20 (1989), 45–59. esp. 45–7 and 52–8.

[3] Stenton, *Anglo-Saxon England*, p. 243, note 1; P. H. Sawyer, *The Age of the Vikings*, 2nd edn (London, 1971), pp. 120–47; Brooks, 'Crucible of Defeat', pp. 49–59.

[4] Cf. S. Coupland, 'From Poachers to Gamekeepers: Scandinavian Warlords and Carolingian Kings', *EME* 7 (1998), 85–114.

Alfred's victory at Edington was doubly favourable given other regions of viking interest: notably East Anglia, where Guthrum's followers were to settle in 879–80; dynastic developments in West Francia attracted other contingents overseas. Only thirteen years later did Alfred's kingdom face comparable attack, on a return of viking forces prompted by famine and East Frankish defeat. The new threat incorporated pan-viking alliance with East Anglia and Northumbria; its action occupied a larger stage, spanning longer distances, more regularly travelled on horseback. Yet Alfred's kingdom had also been transformed in the intervening period, placing critical developments in his years of peace. The first continuation of the *Chronicle* reveals a host of measures, recently adopted, whose effectiveness faced the proof of practice. All built very effectively on West Saxon structures of local defence, yet their implementation was less secure, as a source of further pressure on income, resources and strategic priority. How were these measures secured? All related to much broader aspects of negotiation and interplay with aristocratic agents; communication was central to Alfred's success.

LOGISTICS OF DEFENCE

At the heart of royal security was the network of some thirty proto-urban 'burhs', fortified centres evenly located throughout Alfred's kingdom: no territory lay beyond a day's march. The scheme was probably informed by many precedents: alongside eighth-century Mercian burhs and West Frankish fortifications of the later 860s is the likely influence of Rome, in the 'Leonine City', papal defensive work completed in the early 850s.[5] Organizational mechanisms drew intensively on West Saxon common burdens. The fullest picture emerges from the Burghal Hidage, seemingly written in the latter part of Edward's reign, though probably based on earlier information.[6] To each burh was assigned a garrison for defence and repair, drawn from territory measured in hides. Four men would be needed for each pole (5½ yards) of perimeter wall; each hide would supply one man. The figure of 2400 hides for Winchester would provide for the adequate defence of 9900 feet of wall; its Roman walls measure 9954 feet, a discrepancy of less than one per cent.[7] Comparable matches have been detected at many

---

[5] Nelson, 'Franks and the English', pp. 147–8; D. Hill, 'The Origin of King Alfred's Urban Policies', in *Alfred*, ed. Reuter, pp. 19–33.

[6] Hill and Rumble (eds.), *Defence*; cf. now J. Haslam, 'King Alfred and the Vikings – Strategies and Tactics 876–886 AD', *ASSAH* 13 (2005), 122–54, questionably restricting burghal construction to 878–9.

[7] P. Wormald in *The Anglo-Saxons*, ed. Campbell, p. 153.

other sites, although some assessments remain problematic. Burghal walls consisted of a deep bank of earth, clad with timber revetments at the front and rear, and surmounted by a fighting platform and palisade, also of wood.[8] Intra-mural streets, running continuously behind the wall, enabled efficient deployment against attack.[9] The burhs were not only protective, but supplied permanently manned bases from which sorties could be mounted against local threat. The *Chronicle* consistently refers to *burgware*, burghal 'inhabitants', yet the context often supports reference to the garrison alone. The suffix *–ware* related closely to *waru* ('defence'), accorded prominence in the Burghal Hidage.[10] Resistance of this sort forced invaders northwestwards in 893; viking armies never penetrated far within Alfred's defended kingdom.

The burghal network was complemented by efforts to reorganize army mobilization, the *fyrd*. The *Chronicle* adds by way of explanation that 'the king had divided his *fyrd* into two, so that always half its men were at home, half on service, except for those men who were to guard the burhs'.[11] The most likely implication is that while each burh would be garrisoned on a continuous basis, only half of all other men liable for military service would be required on campaign at any one time, the other half being allowed to remain 'at home', in a system of periodic rotation.[12] Such mechanisms met agrarian as well as military needs. Increased viking mobility forced defenders also to deploy horses, placing a premium on the supply of basic provisions. Viking survivors at Chester in 893 faced the *fyrd*'s ravaging of the surrounding countryside, killing cattle and seizing corn to feed horses. The aim of adequate provisioning seems to have outweighed the difficulty of achieving smooth rotation; men 'at home' would have aided agrarian continuity. The two roles were complementary: in 895 the *fyrd* reportedly camped close to a viking fortress on royal orders, specifically to protect the local corn harvest.

The *Chronicle* assigns two further innovations to Alfred's initiative; whatever the nature of such attributions, both made notable adaptation of established tactics. One was the construction of double riverine fortifications, also deployed in 895 on the river Lea; the vikings were forced overland, abandoning their ships to destruction and requisitioning.

---

[8] C. A. Ralegh Radford, 'The Pre-Conquest Boroughs of England, Ninth to Eleventh Centuries', *PBA* 64 (1980 for 1978), 131–53, at 149–50.

[9] M. Biddle, 'The Evolution of Towns: Planned Towns before 1066', in *The Plans and Topography of Medieval Towns in England and Wales*, ed. M. W. Barley, CBA Research Report 14 (London, 1976), 19–32, esp. 27–9.

[10] K&L, *Alfred*, p. 287, note 10; A. R. Rumble in *Defence*, ed. Hill and Rumble, pp. 178–81.

[11] *ASC* s.a. 893.   [12] Brooks, 'Crucible of Defeat', p. 64; Abels, *Lordship*, pp. 63–6.

Charles the Bald had employed similar tactics on the Marne, Seine and Loire. Only two bridges were actually fortified, at Pont de l'Arche and Les Ponts-de-Cé, but both involved fortifications on either side of the river.[13] Bridge-work had long numbered among the common burdens; as early as 811 a Kentish charter had referred to 'bridge-building against the pagans'.[14] Many Alfredian burhs lay at the mouths of navigable rivers and at vital crossing-points; both locations may have extended an existing strategy. The other innovation, in ship design, is harder to assess, reportedly involving faster 'long ships' of sixty oars or more.[15] Specially constructed on royal orders, such ships differed from a known design of forty oars. Alfred's prototype 'long ships' are accorded only mixed results; by the early eleventh century, when sound evidence next emerges, ship crews were commonly assessed in units of sixty men.[16] Earlier naval engagements had been won in 851, 875 and 885; at the least, this report shows the importance of seaborne forces as a first line of defence.

Alfred's reforms extended across all three common burdens; fulfilment hinged on the co-operation of aristocratic landholders, under co-ordinated local direction. For Asser, the entire process led back to Alfred's nautical helmsmanship, guiding the ship of his kingdom 'through the many seething whirlpools of this present life'.[17] In place of sailors were all bishops, ealdormen, reeves and 'dearest' thegns; the king had secured their passage 'by gently instructing, cajoling, urging, commanding, and (in the end, when his patience was exhausted) by sharply chastising those who were disobedient' in such a way that he converted all participants in power 'to his own will and to the communal benefit of the whole realm'.[18] The image was more than wishful thinking: supported by the intensive environment of Alfred's household, it gains substance from every aspect of documented action. The 'persuasion' that emerges was fundamentally material, rooted in further measures likely to have eased the worst pressures on local resources. Explored in the following sections, such interaction supplies a context for still deeper aspects of material encouragement, in continuous gesture and wise rule.

[13] J. M. Hassall and D. Hill, 'Pont de l'Arche: Frankish Influence on the West Saxon *burh*?', *Archaeological Journal* 127 (1970), 188–95; S. Coupland, 'The Fortified Bridges of Charles the Bald', *Journal of Medieval History* 17 (1991), 1–12.

[14] S 1264 (BCS 332); Brooks, 'Military Obligations', esp. p. 43.

[15] E. and J. Gifford, 'Alfred's New Long-Ships', in *Alfred*, ed. Reuter, pp. 281–9; M. J. Swanton, 'King Alfred's Ships: Text and Context', *ASE* 28 (1999), 1–22.

[16] C. W. Hollister, *Anglo-Saxon Military Institutions on the Eve of the Norman Conquest* (Oxford, 1962), pp. 108–15; cf. Abels, *Lordship*, pp. 109–10.

[17] *VA* 91, lines 28–35.   [18] *Ibid.*, lines 36–45.

The impact of the vikings

On any assessment, royal defence posed a pressing need for manpower. If followed in full, the Burghal Hidage implied a mobilization of some 27,071 men south of the Thames, out of an estimated total population of *c.* 560,000 in 1086, representing perhaps one in five of all adult males.[19] Garrisons of over a thousand are assigned to thirteen of the thirty-one burhs south of the Thames, the largest being Winchester and Wallingford, each at 2400 hides. Yet these were probably but one element of the *fyrd*, separate from rotating contingents who served on campaign. This was a further duty assessed upon land: a Mercian charter of the early ninth century tends to support later evidence for a typical ratio requiring one man from every five hides of land.[20] The Hidage's cut was already deeper at one man per hide; armies may well have incorporated this further assessment. The construction of fortifications probably extended even more widely. Biddle's estimates for Winchester convey an entirely plausible picture of scale, requiring the preparation of some 7900 tons of knapped flints for the new street-plan five miles long.[21] Although *burgware* supplied some necessary labour, Asser refers more generally to 'commands ... not fulfilled because of the people's laziness';[22] while the *Chronicle* for 892 reveals at least one fortification only half-built, occupied by a few *cirlisce men*. Both in construction and service, these burdens fell in practice on landholders, as lords of men and land; as Brooks implies, the entire scheme depended on a supply of labour from rural estates, probably extending to coercion.[23]

Quite understandably, many landlords seem to have shared the reluctance of peasants in their service. The viking attacks had exposed estates to a pressing double jeopardy, in tribute-payments and physical destruction. After viking activity in Kent in the 850s the noble benefactress Ealhburg foresaw the possible suspension of a food-render for as many as three successive years.[24] The extraction of tribute could be equally punitive. In 872 bishop Wærferth is encountered leasing land to fund a payment rendered to the viking army then occupying London; at around the same time the church of Winchester ceded interest in two estates to King Alfred in lieu of its contribution to a West Saxon

---

[19] Brooks, 'Crucible of Defeat', pp. 64–5.
[20] S 1186a (BCS 201; trans. in *EHD*, no. 73); Stenton, *Anglo-Saxon England*, pp. 290–1; Hollister, *Military Institutions*, pp. 38–58; cf. Abels, *Lordship*, p. 108–15 and 126–8, querying the universality of this ratio.
[21] *Winchester Studies I: Winchester in the Early Middle Ages*, ed. M. Biddle (Oxford, 1976), pp. 272 and 450; cf. Nelson, 'Debate: Trade, Industry', pp. 153–4.
[22] *VA* 91, lines 46–7.   [23] Brooks, 'Administrative Background', pp. 143–4.
[24] S 1198 (*St Augustine's*, ed. Kelly, no. 24).

tribute-payment.[25] As Nelson observes, such examples may be associated with a more general increase in instances of land being granted in return for payment.[26] Another problem was the prospect of peasant flight, especially threatening given trends towards manorialism. In West Francia many peasants deserted the lower Seine valley for waged work in Champagne; in 864 Charles the Bald had offered a chance for them to retain their wages, in an effort to reverse the migration.[27] Alfred's law-book is striking: 'If anyone from one district wishes to seek a lord in another district, he is to do so with the witness of the ealdorman in whose shire he previously served'. By Ine's earlier law, any peasant who stole away from his lord was bound to return to his original lord.[28] Such flexibility suggests a comparable problem of peasant vagrancy, which may well have had political implications. Many West Saxons had accepted Danish rule in 878, while Asser refers to individuals 'without captivity with the pagans' in 886. The formulation occurs within clumsy translation of the *Chronicle*, but may suggest the credibility in Asser's eyes of voluntary submission.[29]

Burghal construction was also the context, according to Asser, of royal 'persuasion'.[30] Measures in question combined the attachment of aristocratic interests to successful construction, and more vigorous efforts to assert bonds of lordship. A connection between fidelity and viking defence, suggested by Wallace-Hadrill for West Francia, actually works better in this English context.[31] Alfred's 'treason law' addressed more than thegnly loyalty; its principles were operative in defining a wider package of crimes as offence against the king.[32] This included theft, suggesting threats to livestock and local order; lords themselves bore heightened responsibilities for peace-keeping and organized pursuit.[33] Protection of the king's life formed one element of these broader measures, against *hlafordsearu* or 'lord-treachery', established 'for all ranks, both commoner and noble (*ge ceorle ge eorle*): he who plots against his lord's life is in return to be liable for his life and all that he possesses'.[34] A complex framework of rights and obligations was here underwritten by the inviolability of lordship in general, delicately shared between lord and king. In loyal service men might actively unite against lawless disturbance; quite apart from income in fines and confiscations, landholders had much to gain from such seigneurial participation in local peace.

---

[25] S 1278 (BCS 533 and 534; trans. in *EHD*, no. 94); S 354 (BCS 556).
[26] J. L. Nelson, 'Wealth and Wisdom: the Politics of Alfred the Great', in her *Ruling Families*, no. 2, pp. 38–9.
[27] Nelson, 'The Frankish Empire', p. 46.   [28] *Af* 37, cf. *Ine* 39; also *AGu* 5.
[29] Cf. Keynes, 'Mercians', p. 24, note 108.   [30] *VA* 91.
[31] M. Wallace-Hadrill, *The Long-Haired Kings* (London, 1962), pp. 12–13.
[32] *Af* 4–4.2; Wormald, 'God and King', pp. 338–42. Cf. below, pp. 232–41.
[33] Cf. esp. *VA* 91, lines 55–67.   [34] *Af* 4.2.

Lordly solidarity extended to the burhs themselves, in a concerted apportionment of future revenues. Revealed in detail for the burh of Worcester in the 890s, such arrangements prefigure later attested interests, suggesting a widespread tactic.[35] Beneficiaries were Æthelred and Æthelflæd, as rulers of the Mercians, with bishop Wærferth and his episcopal church. The ealdorman and his wife retained dues on salt from Droitwich in their entirety, but otherwise granted half of all rights pertaining to their lordship to the lord of the church, including land-rents and judicial fines for lesser offences. Similar developments are known from London, associated with its 'restoration' (*instauracio*) within the city's Roman walls. Alfred and Æthelred combined to authorize two adjacent commercial enclosures on a 'trading shore' at Queenhithe; one beneficiary was again bishop Wærferth in 889, the other was assigned to Plegmund and his archiepiscopal church in 898.[36] Many burhs were conceived as trading-centres from the outset: both examples suggest a central role for fiscal and commercial privileges, as compensatory inducement to landlords for the supply of rural labour.[37] Division of the *fyrd* was probably a further concession, staggering requirements of manpower while improving prospects of local defence.

LAND AND LANDHOLDING

Other measures related to land management; their scope must be isolated both from broader ninth-century developments and from problems of retrospection. Generally focused on ecclesiastical landholding, discussion has exposed the difficulties in gauging Alfredian change. At Abingdon in the twelfth century Alfred was remembered as having violently seized the monastery of Abingdon; Robin Fleming once suggested Alfred's centrality in an extensive appropriation of former monastic land, critically transferring resources into royal and secular hands.[38] As Dumville demonstrated, her case was flawed in its dependence on the maximal claims of tenth-century monastic reformers; his account highlights just how little can be known about the fate of many ninth-century communities.[39] Many factors urge a more balanced picture of Alfredian dynamics. 'Secularization' cannot easily be distinguished from

---

[35] S 223 (*SEHD*, no. 13; trans. in *EHD*, no. 99); Brooks, 'Administrative Background', pp. 143–4.

[36] S 346 (BCS 561); S 1628 (BCS 577 and 578); T. Dyson, 'King Alfred and the Restoration of London', *London Journal* 15.2 (1990), 99–109.

[37] Brooks, 'Administrative Background', pp. 143–4.

[38] *Chronicon Monasterii de Abingdon*, ed. Stevenson I, 50; R. Fleming, 'Monastic Lands and England's Defence in the Viking Age', *EHR* 100 (1985), 247–65.

[39] D. N. Dumville, 'Ecclesiastical Lands and the Defence of Wessex in the First Viking-Age', in his *Wessex and England*, pp. 29–54; cf. Blair, *Church*, pp. 291–341.

lay lordship: boundaries were blurred under contemporary conditions. 'Free monasteries' lay under West Saxon royal protection; the benefits of bookland were no longer restricted to ecclesiastical recipients. Many processes could well be masked by such tenurial homogeneity, in place from Æthelwulf's time and compounded by the common burdens, falling equally on all types of land. In landholding also royal strategy was shaped by this distinctive context, negotiated more evenly with disparate lords.

Another change had been the end of synods; evidence for anxiety is notably external. In the 870s archbishop Æthelred had written to Pope John VIII complaining of adversities suffered at the hands of Alfred and other wrong-doers. John's reply was typically bold, urging strenuous resistance; he would believe no aspersion against Æthelred without true investigation.[40] A second letter criticized Alfred himself, warning against the diminution of rights pertaining to Canterbury, if he wished to keep his kingdom secure. Whitelock doubted whether this second message was actually received, yet the most likely window for both letters is John's visit to West Francia in the summer of 878, post-dating Alfred's military recovery. As Brooks observes, such criticisms suggest a reopening of the dispute over Kentish royal monasteries; by the mid-tenth century at least, three of the most important houses had passed into royal gift, while a further three seem to have vanished without trace.[41] If even partially achieved in Alfred's time, this would have added very substantial landed resources to direct royal control.

Such was the position in Kent, especially prone to viking warfare; it need not have been replicated in Wessex or western Mercia. What survives conveys a more equivocal picture of compromise and local agreement.[42] Even the synod of 816 had sanctioned the leasing or limited alienation of ecclesiastical land when justified by famine, viking depredation, or the need to obtain liberty (canon 7). Royal strategy seems to have proceeded just one step further, in encouraging communities to concede small parts of their endowment for royal use. A charter of poor draftsmanship records Alfred himself alienating land from Christ Church, Canterbury in 873; but the favoured solution was leasing, which the synod of 816 had limited to the duration of one life in normal circumstances.[43] The tactic may well have begun in mid-century: a charter of 858 conveyed land to King Æthelbald for his lifetime with reversion to Winchester.[44] In the early 890s Alfred is

---

[40] *C&S*, no. 3 (trans. in *EHD*, no. 222); cf. W. Ullmann, *The Growth of Papal Government in the Middle Ages*, 3rd edn (London, 1970), pp. 219–28.

[41] Brooks, *Canterbury*, pp. 203–6; cf. Blair, *Church*, pp. 298–306 and 322–9.

[42] Dumville, 'Ecclesiastical Lands', pp. 43–6.

[43] S 344 (BCS 536); Brooks, *Canterbury*, p. 159.   [44] S 1274 (BCS 495).

encountered leasing four hides belonging to Malmesbury to his thegn Dudig, for four lives. The precise terms of this charter may be the product of subsequent rewriting, but Edward the Elder secured comparable leases from the community of Winchester.[45] In acceding to yet another request, bishop Denewulf appealed to Edward in writing at the 'unwelcome' scale of royal demand.[46]

There is a revealing comparison with Carolingian *beneficia*, as a formalized mechanism of ecclesiastical concession: West Saxon relationships hinged on piecemeal acts of lease. They also related to measures of secular concession. As Dumville has shown, leasing was intertwined with a broader series of land exchanges, bringing estates of strategic potential into more direct control.[47] Thus in the late 880s or early 890s Alfred can be glimpsed restoring to Winchester reversionary interests which the community had earlier ceded in lieu of tribute-payment; in return the king acquired 100 hides at Cholsey in Berkshire, on the Thames immediately south of the burh of Wallingford.[48] Crucially, the tactic extended to thegnly landholders: other exchanges of the 890s conveyed land at Horn Down, directly between Wallingford and the royal vill at Wantage; and Sutton (Poyntz) in Dorset, on the coast south of Dorchester.[49] Again, the process continued under Edward, who can be observed systematically acquiring estates on the south coast and at strategic points inland, usually by exchange with ecclesiastical communities.[50] The evidence is dominated by Edward's foundation of the New Minster, Winchester. Yet another participant was Ordlaf, ealdorman of Wiltshire, in estates proximate to the burh of Cricklade; transactions included his purchase of Dudig's Alfredian lease from the church of Malmesbury.[51]

As bishop Denewulf's letter reveals, royal policy was not without tensions. Quite apart from the loss of income from committed estates, leasing took land out of its owner's control; exchange depended on a smooth transfer of title and lordship. One such transaction was certainly disputed: Ordlaf's exchange of land at Fonthill roused a residual claim to the estate from Æthelhelm Higa, a layman of uncertain rank.[52] This was the occasion for Ordlaf's written resume of his former title to land; in the event, Æthelhelm's appeal was rejected, and the estate remained

[45] S 356 (BCS 568 and 569); Keynes, 'West Saxon Charters', pp. 1138–9.
[46] S 1444 (BCS 619; trans. in *EHD*, no. 101); cf. S 1285 (*SEHD*, no. 17).
[47] Dumville, 'Ecclesiastical Lands', pp. 43–6.
[48] S 354 (BCS 556); Keynes, 'West Saxon Charters', pp. 1137–8.
[49] S 355 (*Abingdon*, ed. Kelly, no. 18); S 347 (*Glastonbury*, ed. Watkin, no. 1165).
[50] Dumville, 'Ecclesiastical Lands', pp. 45–6.   [51] S 1284, S 1205 and S 1445, cf. S 359.
[52] Keynes, 'Fonthill Letter', pp. 56–8, 64–5, 86–7 and 89–93.

with the bishop and community of Winchester. The outcome hinged on Alfred's own earlier arbitration in this disputed case of bookland: 'if one wishes to change every judgement which King Alfred gave, when shall we have finished disputing?'.[53] As much was implied by Asser in his praise for Alfred's personal assiduity as a 'painstaking judge'.[54] Parties in unresolved cases are pictured hastily seeking his judgement, complemented by further efforts on the king's part to ensure justice in local assemblies, largely conducted in his absence.

As a symbolic generalization, the image is compelling; it bears comparison with Carolingian practices of personal judgement, stressed in both biographies of Louis the Pious.[55] The driving force was the 'investigative' role of *missi*, responsible for groups of Frankish counties; the West Saxon shire system offered tighter structures of communication and local contact.[56] In Alfred's case it is difficult not to see some very direct connection with the law of *hlafordsearu*, widening the scope of 'royal' justice.[57] This too had been a factor in the Fonthill case, repeatedly relevant in moments of royal referral; yet in other respects the dispute may be atypical. As Dumville observes, documented exchanges are characterized by an apparent lack of contention; the terms of leases were also ultimately fulfilled.[58] The surviving dispute record is very limited; probably by many means, vital concessions had been secured without deeper tenurial disruption. Above all, this suggests the power of Alfredian 'justice', as an order upheld over land by complex interaction between king and office-holders. As will be seen, this was a most intensive object of royal 'persuasion', in rhetoric combining judgement with wider principle.

ROYAL INCOME AND URBAN DEVELOPMENT

Integral to defence was the protection of commercial exchange. Through attacks on trading places, viking activity posed a direct threat to royal income; the effect was compounded by heightened costs of tribute and defensive preparation. Partly mediated through land-holding, such burdens were ultimately transmitted to the population at large via mechanisms of taxation and mobilization. Much depended on the capacity of the entire economy to fund these new collective

---

[53] *Ibid.*, pp. 76–7.   [54] *VA* 105 and 106, lines 1–28.

[55] Wormald, *MEL* I, 81–2 and 122–3; F. L. Ganshof, 'Charlemagne's Programme of Imperial Government', in his *The Carolingians and the Frankish Monarchy*, trans. J. Sondheimer (London, 1971), pp. 55–85, at 63–5; MGH Capit. I, no. 33, c. 1; Ansegisus, *Capitularium Collectio*, II.26–7; Thegan, *Gesta Hludowici imperatoris*, c. 13; Astronomer, *Gesta Hludowici imperatoris*, c. 19, both ed. Tremp, pp. 192–4 and 340.

[56] Cf. Werner, '*Missus-marchio-comes*', pp. 195–205 and 227–9.   [57] Wormald, *MEL* I, 144–7.

[58] Dumville, 'Ecclesiastical Lands', p. 46.

needs.[59] Alfredian measures were not the first to address these difficulties, yet involved much deeper restructuring of landscape and commercial activity, underpinning fiscal success. Their rationale again
related to royal 'persuasion', discussed in later chapters; the effect was to
supply very strong economic stimuli.

Already from mid-century are signs of a co-ordinated response to economic and military pressures. One was the tactic of general recoinage,
repeatedly implemented under Alfred's predecessors in *c.* 852, *c.* 862
and *c.* 866, post-dating Offa's second recoinage by over fifty years.[60]
This is likely to have generated considerable income; another dimension
is suggested by progressive debasement from the established standard of
fine silver. By the early 870s, the joint West Saxon-Mercian *Lunettes*
coinage had declined to a fineness of less than one quarter. The dominant
force was probably a long-term decline in silver supply; another is likely
to have been fiscal, in a context suggestive of 'emergency conversion',
offering strong incentives to convert bullion into the latest issue of coin.[61]
Yet the source of such income now faced decline. As undefended coastal
sites, 'wics' were attractive targets; viking action may well have exacerbated a more general downturn in cross-Channel trade. To these conditions came the West Saxon remedy of urban defence, implied by the
reservation of fortress-work in charters from the later 850s. At London
and Winchester there are signs of enhanced function suggesting the re-use
of Roman fortifications.[62] The pair are significant as instances of direct
settlement shift, from *wic* to defended burh. Renewal of Winchester took
commercial activity from *Hamwic*; movement from *Lundenwic* sought the
protection of the city's Roman walls.

Such measures provide a context for wider Alfredian reforms.
Though debasement need not have been inflationary, it may well have
reduced confidence in coin, while jeopardizing any income based on
fixed or customary payments. Such effects suggest a context for Alfred's
own *Cross-and-Lozenge* recoinage, reversing debasement to the former
standard of fine silver. Now redated to *c.* 875–6, the political authority
implied by this action is arresting, predating the battle of Edington.[63] Yet
it is difficult to picture as a straightforward exercise in royal profit-taking.

---

[59] Cf. Maddicott, 'Trade, Industry', pp. 4–17, without emphasis on resource costs.
[60] M. Blackburn, 'Alfred's Coinage Reforms in Context', in *Alfred*, ed. Reuter, pp. 199–215,
at 202–5.
[61] D. M. Metcalf and J. P. Northover, 'Debasement of the Coinage in Southern England in the Age
of King Alfred', *Numismatic Chronicle* 145 (1985), 150–76; cf. Blackburn, 'Alfred's Coinage
Reforms', pp. 202–3.
[62] Above, pp. 23–4.
[63] M. Blackburn, 'The London Mint in the Reign of Alfred', in *Kings, Currency and Alliances*, ed.
Blackburn and Dumville, pp. 105–23, at 119–20; Keynes, 'Mercians', p. 17.

The act mirrors a similar recoinage by Charles the Bald in 864; noble support for the revalued currency would have been central to its implementation.[64] Alfred's revaluation was sufficiently successful to encourage one final recoinage, c. 880, further raising the penny's weight, to a level slightly lighter than its Carolingian equivalent.[65] The effect was to give still greater value, while retaining a relationship favourable to cross-Channel trade. The reform was accompanied by the introduction of a new half-penny, as if to maintain adequate supply of specie. Though examples are scarce, the experiment seems to have been successful.

The benefits were probably shared more evenly between royal and aristocratic interests. The granting of fiscal and commercial privileges had an important monetary dimension in the extension of minting to certain newly established burhs; the principle would be greatly extended under Alfred's successors.[66] This reflected a central role of the burghal network, as the means of protecting commercial exchange. Individual sites followed a variety of common patterns, including some which were purely defensive, yet the majority implied broader functions in organized habitation and protected trade.[67] Some were forts across promontories, such as Malmesbury and Shaftesbury; larger burhs bore the imprint of a rectilinear street-plan, with a high street flanked by back streets. The topography suggests ease of access to the rear of fronted tenements.[68] In several cases the plan formed a blueprint for sites of entirely new establishment, such as Wareham, Wallingford and Cricklade. In others, including Exeter and Bath as well as Winchester, it supplied a new layout behind repaired Roman walls.

What was envisaged is shown by the case of London; by the later 880s Alfred was promoting a 'restoration' of urban activity within the old Roman walls, in a site termed *Lundenburh*.[69] Remarkable excavations at Queenhithe have uncovered the timbers and wares of a late ninth-century beach-market, together with Alfredian coins; they provide tangible evidence for the 'trading shore' to which Worcester and Canterbury were granted privileged access.[70] Fiscal gifts were predicated

---

[64] Nelson, *Charles the Bald*, pp. 33–5 and 207–8, cf. her 'Wealth and Wisdom', pp. 39–43.

[65] Blackburn, 'Alfred's Coinage Reforms', pp. 206–7.

[66] Blackburn, 'London Mint', pp. 121–2; Blackburn, 'Mints, burhs'.

[67] M. Biddle, 'Late Saxon Planned Towns', *Antiquaries Journal* 51 (1971), 70–85.

[68] Biddle, 'Evolution of Towns', p. 28.

[69] B. Hobley, 'Saxon London: *Lundenwic* and *Lundenburh*: Two Cities Rediscovered', in *The Rebirth of Towns in the West AD 700–1050*, ed. R. Hodges and B. Hobley (London, 1988), pp. 69–82; A. Vince, *Saxon London: an Archaeological Investigation* (London, 1990), pp. 13–25; Dyson, 'Restoration of London'.

[70] Anon., 'Bull Wharf: Queenhithe', *Current Archaeology* 14.2 (no. 158) (July 1998), 75–7; J. Ayre and R. Wroe-Brown, 'Æthelred's Hythe to Queenhithe: the Origin of a London Dock', *Medieval Life* 5 (1996), 14–25.

on wider participation in burghal markets; as Jones has suggested, their provision tapped commercializing efficiencies of secure and witnessed trade.[71] After construction, such benefits might be felt more widely among all engaging in market-based exchange. The connection was inherent in the urbanizing scope of Alfredian defence; in some respects unproven, these forces were critical to the burhs' long-term success.

COLLECTIVE SECURITY (1) 'KING OF THE ANGLO-SAXONS'

Defence incorporated the territorial extension of Alfred's rule. West Saxon power had long been in the ascendant in southern Britain, largely at Mercian expense. Ecgberht's royal styling had been twofold, as 'king of the West Saxons and of the people of Kent'; the formulation continued to describe West Saxon power until Alfred's expansion.[72] Viking pressure proved capable of neutralizing rivalries between native kingdoms. Æthelwulf's reign had seen the emergence of a sustained alliance between the West Saxons and Mercians; beyond defensive co-operation against the vikings, it combined offensive action westwards against the Welsh.[73] The alliance found further expression in the harmonizing of West Saxon and Mercian monetary systems, resulting in a uniform currency from the 860s onwards; it was dynastically cemented by the marriage of Alfred's sister, Æthelswith, to the Mercian king, Burgred, in 853, and by Alfred's own marriage to Ealhswith, daughter of a Mercian ealdorman, in 868.

An ambition to establish outright West Saxon overlordship seems first to have emerged after Burgred's departure for Rome in 874, forced by viking defeat. Charter evidence shows Burgred's successor, Ceolwulf, to have held greater power than the 'unwise king's thegn' described in the *Chronicle*, but he may well have accepted unfavourable terms in return for his sudden elevation; as Mercian king he appears a partner at times inferior to Alfred in their co-ordinated coinage.[74] Further upheaval is likely to have accompanied both the division of Mercia with viking forces in 877 and Ceolwulf's mysterious end, possibly in 879. By 883 a certain Æthelred had emerged as ruler of western Mercia, having formally submitted to King Alfred. Whereas Ceolwulf had operated as king, Æthelred was accorded the title of 'ealdorman' and its variants in charters, where Alfred's permission and witness was expressly acknowledged.[75] Alfredian coinage also now enveloped western Mercia. Æthelred's loyalty was amply rewarded: London had formerly lain in Mercian hands,

---

[71] Jones, 'Transaction Costs', esp. pp. 671–3.   [72] Keynes, 'Kent'.
[73] Keynes, 'Mercians', pp. 2–11.   [74] *Ibid.*, pp. 12–19.   [75] *Ibid.*, pp. 19–34.

but coinage implies that the city had turned to Alfred for protection in the late 870s, remaining essentially free from viking encroachment in the 880s, with a brief occupation in 883. The events by which Alfred *gesette* ('occupied') London in 886 seem to have involved formal restoration of its defences, rather than a violent recapture.[76] It was also the occasion for Alfred's entrusting of the city to Æthelred; his marriage to Alfred's daughter, Æthelflæd, sealed this new Mercian relationship.

Now as ealdorman under West Saxon rule, Æthelred's submission was understood to have created a new political order in southern Britain, superseding the bipartite kingdom created by Ecgberht.[77] In charters of the late 880s and early 890s, Alfred is accorded the novel titles *Angul-Saxonum rex* or *Anglorum Saxonum rex* ('king of the Anglo-Saxons'); Asser described the king in similar terms, in contrast to his predecessors. The terms *Angli Saxones* or *Englesaxones* had originally been coined on the Continent to distinguish the Germanic inhabitants of Britain from the *Saxones* in Germany; its adoption may reflect Alfred's Frankish contacts and assistance.[78] Yet this terminology acquired more specific meaning in an Alfredian context, describing the political unity of rule over both Mercians (of 'Anglian' descent) and the 'Saxon' West Saxons. The fusion of two peoples was especially clear in the variant *rex Anglorum et Saxonum*, notably deployed in a charter relating to London.[79] Similar thinking was explicit in the A version of the Second *Ordo*. Departing from its source text, the anointing prayer refers to a king elected to the 'regnum anglorum uel saxonum pariter', deserving the love of 'both these peoples'.[80] The same unity described Alfred's political legacy. Overlordship of the Mercians continued under Edward the Elder, retaining his father's title; the order was inherited intact by Alfred's grandson, Æthelstan. It was only superseded in 927 with Æthelstan's conquest of Northumbria, reflected in his new styling *rex Anglorum*, the first secure deployment of this resonant title.

Alfredian unity was 'Anglo-Saxon': these structures qualify the view attaching Alfred to an insistent harnessing of 'English' identity.[81] In the *Chronicle* and Prose Preface, Alfred's rule was·seen against a wider 'English' past, Bedan in its horizons of spiritual unity. The question concerns the purchase of this available ethnicity. Much has been invested in two specific instances of *Angelcynn* ('Englishkind'): the written treaty

---

[76] *Ibid.*, pp. 21–4; Dyson, 'Restoration of London'.   [77] Keynes, 'Mercians', pp. 34–9.
[78] W. H. Levison, *England and the Continent in the Eighth Century* (Oxford, 1946), p. 92, note 1.
[79] S 346 (BCS 561).
[80] Nelson, 'Second English *Ordo*', pp. 361–6; cf. above, p. 75.
[81] Wormald, 'Bede, the *Bretwaldas*', pp. 120–1 and 127; Wormald, 'Venerable Bede', pp. 24–5; Wormald, '*Engla Lond*', esp. pp. 376–7; Foot, '*Angelcynn*'; cf. now Sheppard, *Families*, pp. 9–50.

established with the Danish king Guthrum, where Alfred is depicted collaborating with *ealles Angelcynnes witan*; and the *Chronicle*'s account of Alfred's 'occupation' of London, where '*all Angel cyn* submitted to him, except those who were in captivity to the Danes'.[82] Yet the force in each case must be judged against the broader scope of *Angelcynn* in earlier usage, already a term of distinction from non-English-speaking peoples. Hence a charter of 855 separated *angelcynnes menn* from *ælðeodige menn* ('foreign men') on the Mercian-Welsh border; in the *Old English Martyrology*, abbot Ceolfrith was buried at Langres in Burgundy with great lamenting *ge Angelcynnes monna ge þiderleodiscra* ('both of Englishmen and locals').[83] The *Chronicle* in particular was referring to the inclusion of Æthelred's Mercians; the events of 886 may well have marked the genesis of 'Anglo-Saxon' rule. *Angelcynn* itself had not been politicized: qualified in deployment, its use reflected a reality of anti-Danish lordship. This was precisely the strength of Alfred's new chosen kingdom, as a community participant in 'Anglo-Saxon' defence; its boundaries were the limits of his uniting rule.

COLLECTIVE SECURITY (2) 'RULER OF ALL THE CHRISTIANS OF THE ISLAND OF BRITAIN'

A final element was pan-Christian leadership: dealings with Mercia have tended to distract from a further transformation in relations with the Welsh. Their kingdoms had long been an area of Mercian political interest. Yet in 853 Æthelwulf had supplied military aid to Burgred in joint action against the Welsh kingdom of Powys; the alliance is revealing of Mercian weakness. It may also be a sign of heightened Welsh resistance. The dominant feature of ninth-century Welsh development was a massive expansion of territory held by the Gwynedd dynasty of Rhodri Mawr ('the Great'); its rule encompassed Powys and Ceredigion, and thus the whole of northern and central Wales.[84] The sole evidence survives in laconic Welsh annals and much later genealogies; often

---

[82] *AGu* Prologue; *ASC* s.a. 886; cf. P. Kershaw, 'The Alfred-Guthrum Treaty: Scripting Accommodation and Interaction in Viking Age England', in *Cultures in Contact: Scandinavian Settlement in England in the Ninth and Tenth Centuries*, ed. D. M. Hadley and J. D. Richards (Turnhout, 2000), pp. 43–64, esp. 58.

[83] S 207 (BCS 489; trans. in *EHD*, no. 91); *Old English Martyrology*, ed. Kotzor II, 219–20, cf. 14. For the latter text's uncertain date, cf. below, p. 118.

[84] J. E. Lloyd, *A History of Wales from the Earliest Times to the Edwardian Conquest*, 2 vols., 3rd edn (London, 1939) I, 322–33; D. N. Dumville, 'The "Six" Sons of Rhodri Mawr: a Problem in Asser's Life of King Alfred', *Cambridge Medieval Celtic Studies* 4 (Winter, 1983), 5–18; K. Maund, *The Welsh Kings: the Welsh Rulers of Wales* (Stroud, 2000), pp. 37–44. Cf. D. Pratt, 'Asser's *Life of King Alfred* in the Context of Anglo-Welsh Relations' (forthcoming).

explained as inheritance by marriage, these acquisitions were more likely driven by force.[85] The last recorded king of Powys, Cyngen, died in Rome in 854 × 855, probably in retirement, but may well have left sons to survive him.[86] Gwynedd's absorption of Powys seems more explicable in a context of extended struggle with Mercian power; Rhodri himself would be killed 'by the Saxons' in 878 (conceivably by Ceolwulf), only to be avenged in 881 at the battle of the Conway, probably fought against ealdorman Æthelred.[87]

The struggle forms an essential backdrop to Asser's recruitment.[88] Rhodri's sons, led by Anarawd, had been active further south, forcing Hyfaidd, king of Dyfed, and Elise ap Tewdwr, king of Brycheiniog, to submit voluntarily to Alfred's lordship and protection, sometime in the early 880s. At about the same time, ealdorman Æthelred had similarly moved southwards, forcing Hywel ap Rhys, king of Glywysing, and Brochfael and Ffyrnfael, kings of Gwent, also to submit to Alfred, in this case for protection against Mercian 'tyranny'. Anarawd and Æthelred were themselves hostile: Alfred's supremacy thus rested on hope of his lordly neutralization of local rivalries, against the common threat of Gwynedd. It was seemingly in the context of these negotiations that Alfred first became aware of Asser, who may well have been bishop of St David's; both monk and priest, he was certainly a figure of importance in the episcopal community.[89] Hyfaidd, king of Dyfed, had posed a threat to the lands and jurisdiction of St David's; Asser's recruitment, reluctantly conceded by the community, had aimed at securing the favour of Hyfaidd's new overlord.[90] By this agreement at least, Asser's service to King Alfred was limited to one half of his time, the rest remaining with St David's.

At around the same time, probably in response to the coalition against him, Anarawd in turn formed an alliance with viking forces settled in Northumbria.[91] Yet he 'received no benefit, only a great deal of harm' from this alliance.[92] In 893 two hostile viking armies based in Essex received reinforcements from the kingdoms of East Anglia and Northumbria; the entire conglomeration was driven northwestwards

---

[85] Dumville, 'The "Six" Sons', pp. 14–16.   [86] *AC* s.a. 854.

[87] *AC* s.a. 854, 877 (for 878) and 880 (for 881); Keynes, 'Mercians', pp. 19–20, note 84.

[88] *VA* 79–81; D. P. Kirby, 'Asser and his Life of King Alfred', *Studia Celtica* 6 (1971), 12–35, but cf. K&L, *Alfred*, pp. 213–14, note 24, where Asser's initial meeting with Alfred is convincingly placed early in 885, rather than late in 883.

[89] K&L, *Alfred*, pp. 51–2.   [90] As Asser pointedly reveals (*VA* 79, lines 53–60).

[91] Kirby, 'Asser and his Life', pp. 15–17 and 31–3; D. P. Kirby, 'Northumbria in the Reign of Alfred the Great', *Transactions of the Architectural and Archaeological Society of Durham and Northumberland* 11 (1958–65), 335–46.

[92] *VA* 80, lines 13–17.

along the boundary of Alfred's kingdom to Buttington, near modern Welshpool, where it was surrounded and defeated by a combined force of West Saxons, Mercians and 'some portion of the Welsh people'.[93] The sources are conspicuously silent on Anarawd's position, but his hostility may be suggested by this partial Welsh support.[94] The location of Buttington, on the border of Powys where Offa's dyke meets the Severn, supplies a plausible context for his decision ultimately to abandon the Northumbrian alliance, and also to commit himself to Alfred in formal submission.[95]

All rulers of the Welsh were now nominally under Alfred's over-lordship; the achievement was central to Asser's *Life*, also written in 893. This context has been neglected in many assessments of Asser's biography which have assumed an intended English readership, centred on the royal household. Weight is attached to the text's royal dedication; Anton Scharer has seen the *Life* either as background reading for prospective royal priests, or a guide to rulership for Alfred's sons.[96] Yet as David Kirby first demonstrated, the *Life* implies a Welsh audience in its very conception, as a Latin translation of the *Chronicle* incorporating among much else a detailed account of recent Anglo-Welsh relations (cc. 79–81); chief concern throughout these chapters is Asser's presentation of his own role to 'our people' at St David's, showing the particular benefits of his West Saxon service, connected with the wider benefits of Alfred's overlordship for the Welsh as a whole.[97] The impression is reinforced by Asser's labelling of protagonists as 'Christians' and 'pagans'; occurring only rarely in the *Chronicle*, the distinction is always prompted by a role for 'non-English' forces, such as Welshmen or Frisians, in anti-viking alliance.[98] Asser's terminology upheld a continuous context of Christian warfare; his efforts reflect the importance of Alfred's Welsh allies in viking pursuit, operating in tandem with forces deployed from West Saxon and Mercian burhs.

In the event, the *Life* gives the impression of being unfinished: this too harmonizes closely with signs of tension in Alfred's western diplomacy.[99]

---

[93] *ASC* s.a. 893.

[94] Cf. Kirby, 'Asser and his Life', pp. 16–17. My interpretation differs in several respects from T. M. Charles-Edwards, 'Wales and Mercia, 613–918', in *Mercia*, ed. Brown and Farr, pp. 89–105.

[95] For the location of Buttington, see F. T. Wainwright, *Scandinavian England*, ed. H. P. R. Finberg (Chichester, 1975), p. 74, note 2.

[96] J. Campbell, 'Asser's *Life of Alfred*', in his *Anglo-Saxon State*, pp. 129–55, esp. 141–3 and 149–50; Scharer, 'History', pp. 186 and 205; Scharer, *Herrschaft*, p. 108; Nelson, 'Monks', pp. 135–6.

[97] Kirby, 'Asser and his Life', pp. 20, 26–7 and 31–3; his case for composition in stages is less convincing (cf. Campbell, 'Asser's *Life*, pp. 152–5).

[98] *ASC* s.a. 893 and 896; K&L, *Alfred*, pp. 230–1, note 12.

[99] K&L, *Alfred*, pp. 56–8 and pp. 242–3, note 72, for lack of completion; cf. Howlett, *British Books*, pp. 365–445.

In the Welsh annals for 894, probably in error for 895, Anarawd is encountered ravaging Ceredigion and Ystrad Tywi 'cum Anglis'.[100] The context may connect with the death of Hyfaidd in 893; there is an arresting possibility of joint action by Anarawd and Alfred in southern Wales.[101] In 896 the south again suffered ravaging, from a viking army based at Bridgnorth.[102] Whatever lay behind these developments, they sit uneasily with claims of Welsh 'protection': one can quite imagine why Asser's rhetoric was abandoned.[103] There is scarcely any evidence for the *Life* ever reaching Wales; the question of court readership would require it to have gained a quite separate purpose in West Saxon context.[104] In many accounts the *Life*'s centrality at court is simply assumed, giving insufficient weight to the priority of vernacular texts in royal communication. Latin biography had been mobilized in Welsh 'persuasion', conveying the court to outsiders through the guiding eyes of Asser's projected intimacy. Many of its details were openly critical of courtly participants, not least the chapter highlighting reluctance in the building of fortifications; while ealdorman Æthelred's 'might and tyranny' ran directly contrary to Mercian unity, strongly represented among Alfred's assisting personnel.[105] The West Saxons themselves received much ambivalent scrutiny, from the laxity of monastic practices to the low status accorded to the wife of their king.[106] In transmission, the *Life* is narrowly preserved, enjoying only limited circulation in later centuries. The context points against a significant courtly after-life; as a window of vision, the *Life* gains clarity from the unguarded nature of its intimate insight.

Asser's purposes are encapsulated in his dedication to Alfred as 'ruler of all the Christians of the island of Britain'. Again, the context was broadly Bedan, in the wider horizons of *Britannia*: within Bede's list of kings who attained *imperium* south of the Humber, all three Northumbrian candidates were accorded rulership of Britain.[107] The list was

---

[100] *AC* s.a. 894; Kirby, 'Asser and his Life', pp. 31–2.

[101] *AC* s.a. 892 (probably for 893); Dumville, 'The "Six" Sons', p. 16; Maund, *Welsh Kings*, p. 44. Cf. Charles-Edwards, 'Wales and Mercia', suggesting Mercian involvement, difficult to square with Venedotian territorial expansion.

[102] *AC* s.a. 895 (probably for 896); *ASC* s.a. 895.

[103] Cf. MacLean, *Charles the Fat*, pp. 228–9, for Notker's *Gesta Karoli*, arguing that its completion may have been similarly overtaken by contemporary events.

[104] The only Welsh reader known to have access is Gerald of Wales: S. Keynes, *Anglo-Saxon History: a Bibliographical Handbook* (Cambridge, 2005), p. 111.

[105] *VA* 91, and 80, lines 6–10. Keynes, 'Mercians', pp. 41–4, cf. Campbell, 'Asser's Life', pp. 141–2.

[106] *VA* 13–15 and 93.

[107] *HE* II.5; Wormald, 'Bede, the *Bretwaldas*', pp. 104–9; S. Keynes, 'Rædwald the Bretwalda', in *Voyage to the Other World*, ed. C. B. Kendall and P. S. Wells (Minneapolis, MN, 1992), pp. 103–23; cf. E. John, *Orbis Britanniae* (Leicester, 1966), pp. 1–46.

appropriated by the *Chronicle* to describe Ecgberht's brief conquest of Mercia in 829. In the A-text, Ecgberht had been the eighth king who was *bretwalda*, possibly meaning 'ruler of Britain'; as opposed to *brytenwalda*, found in all other manuscripts, which probably meant 'wide-ruler'.[108] Neither term is securely attested in other evidence; if the former had any life beyond its solitary occurrence, the context suggests an important 'British' dimension to Ecgberht's West Saxon memory. There may well be a connection with his mysterious subjugation of the Welsh, reported in the *Chronicle* for 830. Alfred's overlordship re-enacted this achievement; as 'ruler of Britain' his role crystallized long-standing ambitions to hegemony over Wales, both exploiting and supplanting those of Mercian power. Efforts in this direction would continue under Edward the Elder, initially through the actions of his sister Æthelflæd, culminating in Æthelstan's more vigorous subjection of the Welsh in 927.[109] Though not entirely successful, Alfred's pacifying unity would inform much later strategy: his rule had shown the power of anti-viking defence.

---

[108] D. N. Dumville, 'The Terminology of Overkingship in Early Anglo-Saxon England', in *The Anglo-Saxons*, ed. Hines, pp. 345–65, at 353.

[109] Lloyd, *History of Wales* I, 331–7; Wainwright, *Scandinavian England*, pp. 321–4; H. Loyn, 'Wales and England in the Tenth Century: the Context of the Athelstan Charters', *Welsh History Review* 10 (1980–1), 283–301.

PART II

Alfredian Discourse and its Efficacy

Chapter 7

THE FIELD OF ALFREDIAN KNOWLEDGE

Part II offers a full exploration of Alfredian royal learning. It begins by establishing its context in educational delivery and ruling discourse; it then moves to situate its role in the complex dynamics of Alfredian power, as the basis for analysis of individual texts. This chapter is concerned with the overall scope of learned innovation, against the backdrop of existing West Saxon practices. As ever, such questions gain much from awareness of parallel structures in the Carolingian world, accentuating the full significance of Alfredian developments in a European context.

ALFREDIAN INNOVATION: ALFREDIAN WISDOM AND THE SHIFT TO VERNACULAR PROSE

Much Alfredian material owes its existence to what has commonly been termed Alfred's 'educational programme', though its scope was not so limited.[1] In effect this amounted to a reorientation of aristocratic education, towards a model placing special weight on the reading of vernacular texts, principally in the form of prose. Texts were mainly translations from Latin originals; reading was serviced by provision of literate instruction. The acquisition of literacy provided access to 'wisdom'; the entire scheme could be presented as a revival, reversing sapiential decline.

Dominating all was the role accorded to Alfred, in an extraordinary array of king-centred evidence. There are many early medieval examples of learned kingship: striking is the inclusion of authorship among royal activities, beyond patronage, reception and consumption. This

---

[1] D. Bullough, 'The Educational Tradition in England from Alfred to Ælfric: Teaching *utriusque linguae*', in his *Carolingian Renewal: Sources and Heritage* (Manchester and New York, 1991), pp. 297–334, at 297–301; cf. esp. Booth, 'Alfred versus Beowulf', not cited, but largely complemented by Discenza, 'Symbolic Capital'.

places Alfred among a much smaller body of rulers identified as the actual authors of texts; each raises very interesting questions of the processes lying behind such production. In Alfred's case a high degree of personal involvement has generally been assumed; the issue is central to all assessment of tone and character, quite apart from questions of agency. Recent doubts expressed by Malcolm Godden have stimulated an alternative approach to these questions, combining authorial image with features of style, content and all else that can be known of royal action.[2] The effect is to strengthen all grounds for accepting Alfred's intensive participation, while clarifying the force of his learned behaviour.

Alfred's distinctive image was central: the entire scheme was presented as a product of his learned interests, seemingly intensive from the mid-880s onwards and closely associated with his assembled body of ecclesiastical helpers. Exhortations to acquire wisdom could appeal to Alfred's own efforts; royal promotion raised the prospect of 'authorized' texts, distinguished by his approval. Alfred's image offered inspiration and endorsement, yet as author as well as reader, it gained a further function, as heightened source of 'wisdom': here was the scheme's greatest potency.

'Royal' texts dominate surviving ninth-century vernacular prose. William of Malmesbury included the translations of Bede and Orosius among works by the king, yet both attributions can be discounted on grounds of dialect and style.[3] The work of Janet Bately has restricted the royal corpus to a smaller body of texts, all translations of biblical or patristic authority: the *Regula pastoralis* of Pope Gregory; the *Consolatio philosophiae* of Boethius; the *Soliloquia* of Augustine of Hippo; and the first fifty Psalms.[4] To these must be added the introduction to Alfred's law-book, excerpting substantial sections of biblical law. Four of the five texts include internal attributions of one kind or another to the king; the principal complication is a degree of input from Alfred's learned helpers, acknowledged in the Prose Preface to the Gregorian translation.[5] Bately has shown that these texts share a range of stylistic hallmarks, distinctive

---

[2] D. Pratt, 'Problems of Authorship and Audience in the Writings of King Alfred the Great', in *Learned Laity in the Carolingian Era*, ed. P. Wormald (forthcoming); cf. M. Godden, 'The Player King: Identification and Self-Representation in King Alfred's Writings', in *Alfred*, ed. Reuter, pp. 137–50; Godden, *Misappropriation*.

[3] *GR* I, 190–1, cf. Thomson's commentary (II, 102–4).

[4] D. Whitelock, 'The Prose of Alfred's Reign', in her *Bede to Alfred*, no. 6, esp. p. 89, hesitant on the Orosius. Bately in *Or*, pp. lxxii–lxxxvi; J. M. Bately, 'Lexical Evidence for the Authorship of the Prose Psalms in the Paris Psalter', *ASE* 10 (1982), 69–95, for the addition of the Psalms.

[5] *CP*, p. 6, lines 20–2.

within contemporary prose, strengthening their integrity as a discrete 'royal' corpus.[6]

There are three further texts whose direct participation in the king's scheme may be strongly suspected. Most straightforward is the translation of Pope Gregory's *Dialogues* by Wærferth of Worcester. According to Asser, Wærferth accomplished his translation 'at the king's command'; its composition probably postdated his entry into royal service, seemingly secured in the early 880s.[7] Wærferth is unmentioned in the text, but there is no reason to doubt Asser's words, which are entirely consistent with the Mercian dialect of the text, and the complex history of its manuscript transmission.[8] The Alfredian connections of the *Anglo-Saxon Chronicle* are equally demonstrable, but more effort has been expended on their precise implications.[9] The text's origins matter less than its fate once completed, in a 'common stock' of annals from which all subsequent copies descend, whose dissemination can be dated to the autumn of 892.[10] Asser's dependence on the *Chronicle* reveals that an early manuscript was known within Alfred's circle, while the character of early additional annals, for 893–6, suggests the responsibility of a writer with special insight into royal policy, seemingly 'close to the events which the annals describe'.[11] The West Saxon translation of Orosius is a further likely participant, though the evidence falls short of conclusive demonstration. The text's handling of geography suggests composition in the later 880s or early 890s;[12] the clearest Alfredian connections are the remarkable accounts of voyages by the Norwegian Ottar and the English merchant Wulfstan.[13] The first had been told by Ottar to 'his lord, King Alfred'; both are highly suggestive, even if early interpolation cannot strictly be ruled out.[14] The relevance of Orosius' original history to Alfred's circle has recently been detected in Asser's *Life*.[15] The translation has often been considered to bear a direct relationship to

---

[6] J. M. Bately, 'King Alfred and the Old English Translation of Orosius', *Anglia* 88 (1970), 433–60, esp. 440–56; Bately, 'Lexical Evidence'; Bately, 'Old English Prose', pp. 118–38. Cf. also E. M. Liggins, 'The Authorship of the Old English Orosius', *Anglia* 88 (1970), 289–322, esp. 292–321; P. P. O'Neill in *Ps(P)*, pp. 73–96.

[7] *VA* 77, lines 1–10. Cf. Bately, 'Old English Prose', p. 103.

[8] Godden, 'Wærferth and King Alfred', pp. 37–41. Cf. Smyth, *Alfred*, pp. 544–89.

[9] J. M. Bately, *The Anglo-Saxon Chronicle: Texts and Textual Relationships* (Reading, 1991); Keynes, 'A Tale of Two Kings', pp. 196–200; Smyth, *Alfred*, pp. 455–526.

[10] K&L, *Alfred*, p. 279.

[11] D. N. Dumville, 'The Anglo-Saxon Chronicle and the Origins of English Square Minuscule Script', in his *Wessex and England*, pp. 55–139, at 69–70; cf. also K&L, *Alfred*, pp. 279–80.

[12] Bately in *Or*, pp. lxxxix–xc.

[13] *Or* I.1, pp. 13–18; C. Fell in *Two Voyagers*, ed. Lund, pp. 16–25.

[14] J. M. Bately, *The Literary Prose of King Alfred's Reign: Translation or Transformation?* (London, 1980), pp. 5–6; Bately, 'Old English Prose', p. 118, note 149.

[15] M. Lapidge, 'Asser's Reading', in *Alfred*, ed. Reuter, pp. 27–43, at 33–4 and 41–2.

the *Chronicle* and the version of Boethius, with reference to a saying attributed to the Emperor Titus, and the treatment of the Gothic kings Alaric and Radagaisus, but Bately considers neither as particularly secure.[16]

Three further texts leave greater room for doubt and speculation. One sometimes neglected is the *Leechbook* of Bald, a West Saxon medical compendium, the first two books of which transmit a text first written for a certain 'Bald', probably a physician.[17] Book II includes a fragmentary chapter of treatments with the explanation 'All this Dominus Elias, patriarch in Jerusalem, ordered to be said to King Alfred', thus recording medical advice sent to the king, in an exchange described by Asser.[18] The inclusion of extraneous material bears comparison with the Orosius; Alfred's medical history strengthens the plausibility of court compilation, though the case is circumstantial. The hazy boundaries of Alfredian prose are encapsulated by two Mercian texts, the translation of Bede and the *Old English Martyrology*. As Bately has emphasized, the *Martyrology* cannot be dated more closely than between *c.* 850 and the very end of the ninth century; for the Bede, the 'only *terminus post quem non* ... is the date of the oldest surviving manuscript fragment, i.e. "s. x in", and the translation can no longer be placed in the ninth century without fresh argument'.[19] Neither text bears any compelling relationship to other prose texts; equally, both might be regarded as likely candidates for inclusion in a scheme of translation.[20] Whatever the case, the pair point suggestively to the role of imported Mercian expertise.

The scope of material is overwhelming: attention to 'court' production is especially valuable, in the importance attached to established practices and broader context. Alfredian change must be assessed against some notable West Saxon continuities. The royal household maintained patterns of itinerancy and attendance which had been fully in place since the mid-ninth century, if not earlier. The scholarly helpers recruited by King Alfred continued the established role of royal priests; in gift-giving, too, Alfredian use of metalwork can be paralleled a generation earlier, while royal fondness for the recitation of vernacular poetry continued a

[16] Bately in *Or*, pp. xc–xci; J. M. Bately, '"Those Books that are Most Necessary for All Men to Know": the Classics and Late Ninth-Century England, a Reappraisal', in *The Classics in the Middle Ages*, ed. A. S. Bernardo and S. Levin (Binghamton, NY, 1990), pp. 45–78, at 63–5. Cf. Whitelock, 'Prose', pp. 73–4 and 82, note 3.
[17] C. E. Wright, *Bald's Leechbook. British Museum Royal Manuscript 12. D. xvii*, EEMF 5 (Copenhagen, 1955), esp. 13–14 and 17–18.
[18] *Leechdoms*, ed. Cockayne II, 288–91; Pratt, 'Illnesses', pp. 67–72.
[19] Bately, 'Old English Prose', pp. 103 and 98, cf. 103–4. For this fragment, see below, pp. 211–12.
[20] Whitelock, 'The Old English Bede', pp. 71–4 and 77; balanced assessment by C. Rauer, 'The Sources of the *Old English Martyrology*', *ASE* 32 (2003), 89–109, at 90–2, 98–100 and 102. For the Latin source, see now M. Lapidge, 'Acca of Hexham and the Origin of the *Old English Martyrology*', *Analecta Bollandiana* 123 (2005), 29–78.

practice apparently learnt in youth. In many respects Alfredian innovation amounted to an intensification of existing trends in West Saxon
cultural production, but collectively these raised the prospect of more
fundamental reorientation, far greater than the sum of its parts.

The most obvious change lay in the promotion of vernacular prose;
there is no reason to doubt the novelty of this selection, if the question is
considered in structural terms. There is every sign that this represented a
major departure in West Saxon context. Naturally one should be wary
of accepting Alfredian rhetoric straightforwardly, yet on this specific
issue royal argument derived much of its force from the unprecedented
nature of measures currently being implemented. In the Prose Preface,
Alfred is found wondering why earlier generations of 'wise men',
thoroughly versed in all books, 'did not wish to translate any part of
them into their own language', with the implication that such translations had been largely unknown.[21] This provides a context for the
dilemma ascribed to 'those serving God', apparently in the 850s and
860s, whose loss of 'wisdom' is attributed to the absence of appropriate
translations amid declining competence in Latin.[22]

The distinctive character of Alfredian 'wisdom' is reinforced by
complementary rhetoric in Asser's *Life*. Much again hinges on Alfred's
own progress; central to Asser's narrative is the weight placed on the
king's unceasing desire for 'wisdom' (*sapientia*). It was in this respect that
Alfred's early upbringing had been so lacking, contrasting with the
processes by which this desire had ultimately been fulfilled, at the hands
of his 'summoned' helpers.[23] The onset of translation was also the
moment of final release. As Keynes and Lapidge note, the extraordinary
occasion on 11 November 887, when King Alfred 'first began through
divine inspiration to read [Latin] and to translate at the same time, all on
one and the same day', is initially presented as a turning-point for the king
alone, yet his resolve 'to instruct many others' emerges as the more
significant development.[24] Perhaps inevitably, Asser's account maximizes
his own role in this decisive incident. The prominence accorded to the
king's prayerbook suggests further contrast with his early education.[25]
Royal concern to secure the copying of a choice passage illustrates
'devout enthusiasm for the pursuit of divine wisdom'; Asser's very
generalized description of the copied passages, as 'rudiments of holy
scripture', throws the capacity to translate Latin into greater relief.[26]

---

[21] *CP*, p. 4, lines 18–25; Whitelock, 'The Old English Bede', p. 61.   [22] *CP*, p. 4, lines 8–18.
[23] *VA* 76, lines 50–62.   [24] K&L, *Alfred*, p. 28.
[25] Cf. S. Lerer, *Literacy and Power in Anglo-Saxon Literature* (Lincoln, NE, 1991), pp. 61–73; Booth, 'Alfred versus Beowulf', pp. 50–5.
[26] *VA* 88, lines 11–17; cf. c. 89, lines 12–15.

Their precise destination is left unclear: Keynes and Lapidge assume that the prayerbook was expanded, but Alfred's resulting *Enchiridion* or 'hand-book' might equally have formed a separate *florilegium*.[27]

INTENDED AUDIENCES AND THE SHIFT TO VERNACULAR LITERACY

There can be no question of the translation programme being confined to the king's immediate circle, nor was readership exclusively eccle-siastical or monastic in composition. The translation of the *Regula pas-toralis*, or *Hierdeboc* ('shepherd-book'), was directed to bishops, but the aspirations of its Preface extended far beyond ecclesiastical instruction.[28] This was encapsulated by the aim of translating 'books ... most necessary for all men to know'; inclusivity continued in the ends such books were to secure 'that all the free-born young men now among the English who have the means to apply themselves to it, may be set to learning (as long as they are not useful for some other employment) until the time that they can read English writings properly'.[29] Though acknowledged, teaching in Latin is presented as a further stage; its reservation for those who are to advance 'to higher order' makes most sense as a reference to ecclesiastical careers.[30]

These provisions have sometimes been interpreted as implying literate instruction throughout Alfred's kingdom, perhaps through the estab-lishment of episcopal schools, with the *Hierdeboc* as central to a new curriculum.[31] Yet the Prose Preface was referring quite specifically to arrangements within the royal household, and the *schola* described by Asser.[32] Parallels with Asser's account are compelling, including the combination of Latin and English. The range of literate skills is at one point extended to writing (*scriptio*); this would be compatible with a

---

[27] K&L, *Alfred*, p. 268 (note 208); Pratt, 'Illnesses', pp. 46–7.

[28] Lay audiences rightly stressed by Booth, 'Alfred versus Beowulf', pp. 49–50; and by Discenza, 'Symbolic Capital', pp. 452–7, though her political context is rather schematic.

[29] '... ðætte eal sio gioguð þe nu is on Angel kynne friora monna, þara þe þa speda hæbben þæt hie ðæm befeolan mægen, sien to leornunga oðfæste, þa hwile þe hi to nanre oðerre note ne mægen, oð ðone first þe hie wel cunnen Englisc gewrit arædan': *CP*, p. 6, lines 10–15.

[30] '... to hierran hade': *CP*, p. 6, line 14 (cf. below, pp. 124, 148 and 153–6); not incompatible with ambiguous use of this terminology at *CP* LII, pp. 411–13 (cf. *Reg. past.* III.28, pp. 466–8), discussed by M. Godden, 'King Alfred's Preface and the Teaching of Latin in Anglo-Saxon England', *EHR* 117 (2002), 596–604, at 599–602, cf. 604.

[31] E.g. Stenton, *Anglo-Saxon England*, p. 272; A. Meaney, 'King Alfred and his Secretariat', *Parergon* 11 (1975), 16–24, at 16; Brooks, 'Crucible of Defeat', p. 16; C. Cubitt, 'Rape, Pillage and Exaggeration', in *Not Angels, but Anglicans: a History of Christianity in the British Isles*, ed. H. Chadwick and A. Ward (Norwich, 2000), pp. 32–9, at 36–7. Cf. Smyth, *Alfred*, pp. 559–66.

[32] *VA* 75, lines 11–21; Bullough, 'Educational Tradition', pp. 297–9; K&L, *Alfred*, pp. 35–6. Cf. Booth, 'Alfred versus Beowulf', pp. 48–9, suggesting Winchester.

more 'restricted' stage of further instruction.[33] As has long been recognized, Asser's account seems to betray specific awareness of the Prose Preface in the statement that pupils of the *schola* had to learn 'ut antequam aptas humanis artibus vires haberent . . . studiosi et ingeniosi viderentur', matching the more natural vernacular phrasing, that youths were to learn only 'þa hwile þe hie to nanre oðerre note ne mægen'.[34]

Restriction within the royal household is strengthened by the aristocratic character of presentation and personnel. The Prose Preface proposed learning for those 'who have the means (*speda*) to apply themselves to it'; royal usage elsewhere supports 'worldly means, prosperity', rather than 'mental capabilities'.[35] For all the talk of 'free men' in the Prose Preface, Asser identifies the most prominent pupil in the *schola* as the king's youngest son, Æthelweard, studying 'with all the nobly born children of virtually the entire area', although 'many' of lesser birth are acknowledged. Additional skills to be acquired included hunting 'and other skills appropriate to noblemen'.[36] The account matches Continental analogies for young aristocrats attached to a ruler's household, to which the term *schola* was applied in its contemporary sense of 'a body bound together by a common set of rules'.[37]

The *schola*'s function is clarified by a further audience, the adult aristocracy. Though highly stylized, Asser's final chapter relates closely to royal legal activities.[38] Unjust 'judges' faced royal chastisement: the reported remedy was highly specific, that 'ealdormen and reeves, terrified and chastened (*correcti*) as if by the greatest of punishments, strove with every effort to apply themselves to learning what is just (*ad aequitatis discendae studium*)'.[39] The ability to read was here virtually essential for all invested with 'offices of power' (*ministeria potestatum*), amounting to 'all ealdormen, reeves and thegns' (*comites . . . omnes, praepositi ac ministri*).[40] Nor was indulgence granted to failure: the king could be pictured endorsing oral recitation of English books, preferably

---

[33] The collocation of both stages at court is insufficiently stressed by Godden, 'Teaching of Latin'; numbers progressing to a full Latin curriculum would thus be small. Asser's words need not imply that Æthelweard had been intended for 'higher order' (cf. the role of Latin in Alfred's upbringing and mid-life instruction).

[34] ' . . . so that, before they had the strength suitable for manly arts . . . they should seem studious and intelligent': *VA* 75, lines 18–21. Lit. 'so long as they are not strong for any other employment': *CP*, p. 6, line 12.

[35] *CP*, p. 6, lines 10–11. *Ps(P)* XLVIII.6, p. 160 (*speda* translating *divitiae*); *Solil* p. 52, line 10; p. 54, line 12 and p. 72, line 23; *Bo* V.i, p. 12, line 3 (*sped* or *speda* meaning 'prosperity'); cf. *Or* I.1, p. 15 (with p. 17, lines 9 and 29): '[Ohthere] wæs swyðe spedig man'. Cf. Bullough, 'Educational Tradition', pp. 319–20 (note 12).

[36] *VA* 75, lines 11–21.   [37] Innes, ' "Place of Discipline" ', p. 62.   [38] Above, pp. 101–2.

[39] *VA* 106, lines 39–42.   [40] *Ibid.*, lines 42–6, cf. 32–9.

by a son or relative. Even this was an extreme measure, only for those too old or sluggish to pursue reading for themselves.[41]

The chapter completes a striking picture of intended audiences, united by the exercise of power. Alfredian wisdom was directed quite specifically to the West Saxon political order in its entirety. As the leading holders of ecclesiastical office, bishops were matched by the king's secular office-holders, his ealdormen and reeves, together with the wider body of king's thegns. Collectively, these were the agents whose constant motion supplied the basis for West Saxon power, united in their capacity as thegns of the king, whose regular contact sustained the active force of royal lordship. Audiences extended beyond current incumbents: pupils in the royal household included sons and heirs of the aristocracy, who would replace their fathers and relatives through natural wastage. Replenishment would have applied equally to the ecclesiastical offices of royal priest, abbot and bishop, for those advancing 'to higher order'. As Booth has noted, the process was a systematic exercise in aristocratic 're-education';[42] it must be understood against the existing backdrop of West Saxon power.

Bishops were prominent recipients; 're-education' is equally applicable if seen in structural terms. In some respects Alfredian developments extended existing trends, towards tighter bonds between the king and his bishops.[43] The shift to vernacular prose seems decisive: there is little sign that earlier material emanating from the household included texts specifically for ecclesiastical consumption. The audience for vernacular poetry was evidently wider; the only texts demonstrably received by ecclesiastics were charters and other documents.[44] Alfredian change here elevated the household, as a source of learned ecclesiastical expertise. The transformation was exemplified by the *Hierdeboc*, characterized as a 'written message' (*ærendgewrit*), and prefaced by royal letter.[45] Bishops were in no way insulated from the implications of literate technology. Episcopal competence may have varied: distribution of the Gregorian translation was justified on the grounds that 'some ... had need thereof who least knew Latin', but this would not have included Plegmund, nor for that matter Wærferth.[46] Yet reading was now supplied uniformly, in 'the language that we can all understand'.

Nor in the case of secular aristocrats was Alfredian education constructed *ex nihilo*. Again, Alfredian developments extended existing trends in royal lordship, towards bonding increasingly dependent on the written

---

[41] *Ibid.*, lines 46–61.   [42] Booth, 'Alfred versus Beowulf', pp. 50–5.   [43] Above, pp. 52–8.
[44] Above, pp. 86–92.   [45] *Verse Preface to CP*, ed. Dobbie, ASPR 6, 110, cf. *CP*, pp. 2–8.
[46] Bullough, 'Educational Tradition', p. 298.

word. Books accompanied bookland in the repertoire of royal gifts. Alfred's gift of an exemplar was placed in this context by bishop Wulfsige, in his preface to Wærferth's translation.[47] It was within lay instruction that the shift to prose acquired its greatest innovatory potential. Via translation, the instruction of secular aristocrats assumed a form closer to that previously reserved for ecclesiastics. There were radical implications in Asser's identification of the skills acquired, as the *liberales artes*.[48] The seven 'liberal arts' amounted to a guiding principle of Christian Latin learning, long known in Anglo-Saxon education via the study of grammar.[49] It was within Latinity that the liberal arts had gained a central position in Carolingian educational theory, popularized by Alcuin.[50]

Such theory probably exerted direct influence: the value of the liberal arts lay specifically in their ability to access divine wisdom, the 'true philosophy' of speculative theology, through the interpretation of scripture.[51] Yet under Alfred wisdom was accessible in the vernacular; the 'liberal arts' were now steps of a general kind, no longer dependent on Latinity.[52] Flexibility continued in attitudes to literacy. *Litteratus* commonly referred to the ability to read and write Latin; the usage is generally cited as symptomatic of the general commitment to Latinity in medieval learning.[53] Yet in Asser's hands *illiteratus* implied an inability to read letters of any form, including the written vernacular.[54] *Literatoria ars* and *litteralia studia* similarly referred to the reading of books in English.[55] Such direct access contrasted with earlier methods of memorization and recitation. Court technology had twofold novelty, offering direct inculcation in 'liberal arts' via the ability to read.

[47] Yerkes, 'Metrical Preface', pp. 512–13; trans. in K&L, *Alfred*, pp. 187–8.

[48] *VA* 75, line 20, and c. 106, line 57. Cf. the king's own desire for the 'liberal arts' (c. 24, lines 6–10, and c. 76, lines 41–3).

[49] P. Riché, *Education and Culture in the Barbarian West: Sixth through Eighth Centuries* (Columbia, SC, 1976), pp. 384–93; Lapidge, 'Anglo-Latin Literature', pp. 1–4; cf. M. Irvine, *The Making of Textual Culture: 'Grammatica' and Literary Theory, 350–1100* (Cambridge, 1994), pp. 272–333.

[50] J. Marenbon, 'Carolingian Thought', in *Carolingian Culture*, ed. McKitterick, pp. 171–92; M.-Th. d'Alverny, 'La Sagesse et ses sept filles. Recherches sure les allégories de la philosophie et des arts liberaux du IXe au XIIe siècle', in *Mélanges dédiés à la mémoire du Felix Grat*, 2 vols. (Paris, 1946) I, 245–78; Riché, *Écoles*, pp. 111–18; Brown, 'Carolingian Renaissance', pp. 28–44, and J. Contreni, 'The Pursuit of Knowledge in Carolingian Europe', in *'The Gentle Voices of Teachers'*, ed. Sullivan, pp. 106–41.

[51] Alcuin, *Disputatio de vera philosophia*, in PL 101: 849–54; Marenbon, 'Carolingian Thought', pp. 172–3; d'Alverny, 'La Sagesse', pp. 245–8 and 250–7; M. Alberi, '"The Better Paths of Wisdom": Alcuin's Monastic "True Philosophy" and the Worldly Court', *Speculum* 76 (2001), 896–910.

[52] Bullough, 'Educational Tradition', p. 298. Cf. Irvine, *Textual Culture*, pp. 415–20.

[53] H. Grundmann, '*Litteratus – illiteratus*: der Wandel einer Bildungsnorm vom Altertum zum Mittelalter', *Archiv für Kulturgeschichte* 40 (1958), 1–66.

[54] Grundmann, '*Litteratus – illiteratus*', p. 36; *VA* 106, line 42, cf. c. 22, line 12.

[55] *VA* 106, lines 44 and 47.

Alfredian priorities were informed by Carolingian trends; yet there were important differences. Royal learning drew more broadly on Insular as well as Frankish expertise. The programme that resulted did not extend Frankish ecclesiastical reform, nor the patterns of activity that had given this movement its momentum.[56] The contrast was not just with the Carolingian commitment to Latinity, though the distinction is striking. Nor was it simply a question of scale. The fundamental divide was between a Carolingian agenda directed towards the Frankish people as a whole; and a more limited and specific Alfredian agenda, directed towards aristocratic orders, and more exclusively reliant on the royal household. Carolingian reform was multi-centric from its outset: Alfred's 'free-born young men' may echo one of Charlemagne's provisions in the *Admonitio generalis*, but the latter had described the establishment of multiple *scolae*, explicitly intended for future ecclesiastics.[57] The strength of ecclesiastical 'correction' was reflected in the range of centrally authorized texts, dominated by biblical, liturgical and canonical texts, together with homiletic and hagiographical material, united by aspirations of ecclesiastical regulation and standardization.[58] Alfredian translations suggest different mechanisms in their focus on texts of patristic authority, insufficient for wider reform.

More striking are parallels in courtly education. The practice of maintaining young aristocrats at court extended back to Merovingian rule.[59] Carolingian innovation affected the character of instruction, regularly characterized as the 'liberal arts'.[60] These had been included by Charlemagne for the instruction of his daughters as well as sons; his cousin Wala had received similar instruction at Pippin's court a generation earlier.[61] Such qualities became prized as a route to possible preferment at royal hands. Former palace chaplains feature prominently as recipients of episcopal and abbatial office throughout the Carolingian period.[62] Donald Bullough advanced strong grounds for lay participation in Charlemagne's *scola palatii*, highlighting the dominance of secular

---

[56] Above, pp. 58–62.
[57] MGH Capit. I, no. 22, c. 73; Ansegisus, *Capitularium Collectio*, I.68; Bullough, 'Educational Tradition', pp. 297–300.
[58] Above, p. 59.
[59] Riché, *Écoles*, pp. 296–7; McKitterick, *Written Word*, pp. 213–16; Innes, '"Place of Discipline"', pp. 62–3.
[60] See esp. Alberi, '"Better Paths of Wisdom"'; R. McKitterick, 'The Palace School of Charles the Bald', in her *Frankish Kings*, no. 6, p. 329.
[61] Einhard, *Vita Karoli*, ed. Holder-Egger, c. 19, cf. 25, pp. 23 and 30; Paschasius Radbertus, *Epitaphium Arsenii* I.6, PL 120: 1572A.
[62] Innes, '"Place of Discipline"', pp. 63–4; J. Fleckenstein, *Die Hofkapelle der deutschen Könige, I: Grundlegung: Die karolingische Hofkapelle*, Schriften der MGH 16.1 (Stuttgart, 1959).

aristocrats at the time of Alcuin's arrival.[63] There were similar arrangements under Charles the Bald. Contemporary references to his household as a *schola* were far from illusory topoi.[64] The *Gesta episco-porum Autissiodorensium* describes 'nobles and magnates of the kingdom' as accustomed to attach their offspring to Charles's court 'for the sake of learning worldly and ecclesiastical behaviour'.[65] No less revealing is Hincmar's advice to Charles's grandson, Carloman. Urging the appointment of sons from established families, Hincmar identified a large portion of the West Frankish order in his reference to 'palace officials' and 'prefects of the realm': wisdom and 'good studies' were prominent qualities for advancement.[66]

This was the context for the story attributed to Charlemagne by Notker the Stammerer, writing in the 880s, combining idealized recollection with contemporary exhortation.[67] The emperor was pictured presiding over learned competition between *pueri* of varying backgrounds. Praising the humble for work 'sweetened with all the condiments of wisdom', he raised the prospect of bishoprics and monasteries, before chastizing those of noble background for their idleness: 'You should know this for certain: if you do not make up for your earlier negligence immediately by vigilant study, you will receive nothing good from Charlemagne'.[68] Notker's text was addressed to Charles the Fat: it is difficult not to see contemporary concerns in this act of memory.

Notker's story supports the broader adaptation of Carolingian methods in Alfredian education.[69] This hinged on the 'liberal arts' in educational theory, and their significance for the laity; both found Alfredian implementation under English conditions. A fundamental variable was again linguistic: Carolingian structures supplied lay education beyond as well as within the royal household, with young nobles receiving tuition also from their parents, from a local religious house, or another aristocratic household.[70] In Alfred's kingdom, the rapid harnessing of the written vernacular allowed literate instruction to acquire

---

[63] D. Bullough, '*Albuinus deliciosus Karoli regis*: Alcuin of York and the Shaping of the Early Carolingian Court', in *Institutionen, Kultur und Gesellschaft im Mittelalter: Festschrift für Josef Fleckenstein zu seinem 65. Geburtstag*, ed. L. Fenske, W. Rösener and T. Zotz (Sigmaringen, 1984), pp. 73–92, esp. 85–92.

[64] McKitterick, 'Palace School', p. 329. Cf. P. Godman, *Poetry of the Carolingian Renaissance* (London, 1985), pp. 56–8, discussed by Nelson, 'Charles le Chauve', pp. 39–40.

[65] Ed. Waitz, p. 400; McKitterick, 'Palace School', p. 329.   [66] *De ordine palatii*, c. 6, p. 96.

[67] *Gesta Karoli Magni Imperatoris*, ed. Haefele, I.3, pp. 4–5; Innes, ' "Place of Discipline" ', pp. 69–70; MacLean, *Charles the Fat*, pp. 199–229, esp. 210–12.

[68] *Gesta Karoli Magni Imperatoris*, ed. Haefele, I.3, pp. 4–5.

[69] Cf. Bullough, 'Educational Tradition', pp. 297–300.

[70] Riché, *Écoles*, pp. 287–313; McKitterick, *Written Word*, pp. 211–27 and 244–70; Nelson, 'Literacy', pp. 11–14; Sullivan, 'Cultural Activity', pp. 68–71.

greater exclusivity. To this extent the closest parallel was with East Frankish exploitation of Germanic vernacular texts.[71] Yet even here the West Saxon evidence is considerably stronger for mechanisms of lay delivery, primarily located within the royal household.[72]

TEXTUAL DISSEMINATION AND THE FIELD OF ALFREDIAN KNOWLEDGE

The role of individual texts poses many difficulties. Precision is restricted by the generalized nature of Asser's testimony; vernacular texts are only slightly more forthcoming on intended readership. The *Hierdeboc* is unusually specific, yet its distribution bears comparison with three further texts, preserved in large numbers of manuscripts, suggesting significant dissemination early in their transmission-history. The 'common stock' of the *Chronicle* indicates distribution from a single source, probably late in 892.[73] Alfred's law-book survives in six whole or fragmentary manuscripts; knowledge of its contents was regularly assumed in later legislation.[74] Wormald has highlighted the Old English Bede, also attested by six witnesses, though its relationship to Alfred is less secure.[75]

Other texts offer internal indications of readership, with more tantalizing evidence for promulgation. Wærferth's translation of the *Dialogues* circulated in two different formats, distinguished by separate prefaces.[76] The first portrayed Alfred as having commissioned the translation from his 'true friends'; the alternative preface by Wulfsige of Sherborne reveals copying from an exemplar received from the king.[77] Wider dissemination is suggested by the practice of addressing an implied plurality of readers: '[h]e who sets out to read me through', as Wulfsige puts it, giving voice to the book.[78] The technique recurs in no less than three of Alfred's texts. The Prose Preface to the Boethius addressed 'each of those whom it pleases to read this book'.[79] The royal Psalms came with introductions explaining their significance for 'each of those who sing it'.[80] The preface to the *Soliloquies* urged 'every man' to follow steps towards temporary and eternal rest.[81]

---

[71] Goldberg, *Empire*, pp. 179–85, cf. 210–12.

[72] *Ibid.*, where the precise means of instruction remains unclear; cf. letter of Ermanrich of Ellwangen to Grimald of St-Gallen (MGH Epist. V, no. 10, pp. 534–79, esp. 534–6), revealing courtly instruction of future ecclesiastics (Goldberg, *Empire*, pp. 171–2).

[73] K&L, *Alfred*, pp. 277–9.   [74] Below, pp. 214–15 and 238–9.

[75] Wormald, 'Engla Lond', pp. 376–7.

[76] Godden, 'Wærferth and King Alfred', pp. 35–40.

[77] GD I, 1; trans. in K&L, *Alfred*, p. 123; Yerkes, 'Metrical Preface', p. 512; trans. in K&L, *Alfred*, pp. 187–8.

[78] Godden, 'Wærferth and King Alfred', pp. 38–40.   [79] *Bo*, p. 1; trans. in K&L, *Alfred*, pp. 132–3.

[80] Below, pp. 247–51.   [81] *Solil* pp. 47–8; trans. in K&L, *Alfred*, pp. 138–9.

All three of these texts have survived very narrowly. This has often seemed unpromising, but on closer inspection the record remains consistent with wider dissemination. The Boethius is known from only two manuscripts, dating from the mid-tenth and early twelfth centuries; the Psalms and *Soliloquies* are each preserved in single manuscripts of the late eleventh and mid-twelfth centuries respectively.[82] Yet the survival of Old English manuscripts became increasingly difficult in the later middle ages; these patterns of transmission are not untypical. There are many indications that the Boethius was widely known from an early stage;[83] there is nothing to match this for the other two, but multiple copies were clearly available in later centuries. The Alfredian introductions to the Psalms survive in a second manuscript, added to the margins of a mid-eleventh-century Psalter, in a form not directly copied from the principal manuscript.[84] Such circulation provides a context for William of Malmesbury's oddly specific inclusion of some portion of the Psalter among works by the king. For the *Soliloquies* also there is a secondary witness, in a short eleventh-century extract.[85]

The possibility has sometimes been raised of 'lost' texts which have failed to survive; the chances are greater for poetry than prose. William of Malmesbury's testimony deserves weight, given the wider availability of Alfredian texts. If claims for authorship are disregarded, his list correlates very closely with surviving texts of prose. The only omission is the *Soliloquia*; the only problematic inclusion is what William identifies as the king's *Enchiridion* or 'hand-book'. Whitelock's solution was to suggest grounds on which William might have mistaken a copy of the Alfredian *Soliloquies* for Alfred's composite 'hand-book', whose construction is otherwise described by Asser.[86] The argument has some attractions, but William's other references to the 'hand-book' rather suggest genuine access to a composite text somehow identified as Alfredian.[87]

There are good reasons for a 'maximum' view of texts participating in 're-education'. In addition to the strong associations which many texts exhibit with King Alfred, the very general scope of 'wisdom' as divine knowledge makes it difficult to exclude any candidate on grounds of content. Alfredian texts provided access to 'wisdom' in a variety of forms, yet collectively these suggest a coherent field or continuum of divine knowledge, ranging from the revelation of scripture to more direct reflection on the role of man and his relationship to God, and thence to

---

[82] Below, pp. 245–6, 303 and 332.   [83] Below, pp. 303–4.   [84] Below, pp. 246 and 261.
[85] Below, pp. 332–3.
[86] Whitelock, 'Prose', pp. 71–3; Whitelock, 'William of Malmesbury', pp. 90–1.
[87] As noted by Thomson in *GR* II, 103–4; cf. Pratt, '*Handbook*'.

the unfolding of this relationship in human history.[88] Scriptural elements were most intensive in the Psalms and law-book introduction; the relationship between man and God dominated the four patristic translations. Historical concerns were uppermost in the Orosius, relentless on the workings of divine providence, and the *Chronicle*, more reticent but anchored by the reference-point of Christ's incarnation.[89] Both the Bede and *Martyrology* could easily have occupied this field, though their status is uncertain.

Again, Carolingian influence might be suspected among texts of Alfredian knowledge; the picture is more equivocal than has sometimes been recognized. Alfredian 'wisdom' followed the common early medieval prioritization of religious over secular learning; general similarities are perhaps only to be expected, for example, in the role of the Psalter as an educational starting-point, the value of patristic writings for normative instruction and theological exegesis, and a role for hagiography within lay devotion.[90] No less typical was the place of legal and historical texts in 'liberal' education.[91] Yet even here are significant differences: one should note the apparent lack of material from the New Testament, striking when compared with translations prepared under East Frankish royal patronage, distinctively focused on the gospels.[92] Specific connections seem less decisive from this perspective. None of the Alfredian Latin source-texts was unavailable in the Carolingian world; more positively, those of Boethius and Augustine may well have been recent imports.[93] Taken as a whole, the supply of texts seems to reflect the wider connections of Alfred's household. The fundamental starting-point for selection were texts which had long been prominent in Insular learning. In addition to the Psalter and Bede's history, the two Gregorian texts were certainly widely known: both were among source-texts for the 'Leiden family' of glosses, generally held to reflect the

---

[88] Whitelock, 'Prose', p. 98: 'to make all this knowledge available to many was surely a great conception'.

[89] Bately, *Translation or Transformation?*, pp. 18–21; W. A. Kretzschmar, 'Adaptation and *anweald* in the Old English Orosius', *ASE* 16 (1987), 127–45.

[90] P. Riché, 'Le Psautier, livre de lecture élémentaire d'après les vies des saints mérovingiens', in *Etudes Mérovingiennes. Actes des Journées de Poitiers 1952* (Paris, 1953), pp. 253–6; Riché, *Écoles*, pp. 288–306; Wallace-Hadrill, *Frankish Church*, pp. 283–6 and 403–11; McKitterick, *Frankish Church*, pp. 80–114 and 155–83; McKitterick, *Written Word*, pp. 217–18, 241–3 and 244–70.

[91] R. McKitterick, 'Some Carolingian Law-Books and their Function', in her *Books, Scribes and Learning in the Frankish Kingdoms, 6th–9th Centuries* (Aldershot, 1994), no. 8; Wormald, *MEL* I, 30–92; Y. Hen and M. Innes (eds.), *The Uses of the Past in the Early Middle Ages* (Cambridge, 2000); R. McKitterick, *History and Memory in the Carolingian World* (Cambridge, 2004).

[92] K&L, *Alfred*, pp. 295–6 (note 12); Goldberg, *Empire*, pp. 179–85; cf. also Bostock, *Handbook*, pp. 157–86 and 190–212, and Edwards, 'German Vernacular Literature', pp. 152–7.

[93] Below, pp. 270–2 and 312–17.

teachings of Theodore and Hadrian, together with Orosius' history.[94] The exemplar of the *Regula pastoralis* seems more likely to have been of English than Continental transmission.[95] Recent investigation of the Orosius has pointed suggestively to Wales.[96] Other developments suggest Irish influence, strongly attested in the translation of the Psalms, and suggested by the law-book.[97]

The Alfredian scheme has often been seen as providing access to a representative cross-section of available Latin learning. For Wallace-Hadrill, Alfredian texts were entirely 'the obvious books for ... self-instruction and general instruction in the social role of Christianity'.[98] As much was claimed by Alfred's Prose Preface, yet such rhetoric masked the selectivity of 'necessary' learning, involving a distinctive blend of foreign and domestic expertise. The combination of Boethius and Augustine was especially shaped by contingent interests in Alfred's circle.[99] Each text must be judged on its own terms in the making of Alfredian knowledge.

---

[94] Lapidge, 'School of Theodore and Hadrian', pp. 150–1.   [95] Below, pp. 142–3.
[96] Lapidge, 'Asser's Reading', pp. 33–4 and 41.   [97] Below, pp. 230–2 and 248–51.
[98] Wallace-Hadrill, *Early Germanic Kingship*, p. 142; cf. Whitelock, 'Prose', pp. 75 and 98.
[99] Below, pp. 264–307 and 308–37.

Chapter 8

THE CONSTRUCTION OF ALFREDIAN DISCOURSE

The role of production embraces many of the most problematic features
of Alfredian kingship. This chapter addresses the role of the texts
attributed to Alfred, and their position in the programme as a whole. As
such, it serves a twofold purpose: a unique context for the king's texts
would also extend the basis for their systematic study. From the degree
of investment in these texts, it is difficult not to regard Alfred's personal
role in their composition as entirely central to their potential value. Yet
much depended on an appropriate medium: one must focus initially on
Alfred's textual image, and the means by which it was sustained.[1]

The value of Alfred's texts was enhanced most directly by the
assertion of his role in composition. Royal authorship attracted much
effort in its repeated establishment. The help of scholarly helpers was
acknowledged for the *Hierdeboc*; even here Alfred's role was firmly
asserted in the Verse Preface.[2] There were no such qualifications for the
Boethius: the authenticity of the Prose Preface has sometimes been
questioned, but Sisam argued convincingly for its basis in Alfredian
material.[3] The first-person of the king intervenes most strongly in the
law-book towards the end of the preface.[4] The *Soliloquies* are more

---

[1] Cf. M. Swan, 'Authorship and Anonymity', in *Companion to Anglo-Saxon Literature*, ed. Pulsiano and
Treharne, pp. 71–83, esp. p. 73, for the relevance of M. Foucault, 'What is an Author?', in *The
Foucault Reader*, ed. Rabinow, pp. 101–20. This chapter draws occasionally from Pratt, 'Authorship',
and Pratt, 'Illnesses' (both by kind permission of Cambridge University Press). On the general theme,
cf. Lerer, *Literacy*, pp. 61–96; A. J. Frantzen, 'The Form and Function of the Preface in the Poetry and
Prose of Alfred's Reign', in *Alfred*, ed. Reuter, pp. 121–36, at 134–6; C. Karkov, *The Ruler Portraits of
Anglo-Saxon England* (Woodbridge, 2004), pp. 34–42; Discenza, *King's English*, pp. 1–29 and 45–50.
[2] *CP*, p. 6, lines 20–2; *Verse Preface to CP*, ed. Dobbie.
[3] *Bo*, p. 1; K. Sisam, *Studies in the History of Old English Literature* (Oxford, 1953), pp. 292–7,
esp. 295–7.
[4] *Af* Int.49.9.

problematic: the only reference to Alfred occurs at the end, and need not be contemporary.[5] Yet the opening of the preface has been lost: his first-person is well established in the portion that survives. The only clear exception is the translation of the Psalms: even here there is no way of knowing whether material has been lost.

These assertions had special significance. It has been insufficiently emphasized that these instances are in fact the *only* examples of projected authorial image among the vernacular texts associated with Alfred's reign. Wærferth's involvement in translating the *Dialogues* is only revealed by Asser. Anonymity was ubiquitous, extending beyond translated texts, such as the Orosius or Bede, to include instances of free-standing composition, such as the *Chronicle*. This contrasts with the Latin output of Alfred's circle, such as Asser's *Life* and an acrostic attributed to John the Old Saxon, where priorities differed.[6] The effect was to reinforce the distinction between 'authorized' texts and those actually of the king. Wærferth's anonymity seems explicable in this light, accompanied in one version by a preface highlighting Alfred's personal commission; another celebrated his gift of an exemplar.[7] When compared with such conspicuous 'authorization', royal texts involved nothing less than the full monopolization of authorship in the person of the king, an extreme extension of West Saxon courtly trends.

Royal texts were further enhanced by their distinctive language and style. Alfred's image as creative translator was no empty label, but received support from the singular textuality to which this image was attached. These observations proceed from Bately's analysis: the texts in Alfred's name are in early West Saxon dialect, so attention focuses on appropriate comparanda, principally the Orosius and the 'common stock' of the *Chronicle*.[8] Even within this broader spectrum of early West Saxon, Bately shows that the 'royal' texts can be further distinguished on the grounds of lexical choice, supplemented by considerations of syntax and style.[9] The evidence of lexis has weight given the general availability of Latin equivalents; Bately's distinctive features include cases of lexical variation as well as lexical consistency.[10] These correspondences are strong given that the *Chronicle* may itself be the work of several compilers, and can be firmly

[5] *Solil* p. 97, lines 17–18, cf. p. 38.
[6] M. Lapidge, 'Some Latin Poems as Evidence for the Reign of Athelstan', in his *ALL* II, 49–86, at 60–71.
[7] *GD* I, 1; trans. in K&L, *Alfred*, p. 123. Yerkes, 'Metrical Preface', pp. 512–13; trans. in K&L, *Alfred*, pp. 187–8.
[8] Esp. Bately, 'Translation of Orosius'; Bately, 'Lexical Evidence'; Bately, 'Old English Prose', pp. 118–38.
[9] Bately, 'Lexical Evidence', esp. pp. 71–94; P. P. O'Neill in *Ps(P)*, pp. 73–96.
[10] Bately, 'Lexical Evidence', pp. 90–3.

distinguished from the style of the Orosius.[11] Certain inconsistencies in usage can also be detected across the 'royal' corpus, together with occasional words usually regarded as characteristic of Mercian dialect, but these are insufficient to undermine the case for common vocabulary.[12] Stylistically, the 'royal' texts bear closest comparison with the Orosius, not least in the overall approach to translation, more heavily reliant on free paraphrase as opposed to the literal rendering of individual Latin sentences.[13] Yet here too the 'royal' texts can be distinguished at this micro-level by certain idiosyncracies of syntax and shared mannerisms.[14]

Taken as a whole, the 'royal' corpus bears ample testimony to the cosmopolitan resources in courtly service. As Mechthild Gretsch has noted, 'Mercianisms' must be judged carefully, given the considerable potential for incorporation of 'Mercian' vocabulary into spoken early West Saxon, but it is difficult not to suspect some connection with the king's Mercian helpers, particularly given the greater prominence of this feature in 'royal' texts.[15] The influence of Irish learning may be strongly suspected in the translation of the Psalms and in aspects of the law-book; both lend significance to the Irish presence in Alfred's household, and thus to the possibility of input which may not have been explicitly acknowledged.[16] Such features complement evidence suggestive of Carolingian expertise, in the concessions made towards the 'Gallican' text of the Psalter, and most definitively in the approach to law represented by the law-book. Both the Boethius and Augustine suggest deep awareness of associated Carolingian scholarship. Yet in each case such elements supplied merely one aspect of treatment, often skewed in translation; uniting all were priorities and imagery distinctive to this corpus, very plausibly identified as 'royal'. The point is strengthened by the predominant dialect, native to Alfred but none of his acknowledged helpers; Bately's analysis suggests speech as a shaping source of unity.

All these features supported still greater enhancement of 'royal' texts at macro-level, in the unity and complementarity of their content. All

---

[11] J. M. Bately, 'The Compilation of the Anglo-Saxon Chronicle, 60 BC to AD 890: Vocabulary as Evidence', *PBA* 64 (1978), 93–129, at 101–29; Bately in *Or*, pp. lxxxiii–lxxxvi.

[12] Bately, 'Translation of Orosius', pp. 452–3; Bately, 'Lexical Evidence', pp. 78–86.

[13] Bately, 'Old English Prose', pp. 118–38.

[14] Bately, 'Translation of Orosius', pp. 444–52; Bately, 'Lexical Evidence', p. 94; syntactical similarities identified by Liggins, 'Authorship', pp. 292–321.

[15] Gretsch, 'Junius Psalter Gloss', pp. 98–106; cf. now C. Schreiber, 'Dialects in Contact in Ninth-Century England', in *Bookmarks from the Past: Studies in honour of Helmut Gneuss*, ed. L. Kornexl and U. Lenker (Frankfurt-am-Main, 2003), pp. 1–31.

[16] P. P. O'Neill, 'The Old English Introductions to the Prose Psalms of the Paris Psalter: Sources, Structure, and Composition', in *Eight Anglo-Saxon Studies*, ed. J. S. Wittig (Chapel Hill, NC, 1981), pp. 20–38; O'Neill in *Ps(P)*, pp. 23–6; K&L, *Alfred*, p. 304 (note 2); *VA* 76, lines 21–6; *ASC* s.a. 891.

texts within the Alfredian programme offered 'necessary' knowledge: the 'royal' texts were further distinguished in supplying forms explicitly concerned with the theory and practice of power, and the behaviour of those privileged to wield it. It is on this basis that they may be regarded as operating within a single discourse, firmly associated with the king. Much of this reflected existing structures in locating power within a framework of office-holding, shared between the king and his thegns. It was this field of office-holding which supplied the basis for an Alfredian form of political thought, articulated textually through distinctive political language. Alfredian discourse was shaped by its commitment to two complementary political languages, governing office-holding in similar ways: first, language derived from Gregory the Great, expounded most fully in the *Hierdeboc* and second, a 'Solomonic' language of office-holding, ultimately from the bible, but endowed with further ninth-century resonances. Both operated across the full range of 'royal' texts, which must be read as a continuous whole.

Alfred's image commands attention in wider European context. Central features of this 'royal' discourse were without parallel in the Carolingian world. What distinguished Alfredian discourse was the extreme exclusivity of its 'royal' delivery, and its commitment to universalizing, and in this sense 'philosophical' explanation, frequently generated independently within the ambiguous constraints of translation. Better parallels among contemporary rulers lay further east, in the learned activities of the eastern Emperor Leo VI (886–912) and Tsar Symeon of the Bulgars (893–927), explored by Jonathan Shepard.[17] The most direct Carolingian comparison is with capitulary-material, often incorporating the ruler's first-person, and in western regions a potent medium for collective 'ministerial' responsibilities.[18] Yet beyond this the 'royal' first-person was relatively scarce, principally restricted to letters. There is very little which might be identified as a universalizing or 'philosophical' discourse of power.[19] For Charles the Bald, fuller theorizing was restricted to papal correspondence.[20] Such reticence is thrown into relief by the intensity of advice-literature in western regions, directed towards rulers by ecclesiastical writers.[21] Even in East

---

[17] J. Shepard, 'The Ruler as Instructor, Pastor and Wise: Leo VI of Byzantium and Symeon of Bulgaria', in *Alfred*, ed. Reuter, pp. 339–58.

[18] Above, pp. 71 and 88. Cf. also Nelson, 'Charles le Chauve', esp. pp. 46–9.

[19] See esp. Nelson, 'Political Ideas', pp. 137–8; Nelson, 'Carolingian Contemporaries', pp. 307–10, effectively qualifying parallels earlier drawn with Alfred in Nelson, 'Charles le Chauve', pp. 41–3.

[20] J. L. Nelson, ' "Not Bishops' Bailiffs but Lords of the Earth": Charles the Bald and the Problem of Sovereignty', in her *Frankish World*, pp. 133–43. Cf. J. L. Nelson, 'The Voice of Charlemagne', in *Belief and Culture*, ed. Gameson and Leyser, pp. 76–88, discussing capitulary-material.

[21] Above, pp. 27 and 59–62; Nelson, 'Political Ideas', pp. 147–8.

Francia, where conditions differed, royal documentary production was more restricted. Vernacular texts associated with Louis the German are either anonymous or attributed to ecclesiastics.[22]

Such contrasts related to regional conditions. The Alfredian programme is too easily interpreted as an autonomous act of will, neglecting forces integral to its construction. Alfred's image amounted to an extreme extension of West Saxon trends. Within the wider community of 'court societies', decisive was the range and quality of West Saxon royal monopolies, and the mechanisms by which these monopolies were sustained. Fundamental was the exceptional degree of contact in the royal household, and its exclusivity with respect to other potential fora, whether assemblies or synods.[23] Royal production owed much to the mono-directional nature of gift-giving, central to the broader ubiquity of West Saxon royal lordship.[24] The absence of advice-literature reflected a distinctive relationship between king and bishops, under ninth-century Southumbrian conditions.[25] In all these respects, Alfred's monopolization of authorship seems less unexpected; incentives for collective investment in the royal word were notably extreme.

LANGUAGES OF OFFICE-HOLDING (I) GREGORIAN LANGUAGE

Alfredian reception of the *Regula pastoralis* lay at the heart of attitudes towards power and authority. Whilst this general point has become increasingly appreciated, the role of such language relates to several areas of debate. Necessarily dominant has been Alfred's image as a suffering king, afflicted by illness.[26] Closely related is Asser's portrait of the king, supplying the most detailed account of this image.[27] Both have been further complicated by an awareness of Frankish parallels, and the possibility of attributing many aspects of Alfredian kingship to specific Carolingian models.[28] Such an approach has much to commend it given the constituency of royal helpers. Yet there are also limitations. The imagery of kingship was intertextual, drawing on closely related material,

---

[22] Goldberg, *Empire*, pp. 36–7 and 179–85.   [23] Above, pp. 28–43 and 52–4.
[24] Above, pp. 38–43.   [25] Above, pp. 26–7 and 44–62.
[26] Scharer, 'History', pp. 187–91; Scharer, *Herrschaft*, pp. 66–82; Nelson, 'Monks', pp. 135–8; P. Kershaw, 'Illness, Power and Prayer in Asser's *Life of King Alfred*', EME 10 (2001), 201–24. Cf. Pratt, 'Illnesses'.
[27] Kershaw, 'Illness, Power'; M. Kempshall, 'No Bishop, No King: the Ministerial Ideology of Kingship and Asser's *Res Gestae Aelfredi*', in *Belief and Culture*, ed. Gameson and Leyser, pp. 106–27; A. Sheppard, 'The King's Family: Securing the Kingdom in Asser's *Vita Alfredi*', *Philological Quarterly* 80 (2001), 409–39; S. DeGregorio, 'Texts, *topoi* and the Self: a Reading of Alfredian Spirituality', EME 13 (2005), 79–96.
[28] Scharer, 'History', pp. 185–206; Scharer, *Herrschaft*, pp. 61–108; cf. Nelson, 'Monks', and Kershaw, 'Illness, Power'.

not least the bible, liturgical texts, patristic writings and legal material, all variously cited in advice-literature; this places important limits on the detection of specific 'sources' or influences.[29] Such problems are acute for the *Regula pastoralis*, also dependent on biblical exempla, and regularly subject to citation on both sides of the Channel. For all these reasons one must focus on the immediate deployment of Gregorian language, before returning to the question of possible precedent.

Not the least factor behind the popularity of Gregory's text was its status as an extended treatment of power, framed as advice to those wielding it.[30] Although originally a manual for episcopal conduct, Gregory's account so blurred the boundaries between ecclesiastical and secular authority that his advice could assume wider application. Ruling was characterized as an act of service, located in the restraining of sin. Gregorian rhetoric harnessed language of secular authority, in the allusive position of *rector* ('ruler'), only to undermine it by appeal to pastoral responsibility.[31] The ruler administered a specific office, as pastor and teacher, held on trust from God, but with obligations firmly within the world.[32] This involved the highest fulfilment of Christ's two injunctions, combining the love of God with the active life of service to fellow men.[33] So heavy were these responsibilities that they could only be undertaken by persons of outstanding virtue. Even then the ruler was implicated in a constant struggle to maintain appropriate balance between spiritual and worldly concerns.[34] As a consequence of his worldly involvement, the ruler was exposed to heightened dangers of sin, arising most fundamentally from the very desire of ruling (*libido dominandi*).[35] His greatest danger lay in yielding to this desire, thus succumbing to the central vice of pride (*superbia*).[36] The threat was frequently characterized in bodily terms, as the impact of fleshly temptation; much advice was concerned to protect the mind from such excesses, and thus to preserve humility.[37]

The most faithful of 'royal' translations, the *Hierdeboc* has often been deemed an 'early' work; such respect must also be judged against the

---

[29] Kempshall, 'No Bishop', p. 107; Wormald, *MEL* I, 124.

[30] R. A. Markus, *Gregory the Great and his World* (Cambridge, 1997); R. A. Markus, 'The Latin Fathers', in *The Cambridge History of Medieval Political Thought c.350–c.1450*, ed. J. H. Burns (Cambridge, 1988), pp. 92–122, at 116–22; cf. also C. Straw, *Gregory the Great: Perfection in Imperfection* (Berkeley, CA, 1988); B. Judic in *Reg. past.*, pp. 15–102; G. R. Evans, *The Thought of Gregory the Great* (Cambridge, 1986).

[31] R. A. Markus, 'Gregory the Great's *rector* and his Genesis', in *Grégoire le Grand*, ed. J. Fontaine, R. Gillet and S. Pellistrandi (Paris, 1986), pp. 137–46.

[32] *Reg. past.* I.1, pp. 128–32.   [33] *Ibid.* I.7, pp. 150–4.

[34] *Ibid.* II.5, II.6 and II.7, pp. 196–230.   [35] *Ibid.* II.6, pp. 210–12; cf. I.8, pp. 154–6.

[36] *Ibid.* I.8 and II.6, pp. 154–6 and 202–18; cf. I.4, I.7 and I.9, pp. 140–4, 150–4 and 156–60.

[37] *Ibid.*

deep impact of Gregorian ideas on Alfredian thinking and behaviour. The rendering showed much sensitivity to Gregory's language, yet frequently in terms bearing specific resonance within the West Saxon political order.[38] Wider application of Gregorian principles receives powerful support from Asser's *Life*. Gregorian 'echoes' in Asser's biography have been much rehearsed; it is important to consider how such features might have arisen. Asser was an acknowledged helper: the possibility has been raised of restricting such features to his authorial artifice.[39] Yet the idiosyncratic portait presupposes a significant basis in observable behaviour. As 'ruler of all the Christians of the island of Britain', the role of *rector* was accorded to the king, yet his exposition of Gregorian principles was selective. Pastoral imagery was notably absent; Kempshall goes too far in suggesting direct connections at every turn.[40] Gregorian dimensions were strongest in learning and suffering.

Alfred's status as a learned king received justification from the Gregorian balancing of action and contemplation. Time and again, Alfred's concerns were presented as combining the heavenly with the worldly, the interior with the exterior, the mental with the bodily. On Alfred's medical history, the king reportedly identified the worst aspect of his hidden illness as the threat that it posed to his obligations *in divinis et humanis rebus* ('in heavenly and worldly affairs').[41] Elsewhere, Alfred's concerns as king were described as the *internae atque externae regiae potestatis sollicitudines* ('the internal and external concerns of regal power'), in addition to his illnesses and viking attacks.[42] Such language continued in the 'summoning' of scholars, reportedly undertaken *quasi . . . nullam aliam intrinsecus et extrinsecus perturbationem pateretur* ('as if . . . he suffered no other disturbance internally and externally').[43] These references compare with a series of chapters in the *Regula pastoralis* on the balancing of spiritual and secular concerns, encapsulated by part II, chapter 7.[44] The theme continued in the first-person preface to Wærferth's *Dialogues*. The act of commission was justified by the 'greatest need', shown by 'holy books', and shared by those 'to whom God has granted such a lofty station of worldly office (*swa micle heanesse woruldgeþinga*), that we sometimes calm our minds among these earthly cares and incline them to divine and spiritual justice (*riht*)'.[45] Not least among such books was the *Regula*

---

[38] Below, pp. 195–209. [39] Kempshall, 'No Bishop', esp. pp. 107–8 and 122–3.
[40] *Ibid.*, esp. pp. 112–22. [41] *VA* 74, lines 64–70.
[42] *Ibid.* 25, lines 7–11. Cf. K&L, *Alfred*, p. 76: 'the cares (both domestic and foreign) of the royal office'.
[43] *VA* 76, lines 36–8. [44] *Reg. past.* II.7, cf. II.6 and II.8, pp. 218–30, cf. 202–18 and 230–6.
[45] *GD* I, 1; trans. in K&L, *Alfred*, p. 123.

The construction of Alfredian discourse

pastoralis; part II, chapter 11 explained 'How much the ruler should be intent on meditations on the holy law'.[46]

These principles were fulfilled in the king's actions. The account of Alfred's division of revenues has been much discussed, chiefly in relation to papal or biblical models; insufficient weight has been given to Asser's own explanation, of a vow undertaken by the king to devote to God 'one half of his service, both by day and night', matching such internal efforts with a similar gift of 'external riches'.[47] Alfred's initial division of revenues into two parts, equally reserved for *secularia negotia* and for God, further extended the principle.[48] A similar division applied to the 'service of his own body and mind', in respect of his promise 'to render to God ... one half of the service of mind and body both by day and night'.[49] It was in this devotional context that Asser described the construction of a candle-lantern on Alfred's instructions, regulating his learned behaviour with improved exactitude.[50]

Gregorian attitudes were also the framework for Alfred's pain and suffering. Time and again, Asser stresses the many obstacles which Alfred faces as king, *inter omnia praesentis vitae impedimenta*, of which three obstacles were especially severe.[51] First, Alfred was regularly afflicted (*perturbatus*) by the effects of a mysterious illness, unknown to all physicians, with symptoms not outwardly visible on his body.[52] The illness supplied an almost constant source of tribulation throughout Alfred's adult life, since its sudden emergence in the aftermath of his marriage in 868. Second, Alfred was equally afflicted by the attacks of vikings, suggestively characterized as *infestationes paganorum*, sustained from land and sea without rest.[53] Third, Alfred received still further *perturbatio*, according to Asser, from the reluctance of his own people to undertake his orders, especially with regard to the building of fortifications.[54]

Several of these details were unique to Alfredian circumstances. Yet the portrayal also related to the ambiguous position of worldly reponsibility within Gregorian thought, as a burden characterized by the greatest dangers and temptations.[55] Alfred's various afflictions must be read against the specific role of adversities within the *Regula pastoralis*, which were actually to be welcomed by the ruler as a means of retaining humility.[56] The beneficial effects lay specifically in their ability to recall

[46] *Reg. past.* II.11, pp. 252–6. Cf. *CP* XXII, pp. 168–72.
[47] Nelson, ' "King Across the Sea" ', p. 51; *VA* 99, lines 1–17.
[48] *Ibid.* 99, lines 17–25, cf. cc. 100 and 102.   [49] *Ibid.* 103, lines 1–11.
[50] *Ibid.* 104; below, pp. 186–7.
[51] *VA* 22, lines 7–8; c. 24, lines 5–6; c. 25, lines 1–2 and 13–14; c. 76, lines 1–2.
[52] See esp. Pratt, 'Illnesses'.   [53] *VA* 25, lines 7–11; cf. c. 76, lines 1–3, and c. 96, lines 4–12.
[54] *Ibid.* 91, lines 25–8.   [55] Esp. *Reg. past.* I.4, pp. 140–5.
[56] *Ibid.* I.3 and II.3, pp. 136–40 and 180–6.

the mind to its own weakness, and away from the dangers of worldly and bodily cupidity.[57] Tribulation of the body in particular was an invaluable counterweight to the temptations of power.[58] Gregory himself had suffered from a painful disease of the internal organs for much of his life, highlighted from an English perspective by Bede.[59]

This was the context for Alfred's own bodily suffering. Of central importance was Alfred's hidden disease, contracted at the time of his marriage; the history of suffering was traced back to the earlier disease, *ficus*, contracted 'in the first flowering of his youth'.[60] Decisive is the explanation given for the initial attack of *ficus*, of a sudden resolve on Alfred's part 'to confirm his own mind in God's commandments' when unable to abstain from bodily desire (*carnale desiderium*), followed by a prayer that God might 'strengthen his mind in the love of His service by means of some illness'.[61] What has often seemed the most problematic aspect of Asser's *Life* was in part the exemplary discipline of a Gregorian ruler.[62] This was not the portrayal of a saint, but a layman wrestling in an extreme manner with implications of worldly responsibility.[63] The struggle against bodily desire presupposed broader restraint. In 871 Alfred was reported to have acceded 'virtually unwillingly' (*quasi invitus*), albeit in the face of viking threat.[64] Reluctant acceptance of power was a defining aspect of 'true humility'; the *Regula pastoralis* had been Gregory's answer to ironic criticism of his reluctance to accept papal office in 590.[65]

Such principles did not stop with the king. The *Hierdeboc* was directed to bishops, but included secular language in its suggestive terminology.[66] The text's principal value lay in its ability to supply a universal language of office-holding, potentially applicable to ealdormen, reeves and thegns as well. Asser presents secular nobles as entirely comparable, listing the king's 'bishops and ealdormen, and his thegns most noble and dear to him, and reeves as well (in all of whom, after the Lord and the king, the power of the entire kingdom is seen to be invested, as is appropriate)'.[67] There was a specific Gregorian echo in Asser's criticism of noble attitudes towards the power, contrasting with the king's own efforts, on the

---

[57] *Ibid.*, I.3, lines 19–46, pp. 138–40, and II.3, lines 15–38, pp. 182–4.
[58] *Ibid.*, cf. I.10, lines 1–11, pp. 160–2, and III.12, lines 115–38, pp. 330–2; cf. esp. Straw, *Gregory*, pp. 107–46.
[59] Scharer, 'History', p. 188.   [60] Pratt, 'Illnesses', pp. 57–63; above, p. 89.
[61] *VA* 74, lines 39–55.
[62] Pratt, 'Illnesses', pp. 81–2; cf. also Kershaw, 'Illness, Power', pp. 215–16; Kempshall, 'No Bishop', pp. 118–22.
[63] Cf. Smyth, *Alfred*, pp. 199–216.   [64] *VA* 42, lines 11–16.
[65] *Reg. past.* I.6, pp. 148–50, cf. Praef., pp. 124–6.   [66] Below, pp. 195–204.
[67] *VA* 91, lines 36–9.

basis that 'nearly all the magnates and nobles of that land had inclined their minds more to worldly than to divine affairs'.[68] The pertinence of Gregorian thinking is strengthened by Asser's direct quotation, three chapters earlier, on responsibilities of alms-giving.[69]

All these concerns built on established attitudes towards office-holding.[70] Consistent was the commitment to worldly authority as a form of service, held on trust from God, and equally extended to thegnly recipients. Such observations attach further significance to the role of textual culture, as a novel means of regulating office-holding according to the 'royal' written word. This was directly reflected in Alfredian deployment of Gregorian language, in the indispensability of divine knowledge. Further novelty may be suggested in the value attached to humility, and concomitant concerns against worldly desire and its bodily implications. The evidence falls short of demonstrating any specific dissemination of the *Hierdeboc* to secular nobles; it may well have been reserved for episcopal recipients.[71] Yet these concerns received prominence throughout the royal corpus, through extensive importation of Gregorian language and the provision of compatible models and exempla.

Now to possible precedents: episcopal application must be separated from the further extension of Gregorian principles to secular activity. For the former, English precedents are sufficiently strong to suggest a significant harnessing of episcopal memory. Attention focuses on Gregory's special status as 'Apostle of the English'; his pastoral theology had supplied a central blueprint for ecclesiastical reform.[72] Gregorian influence has long been recognized in the agenda of Bede, largely continued by Alcuin.[73] Yet the impact of Bede's message remains uncertain; assessments have generally stressed the practical obstacles to reform in eighth-century Northumbria.[74] In Southumbria, in contrast, a similar agenda received sustained support, via the reforming activities of southern synods.[75]

---

[68] *Ibid.* 105, lines 10–14.
[69] *Ibid.* 102, lines 9–14; *Reg. past.* III.20, lines 24–7, p. 384. Cf. *CP* XLIV, p. 320, lines 13–17.
[70] Cf. above, pp. 69–72 and 75–8.   [71] Below, pp. 179–82.
[72] Thacker, 'Bede's Ideal of Reform'; A. Thacker, 'Memorializing Gregory the Great: the Origin and Transmission of a Papal Cult in the Seventh and Early Eighth Centuries', *EME* 7 (1998), 59–84; cf. also A. Scharer, 'The Gregorian Tradition in Early England', in *St Augustine and the Conversion of Early England*, ed. R. Gameson (Stroud, 1999), pp. 187–201; Scharer, *Herrschaft*, pp. 128–33.
[73] Thacker, 'Bede's Ideal of Reform', pp. 146–53; Bede's letter to Ecgberht, c. 3, in *Venerablis Baedae Opera Historica*, ed. Plummer I, 406; MGH Epist. V, nos. 116 and 124, pp. 171 and 181–4.
[74] D. P. Kirby, *Bede's Historia ecclesiastica gentis Anglorum: its Contemporary Setting*, Jarrow Lecture 1992 (Jarrow, 1993), esp. p. 12; Brooks, *Canterbury*, pp. 177–9.
[75] Cf. above, pp. 44–6 and 48–9.

The centrality of Gregorian ideals emerges from a fire-damaged late eighth-century manuscript, London, British Library, Cotton Otho A. i. Reconstructed by Keynes, it originally supplied a comprehensive dossier of the key texts of eighth-century reform.[76] These comprised the canons of the 747 synod of *Clofesho*; letters by Boniface to Cuthbert, archbishop of Canterbury, and to Æthelbald, king of the Mercians, to which the synod had responded; and the charter of privileges issued by Æthelbald at Gumley in 749, a further response to Boniface's criticisms.[77] All had been preceded by a Latin text of the *Regula pastoralis*, in abridgement or epitome, condensed to one third of its original length. The epitome reinforced Gregorian ideals in the attached documents. Boniface's letter to Cuthbert had included a long section on the pastoral responsibilities of bishops, culminating in quotations from Gregory's text.[78] The bishops at *Clofesho* had deliberated on Gregory's homilies, together with the 'canonical decrees of the holy fathers'; their canons placed episcopal example at the heart of wider spiritual renewal.[79]

Only a few fragments of the abridgement can be reconstructed, but its editorial procedure seems clear, preserving the substance of Gregory's recommendations, while omitting exegetical detail.[80] A quotation from Isidore's *Sententiae* in one fragment makes some sense as a text itself dependent on the *Regula pastoralis* and other Gregorian works.[81] The text of the abridgement has no known antecedents; it is tempting to associate its preparation with these reforming activities.[82] The codex as a whole amounted to an ambitious memorialization of Southumbrian reform, specifically reflective of conditions within the heartlands of the Mercian kingdom, with potency as a manual for episcopal conduct. Its construction cannot be securely localized, but remains consistent with possible Mercian production.

The book's significance lies in the Southumbrian context that it provides for Alfred's *Hierdeboc*, and its suggestive status in preserving

---

[76] S. Keynes, 'The Reconstruction of a Burnt Cottonian Manuscript: the Case of Cotton MS. Otho A. I', *British Library Journal* 22.2 (1996), 113–60, esp. 135–41.

[77] *Die Briefe der heiligen Bonifatius*, ed. Tangl, no. 78, pp. 161–71, and no. 73, pp. 146–56; S 92 (BCS 178).

[78] *Ibid.*, no. 78, p. 165, line 23, to p. 169, line 14.

[79] Synod of *Clofesho*, Proœmium and cc. 1, 2, 3, 4, 5, 6, 20, 24 and 25.

[80] Keynes, 'Reconstruction', pp. 119 and 125, and 147 (note 42). The abridgement certainly included parts I, II and III: part II was reduced by about two thirds, part III by more (p. 149, note 68).

[81] *Ibid.*, pp. 123 and 149–50 (note 69).

[82] R. W. Clement, 'A Handlist of Manuscripts containing Gregory's *Regula pastoralis*', *Manuscripta* 28 (1984), 33–44, reports two later manuscripts bearing abridged versions which require further investigation: Metz, Bibliothèque Municipale, 134 (Metz, s. viii–ix; lost in 1944); and Vatican City, Biblioteca Apostolica Vaticana, Reg. lat. 69 (NW Francia, s. ix–x).

what may be a 'Mercian' form of episcopal memory. This background receives support from the portrayal of translation, as an act of adaptive restoration within a project similarly presented in restorative terms. In the Verse Preface, the act was situated in the broadest context of the history of Christianity among the English, received from Rome.[83] The authority of the *Regula pastoralis* was doubly established in this context, as an act of wisdom (*snyttru*), the product of Gregory's exceptional mental equipment, and as a 'written message' (*ærendgewrit*) first brought 'to island-dwellers' (*iegbuendum*) by Augustine. The latter's association with Gregory is striking. The feast days of both saints had been singled out for universal observance at *Clofesho*; the coupling was a distinctive part of southern episcopal identity.[84]

This was the context for Alfredian interest in Gregory's saintly status. Revealing is a story preserved in the margins of a twelfth-century Worcester manuscript, reportedly extracted from the 'true sayings of Alfred, king of the Anglo-Saxons' (*angulsaxonum regis alfredi ueredicis dictis*).[85] Worcester ownership of a text known as the *dicta regis Ælfredi* is confirmed by a further reference in John of Worcester; they may well have been the Alfredian material known to William of Malmesbury, identified by William as the king's *Enchiridion* or 'hand-book'.[86] The story concerns Gregory's attitude to the memory of Pope Siricius (384–9). Siricius is reported to have expelled the learned translator Jerome from Rome for a gesture critical of papal worldliness; a second passage reports with approval Gregory's efforts to pass judgement on his predecessor, symbolically extinguishing the oil-lamp above his tomb. Many aspects remain obscure: the story's Alfredian interest presumably lay in its exemplification of Gregory's papal responsibility, and authoritative approbation of Jerome as biblical translator. The transmission of this material is uncertain: a briefer version appears in the Whitby *Life of Gregory*, but the Alfredian passages are more detailed.[87] With regard to their substance, the evidence again points to Mercian input, in this case to Worcester.[88] Wærferth's translation includes brief additions at the start of each book in which Gregory is twice described

[83] *Verse Preface to CP*, ed. Dobbie.
[84] Synod of *Clofesho*, c. 17; Thacker, 'Memorializing Gregory the Great', pp. 81–2.
[85] Cambridge, University Library, Kk. 4. 6, fols. 233r and 244v; ptd by W. Levison, 'Aus Englishen Bibliotheken II', *Neues Archiv* 35 (1910), 333–431, at 424–7; Whitelock, 'William of Malmesbury', pp. 90–1; Remley, 'Aldhelm', pp. 96–9, drawing close connections with Asser's Latinity; cf. Pratt, 'Handbook'.
[86] *Florentii Wigornensis Monachi Chronicon ex Chronicis*, ed. Thorpe I, p. 272. Thacker, 'Memorializing Gregory the Great', pp. 67–9, follows Whitelock's suggestion of an augmented copy of the *Soliloquies*, but see above, p. 127, cf. pp. 81 and 119–20.
[87] Thacker, 'Memorializing Gregory the Great', pp. 67–9.   [88] *Ibid.*, pp. 68–9.

as 'golden-mouthed'; the unusual nature of this epithet may suggest access to related Gregorian material.[89]

Devotion to Gregory extended to translation. The telescopic focus of the Verse Preface established a special relationship between Gregory, Augustine and the king.[90] The text's ambiguous characterization as an *ærendgewrit* implied a twofold role for Alfred, as direct recipient of the Latin text conveyed by Augustine, and faithful mediator of its 'every word'. Naturally one must be wary of such self-representation, yet the depiction acquires further significance from the text's Latin transmission, explored in detail by Richard Clement.[91] The *Regula pastoralis* is highly unusual in that the earliest phases of its dissemination can be reconstructed from a single witness, Troyes, Bibliothèque Municipale, MS 504 (T), an Italian manuscript of the 590s, seeming to preserve several layers of Gregory's own emendations in the final stages of composition. Two of these layers represent 'editions' (T1 and T2) from which all subsequent manuscripts are descended; the text was initially circulated in one form (T1) before a further stage of revision (T2).[92]

The Alfredian translation was based on a T1 version of the text, in an especially pure form.[93] Only three pre-viking witnesses survive complete, but each preserves a mixture of T1 and T2 readings, as do the majority of medieval manuscripts; closer texts are only found in tenth- and eleventh-century English manuscripts.[94] Yet according to Clement, Continental manuscripts show a preference for the T2 text.[95] In at least one case, moreover, the Alfredian exemplar included a reading which was corrected in T *prior* to the circulation of T1.[96] One may compare the Verse Preface, stressing the authority of Gregory's *ærendgewrit* 'just as [he] had previously set it out'. Both texts are subject to re-editing, so findings must be tentative, yet Clement's case remains strong for dependence on an exemplar rightly invested with significance, by virtue

---

[89] *Ibid.*, p. 68; *GD* I, 94, lines 12–25 and I, 179, lines 1–4.

[90] Cf. N. G. Discenza, 'Alfred's Verse Preface to the Pastoral Care and the Chain of Authority', *Neophilologus* 85 (2001), 625–33.

[91] R. W. Clement, 'Two Contemporary Gregorian Editions of Pope Gregory the Great's *Regula pastoralis* in Troyes MS. 504', *Scriptorium* 39 (1985), 89–97; R. W. Clement, 'King Alfred and the Latin Manuscripts of Gregory's *Regula pastoralis*', *Journal of the Rocky Mountains Medieval and Renaissance Association* 6 (1985), 1–13.

[92] Clement, 'Two Contemporary Gregorian Editions', pp. 96–7; T2 text generally followed by the SC edition, with some variants in the apparatus.

[93] Clement, 'Latin Manuscripts', pp. 8–9.   [94] *Ibid.*, p. 9.

[95] *Ibid.*, pp. 9–10; cf. also E. Dekkers in *Reg. past.*, p. 105.

[96] *CP* II, p. 30, lines 17–18 (Matthew XVIII. 6). Cf. *Reg. past.* I.2, lines 33–4, p. 136 (for the text in T1/T2), and Clement, 'Two Contemporary Gregorian Editions', pp. 94–5, for the pre-T1 text and discussion, without reference to the *Hierdeboc*.

of some special association with Gregory and Augustine.[97] Canterbury would be an obvious possible source, though it would be unwise to rule out other centres in this Southumbrian context.

The ambiguity of translation, as an act of appropriation, receives support from the Prose Preface. Its stylized, even fictive, qualities have long been recognized, as a reductive harnessing of the past. Royal rhetoric included one very pertinent reflection of this background. 'As often as you can, free yourself from worldly affairs so that you may apply that wisdom which God gave you wherever you can': the injunction echoed one of the *Clofesho* canons, reminding priests of the need 'a saecularibus negotiis causisque in quantum praevaleant vacare', within a broader resume of pastoral duties.[98] The echo lends an edge to the entire preface, as an appeal to the effects of wisdom; it accords heightened significance to the opening 'golden age', when kings succeeded 'both in warfare and in wisdom'. The memory has long been recognized as appealing to the age of Theodore and Hadrian, celebrated by Bede; 'happy times' (*gesæliglica tida*) may conceivably reflect knowledge of the Mercian translation.[99] Yet the reference to foreigners seeking wisdom implies a longer period, extending at least as far as the earliest missionary activity on the Continent.[100] Multiple resonances abound, from the obedience of kings 'to God and his messengers', to the material benefits of wise rule, and the availability of teachers. Yet there is no place in this 'royal' memory for the holding of synods, contrasting with their central role in this formative period, under Theodore's leadership.[101] This ecclesiastical history reflected the new status of the Southumbrian episcopate, now primed to receive Gregory's message from the West Saxon king.

In the Frankish world also the *Regula pastoralis* had functioned as an episcopal manual, yet its status was as a symbol of Frankish episcopal identity, within Carolingian ecclesiastical reform.[102] As such the text was frequently associated with texts of canonical authority, carrying

---

[97] See now C. Schreiber, *King Alfred's Old English Translation of Pope Gregory the Great's Regula Pastoralis and its Cultural Context: a Study and Partial Edition* (Munich, 2002), pp. 35–7, for balanced discussion of the question, though without reference to the pre-T1 variant cited above (cf. her commentary, p. 483). Dekkers in *Reg. past.*, p. 109, for future CCSL edition, cf. Clement, 'Latin Manuscripts', p. 12, note 6.

[98] *CP*, p. 4, lines 1–4; synod of *Clofesho*, c. 8; D. Whitelock in *Sweet's Anglo-Saxon Reader*, ed. Whitelock, pp. 5 and 224.

[99] Wormald, 'Venerable Bede', pp. 24–5. *CP*, p. 2, lines 1–12; *HE* IV.2, cf. *OE Bede*, p. 258.

[100] *HE* V.9–V.11, cf. *OE Bede*, pp. 408–22.

[101] Cf. Thacker, 'Memorializing Gregory the Great', pp. 75–8, suggesting Theodore's active promotion of Gregory's cult.

[102] E.g., council of Tours (813), c. 3 (MGH Conc. II.i, p. 287); Notker the Stammerer, *De interpretationibus divinarum* (884 × 890), in PL 131: 998D–999B.

close associations with conciliar and synodal activity.[103] It was retained in episcopal hands: there is no evidence for central dissemination under royal patronage. Possession of Gregory's work was assumed in letters by Alcuin.[104] In the 'reform' councils of 813, the text's application remained a matter of self-regulation.[105] The Mainz proceedings are explicit that bishops considered the *Regula pastoralis* in their own corporate gathering.[106] Such practices contributed to the centrality of Gregorian ideas in more assertive episcopal statements, at the councils of Paris (829) and Aachen (836).[107] Extensive citation served an episcopal agenda of spiritual anxiety and sacerdotal admonition.

Frankish deployment reflected important differences in episcopal cohesion and power.[108] The point is encapsulated by procedures for the inauguration of bishops, elaborated and standardized under Hincmar.[109] Many innovations concerned the process of examination by which any candidate would be questioned in advance of consecration, according to provisions laid down in canons attributed to an early fifth-century council of Carthage.[110] The bishop-elect was required to read a passage from the opening of the *Regula pastoralis,* and to confirm his willingness to observe its precepts. The process would then be repeated with a book of canon law. It has sometimes been suggested that Hincmar 'regularly presented a copy [of the *Regula pastoralis*] to every bishop at consecration', but this may be an over-interpretation of the words *data est ei regula pastoralis,* which need only mean for the duration of the examination.[111] Hincmar's contribution was rather to ritualize the established Frankish association between the text as a bishop's manual and the canons.

---

[103] Council of Tours (813), c. 3 (MGH Conc. II.i, p. 287); council of Chalon-sur-Saône (813), c. 1 (*ibid.*, p. 274); council of Aachen (836), c. 16 (MGH Conc. II.ii, p. 709); cf. Wormald, *MEL* I, 124, regarding the connection as Alcuinian.

[104] MGH Epist. IV, nos. 39 and 113, pp. 82–3 and 163–6; cf. also nos. 116 and 124.

[105] Council of Tours (813), c. 3 (MGH Conc. II.i, no. 38, p. 287); council of Chalon-sur-Saône (813), c. 1 (*ibid,* no. 37, p. 274); council of Mainz (813), Praef. (*ibid.*, no. 36, p. 259); council of Rheims (813), c. 10 (*ibid.*, no. 35, p. 255).

[106] Council of Mainz (813), Preface (MGH Conc. II.i, no. 36, p. 259, lines 25–9).

[107] Council of Paris (829) (MGH Conc. II.ii, no. 50, pp. 596–680); council of Aachen (836) (*ibid.*, no. 56, pp. 705–24).

[108] Here cf. A. Crépin, 'L'importance de la pensée de Grégoire le Grand dans la politique culturelle d'Alfred, roi de Wessex (871–899)', in *Grégoire le Grand,* ed. Fontaine, Gillet and Pellistrandi, pp. 579–87; Kempshall, 'No Bishop', at pp. 106–12; Scharer, 'History'; Scharer, *Herrschaft.*

[109] Nelson, 'Kingship, Law', pp. 139–45; J. Devisse, *Hincmar Archevêque de Reims 845–882,* 3 vols. (Geneva, 1975–6) II, 856–61; H. G. Beck, 'The Selection of Bishops Suffragan to Hincmar of Rheims 845–882', *Catholic Historical Review* 45 (1959), 273–308.

[110] Examination of Willebert, bishop-elect of Châlons-sur-Marne, at the council of Quierzy (868) (MGH Conc. IV, no. 28, pp. 320–3); Hincmar's account (869 × 870) of Hincmar of Laon's inauguration (*c.* 858), in his *Opusculum* (PL 126: 290–3, at col. 292).

[111] S. Potter, 'The Old English *Pastoral Care*', *Transactions of the Philological Society* (1947), 114–25 at 115; Clement, 'A Handlist of Manuscripts', pp. 34–5.

Another innovation required the bishop-elect to recite and sign a written profession of faith and obedience to the see of Rheims, then given to the archbishop. The evidence falls short of any direct connection with the Southumbrian series of episcopal professions, surviving for the period *c.* 798–*c.* 870.[112] No details are preserved of episcopal examination, but a similar role for the *Regula pastoralis* would not be unexpected, magnifying the *Hierdeboc's* significance.[113] Yet any general similarities are outweighed by the singular potency of Hincmar's West Frankish stage-management, amid his intensive intervention in elections and broader efforts to assert metropolitan authority.[114] Written professions supplied valuable ammunition in his struggle against bishops who claimed freedom from metropolitan interference, using the forged decretals of pseudo-Isidore.[115] The profession of Adalbert, bishop of Thérouanne (*c.* 871) committed its signatory to an extensive statement of doctrinal orthodoxy, culminating in a promise of obedience in accordance with all legitimate sources of written ecclesiastical law.[116] There was a marked contrast with Southumbrian practice, frequently invoking secular lordship, with little or no reference to canonical authority.[117] This only further highlights the degree of dislocation in Grimbald's enlistment, upholding Gregory's message in West Saxon royal hands.

With regard to kingship, Alfredian interests have also often been related to Frankish precedent, yet the view must be qualified.[118] Much has been invested in 'Mirrors for Princes'; the approach is taken furthest by Anton Scharer, arguing for a close connection between Asser's *Life* and the *Liber de rectoribus christianis* by Sedulius Scottus.[119] A few of the parallels are indeed striking, yet there is only one decisive case of verbal correspondence, relating to the *Proverbia Grecorum*, a text which was more widely known.[120] Given the intertextuality of royal imagery, the threshold for positive influence must be set high. Sedulius' text must be seen in the broader context of West Frankish court culture; account must also be taken of direct Alfredian access to Gregory's work. Many of the correspondences suggested acquire more immediate significance in

---

[112] Cf. above, pp. 49, 53 and 56.

[113] For possible allusion to a process of examination, cf. *Canterbury Professions*, ed. Richter, nos. 18, 24 and 25, pp. 16, 21 and 22.

[114] Devisse, *Hincmar* II, 635–69 and 846–61; Wallace-Hadrill, *Frankish Church*, pp. 271–303.

[115] P. R. McKeon, *Hincmar of Laon and Carolingian Politics* (Chicago, IL, 1978); Devisse, *Hincmar* II, 738–90.

[116] PL 87: 916–17; Nelson, 'Kingship, Law', pp. 144–6. [117] Above, p. 53.

[118] Scharer, 'History', pp. 185–206; Scharer, *Herrschaft*, pp. 61–108; Kershaw, 'Illness, Power'; Kempshall, 'No Bishop', esp. pp. 106–12.

[119] Scharer, *Herrschaft*; review by D. Pratt in *EME* 14.3 (2006), 346–8.

[120] Scharer, 'History', p. 198; Scharer, *Herrschaft*, p. 96. *VA* 88, lines 37–9; cf. D. Simpson, 'The "Proverbia Grecorum"', *Traditio* 43 (1987), 1–22, at 11.

this light.[121] Evidence for the transmission of advice-literature is actually quite limited in most cases.[122] The only text demonstrably available in pre-Conquest England is a versified version of Smaragdus' *Via regia*.[123] A lost fragment, once identified as part of a Frankish 'constitutional treatise', has emerged as a less promising text attributed to Jerome.[124] Anything is possible given the texts securely attested in Alfred's circle, but these are good reasons for circumspection.

The framework of 'ministerial' rulership is fundamental: it was in this respect that Alfredian thinking bore the strongest impact of Carolingian expertise. English precedents cannot be disregarded: regular study of Gregory's writings had been recommended to King Edwin by Pope Honorius.[125] Gregorian language had been applied to rulers and lords in *De duodecim abusivis*, frequently quoted in Alcuin's letters; divine service was prominent in West Saxon royal anointing.[126] Yet nothing matches the intensity of Alfred's Gregorian posturing, in fulfilling a role explicitly presented as a *ðegnung* or 'ministry', with personal commitment to learned reform. Many of these features bear close comparison with Carolingian trends, in the intensive regulation of behaviour by biblical and patristic norms, together with the significance accorded to Gregorian thought and the Psalter, as key sources of royal 'ministry'.[127] Royal rhetoric criticized the conditions of Alfred's youth: this was a broader change of tone, informed by Carolingian practices.

Yet these dimensions involved important contrasts. 'Ministerial' imagery had distinctive force, dominated by differences in the relationship of bishops and kings.[128] What 'Mirrors for Princes' shared with Alfredian experiences were varieties of learned responsibility, yet these were ecclesiastical and frequently episcopal products. There were differences in the character of royal *ministerium*. Certain assumptions

---

[121] Scharer, *Herrschaft*, esp. pp. 68, 71–2, 81 and 106–7 (tribulation and adversity); pp. 92–3 (nautical imagery, cf. *Reg. past.* I.9, lines 30–6, pp. 158–60; *CP* IX, p. 58, lines 5–8); p. 71 (God as physician, cf. *Reg. past.* III.26, lines 79–91, p. 444; *CP* L, p. 391, lines 17–33).

[122] S. Hellmann in *RC*, pp. 11–18, for the four known witnesses to Sedulius' text, all Continental. Cf. Anton, *Fürstenspiegel*, pp. 168–90, for Smaragdus; A. Dubreucq in *DIR*, pp. 118–31; Devisse, *Hincmar* I, 10–12.

[123] Cambridge, University Library, Gg. 5. 35 (the 'Cambridge Songs' manuscript), fols. 378–379v; Gneuss, *Handlist*, no. 12; Anton, *Fürstenspiegel*, pp. 179–89.

[124] W. P. Stoneman, '"Writ in Ancient Character and of No Further Use": Anglo-Saxon Manuscripts in American Collections', in *The Preservation and Transmission of Anglo-Saxon Culture*, ed. P. E. Szarmach and J. T. Rosenthal (Kalamazoo, MI, 1997), pp. 99–138, at 100–1 and 110, with references. Cf. K&L, *Alfred*, p. 216 (note 43).

[125] *HE* II.17.

[126] Pseudo-Cyprian, *De XII Abusivis Saeculi*, ed. Hellmann; Anton, *Fürstenspiegel*, pp. 88–107.

[127] Pratt, 'Illnesses', pp. 43–7, cf. 81–90. Cf. esp. R. Deshman, 'The Exalted Servant: the Ruler Theology of the Prayerbook of Charles the Bald', *Viator* 11 (1980), 385–417.

[128] Cf. above, pp. 58–62 and 71–2.

continued: the basis of rulership was located in the need to restrain sin; the royal office brought heightened demands of conduct. 'Reges a regendo, id est a recte agendo dicuntur': Isidore's definition received regular explanation by Carolingian writers as the basis for exemplary rule.[129] A king's ability to rule his people depended on more intimate qualities, of self-rulership and rule over his own household, vital safeguards against worldly temptation.[130] A Gregorian framework was upheld by regular deployment of Gregory's own writings, complemented by the presence of Gregorian language in other influential texts, notably Isidore and Pseudo-Cyprian.[131]

Such imagery had been constructed differently: both form and function epitomized the distinctive implications of 'ministerial' discourse, as a product of Carolingian reform. Royal 'ministry' was inseparable from the broader agenda of 'correction', incorporating heavy responsibility for reforming goals.[132] 'Mirrors for Princes' reflected the concern of bishops and other ecclesiastics to shape this agenda; advice reinforced the value of sacerdotal judgement in regulating royal behaviour.[133] As such, these texts sat alongside synodal activity, as statements often primarily of episcopal identity. Jonas of Orléans's *De institutione regia* (c. 831) drew heavily on the council of Paris of 829; the same boundaries were often blurred by Hincmar.[134] Here too Gregorian thought remained an essentially sacerdotal instrument. There are revealing similarities with the *Regula pastoralis* as an episcopal *speculum*; the work was an important model for the entire genre of advice-literature.[135]

Such factors encourage a more qualified view of West Frankish impact. The prominence of the church within 'Mirrors' cannot be sufficiently stressed as a starting-point for the delineation of duty. The regular citation of Gelasius and other pronouncements on the relative powers of bishops and kings encapsulated many preoccupations of

---

[129] Isidore, *Etymologiae*, ed. Lindsay, I.xxix.3; council of Paris (829), Book II, c. 1 (MGH Conc. II. ii, no. 50, p. 649); *DIR* 3, p. 184; *RC* 2, p. 25. Cf. also Hincmar, *De regis persona*, c. 2 (PL 125: 835); Hincmar, *De ordine palatii*, c. 2, p. 44.

[130] Council of Paris (829), Book II, c. 1 (MGH Conc. II.ii, no. 50, pp. 649–51); *DIR* 3, pp. 184–96; *RC* 2 and 5, pp. 25–7 and 34–6; priorities encapsulated by Hincmar's intervention against Lothar II's attempted divorce, acutely assessed by Airlie, 'Private Bodies'.

[131] *DIR* 6, 7 and 10, pp. 212–14, 216, 234–6, cf. c. 3, pp. 188–92; Hincmar, *De regis persona*, cc. 1, 3 and 22, cf. c. 2 (PL 125: 834–5, 835–7 and 848–9); *RC* 2, 4 and 13, pp. 25–6, 32–3 and 59; cf. Pseudo-Cyprian, *De XII Abusivis Saeculi*, pp. 51–3. Deshman, 'Exalted Servant', pp. 402–3 and 406–9, for Hincmar's Gregorian sources.

[132] Cf. above, pp. 58–62.

[133] *DIR* 1 and 2, pp. 176–82; Hincmar, *De regis persona*, Praefatio (PL 125: 833), citing Aggeus II. 12; *RC* 12, pp. 54–8.

[134] Dubreucq in *DIR*, pp. 45–55; Anton, *Fürstenspiegel*, pp. 341–5; Devisse, *Hincmar* II, 990–1004.

[135] Strangely neglected by Anton, *Fürstenspiegel*, cf. also O. Eberhardt, *Via Regia: Der Fürstenspiegel Smaragds von St. Mihiel und seine Litterarische Gattung* (Munich, 1977), pp. 267–311.

sacerdotal advice.[136] In the heavier burden borne by priests was the basis for more assertive accounts of episcopal duty, responsible to God for royal conduct.[137] Notions of ecclesiastical protection were often extended to include respect for autonomous practices as well as military defence. The preservation of ecclesiastical autonomy has long been recognized as a central theme in Hincmar's writings;[138] such attitudes were largely replicated by Sedulius Scottus.[139] As Staubach has highlighted, respect for the church and its privileges were a central expectation of Sedulius' *rector*.[140] Much of his advice was concerned to show the indispensability of such rule to the successful fulfilment of 'ministry'.[141]

There was no comparable 'ecclesiology' within Alfredian discourse. The very terminology of *seo halge cirice* occurred very rarely within the royal corpus, restricted to instances of faithful translation in the *Hierdeboc*.[142] Striking are examples of free-standing rhetoric, such as the Prose Preface or law-book introduction. Royal expression was characterized by the language of 'orders', as in the 'witan ... ge godcundra hada ge woruldcundra', to be compared with reflections on the *ecclesiasticus ordo* in the opening of Fulk's letter, probably echoing the sentiments of his addressee.[143] In both cases such language implied complementarity between office-holders of all kinds; there was no role for royal duties towards ecclesiastics alone.

For secular office-holding also Carolingian influence remains pressing, if equally problematic. There is no reason to suppose a restricted lay curriculum. Asser envisages ealdormen and reeves applying themselves 'to learning what is just', yet the implications of justice extended far beyond the presciptions of written law.[144] Asser implies a wider course

---

[136] Council of Paris (829), Book I, c. 3 (MGH Conc. II.ii, no. 50, pp. 610–11); *DIR* 1, pp. 176–8; council of Aachen (836), Prol. (MGH Conc. II.ii, pp. 705–6); synod of St-Macra at Fismes (881), c. 1 (PL 125: 1071); Hincmar, *De ordine palatii*, c. 2, p. 42; Anton, *Fürstenspiegel*, pp. 205–21, 231–40, 244–5, 278–81 and 319–29; K. F. Morrison, *The Two Kingdoms: Ecclesiology in Carolingian Political Thought* (Princeton, NJ, 1964).

[137] *DIR* 1 and 2, pp. 176–82; Hincmar, *De divortio*, PL 125: 757–8, for Hincmar's classic statement of sacerdotal competence; *RC* 12, pp. 54–8.

[138] Anton, *Fürstenspiegel*, pp. 319–35; J. Devisse, *Hincmar et la loi* (Dakar, 1962), at pp. 72–89; Devisse, *Hincmar* II, 676–9, 688–9 and 717–19, cf. 730–9; Staubach, *Rex Christianus*, pp. 158–68 and 182–7; cf. Morrison, *The Two Kingdoms*, pp. 68–115 and 215–38; Nelson, 'Kingship, Law', pp. 155–71.

[139] Staubach, *Rex Christianus*, pp. 149–87, esp. 158–68.

[140] *RC* 1, 11, 12 and 19, pp. 25–7, 50–8 and 84–8.

[141] *Ibid.* 2, 4, 14, 15 and 18, pp. 25–7, 30–3, 62–72 and 80–4.

[142] E.g., *CP* V, p. 42, line 25; XV, p. 94, line 7; XVII, p. 114, lines 8–9 and 17; XVIII, p. 130, line 3 and p. 134, line 5; and XXII, p. 170, line 2 and p. 172, line 7.

[143] *CP*, p. 2, lines 1–4 and 8–10, and p. 6, line 14; *C&S*, no. 4, pp. 7–8 (trans. in K&L, *Alfred*, pp. 182–3).

[144] *VA* 106, lines 39–46.

of study, omitting reference to a book of law, while describing the recitation of multiple English books.[145] This supports the centrality of royal texts, in conveying knowledge explicitly concerned with the responsibilities of power. The ideal and reality of Carolingian male aristocratic behaviour has attracted much attention; many priorities can be closely paralleled in this fuller evidence for secular norms.[146] These include the combination of devotion with intimate learned engagement, heightened attention to sins arising from worldly involvement, and concomitant stress on avoiding such dangers while maintaining the necessity of worldly contact. One solution was the supplying of protection to defenceless subjects, *pauperes*, widows and orphans; another was just judgement. Such ideals departed significantly from martial features of lay identity; tensions have been detected in many aspects of aristocratic practice.[147]

The restructuring of masculinity was a further product of reform, involving new standards of behaviour.[148] Principal media were 'Mirrors for Laymen' and associated devotional material, offering partial insight into lay experience.[149] Another case is that of Gerald of Aurillac (d. 909), primarily known from the later biography by Odo of Cluny (c. 936 × 942), complicating his accessibility.[150] Much hinges on the effectiveness of 'ministerial' rule in promoting common purpose with secular office-holders, as participants in, and recipients of, parallel duties. Such structures were implicit in the comital *ministerium*, repeatedly cited in West Frankish capitularies.[151] Yet it remains questionable how far this 'royal' agenda shaped everyday perspectives. Notions of office-holding are assigned a prominent role by Innes, but from the evidence cited it is less clear that such processes relied on 'ministerial' rhetoric, as opposed to language of *honores* and *dignitates*, and associated fields of loyalty and honour.[152] This compares with the limited impact of capitulary-legislation

---

[145] *Ibid.* 106, lines 46–54.

[146] Smith, 'Gender and Ideology'; S. Airlie, 'The Anxiety of Sanctity: St Gerald of Aurillac and his Maker', *JEH* 43 (1992), 372–95; Nelson, 'Monks'; Pratt, 'Illnesses', pp. 40–5.

[147] Airlie, 'Anxiety'; Nelson, 'Monks'.

[148] *Ibid.*, esp. pp. 138–42.

[149] Smith, 'Gender and Ideology'; Anton, *Fürstenspiegel*, pp. 83–8 and 212–13; Wallace-Hadrill, *Frankish Church*, pp. 283–6 and 403–11. Cf. an unpublished paper by Rachel Stone, 'Power Corrupts? Carolingian Moralists on Noble Power and Wealth', whose forthcoming PhD dissertation (University of London) will be an important reassessment of this genre.

[150] Airlie, 'Anxiety'; Nelson, 'Review Article: Waiting for Alfred', *EME* 7 (1998), 115–24, cf. Smyth, *Alfred*, pp. 205–16 and 261–80.

[151] Cf. above, pp. 71–2.

[152] Innes, *State and Society*, pp. 257–8 and 262–3, cf. earlier citation of *ministerium* in eighth-century contexts, antedating the reforms of Louis the Pious (pp. 75–6 and 188–90); and ninth-century examples involving *honores* (pp. 221–2 and 237–9).

in eastern regions; even in the west, conditions were less conducive than in Wessex.[153]

One factor was less intensive contact between ruler and aristocracy. The vitality of written law-making should not be underestimated, yet as 'royal' textuality it remained isolated. Nelson has now retreated from similarities in the 'uses of wisdom' under Alfred and Charles the Bald.[154] Royal action must be balanced against sacerdotal responsibilities for aristocratic 'correction'. There was an important counter-tendency towards the effective isolation of royal duties from those expected from subjects.[155] Advice-texts were far from unanimous in assigning specific royal responsibility for subordinate office-holders. Sedulius was notably silent when compared with Jonas of Orléans and Hincmar.[156] The latter elsewhere drew specific connection between comital activity and the plight of *pauperes*, their oppression an offence against God.[157]

Alongside royal mechanisms were 'Mirrors for Laymen', supplying abundant sacerdotal 'correction'. Three examples owed their existence to similar circumstances, of ecclesiastical authorship for a comital recipient, seemingly at his request: Paulinus of Aquileia's *Liber exhortationis*, for Heiric of Friuli (795), Alcuin's *De virtutibus et vitiis*, for Wido of Brittany in 799 or 800, and Jonas of Orléans's *De institutione laicali*, initially composed for Matfrid of Orléans (818×828). The one exception is the *Liber manualis* of Dhuoda (841–3), for her adolescent son, William; even here all were united as manifestations of intra-aristocratic, and in this sense, regional, patronage, isolated from royal sponsorship or intervention.[158] This was magnified by the wider circulation these texts enjoyed through copying and citation, not least in a court context, explicitly acknowledged by Dhuoda.[159] The diffuse quality of production is striking; there is a structural parallel with Gerald's career, largely situated in a regional (Aquitainian) context by his biographer, and not unconnected with circumstances of political fragmentation after the reign of Charles the Fat.[160]

---

[153] *Ibid.*, p. 221; Goldberg, *Empire*, pp. 18 and 210.
[154] Nelson, 'Carolingian Contemporaries', pp. 307–10; cf. Nelson, 'Charles le Chauve', pp. 41–3.
[155] Guillot, 'Une ordinatio méconnue', p. 484, note 131.
[156] *DIR* 5, pp. 204–10, cf. council of Paris (829), Book II, c. 3 (MGH Conc. II.ii, no. 50, pp. 653–4); Hincmar, *De ordine palatii*, c. 3, pp. 50–2; c. 4, p. 66; and Epilogus, pp. 96–8.
[157] Hincmar, *Ad episcopos*, cc. 13–15 (PL 125: 1015–16), with J. Devisse, ' "Pauperes" et "paupertas" dans le monde carolingien: ce qu'en dit Hincmar de Reims', *Revue du Nord* 48 (1966), 273–87, esp. 279: key sentence probably drawn from council of Paris (829), Book II, c. 2 (MGH Conc. II.ii, no. 50, p. 652; cf. *DIR* 4, pp. 198–200).
[158] Dhuoda, *Handbook for her Warrior Son*, ed. Thiebaux; J. L. Nelson, 'Dhuoda', in *Learned Laity*, ed. Wormald (forthcoming).
[159] Airlie, 'Anxiety', p. 379; Dhuoda, *Liber manualis*, ed. Thiebaux, I.1 and I.7, pp. 58 and 70.
[160] Airlie, 'Anxiety', pp. 386–7.

Primary rhetorical concern was with the status of recipients as members of the lay *ordo*, supplying ambiguous reassurance of its compatibility with salvation.[161] Advice privileged the martial and domestic concerns of a *laicus*, as soldier, husband and head of household.[162] Gerald's extreme presentation was exceptional: his saintly status could only be achieved by direct abnegation of marriage and the use of weapons, 'without which', as Notker the Stammerer observed, 'life on this earth cannot be carried on'.[163] The earliest 'Mirrors' preceded comparable advice-literature to rulers; imitation of royal practices was left unclear. 'Ministerial' language is conspicuous by its general absence: in Jonas' text responsibilites of those *qui praesunt* are restricted to a single chapter, on duties to *pauperes*.[164] Dhuoda was unusual in stressing 'useful' royal service; her lessons were largely restricted to court behaviour.[165] Gerald's case is exceptional in its sustained treatment of comital responsibilities, the more striking for its timing and regional detachment.[166]

In general, advice-literature emerges as a relatively poor conduit for ideas of office-holding. There is a striking contrast with the relentless focus of Alfredian discourse, sustained across a body of intimately 'royal' texts. Sacerdotal admonition shows a further Carolingian difference, in the concern for appropriate behaviour within marriage. English tolerance of irregular unions was a source of Continental criticism; while sexual offences are highlighted in the law-book, definitive statements against concubinage and forbidden degrees are lacking when compared with later tenth- and early eleventh-century English legislation.[167] In Alfredian discourse, power itself was the fundamental source of obligation and moral restraint.

LANGUAGES OF OFFICE-HOLDING (2) SOLOMON'S DREAM

This theme has also been much rehearsed. The example of King Solomon is seen to have informed many Alfredian attitudes; again, this has generally been interpreted in terms of the reception of Carolingian

---

[161] *Ibid.*, pp. 376–8; Nelson, 'Monks', pp. 126–7.
[162] Paulinus of Aquileia, *Liber exhortationis*, cc. 5, 20 and 38 (PL 99: 200–1, 212–14 and 239–42); Alcuin, *De virtutibus et vitiis*, c. 36 (PL 101: 638); *DIL*, Praefatio and II.1–16 (PL 106: 124 and 167–99); Dhuoda, *Liber manualis*, ed. Thiebaux, III.1–2, pp. 84–8, for filial obligations.
[163] *Gesta Karoli Magni Imperatoris*, ed. Haefele, II.10, p. 66.
[164] As observed by Stone, 'Power Corrupts?', cf. Smith, 'Gender and Ideology', pp. 62–4. *DIL* II.22 (PL 106: 213–15), cf. II.16, using pastoral imagery for parental responsibilities (PL 106: 197–9).
[165] *Liber manualis*, ed. Thiebaux, III.8, pp. 104–6, cf. also III.4, pp. 92–4.
[166] Airlie, 'Anxiety', pp. 384–93.
[167] M. Clunies Ross, 'Concubinage in Anglo-Saxon England', *P&P* 108 (August 1985), 3–34, at 21–3, 30–2 and 34.

models, with broader conclusions for Alfredian kingship.[168] Yet many questions remain of the novelty and significance of such imagery in a West Saxon context, strengthening the need for focus on Alfredian uses of Solomonic language, as the basis for appropriate comparison.

The value of Solomonic example lay in its ability to supply a further language of office-holding, comparable in use to that of Gregorian language, which placed even greater weight on divine knowledge, characterized as 'wisdom' (OE *wisdom* or *sapientia*). The biblical orientation of this language emerges most explicitly in Asser's account, yet these principles were pervasive in the written vernacular, again restricted to royal texts. Asser's treatment harmonized with this broader context, in applying Solomonic principles to the king, stressing his transition to the role of teacher. Dominant was the king's unceasing desire for wisdom, reportedly his highest priority in the face of all other *perturbationes*, and finally addressed through translation. Intensive Solomonic overtones became explicit at a crucial turning-point. The 'summoning' of helpers was attributed to Alfred's concern at his deficiency in 'divine wisdom'.[169]

It was in this respect that the king was compared to the 'holy, highly esteemed and exceedingly wealthy Solomon, king of the Hebrews', with allusion to circumstances in which the biblical king, 'having come to despise all present glory and riches, sought wisdom from God, and thereby achieved both (namely, wisdom and present glory)'.[170] The incident in question was a dream attributed to Solomon in the aftermath of his accession; the Lord had appeared to the king at night, offering to grant any request he cared to name. Solomon sought an 'understanding heart' (*cor docile*) in order to judge his people (III Kings III. 11–14); in a second version, followed by Asser, he identified *sapientia* and *intelligentia* (II Chronicles I. 7–12).[171] The Lord duly obliged, but added a material bonus, endowing the king also with riches, wealth and glory (*divitiae et substantia et gloria*). The exchange highlighted Solomon's earlier neglect for such potential rewards; the incident was inseparable from his broader reputation as a wise ruler, demonstrated through acts of judgement and more general respect for the Lord's covenant (*pactum*) with the people of Israel, regulated by adherence to the law of God.[172] In III Kings, Solomon's dream preceded his judgement in the case of the two prostitutes.[173] Material benefits emerge at every turn in Solomon's temple and palace, constructed at his command, and his immense riches and wealth,

---

[168] Nelson, 'Wealth and Wisdom', pp. 35–6; Nelson, 'Political Ideas', pp. 157–8; Scharer, 'History', pp. 191–9; Scharer, *Herrschaft*, pp. 83–108; Wormald, *MEL* I, 121–4 and 427–9; Abels, *Alfred*, pp. 219, 239, 248–9 and 256–7; Kempshall, 'No Bishop', pp. 109–10.
[169] *VA* 76–8.   [170] *Ibid.* 76, lines 43–8.   [171] Cf. Wisdom VII.
[172] III Kings III–XI and II Chronicles I–IX.   [173] III Kings III. 16–28.

combining tribute from neighbours with internal taxation.[174] Many of these principles received more abstract treatment in the Sapiential books of the Old Testament; several could be interpreted as Solomon's own writings.[175]

There was notable congruity with Gregorian imagery; this extended to the application of Solomon's dream, as a language similarly extended to all office-holders within the West Saxon order. Wider application is revealed by Asser's chapters on 'royal' justice.[176] Alfred's role as 'an extremely astute investigator in judical matters' was central. The king could be pictured in habitual response to his long-suffering judges, expressing astonishment at their 'arrogance' in enjoying the office and status of wise men, while neglecting the 'study and application of wisdom'; and ironically offering removal from such offices if they will not apply themselves 'much more attentively to the pursuit of wisdom'.[177] This is supported by the law-book or *Domboc* ('judgement-book'): the introduction accorded prominence to Mosaic law as the starting-point for all subsequent law-giving.[178] Solomonic language was distinctive, situating acts of judgement and law-giving against the backdrop of biblical precedent, and its recent emulation in Alfredian written law.

Yet the implications of Solomon extended to principles more general in the exercise of power. Such qualities emerge from the use of Solomonic language in the Prose Preface. The alliterating pair of wisdom and wealth cannot be missed within royal rhetoric, but there has been less agreement on their valency in compositional or philosophical context. Tom Shippey raised the possibility of a popular saying, perhaps that 'wealth without wisdom is worthless'; Paul Szarmach has posited an erudite context with reference to Augustinian attitudes to learning.[179] The concept of wisdom can only have conveyed multiple resonances, not only biblical and patristic but poetic and classical; part of its strength was such simultaneous signification. Yet a strong case remains for the specific impact of Solomonic precedent; once noted by Klaeber, and more recently by Nelson and Scharer, these dimensions supplied the basis of Alfred's written message.[180]

---

[174] III Kings IV. 21–34, VII–VIII, IX. 19 and X; II Chronicles II–V and VIII–IX.

[175] Proverbs, Ecclesiastes, the Song of Songs and Wisdom; cf. III Kings IV. 32–3; J. Wood, *Wisdom Literature: an Introduction* (London, 1967); J. L. Crenshaw, *Old Testament Wisdom: an Introduction* (Atlanta, GA, 1981).

[176] Cf. above, pp. 101–2 and 148–9.   [177] *VA* 106, lines 28–39.   [178] Below, pp. 214–41.

[179] T. A. Shippey, 'Wealth and Wisdom in King Alfred's Preface to the Old English *Pastoral Care*', *EHR* 94 (1979), 346–55, at 353; P. E. Szarmach, 'The Meaning of Alfred's Preface to the Pastoral Care', *Mediaevalia* 6 (1980), 57–86, at 63–70, cf. 78–9.

[180] F. Klaeber, 'Zu König Ælfreds Vorrede zu seiner Übersetzung der *Cura Pastoralis*', *Anglia* 47 (1923), 53–65, at 58; Nelson, 'Wealth and Wisdom', pp. 35–6; Scharer, *Herrschaft*, p. 86.

The letter offered application to episcopal addressees, in an account still more inclusive on the need for wisdom. Royal recollection appealed to four discrete historical periods, explained by a clear relationship between wisdom and worldly success.[181] As many commentators have observed, the setting for this history was notably 'English', in its concern with circumstances 'throughout Englishkind' (*geond Angelcynn*); one must be alive to the deep ambiguity of this perspective, equally blind to the fluctuating power of kingdoms and the recent growth of Alfred's own.[182] Prompted in some sense by Bede, this royal agenda retained Bede's stress on 'English' ecclesiastical, rather than political, unity, sharpened but not eclipsed by the Alfredian extension of West Saxon rule.

This was the Preface's point of departure, from conditions first described by Bede: a portentous period of 'happy times ... throughout Englishkind', ruled by kings who combined internal peace with external expansion.[183] The Solomonic basis for success is apparent in the qualities attributed to those in power, as 'wise men ... both of religious and secular orders' (*witan ... ge godcundra hada ge woruldcundra*), successful 'both in warfare and in wisdom' (*ge mid wige ge mid wisdome*). As Shippey observes, this ideal situation informs comparison with conditions 'now', in the early 890s, almost certainly before 893–6 given the reference to contemporary peace.[184] There was still stronger contrast with a third period, at the time 'when I succeeded to the kingdom' in 871.[185] All the conditions of the first period had been thrown into reverse. A decline of learning (*lar*) was held to have induced a severe reduction in Latinity; a causal connection with viking activity was asserted through unspecified 'punishments' (*witu*), incurred 'when we ourselves did not cherish [wisdom] nor transmit it to other men'.[186]

Already retrogressive, a method seemingly typical of royal story-telling, the effect was to induce further regression to a final period, 'before everything was ravaged and burned', approximating to the decade 855–65 and rightly identified as the turning-point in this historical rhetoric.[187] Propitious conditions had in many respects continued: Alfred's bishops were invited to remember multiple 'churches *geond Angelcynn* ... filled with treasures and books' (*maðma and boca gefylda*), and 'a great multitude of servants of God'. The preface to Ine's

---

[181] Shippey, 'Wealth and Wisdom', pp. 351–3.
[182] Cf. esp. Wormald, 'Venerable Bede', pp. 24–5; Foot, '*Angelcynn*', pp. 30–1.
[183] *CP*, p. 2, lines 2–11; *HE* IV.2.
[184] *CP*, p. 2, lines 11–12; p. 2, line 18, to p. 4, line 1; p. 6, line 9.   [185] *Ibid.*, p. 2, lines 16–18.
[186] *Ibid.*, p. 2, lines 12–16, and p. 4, lines 4–8.
[187] *Ibid.*, p. 4, lines 8–16; Shippey, 'Wealth and Wisdom', pp. 347 and 350–1.

laws shows 'servants of God' as the ecclesiastical order in general. The material implications of *maðmas*, as earthly treasures, provided immediate evidence for continuing prosperity. Yet these are then exposed as masking a pivotal discontinuity, in the inability of God's servants to love wisdom in the manner of their predecessors. Though criticized, the position of this ecclesiastical cohort was partially mitigated by their imagined speech, attributed to their mouths in a rhetorical strategy common in Pope Gregory's writings.[188] The ecclesiastics were pictured freely acknowledging the success of their predecessors, through the love of wisdom, by which 'they obtained wealth and passed on to us'. 'Her mon mæg giet gesion hiora swæð': in a characteristic deployment of hunting imagery, their mid-ninth-century successors were shown helplessly aware of this Solomonic 'track', yet prevented from following it by their inability to read Latin.

One effect was to urge reassessment of Latinity. The predicament played a vital role in the justification of translation, as a means of facilitating wisdom independent of access to Latin. The equation between Latinity and learning (*lar*) was now qualified by the value of wider linguistic knowledge. The absence of translated texts prompts one final regression, to the 'good, wise men' of the first period; their failure to supply such texts is the context for a further speech, here in the royal first-person.[189] These predecessors could not have predicted the future decline of learning: the lack of existing translations reflected their exemplary desire for wisdom, in this case through knowledge of multiple languages, probably alluding to Theodore and Hadrian. Yet, in an implicit departure from this precedent, under present conditions vernacular translation emerges as entirely necessary for the wider pursuit of wisdom, a novel development with value of its own. Translation is shown to be a common consequence of gentile contact with divine scripture, as applicable to Greek and Latin learning as to 'all other Christian peoples'. The effect was to imply a new chapter in the relationship between Bede's *gens Anglorum* and God, signalled by this elevation, however qualified, of its common tongue.

Linguistic elevation was predicated on utility, investing still further significance in the consequences of wisdom. Here too the ecclesiastics' speech was fundamental, illustrating the directness of material benefits. The *wela* in question cannot have been 'spiritual': materiality is supported both by earlier 'treasures' (*maðmas*) and the general context of inherited

[188] Klaeber, 'Ælfreds Vorrede', p. 59; missed by B. F. Huppé, 'Alfred and Ælfric: a Study of Two Prefaces', in *The Old English Homily and its Backgrounds*, ed. P. E. Szarmach and B. F. Huppé (Albany, NY, 1978), pp. 119–37, at 129.
[189] *CP*, p. 4, line 21, to p. 6, line 6.

prosperity.[190] The ecclesiastics' inability to love wisdom was the direct cause of material decline. '[A]nd forðæm we habbað nu ægðer forlæten ge þone welan ge þone wisdom, forðamþe we noldon to ðæm spore mid ure mode onlutan': Shippey's case is persuasive for a change of voice, reflecting on these connections from a contemporary perspective.[191] For the king's addressees, this amounted to an effective invitation to exhibit Solomonic judgement, as the only basis for wealth and success. The recent loss of wealth through viking attack could only be seen as divine punishment for a prior loss of wisdom by ecclesiastics, and the West Saxon order in its entirety. The king's efforts offered the only hope of reversing these forces, towards a secure and prosperous future.

Solomonic language reinforced a wide range of Gregorian assumptions, extending beyond power, as a responsibility exercised before God, to the importance of divine knowledge and necessity of worldly involvement. Wealth and wisdom were a further means of expressing balance between action and contemplation; similarities extended to the weight of dangers associated with worldly involvement. Both languages accorded utmost significance to the action of desire, as the point of greatest vulnerability to temptations: divine knowledge offered immediate regulation and redress. Within Gregorian language, greatest danger was the desire of ruling (*libido dominandi*), threatening to enslave the mind to pride and greed.[192] Within Solmonic language, the significance of desire was further magnified in the exclusive request for wisdom, as opposed to riches, glory and all other benefits. The priority was highlighted by the dilemma of pre-viking ecclesiastics, surrounded by earthly treasures but unable to match this with the love of wisdom alone.

The lesson for addressees was one of self-evident preference: disengagement from worldly affairs as often as possible to enable the application of wisdom.[193] There was a similar lesson for secular office-holding: injustice within Alfred's kingdom was attributed not only to 'ignorance' but to material distractions encourging 'ill-will' (*malevolentia*) on the part of individual judges 'either for love or fear of one party, or for hatred of the other, or even for the sake of a bribe (*aut etiam pro alicuius pecuniae cupiditate*)'.[194] Widely available in learned contexts, and ultimately from Isidore's *Sententiae*, this catalogue assumed additional significance in Alfredian discourse, as temptations only countered by

---

[190] Against P. R. Orton, 'King Alfred's Prose Preface to the Old English *Pastoral Care*, ll. 30–41', *Peritia* 2 (1983), 140–8, at 145–7; cf. Discenza, 'Symbolic Capital', pp. 435, 447–51 and 466–7, ultimately uncertain on the material dimensions of wealth and wisdom.
[191] Shippey, 'Wealth and Wisdom', pp. 347–50.   [192] Cf. above, pp. 135–9.
[193] *CP*, p. 4, lines 1–4. Cf. above, p. 143.   [194] *VA* 106, lines 24–8.

exclusive desire for wisdom.[195] Yet restraint had broader implications, exemplified by Asser's criticism of attitudes towards *pauperes*. 'Nearly all the magnates and nobles ... had inclined their minds (*mentem declina-verant*) more to worldly than to divine affairs': the explanation referred directly to mental dilemma, echoing the hunting metaphor at the heart of the Prose Preface.[196]

Such desire was prominent across the royal corpus, in forms imme-diately Gregorian or Solomonic, or in readily compatible language. This was heightened by the general character of these texts as distinctively 'sapiential', inseparable from their unique status as 'royal' sources of wisdom. The Psalter bore long-established resonances as Old Testament wisdom literature; the excerpts from Exodus in the law-book reflected prevalent biblical associations between wisdom and law. The sig-nificance of the latter text emerges from a series of pronouncements against perverse judgements, including bribes, adapted from Exodus XXIII. 6–8, which more closely resemble Asser's catalogue.[197] The prominence of carnal, fleshly desire within the 'royal' Psalter was enhanced by David's instructive status, largely compatible with that of his son and successor.[198] This was the context for the extensive recep-tion of Neo-Platonic thought, insufficiently stressed as an area of active philosophical engagement. The special value accorded to the Boethius and *Soliloquia* reflected their shared status as monuments of Late Antique philosophical theology, each soliciting the reader's own pursuit of wisdom through the genre of internal dialogue.[199] Extensive departures placed even greater weight on the dangers of worldly desire; such changes were central to the character of 're-education', as an extreme implementation of Solomonic philosopher-rulership.

The significance of Carolingian precedent must be judged against the immediate availability of biblical texts and Solomon's existing promi-nence. Much hinges on the First Coronation *Ordo*: Alfred's Solomon must be seen against the king's established position in West Saxon posturing, already associated with wisdom and justice.[200] Alfredian novelty rested on the use of Solomon's dream, restraining desire through literate engagement, and its specific association with appropriate written law. This is strengthened by comparison with vernacular poetry. Pride and greed rank highly among human weaknesses in poetic contexts, frequently contrasted with aspects of wisdom through which such failings

---

[195] Wormald, *MEL* I, 123; Scharer, *Herrschaft*, pp. 116–17; *capitulare* of 786, c. 13.
[196] *VA* 105, lines 10–13; *CP*, p. 4, lines 16–18.   [197] *Af* Int.43.
[198] Pratt, 'Illnesses', pp. 85–8.   [199] Below, pp. 264–307 and 308–37.   [200] Cf. above, pp. 72–8.

might be overcome.[201] This opposition has long been recognized in *Beowulf*, in the need to combine wise insight with boldness of execution, and thus to resist dangers of pride and greed associated with riches and material prosperity.[202] King Hrothgar's warning to Beowulf was pivotal; Beowulf in turn sought the dragon's treasure for his people alone.[203] Wisdom and self-control were similarly equated in *The Wanderer*; *Precepts* and *Vainglory* warned strongly against pride. Yet there can be no question of any direct connection with Alfredian wisdom; apparent similarities must be qualified by further contrasts.[204]

Firstly, Solomon himself was largely absent from poetry, his appearance principally restricted to the *Solomon and Saturn* dialogues. While this might strengthen O'Neill's identification of these texts as Alfredian, Solomon's role makes no reference to his dream, nor to pride and greed, despite extensive interaction with the Chaldean Saturn.[205] Secondly, in the case of *Beowulf*, such themes were heavily directed towards martial aspects of kingship and conduct, in the collocation of wisdom with physical strength, and the value attached to an avowedly earthly form of 'heroic' glory (*lof*).[206] Hrothgar's advice concerned generous gift-giving in the aftermath of earthly success: there was no room for Alfredian themes of fleshly temptation.[207] Thirdly, heavily focused on lordship, such moralizing remained isolated from any complementary framework of office-holding or delegated responsibility. Beowulf's awareness of his 'people's need' was primarily royal.[208] Attitudes to wealth and judgement were located within inter-aristocratic gift-giving and physical treasure, as opposed to wider 'royal' justice.[209]

The absence of poetic precedent strengthens the case for Carolingian influence, though its precise assessment is far from straightforward. As Wormald has observed, connections between wisdom, just judgement and law-giving find close parallels in the Carolingian world, suggesting precedents for Alfredian legal innovation.[210] Biblical dimensions of rule

---

[201] T. A. Shippey, *Poems of Wisdom and Learning in Old English* (Cambridge, 1976), pp. 7–12 and 46–7; E. T. Hansen, *The Solomon Complex* (Toronto, 1988), pp. 41–80; Clemoes, *Interactions*, pp. 112–16 and 398–408.

[202] R. E. Kaske, 'Sapientia et fortitudo as the Controlling Theme of *Beowulf*', *Studies in Philology* 55 (1958), 423–56.

[203] *Beowulf* 1724–85 and 2795–2808.

[204] Cf. T. D. Hill, 'The Crowning of Alfred and the Topos of *sapientia et fortitudo* in Asser's *Life of King Alfred*', *Neophilologus* 86 (2002), 471–6, also lacking reference to the First *Ordo*.

[205] P. P. O'Neill, 'On the Date, Provenance and Relationship of the "Solomon and Saturn" Dialogues', *ASE* 26 (1997), 139–68, at 154–65. Cf. Hansen, *Solomon Complex*, 147–52; and now K. Powell, 'Orientalist Fantasy in the Poetic Dialogues of Solomon and Saturn', *ASE* 34 (2005), 117–43.

[206] *Beowulf* 24–5, 1534–6 and 3180–2.   [207] *Ibid.* 1747–57.   [208] *Ibid.* 2795–2801.

[209] Cf. *Wanderer* 64–74 and 111–15.   [210] Wormald, *MEL* I, 118–25 and 427–9,

were inextricably connected with widening royal responsibilities for justice, exemplified in dispute settlement by the 'correction' of judicial abuses.[211] These received further force from capitularies, themselves urging judgement in accordance with written law.[212] In addition to Christian imperial models, such functions were frequently related to Old Testament kingship and the upholding of divine law. Charlemagne had received extensive praise for wisdom in the letters of Alcuin; 'Mirrors for Princes' frequently endorsed Solomon's example.[213] It is accordingly significant that such deployment should include reference to Solomon's dream.

The prominence of this incident in the *Liber de rectoribus christianis* is by no means the only example; Scharer's concentration on Sedulius' text takes insufficient account of its wider availability in contemporary discourse.[214] The language was again closely connected with 'ministerial' notions of rulership; its popularization may owe much to Smaragdus' *Via regia*, written for either Louis the Pious or Charlemagne.[215] Solomon's dream was cited from the Book of Wisdom in words attributed to the king: 'Wherefore I wished, and sense was given to me: and I called upon the spirit of wisdom and she came upon me: and I preferred her before realms and thrones, and considered riches to be nothing in comparison to her ... But all good things came to me equally with her, and innumerable virtues through her hands, and I rejoiced in all these things, because wisdom went before me' (Wisdom VII. 7–11). In a catena of quotations, Smaragdus accentuated the regal quality of wisdom, informing just judgement, and its immense value in all senses, combining material riches with spiritual rewards.[216]

Later use confirms the dream's status as a central feature of learned imagery, regularly applied to rulers in contexts of exhortation and literary patronage. For Nelson, 'the explicit linkage of wisdom and wealth was not a Carolingian commonplace': there is in fact abundant evidence for such a connection.[217] In 817, Solomon's preference for wisdom over riches and long life was cited by Agobard as a model of learned judgement in the archbishop's celebrated letter to Louis the Pious, criticizing Frankish legal diversity.[218] Usage intensified in the later ninth century,

---

[211] *Ibid.* I, 123–4.
[212] *Capiulare missorum generale* (802), MGH Capit. I, no. 33, c. 1, with Ansegisus, *Capitularium Collectio* II.26–7; McKitterick, *Written Word*, pp. 26–33 and 37–40.
[213] MGH Epist. IV, nos. 121, 229 and 257; cf. letter of Cathwulf to Charlemagne (*ibid.*, p. 503, lines 12–15).
[214] Scharer, 'History', pp. 191–9; Scharer, *Herrschaft*, pp. 83–7.
[215] Anton, *Fürstenspiegel*, pp. 161–8; Eberhardt, *Via regia*, pp. 195–263.
[216] Smaragdus, *Via regia*, c. 4 (PL 102: 941–5, esp. 942–3).
[217] Nelson, 'Wealth and Wisdom', p. 36.
[218] MGH Epist. V, no. 3, pp. 158–64, at 162, lines 17–20.

amid rivalry between Louis' sons. A letter of Hrabanus Maurus shows an intriguing deployment of Solomon's dream in East Frankish court culture. Goldberg has highlighted Louis the German's wise rulership, associated with his promotion of Germanic translation.[219] Hrabanus' letter occurs in a Latin context, recommending his encyclopaedic *De rerum naturis* for Louis' scrutiny (*c.* 842–6); his exposition alludes beyond Louis's learning to wider promotion of wisdom among his subjects.[220]

Yet the language of Solomon's dream acquired widest currency under Charles the Bald. The connection of wisdom with success offered considerable rhetorical potential; usage shows close correlation with changing circumstances.[221] Amid Charles's early struggles to maintain his realm in the 840s, Lupus of Ferrières recommended Solomon's preference for wisdom as a means of achieving peace.[222] At around the same time, in a poem prefacing Charles's First Bible, made for the king at Tours, the poet Audradus Modicus assured Charles that divine wisdom offered protection against the 'wicked enemy', in concert with the cardinal virtues.[223] 'Those of you equipped with worldly benefits, gape': his advice continued, 'who shone forth richer in riches than Solomon? Rich wisdom, when granted to him, did this, and placed him ahead of all kings'. Sedulius' chapter must be judged against these earlier uses of the dream, now harnessed at the moment of Charles's greatest triumph, after the acquisition of Lotharingia in 869. Yet re-interpretation continued: the dedicatory poem to Charles's Second Bible, made for the king at St-Amand in the early 870s, reflected further reversals after the subsequent loss of Lotharingian territory, together with renewed imperial ambitions.[224] Addressing Lady Wisdom directly, the poet gave reassurance that *Sapientia* would ultimately reward Charles more abundantly than Solomon himself.[225] A final citation was again from St-Amand, in the verse preface addressed to Charles by Hucbald of St-Amand, accompanying a poem on sobriety by Hucbald's late colleague Milo.[226] Hucbald presented Charles's imperial elevation as the ultimate reward for his wisdom, drawing close connections between law-giving and prosperity.

There can be little prospect of a single 'source': the possibility remains of positive connections with Alfredian expertise. The East Frankish

[219] Goldberg, *Empire*, pp. 180–5 and 301–3, cf. 33, 166–7 and 171–2.
[220] MGH Epist. V, no. 37, pp. 473–4, citing Wisdom VII. 7–21 and III Kings III. 9–14.
[221] The relevant passages are printed and translated in the Appendix (below, pp. 353–5).
[222] MGH Epist. VI, no. 33, p. 42, lines 6–8.
[223] P. E. Dutton and H. L. Kessler, *The Poetry and Paintings of the First Bible of Charles the Bald* (Ann Arbor, MI, 1998), pp. 110–13, lines 157–66 and 179–87.
[224] For the role of the Second Bible in Charles's relationship with St-Amand, see McKitterick, 'Charles the Bald and his Library', pp. 42–6.
[225] MGH Poet. III, pp. 255–7, lines 41–9 and 82–96.   [226] *Ibid.*, p. 611, lines 11–12 and 15–20.

evidence is notable, raising the difficulty of distinguishing Grimbald from John the Old Saxon. Yet West Frankish usage was especially intensive; account must also be taken of the dream's Alfredian associations with judgement and law-giving. Here Grimbald's influence seems undeniable: parallels have long been recognized between the law-book introduction and Fulk's letter.[227] Behind both was legal thinking associated with Fulk's predecessor, Hincmar.[228] It is accordingly significant that Hincmar attached special value to royal wisdom, especially given his extensive role in drafting Charles's legislation. Wider use of Solomonic imagery may be attributable to Hincmar's inspirational agency. For Hincmar, wisdom was a defining aspect of all 'true' kingship, specifically displayed in rightful judgement and Christian law-giving.[229] In 858 he mustered Solomon's dream to its defence, in his critical letter to Louis the German.[230] Hincmar defended his position on a number of occasions with reference to Lady Wisdom's words in Proverbs VIII. 15, 'Per me reges regnant et legum conditores iusta decernunt'.[231] Their significance receives support from Charles's Third Bible, produced at Rheims and probably given to the king as a wedding-gift in January 870.[232] The Book of Proverbs was preceded by a full-page illustration of Solomon passing judgement over the two prostitutes, below the scene of his royal anointing.[233]

This strengthens the case for Grimbald, sharpening his connections both with Fulk and Rheims. Wider usage must be set alongside Hincmar's pervasive influence and complex scholarly contacts embracing the West Frankish court itself.[234] Scharer has rightly highlighted connections which brought Rheims into close contact with the schools of Laon and Auxerre, as a possible conduit for wider influences with reference to the scholar Heiric of Auxerre.[235] Fulk's enlistment of two of Heiric's pupils, Remigius of Auxerre and Hucbald of St-Amand, has often been noted, though the chronology is problematic, with 892 as the most likely date for their arrival at Rheims.[236] Yet in Hucbald's case the transfer had been preceded by a further period away from St-Amand at

[227] Whitelock in *C&S*, p. 16; K&L, *Alfred*, p. 305 (note 3); Wormald, *MEL* I, 423–6.
[228] Below, pp. 223–8.
[229] See esp. *De divortio*, Resp. to Quaest. VI (PL 125: 757C); cf. below, pp. 224–6.
[230] MGH Conc. III, no. 41, c. 11, p. 419, lines 32–3.
[231] *De divortio*, Resp. to Inter. V (PL 125: 652D–653A); *Quaterniones*, PL 125: 1051C–D; Epist. 15 (PL 126: 98A–B). Cf. Nelson, 'Kingship, Law', pp. 134–5, note 4.
[232] Staubach, *Rex Christianus*, pp. 234–61.
[233] Fol. 185v; Staubach, *Rex Christianus*, plate 19, with *titulus* further echoing Proverbs VIII. 15 (MGH Poet. III, p. 262, no. XVI); also the frontispiece in Nelson, *Ritual*.
[234] Staubach, *Rex Christianus*, pp. 151–68 and 181–7.   [235] Scharer, *Herrschaft*, pp. 105–8.
[236] Below, p. 273.

the monastery of St-Bertin, where he had been enlisted to teach abbot Rodulf.[237] Placing Hucbald securely at St-Bertin in March 889, Grierson suggested a significantly earlier date for his arrival, on the basis that he would have needed permission from his abbot, bishop Gauzlin, before the siege of Paris, begun 29 November 885. Grimbald was at St-Bertin on 8 September 885; it is quite possible that he met Hucbald prior to his departure.[238] Hucbald's presence is striking given the double use of Solomon's dream at St-Amand; this must be balanced against Hincmar's legacy.

West Frankish usage encapsulated all the distinctive features of 'ministerial' rulership, upholding reform.[239] As Nelson implies, the production of opulent books for Charles the Bald reflected the strength of ecclesiastical structures, one aspect of exclusive bonding between kings and bishops.[240] The preference for complete bibles, together with theological and liturgical texts, captured the ruler's special responsibilities for Christian orthodoxy. The quality of wisdom reflected this ecclesiastical agenda. For Hincmar, the wisdom 'by which kings reign' included special respect for canon law and ecclesiastical jurisdiction.[241] The view found fullest expression in the later 860s, stimulated by dispute with Charles over a defining issue: the settlement of disputes over military benefices on church property.[242] Canon law, supported by laws of Theodosius I and Honorius, required such cases to be resolved in private hearings by bishops or specially chosen judges.[243] The dispute embraced broader areas of concern: the same agenda suffused Sedulius' appeal to Solomonic precedent.[244] Wisdom was repeatedly shown to hinge on respect for the 'privileges and rights of the Holy Mother Church'.[245] The ruler's wisdom was to be measured by his willingness to hold regular synods, issuing judgements compatible with canonical statutes, and humble acknowledgement of ecclesiastical jurisdiction over disputed benefices.[246] God's generous support for such rule cannot be detached from what Sedulius presents as the church's greater contribution to security, adding 'spiritual troops', doubly effective against visible and invisible enemies.[247] Solomon's dream was central to this

---

[237] P. Grierson, 'Grimbald of St Bertin's', *EHR* 55 (1940), 529–61, at 551.
[238] *Ibid.*, p. 542, note 8, cf. pp. 545 and 547.   [239] Cf. above, pp. 58–62.
[240] Nelson, 'Lord's Anointed', p. 124.
[241] See esp. Hincmar's letter to Charles of September 868 (PL 126: 98A–B), citing Proverbs VIII. 12 and 15.
[242] McKeon, *Hincmar of Laon*, pp. 16–38, cf. 275; cf. also Devisse, *Hincmar* II, 726–37.
[243] Hincmar, *Quaterniones*, PL 125: 1051C–D; McKeon, *Hincmar of Laon*, pp. 25–8.
[244] Staubach, *Rex Christianus*, pp. 158–68 and 181–7.   [245] *RC* 19, pp. 84–8.
[246] *Ibid.* 11–13 and 19, esp. 11; in context, the hope was of a supra-regional synod, encompassing West Francia and Lotharingia (Staubach, *Rex Christianus*, pp. 159–61).
[247] *RC* 19, p. 87, lines 10–21; cf. cc. 14–16, pp. 62–77.

message, illustrating the causal relationship between *religiosa sapientia* and material prosperity.[248] Its force must be judged against Charles's regular acknowledgement of ecclesiastical privilege.[249] Though mixed, his record offered considerable hope in a reign punctuated by tactical restorations of church property.[250]

Alfredian uses crystallize many West Saxon differences. West Frankish deployment was restricted when compared with its Alfredian royal deployment, openly extended to all thegns. Solomonic wisdom was transformed from a royal responsibility borne towards the church to a quality shared between all members of the West Saxon order, without special 'ecclesiastical' arrangements. This was exemplified by royal judgement, now detached from respect for synodal authority and firmly at the head of 'royal' justice, potentially all-encompassing.[251] The transformation had clear basis in West Saxon structures, in particular the lack of synodal activity and the settling of bookland disputes at royal assemblies, amid more general blurring of ecclesiastical and secular land tenure.[252] The use of legal theory was highly selective, for West Saxon royal purposes.

The deployment upheld judicial ideals, a further area precluding attribution to specific 'sources'. Carolingian promotion of justice had long been matched by rhetoric of judicial probity.[253] '[E]ither for love or fear of one party, or for hatred of the other, or even for the sake of a bribe': the same formula was central in Carolingian 'correction'.[254] Prominent in the *Admonitio generalis*, the abuses had been further tied to the comital *ministerium* in Louis' *Admonitio* of 823 × 825.[255] There was a specific connection with comital wisdom. A Carolingian prologue to the *Lex Salica* attributed primordial Frankish law-giving to collective pursuit of the 'key of wisdom'; the *Admonitio generalis* stressed the indispensability of 'law ... recorded for the people by wise men (*a sapientibus*)'.[256] The appointment of just judges was a regular part of the royal *ministerium*.[257] 'Give from among you wise and understanding men, and whose conduct is approved among your tribes' (Deuteronomy I. 13): Moses' request for multiple judges among the people of Israel supplied a governing

---

[248] *Ibid.* 4, pp. 30–3.   [249] Nelson, 'Kingship, Law', pp. 146–8, with references.

[250] McKeon, *Hincmar of Laon*, pp. 20–1, 27–8 and 37–8; Devisse, *Hincmar* I, 105–13 and II, 901–5.

[251] *VA* 106.   [252] Cf. above, pp. 44–58 and 99–102.   [253] Wormald, *MEL* I, 122–3.

[254] *VA* 106, lines 24–8; *Af* Int.43.

[255] MGH Capit. I, no. 22, c. 63; Ansegisus, *Capitularium Collectio*, II.6 ('De admonitione ad comites pro utilitate sanctae Dei ecclesiae').

[256] 'Long prologue' to *Lex Salica*, added *c.* 763–4, in MGH Leges nat. germ. IV.ii, pp. 4–5 and 198; MGH Capit. I, no. 22, c. 63.

[257] Smaragdus, *Via regia*, c. 28 (PL 102: 966); *DIR* 5, pp. 204–10, cf. council of Paris (829), Book II, c. 3 (MGH Conc. II.ii, no. 50, pp. 653–4); Hincmar, *De ordine palatii*, c. 3, pp. 50–2; c. 4, p. 66; and Epilogus, pp. 96–8.

archetype.[258] For Jonas of Orléans, the appointment of unjust judges was a fundamental breach of royal responsibility; the reward of salvation offered a positive stimulus, drawing judges away from greed and avarice.[259] King Jehosaphat had given similar instructions to newly appointed judges: 'Take care what you do, for you exercise not the judgement of man, but of the Lord: and whatsoever you judge, it shall redound to you. Let the fear of the Lord be with you, and do all things with diligence; for there is no iniquity with the Lord our God, nor respect of persons, nor desire of gifts' (II Chronicles XIX. 6–7).[260] The 'fear of the Lord' was synonymous with wisdom, the upholding of divine (Mosaic) law.[261] Such principles hinged on the precedent of Israel's covenant, governed by the law of God.[262]

Royal usage intensified under the later Carolingians, in parallel exercises of courtly discipline. Nelson has highlighted the effectiveness of Charles the Bald's capitularies in communication with the West Frankish secular aristocracy, including notions of comital duty.[263] Charles's role owed as much to Roman precedent, his capitularies sometimes drawing on the Theodosian Code, with weight on the *res publica* as the object of collective utility.[264] Yet connections with Charles's palace school, and other sources of education, suggest wider aristocratic participation in royal 'wisdom'.[265] Goldberg has explored some comparable processes in East Francia, less dependent on capitulary-material.[266] The Old High German poem *Muspilli*, preserved in a manuscript owned by Louis the German, illustrated dangers of bribery for aristocrats involved in judgement, by comparison with the Last Judgement.[267] The Latin *Carmen de Timone comite*, addressed to Louis in the early 830s, applauded the efforts of Louis' count of the palace Timo to revive 'the neglected business of the law'.[268] Praising Louis for his philosopher-rulership, the poet stressed *sapientia* as the basis for judgement, warning of the spiritual dangers of avarice.

Alfredian developments also exploited judicial wisdom, yet the effect differed from both these precedents. 'Mirrors for Laymen' again offer an alternative perspective, shaped by comital patronage of ecclesiastical

[258] *DIR* 5, lines 1–42, pp. 204–6.
[259] *Ibid.*, lines 61–74, p. 208 (citation of Isidore, *Sententiae* III.lii.1–3).
[260] *Ibid.*, lines 96–100, p. 210.
[261] Crenshaw, *Old Testament Wisdom*, p. 96; Job XXVIII. 8; Ps. CX. 10; Proverbs IX. 10; Ecclesiasticus I. 16, XIX. 18 and 21, and XXV. 13–15.
[262] Wormald, *MEL* I, 122–4.   [263] Nelson, 'Charles le Chauve', pp. 47–9.
[264] Nelson, 'Translating Images of Authority: the Christian Roman Emperors in the Carolingian World', in her *Frankish World*, pp. 89–98.
[265] Nelson, 'Charles le Chauve', pp. 44–6.
[266] Goldberg, *Empire*, pp. 219–22 and 229–30, cf. 78 and 175–6.
[267] *Ibid.*, pp. 36–7; Bostock, *Handbook*, pp. 135–54; Edwards, 'German Vernacular Literature', pp. 148–50.
[268] MGH Poet. II, pp. 120–4, esp. lines 5–16, 41–56 and 65–78.

writers. Three of the texts had extensive chapters on just judgement, including the standard abuses; among requisite virtues was the 'fear of the Lord' and wisdom.[269] Yet only in one case, Jonas' *De institutione laicali*, is justice associated with any broader framework of Gregorian responsibility.[270] One may wonder at the success of royal efforts to appropriate just judgement as a specifically comital duty. Capitularies must be seen against these competing sources of judicial admonition, the product of intra-aristocratic patronage. Even within royal 'Mirrors' the 'correction' of kings did not always extend to subordinate judicial activity: Sedulius' silence was notable. Royal law-giving had greater priority than wider participation in 'ministry':[271] Solomon's dream had applied to Charles alone.

This highlights a further Alfredian transformation, in the dream's consistent application to subordinate office-holders, not only to eal-dormen, reeves and thegns as 'judges', but also to bishops. Alfredian language was relentless; Carolingian responsibilities could be described in other ways. In *De ordine palatii*, judicial quotations from the Book of Wisdom were reserved for the royal office; counts and judges were warned by Pseudo-Cyprian's sixth abuse, 'a lord without virtue'.[272] Hincmar's quotation from Proverbs VIII, 'Per me reges regnant', was similarly reserved for kings.[273] The extension to subordinate office-holders again reflected West Saxon conditions, not least the extreme royal monopoly in the settling of contentious disputes. The status of royal justice was embedded in the First English *Ordo*: Solomon's dream gave new articulation to these collective concerns, lacking any special treatment of bishops or *ecclesia*.

Such deployment cannot be detached from its transmission, via texts intimately associated with the king. Dependence on Solmonic 'royal' imagery remains highly suggestive of the processes lying behind its manipulation. Alfredian royal authorship was itself a novel means of Solomonic imitation, openly extended to the king's aristocratic audi-ences. The monopolization of authorship enabled more consistent and

[269] Alcuin, *De virtutibus et vitiis*, cc. 20–1, cf. Praef., cc. 1 and 15 (PL 101: 628–9, 614–15 and 624); *DIL* II.24–7 (PL 106: 218–27); Dhuoda, *Liber manualis*, ed. Thiebaux, IV.8–9, pp. 154–60; cf. also R. Newhauser, *The Early History of Greed* (Cambridge, 2000), pp. 116–21, for goals of 'moderation' in this literature.
[270] *DIL* II.24, cf. II.22 (PL 106: 220–1 and 213).
[271] Guillot, 'Une ordinatio méconnue', p. 484, note 131.
[272] *De ordine palatii*, Prologus, p. 36, lines 39–42; cf. c. 3, pp. 50–2, lines 176–203.
[273] Applied to Lothar II in *De divortio*, Resp. to Inter. V (PL 125: 652D–653A); applied to Charles the Bald in *Quaterniones*, and letter of September 868 (PL 125: 1051C–D and PL 126: 98A–B). Cf. episcopal application to Arnulf of Carinthia at the council of Tribur (895), in MGH Capit. II, no. 252, p. 212.

relentless harnessing of aristocratic responsibilities to the needs of royal power. Both Solomonic and Gregorian languages could be deployed to offer a single framework for aristocratic conduct, dependent on the king as exemplary office-holder; pride and greed were appropriated within this exclusive moral framework. The overall effect was to imply closer and more consistent connections between the correction of sin and rightful exercise of power, both achieved through the restraining of worldly desire. The tranformation of Solomon's dream was central to these structures, seamlessly connecting restraint with the operation of justice. The result was a distinctive Alfredian language of wealth and wisdom; its implications hold the key to questions of reception.

THE IMPLICATIONS OF ALFREDIAN DISCOURSE

The role of this language must be judged against all other aspects of royal power. The uses of this discourse related very directly to the implications of vernacular literacy, as the privileged mechanism by which it was transmitted. Though never operating on its own, the ability to read assumed central significance in effecting direct access to wisdom through vernacular prose. The transformative capacity of literacy has long been identified in its status as a mental technology, powerfully open-ended in its effects on thought and behaviour. This was inherent in the character of royal discourse, controlling mental processes as the primary function of the written word; it receives further weight from the single means of authorship. This potential had deep effects on the everyday functioning of the West Saxon order, as a tool of royal power.

The establishment of context is complicated by problems of dating. The only landmarks are St Martin's Day 887, seemingly representing the king's decision to undertake translation, and the dissemination of the *Hierdeboc*, strictly datable to the period 890–6, but probably preceding 893.[274] As Whitelock argued, the Prose Preface need not preclude the existence of other translations, in addition to the *Dialogues*.[275] Yet the *Chronicle* was disseminated in 892; tentative dating of the Orosius to the later 880s or early 890s might still postdate the royal undertaking of 887.[276] It has sometimes been assumed that the king's remaining translations were 'late' works, largely on the basis of Asser's silence, but this seems too general to carry weight.[277] Only the *Dialogues* receive direct reference, but Asser knew the *Chronicle*; multiple English books

---

[274] Above, pp. 121 and 154; Dumville, 'Tenth-Century Reform', p. 187; *CP* p. 6, line 9.
[275] Whitelock, 'Prose', p. 75.   [276] K&L, *Alfred*, pp. 278–9; Bately in *Or*, pp. lxxxix–xc.
[277] Stenton, *Anglo-Saxon England*, pp. 271–6; cf. Whitelock, 'Prose', pp. 74–5. Cf. Smyth, *Alfred*, pp. 237–48, unencumbered by Asser's testimony.

were already available.[278] Alfred's youngest son, Æthelweard, seems to have been unusual in directly benefiting from his *schola*.[279] The suggestion of an ecclesiastical destiny correlates neither with the broader basis of Alfredian education nor with Æthelweard's later career.[280] His fuller education probably reflected his youth amid rapid expansion in the availability of teachers and texts. Edward and Ælfthryth had received youthful instruction comparable to Alfred's own; in adulthood by the later 880s, they could benefit only tardily from *liberalis disciplina*.[281]

There is no reason why the majority, if not all, of the king's texts should not have been available in the years immediately preceding 893. Later viking warfare can only have restricted available time and effort. Asser implies considerable progress in the king's sapiential enterprise: the existence of the law-book is strongly indicated by his final chapter.[282] An earlier *terminus post quem* is provided by Fulk's letter of about 886; Asser's silence must be judged against the wider basis which he describes for the 'study of justice'.[283] By the same token, his reference to multiple books deserves much weight given the singular treatment of power in royal texts. The inclusion of the Boethius in Asser's thinking cannot be proved, but would be supported by its Solomonic content and the Latin text's special status in 'liberal' instruction.[284] Similar criteria would apply to the *Soliloquies*, though allowance must be made for relative chronology. Stylistic variations in the royal corpus have often been noted, suggesting a course of increasing ambition from the most faithful translation, the *Hierdeboc*, to the extreme freedom applied to Augustine.[285] There is evidence for inter-dependence: Gregorian language was influential in the Boethius; ideas generated in a Boethian context made additional appearance in the *Soliloquies*.[286] O'Neill has argued for the priority of both Neo-Platonic texts over the Psalms.[287] Yet the situation was probably more complex: there are signs of counter-fertilization from the *Soliloquies* to the Boethius.[288] According to William of Malmesbury, Alfred had died with barely the first portion of the Psalter translated, but the claim is ambiguous, and might still be a misunderstanding.[289] There is

---

[278] *VA* 77, lines 3–10; c. 75, lines 15–31, and c. 106, lines 46–61.   [279] *Ibid.* 75, lines 11–21.

[280] Pratt, 'Illnesses', pp. 52–3, note 75; cf. Nelson, '"King Across the Sea"', p. 57.

[281] *VA* 75, lines 21–31.

[282] Stenton, *Anglo-Saxon England*, pp. 271–2 and 275–6; Scharer, *Herrschaft*, pp. 112 and 123, note 36; cf. Wormald, *MEL* I, 120–1, 284–5 and 429.

[283] Whitelock in *C&S*, p. 16; *VA* 106, lines 39–54.   [284] Below, pp. 302–7.

[285] Stenton, *Anglo-Saxon England*, pp. 272–5; Whitelock, 'Prose', pp. 75–7; A.J. Frantzen, *King Alfred* (Boston, MA, 1986), p. 10.

[286] Below, pp. 285–92 and 299–301, cf. 319–21; Carnicelli in *Solil*, pp. 32–4.   [287] *Ps(P)*, pp. 83–95.

[288] Whitelock, 'Prose', pp. 76–7. See esp. *Bo* XXVIII.v, p. 121, lines 9–12 (cf. *Cons. phil.* IVp4.27, p. 76), seemingly dependent on *Solil* p. 78, lines 11–14 (cf. *Soliloquia* I.xiii.23, p. 36, lines 1–11).

[289] *GR* I, 192–3, cf. Thomson's commentary (II, 104).

no reason to suppose that translations were undertaken discretely. The impression is of a more continuous process across a range of projects, at least partially completed by the early 890s.

The case is significant in locating the impact of 're-education' in circumstances of peace, prior to 893, strengthening associations with defensive reform. Yet if some connection of this kind has often been postulated, the conjunction is sharpened by the effective West Saxon mobilization from the 850s, apparently achieved by other means. Any answer must return to the royal household, as the intensive locus of power, and the implications of literate engagement in an environment dominated by personal interaction with the king. Contact now involved translated prose: monopolization of authorship brought its construction into the highest sphere of royal intimacy.[290] Asser's account of Alfred's learning reveals familiar exploitation of the 'royal chamber' (*regia cambra*), the king's *bur* to which access was restricted.[291] Yet he shows an equally important role in wider reception, through acts of learned display: 'reading aloud from books in English and above all learning English poems by heart'; 'listening eagerly and attentively to Holy Scripture being read out by his own countrymen, or even ... in the company of foreigners'; combined with teaching, such that 'he did not cease from personally giving, by day and night, instruction in all virtuous behaviour and tutelage in literacy' to noble sons attached to the royal household.[292] As has been observed above, oral interaction is often stressed in assessments of literate culture, exemplified by the performative act of reading.[293] Theatrical qualities were already central to the royal household: the value of innovation lay in a complex textual enhancement of West Saxon theatre, in which the king's own texts supplied the driving dramatic force.

If the household remained centre stage, 're-education' demanded further extension at local level, through no less complex processes of replication. One location was evidently episcopal, facilitated by the *Hierdeboc*. Although allowances were made for loaning and duplication, the Prose Preface was equally insistent on the retention of supplied codices within episcopal churches, barring only their personal use by bishops.[294] Another environment exploited the bonds of the secular

---

[290] See above, pp. 30, 33 and 37, for Alfred's *hræglðegn* and other thegnly officials. For what follows, cf. Elias, *Civilizing Process*, pp. 312–24 and 387–413; Elias, *Court Society*, 89–104, 110–16 and 214–35.

[291] *VA* 88, lines 1–4. Cf. above, pp. 36–7.

[292] *Ibid.* 76, lines 9–10, 26–9 and 32–6.

[293] Above, pp. 78–80; Stock, *Implications of Literacy*, pp. 3–11; Stock, *Listening for the Text*, pp. 19–38; O'Brien O'Keeffe, *Visible Song*, pp. 8–14; Howe, 'Reading'; Orchard, 'Oral Tradition', pp. 101–23; Frantzen, 'Preface', pp. 134–6.   [294] *CP*, p. 8, lines 1–6.

aristocratic household, literally 'at home' (*æt ham*). *Pace* Wormald, Asser indicates considerable support for Alfredian priorities among adult nobles, depicting the co-operation of 'nearly all ealdormen, reeves and thegns', and implying some success in learning to read.[295] No less revealing is his account of regular recitation to the old or sluggish. As Campbell notes, the reference to a servile retainer may imply the use of priests in aristocratic service, who could be unfree; the assumption of a son or other relative gives weight to lay personnel.[296] Local reception of court culture was already a force for cohesion, yet it was here that Alfredian change effected its deepest transformation. The reach of royal lordship received still further power from the communicational capacity of writing. Local acts of reading enabled nothing less than the virtual projection of West Saxon court theatre, conducted at a distance by royal texts alone.

Translation must be situated in these performative structures. The medium offered distinctive opportunities for theatrical projection. Ambiguity of relationship between source and translation gave strong scope for fictionality. Fictive qualities have been much stressed by Malcolm Godden, who has rightly highlighted the complex character of ninth-century translations, often involving the manipulation of multiple voices and *personae*, including those of original Latin authors.[297] Yet the royal monopolization of authorship is neglected; Godden neglects a further layer of imaginative assumption, on which the status of any translation depended. Translation is distinguished by its special relationship to performance, as a written record of imagined reading. This defining property has been overlooked in much theoretical discussion.[298] The early emergence of translation in vernacular languages reflected this imaginative 'literate' appeal. Such effects were heightened in an Alfredian context by weight sometimes attached to the voice of original authors, and by the use of prose. Yet they carried special force when combined with the properties of royal authorship, lacking for anonymity. The imagined reading of translation was endowed with an imagined reader, King Alfred, operating in a specific location, at the heart of his household. The conceit of translation offered potential for an active royal presence, beyond any straightforward goals of replication. In the *Hierdeboc* and biblical translations, this was sustained through ambiguity of the translatory first-person, involving direct exploitation of 'authority' figures,

---

[295] *VA* 106; cf. esp. Wormald, 'Literacy', pp. 96, 105, 108–9 and 113.
[296] Campbell, 'Placing Alfred', p. 13.
[297] Godden, 'Player King'; Godden, *Misappropriation*; cf. Pratt, 'Authorship'.
[298] Cf. R. Copeland, *Rhetoric, Hermeneutics, and Translation in the Middle Ages* (Cambridge, 1991); L. Venuti, *The Translator's Invisibility: a History of Translation* (London, 1995); Stanton, *Culture of Translation*; Discenza, *King's English*, esp. pp. 1–11.

especially heightened in the Psalms. The Boethius and Augustine held still more complex opportunities, as 'internal' dialogues involving ambiguous *personae*, allowing royal reference to reach new heights through suggestive projection. Royal texts offered an exclusive and highly sophisticated form of imagined theatre; re-enactment through reading supplied the virtual presence of the king himself.

Such performance was itself a play within a play, part of the broader drama of West Saxon theatre. Imagined, textual role-playing was subservient to the king's observable role-playing on the stage of the royal household. In many respects Alfred's practice drew on roles long-established within West Saxon kingship, reliant on the exhibition of exemplary lordship and office-holding, conducted against the backdrop of Old Testament kingship. This places still further weight on learned innovation, and the unusual features of Alfred's everyday behaviour.[299] Every aspect of his conduct acquired meaning from the principles of Alfredian discourse, exclusively available in the royal corpus. Contrary to many assessments, Alfred's 'personality' can barely be detached from these structures of power. Virtually all the king's activities related to just three overarching roles, unique to his person: his unceasing pursuit of wisdom, finally released late in his career, and the problematic effects of his mysterious illness, apparently persistent throughout adulthood. To these royal textuality added a third, as 'truthful lord'.[300] All three roles placed Alfred at the heart of novel interplay, incorporating leading members of the West Saxon order, yet visible more widely, beyond the royal *bur*. It was ultimately this role-playing which endowed Alfredian discourse with its considerable power.

Alfred's first role, as a late beginner, incorporated all central aspects of Solomonic imitation, including the framework of wealth and wisdom. Alfred's late involvement in translation, only achieved in mid-life, was by the early 890s presented as the climax of lifelong sapiential desire, negligently hindered in his youth.[301] Alfred's learned behaviour provided a living symbol of humble restraint: his desire for wisdom could playfully be portrayed as 'good greed', while simultaneously the only just route to power and wealth.[302] Such messages depended on wider access to the royal corpus, and direct interaction with all recipients of 're-education', in which the king's experiences were centre stage. Asser

---

[299] Cf. Althoff, *Otto III*, pp. 132–48, for novel aspects of Otto's conduct; Elias, *Court Society*, pp. 89–90 and 119–40, for a courtly ruler's 'ability to achieve large-scale effects by a relatively small expenditure of personal energy'.

[300] Below, pp. 328–32 and 336–7.   [301] *VA* 76, lines 36–70 and c. 88, lines 11–17.

[302] *Ibid.* 78, lines 1–2. Cf. *Solil* p. 84, line 16: 'þæt is swiðe good gytsung', only loosely related to *Soliloquia* II.i.1, p. 46, line 15.

claimed to describe the concern of both young and old in learning letters 'with a view to the character of the aforementioned king (*ad praefati regis notitiam*)'.[303] Younger members of the household were expected to be thankful for their new opportunities so regrettably denied to the king.[304] Adult ealdormen, reeves and thegns were conversely to take heart from the king's own late start, stimulated by recent teaching. The dominance of secular audiences reflected the appeal of Alfred's experiences as a layman.

The role has implications for royal authorship. Here the question of the king's personal involvement assumes vital import.[305] The case for stylistic unity has already been reviewed; the abundant evidence for learning suggestive of royal helpers must be balanced against the singular features of this prose.[306] The distinction between 'authorization' and authorship is pressing given the close interaction between the king and his audiences, combining speech and text. Alfred's image as author was not restricted to the written page, but received enhancement from every aspect of interpersonal contact. The possibility arises of ironic reception of the king's claims, but this must be balanced against Asser's testimony, where personal involvement in translatory activity seems unquestioningly endorsed.[307] Any doubt concerned the precise extent of Alfred's Latin competence, as opposed to any greater questioning of his personal contribution.[308] It is difficult to account for the existence of these texts had Alfred been unable to sustain this image, whenever he was encountered in person. The possibility arises of some dissimulation on the king's part, perhaps reliant on general familiarity with the texts at his disposal, yet it is unlikely that credibility could have been maintained by this means alone. Credibility also depended heavily on the king's existing familiarity to the eyes and ears of aristocratic audiences, now mediated in textual form. Yet the translations that emerged did not merely bear the king's name, but were also endowed at a fundamental level by distinctive textual unity. Alfred's extensive involvement gains much strength from this decisive harmony of texts and context. This was the direct textual extension of Alfred's person, fundamentally dependent on its authenticity and recognition.

The role extended further: Asser portrayed the king admonishing ealdormen and reeves who had neglected wisdom, offering a stark choice between loss of office and more attentive study.[309] In portraying

---

[303] *VA* 106, lines 61–3. [304] *Ibid.* 25 and 106, lines 54–61.
[305] Discussed more fully in Pratt, 'Authorship'. [306] Cf. above, pp. 130–3. [307] *VA* 88–9.
[308] Implicit perhaps in *VA* 88, lines 1–4, and the connection with St Martin: see Pratt, 'Authorship'.
[309] *VA* 106, lines 28–39.

wisdom as the sole criterion for office-holding, Asser implies a novel enhancement of informal competition for appointment, according to a script which paradoxically stressed not only the denial of worldly desire, but direct access to royal learning. Alfredian discourse should not be underestimated as a mask for royal and aristocratic power. Retrospective denigration of the Mercian Ceolwulf as 'unwise' provides a glimpse of this language in action; his attributed status as 'king's thegn' may be equally significant in this aristocratic context.[310] Such encouragement was effective: its success has generally been detected directly, in changing aristocratic attitudes towards the written word. Keynes has advanced a persuasive case for connecting Alfredian developments with further changes in the documentary record from the early tenth century onwards, exemplified by the legislative output of tenth-century English kings.[311] The importance of royal intiative has been observed in the episcopal appointments of Plegmund and Asser; the importance of learning in secular appointments is suggested by Ordlaf of Wiltshire, recorded as the king's leading ealdorman from the early 890s.[312] Ordlaf's engagement with the written word is only known from the Fonthill letter, an unusual survival. Yet it is difficult to detect wholesale changes in personnel: Ordlaf was the grandson of an earlier ealdorman.[313] The West Saxon order had long relied on selective promotion among a tightly knit aristocracy; the pattern continued in late Alfredian and early Edwardian appointments.[314] Attention focuses on the co-operation of existing aristocrats and their children, from the latter years of peace.

Every aspect of Alfredian discourse assumes potency in this immediate context. The treatment of materiality, prominent in both royal languages, correlates with the manifold material pressures at local level from the 880s onwards, within the dynamics of military reform.[315] These were faced by all landholders, over and above the effects of earlier viking warfare. Landed resources had already been squeezed by the pressure of tribute-payments, while viking activity had placed strains on the capacity of the internal economy. Already in decline, coastal 'wics' were gravely threatened by viking raiding; further inland, viking pressure encouraged peasant flight, creating an effective shortage of rural labour. These problems were exacerbated by military burdens, shaped by requirements of the burghal network. Local defence demanded enormous quantities of manpower: landholders faced the difficult task of

---

[310] *ASC* s.a. 874.   [311] Keynes, 'Royal Government', esp. pp. 230–48.
[312] Cf. above, pp. 37–8 and 101–2; Keynes, *Atlas*, table XXII.   [313] S 1284 (BCS 590).
[314] See esp. Keynes, *Atlas*, table XXXV: ealdormen Alfred, Beocca and Sigewulf were all Alfredian ealdormen; Beorhtwulf, Oswulf and Wulfsige were names of Alfredian thegns.
[315] Cf. above, pp. 93–105; Davis, 'Propaganda', pp. 77–81.

balancing priorities at a time when peasant labour was already difficult to pin down. Land-exchanges and leases added to the inconvenience of landholders in possession of strategic land. For episcopal landholding an additional burden arises from the possibility of tactical delay in certain appointments, diverting revenue into royal hands.[316] The context supports Asser's picture of the king's personal 'persuasion' in these difficult circumstances, intensively encouraging collective co-operation.[317]

The dangers of worldly desire were urgent here, implying nothing less than the subordination of all personal considerations to the needs of Alfred's kingdom. This is not to deny a role for other vernacular texts, but their valency must be judged against the intimate action of royal texts, uniquely addressing the responsibilities of power.[318] The *Chronicle* has generally received the greatest weight as a tool of encouragement, together with wider ethnic unity; neither matches the mental immediacy of Alfredian discourse, as a co-ordinated philosophical solution to material pressures. The ambiguous position of 'Englishkind' in royal writing militates against its full politicization in Alfred's hands.[319] The centrality of Alfredian discourse was implicit in Asser's frank account of the difficulties in implementing the burghal scheme. Those reluctant to co-operate are portrayed in 'untimely repentance': 'now they lament their negligent scorn for royal commands, and loudly applaud royal wisdom' ('et regalia se praecepta incuriose despexisse dolent, et regalem sapientiam totis vocibus collaudant').[320] Such approval involved direct acceptance of wider material needs: 'what they had previously refused, they now promise to make every effort to fulfil – that is, with respect to constructing fortresses and to other things of communal benefit to the whole realm (*de arcibus construendis et ceteris communibus communis regni utilitatibus*)'. Summarizing royal 'persuasion', Asser again praises Alfred's success in exploiting and converting his office-holders 'most wisely (*sapientissime*) both to his own will and to the communal benefit of the entire realm (*ad suam voluntatem et ad communem totius regni utilitatem*)'.[321]

The language of communal utility may itself be innovative: West Saxon common burdens were reserved in plainer terms, *praeter expedicionem et pontis arcisve instructionem*.[322] Ultimately deriving from Roman law and Roman political thought, the securing of *communis utilitas* was a

---

[316] See esp. the letter of Pope Formosus, discussed below, pp. 210–12; Whitelock in *C&S*, pp. 35–6.
[317] *VA* 91, lines 28–45.
[318] Esp. Davis, 'Propaganda'; Wormald, 'Bede, the *Bretwaldas*', pp. 120–9; Wormald, '*Engla Lond*', pp. 366–7 and 376–8; Foot, '*Angelcynn*'; cf. also Sheppard, *Families*, pp. 26–50.
[319] Above, pp. 154–5, cf. 106–7.   [320] *VA* 91, lines 67–72.   [321] *Ibid*. 91, lines 36–45.
[322] *Sic vel sim.* S 343, S 345, S 348, S 354, S 355, S 356 (all Alfredian); cf. S 326, S 335, S 336, S 1274 for earlier West Saxon examples.

feature of Carolingian 'ministerial' responsibility, harnessed under Charles the Bald in the context of viking defence.[323] Yet such language acquired distinctive force through its application to the common burdens, enhancing its appeal in royal hands. Other needs included the king's new 'long-ships', designed 'just as it seemed to him that they would be most useful' (*swa him selfum ðuhte þæt hie nytwyrðoste beon meahten*); another was wisdom itself, accessed through books 'most necessary for all men to know' (*þe nidbeðyrfesta sien eallum monnum to witanne*).[324]

The value of Alfredian discourse extended beyond the expression of needs, to include positive counter-appeal to self-interest. Material inducements towards co-operation have been identified: these too relied on Alfredian discourse for their coherence and persuasive force.[325] Much hinges on the message of the law-book, an immediate expression of Solomonic rule. The pivotal law of *hlafordsearu* applied to all orders, *ge ceorle ge eorle*, in a complex framework of faithful obligation.[326] The bonds expressed were not new, any more than was the receipt of monetary compensation (*bot*) by 'worldly lords', or lordly responsibility for the behaviour of commended men. Yet in Alfred's law betrayal of the king could be perpetrated indirectly, through the harbouring of fugitives; Wormald has advanced strong grounds for a significant widening of treachery, to cover crime in general, including theft.[327] The manoeuvre bore resemblance to fuller Frankish provisions of the late eighth and early ninth century, including some role for a general oath of loyalty, though it is less clear by whom and in what circumstances such an undertaking might have been sworn.[328]

These provisions gain significantly as a response to contemporary conditions. The treatment of treachery has long been associated with defence; what needs stress is its potency at local level, where disruption was most acute. *Hlafordsearu* offered enhancement to the existing monopolization of justice, through a widening of offences against the king. Its implications addressed threats to livestock, produce and other moveable property, with heightened responsibilities for lords in peace-keeping and organized pursuit.[329] Though the latter gained from a share in fines and confiscations, the framework contributed more evenly to an adjusted seigneurial order. Transfer of men between lords received greater tolerance; the granting of extensive 'mass days' to freemen and slaves

---

[323] Cf. above, p. 71; Nelson, 'Charles le Chauve', pp. 47–9; Edict of Pîtres (864), MGH Capit. II, p. 328, lines 15–28, cf. cc. 1, 4, 10, 35 and 36 for excerpts from Louis' *Admonitio* (Ansegisus, *Capitularium Collectio* II.18, II.23 and II.24).

[324] *ASC* s.a. 896; *CP*, p. 7, line 7.   [325] Cf. above, pp. 96–105.

[326] *Af* 4–4.2; see below, pp. 232–41.   [327] Wormald, 'God and King', pp. 338–42.

[328] Below, pp. 233–6.   [329] Cf. esp. *VA* 91, lines 58–67.

suggests a comparable economic inducement.[330] *Hlafordsearu* expressed dualistic commitment to lordship, both royal and aristocratic, when such bonds faced intensive threat. As advice to 'judges', the law-book offered further easing of local pressures. Royal concern for *pauperes* had sharper implications against these problems of peasant labour. Principles of good judgement offered wider regulation of 'justice', applicable in any dispute settlement, and decision-making beyond. As a warning against corruption, the law-book cannot be detached from the role of bookland in dispute, whose solitary reference is unusual in written law.[331] Royal good will in land exchanges and leases was a vital source of strategic land.[332]

The counter-appeal of Alfredian discourse was encapsulated by the Solomonic hope of future wealth. Solomon's example was openly equivocal, combining desire for wisdom alone with riches and glory in superabundance. Wealthy restraint received extensive support in the Boethius; wholesale revision of the Latin source-text was shaped by more positive treatment of worldly goods.[333] The language of necessity was equally equivocal: power and wealth were invaluable gifts of wisdom, their possession essential for God's purposes in the world. Future 'wealth' in the Prose Preface was unspecified; part of the value of such posturing may have lain in its universal applicability, amid economic disruption. The irony would have been heightened for recipients if Alfred had indeed derived income from vacant sees.[334] Yet the source of much wealth did not need closer identification, in the burghal programme, simultaneously promoted by fiscal incentives reliant on land and revenue associated with burghal markets.[335] The higher silver content of Alfred's coinage was a further vital component in exchange.[336]

The value of 'wealth' was enhanced by royal posturing: the image of Alfred's formal distribution of revenues is radically sharpened by the intensive division of income at source, in burghal markets, between the king and his office-holders.[337] Yet any stake remained worthless if the burh could not be brought to completion, nor established as a viable market. It was towards precisely this aristocratic dilemma, over the delicate balancing of long- and short-term economic priorities, that the royal language of wealth and wisdom was ultimately directed. Ealdorman Æthelred can be placed at the heart of such developments in

---

[330] *Af* 37–37.2, cf. *Ine* 39; *Af* 43–43.1.   [331] *Af* 41–41.1.   [332] Above, pp. 100–2.
[333] Below, pp. 280–307.   [334] Below, pp. 210–12.
[335] Above, pp. 99 and 104–5; Brooks, 'Administrative Background', pp. 142–5.
[336] Above, pp. 103–4.
[337] *VA* 100–2, with S 346 (BCS 561), S 1628 (BCS 577 and 578) and S 223 (BCS 579; *SEHD*, no. 13; trans. in *EHD*, no. 99). Cf. *Af* 2, with Whitelock in *C&S*, p. 23, note 1, for comparable benefits at source from the king's *feorm*.

London and Worcester; although the precise context is irrecoverable, Ceolwulf's denigration acquires suggestive force against the wise activities of his successor.[338] Not merely symbolic, the value of wisdom lay in its ability to encourage, as well as to articulate, such overarching commitment to burghal construction. The king's own philosophy provided every reason to embrace such future income, as wealth necessarily achieved through all-encompassing restraint of worldly desire. To accept the king's message was to acknowledge a further royal monopoly, sustained through wisdom, over all means to legitimate wealth.

Alfred's second role, as a suffering king, has already been outlined; its full significance emerges in this context of persuasory theatre.[339] The incorporation of Alfred's person was deep and continuous, in the disturbing effects of his second illness, first incurred at the time of his marriage, and intermittent throughout his adult life. The nature of his physical complaint is clarified by the list of remedies sent by the Patriarch Elias, including treatments for constipation, diarrhoea and other aspects of 'internal tenderness'.[340] This only adds weight to the king's reported story, that the second illness had answered his youthful prayer for 'some less severe illness' which (like the 'piles') would not be outwardly visible on his body. The level of detail demands modern medical assessment: a diagnosis of Crohn's disease would match all available symptoms, reinforcing the intimacy of Alfred's suffering, as an unpleasant internal disorder involving bouts of relapse and remission.[341] Asser stresses the intermittent character of Alfred's illness, as well as its periodic severity. There is no reason to suppose any greater restriction on royal activity, which may explain why the king's physical effectiveness also was beyond question. Every aspect of Alfred's devotional behaviour held special significance in these unusual circumstances. There were close parallels with Carolingian trends in the extension of private prayer and confession to laymen; this medical context holds the key to their deployment. Personal sinfulness was long established as a possible cause of illness; such a connection was here encouraged by the unknown cause of Alfred's condition, strongly resistant to medical treatment.

The king's role again acquired meaning from his associated texts. Gregorian dimensions have been observed in the attribution of suffering to

---

[338] *ASC* s.a. 874; cf. Æthelred's prominence in all three examples of fiscal privileges (S 346, S 1628 and S 223). Ceolwulf's precise position in the later 870s remains problematic (Keynes, 'Mercians', pp. 12–19; Blackburn, 'Alfred's Coinage Reforms', pp. 212–14).

[339] Cf. above, pp. 136–8; cf. Pratt, 'Illnesses'.

[340] *Leechdoms*, ed. Cockayne II, 288–91, cf. 174–5.

[341] G. Craig, 'Alfred the Great: a Diagnosis', *Journal of the Royal Society of Medicine* 84 (1991), 303–5; Pratt, 'Illnesses', pp. 72–81.

the onset of Alfred's first illness in his youth, positively requested from God as a means of restraining his bodily desire (*carnale desiderium*).[342] The openness is striking against West Frankish royal humility, shaped by the need for sexual propriety under ecclesiastical admonition.[343] Responsibilities of mental control were thus heightened by bodily suffering. Yet Alfred's pain was situated in a broader drama of Gregorian tribulation, extending far beyond his physical body. This is confirmed by Asser's account of the king's multiple *perturbationes*, but all action depended on the royal vernacular: the *Life* is invaluable for its separate compositional agenda.[344] Prominent throughout the royal corpus, *earfoðu* ('hardships') emerge most strongly in the Psalm translation, in the immediate context of biblical kingship.[345] Royal handling was heavily Davidic, placing weight on the historical circumstances of composition. David's struggles feature prominently in the exegetical introductions; in many cases the context was further specified as *earfoðu ge modes ge lichaman* ('hardships both of mind and body'), together with threats posed by military enemies. Bodily illness received further treatment in several passages of expansion, generally in the context of divine punishment, rather than Job-like testing. Suggestive of the king's own symptoms, these are further distinguished by a strong sexual focus for royal sin.[346] Similar connections recur in the translations of Boethius and Augustine, attentive to dangers of sexual temptation.[347]

Here too the royal corpus was at the heart of everyday interplay between the king and aristocratic audiences, in encounters united by his personal presence. Such universal exposure is again striking against the more restricted deployment of West Frankish royal humility.[348] Translatory additions reinforce Asser's picture of sustained royal anxiety. Even in remission, Alfred was depicted in open loathing at the 'fear and horror' of his pain, rendering him 'virtually useless, as it seemed to him, for divine and human affairs'.[349] The overall effect was to establish potent connections between the king's bodily suffering and that endured by the West Saxon order in its entirety.[350] The material effects of the viking attacks were replicated deep inside the king's body by the equally unpredictable attacks of his mysterious illness. The sinful cause of the king's illness was equally matched by the role accorded to the viking attacks as divine punishment. The king's physical suffering was only

---

[342] *VA* 74, lines 39–60; *Reg. past.* III.12, II, 330–2, lines 115–38; *CP* XXXVI, p. 256, line 19 to 260, line 1; cf. stress on carnal temptation by Lothar II in different circumstances (above, pp. 61–2).

[343] Pratt, 'Illnesses', pp. 43–5; cf. Lothar's vulnerability to West Frankish episcopal criticism (Airlie, 'Private Bodies', pp. 25–7 and 31–5).

[344] *VA* 25, lines 1–13 and c. 91, lines 1–12 and 25–8.

[345] Below, pp. 256–63; Pratt, 'Illnesses', pp. 85–8.   [346] Below, pp. 260–1.

[347] Pratt, 'Illnesses', pp. 75–81.   [348] Above, pp. 64 and 162; Nelson, 'Lord's Anointed', p. 124.

[349] *VA* 74, lines 64–70.   [350] Pratt, 'Illnesses', pp. 81–90.

exacerbated by the reluctance of his people to obey royal orders, among the wider burdens of Gregorian rulership. Alfred's body itself acquired all-encompassing significance, as a microcosmic representation of his kingdom. Yet the value of this transformation lay also in its instructive capacity, in the context of defensive reform. Alfred's own conspicuous sinfulness eased the tone of collective criticism; royal protestations of pain and fear provided constant illustration of the dangers of excessive desire. Thegnly expression of sympathy now bore wider implications of defensive cooperation. Alfred's patent incurability left burghal construction as the only means of alleviating royal pain; the burdens involved were themselves diminished by the king's own sacrificial commitment. To contradict the king in his outright despair was to confirm the 'usefulness' of his pervasive role.

The intensity of Alfred's posturing exemplifies the power of the royal written word. Burghal construction itself cannot be detached from the effects of royal performance. The projection of Alfredian theatre was total and continuous, extending beyond acts of reading to include every aspect of aristocratic conduct under the pressures of viking defence. The centrality of the court was only further enhanced by its projection: the value of the king's role-playing lay in its regular observation at first hand, comprehensively facilitated by the West Saxon royal household. There is no tension between individual and structure: the highly personal character of royal role-playing was itself a product of this court environment, encouraged by the intimate potential of writing. What commands attention is the relentlessness of the king's behaviour, and the urgency of its deployment within such a delicate process of collective encouragement. Every gesture and utterance went hand in hand with the documented range of Alfred's instructions, gifts and concessions, in a single strategy of wise restraint. Though necessarily aided by its courtly generation, this strategy was no less heavily dependent on Alfred's own inspiration and initiative. The case for his centrality within translation is only further strengthened by such wider evidence for extensive royal agency. The efficacy of Alfredian discourse lay firmly in Alfred's own abilities of projection and artifice, adapting every aspect of his person to the collective recognition of urgent material needs.

Chapter 9

ALFREDIAN TECHNOLOGY: BOOKS AND *ÆDIFICIA*

Alfredian theatre privileged reading, essential to the delivery of vernacular prose. Translation offered the imagined reading of a Latin text; its re-enactment was no less dependent on reading and recitation. Much of the novelty of Alfredian theatre lay in its exploitation of literacy as a form of mental technology, extending beyond direct interaction to include more open-ended priorities of wisdom and self-restraint. Such mental effects were in turn dependent on material innovation, geared to the demands of the royal written word. Book production was inescapable, yet innovation extended further, to artefactual production. Alfredian books were matched by a series of novel objects, also implicated in the literate acquisition of wisdom. As a centre of production as well as performance, the royal household was enhanced by the unity of investigative enterprise. The outcome was a co-ordinated system of technology, oriented towards the king's mental goals. The court itself supplied all necessary mechanisms of projection, enhancing the reins of its central control.

BOOKS AND BOOK PRODUCTION

Textual duplication was essential for wider performance. 'Re-education' witnessed the copying of manuscripts on a considerable scale. Multiple copies of the *Hierdeboc* were required for episcopal recipients; comparable processes lay behind the 'common stock' of the *Chronicle* and the law-book. Dissemination of other royal texts is supported by context, prefatory material and transmission-history.[1] Precise mechanisms are clouded by uneven evidence. Knowledge is dominated by just two Alfredian books surviving into the modern era, both copies of the *Hierdeboc*: Oxford, Bodleian Library, Hatton 20 (4113), the codex sent to

---

[1] Cf. above, pp. 126–7.

Wærferth, and London, British Library, Cotton Tiberius B. xi, a copy almost completely destroyed by fire.[2] This tiny corpus must be distinguished from a wider body of early vernacular manuscripts, including the 'Parker' manuscript of the *Chronicle* (Cambridge, Corpus Christi College, MS 173, s. x^{in}), the 'Tollemache Orosius' (London, British Library, MS Additional 47967, s. x^{in}), the 'Otho Bede' (British Library, Cotton Otho B. xi, s. x^{med}) and the manuscript of Bald's *Leechbook* (British Library, Royal 12. D. xvii, s. x^{med}). These manuscripts have often given rise to the identification of Winchester as a major centre of Alfredian book production, but this view has been undermined by Dumville, re-dating the earliest phases of Square Minuscule script to the early tenth century.[3]

If the case for Winchester remains uncertain, Alfred's reported activities point to abundant scribal activity in the royal household. Royal composition necessitated an immediate record: Asser provides details of such a process in the assembling of the king's *enchiridion* or 'hand-book'.[4] The role of Alfred's helpers related to patterns of service by royal priests; his mature efforts involved an extension of scribal service.[5] Yet demand necessitated the participation of other centres. Scribes 'south and north' were highlighted in the *Hierdeboc*'s Verse Preface; copying at a distance was celebrated by Wulfsige of Sherborne.[6] Textual authenticity was stressed in both cases to a privileged examplar (*bysen*), received from the king. The act of copying was itself a duplication of court theatre, its intimacy guaranteed by exclusive distribution.

For the *Hierdeboc* such processes can be closely observed. Sisam's survey is now in need of revision.[7] In addition to Hatton 20 (H), sent to Wærferth, the names of two further Alfredian bishops are mentioned in later copies: Cambridge, University Library, MS Ii. 2. 4 (U), a late eleventh-century manuscript specifying Wulfsige as recipient, and London, British Library, Cotton Otho B. ii (Cii), a fire-damaged late tenth- or early eleventh-century descendant of the copy sent to

---

[2] Ker, *Catalogue*, nos. 324 and 195; Gneuss, *Handlist*, nos. 626 and 375; N.R. Ker, *The Pastoral Care*, EEMF 6 (Copenhagen, 1956).

[3] Dumville, 'Anglo-Saxon Chronicle', pp. 81–98. Cf. M.B. Parkes, 'The Palaeography of the Parker Manuscript of the Chronicle, Laws and Sedulius, and Historiography at Winchester in the Late Ninth and Tenth Centuries', *ASE* 5 (1976), 149–71; Meaney, 'Secretariat'; A. Lawrence, 'Alfred, his Heirs and the Traditions of Manuscript Production in Tenth Century England', *Reading Medieval Studies* 13 (1988), 35–56.

[4] *VA* 88.   [5] Cf. above, pp. 54–8 and 119–20.

[6] *Verse Preface to CP*, ed. Dobbie; Yerkes, 'Metrical Preface', pp. 512–13; trans. in K&L, *Alfred*, pp. 187–8.

[7] Sisam, *Studies*, pp. 140–7; cf. Keynes, 'Power of the Written Word', pp. 193–6; Schreiber, *Alfred's Translation*, pp. 51–82.

Heahstan, bishop of London.[8] The existence of further lost copies is demonstrated by Tiberius B. xi (Ci), known from fragments. This contemporary manuscript once fulfilled functions of great significance: its readings suggest an early version of the text, prior to correction, and included a blank space in the Prose Preface rather than an episcopal name.[9] According to Junius, its first page bore the inscription, 'Plegmunde arcebisc[eop] is agifen his boc. and Swiðulfe bisc[eop]. and Wærferðe bisc[eop]'.[10] As an 'ancient' memorandum, this revealed further dissemination to Plegmund of Canterbury and Swithulf of Rochester, presumably in a form comparable to Wærferth's copy (H). Of two remaining manuscripts, Cambridge, Corpus Christi College, MS 12 (CC) (s. $x^{2/2}$) leaves no space for an episcopal recipient, while in Cambridge, Trinity College MS R. 5. 22 (T) (s. x/xi) the Prose Preface is omitted.[11] Given such sound evidence for copies sent to at least five of Alfred's bishops, distribution is likely to have extended to all other surviving sees in the Canterbury province.

Close connections between Ci and H throw further light on the technology of reproduction. Ker's detailed analysis reveals the activity of five, or perhaps six scribes, here distinguished by code letter:[12]

	Ci (no addressee)	Ci frag. fols.	H (for Wærferth)	H fols.
Prose Preface	B	8, 6+4	A	1r–2v
Verse Preface	C?	–	D	2v
Chapter Headings	A	2+5, 1+3	D (main scribe) E (minor scribe)	3r–5v
Main Text	A	7, Kassel leaf	D (main scribe) E (minor scribe)	6r–98v

A further scribe (X) is postulated by Keynes; the independence of the 'ancient hand' in Ci remains uncertain. All other identifications for Ci are based on surviving fragments, with the exception of the Verse

---

[8] Ker, *Catalogue*, nos. 19 and 175; Gneuss, *Handlist*, nos. 14 and 353; *The Pastoral Care, edited from British Library MS. Cotton Otho B. ii.*, ed. I. Carlson *et al.*, Stockholm Studies in English 34 and 48 (Stockholm, 1975–8).

[9] Carlson in *Pastoral Care*, part I, pp. 26–8; Ker, *Pastoral Care*, pp. 12–19; P. Wormald, 'Alfredian Manuscripts', in *The Anglo-Saxons*, ed. Campbell, pp. 158–9.

[10] 'Archbishop Plegmund has been given his book and bishop Swithulf and bishop Wærferth': Ker, *Pastoral Care*, p. 12.

[11] Ker, *Catalogue*, nos. 30 and 87; Gneuss, *Handlist*, nos. 37 and 180.

[12] Ker, *Pastoral Care*, pp. 12–19; Keynes, 'Power of the Written Word', pp. 194–5.

Preface, where one must rely on Wanley's statement that each preface was written by a different hand.[13]

The two prefaces were written on a separate bifolium in H; Ci probably had the same construction. The implications of this addition remain unclear, but there is no need for any revisionist conclusions. Encouraged by the title at the head of Junius's transcript of Ci, 'Ðis is seo foresprǣc hu S. Gregorius ðas boc gedihte þe man Pastoralem nemnað', Sisam suggested that the Prose Preface may have been an 'afterthought'.[14] Yet as Ker noted, Junius's title is probably a red herring: the same words occur in U, *before* the Prose Preface, to which Junius also had access via Parker's edition.[15] Ci and H indicate a firm consistency of purpose in duplication, entirely compatible with the Prose Preface. Wider access to the *Hierdeboc* is not unlikely, but receives no firm support from the manuscript record. The chapter headings on fol. 3r in H begin without title or incipit; the inclusion of prefatory material had never been in doubt. The two prefaces can only have functioned as a pair, present together in five of the six manuscripts.[16] The outcome was a standardized episcopal 'edition' of the text, bearing strong signs of co-ordination and planning, striking in view of its apparent haste.

In Ci and H, scribal enterprise can be closely reconstructed. Noting the Ci's special status, seemingly retained at 'headquarters', Sisam highlighted the role of its principal scribe (A) as the hand of the Prose Preface in H. On this basis he suggested that the main text of H had been written at a second centre, and that copies had commonly been returned to 'headquarters' for the addition of prefaces.[17] Yet this interpretation is incompatible with Ker's analysis, precluded by the role of scribe D, as the hand of the Verse Preface in H as well as the main text in the same manuscript.[18] Because the added bifolium of H contains work by the sole scribe of Ci's main text (A) and the principal scribe of H's main text, both manuscripts are likely to have been produced in the same environment.

Taken alone, such evidence would support various scenarios of production. Neither manuscript was copied from the other: H preserves a number of inferior readings despite heavy contemporary correction; Ci probably preserved an early version of the text rather than a finalized

---

[13] Ker, *Pastoral Care*, p. 12.
[14] 'This is the preface [explaining] how Saint Gregory composed this book that is called Pastoralis'. Sisam, *Studies*, pp. 144–5; cf. also Smyth, *Alfred*, pp. 241–2.
[15] Ker, *Pastoral Care*, p. 15.
[16] For the Verse Preface, cf. O'Brien O'Keeffe, *Visible Song*, pp. 88–95.
[17] Sisam, *Studies*, pp. 141–3.
[18] Ker, *Pastoral Care*, p. 22; Keynes, 'Power of the Written Word', p. 195.

exemplar.[19] Where *were* Alfred's 'scribes south and north'? Despite the connections in these two survivals, some form of multicentric co-operation must still be assumed. Yet the image of a fixed 'headquarters' is unhelpful given the king's mobility and the intermittent character of much attendance. At all events, Ci's special status must be judged against the character of both manuscripts, indicative of West Saxon execution.[20] Both preserve early West Saxon forms; the script is late Insular minuscule, not the Square Minuscule of early tenth-century manuscripts. The variability of execution is striking: Ker distinguished the confident set hand of scribe A from the work of scribes D and E, which exhibits a number of irregularities, only attaining fluency towards the end of their respective stints.[21] This extends attention beyond named helpers to other scribes, whose skills might well have lain in documentary production. The continuing availability of West Saxon royal priests is indicated by early Edwardian witness-lists, associated with the founding of the New Minster.[22] By the same token, there may be dangers in identifying Winchester as the dominant source of expertise.[23] Wherever Ci and H were executed, the effect would have been the same, in supplying privileged mechanisms of duplication.

The possibility arises of a 'court style', stimulated by centralized demand. Characterization of the *Hierdeboc* as an *ærendgewrit* receives added force from the script of these early copies, probably a direct development from that used in royal documents. Ci and H bear a close relationship to examples of 'West Saxon minuscule' from Æthelwulf's time.[24] In the absence of later West Saxon documents in original form, Ci and H may be the only examples of comparable output. The question is barely clarified by other southern books, a meagre haul dominated by vernacular prose: London, British Library, MS Additional 23211 (Wessex, s. ix^{ex}), comprising fragments of genealogical material and of the *Old English Martyrology*; Durham, Cathedral Library, A. iv. 19, pp. 1–121 (s. ix/x) a liturgical manuscript later transported north; London, British Library, MS Additional 40165A, fols. 6–7 (x. ix^{ex} or s. ix/x), a second *Martyrology* fragment; British Library, Cotton Domitian A. ix, fol. 11r (s. ix^{ex} or x^{in}), fragmentary excerpts from the Old English Bede; and British Library, Royal 5. F. iii (Worcester provenance; s. ix^{ex}

---

[19] Carlson in *Pastoral Care*, part I, pp. 26–33, correcting D. M. Horgan, 'The Relationship between the O. E. MSS. of King Alfred's Translation of Gregory's Pastoral Care', *Anglia* 91 (1973), 153–69, at 155–6 and 160; cf. also Schreiber, *Alfred's Translation*, pp. 75–9.

[20] Keynes, 'Power of the Written Word', pp. 194–6.

[21] Ker, *Pastoral Care*, p. 19.   [22] Keynes, 'West Saxon Charters', pp. 1146–7.

[23] Dumville, 'Anglo-Saxon Chronicle', esp. pp. 71–2 and 97–8.

[24] Keynes, 'Power of the Written Word', pp. 188 and 193–7.

or ix/x), a broken manuscript of Aldhelm's prose *De virginitate*.[25] All are written in the same late Insular minuscule; court connections cannot strictly be ruled out in several cases. Yet the script of Royal 5. F. iii is generally agreed to exhibit 'Mercian' features, while Dumville has noted wide variations in aspect across the remainder of this corpus, distinct from the style of Ci and H.[26] The case is perhaps strengthened for associating 'court' production with the supply of exemplars.

Textual layout remains open to the wider evidence of later copies. There is every indication that translations were copied discretely, with a single text per volume. An early association has sometimes been postulated between the *Chronicle* and law-book, both in the 'Parker' manuscript.[27] Yet the law-book was a subsequent addition to this codex, probably occurring in the 930s.[28] In contemporary usage, texts were also 'books', the Boethian *Froferboc* ('consolation-book') supplementing the *Hierdeboc* and *Domboc*. Such practices reflected priorities of textual integrity, similarly observable in the presentation of texts, incorporating preliminary material only partly derived from their sources. The copying of translated texts was heightened replication, with implicit appeal to Latinate models. The *Hierdeboc* and *Froferboc* borrowed chapter-headings; the law-book followed a similar structure, with 120 chapter divisions.[29] Further introductory material was translated for Gregory and Boethius; in four of the five such prolegomena were supplemented by royal prefaces, framing all reading within an additional 'Latin' conceit.[30]

This may have extended to very basic scribal priorites. William Schipper has noted a consistent preference for 'long lines' in the format of vernacular manuscripts from Alfred's reign onwards, when compared with a greater variety of formats in Latin manuscripts of English pro-duction.[31] Preference for 'long lines' probably related to their use in Latin, especially patristic, exemplars. Much of the potency of Alfredian book-production lay in such artifice, the harnessing of Latinity and Latin-like textuality in conscious elevation of vernacular discourse.

Such appropriation continued in the handling of decoration. No illuminated miniatures survive for Alfredian texts; other vernacular books were probably comparable to Ci and H. This was in marked

---

[25] Ker, *Catalogue*, nos. 127, 106, 132, 151 and 253; Gneuss, *Handlist*, nos. 282, 223, 298, 330 and 462; D. N. Dumville, 'English Square Minuscule Script: the Background and Earliest Phases', *ASE* 16 (1987), 147–79, at 158.

[26] M. Brown in *Making of England*, no. 237; Dumville, 'English Square Minuscule', p. 158.

[27] Parkes, 'Parker Manuscript'; Wormald, '*Lex Scripta*', p. 34.

[28] Dumville, 'Anglo-Saxon Chronicle', esp. pp. 135–9.   [29] Below, pp. 215–16 and 231.

[30] Cf. T. Janson, *Latin Prose Prefaces: Studies in Literary Conventions* (Stockholm, 1964).

[31] W. Schipper, 'Style and Layout of Anglo-Saxon Manuscripts', in *Anglo-Saxon Styles*, ed. C. E. Karkov and G. H. Brown (Albany, NY, 2003), pp. 151–68.

contrast to West Frankish practices, where 'court' productions frequently extended to monarchical representation; a further East Frankish miniature has been interpreted as depicting Louis the German.[32] Alfredian production compared with Latin models of patristic and school texts, frequently without illustration. The *Consolatio* was unusual in its early association with prefatory illustration. In H, decoration was restricted to initials and occasional marginal elements, relating to earlier South-umbrian ornamentation; even this work was unusually restrained.[33] A contrast has been noted with more elaborate, florid forms already available at certain southern centres at the end of the ninth century, apparently influenced by Carolingian sources.[34] It is difficult not to associate such practices with the value attached to wisdom as a form of textual understanding, rooted in access to translated script. Only on one page in H do marginal elements relate to the accompanying text, illustrating a man and a mother with child.[35] The full force of figural depiction was reserved for other media, separate from the written page.

CANDLE-LANTERN, FULLER BROOCH AND 'ÆSTELS'

Book production accompanied parallel developments in the fashioning of portable artifacts. Already in Æthelwulf's time, the royal rings suggest a 'court' style of metalwork. Asser repeatedly refers to 'craftsmen' (*operatores*) assembled by Alfred 'from many races', receiving one third of royal revenue designated for secular affairs.[36] As with the use of royal scribes, the mid-ninth-century rings offer likely precedents for such craftsmen in royal service, possibly attached to the household: their precise location is unknown.

Yet for Asser every aspect of production was in some sense without precedent: 'And what [shall I say] of the treasures (*ædificia*) incomparably fashioned in gold and silver at his instigation?'.[37] The design and commissioning of artifacts emerges as a further royal activity: 'giving instruction to all his goldsmiths (*aurifices*) and craftsmen (*artifices*); ... making to his own design wonderful and precious new treasures (*ædificia nova*) which far surpassed any tradition of his predecessors'.[38] The role mirrored royal authorship, in the exclusivity of creative agency vested in the king. The construction of objects raises especially complex

---

[32] Staubach, *Rex Christianus*, pp. 221–81; Deshman, 'Exalted Servant'; Dutton and Kessler, *First Bible of Charles the Bald*; Goldberg, 'Frontier Kingship', pp. 67–70, cf. 73–7; Goldberg, *Empire*, pp. 285–7.
[33] L. Webster in *Golden Age*, p. 18; E. Temple, *Anglo-Saxon Manuscripts 900–1066* (London, 1976), p. 11.
[34] *Ibid.* [35] Fol. 34v; *Golden Age*, p. 21. [36] *VA* 101, lines 4–7. [37] *Ibid.* 91, lines 19–21.
[38] *Ibid.* 76, lines 5–9.

problems, but again there are grounds for accepting significant royal input. Central is the remarkable corpus of late ninth-century metalwork: every aspect of these artifacts answered the distinctive demands of Alfredian discourse. The iconographic character of 'court' metalwork was now subsumed to the priorities of literate wisdom, establishing material aspects of didacticism, the technological enhancement of Alfredian theatre.

Alfredian discourse extended to craftsmanship. Asser's use of Latin *ædificia* has been noted, describing 'treasures' rather than the usual meaning 'buildings'.[39] The term probably reflected further Solomonic precedent, in the construction of the Temple, as 'aedificium domus Domini et aedificium regis', central within Israel's divine covenant.[40] Yet Alfred's craftsmen were also skilled 'in omni terreno aedificio': such usage related to royal language, pertaining to physical construction.[41] At its heart lay the distinctive preference for OE *cræft*, meaning 'virtue, skill, strength', first noted by Peter Clemoes.[42] *Cræft* and craftsmanship encapsulated royal expectations of power. *Cræftas* were divine gifts, possessed in abundance by those who should rule; wisdom was 'se hehsta cræft', implying practical needs for worldly 'tools' and 'resources'.[43] Royal artifacts exploited similar associations between physical skill and learned improvement. The value of *ædificia* lay in the edificatory or instructive character of their form and function, and the excellence of its execution.

One example of edification has not chanced to survive: Asser's account of Alfred's candle-lantern acquires sharper focus as an instance of wise invention.[44] The king's initiative had responded to practical difficulties in securing accurate division of his time between devotion to God and secular affairs. The royal solution was to furnish six candles of equal weight, with twelve inch marks along their length, thus measuring threefold divisions of hours when burnt continuously through twenty-four hours of day and night. Yet the speed of burning was hastened by draughts: a solution was reached 'ingeniously and wisely' (*artificiose atque sapienter*), in an ornate lantern (*laterna*) of wood and ox-horn, improving accuracy. This construction was architectural: translucent windows

---

[39] Pratt, 'Persuasion', pp. 199–200; cf. Webster, '*Ædificia nova*', pp. 79–81.
[40] R. Deshman, 'The Galba Psalter: Pictures, Texts and Context in an Early Medieval Prayerbook', *ASE* 26 (1997), 109–38, esp. 133; III Kings IX. 1, cf. II Chronicles VII. 11.
[41] *VA* 101, lines 6–7.
[42] Clemoes, 'King Alfred's Debt', pp. 213–17 and 223–38; N. G. Discenza, 'Power, Skill and Virtue in the Old English Boethius', *ASE* 26 (1997), 81–108.
[43] *Bo* XXVII.ii, p. 62, line 24; cf. *Cons. phil.* IIIp4.7, p. 43. *Solil* p. 62, lines 5–10; cf. *Soliloquia* I.iv.10, pp. 17–18. Cf. below, pp. 287–95, 319–20 and 335.
[44] *VA* 104; Pratt, 'Persuasion', pp. 201–6.

ensured the visibility of inch marks; a small door enabled the candle to be changed without permitting draughts.

Such craftsmanship answered textual needs. The twofold division of royal time related to Gregorian priorities of action and contemplation. By their regular divisions Alfred's candles gave hours of equal length, departing from the varying 'temporal hours' measured by sun-dial. The lantern's innovation was inseparable from its heightened significance as a tool of Alfred's personal theatre, constantly present at the household's heart. 'For þam þu onælest min leohtfæt, Drihten, min God, onlyht mine þystru' (Ps. XVII. 29): as a source of physical illumination and mental discipline, the lantern's functions were intimate and literate, implying far more than self-regulation.[45] Performance for aristocratic audiences receives support from the need for worldly disengagement, solicited in the Prose Preface.[46] The operative verb *geæmettian* ('to be unoccupied') recurred frequently in the *Hierdeboc*. The lantern's value lay in this wider projection of daily royal priorities, through courtly extension of the king's time. The everyday theatre of the household now received heightened mechanization from the mental and symbolic rhythms of 'court' time. Its distinctiveness could only have been enhanced by the preference for equal hours, perhaps also by the construction of further lanterns. The power of the king's device depended on its unique association with his person, bathing all actions in continuous Gregorian light.

Surviving artifacts fit seamlessly into this context. The extraordinary Fuller brooch lacks provenance or inscription, yet bears all the hallmarks of royal production.[47] The form was not unusual, as a silver disc-brooch bearing quadripartite bosses; what distinguished the Fuller brooch was its adornment with a sophisticated iconographic scheme, rightly interpreted as the Five Senses. The actions of sensation are conveyed by five youthful male figures. Dominated by the central figure of Sight, they are complemented by sixteen outer roundels, depicting four animate categories: the upper portion of a human, a quadruped, a floral motif and a bird.

The scheme is without precedent in western art; the Senses themselves were widely known from patristic sources, frequently associated with temptation and man's mortal existence. The brooch accorded significance to Sight; its singular treatment is suggestive of philosophical or theological thinking, dominated by the Christian Neo-Platonic metaphor of spiritual vision. Patristic imagery of this kind often accompanied appeal to the 'mind's eyes' (*oculi mentis*), a faculty of spiritual knowledge

---

[45] 'For you kindle my lantern, Lord, my God, lighten up my darkness': *Ps(P)* XVII.27, p. 118 (cf. O'Neill in *Ps(P)*, p. 94). Cf. Matthew V. 15 (cited by Hincmar in MGH Conc. III, no. 41, c. 1, p. 419).
[46] *CP*, p. 4, lines 1–4. [47] *Making of England*, no. 257; Pratt, 'Persuasion', pp. 206–20.

notably favoured by Gregory the Great. The royal translations show sustained interest in this concept, introducing *þa modes eagan* on numerous occasions, beyond the more occasional references in Latin source-texts. The *Soliloquies* offered highly inventive investigation of spiritual perception. Augustine had left the *Soliloquia* unfinished: the royal version effectively 'completes' the work with a new 'Book III', influenced by Augustine's *De uidendo Deo*.[48] Expansions are striking in this framework. When *Ratio* presents the physical senses as inadequate for knowledge of God, the vernacular *Gesceadwisnes* speaks more explicitly of 'outer sensation' (*ðam uttram gewitte*): 'neither eyes, nor ears, nor smell, nor taste, nor touch'.[49] Both figures agree in promising to prepare the soul to 'see God with the eyes of your mind': the translation drew even stronger connection with wisdom, 'the eternal sun', through the exercising of mental virtues (*cræftas*).[50]

The four aspects of creation would be equally explicable here, as examples of shared mortality. An early addition dwells on cycles of death and renewal in nature, even extending to 'men's bodies', showing the eternal quality of resurrection.[51] A later argument asserts the soul's immortality by appeal to 'two eternal creations, that is, angels' and men's souls', endowed by God with eternal gifts.[52] The human busts in the outer roundels would therefore distinguish man's bodily existence from his eternal qualities, shared with angels alone. The treatment of physical sensation would illustrate parallel limits in sensory knowledge, as opposed to the higher qualities of spiritual perception, realizing the gifts of man's eternal soul. The centrality of Sight would show man's potential to acquire divine knowledge or wisdom, however partial in this life, through proper exercise of his 'mind's eyes'.

The coherence of depiction was instructive, rooted in textual understanding. Whether gift or royal possession, the brooch's function was aided by its status as an everyday intimate object, comparable to Alfred's lantern. As an aspect of attire, worn at the shoulder, the brooch offered parallel opportunities for interpersonal reflection, equally dependent on vision and light. Didactic goals receive support from the

---

[48] Below, pp. 321–32.
[49] *Solil* p. 59, lines 5–9. Cf. *Soliloquia* I.iii.8, p. 14, lines 1–3. For the Five Senses, cf. also Alcuin, *De animae ratione*, cc. 8 and 12 (PL 101: 642D and 644D–645A), a text almost certainly known directly in Alfred's circle (c. 8, cf. *Bo* XLII, p. 148, lines 10–12; M. Godden, 'Anglo-Saxons on the Mind', in *Learning and Literature in Anglo-Saxon England: Studies presented to Peter Clemoes*, ed. M. Lapidge and H. Gneuss (Cambridge, 1985), pp. 271–98, at 271–8; cf. below, pp. 323 and 327); and A. Gannon, 'The Five Senses and Anglo-Saxon Coinage', *ASSAH* 13 (2005), 97–104.
[50] *Solil* p. 64, lines 5–8 and p. 78, lines 3–8. Cf. *Soliloquia* I.vi.12, p. 19, lines 18–21 and I.xiii.23, p. 35, lines 5–9.
[51] *Solil* p. 53, lines 17–27. Cf. *Soliloquia* I.i.4, p. 8, lines 1–12.
[52] *Solil* p. 82, lines 14–17, and p. 85, lines 16–19. Cf. *Bo* XL.vii, p. 140, line 30, to p. 141, line 3; XLI.v, p. 146, lines 8–14; XLII, p. 147, line 29, to p. 148, line 2.

role accorded by *Gesceadwisnes* to precious metals; 'unsound eyes' should be directed to gold and silver, then towards fire, before finally the sun.[53] Successful interpretation of the brooch led the observer back to the royal written word, through depiction of man's route to wisdom, playfully situated against sensory gesture. Whether worn by a king's thegn, or on the royal shoulder, the brooch amounted to a central prop within Alfred's personal theatre, demonstrative of royal philosophy.

A third type of object is attested in four examples. Every aspect of the Alfred Jewel suggests intimate royal connections.[54] Alfred's role was proclaimed in the lettering AELFRED MEC HEHT GEWYRCAN ('Alfred ordered me to be made'); the identification is strengthened by the earlier 'Æthelwulf' ring, quite apart from the Jewel's findspot, near Athelney. The Jewel took the form of a reused Roman quartz crystal, offering view to a plaque of cloisonné enamel, bearing the portrait of a seated male figure with blond hair, seemingly holding plant stems. The back reveals a tree-like design on a separate gold plate; the bottom terminates in an animal head of sheet gold, bearing a riveted socket. A close parallel has long been recognized in a second fitting, found at Minster Lovell in Oxfordshire, also executed in gold with enamel.[55]

Discoveries of the 1990s established a stratified corpus. A third fitting, found at Bowleaze Cove, near Weymouth, in Dorset, has dome and socket in gold, but with less lavish decoration.[56] A fourth jewel, found near Warminster in Wiltshire, follows the Alfred Jewel in its reuse of rock crystal; its treatment is closer to the Bowleaze piece, focused on a simple setting of blue glass.[57] A single workshop has generally been suspected for the Alfred and Minster Lovell Jewels: Leslie Webster has extended the case for regarding all four fittings as central products under royal direction.[58] These objects supply remarkable evidence for a new type of portable artifact; the common form is unprecedented in Insular or Continental metalwork, nor are there clear parallels in later Anglo-Saxon production. While the Alfred Jewel has attracted many interpretations, the question must embrace a hierarchy of fittings. Two features were essential: the riveted socket, probably holding a rod of wood or ivory, and the flat back shared by all examples.[59] Arguments for the Alfred Jewel as a book-pointer have often relied on the term *æstel* in the Prose Preface. The

---

[53] *Solil* p. 78, lines 8–23. Cf. *Soliloquia* I.xiii.23, p. 35, line 10, to p. 36, line 15.
[54] *Making of England*, no. 260; Pratt, 'Persuasion', pp. 194–200 and 216–20.
[55] *Making of England*, no. 259.   [56] *Ibid.*, no. 258.
[57] L. Webster, 'Two New Parallels to the Alfred and Minster Lovell Jewels: the Bowleaze and Warminster Jewels', in *'Through a Glass Brightly': Studies presented to David Buckton*, ed. C. Entwhistle (Oxford, forthcoming).
[58] Webster, '*Ædificia nova*', p. 85.   [59] Pratt, 'Persuasion', pp. 197–8.

corpus offers independent support for a delicate handheld device, also capable of being laid flat. The interpretation of *æstel* remains persuasive: each was to be placed 'in' or 'on' the book, without being removed from it; later glosses support the basic meaning 'small spear, pointer'.

The replication of æstels is especially significant given their functional dependence on the written page. The value of æstels lay in their novel function, providing enhanced guidance to the act of reading. Harnessing vision and light to this single purpose, an æstel did not merely aid the eye, but offered intimate demonstration of the relationship between wealth and wisdom. Distributed with the *Hierdeboc*, the gift of an æstel supplied obvious counterpoint to the message of the Prose Preface, of ecclesiastics distracted by abundant wealth. An æstel offered literal direction back to the right 'track', through instructive refashioning of 'treasures'.[60] As the Preface implied, a book-pointer was worthless without books, only magnified by the high cost specified for each æstel, at fifty mancuses.[61] Such a figure could only apply to the more opulent fittings. The surviving sample must represent a small fraction of contemporary models, extending beyond royal and episcopal use to include the secular aristocracy. Here too æstels did not merely dramatize the choice between wealth and wisdom, but encouraged its daily projection at local level, through the personal theatre of reading.

Such effects were enhanced by the iconographic content of individual examples. The complex case of the Alfred Jewel is matched by parallel signification in the Minster Lovell and Warminster pieces, incorporating twofold crosses. The Alfred Jewel has attracted numerous interpretations, but is best approached from the parallels between its male figure and the central field of the Fuller brooch.[62] The askance head and eyes of the jewel's figure must indicate further reference to mental vision, receiving added force from functional deployment against the written page. Yet one should hesistate before identifying him straightforwardly as Sight.[63] Both brooch and jewel must be judged against the ubiquitous use of plant-stems and floral rods in early medieval art, seemingly related to Eastern and Mediterranean models. The brooch's figure bears very close resemblance to an illustrated initial in a tenth-century Beneventan manuscript, probably reflecting a Late Antique image.[64] The jewel's figure may relate more directly to Insular gesture, through the so-called 'Osiris pose' of crossed staffs or rods, familiar from a representation of Christ in the Book of Kells and from Irish high crosses.[65] Webster has

---

[60] *CP*, p. 4, lines 8–18.   [61] *Ibid.*, p. 6, line 24, to p. 8, line 6.
[62] Pratt, 'Persuasion', pp. 200 and 216–20.
[63] Cf. E. Bakka, 'The Alfred Jewel and Sight', '*Antiquaries Journal* 46 (1966), 277–82.
[64] Pratt, 'Persuasion', pp. 218–20.   [65] *Ibid.*, p. 217.

drawn connections between the Alfred Jewel and the lost 'Chosroes Dish', once owned by Charles the Bald, with an image interpreted as Solomon; though compelling, her discussion takes insufficient account of these closer Insular parallels.[66]

Iconography of this kind referred to the flowering rod of Aaron, borne by Christ as eternal priest. First pursued by David Howlett, parallel identification of the jewel's figure would bring suggestive implications of wisdom, through the association with *doctrina et ueritas* on Aaron's breastplate of judgement.[67] The case for Christ is strengthened by the reverse of the jewel, plausibly interpreted as the Tree of Life, a manifestation of wisdom (Proverbs III. 18); and by the animal head beneath, comparable to Christ's triumph 'over asp and viper' (Ps. XC. 13).[68] The crystal would offer extraordinary harmony with the question of God's visibility, seen 'now through a glass darkly (*per speculum in enigmate*), then face to face' (I Corinthians XIII. 12).[69] Solomonic reference is not unlikely in this multivalent context, though could only be subservient to the identity of Christ. The Fuller brooch is again instructive: the prominence of plant stems in both contexts strengthens the likelihood of inventive significance, in the hands of bearers similarly distinguished by the sight of wisdom. Just as each æstel gave substance to Solomonic 'wealth', so Alfredian plant stems made heightened visual reference to worldly advantages and prosperity (*ða woruldsælða*), the undesired consequences of desiring wisdom alone.[70] Both Sight and Christ showed success to depend on inner, mental understanding. The gesture was magnified by the function of the Alfred Jewel, supreme within royal theatre, directing every aspect of reading towards Solomonic re-enactment.

The imagery encapsulates the role of *ædificia*. Not just æstels but all opulent products exemplified the appropriate use of precious resources. Such restrained deployment was justified by their shared function, relentlessly drawing the mind to higher, textual understanding. The intensity of output testifies both to the scale of audience and the extraordinary potency of this personal technology. As 'the greatest treasure-giver of all kings', Alfred's gifts were not merely wise, but invited the continuous exercise of Solomonic desire, heightened by the juxtaposition of books with tangible wealth.[71] *Ædificia* supplied vital connections between royal craftsmanship and burghal construction,

[66] Webster, '*Ædificia nova*', pp. 96–102.
[67] Exodus XXVIII. 4 and XXVIII. 30; Leviticus VIII. 8; D. R. Howlett, 'The Iconography of the Alfred Jewel', *Oxoniensia* 39 (1974), 44–52, at 44–6.
[68] *Ibid.*, pp. 46–7.   [69] Pratt, 'Persuasion', p. 218.
[70] *Ibid.*, p. 220. Cf. below, pp. 281–7 and 300–1.
[71] Yerkes, 'Metrical Preface', p. 513; trans. in K&L, *Alfred*, p. 188.

centrally dependent on aristocratic restraint. Athelney was the site of a royal fortress; Bowleaze Cove lies close to Sutton Poyntz, a prime example of strategic land exchange.[72] Here above all *ædificia* added force to the long-term rewards of burghal income, appropriately secured through wisdom: a message doubly articulated by Alfredian plant-stems. Complementary and interdependent, as tools of lordship, books and *ædificia* gave vital substance to the power of royal *cræft*.

[72] S 347 (BCS 564; *Glastonbury*, ed. Watkin, no. 1165).

Chapter 10

THE *HIERDEBOC* AS A TREATISE OF POWER

The centrality of Gregorian language within Alfredian discourse high-lights the *Hierdeboc*'s significance as a guiding means of 're-education'. Enhanced in translation, Gregory's open-ended treatment of authority informed fundamental assumptions about the role of power. Though directed to episcopal readers, the text's implications extended more widely to present and future participants in power. Gregorian language received further force from its impact on other royal translations. Through reception and wider implementation, the *Hierdeboc* supplied an overarching treatise of contemporary power.[1]

The act of translation must be situated in this context. The fidelity of the king's version, closer to its source than any other royal text, cannot mask its contemporary significance. Royal translation was a gesture of appropriation, mirroring the new relationship between Southumbrian bishops and West Saxon king.[2] Alfred's status as translator simulta-neously reinforced the need for full secular participation. The closeness of translatory treatment reflected not only the directness of Gregory's rhetoric, but his authoritative Southumbrian memory. Yet textual reshaping was not confined to outward presentation: translation deman-ded active engagement with Gregorian thought and language, the more revealing for its focus on rule. The mediation of Gregory was a re-reading through the lens of West Saxon structures, effecting a localized treatment of power.

---

[1] For pertinent earlier studies, cf. Crépin, 'L'importance'; R.W. Clement, 'The Production of the Pastoral Care: King Alfred and his Helpers', in *Studies*, ed. Szarmach, pp. 129–52; N. G. Discenza, 'The Influence of Gregory the Great on the Alfredian Social Imaginary', in *Rome and the North: the Early Reception of Gregory the Great in Germanic Europe*, ed. R. H. Bremmer, K. Dekker and D. F. Johnson (Leuven, 2001), pp. 67–81; Schreiber, *Alfred's Translation*, esp. pp. 11–22; DeGregorio, 'Texts, *topoi*', pp. 87–93.

[2] Cf. above, pp. 139–45.

LANGUAGE AND CONTEXTS

Pope Gregory's deep impact on medieval western Christendom owed much to the character of his pastoral theology. On the subject of power, Gregory's ideas struck a chord with early medieval readers, arising from his own experience of exercising authority, first temporal, then ecclesiastical, in a world which had much in common with later structures.[3] In the fourth and fifth centuries Christianity had been shaped by its relationship to secular culture; by Gregory's time 'the Church had come to swallow up the world', spitting out much of its 'secular' antique inheritance in favour of a culture that was 'radically and almost exclusively scriptural'.[4] At issue was now the best means of saving souls within an ordered community. Integral to Gregory's answer was the role of power, shaping all expected qualities of human agency.

The *Regula pastoralis* offered a comprehensive summary of Gregorian thinking, consistently directed towards practice. Gregory himself conceived the text as a manual for bishops; the timing was also significant, in the first year of Gregory's pontificate (590).[5] Gregorian rhetoric sought to dissuade all but the most securely equipped from accepting such a responsibility, posing grave dangers for the soul. Gregory's recommendations for bishops expressed an internal need for reconciliation to the office which, as later legends would celebrate, he had gone to great lengths to avoid.[6] Earlier in his career, as Prefect of the City of Rome and as a papal representative in Constantinople, Gregory had twice retired to monastic life.[7] The *Regula pastoralis* gave final justification for Gregory's own exercising of authority, informed by his extended career.

Gregory's language further blurred the boundaries between ecclesiastical and temporal. The text was framed as a fourfold process of instruction for anyone coming to the 'summit of rule' (*culmen regiminis*), towards the proper recognition of obligations in living and teaching, guaranteed by the self-regulation of human frailty (*infirmitas*).[8] Gregory's episcopal audience found their duties discussed in deliberately ambiguous language. In addition to the term *rector* ('ruler'), the recipient was barely clarified by his status as *praelatus* ('one placed ahead of others') or *praesul* ('one who directs'), supplemented by the action of *praeesse* ('to be foremost'), exercised over *subditi* or *subiecti* ('subjects').[9] This gave force

---

[3] R. A. Markus, *The End of Ancient Christianity* (Cambridge, 1990), pp. 213–28.
[4] *Ibid.*, p. 225; Markus, *Gregory*, p. 41.
[5] B. Judic, 'Structure et fonction de la Regula Pastoralis', in *Grégoire la Grand*, ed. Fontaine, Gillet and Pellistrandi, pp. 409–17, at 414–17; Judic in *Reg. past.*, pp. 15–22; Markus, *Gregory*, p. 14.
[6] Judic in *Reg. past.*, pp. 16–17, note 3; *Reg. past.* Praef., p. 124, lines 3–5.
[7] Markus, *Gregory*, pp. 8–14 and 20–1.   [8] *Reg. past.*, p. 124, lines 10–19.
[9] Markus, 'Gregory the Great's *rector*', esp. p. 143.

to Gregory's depiction of rulership as an act of service, subverting implications of domination with a framework of care and oversight, as a *pastor* related to his flock.[10] Every aspect of instruction was guided by this recurring juxtaposition. Deployed by Gregory for episcopal benefit, such rhetoric was central to his appeal within early medieval political thinking, extended to secular rulership in normative texts.

The translation must be judged against this dominant rhetoric. 'Hwilum word be worde, hwilum ondgit of andgite': the statement of translatory method repeated a common endorsement of non-literalism, used on a number of occasions by Gregory, and associated with Jerome, understandably influential in medieval translation.[11] The royal corpus would have harnessed a wide range of expertise, not least a high competence in vernacular expression, rooted in learned understanding of text and context. Alfredian posturing bears interesting comparison with Roman attitudes towards translation: in the hands of Cicero and Horace 'non verbum pro verbo' had supplied justification for highly inventive methods of translation, focused on contemporary circumstances of reception, with departures governed by principles of rhetorical *imitatio*.[12] Though implemented most influentially in Jerome's biblical translations, the antithetical model of literalism was provocatively applied to Greek philosophical texts by Boethius and Eriugena.[13] Alfredian preference for flexibility shows the mediatory significance of Jerome's position, whose endorsement of non-literalism for non-biblical texts offered considerable scope for translatory freedom, notionally subservient to the preservation of meaning.[14]

Even in the *Hierdeboc*, royal practice was inventive. Once denigrated as 'unadorned' and 'undistinguished', royal methods have received important revision through comparison with the *Dialogues* and the Old English Bede.[15] Whereas the latter are often quite literal, borrowing or respecting the sentence structures of their source-texts, Bately characterizes the *Hierdeboc* as translation 'sentence by sentence', reliant on syntactical and stylistic rearrangement to achieve clear and balanced prose.[16] Similar processes can be observed at macro-level, in the choice of terms relating to authority. On the one hand, the application of the text became more explicit. Whereas *episcopus* appears rarely in the Latin

---

[10] Markus, 'The Latin Fathers', pp. 119–20.
[11] A. S. Cook, 'Alfred's "Word for Word" Translation', *The Academy* 30 (1886), 108; K&L, *Alfred*, p. 259 (note 164); Copeland, *Rhetoric*, pp. 47–51. For Jerome's Alfredian significance, cf. above, p. 141.
[12] Copeland, *Rhetoric*, pp. 28–35.   [13] *Ibid.*, pp. 48–53.   [14] *Ibid.*, pp. 48–51.
[15] W. H. Brown, 'Method and Style in the Old English Pastoral Care', *Journal of English and Germanic Philology* 68 (1969), 666–84, at 678; Bately, 'Old English Prose', pp. 118–27, esp. 126, note 191.
[16] *Ibid.*, pp. 125–7.

text, *praesul* and *pastor* are frequently rendered as *bisceop*, together with *bisceopdom* and *bisceophad* for the corresponding office of responsibility.[17] The implications of *magisterium* are extended through common use of *lareow* ('teacher', 'preacher') as one variant for Gregory's *rector*, matched by *lareowdom* ('office of teaching') as a substitute for *regimen*.[18]

Yet royal language was rarely unqualified, transcending the mere reproduction of Gregorian rhetoric to acquire special overtones from vernacular terminology. *Rector* is also translated as *reccere*, with *reccendom* for *regimen*; these mingle with terms redolent of the West Saxon order.[19] *Ealdorman* receives striking deployment as a variant for *rector* and *prae-positus*, paired with *ealdordom* ('office of leader').[20] Notions of respon-sibility are enhanced by *scir* ('charge', 'shire') and *scirmenn* ('men with a charge'), replacing *praepositi*.[21] Service acquires immediate overtones from *ðegnung*, the regular equivalent of *ministerium* and *officium*.[22] *Subditi* and *subiecti* find suggestive treatment in *hieremenn*, which could also mean 'retainers'.[23] The elaborate intensification of Gregorian effects combined with a broader resituating of Gregorian rhetoric, within the linguistic framework of West Saxon power. The overall effect accords closely with the *Hierdeboc*'s distribution, but also with the wider appli-cation of Gregorian language, to secular office-holders and the king.

THE ORIGIN AND PURPOSE OF POWER

Such West Saxon language has implications for the force of Gregory's message in royal hands. Gregorian rhetoric focused attention on the precise function of earthly power (*potestas*), in conceptual discussion

---

[17] *Reg. past.* I.7, pp. 150–6 (*episcopus*); *CP* XII, p. 74, line 3; XVIII, p. 128, line 10; XVIII, p. 132, line 3 (*bisceop* for *praesul*); IX, p. 58, line 22 (*bisceophad* for *praesul*); XI, p. 73, line 22 (*bisceopdom* for *pastorale magisterium*); XVI, p. 104, lines 7 and 9 (*bisceop* for *pastor*). Cf. *Reg. past.* II.1, lines 3–4, p. 174; I.9, line 48, p. 160; I.11, line 123, p. 172; II.5, lines 72–3, p. 200.

[18] *CP* XIII, p. 74, line 18; XIV, p. 80, line 1; XV, p. 88, line 3. Cf. *Reg. past.* II.2, line 1, p. 176; II.3, line 1, p. 180; II.4, line 1, p. 186. *CP* II, p. 28, lines 19–20 (*lareowdom* for *locus regiminis*); III, p. 32, line 7 (*lareowdom* for *regimen*). Cf. *Reg. past.* I.2, line 1, p. 132; I.3, line 4, p. 136.

[19] *CP* XIII, p. 74, line 19; XVI, p. 102, line 7; XVII, p. 106, line 5. Cf. *Reg. past.* II.2, line 2, p. 176; II.5, line 50, p. 198; II.6, line 1, p. 202. *CP* III, p. 32, line 4; IV, p. 36, line 11. Cf. *Reg. past.* I.3, line 1, p. 136; I.4, line 1, p. 140.

[20] *CP* V, p. 40, line 9; IX, p. 58, line 18 (*ealdordom* for *regimen*); XVII, p. 106, line 8 (*ealdorman* for *rector*); XVII, p. 116, lines 11–12 (*ealdorman* for *praepositus*). Cf. *Reg. past.* I.5, line 1, p. 144; I.9, line 43, p. 160; II.6, line 3, p. 202; II.6, line 114, p. 210.

[21] *CP* X, p. 60, line 11; XV, p. 90, line 21; XVII, p. 122, line 1 (*scir*); *CP* XVII, p. 108, line 18; XXI, p. 152, line 24 (*scirmenn*). Cf. *Reg. past.* II.6, line 32, p. 204; II.10, lines 41–2, p. 240.

[22] *CP* VII, p. 46, line 20; XIII, p. 74, line 20 (*ðegnung* for *officium*); XVII, p. 120, line 18 (*ðegnung* for *ministerium*). Cf. *Reg. past.* I.7, line 1, p. 150; II.2, line 3, p. 176; II.6, line 162, p. 214.

[23] *CP* I, p. 28, line 5; X, p. 62, line 19; XIII, p. 78, line 15. Cf. *Reg. past.* I.1, line 40, p. 132; I.10, line 39, p. 164; II.2, lines 46–7, p. 180.

fully integrated with practice. The translation implies sustained engagement with this Gregorian teaching. The main effect was a bold refashioning of Gregory's universal treatment of power to construct a new and potent language of West Saxon office-holding, sensitive to the realities of Alfredian rule.

Gregory's central depiction of rulership as an act of service drew on a framework which he had earlier developed in his *Moralia in Iob*.[24] The *Moralia* is explicitly quoted in part II, chapter 6, concerned with the ruler's obligations to be 'a companion to those acting well', and 'rigid against the vices of sinners'. All men are born equal by nature, 'but by the varying order of merits, sin esteems some less than others'. Men cease to be equal only as a result of their own sins: 'but this diversity which has proceeded from vice is ordered by divine judgement, so that because each man cannot stand equally, one is ruled by another'.[25] The Gregorian universe is under constant direction from God, guiding the distribution of earthly power in accordance with its purpose. The most meritorious receive power as a remedy for others; their aim in ruling should be to eradicate sin, reinforcing the fear of divine judgement. Necessary virtues (*uirtutes*) are similarly distributed by divine gift, and must be exercised intensively if the goal of power is to be even partially realized.

The purpose of power supplies the basis for Gregory's account of rightful rule. Rulers should not be pleased to *praeesse* ('to be foremost') over other men, but to *prodesse* ('benefit') them: action will vary greatly according to their individual circumstances. It is here that Gregory presents rulership as a skill or art (*ars*), involving continuous judgement over the gravest matters of responsibility: 'the rule of souls is the art of all arts'.[26] The scope of judgement is captured by the Gregorian metaphor of physicianship. A sinner will need quite different treatment from that required by good men. Power has its origin in present-day sins; it should therefore be wielded only insofar as these sins have disrupted the natural equality which still exists among good men.[27] The ruler should 'consider himself equal to those of his subjects who live rightly', yet sinners should be ruled with fear, as the wild beasts whom they imitate.[28] Such judgement supports the ruler's flexible admonition of subjects, systematically delineated in part III, so that by soothing or chastisement, discipline or mercy, sinners are corrected and the good encouraged.[29]

---

[24] *Moralia in Iob* XXI.xv.22–4, ed. Adriaen, CCSL 143, 143A and 143B, 1081–3; Markus, 'The Latin Fathers', pp. 120–1, for Gregory's distinctive reading of *De civitate Dei* XIX.15.
[25] *Reg. past.* II.6, lines 9–14, pp. 202–4.
[26] '[A]rs est artium regimen animarum': I.1, lines 4–5, p. 128.   [27] II.6, lines 14–17, p. 204.
[28] II.6, lines 1–8 and 28–37, pp. 202 and 204.
[29] II.5, pp. 196–202; II.6, pp. 202–18; II.10, pp. 238–52; III.1–35, pp. 263–518.

The treatment of power supports the stress on humility as a fundamental quality of rulership. The difficulties of Gregorian rulership stems from the equivocal status of worldly involvement, as a source of temptation incompatible with the ruler's true goals. Power brings heightened dangers of sin, not only from wider responsibilities but from internal threats posed by the desire of ruling (*libido dominandi*).[30] The ruler must rule himself: even a wise ruler runs the risk of accepting praise for these qualities, inflating his mind in pride (*superbia*).[31] The proud ruler is pictured looking scornfully on good men, preferring his own delight (*delectatio*) to those benefits that he should be providing for his subjects.[32] '[H]e rules power well, who knows how both to keep it and fight it': the good ruler is locked in constant struggle to remain equal with the good, while correcting the sinful.[33] Every aspect of Gregory's advice relates to the struggle to reconcile effective rulership with continuing humility. It may even be necessary for the ruler to regard himself as secretly equal to the sinners that he corrects.[34] Yet this must be balanced against the *disciplina* necessary for the correction of sinners.[35]

It is here that the secular language of translation reaches its fullest intensity. Previous chapters are dominated by the *lareow* and the *hierde* ('shepherd'); now *ealdorman* and *ealdordom* are introduced as the equivalent of Gregory's *rector*. Clearly, to some extent such language adapted Gregorian rhetoric, stressing to bishops the subversion of conventional authority. Yet the heightened secularity of the vernacular also suggests wider application of these principles. *Cyning* is only rarely employed, largely restricted to biblical examples already cited by Gregory.[36] A rare omission may indicate a concern not to exclude kings from this chapter's implications. 'Antiqui etenim patres nostri non reges hominum, sed pastores pecorum fuisse memorantur': the vernacular reports only 'ðæt ure ealdan fædras wæron ceapes hierdas', avoiding Gregory's explicit denial of the existence of kingship in deepest antiquity.[37]

The vernacular chapter emerges as a comprehensive treatment of *anweald* ('power') and *rice* ('rule'), tailor-made for West Saxon conditions.

---

[30] II.6, pp. 210–12; cf. I.8, pp. 154–6.   [31] II.6, lines 38–45, p. 206.

[32] II.6, lines 48–51 and 143–6, pp. 206 and 212.

[33] '[P]otentiam bene regit, qui et tenere illam nouerit et impugnare': II.6, lines 77–8, p. 208.

[34] II.6, lines 114–20 and 161–3, pp. 210 and 214.   [35] II.6, lines 163–7, p. 214.

[36] *CP* III, p. 32, lines 11–20 (Christ); III, p. 34, lines 14–20 (Saul); III, p. 36, lines 3–7 (David); IV, p. 38, lines 2–5 (Hezekiah); IV, p. 38, lines 13–18 (Nebuchadnezzar). Cf. *Reg. past.* I.3, lines 8–19, pp. 136–8; I.3, lines 32–6, p. 138; I.3, lines 42–4, p. 140; I.4, lines 17–20, p. 142; I.4, lines 28–39, p. 142.

[37] 'For our ancient fathers are remembered to have been not kings of men, but pastors of flocks/ cattle': *Reg. past.* II.6, lines 18–19, p. 204. 'Behold, it is said that our ancient fathers were pastors of cattle': *CP* XVII, p. 108, lines 4–5; Crépin, 'L'importance', pp. 584–5.

The dangers of desire and temptation are reinforced by rich language of control and excess. Multiple *undeawas* ('vices') and *oliccunga* ('flatteries') are united by implications of excessive and unrestrained desire. So deceived, the ruler beomes 'raised up above himself in his mind': 'when he is surrounded externally by immoderate praise (*mid ungemetlicre heringe*), he is internally deprived of righteousness'.[38] Vices threaten through the tempting of desire: 'Let those who are over others take care earnestly that the greater their power is seen to be over other men, the more they are restrained inwardly by humility ... lest the mind, afflicted by the desire (*lustfulnes*) of power is drawn to pride'.[39] Pride bears the imprint of excess in royal preference for *ofermetto*, together with related variants *ofermodgung* and *oferhygd*, extended to other parts of speech by *ofermodgian*, *ofermod* and *ofermodlice*.[40] Such effects are complemented by the alternative *upahæfennes*, with verbs *upahebban* ('to raise up') and *aðindan* ('to inflate') echoing imagery of elevation and swelling.[41] The handling of pride only strengthens the positive effects of *eaðmodnes* ('humility'), repeatedly associated with *gemetgung* ('moderation').[42] Moderation emerges as a vital attribute, also conveyed by the adjective *ungemetlic*, expressing the many balances that the ruler must maintain towards his subjects.[43]

Continuity of self-regulation is encapsulated by the royal handling of virtue, regularly conveyed by *cræft*. The term's significance extended beyond artefactual production to every aspect of appropriate behaviour, an essential quality of rightful rule. As Clemoes showed, royal usage was distinctive in preferring *cræft* to *mægen* ('manly strength'), used for virtue in the Mercian *Dialogues* and Bede.[44] As such, it may be an unusual borrowing from vernacular poetry. In *Elene* and *Guthlac A* and *B*, *cræft* is a moral and spiritual force granted by God, extending to such compounds as *snyttrucræft* ('wisdom-craft'), *modcræft* ('mind-craft') and *leornungcræft*.[45] *The Gifts of Men* places the diversity of human *cræftas* within a moral order

---

[38] *CP* XVII, p. 110, lines 6–9. Cf. *Reg. past.* II.6, lines 44–6, p. 206.

[39] 'Ða þe ofer oðre bioð giemen he geornlice ðætte swæ micle swæ hiera anwald bið mara gesewen ofer oðre menn ðæt hie swae micle ma sie innan geðrycte mid eaðmodnesse ... ðætte ðæt ofsetene mod mid ðære lustfulnesse his onwaldes ne sie getogen to upahæfenesse': *CP* XVII, p. 118, lines 13–21. Cf. *Reg. past.* II.6, lines 136–42, p. 212.

[40] *CP* VII, p. 50, line 3; VII, p. 50, line 12; XVII, p. 108, lines 12–13; XVII, p. 108, line 18; XVII, p. 110, line 1; XVII, p. 110, line 23. Cf. *Reg. past.* I.7, line 28, p. 152; I.7, line 36, p. 152; II.6, lines 27–8, p. 204; II.6, lines 32–3, p. 204; II.6, line 39, p. 206; II.6, line 57, p. 206.

[41] *CP* XVII, p. 110, line 9; XVII, p. 110, line 1; XVII, p. 118, lines 20–1. Cf. *Reg. past.* II.6, lines 44–5, p. 206; II.6, line 39, p. 206; II.6, lines 140–2, p. 212.

[42] *CP* XVII, p. 112, lines 16–18. Cf. *Reg. past.* II.6, lines 72–5, p. 208.

[43] *CP* XVII, p. 124, lines 13–16. Cf. *Reg. past.* II.6, lines 198–201, p. 216.

[44] Clemoes, 'King Alfred's Debt', esp. pp. 223–5; Discenza, 'Power, Skill and Virtue', pp. 87–8 and 93–4.

[45] Clemoes, 'King Alfred's Debt', pp. 213–15.

sensitive to the dangers of pride.[46] Divine distribution extends to the *beadocræftig* warrior, the *searocræftig* jeweller, the *modcræftig smið*, and the horseman *wicgcræfta wis* ('wise in horse-crafts'); yet each is of similar value to God, fearing the effects of greater 'wisdom-craft' in any individual.

The value of *cræft* lay in its ability to connect moral power with continuous expertise, with additional implications of physical construction. Gregorian *ars* and *uirtus* were fused to create a single quality of rulership, established by divine gift but open to improvement through learning and practice. The *Hierdeboc* became a source of such training. Gregory's prefatory letter is slightly recast to include reference to *ðone cræft ðæs lareowdomes* ('the craft of the office of teaching'); the Latin *ars artium* receives novel force as the *cræft ealra cræfta* ('craft of all crafts').[47] The effect was sharpened by the letter's criticism of those who wish to be teachers, 'ðeah þe hi næfre leorningcnihtas næren' ('although they were never disciples').[48] 'But many are honoured with great gifts of many powers and virtues (*monegra mægena and cræfta*), because they ought to teach many, and they receive such gifts in order to help other men': *cræftas* also retain their status as gifts of God, with obligations of teaching and care.[49] The great danger is that rulers grow presumptuous of their special *cræftas*, exalting themselves in over-confidence and pride.[50] The dynamic interrelationship between *cræft* and learning only enhanced the force of Gregory's advice.

The universality of *cræft* receives special weight. A single instance of *dux* prompts extended deployment of secular language, in a catena of biblical quotations focused on pride:

Be ðæm wæs swiðe ryhte gecweden ðurh sumne wisne monn, he cwæð to ðæm oðrum: 'To ealdormenn ðu eart gesett, ne bio ðu ðeah to upahæfen, ac bio swelce an ðinra hieremonna' (Ecclesiasticus XXXII. 1) ... Be ðæm ilcan eft sio Soðfæstnes, ðæt is Crist, ðurh hiene selfne cwæð ... : 'Wiete ge ðætte ðeoda kyningas beoð ðæs folces waldendas, and ða þe ðone onwald begað hie beoð hlafurdas gehatene; ne sie hit ðonne no swæ betweoxn eow, ac swæ hwelc swæ wille betweoxn eow fyrmest beon, se sceal bion eower ðegn, and swæ hwelc swæ wille betweoxn eow mæst beon, sie se eower ðeow' (Matthew XX. 25–7).[51]

---

[46] *Ibid.*, pp. 230–1.   [47] *CP* I, p. 24, lines 15–18. Cf. *Reg. past.* I.1, lines 2–5, p. 128.

[48] *CP*, p. 24, lines 7–13. Cf. *Reg. past.* Praef., lines 27–34, p. 126.

[49] *CP* V, p. 40, lines 11–13. Cf. *Reg. past.* I.5, lines 3–5, p. 144.

[50] *CP* LXV, p. 463, lines 26–8. Cf. *Reg. past.* IV, lines 31–2, p. 536.

[51] 'About this it was very rightly said by a certain wise man, who said to another: "You are established as ealdorman, yet may you not be raised up, but be as one of your retainers" ... About this same matter Truth, that is Christ, through himself said ... : "Know that kings of nations are rulers of the people, and those who exercise power are called lords; may it not be so among you, but whosoever desires to be foremost among you, let him be your thegn, and whosoever desires to be greatest among you, let him be your servant" ': *CP* XVII, p. 118, line 22 to p. 120, line 7. 'Ducem te constituerunt, noli extolli, sed esto in illis quasi unus ex illis ... Hinc per semetipsam Veritas ... dicit: Scitis quia principes gentium dominantur eorum, et qui

Ealdorman, kings, lords: unusually loose translation enables the inclusion of three holders of secular power, all subject to Gregorian service. Yet their authority is not the same. Further expansion contrasts the positions of ealdorman and lord:

And swæðeah oft agyltað ða ealdormenn efnswiðe on ðæm þe he bið to eaðmod ðæm yflan monnum, and læt hiene him to gelicne, and licet wið hie ma geferrædenne ðonne ealdordome. Swiðe ryhte se bið geteald to ðæm licetterum se þe on lareowes onlicnesse ða ðenunga ðæs ealdordomes gecirð to hlaforddome, and gemacað ðæt his ege and his onwald wyrð to gewunan and to landsida on his scire. Ond ðeah hwilum giet swiður hie syngiað on ðæm þe hie healdað ma geferrædenne and efnlicnesse ðonne ealdordom wið ða yflan and ða unryhtwisan.[52]

The position of ealdorman here becomes the dominant example of Gregorian rulership, in terms indicative of West Saxon conditions. The temptations of power are likened to the transformation of *ealdordom* ('office of leader') to *hlaforddom* ('office of lord'), deceitful appropriation of an archetypal position of responsibility. *Scir* is exploited in the image of fear widening *to landsida* ('as a territorial custom'); the alternative danger of *geferræden* ('fellowship') with evil-doers harnesses language of thegnly companionship. The analogy was more than instructive, acquiring force in the immediate context of royal 'persuasion', dominated by notions of service and the effective mobilization of subjects. *Ealdordom*, as a royal office, adds irony in this ostensibly episcopal context.

The need for humility was never far from kingship. The handling of biblical rulers reinforced humble aspects of Alfred's personal theatre.[53] The story of Nebuchadnezzar and Babylon receives notable elaboration as an example of pride, related to 'the great work and beauty of the city (*ceastre*)' and its inner, mental effects.[54] Nebuchadnezzar had been 'very

---

maiores sunt, potestatem exercent in eos. Non ita erit inter uos, sed quicumque uoluerit inter uos maior fieri, sit uester minister; et qui uoluerit inter uos primus esse, erit uester seruus': *Reg. past.* II.6, lines 145–53, pp. 212–14.

[52] 'And yet ealdormen often do wrong equally greatly inasmuch as he may be too humble to evil men, and consider himself as equal to them, and feign more a fellowship with them than the office of leader. Very rightly is he accounted as a deceiver who in the similitude of a teacher turns the ministry of the office of leader to the office of lord, and causes his power and fear of him to become as a habit and a territorial custom in his shire. And yet sometimes they sin yet more in that they maintain more a fellowship and an equality than the office of leader towards the evil and the unrighteous': *CP* XVII, p. 120, line 20, to p. 122, line 3. 'Inter hypocritas enim iure deputatur, qui ex simulatione disciplinae ministerium regiminis uertit in usu dominationis; et tamen nonnumquam grauius delinquitur si inter peruersos plus aequalitas quam disciplina custoditur': *Reg. past.* II.6, lines 161–5, p. 214.

[53] Above, pp. 170–8.

[54] *CP* IV, p. 38, lines 13–19. Cf. *Reg. past.* I.4, lines 28–39, p. 142 (T2 text, but translation closer to T1 in Clement, 'Two Contemporary Gregorian Editions', p. 92).

raised up in his mind as a result of his power and his chance success'.[55]
His loss of worldly rule (*worldrice*) and punishment among beasts is more
fully explained as an extension of self-deceit:

Se ilca se þe wende þæt he wære ofer ealle oðre men, him gebyrede þæt he
nysse self ðæt he man wæs. Swaðeah ... ne tæle ic na micel weorc ne ryhtne
onwald, ac ic tæle þæt hine mon forðy upahebbe on his mode; and þa
untrymnesse hira heortan ic wolde getrymman and gestiran ðære wilnunge
ðæm unmedemum, þæt hira nan ne durre gripan swæ orsorglice on ðæt rice
and ðone lareowdom ... .[56]

The conclusions drawn succinctly summarize the dangers of desire. Saul
similarly supplies instruction as a ruler rising through humility, only to
be cast down for pride.[57] 'Because he perceived that he could do more
than any other man, he supposed that he was also greater than any man':
the translation again focuses on self-deception.[58]

Lessons of divine assistance for the humble are further clarified by the
treatment of David. *Earfoðu* ('hardships') must be seen as beneficial,
granted by God as a reminder of the ruler's *untrymnes* ('infirmity'),
providing inducement to humility, as opposed to the dangers of *orsorgnes*
('freedom from care', translating *prospera*).[59] 'In prosperity (*gesuntfulnes*)
the mind becomes raised up; and in hardships, even if it had previously
been raised up, it is humbled'.[60] David's exemplification of both is
enhanced by language of royal lordship. His forbearance in declining to
slay Saul is cast against a background of harsh exile (*wræc*) and former
loyalty (*treow*).[61] 'Shameless desire' lies at the heart of David's pride in
the slaying of Uriah, 'for ðære scamleaslican gewilnunge his wifes'; the
crime is magnified by Uriah's status as his faithful 'ðegn'. David was
protected from complete downfall only by the return of further 'toils
and hardships'. His humility remains isolated from Nathan's rebuke, in

---

[55] ' ... swiðe upahæfen on his mode for his onwalde and for his gelimpe': *CP* IV, p. 38, line 14.

[56] 'To the same man who thought he was above all other men, it happened that he did not know
himself whether he was a man. Nevertheless ... I do not reproach great work nor right power,
but I reproach that a man raises himself up in his mind as a result; and I would like to strengthen
the weakness of their hearts and restrain the desire of the unfit, so that none of them dares to
seize so freely from care onto the rule and the office of teaching ... ': *CP* IV, p. 38, line 25, to
p. 40, line 6. Cf. *Reg. past.* I.4, lines 44–50, pp. 142–4.

[57] *CP* XVII, p. 112, lines 5–18. Cf. *Reg. past.* II.6, lines 64–75, pp. 206–8.

[58] 'Forðy he ongeat ðæt he ma meahte ðonne ænig oðer, ða wende he ðæt he eac mara wære': *CP*
XVII, p. 112, lines 14–15.

[59] *CP* LXV, p. 465, lines 30–3. Cf. *Reg. past.* IV, lines 64–66, p. 538.

[60] 'On ðæm gesuntfulnessum ðæt mod wirð upahæfen; and on ðæm earfeðum, ðeah hit ær
upahæfen wære, hit bið geeaðmeded': *CP* III, p. 34, lines 4–6. Cf. *Reg. past.* I.3, lines 24–6,
p. 138.

[61] *CP* III, p. 34, line 20 to p. 36, line 10, trans. in K&L, *Alfred*, pp. 127–8. Cf. *Reg. past.* I.3, lines
36–46, pp. 138–40, with I Kings XXIV. 1–23 and II Kings XI. 1–27.

contrast to the extensive Carolingian deployment of this incident, especially under Charles the Bald.[62] The image was depicted in ivory on the front cover of Charles's psalter, reliant on Gregorian and biblical exempla.[63] As a tool of sacerdotal admonition, Nathan's role was bound to be limited, in discourse associated with faithful priestly service.[64]

Further expansion emerges on evil rulers, potentially problematic in a framework attributing power to present-day sins. Much of Gregory's rhetoric hinged on the potentially disastrous effects of shortcomings among those who rule.[65] Not only is the ruler subject to greater temptations, but his sins will bring greater divine punishment, setting a bad example for his subjects.[66] Bad rulers do not receive divine support, but are only permitted and tolerated by God, bearing a relationship to their subjects' sins.[67] Gregory's explanation is unusually oblique: 'The ignorance of shepherds doubtless frequently fits the merits of their subjects; for although the former do not have the light of knowledge through their own sin, nevertheless it is enacted with strict judgement that through their ignorance those who follow also offend'.[68] The translation is more categorical:

Unwise lareowas cumað for ðæs folces synnum. Forðon oft for ðæs lareowas unwisdome misfarað þa hiremen, and oft for ðæs lareowes wisdome unwisum hiremonnum bið geborgen.[69]

Explanations of bad rulership were common among Continental writers, often employing Gregory or Isidore to suggest divine toleration or instrumental punishment, yet in royal hands such theorizing reflected the dynamics of Alfredian rule.[70] The translation incorporated 'unwisdom': this imagery held special force amid concerted criticism of officeholders for their loss of wisdom.[71] Rulership over sin was implicated in the struggle to mobilize manpower, described by Asser; its terms were

---

[62] Deshman, 'Exalted Servant', pp. 406–7; *RC* 12, p. 54.

[63] Deshman, 'Exalted Servant', pp. 404–12 and figs. 17–18.

[64] See *CP* XIX, p. 144, lines 18–20, where the prophet is David's 'own thegn'. Cf. *Reg. past.* II.8, lines 49–50, p. 234.

[65] *Reg. past.* I.1–5 and 11, pp. 128–48 and pp. 252–6. [66] I.2, lines 37–43, p. 136.

[67] I.1, lines 208, p. 130.

[68] 'Quae nimirum pastorum saepe imperitia meritis congruit subiectorum; qui quamuis lumen scientiae sua culpa exigente non habeant, destricto tamen iudicio agitur, ut per eorum ignorantiam hi etiam qui sequuntur offendant': I.1, lines 39–43, p. 132.

[69] 'Unwise teachers come on account of the people's sins. For often as a result of the teacher's unwisdom his subjects transgress, and often as a result of the teacher's wisdom, unwise subjects are spared': *CP* I, p. 28, lines 3–6.

[70] *DIR* 3 and 7, pp. 196 and 218; Hincmar, *De regis persona*, c. 1, PL 125: 834C–835A; Anton, *Fürstenspiegel*, pp. 296–8.

[71] *VA* 106, lines 28–36; *ASC* s.a. 874.

further clarified by the *Domboc*.[72] The protective role of 'wise teachers', additionally stressed in the passage, matched the urgent need for co-operation under the pressures of attack.

Yet opposition to a sinful ruler is denied. Gregory's advice offered overarching commitment to divine order, again shaped by sin. If subjects make heedless judgement against their ruler's actions, they place their own rectitude at risk to the swelling of pride.[73] David's refusal to smite Saul is presented as archetypal of behaviour by good subjects under evil rulers.[74] David's heart struck him even for cutting off the border of Saul's cloak: even the humblest criticism would be a derogation of due dignity.[75] Argument returns to the purpose of power: 'when we sin against men placed foremost (*praepositis*), we go against the order of him who put them foremost over us'.[76] The translation shows notable flexibility: the heading announces the admonishing of ealdormen and subjects (*ealdormen* – *hieremenn*), while the text applies Gregory's defence to lords and servants (*hlafordas* – *þeowas*): ' . . . forðæm ðonne we agyltað wið ða hlafordas, ðonne agylte we wið ðone God þe hlafordscipe gescop'.[77] There was no inherent tension: the shift to lordship was effected through David's example, enhanced as a story of loyalty.[78] Lordship was similarly defended in Alfred's *Domboc*: both statements drew their force from conditions otherwise threatening to local bonds. In the following chapter, *hlafordscipe* was connected with service: its negative treatment always involved contrast with the additional obligations of rulership.[79] Royal language reflected the complementary roles of *hlafordscipe* and *ealdordom* at the heart of West Saxon power.

THE ACTIVE AND CONTEMPLATIVE LIVES

The difficulties inherent in Gregorian rulership were further intensified by royal use of *cræft*. As fundamental attribute for ruling, *cræft* brought temptations towards pride; as continuous expertise, it highlighted the challenges of human judgement. The effect was only to enhance the

---

[72] *VA* 91, lines 25–72.   [73] *Reg. past.* III.4, lines 72–5, p. 280.   [74] III.4, lines 88–90, p. 280.
[75] III.4, lines 97–102, p. 282.
[76] 'Nam cum praepositis delinquimus, eius ordini qui eos nobis praetulit obuiamus': III.4, lines 113–14, p. 282.
[77] ' . . . for when we sin against lords, we sin against God who created lordship': CP XXVIII, p. 200, lines 2–3.
[78] 'Hwæt tacnað us ðonne Saul buton yfle hlafordas? Oððe hwæt Dauid buton gode ðeowas?' ('What then does Saul symbolize for us unless evil lords? Or what David unless good servants?'): CP XXVIII, p. 196, lines 22–3.
[79] See esp. CP XVII, p. 118, lines 2–7 (discussed above), and XIX, p. 142, line 24 to p. 145, line 3. Cf. *Reg. past.* II.6, lines 149–54, pp. 212–14, and II.8, lines 32–5, p. 232.

value of Gregory's advice, as an outline of successful rulership focused on thought and behaviour. *Cræft* hinged on the appropriate resolution of inner tensions, in an all-encompassing approach to the practice of power, ideally suited to West Saxon structures.

Gregory's approach to rulership reflected his own career, pursued between two ideals, the contemplative life dedicated to God and the active life of dutiful work in the world.[80] The struggle did not end with Gregory's papal appointment but received reassessment, as the desirable and necessary means of living a holy life in an imperfect world. The *Regula pastoralis* presented Gregory's acceptance of office as the starting-point for authoritative fulfilment of both ideals. The balancing of action and contemplation supplied an overarching means of preventing the sins of others, while guarding against the ruler's own sins. Gregory discusses the two lives most fully when justifying acceptance of the office of preaching. The active life is epitomized by Isaiah, who desired to preach to others; the contemplative life by Jeremiah, who refused to preach in favour of divine meditation. Each placed greater weight on one of Christ's two injunctions, Isaiah desiring to benefit (*prodesse*) his neighbours through action, Jeremiah seeking the love of God alone.[81] Yet both reached balance in their ministry: Isaiah desired the active life because he knew he had been purged; Jeremiah ultimately accepted God's command.[82] Both examples converge in upholding the twofold fulfilment of Christ's injunctions, and humble acceptance of worldly office when appropriately offered.

The translation shows sensitive treatment of this balancing-act. Though *activa uita* and *contemplatiua uita* are not rendered literally, the vernacular highlights the harmony of Christ's twofold forms of love:

For ðære lufan Isaias wilnode hu he nyttost meahte beon his nihstum on ðys eorðlican life, and forðon he wilnode ðære ðegnunga ðæs lareowdomes. Ieremias ðonne wilnode singallice hine geðidan to ðære lufan his scippendes, and forðæm he forcwæð, and nolde ðæt hiene mon sende to læronne.[83]

This continues in the handling of *contemplatio* and *actio*. Occasionally paraphrased, the former is generally rendered as *sceawung* or *foresceawung*; *actio* is regularly translated as *weorc*.[84] Active and contemplative are

---

[80] Markus, *Gregory*, pp. 8–26; Evans, *Gregory*, pp. 19–25, 80 and 105–9.

[81] Matthew XXII. 36–40; Mark XII. 28–31; *Reg. past.* I.7, lines 13–20, pp. 150–2.

[82] *Ibid.* I.7, lines 24–9, p. 152.

[83] 'Out of love, Isaiah desired to be the most useful to his neighbours in this earthly life, and therefore he sought the ministry of the office of teaching. Yet Jeremiah desired always to subject himself to the love of his Creator, and therefore refused, and did not wish to be sent to teach'; *CP* VII, p. 48, lines 16–18. Cf. *Reg. past.* I.7, lines 18–20, pp. 150–2.

[84] *CP* V, p. 44, line 18 (*smeaung*); XI, p. 64, line 6 (*sceawung*); XVI, p. 96, line 21 (*foreðencende*); XVI, p. 96, line 24 (*foresceawung*); XVI, p. 98, line 24 (*sceawung*); XVI, p. 100, line 14 and line 25. Cf.

otherwise explored through a range of contrasts, between *alta* and *infima*, *celestia* and *carnalia*, *interna* and *exteriora*, or *spiritalia* and *exteriora*, each to be tempered or combined.[85] In things *hiehst* and *nyðemest*, *hefonlic* and *flæsclic*, *innera* and *utera*, *gæstlic* and *eorðlic*, the vernacular reproduces Gregory's balance.[86]

The ideals receive detailed treatment in part II, chapter 5, where the ruler must be 'a neighbour to each in compassion, elevated above all in contemplation', a conduit by which knowledge of the celestial is transmitted to the weak and carnal aspects of his neighbours.[87] Thus Paul contemplated the secrets of the third heaven, but applied his knowledge to the secrets of weak men.[88] Jacob saw angels ascending and descending, and Moses frequently entered and left the tabernacle: preachers should contemplate the Lord, but then descend to the problems of men.[89] The vernacular chapter is introduced with reference to the *lareow*: other evidence suggests wider application to all bound 'mid ðære lufan Godes and monna ægðer ge to ðæm hihstum ðingum ge to ðæm niðemestum'.[90] Moses was especially pertinent, drawn out of the tabernacle by the 'people's need': 'and ðærute he wæs abisgod ymb ðæs folces ðearfe'.[91] Alfred's anxiety at his illness lay in the fear that he be rendered useless 'both in heavenly and worldly affairs'; similar concerns extended to the king's conspicuous divisions of revenues and time.[92] Nobles in general were criticized by Asser for inclining their minds more to secular than to divine affairs.[93] The needs of men acquired sharper definition amid defensive mobilization, Alfred's West Saxon version of 'common benefit'.

The balance is further clarified in part II, chapter 5, 'that the ruler should not diminish his care of internal things when occupied by external things, nor abandon his foresight of external things when concerned with internal things'.[94] Excessive devotion to either concern

---

Reg. past. I.5, line 48, p. 148; II.5, line 2, p. 196; I.11, line 13, p. 164; II.5, line 4, p. 196; II.5, line 23, p. 198; II.5, lines 36 and 45, p. 198. *CP* XI, p. 70, line 8; XII, p. 74, lines 3 and 8; XX, p. 148, line 12; XX. p. 150, line 3. Cf. *Reg. past.* I.11, line 88, p. 170; II.1, lines 3 and 8, p. 174; II.9, lines 8 and 17, pp. 236–8.
[85] *Reg. past.* II.5, lines 23–7, p. 198; II.5, lines 19–21, pp. 196–8; II.7, lines 1–3, p. 218; II.7, lines 114–17, p. 226.
[86] *CP* XVI, p. 98, line 26, to p. 100, line 1; XVI, p. 98, lines 17–21; XVIII, p. 126, lines 8–10; XVIII, p. 134, line 24, to p. 136, line 1.
[87] *Reg. past.* II.5, lines 1–2, p. 196.   [88] II.5, lines 10–16, p. 196.   [89] II.5, lines 39–46, p. 198.
[90] ' . . . by the love of God and men both to the highest and to the lowest things': *CP* XVI, p. 98, line 26, to p. 100, line 1, cf. p. 96, lines 20–1. Cf. *Reg. past.* II.5, lines 24–5, p. 198.
[91] ' . . . and outside he was occupied by the people's need': *CP* XVI, p. 100, line 24 to p. 102, line 1. Cf. *Reg. past.* II.5, lines 44–6, p. 198.
[92] *VA* 74, lines 64–70; cc. 99–104; above, pp. 137, 175 and 186–7.   [93] *Ibid.* 105, lines 8–13.
[94] 'Vt sit rector internorum curam in exteriorum occupatione non minuens, exteriorum prouidentiam in internorum sollicitudine non relinquens': *Reg. past.* II.7, lines 1–3, p. 218.

may lead his subjects to sin. If he is too greatly concerned with worldly tumults, he risks losing the internal knowledge that he should teach to others, as a head unable to guide its feet.[95] The greatest danger lies in *secularia negotia*, which must sometimes be tolerated, but can never be loved.[96] Yet the ruler should also guard against complete devotion to spiritual matters. Not only would this jeopardize the welfare of his subjects (*necessitates subditorum*), but unless he provides his subjects with 'the needs of this present life' (*necessaria praesentis uitae*), they will not receive his instruction willingly.[97]

These principles can again be observed in Alfredian practice. 'Ic ðe bebeode ... ðæt ðu ðe þissa woruldðinga to þæm geæmettige swa ðu oftost mæge, ðæt ðu ðone wisdom þe ðe God sealde ðær ðær ðu hine befæstan mæge, befæste': probably echoing a canon of *Clofesho*, the king's instruction to his bishops expressed concern for the balancing of spiritual and worldly priorities.[98] The chapter deploys very similar language, illustrated by the rendering of II Timothy II. 4 and its accompanying exegesis:

'Nele nan Godes ðeow hiene selfne to ungemetlice gebindan on worldscipum, ðylæs he mislicige ðæm þe he hiene ær selfne gesealde.' Ða ða he lærde ðæt ðære ciricean ðegnas sceoldon stilnesse ðære ðegnunga habban, ða lærde he hie eac hu hie hie geæmetigian sceoldon oðerra weorca.[99]

'To ungemetlice': the message of balance is enhanced by this characteristic qualification. The operative verb *geæmettian* ('to be unoccupied'), together with the adjective *æmtig*, supplied favoured means of expressing Gregorian *uacare*.[100] 'Leisure' in this sense recurs in Asser's account of the court *schola*, where pupils 'scriptioni ... uacabant'; this related to 'hunting and other skills', essential for noble life.[101] There could be no question of otherworldly withdrawal. Spiritual activity was futher regulated by Alfred's candle-lantern: division by two left half of all time devoted to worldly affairs.

Such balancing extended to the king's body. By the early 890s the rationalization of Alfred's illness was firmly Gregorian: as bodily suffering

---

[95] II.7, lines 16–18 and 58–63, pp. 218–20 and 222.   [96] II.7, lines 111–14, p. 226.

[97] II.7, lines 114–22, p. 226.

[98] 'I command ... that you disengage yourselves from these worldly things as most often as you can, so that you use the wisdom that God gave you whenever you are able to use it': *CP*, p. 4, lines 1–4. Synod of *Clofesho* (747), c. 8.

[99] ' "Let no servant of God engage himself too immoderately in worldly matters, lest he displease him to whom he earlier gave himself." When he taught that servants of the church ought to have quietness in their ministries, he taught them also how they had to be disengaged from other works': *CP* XVIII, p. 130, lines 1–5. 'Nemo militans Deo implicat se negotiis saecularibus, ut ei placeat cui se probauit. Hinc Ecclesiae rectoribus et uacandi studia praecipit, et consulendi remedia ostendit': *Reg. past.* II.7, lines 41–4, p. 220.

[100] Klaeber, 'Ælfreds Vorrede', pp. 57–8.   [101] *VA* 75, lines 17–18.

conducive to humility through effects on the ruler's mind.[102] 'What sort of man ought to come to rule': physical affliction dominates Gregory's answer, faithfully conveyed by the vernacular:

Ac ðone mon sciele ealle mægene to biscephade teon, þe on monegum ðrowungum his lichoman cwilmð, and gastlice liofað, and ðisses middangeardes orsorgnesse ne gimð, ne him nane wiðerweardnesse ne ondræt ðisse worlde, ac Godes anne willan lufað.[103]

The sufferings of Alfred's body supplied constant internal hardship. As a means of curtailing sin, conversely, the action of Alfred's illnesses precisely mirrored Gregory's admonition to the sick:

Eac sint ða siocan to manianne ðæt hie ongieten hu micel Godes giefu him bið ðæs flæsces geswinc, forðæmþe hit ægðer ge ða gedonan synna onweg aðwiehð, ge hine eac ðara gelett þe he don wolde, gif he meahte, forðæm ðonne he bið gesargod on ðæs lichoman wundum, ðonne gewyrceað ða wunda on ðæm gebrocedan mode hreowsunge wunda.[104]

Alfred's afflictions led similarly back to his steadfast mind.

Even the limits of suffering were shaped by Gregorian assumptions. 'Not, however, that God would make him unworthy and useless in worldly affairs': not the least priority attributed to Alfred was his physical effectiveness. Yet the king's enduring fear of his affliction rendered him 'virtually useless – as it seemed to him – in heavenly and worldly affairs'.[105] Provocatively exaggerated, the despair was a central gesture in Alfred's personal theatre, playfully inviting contradiction. As an intermittent internal disorder, the king's illness fell far short of ascetic mortification, aiding active duty. The role was never far from urgent royal priorities. Internal and external cares, 'seo innere giemen' and 'seo uterre abisgung', acquired specific resonance from the juxtaposition of medical and military pressure.[106] The 'internal and external cares' of Asser's troubled ruler take their place alongside his illnesses, implicitly contrasted with the 'assiduae exterarum gentium infestationes'.[107]

---

[102] Above, pp. 137–8; cf. Straw, *Gregory*, pp. 107–46.
[103] 'But one ought to draw with all might to the office of bishop the man who afflicts his body with many sufferings, and lives spiritually, and does not concern himself with freedom from the care of this world, nor fears any adversity in this world, but loves God's will alone': *CP* X, p. 60, lines 6–9. Cf. *Reg. past.* I.10, lines 2–5, pp. 160–2.
[104] 'The sick are also to be admonished to understand how great a gift of God the hardship of the flesh is for them, because it both washes away the sins committed, and prevents those he would wish to do, if he could, because when he is afflicted by the wounds of the body, these wounds cause wounds of repentance in the afflicted mind': *CP* XXXVI, p. 256, lines 19–24. Cf. *Reg. past.* III.12, lines 115–19, p. 330.
[105] *VA* 74, lines 53–4 and 68–9.
[106] *CP* XVIII, p. 126, lines 8–10. Cf. *Reg. past.* II.7, lines 1–3, p. 218.
[107] *VA* 25, lines 7–11; c. 91, lines 9–10.

Asser's ship-metaphor in the same chapter bears comparison with Gregorian usage, leading the translation to characterize 'ðæt rice and se ealdordom' as 'ðæs modes storm, se symle bið cnyssende ðæt scip ðære heortan mid ðara geðohta ystum'.[108] The desire for wisdom was repeatedly situated 'inter omnia praesentis vitae suae impedimenta': in a further chapter, Gregorian contemplation is explicitly recommended against 'sio uterre abisgung ðissa worldðinga', only eased by the study of scripture and holy law.[109]

The struggle against tribulation only magnified royal effort and commitment, in all spheres of activity. The status of wisdom was reinforced as the only source of stability; the parallel between body and kingdom drew Gregorian office-holding still further onto Alfred's courtly stage. Here explicit, the dangers of worldly desire were communicated more widely to observers of the king. The translation not only lent further substance to Alfred's image, but supplied a vital framework for this and all other instances of instructive restraint. Carefully adapted to local circumstances, the *Hierdeboc* succeeded through its relationship to collective perception, as an overarching guide to Alfredian power.

THE *HIERDEBOC* AND THE SOUTHUMBRIAN EPISCOPATE

The question remains of the *Hierdeboc*'s episcopal recipients, and its impact on their position under West Saxon rule. Even as a symbol, Alfred's gift was profound, as a text extended to every bishop under his authority. The power underlying the dissemination has been explored, in the enhanced significance of the household for episcopal behaviour, its value in many episcopal appointments, and, above all, the harnessing of bishops as agents under royal lordship. In all these areas there is good evidence for the further strengthening of power in Alfred's final decade. More uncertain are the attitudes of bishops themselves, and the nature of their practice under competing pressures.

On any interpretation, this was a difficult period for the Southumbrian episcopate. Resources and infrastructure had been weakened by warfare and defensive reorganization; bishops were now subject to direct royal criticism in the language of pastoral reform. Viking impact in this sphere remains controversial: effects can only have been regionalized, while the fate of many religious communities is clouded by evidential retrospection. Several recent studies have refuted any picture of blanket disintegration, while illustrating the many difficulties in

---

[108] ' ... the storm of the mind, which is always tossing the ship of the heart with the waves of thoughts': *CP* IX, p. 58, lines 5–6. Cf. *Reg. past.* I.9, lines 33–5, p. 160.
[109] *VA* 25, lines 1–2, p. 21. *CP* XXII, p. 168, lines 12–14. Cf. *Reg. past.* II.11, lines 12–13, p. 252.

establishing local institutional continuity.[110] At all events, two glimpses tend to confirm the vulnerability of ecclesiastical resources to external pressures: both are episcopal. A letter by Denewulf, bishop of Winchester, of the early tenth century appeals to the poor condition in which an estate had been acquired, 'without livestock and left unoccupied by heathen men'.[111] An early Edwardian charter for Sherborne, where Asser remained bishop, offers unusually specific reflection on the passing of all temporalities, 'whether by the evident disasters of war, by the burnings of cities and lands, by the seizures of robbers, by the growth of infirmities, and by other innumerable existing causes'.[112]

Such problems will have been greater in regions under viking control, though the picture is barely recoverable. The see of Leicester was relocated to Dorchester on Thames by the later ninth century; episcopal lists also imply major breaks of succession for Lindsey and the two East Anglian sees of *Dummoc* and Elmham.[113] Though retrospective, the lists receive support from the criticisms of Pope Formosus, discussed below, and from later circumstances in East Anglia. Theodred, bishop of London before 953, reportedly held authority in Suffolk, coinciding with the apparent revival of Elmham alone in the mid-tenth century.[114] Vast regions in Alfred's time may be imagined without episcopal provision: the situation presumably related to the circumstances of viking conquest, though the case is extreme when compared with greater continuity in the north.[115]

Royal policy itself presented bishops with hard choices. The *Hierdeboc* suggested pastoral invigoration, a rekindling of zeal by royal flame. Yet Gregorian rhetoric now incorporated 'active' burdens on land, equally directing resources to defensive needs. In addition to the common burdens, the burghal programme drew further costs from strategic leasing and land exchange. Denewulf's letter conceded an estate of seventy hides in Edward's lifetime; Asser's charter yielded Plympton, Devon, for land elsewhere.[116] Were such gifts always appropriately compensated? The 'wealth' of burghal revenue depended on many local variables. Further tensions might be detected in episcopal appointment. Plegmund's appointment as archbishop in 890 fell two years after the death of his predecessor Æthelred.[117] One explanation might be Grimbald's presence

---

[110] Dumville, 'Ecclesiastical Lands'; J. Barrow, 'Survival and Mutation: Ecclesiastical Institutions in the Danelaw in the Ninth and Tenth Centuries', in *Cultures in Contact*, ed. Hadley and Richards, pp. 155–76; Blair, *Church*, pp. 291–341.

[111] S 1444 (BCS 619; trans. in *EHD*, no. 101). [112] S 380 (BCS 610).

[113] Dumville, 'Ecclesiastical Lands', p. 31; Barrow, 'Ecclesiastical Institutions', pp. 156–61; Blair, *Church*, pp. 316–17.

[114] Barrow, 'Ecclesiastical Institutions', pp. 158–9.

[115] *Ibid.*, pp. 160–1 on York; Kirby, 'Northumbria', pp. 337–40. [116] S 1444; S 380.

[117] Brooks, *Canterbury*, pp. 152–3; Whitelock in *C&S*, pp. 35–6.

in royal service, whose refusal to accept the see was claimed in later Winchester tradition; another factor may have been fiscal, in the vulnerability of episcopal income. Other appointments are more poorly documented: the example is striking when compared with the likely termination of Danelaw sees. Alfredian influence in East Anglia is unlikely to have been negligible; Barrow has raised the possibility of active royal resistance to new Danelaw appointments, restricting episcopacy to regions under West Saxon control'.[118]

How did bishops respond? A chain of correspondence offers almost the only evidential window. Further letters from Fulk of Rheims strengthen the significance of Plegmund's appointment against the backdrop of Grimbald's enlistment. Bishops and priests with 'secretly introduced women', incest, defilement of nuns: Fulk's concerns echoed earlier criticism of English sexual practices, symbolic in his hands of English laxity in canonical observance.[119] Its new defender would be Plegmund, now armed from Rheims with 'holy authorities of canonical censure'.[120] Fulk's interest was matched by renewed papal attention, in the remarkable letter of Pope Formosus (891 × 896), threatening English bishops with excommunication. Formosus' target was episcopal inaction against a reported backdrop of 'pagan' resurgence. Narrowly averting anathema, Plegmund is credited with news of efforts 'to renew the seed of the word of God'.[121] Criticism fell on a failure of apostolic succession: 'Let there be no delay in appointing another, when any priest departs from this life, but as soon as the brother's death is announced . . . , after canonical election let another consecrated [bishop] succeed'.[122] Formosus sent Plegmund his pallium; the letter may well be another product of such contact.[123]

Rightly understood against the evidence for vacant sees, Formosus' criticisms are sharpened by a single scrap of Southumbrian documentation. London, British Library, Cotton Domitian A. ix, fol. 11r preserves a single page of excerpts from the Old English Bede, written in late Insular minuscule of the late ninth or early tenth century.[124] Though the passages are discrete, the leaf probably preserves the final page of a section or volume. The text begins with the final two chapters of the synod of Hertford (672 or 673): the ninth, on the need for more bishops with

[118] Barrow, 'Ecclesiastical Institutions', p. 158; J. Campbell, 'The East Anglian Sees before the Conquest', in his *Anglo-Saxon State*, pp. 107–27, at 116–18.
[119] Letter to Alfred (*c.* 890×891), in *C&S*, no. 5; trans. in *EHD*, no. 224.
[120] Letter to Plegmund (*c.* 890×891), in *C&S*, no. 6; trans. in *EHD*, no. 225.
[121] *C&S*, no. 8; trans. in *EHD*, no. 227. [122] *C&S*, p. 37. [123] *Ibid.*, p. 12.
[124] Ker, *Catalogue*, no. 151; Gneuss, *Handlist*, no. 330; Dumville, 'English Square Minuscule', p. 158 and plate II; J. Bately, *The Tanner Bede*, EEMF 24 (Copenhagen, 1992), 37–9.

increase of the faithful; and the tenth, restating the bonds of marriage.[125] These are followed by reports of Augustine's Frankish consecration; and the consecration of Mellitus, bishop of London, 'ærest on Ongelðiode' at Augustine's hands. At the least, the excerpts are arresting, as evidence uniquely oriented towards Formosus' criticisms, somehow concerned with the diocese of London. Questions of primacy seem unlikely: *pace* Nelson, her suggestion of some project to elevate London goes far beyond the known circumstances of Grimbald's recruitment.[126] Even if Grimbald had been intended for a bishopric, Fulk's later letters focus on Canterbury alone. The more likely context concerns the extent of London's reach in the absence of East Anglian bishops. The division of sees later in Plegmund's career was essentially restricted to Wessex.[127] For all Fulk's aspirations, the Domitian excerpts show the centrality of specifically 'English' canonical precedent, the authority of which had been questioned by Fulk and earlier popes for its marital permissiveness. Whatever was said to Formosus, the vacancies in question endured.

For bishops, also, oversight could be selective. London's significance must be judged against its status as a notable venue for episcopal contact, in 'special' royal assemblies.[128] Episcopal status was effectively restricted to thegns of the king. In the end, bishops had enough to gain, if much to lose, from the protective force of royal lordship. As much is suggested by Denewulf's letter, in many respects the counterpart to Alfred's Prose Preface. Addressed to Edward 'min leof', this is in fact the earliest surviving letter from thegn to king, matched in the secular sphere by the later Fonthill letter.[129] The reluctant lease of Beddington is reinforced by an inventory of livestock, with request of its safe return. Bishop and community then openly beg 'that in charity for the love of God and for the holy church you desire no more land of that foundation, for it seems to them an unwelcome demand'.[130] A complex concession was here delicately underwritten by pre-emptive personal appeal. The strength of the document lies in its subsequent preservation, with Beddington in Winchester's possession. As Dumville notes, the case is typical of such

---

[125] Ptd by J. Zupitza, 'Drei alte Excerpte aus Alfreds Beda', *Zeitschrift für deutsches Altertum* 30 (1886), 185–6; cf. Miller in *OE Bede*, pp. xx–xxi.

[126] Nelson, 'Political Ideas', pp. 156–7; J. L. Nelson, 'Fulk's Letter to Alfred Revisited', in her *Ruling Families*, no. 5, p. 143. Cf. Theodred's probable German origin (acceded 909×926).

[127] See Brooks, *Canterbury*, pp. 210–13.

[128] More likely than a 'provincial synod' (Brooks, *Canterbury*, p. 154). S 346 (BCS 561); S 1628 (BCS 577); cf. above, pp. 35 and 52.

[129] S 1444 (BCS 619; trans. in *EHD*, no. 101); S 1445, with Keynes, 'Fonthill Letter', p. 55.

[130] ' ... ðæt to ælmæssan for Godæs lufan and for ðæræ haligan ciricean þæt ðu þære stowæ londæs maræn ne willnie, for ðam þe him ðyncð ynbædune hæs': S 1444 (BCS 619; trans. in *EHD*, no. 101).

concessions, with scrupulous observance of their respective terms.[131] Here, above all, shared discourse was central, in the recognition of need, directly encouraged by the king's translation. Worldly, royal, grounded in service: in land as in action, the ideals of the *Hierdeboc* were amply fulfilled.

[131] Dumville, 'Ecclesiastical Lands', p. 46.

Chapter 11

THE *DOMBOC* AS A REORIENTATION OF ROYAL LAW

Often neglected, the law-book or *Domboc* gains much from approach within the broader structures of royal thought. Alfred's law-giving was a central act of Solomonic imitation, informed by biblical wisdom. A counterpart in many ways to the *Hierdeboc*, the *Domboc* fulfilled a similar function for secular office-holders as a defining text of 're-education'. The centrality of lordship matched shared interests in loyalty and common needs. As a guide to judgement, its contents echoed wider principles of probity and restraint. What distinguished law-giving was its combination of learned expertise with more immediate articulation of collective priorities. Yet the *Domboc* is not without difficulties as a tool of learning. One problem arises from its novelty in a field otherwise represented by much earlier legal texts. This is compounded by the *Domboc's* character, sometimes seen as 'disorganized', and on any assessment problematic. A third factor is the question of Frankish influence, certainly detectable on many grounds, the precise implications of which remain uncertain. All these issues have been treated at length by Wormald, yielding much on the text's legal import, yet in work often insistently committed to a particular view of early medieval law.[1] Necessarily engaging with his findings and broader assumptions, what follows offers an alternative perspective on the *Domboc's* learned treatment of law and judgement.

WRITTEN LAW: AUTHORITY AND STATUS

In scale and structure, Alfred's *Domboc* had high ambitions. Like the *Hierdeboc*, its transmission was consistent. All six surviving manuscripts

---

[1] News of Patrick Wormald's death arrived as this chapter approached completion. Hope remains that the second volume of *MEL* will be published in some form. This chapter takes account of his 1998 paper '*Anglicarum legum conditor*: King Alfred as Law-maker', which was to form an early section in his second volume.

probably once included the *Domboc* in the same basic 'edition'.[2] After a table of 120 rubrics, providing headings for the text's 120 sections, the reader is confronted with excerpts from Exodus, chapters 20 to 23, comprising the Decalogue and some sixty-six verses of Mosaic law.[3] Attention moves to the treatment of law in the New Testament, and the conversion of many peoples, including the English.[4] Only at this stage is the first-person identified as that of the king, in an account of editorial principles.[5] There follows up to section XLIII a series of pronouncements which one might characterize as Alfred's 'miscellaneous laws', attributed to his initiative.[6] These are concluded with a list of compensation payments for bodily injuries, from head to toe.[7] The final sections XLIIII to CXX offer a long series of laws attributed to Alfred's West Saxon predecessor, Ine (688–726).[8]

The weighty introduction, from Moses to Alfred, captures the scope of royal aspiration. No other Anglo-Saxon king prefaced his laws with anything other than a brief statement of their issuing. The problem is not, as Attenborough once claimed, that the introduction has 'no bearing on Anglo-Saxon law', but rather that it seems alien to Anglo-Saxon legal tradition.[9] The picture can at once be amended when placed in a wider European context. As many commentators have stressed, the recording of law offered exceptional opportunities for enhanced legal statement.[10] Law as written text gave force to shared identity, in multiple accounts of ethnic or corporate unity.[11] Subsequent texts drew force from their relationship to earlier constructions; acts of reissue or compilation could be equally effective in contexts of continuity or disruption. Biblical and Roman models combined to supply key fields of reference, as legal dispensation

---

[2] Wormald, *MEL* I, 267–9; M. R. Richards, 'The Manuscript Contexts of the Old English Laws: Tradition and Innovation', in *Studies*, ed. Szarmach, pp. 171–92; Ker, *Catalogue*, nos. 39, 65, 100, 136, 163 and 373. The text in British Library, Cotton Nero A. i, fols. 3–57 (medieval provenance uncertain, s. xi^{med}) was probably originally complete because it starts with the table of rubrics. British Library, Burney 277, fol. 42 (Kent, s. xi$^{2/2}$) is presumably the remnant of a complete text since each section is numbered. Cambridge, Corpus Christi College MS 383 (St Paul's, London, s. xi–xii) is now acephalous; the rubrics are incorporated into the main text, as a result of which the opening table of rubrics may have been omitted.

[3] *Af* Int.1–49.   [4] *Af* Int.49–49.8.   [5] *Af* Int.49.9–49.10.   [6] *Af* 1–77.   [7] *Af* 44–77.

[8] *Ine* 1–76.

[9] *The Laws of the Earliest English Kings*, ed. F. L. Attenborough (Cambridge, 1922), p. 35.

[10] Wormald, '*Lex Scripta*'; cf. esp. H. Nehlsen, 'Zur Aktualität und Effektivität germanischer Rechtsaufzeichnungen', in *Recht und Schrift im Mittelalter*, ed. P. Classen (Sigmaringen, 1977), pp. 449–502; C. Schott, 'Zur Geltung der Lex Alamannorum', in *Die historische Landschaft zwischen Lech und Vogesen*, ed. P. Fried and W.-D. Sick (Augsburg, 1988), pp. 75–105.

[11] I. N. Wood, 'Ethnicity and the Ethnogenesis of the Burgundians', in *Typen der Ethnogenese unter besonderer Berücksichtigung der Bayern I*, ed. H. Wolfram (Vienna, 1990), 53–70; P. Amory, 'The Meaning and Purpose of Ethnic Terminology in the Burgundian Laws', *EME* 2 (1993), 1–28; R. Collins, *Early Medieval Spain: Unity in Diversity, 400–1000*, 2nd edn (Basingstoke, 1995), pp. 24–30 and 121–8; Ó Corráin, 'Nationality and Kingship in pre-Norman Ireland', pp. 13–19.

fused with the responsibilities of Christian kingship. There was nothing specifically 'Carolingian' about such patterns, though a notable feature of reforming rule.[12] Late eighth- and ninth-century Frankish developments must take their place as a particularly intensive episode of legal reinvention.[13] Charlemagne's pronouncements brought ethnic law under 'corrective' scrutiny, with *Lex Salica* as the special focus for Frankish identity.[14] Diverse in character, capitulary-material could also appeal to the Franks' collective legal status, aiding its selective reissue under ninth-century descendants.[15] Both forms of Frankish law may have offered much in an Alfredian context; their role must equally be balanced against Irish and notably Insular precedent.[16] The *Domboc*'s introduction placed law-giving in a wider field.

The character of written law must be judged against its status. To modern eyes the scope of Anglo-Saxon collections can often seem haphazard. Texts are generally lacking in systematic order, leaving methods of procedure difficult to discern. The implications of clauses can be opaque, while whole areas lie almost entirely outside the surviving corpus.[17] As well as kindred structure and inheritance these include many aspects of slavery, social organization and procedures of dispute settlement. Other sources are problematic: accounts of legal disputes fail to refer to extant written law.[18] The *Domboc* presents the additional feature of internal contradiction, between certain laws of Alfred and those attributed to Ine. This is compounded by the rubrication system, whose presence in all six manuscripts suggests that it is original.[19] Not only do the rubrics often supply very limited information, insufficient to locate an appropriate written law; several sections contain further pronouncements, unrelated to the rubric.[20] The *Domboc* and its features have always been central in Wormald's view of written law. The existence of barbarian legislation 'projected an image of society which corresponded to the ideological aspirations, as well as the practical needs, of . . . its articulate classes'.[21] The actual drafting of law, he suggests, may have aimed 'simply to get

---

[12] Cf. P. Wormald, 'The Emergence of the *Regnum Scottorum*: a Carolingian Hegemony?', in *Scotland in Dark Age Britain*, ed. B. E. Crawford (St Andrews, 1996), pp. 131–60.

[13] Earlier legal production surveyed by I. N. Wood, *The Merovingian Kingdoms 450–751* (London, 1994), pp. 102–19; cf. R. Kottje, *Studien zum Einfluß des alten Testamentes auf Recht und Liturgie des frühen Mittlelalters (6.–8. Jahrhundert)* (Bonn, 1970).

[14] McKitterick, *Written Word*, pp. 40–60; *MEL* I, 33–48.

[15] Nelson, 'Legislation and Consensus', esp. pp. 98–9 and 109–10.   [16] Below, pp. 222–38.

[17] Wormald, '*Lex Scripta*', p. 11.   [18] *Ibid.*, p. 21.

[19] Above, p. 215, note 2; Wormald, '*Lex Scripta*', p. 15; *MEL* I, 268–9. Cf. R. J. E. Dammery, 'The Law-Code of King Alfred the Great', 2 vols. (unpubl. PhD dissertation, Cambridge University, 1990) I, 181–212, claiming the rubrics as a later addition (cf. below, pp. 219 and 231).

[20] Dammery, 'Law-Code' I, 184–99; *MEL* I, 267–8.

[21] Wormald, '*Lex Scripta*', p. 34.

something into writing that *looked* like a written law-code, more or less regardless of its actual value to judges sitting in court'.[22] The multivalency of legal texts cannot be doubted, but Wormald's corollary is more problematic, his position extreme in the wider debate over the uses of early written law.[23] While acknowledging the difficulties posed, many commentators have taken a more positive view of the impact of law in writing.[24] That such texts conveyed political messages need not undermine their potential relevance as sources of normative legal statement. At the same time, the image of judicial 'ready reference' may set an unnecessarily exacting standard of informed deployment.[25] It is important to observe what all views share, in the continuing importance of orally transmitted custom and law-making, alongside written texts.[26] The question remains how far 'ideological', or rather heightened symbolic, features might be detached from impact upon law in practice. Problematic aspects of legislation may make greater sense against the continuing backdrop of orality. Ninth-century Anglo-Saxon legal expertise derived fundamentally from customary experience, by definition difficult to recover. Some of its character may be preserved in the notion of *folcriht*, apparently referring to commonly accepted practices of justice.[27] Texts themselves might be understood against their selectivity, combining 'custom, policy and judgement' for coherent purposes.[28] The goals of writing lay neither in codification nor overarching revision, but might usefully be imagined against forces operating on the contemporary ruling community.

The scope of legislation extended far beyond mechanisms of dispute settlement, but here too utility cannot be discounted. Surviving dispute-records are heavily skewed towards cases involving land, rarely covered

---

[22] *Ibid.*, p. 13.

[23] Comparable to Nehlsen, 'Aktualität'; Schott, 'Geltung': debate usefully reviewed by W. Sellert, 'Aufzeichnung des Rechts und Gesetz', in *Das Gesetz in Spätantike und frühem Mittelalter 4. Symposion der Kommission 'Die Funktion des Gesetzes in Geschichte und Gegenwart'*, ed. W. Sellert (Göttingen, 1992), 67–102.

[24] *Ibid.*, pp. 87–102; R. Kottje, 'Die Lex Baiuvariorum – das Recht der Baiern', in *Überlieferung und Geltung normativer Texte des frühen und hohen Mittelalters*, ed. H. Mordek (Sigmaringen, 1986), pp. 9–23; H. Siems, 'Zu Problemen der Bewertung frühmittelalterlicher Rechtstexte', *Zeitschrift der Savigny-Stiftung für Rechtsgeschichte (Germanistische Abteilung)* 106 (1989), 291–305, at 301–5; McKitterick, *Written Word*, pp. 23–75; H. Mordek, 'Kapitularien und Schriftlichkeit' and 'Leges und Kapitularien', in his *Studien zur fränkischen Herrschergesetzgebung* (Frankfurt, 2000), pp. 307–39 and 341–52.

[25] Cf. Siems, 'Zu Problemen', pp. 303–5.

[26] Wormald, '*Lex Scripta*', pp. 17 and 37–41; cf. McKitterick, *Written Word*, pp. 37–40.

[27] Alfred's will, in *SEHD*, no. 11, p. 17, line 4; *I Edward* Prologue; *II Edward* 8; *II Æthelstan* 2, 8, 9 and 23; *II Edmund* 7; *I Edgar* 7; *III Edgar* 1.1; *VI Æthelred* 8.1; *II Cnut* 1.1.

[28] Cf. Wormald, '*Lex Scripta*', p. 13.

in written law.[29] Even within this corpus many connections can be drawn with recorded procedure.[30] 'Ready reference' may be difficult to envisage in many instances of written law, yet, as Alfredian developments demonstrate, the role of texts was not narrowly confined.[31] As a complex appeal to 'justice', selective and admonitory, the act of writing consistently depended on a shared understanding of common legal practices. Whatever its impact, law as text laid quite specific claims upon collective legal behaviour.

THE CONSTRUCTION OF ALFREDIAN JUDGEMENT

The selection of law was central to the *Dombocs*'s construction. Every clause is seen to result from Alfred's own modest judgement. The operative moment is the king's first emergence, after the account of earlier law-making. The account ends with the establishment of judgements (*domas*) among the English (*geond Angelcynn*), curiously attributed to 'synods' (*seonoðas*), and thus recorded 'in many synod-books (*on monega senoðbec*), here one judgement, there another'.[32] The king alone is represented as having gathered together judgements, and given orders to have recorded in writing 'many of those that our predecessors kept that pleased me'. Some judgements proved to be unsatisfactory: 'many of those that did not please me I rejected with the advice of my wise men (*mid minra witena geðeahte*); and ordered to be kept in another way'.[33] The whole process is ironically associated with the durability of writing: 'For I dared not presume to establish in writing at all many of my own, since it was unknown to me what would please those who came after us'.[34] In addition to Ine, predecessors included Offa, king of the Mercians, and Æthelberht of Kent. Yet Alfred's text only included those judgements 'which seemed most right to me'. Only then was the collection shown to his 'wise men', receiving unanimous approval.[35]

The practice of composition was probably more complex, but need not have been intolerably far from this representation. Renewing and correcting were commonly claimed activities in the prefaces of legal texts; it should not be surprising if they mask greater variety of treatment.[36] Up to section XLIII at least, one must envisage a strong element

---

[29] Cf. Mordek, 'Leges', pp. 348–51, on the limited weight of documentary silence.
[30] Keynes, 'Fonthill Letter', notwithstanding problems raised by Wormald, *MEL* I, 148, 150 and 482; cf. Wormald, 'Charters, Law', pp. 303–10.
[31] Keynes, 'Royal Government', pp. 230–1. [32] *Af* Int.49.7–49.8. [33] *Af* Int.49.9.
[34] *Ibid.*: 'Forðam ic ne dorste geðristlæcan þara minra awuht fela on gewrit settan, forðam me wæs uncuð, hwæt þæs ðam lician wolde ðe æfter us wæren'.
[35] *Af* Int.49.10. [36] *MEL* I, 277–8.

of original writing, often only loosely related to earlier written laws. The nature of intervention is equally problematic. In her seminal study of royal style, Bately expressed reservations over the *Domboc*, noting an unusual concentration of typical usage only in the first-person section of the introduction.[37] Taking a more positive view, Wormald has stressed the extent to which apparent lapses of vocabulary can be paralleled in the *Hierdeboc*.[38] It is an interesting question how far variations might be attributable to chronological development, as opposed to the input or influence of royal helpers. The former is quite possible: the *Domboc* should probably be dated between 886 (Fulk's letter) and 893 (Asser's *Life*); Wormald conversely sees the *Domboc* as post-893.[39] At all events, the close correlation between lexis and first-person warns against any straightforward consistency with other sections.

Clouded by the limited corpus of earlier written law, compilation and drafting must often be assumed from the *Domboc*'s own contents. Much hinges on the status of the 'Ine appendix', found in three manuscripts in early modern times, and probably once present in all six.[40] The original inclusion of Ine has sometimes been doubted, inspiring alternative interpretations of the appendix, either as a post-Alfredian addition, or a nonintegral part of the *Domboc* applicable only to Wessex.[41] According to such arguments, the acknowledged use of Ine would refer only to his impact on Alfred's miscellaneous laws. The case for internal contradiction may be overstated; in any case, Alfred's laws might equally have held precedence. Certainly, Alfred doubles the fine and alters compensation for the destruction of trees, and reduces the fines for *burgbryce* of both bishop and ealdorman so that they are level.[42] Yet pronouncements on church sanctuary may differ from Ine merely because the latter dealt with criminals subject to penalties of death and scourging.[43] Other miscellaneous laws both complement and depend on Ine. Whereas Ine treats fighting in the house of a king, ealdorman, *gafolgelda* or *gebur*, and in a monastery, Alfred addresses that in the presence of an archbishop, ealdorman or bishop, at a meeting where an ealdorman is present, and in the house of a *ceorlisc monn*.[44]

Alfred's miscellaneous laws and Ine are sufficiently complementary to suggest that the former were additional to the latter.[45] Whereas Ine

---

[37] Bately, 'Translation of Orosius', pp. 452–3. [38] *MEL* I, 273–7.

[39] Above, p. 167; Scharer, *Herrschaft*, pp. 112 and 123, note 36; cf. *MEL* I, 281 and 286.

[40] See above, p. 215, note 2.

[41] Dammery, 'Law-Code' I, 236–69; F. Palgrave, *The Rise and Progress of the English Commonwealth*, 2 vols. (London, 1832) I, 47.

[42] *Af* 12; cf. *Ine* 43. *Af* 40; cf. *Ine* 45. [43] *Af* 2 and 5; cf. *Ine* 5.

[44] *Ine* 6 (cf. *Af* 7); *Af* 15, 38 and 39. Differences in value may depend on the slightly different contexts for fighting, and the distinction between compensation and fine.

[45] *MEL* I, 268–9 and 278–80.

concentrates on theft, trading and agricultural matters, Alfred pro-
nounces extensively on homicide, sexual offences and bodily injuries, all
lacking in Ine.[46] There are also two instances of theft which the
appendix does not cover.[47] The one pronouncement on merchants
complements a similar law of Ine, incorporating a role for the king's
reeve.[48] Ine's collection supplied a vital starting-point, its nature also
problematic: as Wormald suggests, the inclusion of duplicate laws and
other incongruities may be signs of later accretion.[49] By the same token,
the presence of these features in the *Domboc*, together with laws
superseded by Alfred, strengthens the case for faithful transmission of a
received text, without editorial intervention.[50]

Æthelberht's impact may be more clearly judged: the picture is of
borrowing and adaptation, within the general task of supplementing Ine.
The largest debt arises from the long list of compensation payments for
bodily injuries, a subject lacking in Ine.[51] Values are often altered on a
basis which cannot easily be determined; the list is also extended.[52]
Further miscellaneous laws cover the culpability of lending a weapon
and the binding of a free man.[53] Both expanded on terser pronouncements in Æthelberht: neither subject was in Ine. Alfred's fine for vio-
lating the king's *mundbyrd* or 'protection' may be especially significant.[54]
The value of fifty Kentish shillings in Æthelberht compares with
five pounds of silver pennies in Alfred (i.e. 1200 pennies = 240 West
Saxon shillings). The earlier West Saxon value was probably 120 shillings; the apparent increase matches the greater premium placed on
the king's life.[55] Again, the king's *mundbyrd* or *borg* is unmentioned in
Ine, but further employed by Alfred on the protection of church
sanctuary.[56]

Alfred's debt to Offa is complicated by the lack of surviving laws in his
name. The loss of such a text is quite possible: Wormald's search focused
on the capitulary of 786, attested by Offa at a Southumbrian synod.[57]
The *Domboc* suggests access either to a version of the Latin text, or
to a hypothetical set of vernacular laws reinforcing some of the 786

---

[46] *Ine* 7, 10, 12, 16–18, 22, 28–9, 35–7, 46–8, 57, 72–3 and 75; *Ine* 25, 53, 55–6, 58–60, 67, 69 and
70.1. *Af* 9, 13, 17, 19, 21, 26–8, 30–1 and 36; 8, 10, 11, 18 and 29; 23–4 and 44–77. On
homicide, cf. only *Ine* 16 and 35 relating to theft, 23 and 74 on inter-ethnic murder, and 54 on
exculpatory oaths. On marriage, cf. only *Ine* 27 and 31.
[47] *Af* 6 and 16.   [48] *Af* 34; cf. *Ine* 25.
[49] Wormald, ' "Inter Cetera Bona" ', p. 191; *MEL* I, 104–5.   [50] *MEL* I, 278.
[51] *Æthelberht* 33–72 cf. *Af* 44–77.
[52] Dammery, 'Law-Code' I, 248–55; *Af* 47.1, 56.1 and 66.1.
[53] *Æthelberht* 18 cf. *Af* 19; *Æthelberht* 24 cf. *Af* 35.
[54] *Æthelberht* 8 cf. *Af* 3.   [55] *MEL* I, 279, with note 77.   [56] *Af* 5.
[57] Wormald, 'In Search of King Offa's "Law-Code" ', in his *Legal Culture*, pp. 201–23.

provisions.[58] The key evidence is the capitulary's pronouncement against the killing of kings, the closest Insular precedent for Alfred's law of *hlafordsearu*.[59] Both texts coincide on the disinherited offspring of adulterous nuns; there are parallels also between Alfred's 'oath and pledge' and the 786 chapter on vows and promises.[60] Ine dealt only with pledges given before a bishop.[61] The question is whether such features are sufficient to distinguish direct access to the 786 capitulary. As Wormald observes, Mercian vocabulary in the *Domboc* need not have arisen from a written source; at the same time, one instance (*lefnes*) coincides with the law on adulterous nuns.[62] The lingering possibility remains of a vernacular text related to the canons, whose scope could not now be determined.

A picture emerges of compositional procedure. Construction began with a received text of Ine: this inspired a significant number of laws in Alfred's name, amplifying or updating earlier pronouncements, and filling gaps in coverage.[63] Laws of Æthelberht and in some sense of Offa provided assistance, but were not included in their entirety. As Wormald suggests, the inclusion of Ine might be hinted at if 'ða oþre forlet' in the introduction meant 'I left the others alone'.[64] Some forty laws cannot easily be seen in these terms: a small number may be attributable either to Mosaic influence or to the impact of extra-English legislation; others may record 'leading cases', individual instances of judgement.[65] The corpus includes a core of laws which may have recorded new principles, notably aspects of *hlafordsearu*, the punishment of offences committed against churches or in holy seasons, and the regulation of feud. It is difficult to see the initial first-person as anything other than a general statement of procedure.[66] The referent of 'þas' ('these') has become a distraction: whether it looks forward in the same sentence, or back (to 'synod-books') there is no difficulty in accepting cognizance of extra-English law.[67] The question is primarily grammatical, the latter involving an awkward change of object.[68] One of Alfred's laws begins 'eac we beodað' ('also we command'): the most economical solution is to

---

[58] Wormald, 'Offa's "Law-Code"', pp. 220–1; cf. also Whitelock in *C&S*, pp. 17–18; K&L, *Alfred*, pp. 305–6 and 308–9; Dammery, 'Law-Code' I, 238–47; Cubitt, *Councils*, pp. 168–70.

[59] *Capitulare* of the papal legates (786), c. 12, cf. *Af* 4.

[60] *Af* 8.2, cf. *capitulare*, c. 16; Wormald, 'Offa's "Law-Code"', pp. 215–17. *Af* 1 and 33, cf. *capitulare*, c. 18.

[61] *Ine* 13.   [62] Wormald, 'Offa's "Law-Code"', pp. 203–4; *Af* 8, cf. 20.   [63] *MEL* I, 279–81.

[64] *Ibid.*, 278–9.   [65] *Ibid.*, 282.   [66] Against Wormald, *MEL* I, 278–80.

[67] Forwards according to Liebermann, *Gesetze* III, 50; E. G. Stanley, 'On the Laws of King Alfred: the End of the Preface and the Beginning of the Laws', in *Alfred the Wise*, ed. Roberts and Nelson, pp. 211–21, at 211–12, note 2. Cf. M. H. Turk, *The Legal Code of Alfred the Great* (Halle, 1893), pp. 38–9, followed by Wormald, *MEL* I, 279.

[68] This (and no more) need be the import of Liebermann's gloss, 'denn nicht jenen ganzen Stoff aller Synodbücher der Vergangenheit liess Ælfred abschrieben', sc. but only those that pleased

221

read the entire sentence as an account of construction, with the inclusion of laws 'ordered to be kept in another way'.[69] 'Ac' ('but') need only be connective, the latter sentence merely amplifying the treatment of Alfred's key (English) sources.

To whom did this *Domboc* apply? The common tendency has been to regard such laws as 'English', at least in aspiration, through their respect for non-West Saxon legal traditions.[70] Such associations were certainly current later in the tenth century, when the 'kingdom of the English' was finally created. Yet this after-life should be distinguished from the circumstances of composition. The adding of Alfred's laws to the 'Parker' manuscript was an act of the 930s, postdating Æthelstan's conquest of Northumbria.[71] The *Domboc* captured the more limited unity of later Alfredian conditions. Central was not so much Alfred's styling as 'Westseaxna cyning', probably a measure of tactfulness, as the peoples whose legal past was conspicuously included. West Saxon, Kentish, Mercian: the elements correspond precisely with constituent peoples under Alfred as 'king of the Anglo-Saxons', inherited by his son.[72] A law of Edward ordered payment of compensation according to the *Domboc* ('swa seo domboc sæcge') if an offence was committed *herinne*. In the east or north payment was to follow *friðgewritu*, now-lost written peace agreements then in force in Northumbria and East Anglia.[73] The area in question was again Alfred's 'Anglo-Saxon' polity. 'We' in Alfred's time were not the 'English', but those whose laws might usefully contribute to a shared agenda.[74] Behind 'English' law lay the ambiguity of Alfred's own ethnic fusion.

THE HISTORICAL PROJECTION OF SECULAR LAW

Compositional judgement was set on the deepest historical stage, extending from Moses to Alfred. The unfolding of judgement is traced from Mosaic law to Christ's teaching in the gospels, and thence via the council of Jerusalem (Acts XV. 1–29) to law-giving among Christian peoples after conversion.[75] Alfred's laws are placed within a continuum of divine law-giving, extending to the authority of his written sources.[76]

---

him. Cf. Wormald, 'Offa's "Law-Code" ', p. 215: 'a denial on principle that Alfred had been influenced by "Synodbücher" '.

[69] *Af* 42.

[70] Thus esp. Wormald, '*Engla Lond*', pp. 366–7 and 376–7; *MEL* I, 281 and 426–9.

[71] Dumville, 'Anglo-Saxon Chronicle', pp. 135–9; *MEL* I, 166–7.

[72] Keynes, 'Mercians', pp. 24–6 and 34–9.

[73] *II Edward* 5.2 cf. *Ine* 30 or *Af* 4; *ASC* s.a. 906 (MSS ABCD); Keynes, 'Royal Government', p. 234, note 36.

[74] *Af* Int.49.9.   [75] *Af* Int.1–49.7.   [76] *Af* Int.49.7–49.9.

There were many European precedents for enhanced biblical allusion. The *Admonitio generalis* cast Charlemagne in the role of Josiah, complete with reinvented Decalogue.[77] The prologue to Bavarian law traced a comparable path from Moses to Christian present.[78] Irish vernacular law offers a separate case of Mosaic cross-fertilization.[79] Such examples highlight the extreme scale of Alfred's Mosaic borrowing, amounting to one fifth of his text.[80] Yet the preface went further, to establish legal legitimacy, in a level of detail largely unparalleled in secular law. Only in Ireland, perhaps as late as the eleventh century, did written law circulate with a comparable account of legal and juristic principle.[81] The question arises of its significance for Alfred's collection.

An initial clue proceeds from similarities between the introduction and Fulk's letter to Alfred, explaining the terms of Grimbald's recruitment (*c.* 886).[82] There can be little doubt of some significant connection with Alfred's constructed history. At the same time, Fulk's letter deployed legal principles otherwise associated with his predecessor, Hincmar. This feature confirms the letter's authenticity, never much in doubt; more importantly, it provides a further context for Grimbald's role in Alfred's service, with reference to Hincmar's formidable legacy in legal expertise.[83] Here as elsewhere West Frankish texts give an indication of Alfred's own scholarly resources, in a series of connections usefully outlined by Wormald. A crucial issue is the meaning and status of Alfredian usage under English conditions.

The legal framework within which Hincmar's writings were generated were very far from that of Alfred's kingdom. His own career had exploited written law of all kinds, in a West Frankish order receptive to the stabilizing effects of archiepiscopal intervention.[84] Hincmar emerges as a distinguished champion of canonical rectitude, vigorously defending the powers of his metropolitan against the twin hazards of papal and

---

[77] McKitterick, *Frankish Church*, pp. 1–2.

[78] *MEL* I, 43–4 and 418, but cf. Kottje, 'Lex Baiuvariorum'.

[79] D. Ó Corráin, 'Irish Vernacular Law and the Old Testament', in *Irland und die Christenheit: Bibelstudien und Mission*, ed P. Ní Chatháin and M. Richter (Stuttgart, 1987), pp. 284–307; D. Ó Corráin, L. Breatnach and A. Breen, 'The Laws of the Irish', *Peritia* 3 (1984), 382–438, esp. 394–416; B. Jaski, 'Early Medieval Irish Kingship and the Old Testament', *EME* 7 (1998), 329–44.

[80] *MEL* I, 418.

[81] D. A. Binchy, 'The Pseudo-Historical Prologue to the *Senchas Már*', *Studia Celtica* 10–11 (1975–6), 15–28; Ó Corráin, Breatnach and Breen, 'Laws of the Irish', pp. 384–94.

[82] *C&S*, no. 4 (trans. in *EHD*, no. 223; K&L, *Alfred*, 182–6).

[83] Authenticity reasserted on other grounds by Nelson, 'Fulk's Letter' (cf. Nelson, '"King Across the Sea"', pp. 48–9); Wormald, *MEL* I, 423–6.

[84] Devisse, *Hincmar*, pp. 31–104, 281–360, 725–824 and 965–1054; Wallace-Hadrill, *Frankish Church*, pp. 292–303; Nelson, 'Kingship, Law'.

episcopal encroachment.[85] In the secular sphere, his practice upheld written law as the basis for successful kingship, in a context which gave prominence to Roman and canonical precedent in addition to capitulary-legislation.[86] All activities were united by issues of ecclesiastical autonomy, under West Frankish kingship symbolically committed to respect for the church.[87] Hincmar's legal theorizing reflected its status as a tool of persuasion, extended most fully in disputes over Lothar II's divorce and that involving the archbishop's nephew Hincmar of Laon, both revealing of these conditions.

Hincmar's pronouncements must be seen within favoured modes of argumentation, readily adapted to circumstances.[88] In general, he distinguished between two types of law, the *leges saeculi* or *mundanae*, created by rulers, and the *divinae et apostolicae leges* or *lex Dei* for the regulation of the church as an all-inclusive spiritual body. Both types of law shared inherent characteristics of repression. 'Lex propter transgressiones posita est' (Galatians III. 19): 'lex non est posita iustis sed iniustis' (I Timothy I. 9); his favourite quotations reflected a widely held patristic view of law as remedy for sin.[89] As Hincmar learned from Leo the Great, 'the law is said not to be imposed on the just man, because he fulfils the norm of the precept by the judgement of his own will'.[90] Such reasoning underpinned Hincmar's celebrated argument against Lothar II, who had claimed entitlement to act as he pleased, that only a true king, who lived up to his title by ruling rightly, lay outside earthly law.[91]

Hincmar's arguments for legal contingency were forged solely in relation to divine law.[92] His case was inseparable both from his wider commitment to the general conciliar canons, and from attempts to assert their superiority over papal decrees, cited as authoritative by his Laon suffragan. Hincmar interprets 'lex propter transgressiones posita est' to mean law is 'fitting for its persons and times', and must therefore be subject to change. Papal decrees contradict both themselves and the canons because they were issued at different times for a variety of purposes. It was for precisely this reason that bishops were assembled by

---

[85] Devisse, *Hincmar* II, 565–669; McKeon, *Hincmar of Laon*.

[86] Devisse, *Hincmar* II, 549–64 and 671–723; Nelson, 'Kingship, Law'.

[87] Above, pp. 58–62, 147–8 and 162–3.

[88] Devisse, *Hincmar et la Loi*, pp. 72–92; Devisse, *Hincmar* II, 549–64; K. F. Morrison, *The Two Kingdoms*, pp. 84–98 and 129–32; Wallace-Hadrill, 'Via Regia', pp. 35–8; Anton, *Fürstenspiegel*, pp. 290–319; Nelson, 'Kingship, Law'.

[89] Report to archbishop Gunthar of Cologne of 860 on Boso's attempted divorce (MGH Epist. VIII, no. 135, p. 85, lines 8–12); *Opusculum*, cc. 25, 31 and 34 (PL 126: 385C, 622D and 627–8); *De divortio*, Resp. to Inter. XII, PL 125: 700D and Resp. to Quaest. VI, col. 757C–D.

[90] 'Justo quippe ideo dicitur lex non esse posita, quia normam praeceptionis implet judicio voluntatis': *Opusculum*, c. 34, PL 126: 627B.

[91] *De divortio*, Resp. to Quaest. VI, PL 125: 757C.   [92] Cf. Wormald, *MEL* I, 423–5.

popes to general councils where, inspired by the Holy Spirit, they created canons which would last forever.[93] Hincmar reinforced his account by comparison with biblical law. The law of nature (*lex naturae*) was followed by the (Mosaic) 'law of the letter' (*lex litterae*), which fitted the 'hardness of the people' (*duritia populi*), established on account of sins. This in turn was not destroyed but fulfilled by the 'law of the Gospel (*lex Evangelii*), later in time but prior in grace, which was extended by the apostles and their successors through the passing of times'.[94] Papal decrees were therefore as contingent as Mosaic law, or the Epistle from Jerusalem, directed towards Gentiles still practising circumcision (Acts XV. 23–9).

Hincmar's treatment of secular law also proceeded from his repressive conception of law, though with alternative stress on durability. The imposition of law against sins and unjust men fused with 'ministerial' assumptions locating the basis of rulership in the prevention of evil.[95] The issuing and upholding of laws were duties directly incumbent on the royal office, the only means by which a king could live up to his name.[96] The prevention of sin bore quite specific obligations to uphold laws consonant with the divine law of the church. In *De ordine palatii*, the king is portrayed striving to respect both types of law, yet if this were not possible, willingly acceding to the 'justice of God'.[97] The 'wisdom by which kings reign' had left an abundance of such judgements already in writing. Charles the Bald's rule had from the first hinged on his undertaking to keep 'for each their due law, just as their ancestors had in the time of my predecessors'.[98] Hincmar himself contributed strongly to such assurances, promoting Ansegisus' collection of capitularies as the primary source for Charles's written law.[99]

Two examples must suffice to show Hincmar's rhetoric in action. His criticism of Lothar II amounted to a vigorous defence of ecclesiastical judgement, citing an earlier law of Louis the Pious.[100] Although Lothar might defend himself by whatever laws or customs he chose, the only secular laws which counted in a Christian realm were those consonant

---

[93] *Opusculum*, c. 25, PL 126: 385C–D; discussed by Devisse, *Hincmar* II, 552–4.
[94] *Opusculum*, c. 20, PL 126: 354D–355A; cf. c. 25, PL 126: 386B–387D, esp. col. 387, for a similar parallel between the general conciliar canons and Christ's fulfilment of Old Testament law.
[95] Report to Gunthar, MGH Epist. VIII, no. 135, p. 85, lines 8–18.
[96] *De ordine palatii*, c. 2, lines 113–15, p. 44; report to Gunthar, MGH Epist. VIII, no. 135, p. 85, lines 8–18.
[97] *De ordine palatii*, c. 5, lines 345–59, pp. 70–2; cf. c. 3, lines 150–69, pp. 48–50.
[98] J. L. Nelson, 'The Intellectual in Politics: Context, Content and Authorship in the Capitulary of Coulaines, November 843', in her *Frankish World*, pp. 155–68.
[99] Nelson, 'Kingship, Law', pp. 148–9; Nelson, 'Literacy', pp. 28–9.
[100] *De divortio*, Resp. to Inter. V, PL 125: 652D–653A; Anton, *Fürstenspiegel*, pp. 307–9.

with Christianity.[101] Only a true king issues laws which are of God, 'through whom kings reign and lawgivers discern just things' (Proverbs VIII. 15);[102] Lothar's sin obliged Hincmar to bind him to laws issued by worthier predecessors, who had respected divine commandments.[103] Hincmar's *Quaterniones* of 868 made comparable protest to Charles the Bald, within strident defence of the *libertates ecclesiae*. Urging special treatment of disputes over benefices, Hincmar's precedents included holy canons and laws of Theodosius I and Honorius, again citing Proverbs VIII. 15.[104] Earlier laws still applied, not merely because they were fitting, but by the force of Charles's promises to preserve the laws of his predecessors, which Hincmar could portray as inviolable *subscriptiones*.[105] Legal preservation was again in service to divine law.

The special force of written law, the priority of divine law, respect for the laws of predecessors: the prominence of such features in the *Domboc* widens the case for specific Hincmarian contact.[106] Less clear is the degree of adherence to Hincmar's carefully guarded principles. Fulk's epistle offered sustained criticism of English practices, traced to unacceptable neglect of canon law.[107] In keeping with earlier foreign criticism, Fulk's starting-point is the limited character of Gregory's injunctions to the newly converted English; Hincmar's teachings are trained on this target. Just as the Epistle from Jerusalem forbade circumcision but retained Jewish abstinence 'from sacrifices, fornication, from things strangled and from blood', so early English practices had once been fitting 'in tempore, hoc est pro captu audientium', but both time and the church had moved on.[108] The Epistle from Jerusalem had long been superseded by the 'holy canons', issued by councils of the early church.[109] So also should the English be amended to full canonical observance: Grimbald's agency was to achieve this.[110] Fulk's intentions sit uneasily with known episcopal action, not least the absence of synods. The Domitian excerpts show notable recourse to early English canonical provision.[111] The *Domboc* makes special treatment of sanctuary and

---

[101] *Ibid.*, Resp. to Inter. IV, PL 125: 658B.   [102] *Ibid.*, Resp. to Quaest. VI, PL 125: 757C.
[103] *De divortio*, Resp. to Inter. XII, PL 125: 699D–700A, discussed by Nelson, 'Kingship, Law', pp. 162–3 (cf. *MEL* I, 278).
[104] *Quaterniones* (the first part of *Pro ecclesiae libertatum defensione*), PL 125: 1051C–D; Nelson, 'Kingship, Law', pp. 163–6; Nelson, 'Translating Images of Authority', esp. pp. 91–3; Anton, *Fürstenspiegel*, pp. 330–4; McKeon, *Hincmar of Laon*, pp. 24–6, cf. 170 and 274–5 for the date.
[105] *Quaterniones*, PL 125: 1040; cf. Hincmar's letter to Charles later in the same year, also citing Proverbs VIII. 15 (Ep. 15, PL 126: 98A–B), with Anton, *Fürstenspiegel*, pp. 297–8, and Nelson, 'Kingship, Law', pp. 134–5, note 4.
[106] *MEL* I, 423–6. Cf. the relevance of Solomonic wisdom, discussed above, pp. 158–66.
[107] Cf. above, pp. 51–2.   [108] *C&S*, no. 4, p. 8, line 19, to p. 9, line 5.
[109] *Ibid.*, p. 9, lines 19–25.   [110] *Ibid.*, p. 9, line 25, to p. 10, line 2; cf. esp. p. 11, lines 19–24.
[111] Above, pp. 211–12.

'holy' offences, but cannot easily be read as an English deployment of canon law.

This impression is reinforced by the Alfredian introduction, far from slavish in its handling of Hincmarian legal theory. The account of divine law is largely replicated, but within a different framework of English law-giving. The connections suggest a context close to the reception of Fulk's letter. The text began with 'ða domas þe se ælmihtega God self sprecende wæs to Moyse'; these in turn Christ said he came 'not to break or to forbid, but to augment with all good things' (a loose adaptation of Matthew V. 17, cited by Hincmar in a similar context).[112] Next came the Epistle from Jerusalem, whose approach of compromise and relaxed simplicity is related, as by Hincmar and Fulk, to necessities of conversion.[113] Then the text turns to the injunctions of church councils, summoned after the conversion of many peoples, here termed 'seonoðas'.[114] Yet both archbishops had used such history to bolster the 'holy canons', Hincmar to establish the contingent nature of papal decrees, Fulk to criticize English negligence. The introduction was instead developing precise connections with English secular law.

The operative passage is that describing conciliar activity, after 'many peoples had received the faith of Christ'. Fulk's account had appealed to the summoning of general councils 'non solum ex vicinis civitatibus vel provinciis, sed etiam ex transmarinis regionibus', implying that the English had sent delegates (and should now be bound by the resulting canons).[115] The introduction follows Fulk with 'monega seonoðas' assembled 'geond ealne middangeard', but then relates these (general?) councils to local English practice, in synods assembled 'geond Angelcyn'.[116] Such synods are credited with the full establishment of monetary-compensation (*fiohbot*), whose extraction lay at the heart of Anglo-Saxon law. These decisions lay preserved 'in many synod-books' (*in monega senoðbec*): it was upon such judgements, establishing 'compensation for many offences' (*monegra menniscra misdæda bote*), that the *Domboc* itself had drawn.[117] The role of 'synod-books' is especially problematic. 786 might be one precedent; very little can be known about source-manuscripts at royal disposal.[118] Yet the term *synodus* in an English

---

[112] *Af* Int.49. Hincmar, *Opusculum*, c. 22, PL 126: 387C.   [113] *Af* Int.49.1–49.6.

[114] *Af* Int.49.7.   [115] *C&S*, p. 9, lines 17–23.

[116] 'Siððan ðæt þa gelamp, þæt monega ðeoda Cristes geleafan onfengon, þa wurdon monega seonoðas geond ealne middangeard gegaderode, and eac swa geond Angelcyn, siððan hie Cristes geleafan onfengon, halegra biscepa and eac oðerra geðungenra witena' ('After this, when it happened that many peoples had received the faith of Christ, many synods of holy bishops and also other distinguished wise men were assembled throughout all the earth, and likewise throughout the English, after they had received the faith of Christ'): *Af* Int.49.7.

[117] *Af* Int.49.7.   [118] Wormald, 'Offa's "Law-Code"', p. 221; *MEL* I, 106–7 and 280–1.

context had been reserved for provincial councils.[119] Diplomatic usage was precise in distinguishing *synodus* from royal *concilium*, of which there is every impression in Ine's preface.[120] At the same time, monetary-compensation, together with feud and much else, can only have been pre-Christian in origin.[121] For the introduction, the establishment of *bot* was an act of Christian mercy, respecting holy sanction in the aftermath of conversion.

Both peculiarities make sense, however, when judged against Fulk's earlier position. Critical of English practices, his letter had aimed at their comprehensive 'updating' in line with 'holy canons'. Alfred's history now effected an inventive vindication of native observance, via the medium of secular law. Contrary to Fulk's criticism, English practices were already in accordance with ecclesiastical canons, and had long been so, through the primordial establishment of monetary-compensation by native 'synods'. Alfred's sources already supplied 'wise' judgement consonant with Christian teaching; little amendment would be needed for his own laws to satisfy these 'Solomonic' principles. The judgements in question did not merely accord with divine law, they were themselves divine, established by synods within the additional burdens of canonical legislation. Yet Alfred's own assembly had been royal, involving the entirety of his 'wise men'.[122] Drawn from multiple 'synod-books', the *Domboc* now offered law from a single source, in partially imagined appropriation. All Hincmarian distinction between divine and secular was now radically blurred by the synodal origin of merciful compensation. The effect was to place native law, and Alfred's judgements, directly at the head of God's own legal continuum.

Nor is such a response surprising. The 'divine' character of royal law has emerged as a central fact of the enlarged tenth-century 'English' polity, exploited to the full by archbishop Wulfstan under renewed viking pressures.[123] Its Alfredian emergence has generally been attributed to the impact of Frankish models, over a biblical agenda borrowed from Bede.[124] Yet its precise formulation, subtly recasting Hincmarian theory, strengthens the significance of internal practices whose operation

---

[119] See evidence cited by Cubitt, *Councils*, pp. 4–7, notwithstanding her discussion, the principal exceptions being the Northumbrian synod of Whitby, whose status is uncertain; and Willibald, *Vita Sancti Bonifatii*, c. 4, whose 'synodale concilium' need not precisely reflect English terminology. Cf. King Edmund's 'micel sinoð' of 941 × 946 (*ibid.*, pp. 238–9), postdating Alfredian transition (cf. below, p. 348).
[120] S 168 (BCS 335) and S 1436 (BCS 384), with Cubitt, *Councils*, p. 6, cf. 5.
[121] *MEL* I, 422, with note 26.   [122] *Af* Int.49.10.
[123] Esp. Wormald, 'Lex Scripta', p. 34; Wormald, 'Engla Lond', pp. 375–7; *MEL* I, 426–9, 448–65 and 481.
[124] *MEL* I, 416–29.

received such learned defence. The reception of Frankish learning must be judged against the existing character of West Saxon kingship, already harnessing 'chosen' status in a distinctive blend of devotional ritual.[125] Mechanisms of covenant and divine aid gave service to West Saxon dynastic triumph, symbolically renewed by royal anointing and specially related to the operation of justice and law. Solomonic posturing, the role for ealdormen in the transmission of royal sceptre, the 'three precepts' issued by new king to his subject people: all elements combined to express the existing status of West Saxon royal justice, specifically devoted to the forbidding of 'thefts' and the upholding of God's 'equity and mercy'.[126] Rather than Frankish or Bedan borrowing in this respect, the *Domboc* emerges as a further 'strengthening' of West Saxon kingship, the textual extension of 'chosen' status within a single framework of royal and divine justice.

Other features also acquire force. The conspicuous amendment facilitated by the Ine appendix contrasts significantly with Hincmarian treatment of secular law. Alfredian revision makes more sense against the backdrop of divine contingency, comparable to the status of papal decrees. The introduction takes care to show the special relevance of biblical precedent for native legal judgement, rooted in the law of Christ. Not only is his teaching shown to have hinged upon 'mercy and humility'; it also supplies the 'Golden Rule', cited in its negative form at the end of the Epistle from Jerusalem. 'Do not do to other men that which you wish that other men would not do to you':[127] the addition differs from Hincmar and Fulk, following an Old Latin variant which also occurs in some Vulgate texts.[128] 'From this one judgement a man can learn to judge every man rightly; he needs no other judgement-book (*ne ðearf he nanra domboca operra*)': the 'Rule' supplied a defining basis for all textual activity, supported by the only rubric applying to the introduction.[129]

---

[125] Above, pp. 63–78. [126] Above, pp. 75–8.

[127] 'Þæm halgan Gaste wæs geðuht and us, þæt we nane byrðenne on eow settan noldon ofer þæt ðe eow neddearf wæs to healdanne: þæt is ðonne, þæt ge forberen þæt ge deofolgeld ne weorðien, ne blod ne ðicggen ne asmorod, and from diernum geligerum; and þæt ge willen, þæt oðre men eow ne don, ne doð ge ðæt oþrum monnum' ('It seemed to the Holy Spirit and to us, that we would not set any burden upon you beyond that which was necessary to restrain you: that is, therefore, that you should forbear from worshipping idols, from tasting blood or things strangled, and from secret fornications; and do not do to other men that which you wish that other men would not do to you'): *Af* Int.49.5.

[128] Acts XV. 29 (cf. Matthew VII. 12, Luke VI. 31, Tobit IV. 16), in *Novum Testamentum*, ed. Wordsworth and White III, 139–40, cf. *Bibliorum Sacrorum latinae uersiones antiquae*, ed. Sabatier III, 552–3; *MEL* I, 423. As a Vulgate reading, it is principally attested in the edition of Theodulf, but since it also occurs in the Book of Armagh (s. ix$^{1/2}$), this may be further evidence for Irish influence (discussed below); cf. K&L, *Alfred*, p. 53, on Asser.

[129] 'Be þon ðæt mon ne scyle oþrum deman buton swa he wille, ðæt him mon deme' ('How a man ought not to judge others except as he would wish to be judged'): *Af* Rubric I, with Int.49.6.

Hincmar's repressive conception of law was here applied to every man, clarifying the *Domboc*'s own status as a source of additional judgement, only imposed against sin.

The case extends to Mosaic law, accorded such respect within divine law-giving: the excerpts suggest the additional impact of Irish learning. Rather than direct recourse to the Vulgate, the translation probably followed the *Liber ex lege Moysi*, an Irish compilation of Old Testament law attributed to the later seventh century.[130] Although the translation omits certain laws present in the *Liber*, and rejects all excerpts from Leviticus, Numbers and Deuteronomy, no law is introduced which the *Liber* ignores.[131] The *Liber* would also account for the peculiar treatment of the Tenth Commandment and misplaced verse-order at the start of chapter 22.[132] Manuscripts show the *Liber* circulating with other Irish canonical texts, including the *Collectio Canonum Hibernensis*, with all four examples written in or near Brittany.[133] Although two of these were subsequently imported into England, one was probably written after Alfred's death, and neither contains a text which could have been translated directly.[134] Asser includes Irishmen and Bretons among visitors submitting to Alfred's lordship; the Psalm translation shows further signs of Irish scholarly activity.[135]

An important principle has been suggested for the *Liber* in the exclusion of laws clearly invalidated by the coming of Christ.[136] The *Domboc* shows comparable respect for Old Testament precedent, heightened by inventive translation, far removed from Hieronymian

---

[130] P. Fournier, 'Le Liber ex lege Moysi et les tendances bibliques du droit canoniqe irlandais', *Revue Celtique* 30 (1909), 221–34, at 230–2; R. Kottje, 'Der Liber ex lege Moysis', in *Irland und die Christenheit*, ed. Ní Chatháin and Richter, pp. 59–69; *MEL* I, 419–21.

[131] *Liber*: Exodus XX. 1–17 and 23–6, XXI–XXII, XXIII. 1–19. Cf. *Af* Int.1–48: Exodus XX. 1–3, 7–17 and 23, XXI, XXII. 1–11 and 16–31, XXIII. 1, 2, 4, 6–9 and 13.

[132] The Second Commandment is omitted, supplemented by a new Tenth Commandment ('Do not make golden or silver gods'), leaving images of God unmentioned: *Af* Int.10, cf. Exodus XX. 23. A similar cautious acceptance of the veneration of images had been promoted by Hincmar. Cf. Turk, *Legal Code*, pp. 34–5; F. Liebermann, 'King Alfred and Mosaic Law', *Transactions of the Jewish Historical Society of England* 6 (1908–10), 21–31, at 25–6. *Af* Int.24–5; cf. Exodus XXII. 1–5; Corráin, Breatnach and Breen, 'Laws of the Irish', pp. 413–17; cf. Kottje, 'Liber', pp. 65 and 68–9.

[133] Kottje, 'Liber', pp. 61–6.

[134] London, British Library, Otho E. xiii, fols. 3v–10r (probably NW Francia, later at St Augustine's, Canterbury, s. x^{in}); Cambridge, Corpus Christi College MS 279, pp. 106–55 (written at Tours or under Turonian influence, later at Worcester, s. ix$^{2/2}$). Both texts are corrupt and include numerous minor departures from the Vulgate, not reproduced in the *Domboc*.

[135] *VA* 76, line 22, p. 60; *ASC* s.a. 891; D. N. Dumville, *Liturgy and the Ecclesiastical History of Late Anglo-Saxon England: Four Studies* (Woodbridge, 1992), pp. 133 and 148–9; D. N. Dumville, *English Caroline Script and Monastic History: Studies in Benedictinism, A.D. 950–1030* (Woodbridge, 1993), p. 48, for Breton contributions to learning. Cf. below, pp. 248–51.

[136] Kottje, 'Liber', pp. 60–1.

literalism. Even biblical texts could receive flexible treatment, openly exploiting comparative potential. Israel offered a parallel society reliant on land, livestock and slaves: selections dealt with common problems.[137] The effect was sharpened in translation, playfully expressing laws as if they were contemporary, even in cases requiring heavy licence. A *servus hebraeus* becomes a *cristen þeow*; a compensation-payment in 'sheckels' is converted into local 'shillings'.[138] The exclusion of asses matched Anglo-Saxon dependence on oxen, while a suggestion of polygamy was judiciously avoided.[139] Rephrasing of longer provisions imitated the structure of contemporary written law. Additional clauses clarify the scope of offences, placing limits on culpability. A man who sells a freeman into slavery is to die only if 'he cannot account for himself' (*he hine bereccean ne maege*).[140] One killing another 'either unwillingly or involuntarily' is to be 'worthy of his life and lawful compensation (*folcryhtre bote*)' if he seeks refuge (*friðstow*).[141] Anyone killing a thief after sunrise is to be accounted guilty 'unless he was acting under compulsion'.[142] A man accused of concealing goods entrusted to him is not to be brought *ad deos* ('before judges'), but simply to *geladian* himself, a technical verb for exculpation.[143] The following law is recast as a subclause to the previous injunction, to apply only if the goods were live cattle; different outcomes depend on the availability of *gewitnesse*, clarifying more allusive provisions.[144]

The imitation was two-way, embracing the entire structure of the *Domboc* in its division into 120 sections. As Wormald points out, the figure was not only Mosaic, as the law-giver's age at death, but offered further connection with the early church, as the number of brethren upon whom the Holy Spirit descended after Christ's ascension in Acts I and II.[145] A few of Alfred's own laws may bear the imprint of Mosaic inspiration: at any rate, the killing of pregnant women and beastly injuries were shared concerns.[146] There can be no question of the Mosaic excerpts actually applying to Alfred's kingdom. The effect was rather to supply a convincing impression of what law would look like without the benefits of Christian augmentation. One area was Christian mercy, as the introduction later

---

[137] *MEL* I, 419–21; Liebermann, 'Mosaic Law'.

[138] Exodus XXI. 2 and 32; cf. *Af* Int.11 and 21.

[139] Exodus XX. 23, XXI. 33, XXII. 4, 9 and 10, XXXI. 4–5, XXXI. 12. Cf. *Af* Int.10, 22, 25, 28, 42 and 48. Exodus XXI. 10, cf. *Af* Int.12.

[140] Exodus XXI. 16; cf. *Af* Int.15.

[141] Exodus XXI. 13; cf. *Af* Int.13 (also *ungewealdes* in *Af* 13).   [142] Exodus XXI. 3; cf. *Af* Int.25.

[143] Exodus XXII. 7–9; cf. *Af* Int.28.

[144] Exodus XXII. 10–11; cf. *Af* Int.28. Cf. also *Af* Int.17 (Exodus XXI. 20–1).

[145] *MEL* I, 417–18.

[146] *Ibid.*, 282; *Af* 9 cf. *Af* Int.18 (Exodus XXI. 22–3); *Af* 24 cf. *Af* Int.21 (Exodus XXI. 28–32).

specified.[147] For all the added caveats, no doubt could be left of Mosaic severity. Bodily injuries remain starkly 'eye for eye, tooth for tooth'.[148] Punishments of death abound, imposed without qualification for wilful murder, slaying or merely cursing a parent, copulation with cattle and offerings to false gods.[149] It is for 'wise men' to decide whether a lord should be killed even for failing to enclose a dangerous ox.[150] Contrasts were many with Alfredian justice. Fundamental was the absence of kingship, necessarily lacking from patriarchal law.

Every aspect of comparison asserted 'chosen' status under royal justice. The role of mercy was integral to this status, as the additional property of a *populus Christianus*, as was kingship, exclusively informed by synodal norms.[151] Here again was the determining force of local conditions, the established strengths of West Saxon kingship. Such extreme biblicism clearly matched the existing qualities of the First *Ordo*, complementary in its literal recreation of anointing.[152] The role of mercy was highlighted in the third precept, 'that the clement and merciful God may therefore grant us his mercy'; both precepts and sceptre upheld the special benefits of royal law.[153] Precisely such benefits were being exported under Alfred from their single dynastic source; the same now received heightened expression in textual form.

THE DEFENCE OF LORDSHIP

The origin asserted for Alfred's sources incorporated generous limits of Christian mercy. The payment of *bot* had been declared by synods 'for almost every misdeed', enabling its plentiful reception by 'worldly lords' for first offences, without taint of sin:

[B]uton æt hlafordsearwe hie nane mildheortnesse ne dorston gecweðan, forþam ðe God ælmihtig þam nane ne gedemde þe hine oferhogdon, ne Crist Godes sunu þam nane ne gedemde þe hine to deaðe sealde, and he bebead þone hlaford lufian swa hine.[154]

---

[147] *MEL* I, 422–3; M. Treschow, 'The Prologue to Alfred's Law Code: Instruction in the Spirit of Mercy', *Florilegium* 13 (1994), 79–110.

[148] Exodus XXI. 24; *Af* Int.19. Cf. *Af* 44–77.

[149] Exodus XXI. 12, 15, 19 and XXII. 20; *Af* Int.13, 14 and 31–2.

[150] Exodus XXI. 29; *Af* Int.21.

[151] Cf. *MEL* I, 422–3: 'But he did not need three chapters of (in parts ferocious) Mosaic law to make the point that judicial mercy was a by-product of conversion'.

[152] Above, pp. 75–8. Cf. Wormald's insistent connecting of biblicism with 'English' ethnicity (*MEL* I, 418–19 and 426–7).

[153] Above, pp. 76–8.

[154] 'Only for lord-treachery did they not dare to declare any mercy, because almighty God judged none to those who despised him, nor did Christ, God's son, judge any to the one who betrayed him to death; and he commanded each to love his lord as Himself': *Af* Int.49.7.

The chain of references might seem fanciful, did they not have clear connection with Alfred's own laws. Mercy had ceased only with outright treachery, located in the field of lordship. God himself had judged no mercy to those who despised him, perhaps a reference to Exodus XXII. 20, punishing by death those who made offerings to foreign gods.[155] Nor had Christ overruled Mosaic law in this case, with his curse on Judas, fulfilled in Acts I. 16–19: 'Woe to that man by whom the Son of man is betrayed; it were better for him, if that man had not been born'.[156] 'And he commanded each to love his lord as himself': Christ had in fact enjoined love of the Lord God and of each neighbour 'sicut te ipsum'. 'Swa hine' conveys both 'as oneself' and 'as Christ Himself', in playful amalgamation of the two injunctions, the latter meaning intensified by the double implications of *hlaford*.[157]

'Butan æt hlafordsearwe': the exclusion coincides with Alfred's law of the same name, supporting immediate continuity of divine principles, the uniting statement of Alfredian judgement. Matching divine mercy, *hlafordsearu* bears almost the only punishment by death in the entire collection. Firstly, anyone plotting against the king's life, either 'by himself, or through the harbouring of fugitives or his men' ('ðurh hine oððe ðurh wreccena feormunge oððe his manna') is to lose his life and possessions, unless he is able to exculpate himself by an oath equivalent to the king's wergild. Secondly, the same liability is established 'for all orders', *ge ceorle ge eorle*, for anyone plotting against the life of his lord, with parallel exculpation to the value of his lord's wergild.[158] The punishments here articulated lie at the heart of Wormald's view of later English law, postulating a single system of justice behind the more disparate written evidence.[159] Several variations on the law of *hlafordsearu* were issued by later kings;[160] certain laws of Edward and Æthelstan regard a man who harbours fugitives as having broken 'his oath and his pledge' (*his að and his wedd*).[161] Alfred's own laws begin with provisions for each man keeping 'his oath and his pledge', as a matter of the greatest need ('þæt mæst ðearf is').[162] In an illuminating conjecture, Wormald suggests

---

[155] *Af* Int.32.
[156] Matthew XXVI. 24, Mark XIV. 21; cf. reference to 120 disciples in Acts I. 15.
[157] Matthew XXII. 26–40; Turk, *Legal Code*, pp. 32–3.   [158] *Af* 4–4.2.
[159] Esp. Wormald, 'Frederic William Maitland and the Earliest English Law', in his *Legal Culture*, pp. 45–69; Wormald, 'God and King'; Wormald, '*Engla Lond*', pp. 366–71; *MEL* I, 144–50, 282–4, 448–9 and 481–3.
[160] *II Æthelstan* 4; *III Edgar* 7.3; *V Æthelred* 30; *VI Æthelred* 37; *II Cnut* 26 and 57.
[161] *II Edward* 4–5.2 (decrees issued at Exeter). *IV Æthelstan* 3–3.2 (decrees issued at Thunderfield) and *V Æthelstan* Prologue 3 (decrees issued at Exeter) record two very similar laws necessary because 'ða aðus and þa wedd and þa borgas' given at Grately had been broken (*II Æthelstan* issued at Grately).
[162] *Af* 1–1.8.

Alfredian reference to a general oath of loyalty, exacted from all subjects, closely related to Frankish arrangements in a form established under Charlemagne.[163] The oath in question may have been that of 802, required from all freemen over the age of twelve, which equated fidelity with a whole range of obligations in respect of God, ruler and justice.[164] It was also sworn 'sicut per drictum debet esse homo domino suo'; later West Frankish provisions show that this implied specific obligations against theft.[165] Nearly the same formula appears in an oath required from 'omnes' in 943, pledging loyalty to King Edmund 'sicut homo debet esse fidelis domino suo'.[166] This in turn may be the context for Cnut's oath, required from every man over twelve, 'that he will not be a thief nor a thief's accomplice'.[167]

The effect was to equate crime in general, including theft, with *hlafordsearu* against the king.[168] The most explicit expression again belongs to Cnut, in his law delineating 'botleas' offences, without compensation in secular law, setting lord-treachery alongside house-breaking, arson, open theft and manifest murder.[169] Proven thieves risked death and forfeiture, with any thief in flight deemed an outlaw (*utlah*) who could be killed on sight.[170] For Wormald, general oath-taking was central to local peace-keeping and enforcement. In addition to non-assistance, under punishment as *hlafordsearu* for the harbouring of fugitives, obligations extended to include positive action, whenever necessary, against local offenders. Laws of Edward are explicit in treating failure to pursue thieves as a breach of 'oath and pledge', punished in the *Domboc* by forty days' imprisonment.[171] Refusal to ride was disobedience

---

[163] Esp. Wormald, '*Lex Scripta*', p. 12; Wormald, 'Ninth Century', p. 155; Wormald, '*Engla Lond*', pp. 366–7. Cf. earlier case for general oath focusing on *II Edward* 5: Stubbs, *Constitutional History* I, 225–6; Liebermann, *Gesetze* II, 413 ('Frieden' 4); J. Goebel, *Felony and Misdemeanor: a Study in the History of Criminal Law* (New York, 1937), p. 424; Campbell, 'Observations on English Government', p. 162.

[164] MGH Capit. I, no. 33, cc. 2–9, pp. 92–3; MGH Capit. I, no. 34, c. 19, pp. 101–2, cf. earlier oath of 789 (MGH Capit. I, no. 23, c. 18, p. 63). Detailed regulations for the re-taking of the 789 oath in 792 × 793 reveal that those who refused to swear were to be kept in custody or brought to the king (MGH Capit. I, no. 25, c. 4, p. 67). F. L. Ganshof, 'Charlemagne's Use of the Oath', in his *Frankish Monarchy*, pp. 111–24; C. E. Odegaard, 'Carolingian Oaths of Fidelity', *Speculum* 16 (1941), 284–96; M. Becher, *Eid und Herrschaft: Untersuchungen zum Herrscherethos Karls des Grossen* (Sigmaringen, 1993), pp. 78–216.

[165] MGH Capit. II, no. 260 (853), cc. 4–8, pp. 272–3, with oaths (p. 274); esp. c. 4 on oath-taking by each 'Francus', cited from Ansegisus, *Capitularium Collectio*, III.23; MGH Capit. II, no. 261 (854), p. 278, giving text of oath 'sicut Francus homo per rectum esse debet suo regi' (Wormald, '*Engla Lond*', pp. 66–7, note 23; cf. Goebel, *Felony*, pp. 98–122); strangely overlooked by Ganshof and Becher as evidence for earlier Frankish arrangements (cf. *Eid and Herrschaft*, pp. 18–19).

[166] *III Edmund* 1 (decrees issued at Colyton in 943). [167] *II Cnut* 21.

[168] Wormald, 'Charters, Law', pp. 307–8; '*Engla Lond*', p. 367; 'God and King', pp. 338–42; 'Maitland', pp. 61–3; *MEL* I, 144–50; cf. Goebel, *Felony*, pp. 359–60 and 424–5.

[169] *II Cnut* 64. [170] *IV Æthelstan* 6–6.3; *II Æthelstan* 20.3–20.6. [171] *II Edward* 4–5.2, cf. *Af* 1.

to the king, fined 120 shillings for 'ðæs cynges oferhyrnesse'.[172] A further element were structures of surety (*borg*), guaranteeing adherence to these legal duties. Cnut's law on oath-taking is preceded by that requring all freemen to be brought within hundred and tithing, groups of ten men collectively responsible for peace-keeping and good conduct.[173] West Frankish provisions of the mid-ninth century show the general oath being sworn by 'centenarii' and 'decani', evidence often neglected in accounts of earlier Frankish oath-taking.[174] The operation of tithings first emerges in regulations dating from Æthelstan's reign; attributing their genesis to Alfred, Wormald's case again rests on constancy of 'oath and pledge'.[175]

The significance of Wormald's interpretation lies in the framework provided for tenth-century 'English' justice, characterized by a strong sense of offence against the king.[176] The system as a whole complements his case against jurisdictional immunities in Anglo-Saxon England, supporting a single structure of 'royal' courts.[177] Oath and surety suggest mechanisms at local level of mutual self-help, in a picture prefiguring many post-Conquest features of peace-keeping and later common law.[178] His evidence for punishment by forfeiture contributes to the apparent strengths of later English kingship.[179] The Frankish context for his system points to the continuing importance of foreign contacts and imported learning through the tenth century and beyond.[180] For the *Domboc* also, the treatment of treachery betrays cross-Channel awareness, with the collection of Ansegisus as a likely written conduit, supplementing royal personnel.[181]

The question remains how far one should envisage an integral system, erected under Alfred alone.[182] The 'criminalization' of treachery cannot be doubted: an initial point concerns the implications of 'oath and pledge'. Association with loyalty is shown in detail for Æthelred's return

---

[172] *II Æthelstan* 20.2, cf. *I Edgar* 2–3.   [173] *II Cnut* 20.

[174] MGH Capit. II, no. 260 (853), p. 274; MGH Capit. II, no. 261 (854), p. 278; Wormald, '*Engla Lond*', pp. 66–7, note 23; Wormald, 'Maitland', p. 56.

[175] '*Engla Lond*', pp. 366–7; 'Maitland', pp. 54–6; *MEL* I, 5 and 137, cf. 7–8, 10, 13–14, 18, 363, 406. There can be no direct connection with Æthelwulf's decimation (cf. Stubbs, *Constitutional History* I, 92).

[176] 'God and King'; '*Engla Lond*'; *MEL* I, 430–65.   [177] 'Lordship and Justice'.

[178] 'Maitland'; *MEL* I, 5 and 137.   [179] 'God and King'; '*Engla Lond*'.

[180] *MEL* I, 286–366 and 430–65.

[181] *MEL* I, 277 and 280; Ansegisus, *Capitularium Collectio*, III.1, 8, 23 and 88 (English transmission of Ansegisus a projected element for *MEL* II); cf. Oxford, Bodleian Library, Hatton 42 (4117), fols. 188–204: Book I only (W. Francia, s. ix^med; in England by s. x^in, later Worcester provenance); and source-texts for Wulfstan's 'Handbook' (*Wulfstan's Canon Law Collection*, ed. Cross and Hamer).

[182] Cf. response to Wormald by P. Hyams, 'Feud and the State in Late Anglo-Saxon England', *Journal of British Studies* 40 (2001), 1–43, esp. pp. 12–17, 30–4 and 36, elements of which would need revision in light of MGH Capit. II, no. 260 (853), pp. 270–6.

in 1014; at the same time, usage is regularly associated with agreements reached at royal assemblies.[183] It is questionable whether oath-taking must be seen as truly general, especially earlier in the period. 'His að and his wæd ... ðe eal ðeod geseald hæfð': Edward's formula bears comparison with the peace between Alfred and Guthrum, similarly concerning 'eal seo ðeod' in East Anglia, where oaths were sworn by participants in the peace both 'for themselves and for their subordinates (*gingran*), both living and unborn'.[184] After earlier agreement at Grately, Æthelstan's decrees at Exeter appeal explicitly to oaths, pledges and sureties 'that were given there', by implication at the assembly.[185] Grately itself had included provision for the oral promulgation of royal wishes in local assemblies.[186]

The point relates closely to the emergence of tithings, not explicitly mentioned in Ansegisus. The strength of Frankish precedent must be balanced against the many possibilities of post-Alfredian innovation. William of Malmesbury's attribution of tithings to Alfred warrants greater respect than has often been allowed, yet his claim might equally reflect awareness of later Anglo-Saxon law.[187] A case remains for systematization under Æthelstan, amid more intensive recourse to Frankish legislation under Alfred's son and grandson.[188] Laws of Edward and an early decree of Æthelstan appear to envisage surety provided by relatives, guaranteeing legal duties under the necessary oversight of the miscreant's lord.[189] These arrangements might be contrasted with an apparent tightening of seigneurial responsibility later in Æthelstan's reign, with surety (*fideiussio*) assigned to lords 'against every theft', delegated to reeves for large estates.[190] Tithings of the London peace-guild, bound by pledge, may show the same process in greater detail.[191] The case for change receives support from the general context of Æthelstan's later assemblies, otherwise concerned to restrain powerful kindreds as the primary hindrance to earlier agreements.[192] Even at this stage the tithing left room for relatives; only in Cnut's laws is the term treated synonymously with *borg*.[193]

[183] *ASC* s.a. 1014 (MSS CDE); *IV Æthelstan* 3.2; *ASC* s.a. 918 (Mercian Register; MSS BCD), s.a. 927 and 947 (MS D).
[184] *II Edward* 5; *AGu* Prologue (MS B; cf. Liebermann, *Gesetze* III, 84).
[185] *V Æthelstan* Prologue 3.   [186] *II Æthelstan* 20.3.
[187] *GR* I, 188–9, cf. Thomson's commentary (II, 98).
[188] The view was expressed by Goebel, *Felony*, pp. 359–60 and 425–6, in full awareness of Frankish parallels (cf. *MEL* I, 25–6).
[189] *II Edward* 3, cf. 6; *II Æthelstan* 2–2.2. Cf. *Ine* 22.
[190] *III Æthelstan* 7–7.3; cf. *III Edmund* 7, *I Æthelred* 1, *II Cnut* 31.   [191] *VI Æthelstan* 3–11.
[192] *IV Æthelstan* 3, *V Æthelstan* Prologue 1 (kindreds); *IV Æthelstan* 3.2, *V Æthelstan* Prologue 1 and 3 (earlier peace not kept); *III Æthelstan* 3; *IV Æthelstan* 6 (amnesties for theft).
[193] *VI Æthelstan* 1.4 (lord or kinsmen to stand surety in case of wrongdoing), 8.2 (asserts peace-guild against powerful kindreds), 9 (proven thieves may be liberated by lord or relatives); *II Cnut* 20, cf. earlier laws requiring all to have surety (*III Edgar* 6; *IV Edgar* 3; *I Æthelred* 1).

The Domboc *as a reorientation of royal law*

The question arises of Alfredian novelty, especially pressing given the shortage of earlier written law. The first precept of the First *Ordo* already upheld the keeping of peace among a Christian people. By the second precept, West Saxon kings were already committed to forbidding 'all thefts (*rapacitates*) and injustices among all orders'.[194] Retained in the Second *Ordo*, both precepts expressed fundamental principles of tenth-century royal law.[195] Other evidence supports royal history on the authority of lords in native law.[196] Laws of Ine imply active co-operation with royal officials in the punishment of thieves, with payment of wergild by anyone convicted of harbouring a fugitive.[197] Charter reservation clauses of the eighth and early ninth century strengthen an important role for lords in local peace-keeping, receiving fines for convicted theft and other rights of punishment, while otherwise responsible in respect of compensation for thefts committed by their men.[198] The 'botleas' char-acter of treachery underpinned all operation of lordship; this in turn had found application to kingship in the capitulary of 786, with appeal to royal status as *christus Domini*, citing Judas, Esther II. 22 and David's refusal to strike Saul as models against the 'killing of lords' (*internecio dominorum*).[199] In Wessex, above all, royal lordship formed the basis for kingship, inten-sively exercised over thegns of the king.[200]

Far from unexpected in this context, some extension of treachery might well be imagined earlier in the ninth century, with little hope of its detection. Yet there are grounds for associating change with Alfred.[201] The *Domboc* threatened forfeiture as well as death: Alfred's reign coincides not only with the earliest examples of forfeited land, but with efforts to safeguard land on loan by its terms of lease.[202] For Wormald such evidence is confirmatory of oral law-making, his system only partially observable in Alfred's laws.[203] Yet his case is weakened if swearing in tens began under Æthelstan. Alfredian innovation might on this basis be understood to have embraced a general obligation to pursue thieves, expressed by oath-taking which may well have been surrogate in many cases, together with widened parameters of treachery against the king. While the latter acquired punishment by forfeiture, the former received penalty of imprisonment, with outlawry for flight. Both measures gained force from the role of local lords, with enhanced responsibilities

---

[194] Above, p. 76. [195] Nelson, 'Second English *Ordo*', p. 363; *MEL* I, 446–8.
[196] Cf. *Af* Int.49.7. [197] *Ine* 30 cf. 28. [198] Goebel, *Felony*, pp. 347–58; *MEL* I, 108; *Ine* 22.
[199] *Capitulare* of the papal legates (786), c. 12.
[200] Cf. prominence of Judas as betrayer in S 298 of 846 (BCS 451; trans. *EHD*, no. 88).
[201] 'Lex Scripta', pp. 9–10; *MEL* I, 282–5.
[202] Esp. Wormald, 'Handlist'; 'Charters, Law', pp. 306–8; 'God and King', pp. 337–42 and 350–3; *MEL* I, 144–8, 306–7; Keynes, 'Fonthill Letter', pp. 85–6.
[203] *MEL* I, 283–4, cf. 481–3.

for local pursuit and the conduct of their men. This is not very far from Alfred's own written laws, only lacking in the place of theft.

Nor can their precise terms have derived from Ansegisus, a point more striking against the collection's deeper influence under Alfred's successors.[204] The king's life receives special protection, while the stress on non-royal lordship may bear closer comparison with Continental Saxon law.[205] The impression is of broader reflection on European precedent, driven above all by internal conditions. The protection of lords correlates with ninth-century developments in seigneurial control; the package as a whole reasserted much at a time when local bonds faced serious threat.[206] Quite apart from cases of outright defection, viking pressure and military reorganization combined to create an effective shortage of labour, only matched by localized loss of livestock, produce and equipment.[207] Treatment of treachery provided further 'persuasion', towards the higher needs of burghal defence. The response of law-giving offered much to local lordship, collectively invested in peace-keeping and protection of property, at a time when both may have been in short supply. Heightened punishments left little room for non-cooperation, while further promoting income from portions of fines and forfeitures.[208] The overall effect was a novel royal monopoly over crime and punishment, actively harnessing shared seigneurial concern.

THE *DOMBOC* IN PRACTICE

Questions remain of the impact of Alfredian innovation, and of the *Domboc*'s own significance as law in writing. Each presents severe problems given the limited evidence for dispute settlement, skewed towards aristocratic cases involving land. Some significant shifts in legal practice cannot be doubted, in all likelihood extending to the lowest levels of society. Less clear is the precise contribution of written law, the more problematic in view of its distinctive form, combining introductory principle with specific legal decree.

Some important role for such textuality is suggested by its transmission, entirely consistent with early access to ealdormen, reeves and thegns. One would not expect any contemporary copies in secular hands to have

---

[204] Cf. Ansegisus, *Capitularium Collectio*, III.1, 8, 23 and 88.
[205] *Af* 4.2; F. S. Lear, *Treason in Roman and Germanic Law* (Austin, TX, 1965), pp. 247–9.
[206] Above, pp. 19–22, 98 and 174–5; cf. esp. *AGu* 5.
[207] *VA* 91, lines 58–67; cf. F. M. Stenton, 'Thriving of the Anglo-Saxon Ceorl', in his *Preparatory to Anglo-Saxon England*, ed. D. M. Stenton (Oxford, 1970), pp. 383–93, at 386–8.
[208] Not all forfeited land was due to the king, but principally bookland: Keynes, 'Fonthill Letter', pp. 85–6; *II Cnut* 77, cf. *I Edgar* 2.1–3.

survived. Though all are later manuscripts, the six principal witnesses attest to the ready availability of exemplars across southern England in the tenth and eleventh centuries.[209] Textual variation is sufficient to suggest at least four lines of transmission, with additional lost copies; still further readings may be preserved by Nowell and Lambarde.[210] This lends powerful substance to the centrality of Alfred's laws under later kings, repeatedly cited in later decrees as 'seo domboc'.[211] Texts in question include *I Edward*, specifically addressed to reeves, and *III Æthelstan*, a report by the bishops and thegns of Kent; access to the *Domboc* was regularly assumed for secular aristocratic audiences.[212] The consistency of rubrication has been noted, bearing parallels with the *Hierdeboc*. The *Domboc* too shows every sign of centralized dissemination, expanding the work of royal scribes.

Conventionally detected in aristocratic conduct, two early instances suggest the scope and complexity of Alfredian treachery. A charter of 901 records the regranting of an estate once forfeited by Wulfhere, ealdorman of Wiltshire, and his wife, 'when he deserted without permission both his lord King Alfred and his country, in spite of the oath which he had sworn to the king and all his leading men'.[213] The Fonthill letter describes the protagonist Helmstan forfeiting his *yrfe* ('property'), seemingly in consequence of his status as a proven and inveterate thief, and subsequently pronounced an outlaw (*flyma*) by King Edward.[214] Both cases raise problems of detail. Wulhere's treachery has generally been associated with 878, as an attested instance of defection, yet his judgement by 'West Saxons and Mercians' would fit more naturally into the 880s; his successor Æthelhelm first appears in 887.[215] Wulfhere's oath-taking might conceivably be associated with 886, the apparent genesis of kingship over 'Anglo-Saxons', and a possible context for some general oath of loyalty.[216] Helmstan's forfeiture presents difficulties as a straightforward breach of 'oath and pledge'; the case as a whole suggests genuine uncertainty in aspects of its application.[217]

---

[209] *MEL* I, 265–7; Richards, 'Manuscript Contexts'.

[210] Turk, *Legal Code*, pp. 19–25; Liebermann, *Gesetze* III, 30–2; Dammery, 'Law-Code' I, 112–72; Wormald, *MEL* I, 265–7; Wormald, 'The Lambarde Problem: Eighty Years On', in his *Legal Culture*, pp. 139–99.

[211] *I Edward* Prologue cf. definitive later references: *II Edward* 5 (*Af* 1); *II Edward* 5.2 (*Ine* 30 or *Af* 4); *II Æthelstan* 5 (*Af* 6); *II Edgar* 3 (*Ine* 4); *II Edgar* 5 (*Ine* 3).

[212] Keynes, 'Royal Government', pp. 232–3.

[213] S 362 (BCS 595; trans. *EHD*, no. 100); Wormald, 'Ninth Century', p. 155.

[214] S 1445 (BCS 591; trans. *EHD*, no. 102; Keynes, 'Fonthill Letter').

[215] *ASC* s.a. 887; Keynes, 'Mercians', p. 31, cf. Nelson, ' "King Across the Sea" ', pp. 52–5, esp. 53, note 41.

[216] K&L, *Alfred*, p. 266, note 200; Scharer, *Herrschaft*, pp. 111–12.

[217] Keynes, 'Fonthill Letter', esp. pp. 80–9; *MEL* I, 144–8.

While evidence for change, both cases suggest limits to the legal impact at aristocratic level. Both Wulfhere and Helmstan were thegns of the king, already bound to their lord by oaths of service. Wulfhere's act seems to have involved quite open disloyalty. Helmstan's case also hinged at more than one point on his status as the 'king's man', allowing special appeal to King Alfred's grave. Punishment also could be flexible: Wulfhere's fate is unknown, but his forfeiture is unlikely to have been complete: his grandson Wulfgar re-emerges as ealdorman under King Æthelstan.[218] Helmstan's outlawry was revoked by royal judgement, and his property at least partially restored, owing much to the protection of his godfather, ealdorman Ordlaf.[219] The limited impression is of necessary adjustment to the wider reach of treachery, tempered by the existing strength of royal lordship. Even in the case of forfeiture, royal judgement extended a monopoly already established, over disputes concerning bookland. Thegnly oath-taking was in any case personal, and its judgement direct. One may wonder how far such cases hinged on the articulation of law in writing.

Attention again shifts to experiences among lower orders of society, largely unattested in dispute-records but seemingly shaped by local aristocratic judgement. Settlements in assembly received procedural guidance from presiding office-holders, while peace-keeping involved local lordship and responsibilities for the conduct of men.[220] There is no need to envisage 'ready reference' in either arena to appreciate the transformatory power of written law.[221] The attractions of Frankish peace lay in its ready adaptation to existing structures. Alfredian innovation harnessed much that was familiar, yet redefined by novel description. Additional treatment of crime and forfeiture received force from novel and 'wise' justification. The value of written law lay precisely in such mental effects on aristocratic perception. Central to local peace, the role was especially significant given apparent limits in general oath-taking. The *Domboc*'s introduction and laws were complementary in evoking a single mental framework. The scale of introduction matched its pivotal role in expressing universal principles of royal law, applicable to every aspect of dispute and redress.[222] All payment to lords found uniting justification as Christian mercy. Transcending the limits of mercy, all remaining offences found definition as *hlafordsearu*, incapable of compensation, understood to extend in the king's case to

---

[218] *Charters*, ed. Robertson, p. 308.   [219] Keynes, 'Fonthill Letter', pp. 85–95.

[220] Goebel, *Felony*, pp. 347–61.

[221] Cf. Wormald's conclusion (*MEL* I, 481, cf. 483), ultimately struggling to explain the use of writing.

[222] Cf. Wormald's emphasis on 'English' ethnicity (*MEL* I, 418–19 and 426–7).

crime in general, including murder, theft and the harbouring of offenders. The appeal of royal law lay in its rational implementation of Christ's teaching, the merciful restraint of sin. Conduct according to the 'Golden Rule' left no need for written judgement.[223]

The best evidence for such impact lies not in dispute settlement but the character of later legislation, extensively dependent on Alfredian legal principles. Continuity was not merely textual, through recopying and citation; it drew also upon shared understanding of royal law, taken for granted in many instances of royal decree.[224] The only doubts concern the extent of royal peace, itself evidence for comprehension of its desirable implications.[225] Such was the legacy of Alfred's own, overtly textual, form of legal theatre. Alfredian principles drew every aspect of legal procedure into collective performance; its implications extended beyond formal settlement to every act of merciful restraint. Pursuit of thieves, outlawry, punishment for treachery: all were sustained by the king's own uniting projection, as object of betrayal and source of peace. Judgement at every stage summoned Alfred's own virtual presence, in all manifestations of courtly experience.

The *Domboc* was central to such theatre; even if not physically present, it was understood to be active against every breach of rightful self-judgement.[226] The action of local assemblies might occasionally provoke appeal to the king: here too, the *Domboc* could hardly be forgotten, as a known framework of legal principle. Through written law, Alfredian theatre found its deepest projection, extending beyond aristocratic agents to incorporate all subjects of Alfred's kingdom. Yet the only requirement for participation was Alfred's own protective lordship, a point proclaimed in the limits of law for every righteous man. Of 'Anglo-Saxon' generation, such qualities were equally paramount under later 'English' justice. Behind both lay the efficacy of more open-ended Alfredian performance: avowedly seigneurial, rooted in arenas of local peace. Both features were central to everyday aristocratic practice: together, these processes upheld what was indeed an intensive and literate reorientation of royal law, textually guided to the evolving needs of Alfred's kingdom.

---

[223] *Af* Int.49.6.   [224] *MEL* I, 286–366, esp. 286–308.
[225] *IV Æthelstan* 3.2; *V Æthelstan* Prologue 1 and 3.
[226] *Af* Int.49.6; cf. H. Mordek, 'Frühmittelalterliche Gesetzgeber und iustitia in Miniaturen weltlicher Rechtshandschriften', *Settimane* 42 (1995), 997–1052, and Mordek, 'Schriftlichkeit', pp. 320–30, for parallel representations of law as 'book'.

Chapter 12

TRIBULATION AND TRIUMPH IN THE FIRST FIFTY PSALMS

As songs largely attributed to King David, the Psalter offered special opportunities for expression within the framework of Alfredian discourse. David supplied a potent example of learned kingship, dominated by the demands of Israel's covenant, prefiguring many aspects of Solomonic rule. As a model for kingship, David received additional force from his significance in Gregory's writings, frequently cited as the archetype of humble responsibility. Such features offered unique potential for translation at royal hands, re-enacting Davidic composition. In form as well as translatory method, the vernacular Psalms show every sign of such enhanced exploitation, extending to subjects otherwise associated with the highest sphere of royal intimacy. The outcome was a highly complex form of literary performance, incorporating many layers of imagined reading. United by royal direction, the effect was to reinforce many aspects of Alfredian restraint.

PSALMODY AND ROYAL DEVOTION

Royal translation of the Psalter is not unexpected given the text's clear significance in Alfred's devotional practice. The Psalter's selection relates most directly to his personal prayerbook, containing material necessary for the divine Office, certain Psalms and many prayers.[1] Possessed by the king from an early age, the *libellus* captures the extreme nature of Alfred's piety, incorporating nocturnal visits to churches for prayer.[2] The daily Office was an obligation normally fulfilled only by ecclesiastics, following a weekly cycle during which all 150 Psalms would be chanted.[3]

---

[1] *VA* 24, lines 1–6; c. 88, lines 6–10. [2] *Ibid.* 74 and 76, lines 12–16.
[3] P. Salmon, *L'office divin au moyen âge*, Lex orandi 43 (Paris, 1967); S. J. P. van Dijk, 'The Bible in Liturgical Use', in *The Cambridge History of the Bible II*, ed. G. W. H. Lampe (Cambridge, 1969), 220–52, at 230–48; A. Hughes, *Medieval Manuscripts for Mass and Office: a Guide to their Organisation and Terminology* (Toronto, 1982), pp. 50–2 and 230.

Alfred's regime may be best explained by the impact of his mysterious illness, reportedly incurred in response to sin.[4] At the same time, his reign coincides with signs of wider activity, suggested by the likely presence in England of two Carolingian Psalters, both customized for personal use.[5] An Alfredian focus for such developments may be strengthened by the Book of Nunnaminster, an early prayerbook of Mercian origin, closely associated by inscription with Alfred's wife, Ealhswith.[6]

As the imported Psalters imply, Alfred's piety harnessed trends long familiar in the Carolingian world, dependent on ecclesiastical reform.[7] The hope of salvation for laymen combined with challenging 'correction' of their conduct in marriage and warfare. Frequently recommended in 'Mirrors for Laymen', private prayer and secret confession offered new release under a heightened fear of sin.[8] Closely connected with 'ministerial' rulership, such mechanisms acquired special potency in royal hands, matching exemplary vulnerability to personal sin.[9] Repentance might be willingly accepted; by the later ninth century, royal prayer supplied regular confirmation of humble and exemplary rule. The case of Charles the Bald has often seemed diagnostic of direct influence in this respect; parallels are certainly striking with several aspects of Alfredian behaviour.[10] Alfred's *libellus* bears close comparison with Charles's surviving prayerbook or *Enchiridion*, also containing prayers for the Hours, many prayers, and directions for use of the Psalms.[11] Charles, like Alfred, found portrayal as a suffering ruler, in a framework informed by Gregorian thought.[12] Sedulius Scottus commended Job-like testing as a source of strength: learned interpretation fluctuated with Charles's own moments of tribulation and triumph.[13] On one occasion also Charles faced serious illness, at a critical moment in 858; according to Heiric of

---

[4] Pratt, 'Illnesses', pp. 57–72.

[5] Cambridge, Corpus Christi College, MS 272 ('Psalter of Count Achadeus', diocese of Rheims, March 883 × May 884); London, British Library, Cotton Galba A. xviii (' "Æthelstan" Psalter', northern Francia, s. ix$^{1/2}$, with subsequent augmentations; in England by s. x^{in} at the latest); Pratt, 'Illnesses', pp. 48–9.

[6] M. P. Brown, *The Book of Cerne: Prayer, Patronage and Power in Ninth-Century England* (London, 1996), pp. 157–61, 168 and 178–81.

[7] Wallace-Hadrill, *Frankish Church*, pp. 283–6 and 403–11; Smith, 'Gender and Ideology'; Airlie, 'Anxiety'; Nelson, 'Monks'.

[8] *DIL* I.12 (PL 106: 145–7); Dhuoda, *Liber manualis*, ed. Thiebaux, II.3 and XI.1, pp. 80–1 and 232–3.

[9] Pratt, 'Illnesses', pp. 43–5.

[10] Scharer, 'History', pp. 190–206; Scharer, *Herrschaft*, pp. 71 and 104–7; Kershaw, 'Illness, Power', pp. 219–24.

[11] Deshman, 'Exalted Servant'; Pratt, 'Illnesses', p. 46.

[12] Staubach, *Rex Christianus*, pp. 191–7, cf. 320–34 on Herculean imagery; cf. Appendix, below, no. 5, p. 355. Deshman, 'Exalted Servant', pp. 390–1, 394–5 and 402–4.

[13] *RC* 16, pp. 72–5.

Auxerre, his bloodless victory showed 'Davidic propriety in the arts of war and peace'.[14] Were such practices directly transferable to Alfred's kingdom? Charles's Psalter, depicting Nathan on its front cover, shows the essential context of West Frankish episcopal correction.[15] Nor was such posturing unique: again, a wider scope is suggested by East Frankish practice, examined by Goldberg.[16]

Alfred's behaviour must in any case be judged against the Psalter's established significance in West Saxon devotion. Davidic aspects of kingship found clear expression in the short sceptre (*sceptrum*), the pre-eminent item of regalia in the First *Ordo*.[17] With a role for *principes* as well as bishops, its investiture gave force to royal justice. Æthelwulf's decimation had been sealed with psalmody, each ecclesiastical community performing fifty Psalms every Saturday, within a programme of prayer again reserving special treatment for bishops and ealdormen.[18] Psalmic commemoration was a practice more usually associated with lay donation, often measured in fifties; individual psalms might also be specified, in terms suggestive of the donor's preferences.[19] Yet such piety had limits: a canon of 747 commends the recitation of psalms to all *fideles*, regardless of linguistic ability, citing licentious exploitation of measures achieved by proxy.[20] Such aspiration provides a context for Alfred's own upbringing in the royal household, with an early role for psalms and prayers. The Latin Psalter had long functioned as a founding text in ecclesiastical education, commonly learnt by heart.[21]

Carolingian parallels seem similarly qualified by this context. There is no special role for bishops; royal translation took to extremes the king-centric character of existing practice. By contrast, Charles's suffering image had been actively promoted by West Frankish ecclesiastical writers; as David to Nathan, his behaviour showed sacerdotal regulation of the royal *ministerium*.[22] This was the significance of Carolingian royal

---

[14] '[M]ansuetissimus rex Carolus, belli pacisque artibus Davidicae semper modestiae comparandus': Heiric of Auxerre, *De miraculis Sancti Germani episcopi Autissiodorensis libri II*, ed. Duru, II.100 and 102, pp. 166–7; Nelson, *Charles the Bald*, pp. 188–9.
[15] Deshman, 'Exalted Servant', pp. 404–7, with figs. 17–18; De Jong, 'Power and Humility', pp. 31 and 51–2.
[16] Goldberg, 'Frontier Kingship', pp. 67–71, with fig. 5, for the Psalter of Louis the German; cf. MacLean, *Charles the Fat*, pp. 225–6.
[17] Above, p. 77.   [18] Above, pp. 68–70.
[19] Grant by ealdorman Oswulf and his wife Beornthryth, specifying 'two fifties', 805×810: S 1188 (*SEHD*, no. 1), cf. S 1198 (*SEHD*, no. 6); fifty Psalms also specified in *VI Æthelstan* 8.6. Cf. more elaborate liturgical commemoration of Æthelred and Æthelflæd in S 223 (*SEHD*, no. 13).
[20] Synod of *Clofesho* (747), cc. 26–7; Thacker, 'Monks, Preaching', p. 162.
[21] McKitterick, *Written Word*, pp. 217–18, 244–57 and 268–9; Riché, *Écoles*, pp. 297–305; Riché, 'Le Psautier'.
[22] Nelson, 'Kingship, Law', pp. 164–5; Deshman, 'Exalted Servant', pp. 406–8; *RC* 12, p. 54.

sin: though not always detrimental, its effects lay open to wider episcopal judgement. Alfred's translation openly exploited the involvement
of his person, not least through additions stressing personal sinfulness.
Frequently of a sexual nature, such extreme disclosure matched the
universality of Alfred's royal office, unencumbered in this respect by
Carolingian reform.[23] Just as important was the relative reach of royal
posturing, in Charles's case largely conducted for select ecclesiastical
audiences. The restricted character of West Frankish practice is epitomized by Charles's actions in 858.[24] Heiric's praise for the king celebrated his special relationship with the monastery of St-Germain,
Auxerre, to which Charles had withdrawn; his political recovery had
followed personal participation in the translation of St Germanus' body
to a grander tomb, accompanied by the singing of Psalms.[25] Only in East
Francia were conditions conducive to the wholesale participation of
secular aristocrats, carefully cultivated in rituals under Louis the German.[26] Even here behaviour was primarily oral and demonstrative,
reliant on oath-swearing, prayer and procession. Alfred's Psalms offered
instruction to all recipients of royal learning, both ecclesiastical and lay.
Wise priorities placed his text at the heart of collective ritual; 'personal'
aspects of translation gave heightened meaning to Alfred's own actions.

APPARATUS AND VOICE

Alfred's Psalms are only known from their transmission in a single late
eleventh-century manuscript, Paris, Bibliothèque Nationale de France,
lat. 8824, a bilingual bicolumnar Psalter compiled from four previously
unrelated items.[27] In the left column the scribe, Wulfwine, placed the
early Latin version of the Psalter known as the *Romanum*, sometimes
attributed to Jerome, as the revision requested by Pope Damasus in 384.
This text had been the standard edition of the Psalter in England for
at least three centuries after Augustine's arrival.[28] For his right column,
Wulfwine possessed a metrical version of the entire Psalter, translated

---

[23] Above, pp. 176–8.
[24] Nelson, ' "King Across the Sea" ', p. 67; cf. Scharer, *Herrschaft*, pp. 106–7.
[25] Heiric of Auxerre, *De miraculis Sancti Germani*, ed. Duru, II.101, pp. 166–7; Nelson, *Charles the Bald*, pp. 188–9.
[26] Goldberg, 'Frontier Kingship', esp. pp. 55–73; Goldberg, *Empire*, pp. 186–200, cf. 131–2 and 285–7.
[27] B. Colgrave, *et al.*, *The Paris Psalter*, EEMF 8 (Copenhagen, 1958); Ker, *Catalogue*, no. 367; O'Neill in *Ps(P)*, pp. 1–22.
[28] R. Weber in *Le Psautier romain*, ed. Weber, pp. viii–ix; C. V. Leroquais, *Les psautiers manuscrits latins des bibliothèques publique de France*, 3 vols. (Mâcon, 1940–1) I, xxvii–xxxv; K. van der Horst, 'The Utrecht Psalter: Picturing the Psalms of David', in *The Utrecht Psalter in Medieval Art*, ed. K. van der Horst, W. Noel and W. C. M. Wüstefeld (Utrecht, 1996), pp. 23–84, at 37.

perhaps in the mid-tenth century from a Roman text that differed in some respects from his own.[29] These renderings are often judged to have been incompetent: for Psalms I–L only, they were replaced by the West Saxon prose translation now known to be Alfred's. This too was based on a Roman text, but on over 140 occasions shows knowledge of Jerome's 'Gallican' version of the late 380s.[30] The Gallican text had first been promoted for liturgical use in ninth-century Francia; these variants suggest the importance of Alfred's Continental helpers. Integral to this translation was a set of Introductions to Psalms II–L, generally relating the contexts of each Psalm to David, to a later event in the Old Testament, to 'ælc rihtwis man', and to Christ.

Little else is known of Alfred's text. In the later eleventh century at the New Minster, Winchester, the same set of Introductions was added to the margins of a mid-eleventh-century Psalter, London, British Library, Cotton Vitellius E. xviii, in a form which cannot be explained as a direct copy of the Paris text.[31] This seems to demonstrate that Alfred's translation never went beyond Psalm L, a feature also reported by William of Malmesbury.[32] Division of the Psalter into 'fifties' had been common in England from at least the eighth century, in all like-lihood under the influence of the Irish, who may have obtained the idea from Hilary, Augustine and Cassiodorus.[33] This was another practice already familiar in West Saxon court devotion.

The Latin Psalters presented any translator with inherent problems of communication and understanding. Allusive qualities of the Hebrew court poetry were only further amplified in Latin, both at verse level and in the implications of whole Psalms.[34] The prevailing tradition of exegesis in the medieval West, represented by Augustine and Cassiodorus, found meaning not in the Old Testament context in which the Psalms had been composed, but through allegorical and mystical interpretations relating such details to Christ and the Church, an approach first popularized by the school of Alexandria.[35] The Psalter's meaning hinged on the liberal

---

[29] Ed. Krapp, ASPR 5.
[30] O'Neill, '"Solomon and Saturn" Dialogues', pp. 163–4; O'Neill in *Ps(P)*, pp. 32–4.
[31] Ker, *Catalogue*, no. 224; Colgrave, *The Paris Psalter*, p. 16; O'Neill in *Ps(P)*, pp. 28–30.
[32] *GR* I, 192–3; Whitelock, 'Prose', pp. 70–1 and 77.
[33] D. H. Wright, *The Vespasian Psalter*, EEMF 14 (Copenhagen, 1967), 47–8; M. McNamara, 'Psalter Text and Psalter Study in the Early Irish Church (AD 600–1200)', *Proceedings of the Royal Irish Academy* 73, section C, no. 7 (1973), 201–98, at 269–70.
[34] E.g. Ps. XIII on those of the Lord's people who no longer believe in him; Ps. XXIII on the lifting up of princely gates; Ps. XLIX, the highly cryptic prophecy of the Lord's coming.
[35] P. Salmon in *Les Tituli Psalmorum*, ed. Salmon, pp. 10–27; M.-J. Rondeau, *Les Commentaires patristiques du Psautier (IIIe–Ve siècles)*, 2 vols., Orientalia Christiana Analecta 219–20 (Rome, 1982–5); M. Gibson, 'Carolingian Glossed Psalters', in *The Early Medieval Bible, its Production, Decoration and Use*, ed. R. Gameson (Cambridge, 1994), pp. 78–100, at 96–8.

arts: attributing their genesis to divine expression in scripture, Cassiodorus presented Psalter exegesis as ideal training in the recovery of symbolic speech.[36] A preface to the Psalter found in many manuscripts is typical in its view of the *Origo psalmorum*. An historical origin is acknowledged in the Psalms' first composition and perfomance by David, together with his musicians Asaph, Eman, Ethan and Idithun, 'but all the Psalms which are written are not read according to history, but are understood as if according to prophecy'. All Psalms with the biblical title 'For David himself' properly relate to the 'sacraments of Christ, because David himself was called "Christus", that is, anointed'.[37] The preface formed a key source for Carolingian depictions of David and his musicians, including several codices owned by Charles the Bald.[38]

The royal translation is notable for its restrained regard for Christological and other interpretative material in the dominant commentary tradition. The approach was quite different from the later Old High German translation by Notker Labeo of St-Gallen, whose version included sections of original Latin text, together with explanatory vernacular passages mainly derived from Augustine and Cassiodorus.[39] Royal priorities generally offered expanded elucidation of Psalmic ambiguity, in a form which was self-contained. The translation of scripture again transcended any straightforward literalism. The rendering of Psalm XLIV is exceptional in supplying allegorical explanations for every significant noun; its topic, the marriage of a king and queen, was unusual and suggestive of Christ's relationship to the Church. The interpretation mainly coincides with that of Augustine, but on a few occasions either follows Cassiodorus or goes another way.[40] Rather than direct dependence on written commentaries, such features may imply more active interaction with scholarly helpers.[41] Occasional interpolations in other psalms more usually clarify contextual sense than mystical significance.

Direct translation was complemented by discrete interpretation, in the Introductions preceding each Psalm. O'Neill has argued convincingly for common authorship: the Introductions complement the Psalm renderings,

---

[36] *Expositio Psalmorum*, ed. Adriaen, CCSL 97–8, Praef. XV, 19–20; J. J. O'Donnell, *Cassiodorus* (Berkeley, LA, 1979), pp. 156–62.

[37] *The Vespasian Psalter*, ed. Kuhn, p. 301, cf. PL 30: 295–6; Wright, *The Vespasian Psalter*, pp. 49–50.

[38] H. L. Kessler, *The Illustrated Bibles from Tours* (Princeton, NJ, 1977), pp. 96–110; Dutton and Kessler, *First Bible of Charles the Bald*, pp. 59–60, with plate II.

[39] Bostock, *Handbook*, pp. 281–98.

[40] O'Neill in *Ps(P)*, pp. 254–8, cf. 34–6; Augustinian influence might be connected with the seventh-century *Glosa Psalmorum ex traditione seniorum* (ed. Boese I, 187–94).

[41] None of the commentaries listed by O'Neill (pp. 34–6 and 352–3) would explain the interpretation of Psalm XL any more precisely than would direct access to Augustine or Cassiodorus.

sometimes supplying distinctive interpretations which are taken further in the Psalm itself.[42] A typical Introduction is that preceding Psalm XIX:

Dauid sang þysne nigonteoðan sealm, and sæde on ðæm sealme hu his folc him fore gebæde on his earfoðum; and eac Ezechias folc gebæd for hine, þa he wæs beseten mid his feondum on þære byrig; and swa doð ealle Cristene men þe þysne sealm singað: hy hine singað for heora kyningas; and eac þa Apostolas hine sungon be Criste, þa hine man lædde to rode.[43]

Though consisting of four elements, the approach differs significantly from the standard patristic division of biblical exegesis into four modes: the anagogical, pertaining to eschatological matters; the historical; the allegorical or mystical, pertaining to Christ or the Church; and the moral or tropological, providing advice for every Christian.[44] The Psalm is first explained historically, as David's instruction to his people to pray for him in his hardships, but then afforded a second historical interpretation, relating to a post-Davidic event in the Old Testament, in this case to Hezekiah during his struggle against his enemies. Only then is the tropological explanation added that the Psalm should be sung by 'all Christian men' for their kings; mystically, it had been sung by the Apostles as Christ was led to the cross.

In effect, the second historical interpretation replaces the more usual anagogical; as O'Neill has shown, this distinctive fourfold scheme existed uniquely in Irish psalm exegesis by about 800.[45] An early ninth-century commentary, the *Old Irish Treatise on the Psalter*, expounds a virtually identical scheme, but not enough survives to reveal how it was implemented in practice.[46] Related material on the Psalter in the *Reference Bible*, a Hiberno-Latin commentary compiled *c.* 800, provides one such introduction for Psalm I, where no Alfredian Introduction survives.[47] The Irish fourfold scheme developed from a distinctive framework of historical interpretation in early Irish exegesis, stressing twofold historical readings.[48]

[42] O'Neill, 'Introductions', pp. 21–6; O'Neill in *Ps(P)*, pp. 27–8 and 73–96.
[43] 'David sang this nineteenth Psalm, and said in it how his people should pray for him in his hardships; and likewise Hezekiah's people prayed for him, when he was besieged by his enemies in the city; and so do all Christian men who sing this Psalm: they sing it for their kings; and likewise the Apostles sang it for Christ, when he was led to the cross': *Ps(P)* XIX, pp. 120–1.
[44] O'Neill, 'Introductions', pp. 26–7; H. de Lubac, *Medieval Exegesis I: the Four Senses of Scripture*, trans. M. Sebac (Grand Rapids, MI, 1998).
[45] O'Neill, 'Introductions', pp. 27–9; O'Neill in *Ps(P)*, pp. 24–5 and 42–3.
[46] O'Neill in *Ps(P)*, p. 24; McNamara, 'Psalter Text', pp. 229–30; M. McNamara, 'Tradition and Creativity in Early Irish Psalter Study', in *Irland und Europa: Die Kirche im Frühmittelalter*, ed. P. Ní Chatháin and M. Richter (Stuttgart, 1984), pp. 338–89, at 363.
[47] O'Neill, 'Introductions', p. 29; McNamara, 'Psalter Text', pp. 227–9.
[48] McNamara, 'Tradition and Creativity', pp. 375–7, cf. 358–60 and 364–6; M. McNamara, 'The Psalms in the Irish Church: the Most Recent Research on Text, Commentary, and

This radical approach to the Psalms had arisen in Ireland under the influence of Theodore of Mopsuestia (*c.* 350–428), whose commentary on the Psalms was known in the form of a Latin translation by Julian of Æclanum (*fl.* 454).[49] A suggested role for Theodore of Tarsus in the transmission of Theodore's commentary fails on a number of grounds.[50] Partly transmitted as an Epitome for Psalms XVI–CL, virtually all the surviving fragments of Julian's translation have Irish connections.[51] An important proponent of the Antiochene school, opposed to the Alexandrine approach, Theodore viewed the Psalms in their immediate Davidic context, and often interpreted them as prophecies pertaining to some later Old Testament event.[52]

Though matching the Irish fourfold scheme, the royal Introductions did not depend on a single source, but were constructed from related material. What was available resembled sections known as the *Argumenta* and *Explanationes* in a composite text, printed by Migne among Bede's works under the title *In Psalmorum Librum Exegesis*.[53] The commentary also included in this text was composed in the twelfth century, and unconnected with the other elements, known from two Continental manuscripts of the ninth century.[54] Introducing each Psalm, the *Argumenta* have three component parts:

a) an historical interpretation, relating either to David or to some post-Davidic event in the Old Testament, largely borrowed from a recension of Julian's translation of Theodore of Mopsuestia, in which the loss of commentary for Psalms I–XVI was made good by the insertion of a separate Antiochene commentary, of Irish transmission and probable origin.[55]

b) a mystical interpretation, sometimes with liturgical note, based on the so-called Columban Series of Psalm *tituli*.[56]

Decoration – with Emphasis on the So-Called Psalter of Charlemagne', in *The Bible as Book: the Manuscript Tradition*, ed. J. L. Sharpe III and K. van Kampen (London, 1998), pp. 89–103.

[49] O'Neill in *Ps(P)*, pp. 37–40; L. de Coninck in *Theodori Mopsuesteni Expositionis in Psalmos Iuliano Aeclanensi Interprete in Latinum Uersae Quae Supersunt*, CCSL 88A, i–xlv; McNamara, 'Psalter Text', pp. 255–7; McNamara, 'Tradition and Creativity', pp. 340–4.
[50] O'Neill in *Ps(P)*, p. 41; cf. G. T. Dempsey, 'Aldhelm of Malmesbury and the Paris Psalter: a Note on the Survival of Antiochene Exegesis', *JTS* 38 (1987), 368–86.
[51] De Coninck in *Theodori Mopsuesteni*, ix–xv.
[52] B. Bischoff and M. Lapidge, *Biblical Commentaries from the Canterbury School of Theodore and Hadrian* (Cambridge, 1994), pp. 19–24, cf. 243–9.
[53] O'Neill, 'Introductions', pp. 30–1; PL 93: 477–1098.
[54] Dempsey, 'Aldhelm of Malmesbury', pp. 371–2, with references (correcting K&L, *Alfred*, p. 302); B. Fischer, 'Bedae de titulis psalmorum liber', in *Festschrift Bernhard Bischoff zu seinem 65. Geburtstag*, ed. J. Autenrieth and F. Brünholzl (Stuttgart, 1971), pp. 90–110; *Argumenta* ptd in *Liber Psalmorum*, ed. Bright and Ramsay.
[55] McNamara, 'Tradition and Creativity', pp. 346–7, 358–60 and 384–9; O'Neill in *Ps(P)*, p. 39 and 41–2.
[56] Fischer, 'Bedae', pp. 94–5; Series I in *Les Tituli Psalmorum*, ed. Salmon, pp. 55–74, of probable Irish origin.

c) a moral or, more often, mystical interpretation deriving from Jerome or Arnobius, and present for only twelve of Psalms I–L.[57]

The *Explanationes* provide information on the Psalm's biblical *titulus*, its contents and divisions, drawn mainly from Cassiodorus.[58] As Fischer has suggested, only the *Explanationes* need be by Bede, often occurring separately in Continental Psalters under the title *Bedae de titulis psalmorum liber*.[59] The *Argumenta* are nowhere ascribed to Bede, and were probably compiled in Ireland.[60]

Collectively, all evidence points to the impact of Irish learning on Alfred's translation, both for the fourfold interpretative scheme and for access to the *Argumenta* and *Explanationes*, known to have been associated in Ireland by the early ninth century.[61] Access can also be shown to additional Theodorean commentary material, probably also of Irish transmission.[62] The effect is to magnify the significance of 'Irishmen' under Alfred's lordship, whose role may also be suspected in Mosaic elements of the *Domboc*.[63] As O'Neill has shown, the Introductions provide valuable evidence for royal understanding of the Psalms, in the active construction of fourfold interpretations, apparently more systematic as the work progressed, from the maximum of only three interpretations offered by the *Argumenta*.[64] Section a) could supply only one of the two historical clauses, while b) and c) might present a choice of mystical clauses, if c) did not provide a moral interpretation instead. Such a transformation involved much fresh vernacular composition; the account of Bright and Ramsay, revised by O'Neill, permits some broader observations.[65]

Above all, the royal Introductions gave priority to the first historical or Davidic clause, as the guiding source of all interpretation. When *Arg.* a) was purely Davidic the Introduction generally failed to include a second historical clause;[66] when *Arg.* a) referred to a post-Davidic event, the Introduction added a new Davidic clause of independent composition. Such changes had the effect of attributing all Psalms to Davidic authorship,

---

[57] Fischer, 'Bedae', pp. 93–4; O'Neill, 'Introductions', p. 31; O'Neill in *Ps(P)*, p. 35.

[58] Fischer, 'Bedae', pp. 99–100. [59] *Ibid.*, pp. 108–9, cf. pp. 101–3.

[60] *Ibid.*, p. 107, cf. pp. 95–7.

[61] O'Neill in *Ps(P)*, pp. 41–4; the *Old Irish Treatise on the Psalter* quotes both *Arg.* a) and *Explanatio* on Psalm I (R. L. Ramsay, 'Theodore of Mopsuestia in England and Ireland', *Zeitschrift für Celtische Philologie* 8 (1912), 452–97, at 462–3).

[62] O'Neill in *Ps(P)*, pp. 37–40. [63] *VA* 76, lines 21–6; *ASC* s.a. 891. Cf. above, pp. 230–2.

[64] O'Neill, 'Introductions', pp. 32–8; O'Neill in *Ps(P)*, pp. 23–8.

[65] J. W. Bright and R. L. Ramsay, 'Notes on the Introductions of the West-Saxon Psalms', *JTS* 13 (1912), 520–58.

[66] O'Neill, 'Introductions', p. 32, citing Ps. II, X, XI, XVI, XVII, XXI, XXXV, XXXVI, XXVIII, XLVII and XLVIII.

regardless of biblical *tituli* attributing Psalms XLI, XLV and XLIX to the sons of Chore and Asaph.[67] On most occasions the new Davidic clause was fashioned from the theme of post-Davidic interpretation in *Arg.* a). Thus for Psalm XIX (quoted above), the interpretation that David had sung 'how his people should pray for him in his hardships' depends on the Psalm's characterization in *Arg.* a), as the people's prayer for Hezekiah when besieged by the Assyrians.[68] Events in David's life remain notably unspecified, with contexts concentrating on experiences of 'hardships' (*earfoðu*) and 'infirmity' (*mettrumnes*), and struggles against enemies and persecution.[69] Yet these Davidic experiences are then presented as foreshadowing not only Hezekiah's struggles and the Babylonian captivity, but also the actions of 'every righteous man' and Christ. In the tropological clause for Psalm XIX, a kingly theme is continued, rejecting alternative exegesis available in *Arg.* b).[70] It may simply have been fortuitous that *Arg.* c) supplied a suitable mystical explanation, compatible with Christ's own kingship.[71] Both tropological and mystical clauses generally supply only brief extension of each Davidic theme to the struggles of every Christian and the experiences of Christ at the hands of the Jews.[72]

The value of fourfold interpretation lay in this directness of connection, between the Psalm's meaning for contemporaries and original Davidic circumstances. Other solely mystical and tropological *tituli* would have been available; royal preference followed existing trends in West Saxon biblicism, giving systematic voice to the transferability of Psalmic experience.[73] As Athanasius had observed, quoted by Cassiodorus, 'Whoever recites the words of a Psalm seems to be repeating his own words, to be singing in solitude words composed by himself; it does not seem to be another speaking or explaining what he takes up and reads'.[74] Translation offered opportunities for still deeper blurring of David's identity, in many cases encouraged by immediate parallels with Alfred's own experiences. With Christ firmly asserted in each mystical clause, Psalm-texts could be freely treated as wisdom from the second king of Israel.

---

[67] *Ibid.*, p. 33, citing Ps. IV, VI, XII, XV, XIX, XX, XXII–XXIV, XXVII–XXX, XXXII, XXXIII, XXXVII, XLI, XLV and XLVI.

[68] 'Pro Ezechia rege suo populus pariter ab Assyriis obsessus orat': *Arg.* a). Cf. second historical clause in *Ps(P)* XIX, p. 120.

[69] Only for Ps. III, VII, X, XXV, XXXV, XXXVIII and L is there mention of specific events in David's life.

[70] 'Aliter, propheta operantem hortatur': *Arg.* b).

[71] 'Item, Christo eunti ad crucem dicit ecclesia, ut Arnobio placet': *Arg.* c).

[72] O'Neill, 'Introductions', pp. 33–4.

[73] Apart from *Arg.* b) and c), and the Columban Series of Psalm *tituli* from which *Arg.* b) are derived, the so-called 'Series of St Augustine of Canterbury' was also known in Anglo-Saxon England (Series II in *Les Tituli Psalmorum*, ed. Salmon, pp. 81–93).

[74] Cassiodorus, *Expositio Psalmorum*, ed. Adriaen, Praef. XVI, p. 22.

GOD, *RIHTWISNES* AND SINFUL ENEMIES

Psalm translation provided a further opportunity to explore 'chosen' status, mediated by the king and regulated by adherence to God's law. Extending the framework of the Prose Preface and *Domboc*, the Psalms depicted a similar world, fundamentally divided between 'iusti' and 'impii', *þa rihtwisan* and *þa unrihtwisan*, determined by attitudes towards *Godes æ*, or *wisdom*.[75] As prayers by David to God, generally in the context of his struggles against the Philistines or rivals within Israel, the Psalms offered a multitude of contemporary parallels. David's anointed status, his 'cities' and court-centred devotion were all secondary to such martial struggle, strongly suggestive of Alfred's own leadership in viking warfare. Yet in the diversity of Psalmic tone and expression, attributed to a variety of historical circumstances, the connection between *rihtwisnes* and victory was not always straightforward. Certain Psalms may have held resonance for different aspects of Alfredian rule.

Most significantly, Psalms XI and XIII were each related to sapiential decline, mirroring royal priorities. In each case *Arg.* a) was interpreted quite loosely to provide of a context of lamentation by David and 'every righteous man', that 'on his dagum sceolde rihtwisnes and wisdom beon swa swiðe alegen'.[76] In Psalm XI such comparison was further encouraged by an addition to the opening verse, that the decline of holiness had occurred 'now, in these times': 'Gehæl me, Drihten, for þam haligdom is nu on þisum tidum fullneah asprungen, and soðfæstnes ys swyðe gelytlod'.[77] The Psalmist blames this decline upon the deceitful and loquacious, whose 'double heart' is characteristically expanded, contrasting evil intentions with empty speech: 'They speak empty things to their

---

[75] 'Eadig byð se wer þe ne gæð on geþeaht unrihtwisra, ne on þam wege ne stent synfulra, ne on heora wolbærendum setle ne sitt; ac his willa byð on Godes æ, and ymb his æ he byð smeagende dæges and nihtes' ('Blessed is the man who does not go in the counsel of the unrighteous, nor stands on the way of the sinful, nor sits on their pestilential seat; but his will is in God's law, and he meditates on this law day and night'): *Ps(P)* I.1–2, p. 100. 'Se muð þæs rihtwisan smeað wisdom and his tunge sprycð rihte domas. Seo æ his Godes bið on his heortan, and ne aslit his fot' ('The mouth of the righteous man will meditate upon wisdom and his tongue will speak right judgements. The law of his God will be in his heart, and his foot will not slip'): XXXVI.30–1, p. 144 (cf. Ps. XXXVI. 31–2). 'David sang þysne tu and feowertigoþan sealm, and healsode God on þyssum sealme þæt he demde betwuh him and his feondum þe nane æ Godes ne heoldon' ('David sang this forty-second Psalm, and beseeched God in this Psalm that he should judge between him and his enemies who did not keep God's law'): XLII, p. 152, largely dependent on Ps. XLII. 1.

[76] '[T]hat in his days righteousness and wisdom should be so greatly diminished': *Ps(P)* XI, p. 110. Cf. *Arg.* a); 'Ex persona Dauid canitur, quod in tempore eius omnis defecerit sanctus et deminutae sint ueritates a filiis hominum'.

[77] 'Save me, Lord, for holiness is now very nearly dead in these times, and truth is greatly lessened': *Ps(P)* XI.1, p. 110. Cf. Ps. XI. 2: 'Saluum me fac Domine quoniam defecit sanctus quoniam deminutae sunt ueritates a filiis hominum'.

neighbours, they speak deceits with their lips, for they do not have in their minds what they speak with their mouths, but intend evil, although they may sometimes speak rightly'.[78] There are obvious parallels with Gregorian rulership over sin; here the Lord is willing to overlook such misdeeds in favour of the 'groaning of the needy' (*granung þæra þearfena*).[79] The Psalm ends with possible influence from Theodorean commentary, evoking righteous martial leadership: 'Although the unrighteous roam outside us on every side, and there is much more of them than us, nevertheless you multiply us against them, and protect us against them'.[80]

In Psalm XIII, criticism is again directed towards the deceitful, whose duplicity receives similar expansion, likened to tombs 'pleasant outside and foul within'.[81] The translation follows additional Theodorean material; its effects highlight the pertinence of historical exegesis.[82] The act of feet shedding blood becomes explicitly culpable, pursued *unþearfes* ('unnecessarily') and 'for yflum willum'; similar qualifications occur in the *Domboc*.[83] To sinful failure is added the certainty of righteous success: 'Why do they not understand that fear and mishaps will come to them when they least expect? (cf. Matthew XXIV. 50 and Luke XII. 46). Why do they not understand that God is with the righteous people?'.[84] Unexpected retribution was a further element in Gregorian rhetoric.[85]

In a similar vein, Psalm II describes how a king, by alleviating God's anger, might lead his people to victory. In royal hands its composition is attributed to circumstances when David 'seofode … and mænde to Drihtne be his feondum, ægðer ge inlendum ge utlendum, and be eallum his earfoðum'.[86] Lacking specific support in *Arg.* a), involvement

---

[78] 'Idla spræca hi sprecað to heora nyhstum, facen hi sprecað mid heora weolorum, for þam hi nabbað on heora mode þæt hi on heora muðe sprecað, ac þencað yfel, þeah hi hwilum tela cweðen': *Ps(P)* XI.2, p. 111. Cf. Ps. XI. 3.

[79] *Ps(P)* XI.5–6, p. 111. Cf. Ps. XI. 6 (likely influence of Gallican version).

[80] 'Ðeah þa unrihtwisan us utan began on ælce healfe, and heora sy mycle ma þonne ure, þeah þu us tobrædst ongean hy, and wið hi gefriðast': *Ps(P)* XI.9, p. 111. Cf. Ps. XI. 9 (with O'Neill in *Ps(P)*, p. 186): 'In circuitu impii ambulant secundum altitudinem tuam multiplicasti filios hominum'.

[81] *Ps(P)* XIII.5, p. 112. Cf. Ps. XIII. 3.   [82] O'Neill in *Ps(P)*, pp. 187–9.

[83] *Ps(P)* XIII.6, p. 112. Cf. Ps. XIII. 3. *Af* Int.13 and Int.25, 12, 13, 18, 20 and 40.2.

[84] 'Hwi ne ongitað hi þæt him cymð, þonne hi læst wenað, ege and ungelimp? Hwy ne ongitað hi þæt God byð mid þam rihtwisan folce?': XIII.9–10, p. 112. Cf. Ps. XIII. 5–6 (with O'Neill's commentary in *Ps(P)*, p. 189).

[85] Matthew XXIV. 50 in *CP* XVII, p. 120, lines 9–20, esp. 14–16: 'Ðonne cymð his hlaford on ðæm dæge þe he ne wend, and on ða tiid ðæt he hiene ær nat' ('Then his lord will come on the day that he does not expect, and at the time that he does not know beforehand'). Cf. *Reg. past.* II.6, lines 154–65, p. 214.

[86] '[L]amented and complained to the Lord about his enemies, both in his own land and from without, and about all his hardships': *Ps(P)* II, p. 100. Cf. *Arg.* a): 'Generalem Dauid querimoniam facit ad Deum quod, regno sibi desuper dato, et gentes et populi Israel inuiderint, communem ad omnes correptionem dirigens'.

of internal and external enemies harmonizes with the use of Gregorian language to describe Alfred's multiple cares of office.[87] 'Eorðcynincgas and ealdormenn' have risen up against the Lord's anointed, but again an expansion emphasizes empty speech: ' "What does their talk benefit them", says the prophet, "although they speak in such a way? For God, who is in heaven, reproaches them and the Lord confounds them" '.[88] For God has established the Psalmist as king, 'in order to teach His will and His law' (*to þam þæt ic lære his willan and his æ*).[89] In return for the Psalmist's teaching, God promises to extend his 'power (*anwald*) over the boundaries of other peoples', that he may rule them with an 'iron rod', and may destroy them 'as a potter can a pot'.[90] Equally directed to *kyningas* and *domeras* ('judges'), the Psalm's conclusion encapsulates contemporary expectations of office-holding: 'Serve the Lord and fear him, rejoice in God, and yet with fear. Receive learning (*lare*) lest God becomes angry with you, and lest you stray from the right way.'[91] *Lar* had also dominated the Prose Preface.

Psalm XVII relates the same principles to military conflict. Inspired by *Arg.* a), the Introduction presents its performance by each man as thanksgiving to God for his 'protection' (*mundbyrd*), 'when he has released him from certain hardships, either him or another for whom he sings it'.[92] The Psalmist recalls how, when surrounded by 'sorrow and manifold punishments (*witu*)', the Lord had responded to his lamentation by revealing his power in earth, fire, thunder and flood.[93] Dependence on Theodorean commentary is again pertinent.[94] Augustine and Cassiodorus had related the destruction of mountains to Christ's first and second comings; for the translation it becomes 'the might of my proud enemies (*þæt mægen minra ofermodena feonda*) ... because God was angry with them (*for þam him wæs God yrre*)'.[95] Similarly, the darkness induced by God had signified for Augustine and Cassiodorus various divine mysteries; the translation portrays God as having 'unleashed darkness between Him and

---

[87] *VA* 25, lines 10–13; above, pp. 204–9, cf. 136–7.

[88] 'Hwæt forstent heora spræc (cwæð se witega) þeah hi swa cweðen, for þam se God þe on heofonum ys hig gehyspð, and Drihten hyg gescent': *Ps(P)* II.4, p. 100. Cf. Ps. II. 4 (with O'Neill in *Ps(P)*, p. 168): 'Qui habitat in caelis inridebit eos et Dominus subsannabit eos'.

[89] *Ps(P)* II.6, p. 100. Cf. Ps. II. 6.   [90] *Ps(P)* II.8–9, p. 101. Cf. Ps. II. 8–9.

[91] 'Ongytað nu, kyningas, and leorniað ge domeras þe ofer eorðan demað. Þeowiað Drihtne and ondrædað hine, blissiað on Gode, and ðeah mid ege. Onfoð lare þy læs eow God yrre weorðe, and þy læs ge wendon of rihtum wege': *Ps(P)* II.10–12, p. 101. Cf. Ps. II. 10–12.

[92] '... þonne he hine of hwylcum earfoðum alysed hæfð, oþþe hine oððe þæne þe he hine fore singð': *Ps(P)* XVII, p. 116. Cf. *Arg.* a): 'Hunc psalmum Dauid prope ultimum uitae suae tempus, ut ipse titulus indicat, pro gratiarum actione cantauit'.

[93] *Ps(P)* XVII.1–15, pp. 116–17, esp. XVII.5. Cf. Ps. XVII. 2–16.

[94] O'Neill in *Ps(P)*, pp. 196–200.

[95] *Ps(P)* XVII.7, p. 117. Cf. Ps. XVII. 8, with O'Neill in *Ps(P)*, p. 197.

my enemies, that he would never be seen by them, and yet He was very bright in his temple'.[96] The Psalmist proceeds to assert his righteousness in the eyes of the Lord, having upheld his 'ways' and 'commandments' (*bebodu*).[97] This is the context for further intervention: 'in Deo meo transgrediar murum' receives remarkable expansion as 'through my God's help, I will go out over the wall of my burh (*ofer minre burge weall*), though it is surrounded outside by enemies'.[98] Though prompted by Theodore, the burghal reference is Alfred's own, bearing close resemblance to at least one account of West Saxon defensive tactics.[99]

A similar scenario is invoked in Psalm XLV, sung by David after God had delivered him from 'many hardships (*earfoðum*)'; and by the men of Judah and Benjamin, described as two 'shires' (*scira*), after God had pre-served them from the onslaught of Phacee, son of Romelia, and Rasin, king of Syria (IV Kings XVI; II Chronicles XXVIII; Isaiah VII. 1).[100] Cassiodorus and Augustine had interpreted the trembling of the earth as a sign of vigorous preaching, and the troubled mountains as worldly powers in general. The translation returns again to 'our enemies':

Ure fynd coman swa egeslice to us þæt us ðuhte for þam geþune þæt sio eorþe eall cwacode; and hy wæron, þeah, sona afærde fram Gode swyþor þonne we, and þa upahafenan kynincgas swa þaer muntas wæron eac gedrefde for þæs Godes strenge.[101]

Though largely following Theodorean material, such preference accent-uates the Psalmist's military struggle.[102] The *ciuitas Dei* had been under-stood ecclesiologically by Augustine and Cassiodorus; for Alfred it becomes 'seo Godes burh on Hierusalem', which these enemies can never overturn while God is constant in her midst.[103] 'Dedit uocem suam

[96] 'And let þystru betwuh him and minum feondum þæt he nære næfre gesewen fram him, and he wæs, þeah, swiðe leoht on his temple': *Ps(P)* XVII.11, p. 117. Cf. Ps. XVII. 12 (with O'Neill in *Ps(P)*, p. 197): 'Et posuit tenebras latibulum suum in circuitu eius tabernaculum eius'.

[97] *Ps(P)* XVII.20–25, p. 35. Cf. Ps. XVII. 21–7.

[98] *Ps(P)* XVII.28, p. 118. Cf. Ps. XVII. 30, with *Theodori Mopsuesteni*, ed. De Coninck, p. 96: 'Si tamquam muro inimicorum circumder insidiis, tibi innitens effugere potero omnes insidias atque transcendere'.

[99] *VA* 54, lines 17–23, for victory gained by king's thegns and their followers by incursion from the fortress of Countisbury, Devon, in 878.

[100] *Ps(P)* XLV, p. 156; Introduction based on a fuller version of *Arg.* a) (O'Neill in *Ps(P)*, p. 259).

[101] 'Our enemies came to us so terribly that it seemed to us, because of the noise, that the whole earth trembled; and yet they were immediately frightened by God more than we were, and the kings, raised up like mountains, were troubled because of God's strength': *Ps(P)* XLV.3, p. 156. Cf. Ps. XLV. 3–4: 'Propterea non timebimus dum conturbabitur terra et transferentur montes in cor maris. Sonauerunt et turbatae sunt aquae eius, conturbati sunt montes in fortitudine eius'.

[102] O'Neill in *Ps(P)*, p. 260.

[103] *Ps(P)* XLV.4, p. 157. Cf. Ps. XLV. 6, with O'Neill in *Ps(P)*, p. 260, for possible influence of the *Glossa in Psalmos*, ed. McNamara, p. 102.

Altissimus et mota est terra': the translation expands with 'the Most High sent his word, and our land and our people was changed for the better, and they and their land for the worse'.[104] Unparalleled in commentary material, the addition focused on divine protection.[105] The mood of triumph extends to the opening of Psalm XLVI, where Theodorean material inspires an added taunt against 'hostile peoples', 'Wepað nu and heofað, eall orlegu folc, for þam ure God eow hæfð ofercumen', before the original opening, 'O clap your hands all you peoples'.[106]

HARDSHIPS AND DIVINE JUSTICE

Other Psalms struck different notes of internal reflection. David's career had included exile and moments of reversal; his biblical reputation had otherwise been shaped by a propensity to sin, exemplified by his adulterous relationship with Bathsheba, wife of the king's supporter Uriah. Many Psalms could be located in such contexts of lamentation and confession, while tradition from at least Cassiodorus' time had established a group of seven regarded as 'penitential'.[107] Translation necessarily involved themes of suffering and sin, yet both attracted extensive instances of translatory intervention. Such handling bears close relationship to Alfred's conspicuous struggle against hindrances and disturbances, not least among which were the effects of Alfred's mysterious illness, attributed to youthful sin.[108] The effect was to strengthen both royal presence in the Psalter and the contemporary significance of Davidic hardships.

Parallels with David were stressed by many Introductions. The Davidic clause is often highly generalized, relating either to 'enemies' or unspecified 'hardships' (*earfoðu*), suggesting limits of historical engagement. On other occasions the hardships are explicitly those 'of mind and body' (*ge modes ge lichaman*). In three out of four cases the detail lacks support in commentary material; the motif is otherwise characteristic of royal style, found in the Boethius and *Soliloquies*.[109] The character of enemies also finds qualification, in Psalm XII, sung by David 'be his

---

[104] '... se hyhsta sende his word, and gehwyrfed wæs ure land and ure folc to beteran, and hi and heora land to wyrsan': *Ps(P)* XLV.5, p. 157. Cf. Ps. XLV. 7.

[105] O'Neill in *Ps(P)*, p. 260.

[106] 'Weep now and lament, all hostile peoples, for our God has overcome you': *Ps(P)* XLVI.1, p. 158. Cf. Ps. XLVI. 2, with O'Neill in *Ps(P)*, p. 261.

[107] Ps. VI, XXXI, XXXVII, L, CI, CXXIX and CXLII; cf. comparable themes in XXI, XXIV and XXXVIII.

[108] Pratt, 'Illnesses', pp. 57–63 and 84–88.

[109] *Ps(P)* III, XVII, XXX and XLI, pp. 101, 130, 133 and 150; parallel with Latin sources only for III (O'Neill in *Ps(P)*, p. 169). Cf. *Ps(P)* XVIII.8 and XXX.22, pp. 120 and 134.

feondum, ægþer ge gastlicum ge lichamlicum', and in Psalm X, sung by
the righteous 'be heora feondum, ægðer ge gesewenlicum ge ungese-
wenlicum'.[110] Neither would be urged by commentaries: both matched
the character of Alfred's own suffering, with parallels between attacks of
vikings and illness.[111] The pattern continued in Psalm XXVII, sung for
protection against hardships 'both of mind and body' and enemies 'both
visible and invisible'.[112] Its Davidic theme was borrowed from *Arg.* a), as a
petition by Hezekiah in time of illness. Replicated elsewhere, the theme
suggests Hezekiah's significance as a model of infirmity.[113]

The role of hardships is pressing given their special position. Tri-
umphant Psalms compare with others less confident of divine intentions.
In several of the first fifty, the Psalmist presents his troubles as a sign that
the Lord has either forgotten his cause, or remained silent; divine aid is
invoked to support the righteous.[114] Still more distant are a few
involving fervent declarations of righteousness, amid hardships which
seem undeserved. The Introduction to Psalm XVI follows *Arg.* a) in
stressing the Psalmist's innocence towards enemies attacking 'without
offence' (*butan scylde*).[115] The translation makes this explicit, interpreting
a test by fire as 'by the fire of many hardships (*mid þam fyre monegra
earfoða*), just as gold and silver': 'ne ic furðum nanum menn ne sæde eal
þa earfoða þe hi me dydon'.[116] A similar scenario is invoked by Psalm
XXXIV, a lamentation of 'mishaps' (*ungelimp*). The Psalmist tells how
false witnesses arose against him, rewarding his good with evil.[117] When
he turned to fasting, his prayers were turned back on him; an addition
explains that 'the judge would not receive the things that I sent him'.[118]

Psalm XLIII offers notable depiction of unjust suffering at the hands of
'foreign peoples' (*þa elðeodegan folc*). The opening section is remodelled to
emphasize past victories gained over such enemies by 'our predecessors'

[110] *Ps(P)* XII, p. 111. Cf. *Arg.* a) and b) for the second historical and mystical clauses only. *Ps(P)* X, p. 110. Cf. *Arg.* a) on David's flight from Saul.
[111] Cf. O'Neill's difficulties in explaining such additions (*Ps(P)*, pp. 183, 186 and 216–17); *VA* 91, lines 1–12.
[112] *Ps(P)* XXVII, p. 130. Cf. *Arg.* a) for second historical clause.
[113] *Ps(P)* V, XV, XXVII and XXIX, pp. 103, 114, 130 and 132.
[114] Ps. IX, XII, XXVII, XXX, XLI and XLII.
[115] *Ps(P)* XVI, p. 115 (with O'Neill in *Ps(P)*, p. 93).
[116] 'Nor even have I mentioned to any man all the hardships that they did to me': *Ps(P)* XVI.3–4, p. 115. Cf. Ps. XVI. 4 (with O'Neill in *Ps(P)*, p. 194): 'ut non loquatur os meum opera hominum'.
[117] *Ps(P)* XXXIV.12, pp. 139–40. Cf. Ps. XXIV. 11–12.
[118] '... for þam heora nolde onfon se dema, þe ic hi to sende': *Ps(P)* XXXIV.13, p. 140. Cf. Ps. XXXIV. 13 (with O'Neill in *Ps(P)*, p. 230): 'et oratio mea in sinu meo conuertebatur'. Cf. regular characterization of God as 'se dema' in *CP*.

(*ure foregengan*), through confident trust in the Lord.[119] Yet past mechanisms have now failed: as the translation relates, the Lord no longer goes 'on fyrd' with his people, with disastrous military effects.[120] As the Psalmist protests, 'we have not forgotten you, nor committed the error of abandoning your law, nor have our minds gone backwards from you ... why do you forget our miseries and our toils?'.[121] The question is arresting against Alfredian developments in law and wisdom, the whole force of which was the promise of improved defence. One may wonder at perspectives in 892, facing the return of viking forces amid far-reaching reform.[122] Yet there was no fatal tension with contemporary aspirations. Psalm XLIII ended with an invocation of divine support; XVI and XXXIV offered grounds at least for future hope.[123] As striking is the relative degree of fidelity.

Hardships more usually featured in the Psalter as an instrument against sin. There is a suggestive contrast in royal handling, with more regular intervention and comment. Though sometimes relevant, Theodorean material is insufficient to explain the selective nature of additions, focused on sinfulness. The dominant explanation was 'penitential', of hardships as a sign of divine displeasure, justly reducing their recipient to humility.[124] Learned tradition asserted David's composition of such Psalms, especially Psalm L, to confess his sin against Uriah and secure divine annulment of

---

[119] 'Drihten, we gehyrdon mid urum earum and ure fæderas hit us sædon: þa weorc þe þu worhtest on hiora dagum and on hiora foregengena dagum. Þæt wæs, þæt þin hand towearp þæ elðeodegan folc and plantode and tydrede ure foregengan. Þu swenctest þa elðeodgan folc and hy awurpe. Ne geeodon ure foregengan na ðas eorðan mid sweorda ecgum, ne hy mid þy ne geheoldon, ne heora earmas hy ne geheoldon ne ne gehældon, ac þin swiðre hand and þin earm and þæt leoht þines andwlitan, for þam hy þe þa licodon, and þe licode mid him to beonne' ('Lord, we have heard with our ears and our fathers said it to us: the works that you performed in their days and in the days of their predecessors. That was, that your hand destroyed the foreign peoples and planted and begat our predecessors. You afflicted the foreign peoples and cast them out. Our predecessors did not gain the earth with the blades of swords, nor keep it with them, nor did their arms keep them nor save them, but your greater hand and your arm and the light of your face, for they then pleased you, and it pleased you to be with them'): *Ps(P)* XLIII.1–5, p. 153. Cf. Ps. XLIII. 2–4, with O'Neill in *Ps(P)*, pp. 251–2: changes not obviously driven by commentary material.

[120] ' ... þeah þu, Drihten, us nu adrifen hæbbe fram þe and us gebysmrod, and mid us ne fare on fyrd, swa þu geo dydest' ('yet you, Lord, have now driven us away from you, and reviled us, and do not go in the army with us, as you did formerly'): *Ps(P)*: XLIII.11, p. 153 (with O'Neill in *Ps(P)*, p. 252). Cf. Ps. XLIII. 10, with *Theodori Mopsuesteni*, ed. De Coninck, p. 196: 'Pro copiis militaribus, sicut hodie *uirtutem regis* appellare solemus exercitum. Neque enim te ducem nostrum ut olim sentimus in bellis, non in nobis propugnans'.

[121] 'Eall þas earfoðu becoman ofer us, and ne forgeate we þeah na þe, ne þæt woh ne worhton þæt we þine æ forleten, ne ure mod ne eode on bæclincg fram þe ... hwy forgytst þu ure yrmða and ure geswinc?': *Ps(P)* XLIII.19 and 25, p. 154. Cf. Ps. XLIII. 18–19 and 24.

[122] Cf. K&L, *Alfred*, pp. 41–2.

[123] *Ps(P)* XVI.13–15, p. 116 (expanding on Ps. XVI.14–15); *Ps(P)* XXXIV.21–4, p. 140 (cf. Ps. XXXIV.21–6); *Ps(P)* XLIII.24–7, p. 154 (cf. Ps. XLIII.23–6).

[124] Ps. VI, XXXI, XXXVII, L, CI, CXXIX and CXLII; cf. also XXI, XXIV and XXXVIII.

the Lord's vow to raise up evil from his own house.[125] The version of Psalm L unfortunately coincides with a missing leaf. Though the Introduction mentions Nathan's chastisement, its clause for every righteous man offers the much narrower theme of sin and repentance.[126] Both here and elsewhere, such Psalms coincide with the Gregorian view of David, as worthy recipient of instructive chastisement.[127] As an act of pride, the slaying of Uriah showed the temptations of 'freedom from care' (*orsorgnes*), corrected by subsequent 'toils and hardships'.[128] 'I said in my splendour, and my freedom from care, "There will never be a change from this", for you gave me in your good will beauty and might'. Psalm XXIX. 7–8 had been cited by Gregory with just this message: 'When you turned your face from me I soon became troubled'.[129] The transitory nature of *orsorgnes* found further reflection in Psalms XXXVI and XLVIII, in each case relating to physical wealth. Both bear comparison with fuller treatment of such themes in the Boethius.[130]

'Penitential' Psalms provided timely illustration of God's anger; they also aroused interest in sinful causation. In Psalm XXIV, the Psalmist begs the Lord in his mercy to forgive his sins, including 'sins of my youth and my ignorance' (*delicta iuuentutis et ignorantiae*). The vernacular adds 'those that I did unwittingly, that is, those that I supposed were not sins'; though paralleled in Cassiodorus, the explanation coheres with Alfred's own reported retrospection.[131] 'Abandoned alone, wretched', the Psalmist requests 'a certain help and consolation (*sum frofor*)' from the Lord against his enemies, appealing to his humility and hardships.[132] Psalm XXXI offered similar confession of sin: an expansion explained the basis for prayer by the holy 'in tempore opportuno', 'because then and during all their good deeds the flood of great waters will never approach them, that is, these present hardships and also those to

---

[125] II Kings 12.   [126] *Ps(P)* L, p. 163.   [127] Cf. above, pp. 202–4.

[128] *CP* III, p. 34, lines 3–14 and line 20, to p. 36, line 3. Cf. *Reg. past.* I.3, lines 24–32 and 36–40, pp. 138–40.

[129] 'Ic cwæð on minum wlencum and on minre orsorhnesse: "Ne wyrð þises næfre nan wendincg," for þam þu me sealdest on ðinum goodan willan wlite and mægen. Þa awendest þu þinne andwlitan fram me, þa wearð ic sona gedrefed': *Ps(P)* XXIX.6–7, p. 132. Cf. *CP* LXV, p. 464, lines 14–20 (a slight expansion on *Reg. past.* IV, lines 51–6, p. 538).

[130] Below, pp. 280–302.

[131] 'Þa scylda mines iugoðhades ne gemun þu, Drihten, ne huru þa þe ic ungewisses geworhte (þæt synt, þa þe ic wende þæt nan scyld nære), ac for þinre myclan mildheortnesse beo þu min gemyndig, Drihten' ('Do not remember the sins of my youth, Lord, nor even those that I did unwittingly (that is, those that I supposed were not sins), but for your great mercy's sake be mindful of me, Lord'): *Ps(P)* XXIV.6, p. 126. Cf. Ps. XXIV.7 (with O'Neill in *Ps(P)*, p. 212): 'Delicta iuuentutis et ignorantiae meae ne memineris secundum magnam misericordiam tuam; memor esto mei Deus, propter bonitatem tuam Domine'.

[132] *Ps(P)* XXIV.15, 17–18 and 20, p. 127. Cf. Ps. XXIV. 16, 18–19 and 21.

come'.[133] The future hardships lack parallel in commentary material.[134] Psalm XXI voiced David's lamentation of 'his hardships and his ene- mies', only loosely relating to *Arg.* a). God's failure to respond receives vernacular explanation: 'for I do not reproach you at all that you do not hear me, but I blame it on my own sins'.[135] Though paralleled in Theodore, the addition gave a firmly sinful cause to divine inaction.

Other renderings emphasize a sexual dimension for royal sin. Psalm XV had been sung by David 'be his earfoðum, ægðer ge modes ge lichaman', only loosely related to *Arg.* a). It too was a petition for support, appealing to earlier rewards for righteousness. A key expansion concerns verse 7, 'Benedicam Dominum qui mihi tribuit intellectum: insuper et usque ad noctem increpauerunt me renes mei': in royal hands, 'Ic bletsige þone Drihten þe me sealde andgit. Ac þeah he me þara uterrena gewinna gefreode, þeah winnað wið me þa inran unrihtlustas dæges and nihtes, þæt ic ne eom, þeah, eallunga orsorh'.[136] Again, there is a relationship to Theodore, 'ita me earum [sc. temptations] exercet angoribus, ut sensus uel cogitationes … sint mihi utiles et uice me magisterii efficacis erudiant'.[137] Yet there were important departures, on the wrongfulness of inner desires and the Psalmist's constant tribulation, as a causal outcome.

Similar connections are traced by Psalm XXXVII, a lamentation of 'mishaps' (*ungelimp*) earlier merited by David's sins.[138] The Lord is implored to restrain his anger 'for your arrows are fastened into me'. An addition explains 'þæt synt, þa earfoðu þe ic nu þolie'; though paralleled in Theodore, the aside continues a near-obsession with suffering.[139] 'For þæm eall min lichama is full flæsclicra lusta, for þam nis nan hælo on minum flæsce': the translation departs significantly from the Gallican variant, 'Lumbi mei impleti sunt [*Ro.* anima mea conpleta est]

---

[133] 'For þæm gebiddað ealle halige to þe on tilne timan; for þæm þonne and for eallum heora goodum dædum ne genealæcð him na þæt flod þæra myclena wætera (þæt synt, þas andweardan earfoþa and eac þa toweardan)': *Ps(P)* XXXI.7, p. 135. Cf. Ps. XXXI.6.

[134] O'Neill in *Ps(P)*, p. 225.

[135] ' … for ðæm ic þe na ne oðwite þæt þu me ne gehyrst, ac minum agnum scyldum ic hit wite': *Ps(P)* XXI.2, p. 122. Cf. Ps. XXI. 3: 'et nocte et non ad insipientiam mihi'. *Theodori Mopsuesteni*, ed. De Coninck, p. 109: 'Cum die nocteque clamans non mererer audiri, reputaui hoc admisso meo'.

[136] 'I will extol the Lord, who has given me understanding; but although he has freed me from outer strifes, nevertheless the inner wrongful desires strive against me, day and night, so that I am never entirely free from care': *Ps(P)* XV.7, p. 114.

[137] 'I am so oppressed by the anguish of temptations that senses or thoughts are useful to me and educate me in the place of powerful teaching': *Theodori Mopsuesteni*, ed. De Coninck, p. 80.

[138] *Ps(P)* XXXVII, pp. 144–5, with O'Neill in *Ps(P)*, p. 237.

[139] 'That is, the hardships that I now endure': *Ps(P)* XXXVII.1–2, p. 145. Cf. Ps. XXXVII. 2–3, with O'Neill in *Ps(P)*, p. 238.

inlusionibus et non est sanitas in carne mea'.[140] The role of desire coincides with Theodore; again, the vernacular stresses bodily effects.[141] A later expansion concerns the Psalmist's abandonment by friends, kinsmen and neighbours, who have 'now united with my enemies'; 'those who were nearest to me, when I was most free from care (*orsorgost wæs*), now stand very far from me'.[142] The interpretation reflects Theodore, but the prosperous context is Alfred's own.[143] Again, the scenario coincides suggestively with royal experiences in 878, in the vivid depiction of Alfred's return, 'as if restored to life after suffering such great tribulations'.[144] Such parallels only strengthen the association between viking warfare and imagined hardships, in a framework of divine punishment.

ALFRED'S PSALMS AND ALFREDIAN THEATRE

Many features point to a key role for the first fifty Psalms in Alfredian 're-education'. The text's transmission is not inconsistent with multiple early copying. A lost copy was seemingly available to William of Malmesbury, while the Introductions are separately transmitted in the Vitellius Psalter.[145] Even the most economical interpretation of Paris and Vitellius texts would require two earlier exemplars at different West Saxon centres in the eleventh century.[146] The sapiential character of the Psalms establishes a strong case for inclusion among essential sources of Alfredian wisdom. Extension to lay recipients receives support from signs of an existing role for the Latin Psalter in early lay education.[147] Yet the royal Psalms could not easily have contributed to Latin understanding: far from Cassidorus' idealized grammatical training, the translation supported Alfredian vernacular study of the 'liberal arts'.[148] The text was a 'book' in its own right, self-sufficient in its didactic goals. The fourfold framework was matched by the renderings, resolving much ambiguity to convey a single train of thought, more sustained than any Latin Psalter, with or without interpretative *tituli*. Such qualities

---

[140] 'For all my body is full of fleshly desires, for there is no health in my flesh': *Ps(P)* XXXVII.7, p. 145. Cf. Ps. XXXVII. 8.

[141] '[N]am lumbi adhaerent renibus, in renibus uero concupiscentialis motus nascitur': *Theodori Mopsuesteni*, ed. De Coninck, p. 174.

[142] 'Mine frynd and mine magas and mine neahgeburas synt nu gemengde wið mine fynd, and standað nu mid him ongean me, and synt me nu toweardes; and þa þe me nyhst wæran, þa ic orsorgost wæs, standað me nu swiðe feor': *Ps(P)* XXXVII.10, p. 145. Cf. Ps. XXVII. 12 (Gallican version).

[143] *Theodori Mopsuesteni*, ed. De Coninck, p. 239; O'Neill in *Ps(P)*, p. 239.

[144] *VA* 55, lines 12–14.   [145] *GR* I, 192–3.   [146] O'Neill in *Ps(P)*, pp. 28–30.

[147] *VA* 24, cf c. 75, lines 26–31.   [148] Cf. above, pp. 123 and 246–7.

suggest the importance of readers literate only in the vernacular, sustaining utility for all audiences, with or without learned teachers.

The case is strengthened for reception in both arenas of delivery: not only at court but 'at home', through the mechanisms described by Asser. Performance related multiple voices to individual experience: the text went further, casting David in terms suggestive of Alfred alone. Psalmody now supplied a royal presence; its implications extended far beyond literate performance in the relentless operation of Alfredian theatre. Shared struggle against viking enemies was now heightened by participation in a single drama of defensive warfare, under David's own leadership. Though doubtless encouraged by viking paganism, key parallels threw greater emphasis on David himself, and his people's standing in divine judgement. Every action now contributed to this collective cause, renewed by the sight of Alfred's own commitment, in prayer and suffering.

This was a vernacular enhancement of existing devotion, already strongly martial. King Æthelred had insisted on hearing Mass before battle; for Asser, such actions demonstrated the 'faith of the Christian king', his victory attributed to divine support for 'Christians' against *pagani*, 'acting wrongfully'.[149] Christian warfare had resonance in the context of 'extra-English' alliance, but its roots were domestic.[150] Alfred's Psalms are merely one sign of added intensity. Action against a viking army at London in 883 included alms-giving to Rome and probably also to Jerusalem; such prayers had reportedly been answered.[151] The Second *Ordo* added a Davidic *uirga equitatis* to the *sceptrum* of the First *Ordo*; the new anointing prayer recalled divine support for 'your humble boy David', including deliverance from Goliath, Saul and 'all his enemies'.[152] Weaponry too could bear the imprint of religious sanction, to judge from the Abingdon sword.[153] To all such posturing the Psalms added a single framework, connecting all actions to the royal text. Within, it conveyed novel expectations, of Alfredian wisdom and the benefits of righteous adherence to God's law.

Still more significant was the connection between hardships and sinfulness, partly Gregorian within inventive historicism. Both supported Alfred's role-playing as a suffering king, inextricably connected with his struggle against illness. For Charles the Bald, humiliation had been interpreted as Job-like testing; Alfredian suffering differed significantly as a sign of divine punishment, openly emphasizing sin.

---

[149] *VA* 37, lines 12–22; c. 39, lines 7–14.   [150] Above, pp. 63–9 and 77–8, cf. 109–11.
[151] *ASC* s.a. 883 (MSS BCDEF); Pratt, 'Illnesses', pp. 69–70.
[152] *Ordines Coronationis Franciae*, ed. Jackson I, 180–1 and 187–8.   [153] Above, p. 65.

Alfred's role bears more comparison with the acknowledged sinfulness of Lothar II, an image comprehensively exposed by Hincmar on Charles's behalf.[154] Similar posturing acquired different force in Alfredian theatre, free from the scope of sacerdotal correction. Central was the prominence of enemies and illness as twin sources of David's chastisement.[155] Both found abundant demonstration in viking warfare and Alfred's bodily suffering; key Psalms upheld a single cause of divine displeasure, in Davidic excess of fleshly desire. Added in translation, such passages gained resonance from Alfred's own explanation of his bodily infirmity, as a response to *carnale desiderium* in his youth.[156] David himself gave central expression of Alfredian discourse. For body as for kingdom, all hope of deliverance lay in worldly restraint.

The centrality of suffering exemplifies the extreme character of courtly projection, reliant on intimate familiarity with Alfred's person. The sinful cause of Alfred's affliction owed much to its persistence in the face of royal piety, even resisting treatments received from Jerusalem.[157] Yet his sinfulness acquired deeper, instructive force from the symbolic parallel between body and kingdom. Attacks of royal illness gave exposure to hardships which were kingdom-wide; self-recrimination showed troubled participation in carnal restraint.[158] War-leadership now combined with internal struggles of mind and body, matching military priorities of defensive preparation.[159] Not without irony did Asser present Alfred's sacrifice as Christ-like, as repentent thief on the cross of his kingdom.[160] As the script of David's struggles, the royal Psalms were central to such projection, enhanced by the context of royal devotion. The power of vernacular psalmody lay in its direct solicitation of divine aid for Alfred and his kingdom, as authentic replication of royal prayer. The sharing of hardships between king and audience lent vital substance to Alfred's bodily power. Through collective action in defence and combat, David's suffering would indeed redeem.

---

[154] Pratt, 'Illnesses', pp. 44–5 and 83; Airlie, 'Private Bodies', pp. 24–6 and 31–5.
[155] Pratt, 'Illnesses', pp. 85–8; *VA* 91, lines 1–12.
[156] *VA* 74, lines 39–55.   [157] Pratt, 'Illnesses', pp. 63–7, 80–1 and 86.
[158] *Ibid.*, pp. 85–9.   [159] Above, pp. 136–8, 176–8 and 206–9.
[160] *VA* 89, lines 1–15; cf. c. 91, lines 1–12.

Chapter 13

THE SEARCH FOR A SATISFACTORY
CONSOLATION

The version of Boethius' *Consolatio philosophiae* captures the height of royal ambitions. A revered monument of Late Antique theology and philosophy, the Latin text offered extensive enquiry into fundamental problems of human existence, supremely enacted in didactic dialogue. Individual suffering, the operation of fate and providence, the nature of good and evil: all found treatment, and answers, amid Boethius' own desperate predicament, imprisoned and awaiting death under his former master, Theoderic, Ostrogothic ruler of Italy (490–526). Surpassing all but the *Soliloquies* in translatory freedom, royal treatment of Boethius has aroused much enquiry, complicated by a possible role for Latin commentary material; while at macro-level, critics have placed varying constructions on argumentative departure. On any interpretation, royal methods cannot be detached from the esoteric qualities of Boethian source-text, distant from Gregory's humble biblicism. Philosophy remained inherently remote from man, tenuously disclosed through stages of enlightenment. The act of translation required extensive engagement with Boethian philosophy; many features imply special interest in pertinent questions, not always closely related to original Latin argument.

In many cases departures cannot be explained by a textual source; they acquire logic and coherence rather as expressions of Alfredian discourse, amid active theorizing on the responsibilities of power. An austere invitation to philosophy, Boethian Neo-Platonism offered much potential as royal wisdom, yet the extremity of its consolation matched Boethius' own circumstances, in full flight from the world. Partly anticipating later arguments, royal intervention extended beyond faithful communication to the bold refashioning of setting and outlook, dominated by Gregorian and Solomonic justifications of humble office-holding. Boethian philosophy gained worldly force as an active source of power and prosperity, distributed to the wise for the needs of men. Wisdom alone brought true recognition of divine purposes, avoiding all desire for wealth as foolish greed. Both extremes gained force from the very principles of divine providence, while Boethian misfortune found novel explanation as a consequence of greed. Distant in many respects from Boethian self-discovery, such theorizing offered a distinctive 'royal' theodicy, with greater scope for human control. Neo-Platonism gained active implications for all in positions of power: the outcome was the fullest expression of Alfredian discourse, the intensive dramatization of Solomonic desire.

THE *CONSOLATIO PHILOSOPHIAE* IN CONTEXT

Much hinges on the complex status and rhetoric of the Boethian source-text, often neglected in discussion. Despite immense popularity among medieval audiences, the *Consolatio* posed enduring problems of inter-pretation. Many proceeded from the context of its production, just two generations before Pope Gregory, but in a very different intellect-ual environment, more strongly committed to 'secular' learning and the inheritance of philosophy and mythology that bound Greece to Rome.[1] This was the culture which the Roman aristocrat Boethius (early 480s–525 × 526) shared with Catholic senatorial families, and had himself extended by his life's work in compiling Latin manuals and translations of Greek learning. Such literary endeavours had combined with an extraordinary career in Theoderic's administration, culminating in 522 with his appointment as *magister officiorum* and a grandiose joint-consulship for his sons. His subsequent accusation of treason showed the vulnerability of Theoderic's Arian rule in relations with Byzantium.[2]

Composed while under house arrest at Pavia, Boethius' *Consolatio* offered both a means of escape and a final act of defiance, recorded for contemporaries as well as posterity.[3] Boethius sought consolation not from revealed truths of divine grace and salvation, but from the dis-cipline of philosophy, the prime object of his studies, latterly besmirched by his enemies. By including nothing that was specifically Christian or pagan, Boethius constructed a Neo-Platonic natural theology, set apart from revelation; such a perspective presupposed the sort of Christian assumptions that Boethius shared with his audience.[4] As with Augustine, whose early dialogues prefigured much Boethian thought, faith and

---

[1] Markus, *Ancient Christianity*; J. Matthews, 'Anicius Manlius Severinus Boethius', and H. Kirby, 'The Scholar and his Public', in *Boethius: his Life, Thought and Influence*, ed. M. Gibson (London, 1981), pp. 15–43 and 44–69; E. Reiss, *Boethius* (Boston, MA, 1982); J. Marenbon, *Boethius* (Oxford, 2003).

[2] H. Chadwick, *Boethius: the Consolations of Music, Logic, Theology, and Philosophy* (Oxford, 1981), pp. 29–46; J. Moorhead, *Theoderic in Italy* (Oxford, 1992), pp. 54–65, 114–30 and 194–211.

[3] Chadwick, *Boethius*, pp. 255–6.   [4] *Ibid.*, pp. 247–53.

reason were ultimately complementary; this was encapsulated by Boethius' ambiguous treatment of the personified Philosophia, the bringer of consolation to his alter ego.[5] As Courcelle noted, all authorities actually mentioned by Philosophia predated the birth of Christ, yet Boethius also alluded to works by Plotinus, Porphyry, Proclus, Augustine and others.[6] Her status may therefore extend to the Neo-Platonism common to all Neo-Platonists after Christ, suggested also by the ladder on her clothing from 'practical' to 'theoretical' philosophy. Yet similarities are more than superficial with the biblical Lady Wisdom.[7] The only explicit biblical reference concerns divine governance of the universe in terms borrowed from the Book of Wisdom; the Prisoner's delight hints at the deeper compatibility of philosophy and revelation.[8]

Boethius' dazzling script forces the reader at every turn to consider the place of scenes within the *Consolatio* as a whole. Redressing the Prisoner's bewilderment, Philosophia holds all didactic authority; as Curley has shown, her performance reflects the very nature of Boethian knowledge, divided into four hierarchical 'faculties', first mentioned in Book V.[9] In Book I, the weary Prisoner can only be approached through *sensus*, shared with the lowest animals. In Book II, Philosophia exploits *imaginatio* through the device of imagined speech; Books III and IV appeal to *ratio*, possessed by humans alone, to assert human participation in the highest good. Only in Book V does Philosophia attain the highest faculty of *intellegentia*, possessed by God alone, to convey glimpses of divine understanding. In every scene, the Prisoner's innocence remains centre-stage: Philosophia's medicines do not merely vindicate divine justice, but offer deeper mental 'therapy'.[10]

Central to the Prisoner's complaint is the juxtaposition of *fortuna* and *uirtus*; proper understanding of this relationship supplies Boethius' theodicy with much rhetorical force.[11] The Romans had worshipped Fortuna as a goddess, represented by a capricious spinning wheel, yet her

[5] E. T. Silk, 'Boethius's Consolatio Philosophiae as a Sequel to Augustine's Dialogues and Soliloquia', *Harvard Theological Review* 32 (1939), 19–39; H. Chadwick, 'Introduction', and A. Crabbe, 'Literary Design in the De Consolatione Philosophiae', in *Boethius*, ed. Gibson, pp. 1–12, at 11–12, and 237–74, at 251–63; Chadwick, *Boethius*, pp. 249–51, cf. 220.

[6] P. Courcelle, *La Consolation de Philosophie dans la tradition littéraire: Antécédents et postérité de Boèce* (Paris, 1967), pp. 24–5.

[7] M.-Th. d'Alverny, 'Le symbolisme de la Sagesse et le Christ de saint Dunstan', *Bodleian Library Record* 5 (1956), 232–44, at 235–40; Crabbe, 'Literary Design', pp. 238–9.

[8] *Cons. phil.* IIIp12.22–3, p. 62, cf. Wisdom VIII. 1; Chadwick, 'Introduction', p. 10; Chadwick, *Boethius*, pp. 237–8.

[9] T. F. Curley, (III), 'How to Read the Consolation of Philosophy', *Interpretation* 14 (1986), 211–63, esp. 216–19; T. F. Curley, 'The Consolation of Philosophy as a Work of Literature', *American Journal of Philology* 108 (1987), 343–67.

[10] Curley, 'How to Read', pp. 214 and 219–20.   [11] Frakes, *Fate*.

power remained capable of human curtailment.[12] As a woman, she lay open to the attractions of a manly man, a *uir uirtutis*, a vulnerability famously exploited by Machiavelli.[13] Yet another view, voiced by certain Stoic writers, raised the possibility of complete escape from Fortuna's clutches, by pursuing *uirtus* alone, an inner source of stability which she could never seize.[14] With the decline of Fortuna's cult in Late Antiquity, ecclesiastical writers contested her linguistic residue.[15] The world could only be governed by God: *fortuna* was either nothing at all, or a popular misidentification of *prouidentia*.[16] Augustine was typical in attacking *fortuna* as a word of the *uulgus*, who blamed *fortuna* or *fatum* for events or their own sins.[17] Neither Fortuna nor *uirtus* explained Roman greatness, but the secret judgement of divine providence.[18]

Boethian rhetoric effected partial rehabilitation of Fortuna, only to expose the true nature of providential control.[19] The Prisoner's error is to assign blame for his downfall, on an adverse change of deceitful Fortuna.[20] The bulk of Book I covers the Prisoner's defence, protesting the innocence of actions which had protected the Roman senate, and had upheld principles of philosopher-rulership.[21] Philosophia herself is questioned for failure of support, and Fortuna seen to have shamelessly harmed an innocent man, whose *uirtus* she should by rights have rewarded.[22] This is the basis for Philosophia's diagnosis of sickness: the Prisoner has forgotten his own self in longing for external goods; he does not know the purpose of things in judging his wicked enemies to be prosperous, and has forgotten by what government the world is ruled

[12] H.R. Patch, 'The Tradition of the Goddess Fortuna in Roman Literature and in the Transitional Period', *Smith College Studies in Modern Languages* 3 (1922), 131–77; H.R. Patch, *The Goddess Fortuna in Mediaeval Literature* (Cambridge, MA, 1927), pp. 10–14; A. Doren, 'Fortuna im Mittelalter und in der Renaissance', *Vorträge der Bibliothek Warburg* 2 (1922–3), 71–115, at 73–5; Frakes, *Fate*, pp. 10–20.
[13] Q. Skinner, *Machiavelli* (Oxford, 1981), pp. 24–31; Q. Skinner, *The Foundations of Modern Political Thought*, 2 vols. (Cambridge, 1978) I, 94–101; H.F. Pitkin, *Fortune is a Woman: Gender and Politics in the Thought of Niccolò Machiavelli* (Berkeley and Los Angeles, CA, 1984), esp. pp. 138–69.
[14] Frakes, *Fate*, pp. 16–17.
[15] *Ibid.*, pp. 20–5; Patch, *Goddess Fortuna*, pp. 14–18; Doren, 'Fortuna', pp. 75–8.
[16] Jerome, *Commentarius in Ecclesiasten*, ed. de Lagarde, CCSL 72, 325; Jerome, *Commentarius in Esaiam*, ed. Adriaen, CCSL 73 and 73A, 219, cf. 753–4; Lactantius, *Divinae institutiones*, III.29, PL 6: 440B–444A; Augustine, *De civitate Dei*, ed. McCracken et al., VII.3 (II, 384–9). Cf. Frakes, *Fate*, pp. 22–4.
[17] Augustine, *Retractationes*, ed. Mutzenbecher, CCSL 57, I.1, 7; Augustine, *Sermones de Vetere Testamento*, ed. Lambot, CCSL 41, nos. XVIIB, XX and XXIX, 231–2, 263 and 374.
[18] Augustine, *De civitate Dei*, ed. McCracken et al., IV.33 and V.1 (II, 124–5 and 132–5).
[19] Chadwick, *Boethius*, pp. 225–47; Frakes, *Fate*, pp. 31–63; G. O'Daly, *The Poetry of Boethius* (London, 1991), pp. 104–235.
[20] *Cons. phil.* Im1.17–20, p. 1.   [21] Ip4.2 to end of Im5, pp. 7–12.
[22] Ip4.4–9, p. 7; Ip4.34, p. 10; Im5.28–9 and 34–6, p. 12.

in supposing Fortuna to fluctuate without a ruler.[23] Book II brings palliative 'lotions' to such sickness, harnessing the full Roman imagery of Fortuna. Those who choose Fortuna as a mistress must accept her nature: that she is constant only in mutability.[24] The Prisoner's folly receives force from Philosophia's mocking prosopopoeia, adopting Fortuna's own voice. All that has been taken are Fortuna's own servants: wealth, honours and other advantages subject to her *ius*.[25] Men must accept the rules if they choose to ride on her wheel.[26] Yet the game is undercut by Philosophia's Stoic emphasis on the external qualities of Fortuna's goods, alien to the good of their possessor.[27] The Prisoner's pursuit of glory and fame may well have been virtuous, but even if achieved, would hardly benefit his mind in heaven.[28]

Book III brings more bitter remedies, in the search for man's true goal, the *summum bonum*. All men strive by nature to attain happiness as the highest of all goods, but pursue it along different paths.[29] Riches, worthy offices (*dignitates*), kingdoms (*regna*), glory and pleasures: each is sought for its goal of sufficiency, respect (*reuerentia*), power (*potentia*), fame and joy, yet all are exposed by Philosophia as 'false goods' (*falsa bona*), failing to deliver the end for which they are sought. Sufficiency, respect, power, fame and joy emerge as qualities which cannot be attained separately, but only in concert, as aspects of true happiness (*uera beatitudo*), identified as the Platonic form of perfect good.[30] As the entity beyond which nothing better can be thought, this perfect good is also God.[31] God himself is the 'unity' of goals that all men desire: the entire universe participates in this goodness.[32] The Prisoner can merely restate his sorrow, that evils exist and go unpunished.[33] Philosophia's solution in Book IV is again Platonic, that the lack of an appropriate will to act negates any power to perform such an action.[34] By nature, every human will hastens towards happiness and the good; it is only good men who accomplish what they seek, through virtues, 'the natural function of obtaining good'.[35] Not only are evil men entirely powerless; incapable of divine performance, evil is nothing at all.[36] Merely bestial in existence, evil men are paradoxically more unhappy (*infeliciores*) for every desire they achieve, and only happier for the benefits of just punishment.[37]

The Prisoner's language marks detachment from 'popular' *fortuna*, yet his query expresses confusion at rewards often received by evil men,

[23] Ip6.18–19, pp. 15–16; Curley, 'How to Read', pp. 214–5.   [24] IIp1, pp. 17–19.
[25] IIp2.3–8, pp. 19–20.   [26] IIp2.9–10, p. 20.   [27] IIp5.24–8, p. 28; IIp6.3 and 13, p. 30.
[28] IIp7.1 and 21, pp. 32 and 34.   [29] IIIp2.2–12, pp. 38–9.
[30] IIIp9.1–21, pp. 49–50; IIIp9.22–33, pp. 50–1; Chadwick, *Boethius*, p. 233.
[31] IIIp10.1–5, p. 53; IIIp10.6–17, pp. 53–4.   [32] IIIp11.5–9, p. 57.   [33] IVp1.1–5, pp. 64–5.
[34] IVp2.5–9, p. 67.   [35] IVp2.10–13 and 23, pp. 67 and 68.
[36] IVp2.14–30, pp. 67–9; IVp2.39–46, pp. 69–70; cf. IIIp12.25–9, p. 62.
[37] IVp3.11–23 and IVm3, pp. 71–3; IVp4.3–9, p. 74; IVp4.14–21, pp. 74–5.

little different from accidental chance (*a fortuitis casibus*).[38] Philosophia's answer invokes a deeper relationship between *prouidentia* and *fatum*. The causes of all mutable things are indeed generated by the divine mind, but by means identified as 'providence' when seen by divine *intellegentia*, and 'fate' when seen by men in temporal events.[39] Whatever men see as fate remains subject to providence, as central pivot to a series of revolving spheres.[40] Only by drawing closer to the pivot can man escape the 'necessity of fate'; the Prisoner's confusion stems from the inadequacy of human reason.[41] Seen as providence divine action is inherently just, but both prosperity and hardships play necessary roles in the restraint of vice and the cultivation of virtues. Man's weakness only enhances the role of testing for certain good men.[42] It is on this basis that Philosophia can expound the true nature of *fortuna*, now relegated to the language of popular speech.[43] All *fortuna* is in fact good, as the product of God's justice in promoting virtue.[44] Such language might seem conventionally Stoical, with *uirtus* denoting inner moral strength, yet Boethian theology adds a twist to Fortuna's control.[45] Men can indeed fashion their *fortuna* through unconquerable virtue, always promoted by God alone.[46]

The role of providence leads to concluding questions in Book V, concerning chance (*casus*) and free will, no less pertinent to the Prisoner's circumstances. Chance, as a causeless event, cannot exist; certain events may be unexpected, but all proceed from the single source of providence.[47] Man's freedom in this order is seen to depend on rational contemplation of the divine mind. The only prisons are those made by men themselves, chained to the earth in ignorance and vice.[48] In all other cases men retain liberty of will, unconstrained by divine foreknowledge (*praescientia*) of future events. Philosophia's solution hinges on the superior quality of divine *intellegentia*, the highest of four Boethian 'faculties' of knowledge, surpassing human reason.[49] Just as a human spectator imposes no necessity on the events of a chariot race, so divine foreknowledge imposes no necessity on future events, whether conducted voluntarily or involving certain outcomes, such as the sun's daily rising.[50] Only God is eternal in existing outside time; his foreknowledge sees the infinite motion of temporal events in an immediate present, 'by a single stroke of mind'.[51] Consolation itself lay ultimately

---

[38] IVp5, pp. 77–8.   [39] IVp6.7–12, pp. 79–80.   [40] IVp6.13, p. 80.
[41] IVp6.14–16, pp. 80–1; IVp6.17 and 24–34, pp. 81 and 82.
[42] IVp6.35–42, pp. 82–3; IVp6.43–52, pp. 83–4.   [43] IVp7.6–7, p. 86; cf. IVp6.19, p. 81.
[44] IVp7.15, p. 87; cf. IVp7.2–15, pp. 86–7.
[45] IVp7.17–19, p. 87; IVm7, pp. 87–9; O'Daly, *Boethius*, pp. 220–34.   [46] IVp7.22, p. 87.
[47] Vp1, pp. 89–90.   [48] Vp2, p. 91.   [49] Vp4.24–39, pp. 97–9, and Vp5, pp. 100–1.
[50] Vp4.15–23, p. 97; Vp5.12, p. 101; Vp6.21–4, p. 104, and Vp6.32–6, p. 105.
[51] Vp6.2–43, pp. 102–6; Vm2.12, p. 92; cf. Vp6.22, p. 104, and Vp6.40, pp. 105–6.

in such just judgement of human actions, undertaken freely, re-affirming commitment to virtues in hope and prayer.[52] God's ways could never be fully comprehended, but Boethius' script had not been in vain.

ROYAL TRANSLATION AND CAROLINGIAN EXPERTISE

Unlike other royal source-texts, the *Consolatio philosophiae* stands apart for its lack of attestation in earlier Insular learning. The earliest secure evidence for the text's circulation coincides with Alfredian developments. Early Insular transmission of the *Consolatio* has been suggested by Fabio Troncarelli, but all aspects of his case can be satisfactorily explained by other means.[53] Attempts to detect distant influence on Insular authors serve only to reinforce consensus that the text was unknown to Aldhelm and Bede. Alcuin's inclusion of Boethius among authors available at York probably refers to another of his logical works; Italy is the more likely source for Alcuin's text.[54] Nor must Insular transmission be inferred from the text's copying at certain Continental centres founded by Insular missionaries, or from lost exemplars which may have exhibited Insular features.[55] Early references to the ideal of philosopher-rulership might seem more promising, but in each case either Jerome or Prudentius are more likely sources, or the passage is a later interpolation.[56]

Such considerations only strengthen the relevance of Carolingian interest in Boethius' text, where Alfred's Continental helpers might again have supplied special expertise. The *Consolatio* circulated widely in ninth-century manuscripts, revered for its theological and philosophical insights, as an eclectic textbook in the liberal arts.[57] Together with Martianus Capella's *De nuptiis Philologiae et Mercurii*, employed for comparable purposes, its lessons gave a Neo-Platonic edge to Carolingian liberal training.[58]

---

[52] Vp6.44, 46 and 47, p. 106; cf. Vp3.29–36, pp. 94–5.

[53] F. Troncarelli, *Tradizioni perdute: La Consolatio Philosophiae nell'alto medioevo*, Medioevo e Umanesimo 42 (Padua, 1981), pp. 107–34, esp. 132–4.

[54] *Ibid.*, pp. 112–27. Cf. D. K. Bolton, 'The Study of the Consolation of Philosophy in Anglo-Saxon England', *Archives d'histoire doctrinale et litteraire du Moyen Age* 44 (1977), 33–78, at 33–4; J. Beaumont, 'The Latin Tradition of the De Consolatione Philosophiae', in *Boethius*, ed. Gibson, pp. 278–305, at 279; M. Gibson, 'Boethius in the Carolingian Schools, *TRHS*, 5th ser. 32 (1982), 43–56, at 45.

[55] Cf. Troncarelli, *Tradizioni perdute*, pp. 107–12 and 128–32.

[56] Bolton, 'Study of the Consolation', p. 33, note 2; M. Lapidge, 'Byrhtferth of Ramsey and the Early Sections of the *Historia Regum* attributed to Symeon of Durham', in his *ALL* II, 317–42, at 334–5 and note 45.

[57] Gibson, 'Carolingian Schools'; Beaumont, 'Latin Tradition'; F. Troncarelli, *Boethiana Aetas: Modelli grafici e fortuna manoscritta della Consolatio Philosophiae tra IX e XII secolo*, Biblioteca di scrittura e civiltà 2 (Alessandria, 1987).

[58] Brown, 'Carolingian Renaissance', pp. 36–8; J. Marenbon, *Early Medieval Philosophy (480–1150): an Introduction* (London, 1983), pp. 10–12.

The role owed much to Alcuin's impact on Carolingian education, evident in his theorizing introduction to the liberal arts, the *Disputatio de vera philosophia*, frequently alluding to Boethian arguments.[59] Pupils ask how they may reach the highest *felicitas*; its attainment is shown to reside not in transitory 'false goods' but the one true good which alone endures.[60] The source of the soul's splendour is specifically 'wisdom', only attainable through biblical study.[61] Philosophia's mystical clothing now consorted with the biblical house of Wisdom, supported by seven columns (Proverbs IX); ascent via 'practical' philosophy now denoted the liberal arts as necessary steps towards divine Wisdom.[62] The role for Boethius offers an arresting perspective on his Alfredian deployment, in vernacular 'liberal' training. Alfredian 'liberal arts' supplied access to royal translation: the effect was only to enhance the status of its Boethian wisdom, no longer subservient to exegetical Latinity.

Yet behind such manoeuvres lay detailed study of the Latin source-text. Quite what this involved has long been complicated by possible connections with Latin commentary material, extensively generated in Carolingian study and widely available by the late ninth century.[63] Partially unresolved, the issue remains problematic in formulation and methodology. Though commentary traditions did develop, behind much material lay complex processes of glossing and accretion to form continuous commentaries, themselves unstable.[64] The resulting traditions are sufficiently amorphous as to defy comprehensive editing. Only a handful of fifty or so pertinent manuscripts have been assessed in an Alfredian context; several early glossed manuscripts await detailed examination.[65] Further problems arise in satisfactorily demonstrating the influence of a particular gloss on royal translation. Points of similarity are inherently likely between two explanations of a common base text, without necessarily implying a direct relationship. Attention has focused

---

[59] Marenbon, 'Carolingian Thought', pp. 172–3; d'Alverny, 'La Sagesse', pp. 245–8 and 250–7; Courcelle, *La Consolation*, pp. 33–46.

[60] Alcuin, *Disputatio de vera philosophia*, PL 101: 850C (cf. *Cons. phil.* IIIp2.4–7, p. 38 and IIIp3.1, p. 41).

[61] *Ibid.*, PL 101: 852B.   [62] *Ibid.*, PL 101: 853B–D.

[63] G. Schepss, 'Zu König Alfreds Boethius', *Archiv für das Studium der neueren Sprachen und Literaturen* 94 (1895), 149–60; B. S. Donaghey, 'The Sources of King Alfred's Translation of Boethius' Consolation of Philosophy', *Anglia* 82 (1964), 23–57; Otten, *Boethius*; Troncarelli, *Tradizioni perdute*, pp. 137–96; J. S. Wittig, 'King Alfred's Boethius and its Latin Sources: a Reconsideration', *ASE* 11 (1983), 157–98; Frakes, *Fate*, pp. 65–8.

[64] Marenbon, *Early Medieval Philosophy*, pp. 71–3.

[65] Wittig, 'Alfred's Boethius', pp. 162–3 and note 21; Troncarelli, *Boethian Aetas*, nos. 19, 66 and 95; E. J. Daly, 'An Early Ninth-Century Manuscript of Boethius', *Scriptorium* 4 (1950), 205–19; F. Troncarelli, 'Boezio nel circolo d'Alcuino: le più antiche glosse carolinge alla Consolatio Philosophiae', *Recherches Augustiniennes* 22 (1987), 223–41.

on classical and mythological material, where similarities might be harder to regard as coincidental. Only the case of Orpheus and Eurydice has been investigated exhaustively, pointing away from regular dependence;[66] without such control, hostages are inevitably given to the discovery of more relevant material in other manuscripts.

Partly as a result of these problems, the extent of scholarly disagreement over this question has sometimes been exaggerated. Neither Schepss nor Otten, the main proponents of royal access to commentary material, believed that glosses had influenced any more than a few passages containing difficult arguments or unfamiliar ancient material.[67] Otten, in particular, wholly accepted the impression of translatory approach that emerges from more recent studies by Wittig, Bately and Irvine, also paralleled in the royal Psalms.[68] Certain passages imply additional research, but the inclusion of material depended primarily on its contextual relevance to what was often a distinctive reading of the source-text.[69] Such independence is especially significant given the preponderance of glossed texts among Latin manuscripts. Of some seventeen manuscripts known from the ninth century and earlier, thirteen bear contemporary glosses;[70] an even greater proportion is evident in the substantial corpus from tenth- and eleventh-century England.[71] Direct access to commentary material is further suggested by the translation's opening section, on the circumstances of Boethius' imprisonment, reflecting knowledge of certain Latin *Vitae* similarly positioned in glossed manuscripts.[72]

The value of commentary material lies not in fully explaining expansions and departures, but placing these changes in interpretative context. The commentary traditions must be approached as information which might well have adorned a Latin exemplar, yet also in a wider sense as evidence for the text's intensive scrutiny in scholarly enquiry. Each tradition incorporated and discussed glosses which were already in circulation. Whether or not these commentaries were fully compiled before the late ninth century, surviving texts convey an invaluable impression of available expertise. This chapter relies on a limited study

---

[66] Wittig, 'Alfred's Boethius', on IIIm12.
[67] Schepss, 'Alfreds Boethius', p. 155, and Otten, *Boethius*, pp. 155–7 and 284–5.
[68] Above, pp. 245–61.
[69] Bately, 'Those Books', pp. 50–5 and 65; Wittig, 'Alfred's Boethius', esp. p. 166; S. Irvine, 'Ulysses and Circe in King Alfred's Boethius: a Classical Myth Transformed', in *'Doubt Wisely'*, ed. Toswell and Tyler, pp. 387–401, esp. 387–91.
[70] Troncarelli, *Boethiana Aetas*, nos. 14, 19, 51, 56, 66, 78, 80, 95, 97, 99, 111, 122, 133; cf. nos. 4, 29, 110 and 134.
[71] *Ibid.*, nos. 5, 26, 39, 44, 69, 70, 72, 73, 75, 77, 85, 87, 88, 93, 105, 118, 133; Bolton, 'Study of the Consolation'.
[72] Below, p. 282.

of the three main commentary traditions. The first, known as the 'Anonymous of St Gallen', preserves teachings disseminated from St Gallen, a major centre of Boethian scholarship.[73] It is attested in two versions, to which their editor Petrus Tax has kindly granted access: a short version surviving as tenth-century glosses in two manuscripts, Naples, Biblioteca Nazionale, IV. G. 68 (= N) and St Gallen, Stiftsbibliothek, 844 (= G); and a longer reworking as a continuous commentary, best attested in the tenth-century St Gallen manuscript, Einsiedeln, Stiftsbibliothek, 179 (= E1).[74]

Certain 'Anonymous' glosses are also represented in a second tradition, attributed to Remigius of Auxerre (c. 841–c. 908). A work of compilation and synthesis, Remigius' commentary soon surpassed the 'Anonymous' in scholarly popularity.[75] Variously attested in later English manuscripts, the Remigian tradition gains further relevance from Remigius' presence at Rheims in the late ninth century, where he had been enlisted by Fulk, together with Hucbald of St-Amand.[76] The precise date is unfortunately uncertain. Lutz claims to detect Remigius at Rheims in 884×885, but the document is not securely dated; Hucbald at least is unlikely to have left St-Bertin before the death of his patron abbot Rodulf in 892, the point at which both recruitments are included in Flodoard's narrative.[77] Though the latter would postdate Grimbald's departure by several years, Alfredian contact with Rheims evidently continued into the early 890s.[78] Partial access to this tradition is afforded by various published extracts; these have been supplemented by four representative manuscripts, each consulted on microfilm.[79] The continuous commentary in Krakow, Biblioteka

---

[73] Courcelle, *La Consolation*, pp. 259–63 and 275–8; Beaumont, 'Latin Tradition', pp. 282–4; Frakes, *Fate*, pp. 65–7.

[74] Troncarelli, *Boethiana Aetas*, nos. 99 and 122; ninth-century main text of N West Frankish, perhaps written at Tours; gloss hand of G probably the same as that for E1 (Petrus Tax, pers. comm.).

[75] Courcelle, *La Consolation*, pp. 241–69 and 278–90; Bolton, 'Study of the Consolation'; Beaumont, 'Latin Tradition', pp. 285–95; Frakes, *Fate*, pp. 67–8; C. Jeudy, 'L'œuvre de Remi d'Auxerre: État de la question' and 'Remigii autissiodorensis opera (Clavis)', in *L'École Carolingienne d'Auxerre de Murethach à Remi 830–908*, ed. D. Iogna-Prat, C. Jeudy and G. Lobrichon (Paris, 1991), pp. 373–96, at 388, and 457–500, at 485.

[76] Manitius, *Geschichte* I, 504–19; G. Schneider, *Erzbischof Fulco von Reims (883–900) und das Frankenreich* (Munich, 1973), pp. 239–44; Jeudy, 'Remigii autissiodorensis opera', pp. 459–60.

[77] C. Lutz in *Remigii Autissiodorensis Commentum in Martianum Capellam*, ed. Lutz I, 7–8, note 9; evidence usefully laid out in Manitius, *Geschichte* I, 505–6, cf. above, pp. 161–2. Courcelle conveniently dated Remigius' commentary to 901–2 (*La Consolation*, pp. 254–9), but cf. Wittig, 'Alfred's Boethius', p. 159, note 12, and 160, note 14.

[78] *C&S*, nos. 5 and 6 (trans. in *EHD*, nos. 224 and 225).

[79] H. F. Stewart, 'A Commentary by Remigius Autissiodorensis on the De Consolatione Philosophiae of Boethius', *JTS* 17 (1915), 22–42; E. T. Silk, *Saeculi Noni Auctoris in Boetii Consolationem Philosophiae Commentarius* (Rome, 1935), pp. 312–43 only (the remainder now agreed to be a twelfth-century compilation); Bolton, 'Study of the Consolation', pp. 60–78.

Jagiellonska, Berl. Lat. Q. 939 (Cologne and Tegernsee, s. x$^{4/4}$), fols. 60v–112r (= Ma) has been employed as a guide to three other manuscripts bearing Remigian glosses: Paris, Bibliothèque nationale de France, lat. 15090 (St-Evre, Toul, s. x) (= P7); Trier, Stadtbibliothek, 1093/1694 (Echternach, s. x$^{4/4}$) (= T); and Paris, Bibliothèque nationale de France, nouv. acq. lat. 1478 (Cluny provenance, s. x–xi) (= P10).[80]

A third tradition is principally attested in Vatican, Biblioteca Apostolica, lat. 3363 (= V), written in the Loire valley in the mid-ninth century, with three layers of later Insular annotation, the earliest of which has been partially published by Troncarelli as the 'Vatican Anonymous'.[81] This first Insular hand was once identified as originating from Wales or south-west England and thus wishfully attributed to Asser, but the glosses show few points of similarity with Alfred's translation.[82] Dumville has tentatively identified the hand as Phase II English Square Minuscule of the 930s.[83] There can be no connection with William of Malmesbury's claim that Asser had expounded the sense of Boethius 'in clearer words'.[84] The report may merely be an extrapolation from Asser's account; as Lapidge notes, its status is not enhanced by Asser's lack of Boethian allusion, though the point is inconclusive.[85] Traces of the 'Vatican Anonymous' also survive in later English manuscripts; it shares certain glosses with Remigius, but its relationship with other traditions has yet to be satisfactorily established.[86]

All three commentaries reflect the text's central place in Carolingian scholarship. Certain limits in the impact of commentary material may have proceeded from the relationship with the liberal arts, as keys to exegetical understanding. The majority of glosses are grammatical; other comments relate Boethius' text to the specific disciplines of rhetoric, music or astronomy. Yet all arts were subservient to divine wisdom; wherever possible, glosses explained Boethius' Neo-Platonism in explicitly Christian terms. Only a few passages posed serious difficulties, on the world soul, possible intermediaries between *prouidentia* and *fatum* and the perpetuity of the world; in each case the reference was either

---

[80] Krakow manuscript formerly Maihingen, Bibliothek Wallerstein, I. 2. IV. ms. 3; Troncarelli, *Boethiana Aetas*, nos. 40, 45, 61 and 68; Wittig, 'Alfred's Boethius', pp. 187–8; Jeudy, 'Remigii autissiodorensis opera', pp. 486–7.

[81] Troncarelli, *Tradizioni perdute*, pp. 137–96, with his 'Boezio nel circolo d'Alcuino', p. 239, note 41.

[82] Wittig, 'Alfred's Boethius', pp. 160–2, 170 and 172, notes 20, 37 and 41. Cf. also M. B. Parkes, 'A Note on MS Vatican, Bibl. Apost., lat. 3363', in *Boethius*, ed. Gibson, pp. 425–7.

[83] Dumville, 'English Square Minuscule', pp. 173–7.

[84] *GR* I, 190–1, with Thomson's commentary (II, 102).   [85] Lapidge, 'Asser's Reading', p. 40.

[86] Bolton, 'Study of the Consolation', p. 40. F. Troncarelli, 'Per una ricerca sui commenti altomedievali al De Consolatione di Boezio', in *Miscellanea in memoria di Giorgio Cencetti* (Turin, 1973), pp. 363–80, at 371–8, argues for Remigian dependence on the Vatican commentary, on assumptions open to question.

reluctantly condemned, or cleverly reconciled with Christian authority.[87] The treatment of Philosophia was central to re-interpretation. All Carolingian readers understood Philosophia as the biblical Lady Wisdom, with all that this implied about the status of her words. For the 'Anonymous of St Gallen' and Remigius, Philosophia represented not only divine *Sapientia*, but Christ himself, whom Paul had identified as the wisdom of God.[88] Both interpret her sceptre as the 'riches and glory' carried in Wisdom's left hand in Proverbs III. 16;[89] and follow Alcuin in regarding her finely woven garments as the liberal arts.[90] For Remigius, her books are the 'fiery law' held in the right hand of the Lord.[91] The 'Anonymous' goes further, interpreting the immense variability of her height with reference to Christ's descent to man, his lofty teaching on earth and heavenly ascent.[92] Wisdom herself became Boethian in Carolingian depictions; in two early ninth-century bibles her iconography incorporated the sceptre and book of Philosophia.[93] Paschasius Radbertus invoked Philosophia's clothing in explaining why the 'clothing of souls', Christ's teaching as wisdom, should not be defiled.[94] An anonymous Irish poet, perhaps Sedulius Scottus, praised archbishop Gunthar of Cologne

---

[87] IIIm9.13–17, p. 52; IVp6.13, p. 80; Vp6.9–14, pp. 102–3. Courcelle, *La Consolation*, pp. 275–90; Beaumont, 'Latin Tradition', pp. 288–95.

[88] I Corinthians I. 24; Ecclesiasticus I. 5; cf. John I. 1.

[89] SCEPTRUM (Ip1.6, p. 2): 'quo potestas eius exprimitur. vt. Attingens. a fine v[sque] a[d] f[inem] f[ortiter] (Wisdom VIII. 1; cf. IIIp12.22–3, p. 62). Et dominabitur a m[are] u[sque] a[d] m[are] (Ps. LXXI. 8). Et in sinistra illius d[iuitiae] e[t] g[loria] (Proverbs III. 16). Significat. quod semper sapientia iure dexterior. atque prior sit omni potestati. ut vbicumque se inserit. apta facultas numquam deerit': E1 (p. 98b). 'Per sceptrum mundana gloria intelligitur quae per sapientiam regitur. In sinistra tenetur quia: In sinistra illius diuitiae et gloria (Proverbs III. 16). Sceptrum namque primum uirga est, deinde inauratur et per disciplinam peruenitur ad gloriam': Stewart, 'Remigius', pp. 26–7; Silk, *Commentarius*, p. 316.

[90] VESTES ERANT TENUISSIMIS FILIS (Ip1.3, p. 2): 'id est liberales artes. subtilibus enim compositae rationibus': E1 (p. 97b), G (p. 14), N (fol. 5v). 'Vestes liberales artes uel doctrinae ingenia uel diuersae disciplinae. Vestes philosophiae tenuissimis filis perfectae esse dicuntur, quia VII liberales artes adeo subtilissimae sunt ut nec origo earum nec finis aduerti possit': Stewart, 'Remigius', p. 26; Silk, *Commentarius*, p. 315.

[91] LIBELLOS (Ip1.6, p. 2): 'Libelli quos in manu dextera gestabat ipsi sunt in quibus liberales artes continentur. Unde et legitur: In dextera eius ignea lex (Deuteronomy XXIII. 2). Aut libellos disertam doctrinam uel theoricam uitam accipimus': Stewart, 'Remigius', p. 26; Silk, *Commentarius*, p. 315.

[92] AD COMMUNEM SESE HOMINUM MENSURAM COHIBEBAT (Ip1.2, p. 2): 'quia sapientia dei cum esset aequalis deo patri semetipsam exinaniuit. formam serui accipiens': E1 (p. 97b). NUNC UERO PULSARE CAELUM SUMMI UERTICIS CACUMINE UIDEBATUR (Ip1.2, p. 2): 'Ob altitudinem doctrinarum dicit. et mysteria uerborum. quibus in carne adhuc auditores instruxit': *ibid.* IPSUM … CAELUM PENETRABAT (Ip1.2, p. 2): 'Nam post praedicationem suam. et post miraculorum signa. postque crucis tormenta. post resurrectionem eius. videntibus discipulis eleuatus ascendit in caelum. et sedit a dextris dei': *ibid.*

[93] W. Koehler, *Die karolingischen Miniaturen: I. Die Schule von Tours* (Berlin, 1930–3), plates 58c and 43c.

[94] *Expositio in Matthaeum*, PL 120: 378B–379B, on Matthew IX. 16–17.

through the mouth of a Boethian apparition, called '*sophia* in Greek, *sapientia* in Rome'.[95] A similar mysterious lady uttered Sapiential citations to the young St Lebuin, according to Hucbald of St-Amand.[96]

Philosophia's ubiquity stands in contrast to the fate of Fortuna in learned discourse. The familiar, wholesale adoption of Boethian Fortuna by medieval writers and artists seems to have begun only in the eleventh century.[97] Ninth-century writers inspired by Boethius regularly deployed alternative terminology, of vicissitudes and tumults, immutability (*nil non mutabile*) and instability (*instabilitas*), earthly inconstancy (*inconstantia mundana*) and transitoriness (*transitorium regnum*), chance (*casu, forte malo*) and lot (*sors impia*).[98] A notable exception is the early tenth-century *Chronicon* of Regino of Prüm, precociously deploying *fortuna* as a mutable manifestation of divine control.[99] The general silence of *fortuna*, broken only in sparse references by Alcuin and Einhard, suggests the concept as problematic.[100] The point is borne out by the commentary traditions, forced to engage with Boethian terminology. As Frakes has noted, the commentaries accept without question the characterization of Fortuna presented in her speech, which they correctly understand to have been spoken by Philosophia.[101] Yet glosses missed by Frakes show this acceptance to have been double-edged, undercut by awareness of Boethius' later rhetoric. Regularly anticipated in earlier glosses, Philosophia's ascent to higher concepts was heightened by Fortuna's relegation to 'popular' speech, surmounted by *prouidentia* and *fatum*. Thus when 'Fortuna' claims 'wealth, honours and others of such things' to be 'of her power' (*mei iuris*), the 'Anonymous of St Gallen' remarks 'sed magis dei'.[102] Remigian glosses are even more explicit in regarding Book II as Philosophia's demonstration 'that *fortuna*

---

[95] *Encomium Guntharii*, in MGH Poet. III, 238–40, lines 1–24.

[96] Hucbald of St-Amand (writing at St-Amand, *c.* 910), *Vita Sancti Lebuini*, PL 132: 880D–881D.

[97] H. R. Patch, *The Tradition of Boethius: a Study of his Importance in Medieval Culture* (New York, 1935), pp. 97–113, esp. pp. 97–100; Courcelle, *La Consolation*, pp. 135–43 and plates 65, 69 and 70; Doren, 'Fortuna', pp. 72 and 85–92.

[98] Examples from Alcuin, *Disputatio de vera philosophia*, PL 101: 851B–C; Alcuin's poem on Lindisfarne, in Godman, *Poetry of the Carolingian Renaissance*, no. 10, pp. 126–39, lines 7, 15, 26, 97–8; M. W. Herren, 'The De imagine Tetrici of Walahfrid Strabo: Edition and Translation', *Journal of Medieval Latin* 1 (1991), 118–39, at line 25 (p. 132); Hrabanus Maurus, *Ad Bonosum*, in MGH Poet. II, 193–6, lines 29–30.

[99] Ed. Kurze, esp. s.a. 874 and 887, pp. 107–8 and 127–8; H.-H. Kortüm, 'Weltgeschichte am Ausgang der Karolingerzeit: Regino von Prüm', in *Historiographie im frühen Mittelalter*, ed. A. Scharer and G. Scheibelreiter (Vienna, 1994), pp. 499–513; MacLean, *Charles the Fat*, pp. 170–1 and 191–2.

[100] Alcuin, *Disputatio de vera philosophia*, PL 101: 851B (cf. *Cons. phil.* IIp4.23, p. 25); Einhard, *Vita Karoli*, ed. Holder-Egger, cc. 8 and 19, pp. 11 and 25.

[101] Frakes, *Fate*, pp. 70–1.

[102] MEI SUNT IURIS (IIp2.6, p. 19): 'sed magis dei': G (p. 42), N (fol. 19v).

is nothing' (*fortunam nihil esse*). As a later gloss explains, 'Now I wonder even more because I know that *fortuna* is nothing, and that all things happen by God's providence'.[103] The view mirrored an earlier patristic proscription of Fortuna, as a word without meaning.[104] Aldhelm had similarly condemned her rulership as an ancient error.[105] Fortuna's bold return in the later middle ages, no longer displaced but controlled by God, warrants further treatment from this prior context, part of broader changes in attitude to classical rhetoric.

The uses of Boethius extended further: Carolingian education provides a context for 'courtly' deployment of Boethian allusion, adapted by ecclesiastical writers to the needs of sapiential rulership. Usage was typically inventive: the eclectic sophistication of Boethian wisdom masked tensions with worldly royal practice. The Prisoner's downfall as studious consul stood in contrast to Carolingian expectations of learned rulership, biblically associated with future success. Worldly authority itself, with riches and glory, found portrayal in the *Consolatio* as 'false goods', posing formidable obstacles to sapiential attainment. Both themes were combined in Philosophia's final depiction of divine justice, undermining any connection between prosperity and divine approval. Perhaps for these reasons, early attention focused almost exclusively on philosopher-rulership, ironically detached from the Prisoner's complaint.[106] For Alcuin the Platonic image supplied convenient praise for Charlemagne's prosperous imperial rule, that kingdoms would be 'happy' (*felicia*), 'si philosophi, id est amatores sapientiae regnarent, vel reges philosophiae studerent'.[107] Transition was seamless to a biblical context for Wisdom's power: 'For it is she who exalts the humble man and makes the powerful man glorious and is praiseworthy in every person' (cf. Proverbs XXIX. 23; Ecclesiasticus X. 17–19 and XI. 1).[108]

Usage intensified under 'ministerial' rulers, with heightened responsibilities of self-control. Louis the Pious received Plato's advice from Walahfrid Strabo, in a poem otherwise darkly commenting on Theoderic's memory.[109] The same saying was harnessed by Paschasius

---

[103] IN TUMOREM (Ip5.12, p. 14): 'Cum aliquis tumor subtus cutem intumuerit atque induruerit. non statim a medico inciditur. Sed ut molescat fomenta adhibet et medicamina molliora. Ita philosophia primum ostendit ei fortunam nihil esse. deinde quid sit summum bonum': Ma (fol. 71v), P7 (fol. 15r), T (fol. 123v). QUONAM MODO (IIp4.29, p. 25): 'Ostendens superius instabilitatem et mutabilitatem fortune. ostendit nunc qualiter ipsa fortuna contemni et mentis tranquillitas haberi possit': Ma (fol. 76v), P7 (fol. 23v), T (fol. 128v), P10 (fol. 15v). MIRARER (IVp5.5, p. 78): 'Nunc autem plus miror quia scio fortunam nihil esse. sed omnia dei prouidentia fieri': Ma (fol. 98v), P7 (fol. 64r), T (fol. 153v), P10 (fol. 43v).
[104] Above, p. 267.   [105] Aldhelm, *Aenigmata*, ed. Glorie, CCSL 133, 388–9.
[106] Courcelle, *La Consolation*, pp. 60–6; Anton, *Fürstenspiegel*, pp. 98, 247 and 255–7.
[107] MGH Epist. IV, no. 229, p. 373, lines 1–8.   [108] *Ibid.*, cf. no. 121, p. 177, lines 21–2.
[109] Herren, 'De imagine Tetrici', lines 256–7, p. 139.

Radbertus in parallel denigration of former palace enemies.[110] Such claims add force to an even wider scope of Boethian engagement at the court of Charles the Bald.[111] Though obviously pertinent given Grimbald's recruitment, its value lies as much in the clarity of response to West Frankish conditions.[112] In the hands of Sedulius Scottus, supplemented by the work of craftsmen under court patronage, Boethian therapy augmented the repertoire of sacerdotal admonition. The special status of ecclesiastical land, upheld by regular synods, and royal responsibilities towards the church: all were central to an artful alleviation of royal suffering, adapted from Boethian imagery. Immediately preceding Sedulius' Solomonic appeal, such advice offered a uniquely West Frankish response to worldly transience, reinforcing the benefits of Solomon's dream. The *ars et industria* of Sedulian rulership is shown to depend on implications of resemblance between this earthly kingdom and 'the whirling of a spinning wheel'.[113] Because 'the glory of this earthly realm' suddenly rises and falls, its *honores* are merely imaginary and fleeting, a pale imitation of the true realm which alone endures. How then could this earthly kingdom be brought to some semblance of heavenly *stabilitas*? Not through military force, answered Sedulius, for the victory of the good is never certain; nor through peace, which might hold among good men, but is frequently destabilized by the wicked. The only solution was wholehearted trust in divine mercy (*clementia*): only the Lord could achieve such stability, as source and object of 'ministerial' duty. Divine foreknowledge enabled consistent support for faithful *ministri*, as David had replaced Saul. Such service lay specifically in just implementation of divine precepts, eliciting stability with 'great and glorious reward'.

Not the least significance of Sedulius' advice is the repeated compromising of Boethian allusion. Fortuna is absent, and though a 'spinning wheel' endures, its presence accompanies direct reversal in the principles of divine control. Apparent disorder is no longer justified by the promotion of *uirtus*; God's actions include worldly aid for his faithful servants, taking direct account of human merits. Such control matched Charles's own portrayal by Sedulius at the 'wheel of his rule', raising the humble and repressing the proud.[114] Wisdom herself enjoyed protective 'sport' in a poem of praise for archbishop Gunthar.[115] The highest good was no

---

[110] Paschasius Radbertus (writing at Corbie in late 820s), *Vita Sancti Adalhardi*, c. 30, PL 120: 1523C.
[111] Staubach, *Rex Christianus*, pp. 141–8 and 196–7 (cf. Otten, *Boethius*, p. 31).
[112] Cf. Scharer, *Herrschaft*, pp. 88–9 and 104–5, otherwise attentive to possible Alfredian connections.
[113] *RC* 3, p. 27, line 27, to p. 29, line 25.
[114] *Caesar erat Karolus*, in MGH Poet. III, no. 28, p. 193, lines 20–4; Staubach, *Rex Christianus*, pp. 212–15.
[115] *Encomium Guntharii*, in MGH Poet. III, p. 239, lines 19–22; cf. Boethian 'ludere' for Fortuna's seeming control (IIm1.7, p. 19).

longer the only hope: similar immutability might be achieved on earth, through prudent fulfilment of royal ministry. The goal was tailor-made for Charles's political priorities, deriving further force from the existing stress on his many adversities, the extended testing of Davidic humility. Such was the need for royal trust, lying neither in arms nor peace, but in the 'spiritual armaments' of ecclesiastical prayer and support, even more effective than the human contribution of military benefices.[116] The appeal harmonized directly with the rewards of *religiosa sapientia*, recently demonstrated in Charles's acquisition of Lotharingia.[117] Behind both lay the distinctive power of West Frankish royal posturing, no less dependent on ecclesiastical resources, in just defence of land and church.

Herculean imagery at Charles's court offers a further aspect of Boethian allusion. The throne preserved in the Vatican as the 'Cathedra Petri' has been convincingly identified as the work of Carolingian craftsmen.[118] Herculean imagery stands out in a series of ivory panels between its front legs, depicting the twelve labours and six grotesque monsters. Produced for court use in the late 860s, both throne and panels reached Rome at an early stage, probably in the context of Charles's imperial coronation. Matters still hotly debated remain the precise context of construction, and the iconographic relationship between the panels and the rest of the throne. Close parallels with Charles's own depiction in manuscripts suggest a sophisticated scheme of 'ministerial' representation, relating wisdom and other virtues to the theme of martial and spiritual struggle.[119] The case for Boethian reference involves Book IV, metre 7, one of only two possible 'sources': its relevance is strengthened by the context of Sedulius' writings and court poetry by Eriugena.[120] Behind the comparison frequently drawn between royal anger and a raging lion, both of which had to be fought, lay Stoic and Christian interpretation of Hercules' labours as the victory of *uirtus* and self-restraint over various vices.[121] Boethian handling commended the pursuit of a celestial path of virtue, implicitly adapted to kingship in the bestial existence of *impii reges*.[122] Yet other

---

[116] Above, pp. 69 and 162–3, cf. 25–7. [117] *RC* 4, pp. 30–2.

[118] L. Nees, 'Charles the Bald and the Cathedra Petri', in *Charles the Bald*, ed. Nelson and Gibson, pp. 340–7; L. Nees, *A Tainted Mantle* (Philadelphia, PA, 1991), pp. 147–301; Staubach, *Rex Christianus*, pp. 283–334.

[119] See esp. Staubach, *Rex Christianus*, pp. 296–9 and 303–34.

[120] Cf. Nees, *A Tainted Mantle*, who bases his interpretation largely on Theodulf of Orléans's poem *Ad iudices* (c. 799); cf. N. Staubach, 'Herkules in der Karolingerzeit', in *Gli umanesimi medievali*, ed. C. Leonardi (Florence, 1998), pp. 676–90.

[121] Staubach, *Rex Christianus*, pp. 320–5; *RC* 2, p. 27, line 16; c. 3, p. 59, lines 10–16; c. 13, p. 61, line 23; and esp. c. 13, p. 60, lines 6–8, from Lactantius, *Divinae institutiones* I.9 (Staubach, *Rex Christianus*, p. 324, note 165).

[122] *Iohannis Scotti Eriugenae Carmina*, ed. Herren, no. 2, pp. 64–7, lines 39 and 59–60, with Staubach, *Rex Christianus*, pp. 56–61: 'virtutis iter' cf. *Cons. phil.* IVm7.32–3, p. 88, and

poems invoked Hercules for his manly and martial strength, recalling Charles's own struggles against visible and invisible enemies.[123] Addressing royal adversity, the entire scheme offered parallel hope for its elevated occupant, after virtuous testing.[124] Earthly triumph lay similarly dependent on acts of royal wisdom. Again distant from Boethian context, such imagery expressed the guiding power of West Frankish ecclesiastical expectation.

ALFREDIAN ADAPTATION: 'MIND', WISDOM AND 'WORLDLY BLESSINGS'

Alfredian handling gains much from parallel West Frankish deployment. The vernacular text offers a further case of courtly adaptation, remarkably sustained within inventive translation. The Prisoner's downfall, the role of 'false goods', the operation of divine justice: all found novel treatment in a text often far removed from Boethian consolation. Several changes precisely mirrored West Frankish manoeuvres. Philosophia received biblical guise, as the persona of *Wisdom*; far from cosmetic, the transformation enabled explicit account of Solomonic kingship. Fortuna too was effectively abandoned as a concept, in a sustained reorientation of divine priorities, towards active aid for humble rule. At the least, such parallels reinforce the value of Alfred's Carolingian personnel, with Grimbald again the most likely conduit; they also strengthen the case for direct awareness of sapiential language in West Frankish courtly repertoire.

Yet the relationship was selective, shaped by West Saxon needs in the complex processes of translation. There can be no question of textual dependence, still less of isolating channels of connection. The problems relating to West Frankish Solomonic language have been noted; for the *Consolatio* also, the 'Cathedra Petri' points to an important breadth of familiarity and reference.[125] Nor could such influence have extended far beyond the elements outlined. Many of the translation's features confirm the distinctive force of Alfredian discourse in key aspects of departure. The character of Solomonic intervention is especially diagnostic, far from the isolation of West Frankish royal ministry. Ecclesiastical obligations are unmentioned: the Prisoner's handling reinforces hopes of wider access to

---

IVp7.21, p. 87. Here dependent on Pseudo-Dionysius, Eriugena's theme of deification recurs in *Cons. phil.* IIIp10.22–5, pp. 54–5, and IVp3.1–9, pp. 70–1, and on the throne (Staubach, *ibid.*, pp. 294–7). *RC* 8, p. 43, lines 5–12, and p. 45, lines 14–19; cf. *Cons. phil.* IVp3.11–21 and IVm3, pp. 71–3.

[123] Staubach, *Rex Christianus*, pp. 325–9 and 297–9.

[124] Cf. 'Post inclitos labores / Ac laurea trophea ... Feliciter regentem / Cum sors beata comat': *RC* 13, p. 61, with possible pun (cf. *comare*, 'to have hair').

[125] Staubach, *Rex Christianus*, p. 315, for carvings of Hercules on the throne's gable.

wisdom, as the basis for all in authority. Such concerns are matched by the general status of power and wealth, reinterpreted in Solomonic terms. Gregorian departures combine to show dangers of greed, over and above their Neo-Platonic emphasis, and explicitly compatible with rightful use. The effects are crystallized in the example of an earthly king.[126] Though he rejects all avarice, his desire for wisdom justifies control of an entire people, and all necessary resources. Here, above all, imported elements were secondary to West Saxon priorities, demanding access to wisdom as a collective remedy for viking punishment. There could be little room for Job-like testing; royal handling went so far as possible to restate the retributive benefits of sapiential rulership. The adaptation of Boethius answered the needs of Alfredian kingship; main determinants of departure were the languages of royal power, already embedded in courtly practice.

Such changes involved coherent reorientation of the text's philosophical and dramatic setting. Alfred's *Froferboc* ('consolation-book') betrays full awareness of its overarching arguments, gaining further clarity from internal signposting. Important claims are recapitulated; other additions tie earlier points to the proceeding discussion.[127] The nature of output is complicated by the translation's survival in two recensions: one entirely in prose, and a second version in which the majority of Boethian metres are replaced by sections of verse, almost entirely derived from the corresponding prose renderings.[128] The status of the latter version remains unclear. Though royal versification is claimed in the prose preface, the text suggests signs of post-Alfredian intervention.[129] The metrical preface draws a distinction between 'Alfred', with efforts described in the past tense, and a first-person 'ic', now taking up the poem; the king's verb *spellian* bears associations with speech and prose. Contrary to some discussions, only the prose version can be securely regarded as a contemporary royal product.[130]

As Frakes has shown, the main focus for change is Fortuna herself, effectively deconstructed into a series of complementary voices and terms.[131] As

[126] *Bo* XVII, pp. 40–1; discussed below, pp. 290–5.
[127] *Bo* XVI.iii, p. 37, lines 21–6; XVI.iii, p. 38, lines 20–8; XXIV.i–ii, p. 52, line 28, to p. 53, line 14; XXVII.iii–iv, p. 63, line 14, to p. 64, line 9. Cf. *Cons. phil.* IIp6.13, p. 30; IIp6.18, p. 31; IIIp2.3–4, p. 38; IIIp4.11–13, p. 43. *Bo* XXXIV.v–vi, p. 86, line 12, to p. 87, line 12; XXXV.iii, p. 97, lines 13–29; XXXVI.vii, p. 109, lines 20–5. Cf. *Cons. phil.* IIIp10.27–9, p. 55; IIIp12.15–16, p. 61; IVp2.32–3, p. 69.
[128] M. Godden, 'Editing Old English and the Problem of Alfred's Boethius', in *The Editing of Old English*, ed. D. G. Scragg and P. E. Szarmach (Cambridge, 1994), pp. 163–76.
[129] As admitted by B. Griffiths, *Alfred's Metres of Boethius* (Pinner, 1991), pp. 38–9, despite his inclination to accept its testimony (pp. 42–3); the possibility was raised but dismissed by Sisam, *Studies*, pp. 295–7.
[130] Cf. Godden, 'Editing Old English', pp. 166–8; D. Anlezark, 'Three Notes on the Old English Meters of Boethius', *Notes and Queries* 51:1 (2004), 10–15.
[131] Frakes, *Fate*, pp. 81–99.

a word for earthly fluctuation, she is replaced by *wyrd*, also employed to render *fatum*. As grantor of worldly goods her role passes to *Wisdom*, while her deceitful qualities are transferred to the goods themselves, conveyed by the allusive compound, *ða woruldsælða* ('worldly blessings'). Such moves combine with quite radical resculpting of the Prisoner's opening predicament. All supporting context is supplied by the translation's own opening section, inspired by Latin *Vitae.*[132] The royal history accepts Boethius' treason without question, as action against Theoderic's unjust rule, apparently following *Vitae I* and *II.* Such a view was typical, suggesting tensions with Theoderic's alternative status as a Germanic hero, manifest in Charlemagne's appropriation of an equine statue from Ravenna, and also represented in Anglo-Saxon poetry.[133]

Only the stress on Theoderic's religious persecution is unparalleled: his description as an 'Arian heretic' may depend on the *Liber Pontificalis* or Bede's *Martyrology.*[134] A story in Gregory's *Dialogues* is the likely source for his 'horrible' death and alleged involvement in the death of Pope John.[135] *Vita II* justifies Boethius' actions as an attempt to restore Roman *libertas*, recently removed by Gothic invasion.[136] In the royal text, the invasion is that of Alaric and Radagaisus, a century earlier than Theoderic's own; such confusion may reflect knowledge of Orosius' history, which ends with this event.[137] *Vita I* mentions 'letters secretly sent to the Greeks' by Boethius, urging their defence of Rome and the senate.[138] The royal text invoked similar 'letters' by which Boethius had sought Greek help in restoring Romans to former 'rights', once enjoyed under 'the Caesars, their former lords'.[139] The Greek 'Caesar' was 'of the same kin as their former lords': the story is transformed by these implications of lordship and betrayal, yet its force remains open, omitting reference to Boethius' fate.[140]

---

[132] *Philosophiae Consolationis Libri Quinque*, ed. Peiper, pp. xxx–xxxiv; Troncarelli, *Tradizioni perdute*, pp. 21–9, for the ninth-century origin of Peiper's *Vitae I–V*.

[133] M. W. Herren, 'Walahfrid Strabo's De Imagine Tetrici: an Interpretation', in *Latin Culture and Medieval Germanic Europe*, ed. R. North and T. Hofstra (Groningen, 1992), pp. 25–41, at 26; F. P. Magoun and H. M. Smyser, *Walter of Aquitaine: Materials for the Study of his Legend* (New London, CT, 1950), pp. 1–2; K. Kiernan, 'Deor: the Consolations of an Anglo-Saxon Boethius', *Neuphilologische Mitteilungen* 79 (1978), 333–40, at 338; cf. K. Malone, *Widsith* (London, 1936), pp. 191–2.

[134] *Le Liber Pontificalis*, ed. Duchesne I, 275–6; Bede, *Martyrologium*, ed. Dubois and Renaud, p. 96, drawing on the *Liber Pontificalis* and Gregory's *Dialogi*.

[135] *Grégoire le Grand: Dialogues*, ed. de Vogüé, IV.31 (III, 104–6), used for Pope John's entry in the *Old English Martyrology*, ed. Kotzor II, 105–7; *GD* I, 305–6.

[136] *Vita II*, ed. Peiper, p. xxxi.

[137] *Bo* I, p. 7, lines 1–6. Orosius, *Historiae aduersum paganos*, ed. Zangemeister, CSEL 5, VII.37, 536–42; *Or* VI.xxxvii–xxxviii, pp. 155–6; cf. Bately, 'Those Books', pp. 59–61.

[138] *Vita I*, ed. Peiper, pp. xxx–xxxi.   [139] *Bo* I, p. 7, lines 7–21.

[140] Boethius' death recorded in *Vita II*, ed. Peiper, pp. xxxi–xxxii; cf. Chadwick, *Boethius*, p. 55, for the popular account of Boethius' execution.

The context supplies a rationale for the *Froferboc*'s early sections, exceptionally free in the treatment of speech and gesture. In royal hands, the Prisoner finds little opportunity for complaint. Almost every detail of his long defence is omitted; his role is swiftly recast as that of *Mod*, a figure largely extricated from sixth-century context, as a speaking 'Mind'. Reflecting Latin *mens*, the designation differed notably from *mod*'s poetic usage as emotive 'mood' or 'passion'.[141] Even in its original form, Boethian rhetoric harnessed the universalizing effects of first-person dialogue; these were only enhanced by *Mod*'s novel status.[142] Matched by Philosophia's own mutation into *heofencund Wisdom*, with subtle transfer of gender, the changes effected a scenario close to Alfred's other translated dialogue.[143] Similar ambiguity was exploited in the *Soliloquia*, where 'Reason' might be either internal or external to her first-person speaker.[144] Almost the only context for *Mod*'s career is his former devotion to wisdom, so deep that he had been 'chosen as a judge (*domere*)'.[145] It is from this height that *Mod* has fallen: in an inversion of Boethian innocence, his loss emerges as self-induced, the direct consequence of sin and folly.

The shift is prepared by *Mod*'s limited lament: the failure of philosopher-rulership is effectively concealed. For *Mod*, Plato's saying amounts to the more general claim, 'that no power was right except with right virtues (*butan rihtum þeawum*)'.[146] This becomes a context for *Mod*'s guilt, fully exposed in the royal response to Fortuna, initially rendered as *þa woruldsælþa*: the mutation enables subtle transfer of deceitful responsibility.[147] Though 'worldly blessings' may be inconstant, this status is traced to human weakness, in the dominant vice of greed. 'Gif þu nu witan wilt hwonan hi cumað, þonne meaht þu ongietan þæt hi cumað of woruldgidsunga'.[148] Rather than the 'changing faces of [Fortuna's] blind power', sinful *Mod* has discovered the 'unstable faith (*truwa*)' of his own 'blind desire'.[149] His weakness enhances the context of earthly fidelity, playfully adapted from Fortuna's role as *domina*. *Mod* has willingly accepted his thegnship of *þa woruldsælþa*: 'if you desire to be their thegn,

---

[141] Godden, 'Mind', esp. pp. 274–7 and 285–95.   [142] Pratt, 'Authorship'.
[143] *Bo* III.i, p. 8, line 15, to p. 9, line 8. Cf. *Cons. phil.* Ipr and Ip2, pp. 2–3 and 4.
[144] *Soliloquia* I.i.1, p. 3, lines 2–5. Cf. *Solil* p. 48, lines 13–17.
[145] *Bo* VIII, p. 20, lines 12–13. Cf. *Cons. phil.* IIp3.5–7, p. 21–2.
[146] *Bo* III.iv, p. 9, lines 19–24. Cf. *Cons. phil.* Ip4.4–5, p. 7.
[147] *Bo* VII.i–ii, pp. 14–17. Cf. *Cons. phil.* IIp1, pp. 17–19.
[148] 'If you now wish to know from where [worldly blessings] come, then you can understand that they come from worldly avarice'; *Bo* VII.i, p. 15, lines 7–9 (an unparalleled addition). Cf. *Cons. phil.* IIp1.4, p. 17.
[149] 'Nu ðu hæfst ongiten ða wanclan truwa þæs blindan lustes': *Bo* VII.i, lines 29–30, p. 15. Cf. *Cons. phil.* IIp1.11, p. 18: 'Deprehendisti caeci numinis ambiguos uultus'.

then you must suffer gladly what pertains to their service and their ways and their will'.[150] Yet even at this stage, additions suggest means of safeguarding against such destructive consequences. *Mod* had once been protected by *Wisdom*'s teachings: 'I knew that you rejected [worldly blessings] when you had them, although you used them. I knew that you often said my sayings against their requests'.[151] 'Worldly blessings alone are not to be thought about when one has them, but each wise mind bewares what end they may have, and guards against both their threats and allurements'.[152]

This extends in the remarkable handling of Fortuna's prosopopoeia, doubly transforming the imaginary voice. The metre describing her wheel is omitted: in a supreme act of invention, her speech is adapted for *Wisdom*, effecting his own transformation as true source of all human goods.[153] Fundamentally biblical in character, the role mirrors several speeches by Lady Wisdom, promising rich benefits to the wise while mocking the folly of those destroyed by their own prosperity.[154] Cru-cially, *Wisdom* claims responsibility for *Mod*'s former advancement, identified as 'wealth and honour (*ge þinra welona ge þines weorþscipes*), both of which came from me when they were lent':[155]

Dysine and ungelæredne ic þe underfeng þa þu ærest to monnum become, and þa þe getydde and gelærde, and þe þa snyttro on gebrohte, þe þu þa woruldare mid begeate, þe þu nu sorgiende anforlete. Þu meaht þæs habban þanc þæt þu minra gifa wel bruce. Ne miht þu no gereccan þæt þu þines auht forlure.[156]

---

[150] *Bo* VII.ii, p. 16, lines 21–4. Cf. *Cons. phil.* IIp1.16–17, p. 18.

[151] '... ic wisse þæt þu hi onscunedest ða ða þu hi hæfdest, ðeah þu hiora bruce. Ic wisse þæt ðu mine cwidas wið hiora willan oft sædest': *Bo* VII.i, p. 15, lines 14–16. Cf. *Cons. phil.* IIp1.5, p. 17: 'Solebas enim praesentem quoque, blandientem quoque uirilibus incessere uerbis eamque de nostro adyto prolatis insectabare sententiis'.

[152] 'Ne sindon þa woruldsælþa ana ymb to þencenne þe mon þonne hæfð, ac ælc gleaw mod behealt hwelcne ende hi habbað, and hit gewarenað ægðer ge wið heora þreaunga ge wið olecunga': *Bo* VII.ii, p. 16, lines 19–21. Cf. *Cons. phil.* IIp1.15, p. 18: 'Neque enim quod ante oculos situm est suffecerit intueri, rerum exitus prudentia metitur; eademque in alterutro mutabilitas nec formidandas fortunae minas nec exoptandas facit esse blanditias'.

[153] *Bo* VII.iii–iv, pp. 17–19. Cf. *Cons. phil.* IIp2.2–IIm2, pp. 19–21.

[154] Proverbs I. 20–33; VII. 1–27; and IX. 13–18; Ecclesiasticus IV. 15–22; XXIV. 5–47; XXXII. 1–28; XXXIII. 1–33; XXXIX. 1–41; and XL. 1–32. *CP* XXXVI, p. 246, line 14, to p. 248, line 4. Cf. *Reg. past.* III.12, lines 12–20, pp. 322–4.

[155] *Bo* VII.iii, p. 17, lines 5–8. Cf. *Cons. phil.* IIp2.2, p. 19.

[156] 'I received you foolish and untaught when you were first born, and then I trained and taught you, and brought you to the wisdom with which you attained the worldly honour that you, now grieving, have lost. You can have thanks that you well enjoyed my gifts. You cannot say that you have lost anything of your own': *Bo* VII.iii, p. 17, lines 11–16. Cf. *Cons. phil.* IIp2.4–5, p. 19: 'Cum te matris utero natura produxit, nudum rebus omnibus inopemque suscepi, meis opibus foui et, quod te nunc impatientem nostri facit, fauore prona indulgentius educaui, omnium quae mei iuris sunt affluentia et splendore circumdedi. Nunc mihi retrahere manum libet: habes gratiam uelut usus alienis, non habes ius querelae tamquam prorsus tua perdideris'.

Yet *Wisdom*'s ways are directly perverted by worldly avarice; again, the context is biblical, in Lady Wisdom's ambiguous splendour, often likened to the riches within her gift.[157] The name that *Wisdom* should rightly have is 'wealth and honour' (*wela and weorðscipe*), but 'worldly men ... have taken it from me, and betrayed me to their arrogances, and considered me as false riches (*to heora leasum welum*), so that I cannot fulfil my services with my servants as all other creatures can'.[158] *Wisdom*'s servants are 'every true wealth and every true honour' (*ælc soð wela and soþ weorðscipe*), 'wisdomas and cræftas and soðe welan' : the 'true goods' of later argument, their inclusion supports a quite different picture of earthly involvement.[159] Fortuna's wheel now lies at *Wisdom*'s just 'play': 'with these servants I turn the whole of heaven', bringing 'humility to the heavens, and heavenly goods to the humble'.[160] By the latter, he offers secure escape from 'this stormy world' into heaven, 'just as the eagle ... goes up above the clouds in stormy weather, so that the storms cannot harm it'. *Mod* too may ascend, but his invitation is strictly conditional, expected 'to seek the earth again with us, in order to help good men (*for godra manna þearfe*)'.[161] The image mirrors expectations in *Hierdeboc*, similarly arising from 'gifts of many virtues and talents (*mægena and cræfta*)', of humble acceptance of rulership 'for oðerra monna ðearfe'.[162] Boethian escape is fundamentally qualified by Gregorian obligation.

Note the vernacular idiom 'to monnum becuman', 'to be born', following the Latin sense: cf. Frakes, *Fate*, pp. 103–4; Nelson, 'Political Ideas', p. 145.

[157] Proverbs III. 13–16; VIII. 10–11 and 18–19; XIV. 24; Wisdom VIII. 5; Ecclesiastes VI. 12–13; Ecclesiasticus I. 20–6.

[158] 'Þone naman ic scolde mid rihte habban þæt ic wære wela and weorðscipe, ac hy hine habbað on me genumen, and hi me habbað gesealdne hiora wlencum and getehhod to heora leasum welum, þæt ic ne mot mid minum ðeowum minra þegnunga fulgangan swa ealla oþra gesceafta moton': *Bo* VII.iii, p. 17, line 31, to p. 18, line 5, close to Proverbs VIII. 18–21 (cf. VIII. 15: 'Per me reges regnant'). Cf. *Cons. phil.* IIp2.8, p. 20: 'nos ad constantiam nostris moribus alienam inexpleta hominum cupiditas alligabit?'.

[159] *Bo* VII.iii, p. 17, lines 18–19; XVI.iii, p. 39, lines 4–9; XXXIV.i–xii, pp. 82–94. Cf. *Cons. phil.* IIp2.6, p. 19; IIp6.19, p. 31; IIIp10, pp. 53–6; Otten, *Boethius*, pp. 24 and 26–7.

[160] 'Da mine þeowas sindon wisdomas and cræftas and soðe welan ... mid þæm þeowum ic eom ealne þone hefon ymbhweorfende, and þa niðemystan ic gebringe æt þæm hehstan, and þa hehstan æt ðæm niðemæstan; ðæt is þæt ic gebringe eadmodnesse on heofonum, and ða hefonlican god æt þæm eaðmodum': *Bo* VII.iii, p. 18, lines 5–11. Cf. *Cons. phil.* IIp2.9, p. 20: 'Haec nostra uis est, hunc continuum ludum ludimus: rotam uolubili orbe uersamus, infima summis, summa infimis mutare gaudemus'.

[161] 'Ac þonne ic up gefere mid minum þeowum þonne forseo we þas styrmendan woruld swa se earn ðonne he up gewit bufan ða wolcnu styrmendum wedrum, þæt him þa stormas derigan ne mægen. Swa ic wolde, la Mod, þæt þu þe fore up to us gif þe lyste, on þa gerad þæt þu eft mid us þa eorðan secan wille for godra manna þearfe': *Bo* VII.iii, p. 18, lines 11–16. Cf. *Cons. phil.* IIp2.10, p. 20: 'Ascende si placet, sed ea lege, ne uti cum ludicri mei ratio poscet descendere iniuriam putes'. Cf. Isidore, *Etymologiae*, ed. Lindsay, XII.vii.11, and Proverbs XXIII. 5.

[162] *CP* V, p. 40, lines 11–13; XVI, p. 100, line 16, to p. 103, line 11. Cf. *Reg. past.* I.5, lines 3–5, p. 144; II.5, lines 39–54, pp. 198–200. Cf. above, pp. 205–9.

Mod's sins here acquire force. His downfall is attributed to pride, an excessive trust in his own 'righteousness and good will', expecting full reward for good works in this world.[163] The explanation matches Davidic self-assessment in Psalm XXIX. 7–9, cited in the *Hierdeboc*: ' "I supposed in my pride and my abundance, when I was full both of wealth and good works, that there would never be an end to it. . . . Lord, you turned your face from me, then I became troubled" '.[164] The point is reinforced by further invention, belatedly mimicking Fortuna's prosopopoeia with an imagined speech by *þa woruldsælða*, also protesting innocence.[165] Again later arguments are anticipated, in *Mod*'s mistaken identification of good, setting *þa woruldsælða* on the throne rightly occupied by his creator.[166] Yet criticism extends to his active hindering of the creator's will. 'Worldly blessings' are in fact the more deceived by *Mod*'s actions, prevented from fulfilling the creator's purposes: 'For he lent us to you to use in accordance with his commandments, not at all to complete the will of your unrighteous avarice'.[167] The fault has been *Mod*'s alone, openly acknowledged in his response, confessing himself 'guilty in every way'.[168]

As many commentators have observed, the exchange amounts to a universal theory of possession, based on rightful use.[169] Though patristic precedents have been cited, none comes very close to this distinctive treatment.[170] Its precise force must be seen in the wider context of *Mod*'s criticism, consistently re-ordered in a dazzling expression of Alfredian discourse. The entire scenario gave sustained re-enactment of Solomonic principles, artfully harnessed to earthly bonds of lordship. Beyond Boethian righteousness lay this deeper account of divine betrayal, explicitly effected by avarice and greed. Central object was the figure of *Wisdom*: initially ambiguous as *Mod*'s 'foster-mother', as Nelson observes, he soon assumes his role as 'a model of good lordship'.[171] Generous giving, conditional lending to faithful servants: every feature matched West Saxon royal practice. Developing wisdom's vernacular gender, the effect is redolent of Christ's own sapiential status, though an identification is

---

[163] *Bo* VII.iii, p. 18, lines 21–5. Cf. *Cons. phil.* IIp2.14, p. 20.
[164] *CP* LXV, p. 465, lines 14–20; cf. *Reg. past.* IV, lines 51–6, p. 538. *Ps(P)* XXIX.6–7, p. 132.
[165] *Bo* VII.v, p. 19, lines 11–23. Cf. *Cons. phil.* IIp2.2 and 8, pp. 19 and 20.
[166] *Bo* VII.v, p. 19, lines 13–16.
[167] '. . . forðæmðe ure ðe onlænde æfter his bebodum to brucanne, nallas þinre unrihtgitsunga gewill to fulfremmanne': *Bo* VII.v, p. 19, lines 21–3.
[168] *Bo* VIII, p. 19, lines 26–8 (an unparalleled addition). Cf. *Cons. phil.* IIp3.2, p. 21.
[169] Otten, *Boethius*, pp. 21–35 and 97–9; Frakes, *Fate*, pp. 100–11; Discenza, 'Power, Skill and Virtue', pp. 100–3; Discenza, *King's English*, pp. 94–100.
[170] Otten, *Boethius*, pp. 32–3; Nelson, 'Political Ideas', p. 144 and note 84.
[171] *Bo* III.i, p. 8, line 15, to p. 9, line 8. Cf. *Cons. phil.* Ip1 and Ip2, pp. 2–3 and 4. Nelson, 'Political Ideas', p. 145.

never made explicit.[172] *Wisdom*'s gifts of 'wela and weorðscipe' are precisely those received by Solomon, yet *Mod* has forgotten the effects of his training.[173] Not only has he accepted the lordship of *þa woruldsælða*; his betrayal is double, preventing fulfilment of divine will.[174] Every gesture shows the guiding force of Solomonic desire. 'Worldly blessings' had been *Wisdom*'s gifts, for the wider needs of men; commands in question included the twofold nature of Christian love.[175] Wrongfully directed towards these benefits, *Mod*'s desires have brought exile and ruin.[176] *Wisdom*'s rightful name, 'wela and weorðscipe', captures the reversal of Solomonic priorities; gifts were dependent on such true recognition. Among much refashioning of Boethian context, the framework asserted positive support for wisdom in earthly rule. This was an Alfredian drama of obligation and benefit, focused on power and sapiential control.

CRÆFT, TOOLS AND RESOURCES

Philosophia's 'stronger lotions' prompt more restrained treatment, often faithful to interlocutory exchange. Contrary to several interpretations, the received content did not strictly condemn Fortuna's gifts, nor earthly possession, but exposed their many dangers as objects of human trust.[177] *Diuitiae, dignitates et potentia, gloria*: each were pursued by men in error, anticipating benefits to their goodness, when such *bona* were external.[178] Now prefaced by *Mod*'s betrayal, the same arguments reinforced all preceding emphasis on the dangers of worldly desire. *Þa woruldsælða* could never be good in themselves, but owed any goodness to their possession by good men.

The harmony was especially strong for *ðas woruldæhta and welan* ('worldly possessions and riches'); Boethian argument supported repeated condemnation of *seo gitsung*.[179] 'All riches are better and more precious when given than kept'; the dangers of miserliness combine with royal language of excess and moderation.[180] 'Why are you

---

[172] I Corinthians I. 24; Ecclesiasticus I. 5; John I. 1; F. A. Payne, *King Alfred and Boethius* (Madison, WI, and London, 1968), pp. 126–8.

[173] *Bo* III.i, p. 8, lines 20–1. Cf. *Cons. phil.* Ip2.3, p. 4.

[174] *Bo* VII.ii, p. 16, lines 3–4, and lines 24–8; VII.v, p. 19, lines 11–23. Cf. *Cons. phil.* IIp1.12 and 17, p. 18; IIp2.2 and 8, pp. 19 and 20.

[175] *CP* VII, p. 48, lines 12–14; cf. *Reg. past.* I.7, lines 15–16, p. 150; Matthew XXII. 36–40; Mark XII. 28–31. Cf. above, pp. 205–6.

[176] *Bo* II, p. 8, lines 6–9. Cf. *Cons. phil.* Im1.1–4, p. 1.

[177] Neither Boethius nor Philosophia regards the material realm as 'necessarily evil'; cf. Otten, *Boethius*, p. 30; Frakes, *Fate*, pp. 42–7 and 112–13; Payne, *Boethius*, pp. 62 and 131.

[178] *Cons. phil.* IIp5 to IIm8, pp. 26–36. [179] *Bo* XIII–XIV, pp. 27–9. Cf. *Cons. phil.* IIp5, pp. 26–8.

[180] '... nu is forþam ælc feoh betere and deorwyrðre geseald þonne gehealden': *Bo* XIII, p. 28, lines 7–8. Cf. *Cons. phil.* IIp5.5, p. 26.

nevertheless inflamed with such empty joy; why do you love those alien goods so immoderately (*swa ungemetlice*), as if they were yours?'.[181] The qualification extends in an unusual addition, delineating a precise 'limit' (*þæt gemet*) of 'present blessings':

Gif þu þonne þæt gemet habban wille, and þa nydþearfe witan wille, þonne is þæt mete and drync and claðas and tol to swelcum cræfte swelce þu cunne þæt þe is gecynde and þæt þe is riht to habbenne.[182]

The dangers lie in desiring 'ofer gemet', measured by these earthly 'necessities'. Discussion has assumed dependence on commentary material; Frakes gives a list comprising *potus, cibus, uestimentum*.[183] Yet the 'Anonymous of St Gallen' mentions only *cibus*, while Remigius relates the argument to those 'nimio potu ciboque utentes'.[184] Only the twelfth-century commentary published by Silk includes *uestimentum*.[185] The passage is better regarded as an independent response, though not atypical of ninth-century attitudes.[186] Alcuin had used the same passage in a comparable definition of *moderatus usus*. 'As much as bodily necessity requires, and the study of wisdom demands': Alcuin's 'Teacher' offers a studious limit for consumption, citing a favourite quotation, 'Ne quid nimis', ultimately derived from Terence.[187] The royal position is more suggestive of Christ's own statement: 'be not anxious for your life, what you shall eat, nor for your body, what you shall wear. Surely life is more than food, and the body

---

[181] *Bo* XIV.i, p. 29, lines 25–7. Cf. *Cons. phil.* IIp5.14, p. 27.

[182] 'If you nevertheless want to have a limit, and want to know what things are necessary, these are food and drink and clothes and tools for such craft as you know is natural to you and is right for you to have': *Bo* XIV.i, p. 30, lines 7–10. Cf. *Cons. phil.* IIp5.15, p. 27: 'Terrarum quidem fructus animantium procul dubio debentur alimentis; sed si, quod naturae satis est, replere indigentiam uelis, nihil est quod fortunae affluentiam petas' ('Indeed the fruits of the earth, without doubt, are bound to the support of living things; but if you want to satisfy your need, which is enough for nature, there is no need to seek fortune's abundance').

[183] Frakes, *Fate*, p. 112, followed by Nelson, 'Political Ideas', p. 143 and note 82.

[184] INIUCUNDUM (IIp5.16, p. 27): 's[cilicet] in cibis': E1 (p. 122b). TERRARUM QUIDEM FRUCTUS (IIp5.15, p. 27): 'Argumentum contra nimio potu ciboque utentes. Omnis superfluitas cibi atque potus generabit nausiam fastidiumque aut infirmitatem corporis (Quia ille felix est qui cibis cum temperamento utitur. Superfluitate reiecta modum nature custodire contendit – T only)': T (fol. 129v), P7 (fol. 25r). REPLERE INDIGENTIAM UELIS (IIp5.15, p. 27): 'Hoc diogenes cinicus adimpleuit. qui amore sapientie omnia reliquit. et uidens aliquando pastorem concauis manibus aquam bibentem proiecit uasculum quo hactenus hauserat. Nesciebam, inquiens, quod ita nature possem satisfacere. atque sic postmodum bibere solitus erat': Ma (fol. 77r), T (fol. 129r), P7 (fol. 25r), P10 (fol. 16v).

[185] Silk, *Commentarius*, p. 92; Otten, *Boethius*, p. 27; Frakes, *Fate*, p. 112.

[186] Cf. Newhauser, *Greed*, pp. 116–24; R. Newhauser, 'Towards *modus in habendo*: Transformations in the Idea of Avarice', *Zeitschrift der Savigny-Stiftung für Rechtsgeschichte (Kanonistische Abteilung)* 106 (1989), 1–22.

[187] Alcuin, *Disputatio de vera philosophia*, PL 101: 850C–851A (cf. Terence, *Andria*, line 61), with allusion also to Juvenal's empty wayfarer (cf. *Cons. phil.* IIp5.34, p. 28).

more than clothing'.[188] Every detail matched aspects of contemporary royal
practice. 'Cibo, potu et vestimento' had been the scope of Æthelwulf's
sustenance for *pauperes*.[189] Alfred upheld a similar reputation for alms and
alms-giving; 'tools' now extended to the needs of ruling *cræft*.

Much harmony continues for *se weorðscipe and se anweald* ('honour and
power'), yet with additions of emphasis.[190] The vernacular incorporates
'wela', in the doublet 'wela and anweald', further employed in later
sections.[191] As Godden notes, such terminology may reflect the wider
scope of *dignitates*, as trappings and prosperity; adjectival usage consistently distinguishes the 'powerful man' (*rice*) from the 'wealthy'
(*welig*).[192] Yet the overall effect is not to weaken, but to reinforce the
connections between wealth and political responsibility. 'Se eower
wela ... and se eower anweald, þe ge nu weorðscipe hatað': *Wisdom*'s
words continue the irony of sapiential misidentification.[193] Royal
expansion focuses on power in the hands of the virtuous, raised only
briefly by Philosophia as the sole source of *honor*.

Forþampe se anwald næfre ne bið good buton se god sie þe hine hæbbe ... Forþam
hit bið þætte nan man for his rice ne cymð to cræftum and to medemnesse, ac for
his cræftum and for his medumnesse he cymð to rice and to anwealde. Ði ne bið
nan man for his anwealde na þe betera, ac for his cræftum he beoð good, gif he
god bið, and for his cræftum he bið anwealdes weorðe, gif he his weorðe bið.[194]

Cræft, the basis of rule in the *Hierdeboc*, reinforces its active implications.[195] Already assigned to *Wisdom*'s gift, *cræftas* confer not only
worthiness of power, but direct ability to attain it. This is then exemplified by wisdom:

Leorniað forðæm wisdom, and þonne ge hine geleornod hæbben, ne forhycgað
hine þonne (cf. Proverbs IV. 5). Þonne secge ic eow buton ælcum tweon þæt
ge magon þurh hine becuman to anwealde, þeah ge no þæs anwealdes ne

[188] Matthew VI. 25, cf. 19–34. Cf. Asser, *VA* 76, lines 49–50, citing Matthew VI. 33 immediately
after Solomonic allusion.
[189] *VA* 16, lines 18–25.   [190] *Bo* XVI.i–iii, pp. 34–9. Cf. *Cons. phil.* IIp6, pp. 29–31.
[191] *Bo* XVI.i, p. 34, lines 20–1. Cf. *Cons. phil.* IIp6.1, p. 29.
[192] M. Godden, 'Money, Power and Morality in Late Anglo-Saxon England', *ASE* 19 (1990), 41–65,
at 45–6.
[193] *Bo* XVI.i, p. 34, lines 20–1, cf. VII, p. 17, line 31, to p. 18, line 5.
[194] 'For power is never good, except if he is good who has it ... It is because of this that no man
comes to virtues and dignity because of his rule, but rather comes to rule and to power because
of his virtues and dignity. From this, no man is better because of his power, but rather is good
because of his virtues, if indeed he is good, and is worthy of power because of his virtues, if
indeed he is worthy'; *Bo* XVI.i, p. 35, lines 10–18. Cf. *Cons. phil.* IIp6.3, p. 30: 'At si quando,
quod perrarum est, probis deferantur, quid in eis aliud quam probitas utentium placet? Ita fit ut
non uirtutibus ex dignitate sed ex uirtute dignitatibus honor accedat'.
[195] Above, pp. 199–201 and 204–5; cf. also Discenza, *King's English*, pp. 105–22.

wilnigan. Ne þurfon ge no hogian on þam anwealde, ne him æfter þringan. Gif
ge wise beoð and gode, he wile folgian eow, þeah ge his no ne wilnigen.[196]

Gregorian duty fuses with Solomonic benefit; there is no more succinct
expression of royal language. At its heart was wisdom's own status as 'se
hehsta cræft', prominently depicted in a later addition, its force embracing
the four 'cardinal' *cræftas* of *wærscipe* ('prudence'), *gemetgung* ('moderation'), *ellen* ('courage') and *rihtwisnes* ('justice').[197] Again, the reference
was sapiential: recent discussion has overlooked the compelling context
of Wisdom VIII. 7, 'labores huius magnas habent virtutes; sobrietatem
enim et sapientiam docet et iustitiam et virtutem'.[198] The highest *cræft* was
itself Solomonic, dependent on wise restraint. As a route to power, its
message reinforced all earlier lessons of *Mod*'s sinfulness. Within the
chapter, the inclusion offered a counter-weight to all later exempla,
focused on power in evil hands.[199] The savagery of the Egyptian Busiris,
the respective Roman crimes of 'Liberius', Regulus and Nero: all reinforced the dangers of earthly temptation.

Only in this context can one approach the remarkable handling of *gilp*
('glory'), the climax of all concern.[200] Often quoted in isolation, its
opening acquires full force in these contexts of desire and rightful use.
The lengthy addition coincides with the Prisoner's own protest, denying
any ambition for *mortales res*, that he had merely sought an 'opportunity'
(*materia*) for beneficial employment of his *uirtus*.[201] The denial itself is
largely replicated in *Mod*'s words against 'seo gitsung and seo gemægð
þisses eorðlican anwealdes'; the latter element finds quite different
exposition, on the basis of earthly need.[202] 'Tol ... and andweorc'
('tools and resources'), the latter bearing a convenient relationship to
materia: both had still been desired by *Mod* 'for the work that was
commanded to me to perform'.[203] The task itself was that of honourable

---

[196] 'Therefore study wisdom, and when you have learned it, do not reject it. For I say to you
without any doubt that you can come to power through wisdom, although you do not desire it.
You need not care for power, nor strive after it. If you are wise and good, it will follow you,
although you do not desire it': *Bo* XVI.i, p. 35, lines 18–24 (an unparalleled addition).

[197] *Bo* XXVII.ii, p. 62, lines 24–6; also XXXII.i, p. 72, lines 13–15. Cf. *Cons. phil.* IIIp4.7, p. 43;
IIIp8.7, p. 48.

[198] '[Wisdom's] labours have great virtues; for she teaches moderation and wisdom and justice and
courage'. Cf. P. E. Szarmach, 'Alfred's Boethius and the Four Cardinal Virtues', in *Alfred the
Wise*, ed. Roberts and Nelson, pp. 223–35. The cardinal virtues were well known in the early
middle ages: S. Mahl, *Quadriga Virtutum* (Cologne and Vienna, 1967); cf. Otten, *Boethius*,
pp. 28–9; Clemoes, 'King Alfred's Debt', pp. 222–3.

[199] *Bo* XVI.ii–iv, pp. 36–40. Cf. *Cons. phil.* IIp6.8–IIm6, pp. 30–2.

[200] *Bo* XVII–XIX, pp. 40–7. Cf. *Cons. phil.* IIp7–IIm7, pp. 32–5.   [201] *Cons. phil.* IIp7.1, p. 32.

[202] *Bo* XVII, p. 40, lines 5–9.

[203] '... buton tola ic wilnode þeah and andweorces to þam weorce þe me beboden was to
wyrcanne': *Bo* XVII, p. 40, lines 9–10.

rulership, guiding 'power' (*anwald*) granted on trust, for 'nan mon ne mæg nænne cræft cyðan ne nænne anweald reccan ne stioran butun tolum and andweorce'.[204] The 'king' who emerges need not be *Mod* himself; the argument nevertheless gains much from the royal example.[205] *Gebedmen and fyrdmen and weorcmen* ('praying-men and fighting-men and workmen'): the king's 'tools' are indeed considerable, as three 'orders' or *geferscipas* ('companies') of men, matched only by the scale of necessary 'resources'.[206] 'Land to dwell on, and gifts, and weapons, and food, and ale, and clothing, and whatever else that the three orders need': all would nevertheless fall within the 'limit' already assigned to rightful need.[207] Yet without such 'provisions' (*biwist*), the king's 'tools' cannot be maintained, nor can he fulfil his commanded task. *Mod*'s actions had been of a similar nature, seeking 'resources' with which to exercise his power, lest his 'cræftas and anweald' (doubly rendering *uirtus*) became 'forgotten and hidden'.[208]

The status of the passage should not be in doubt. *Wisdom*'s reply is notably equivocal, ridiculing not the pursuit of glory through virtue, but merely 'wilnung leases gilpes and unryhtes anwealdes and ungemetlices hlisan godra weorca ofer eall folc'.[209] The section is reoriented by the earlier intervention. Warnings against desire for fame are repeatedly restricted to men acting 'ungemetlice'.[210] *Mod* is rebuked for assuming his 'honour' (*ar*) will be eternal, but criticism falls short of such 'good fame' (*god hlisa*), merely preserved 'after your days'.[211] *Wisdom*'s subsequent song openly restricts its force to those desiring 'idle fame and unuseful glory' (*þone idelan hlisan and þone unnyttan gilp*).[212] The distinction mirrors that already established in the good use of power; the passage is pivotal in elucidating the scope of rightful worldly involvement.

Such equivocation has long been recognized in the *Froferboc*; the extent of departure has sometimes been overstated. Worldly goods are not straightforwardly 'revalued': in Book III, Boethian arguments are followed quite faithfully on the 'falsity' of each good, failing to deliver

---

[204] '... no man can make known any craft, nor rule nor guide any power, without tools and resources': *Bo* XVII, p. 40, lines 12–14 (*cyðan* cf. Latin *tacita*).
[205] Against Godden, 'Player King', pp. 143–4; cf. Discenza, *King's English*, pp. 84–5, 96–100 and 182 (note 87).
[206] *Bo* XVII, p. 40, lines 15–18.
[207] '... land to bugianne, and gifta, and wæpnu, and mete, and ealo, and claþas, and gehwæt þæs ðe þa þre geferscipas behofiað': *Bo* XVII, p. 40, lines 21–3.
[208] *Bo* XVII, p. 40, lines 25–7 (cf. Latin *tacita consenesceret*).
[209] '... the desire for false glory and unrighteous power and immoderate fame for good works among all people': *Bo* XVIII.i, p. 41, lines 12–14. Cf. *Cons. phil.* IIp7.2, p. 32.
[210] *Bo* XVIII.i, p. 41, line 13; p. 42, line 18; XVIII.ii, p. 42, line 25; p. 43, line 19.
[211] *Bo* XVIII.iii, p. 44, lines 8–13. Cf. *Cons. phil.* IIp7.14–15, p. 33.
[212] *Bo* XIX, p. 46, lines 2–5. Cf. *Cons. phil.* IIm7.1–4, p. 34.

the goal for which it is sought.²¹³ A clear distinction is maintained between such 'false blessings' (*þa leasan gesælða*) and 'true blessings' (*þa soðan gesælða*), only manifest in 'þæt hehste good'.²¹⁴ Frakes's claim is unsustainable that these sections express a concept of 'true earthly goods'; such formulations as *se soða weorðscipe, godcunde anwald* and *sio hehste blis* remain unique qualities of 'þæt hehste good'.²¹⁵ What the translation upheld was more qualified: the goodness of certain 'blessings' in the hands of good men, significant enough given royal discourse of worldly obligation. Later instances derive force from *Mod*'s intervention. *Mod*'s 'good fame' had demanded humble restraint: a later addition urges praise 'as more famous and righteous' upon 'those who become who they are *mid cræftum*'.²¹⁶ 'Wela' and 'anweald' had been similarly promised to those who did not desire it.²¹⁷ All matched the spheres of Solomonic benefit. *Mod*'s words directly echoed the sapiential claim of 'everlasting memory': 'Propterea habebo per hanc inmortalitatem et memoriam aeternam his qui post me futuri sunt relinquam'.²¹⁸ To these could be added the gift of 'true friends' (*ða getriewan friend*), justified as 'the most precious thing of all these worldly blessings'.²¹⁹ Its unique quality was again selflessness: 'Forþamðe ælces oðres þinges on þisse worulde mon wilnað, oððe forþamþe he mæg þurh þæt to anwealde cuman, oððe to sumum woruldluste, butan þæs getreowan freondes'.²²⁰ The measure in each case was ultimately God's own, in active distribution of *cræft*; *Mod*'s intervention offered earthly precision, by appeal to the limits of need. Hence the centrality of wisdom, 'forðæm ne mæg non mon nænne cræft bringan buton wisdome'.²²¹ Its effects were now twofold: as sole object of desire, restraining all others through continuous earthly judgement.

The model was *Mod*'s royal example; its features might seem unspecific, incorporating archetypal functions in the need for 'praying-men and

---

²¹³ *Bo* XXII–XXXV, pp. 50–103. Cf. *Cons. phil.* IIIp1–IIIm12, pp. 37–64.

²¹⁴ See esp. *Bo* XXIII, p. 52, lines 9–13. Cf. *Cons. phil.* IIIm1.11–13, p. 38; Otten, *Boethius*, p. 122, for the possible relevance of the Remigian tradition.

²¹⁵ Cf. Frakes, *Fate*, pp. 117–19; Payne, *Boethius*, p. 69, citing *Bo* XXXIII.i, p. 74, lines 20–5; royal terminology seems more faithful to Boethian distinctions (cf. *Cons. phil.* IIIp9.2, p. 49).

²¹⁶ *Bo* XXX.i, p. 68, line 31, to p. 69, line 4. Cf. *Cons. phil.* IIIp6.7, p. 46.

²¹⁷ *Bo* VII.iii, p. 17, lines 5–8; XVI.i, p. 35, lines 18–24.

²¹⁸ 'Moreover by the means of her I shall have immortality: and shall leave behind me an everlasting memory to them that come after me': Wisdom VIII. 13.

²¹⁹ *Bo* XXIV.iii, p. 54, lines 8–20 (a significant expansion). Cf. *Cons. phil.* IIIp2.9, pp. 38–9; R. Thomas, 'The Binding Force of Friendship in King Alfred's *Consolation* and *Soliloquies*', *Ball State University Forum* 29.1 (1988), 5–20.

²²⁰ 'For one desires every other thing in this world, either because one can come to power through it, or to certain worldly desires, except each true friend': *Bo*. XXIV.iii, p. 54, lines 13–15.

²²¹ '. . . for no man can bring forth any craft without wisdom': *Bo* XVII, p. 40, line 28, to p. 41, line 1.

fighting-men and workmen', prefiguring later medieval language of the 'three orders'.[222] Long recognized as a precocious deployment, the image must now be judged against earlier West Frankish usage, associated with the school of Auxerre.[223] In the hands of Haimo, writing around 850, a trifunctionality of *sacerdotes*, *milites* and *agricultores* was fashioned from the memory of Roman division into *senatores*, *milites* and *plebes*, available in Isidore.[224] The usage of Haimo's pupil, Heiric, was still closer, substituting *oratores* for *sacerdotes*, together with *belligerantes* and *agricolantes*.[225] Alfredian proximity cannot be coincidental; the case for an Auxerre connection here is if anything stronger than that for Remigian influence, though precision is precluded by the wider audience for Heiric's *Vita Sancti Germani*, addressed and presented to Charles the Bald.[226] As Nelson notes, *oratores* and *bellatores* recur in the *Miracula Sancti Bertini*, written late in the 890s; the context is suggestive, though such terminology was not itself unusual.[227] Whatever the case, there can be no question of passive reception: every aspect of West Frankish usage reflected ecclesiastical priorities. Haimo's scheme described constituent parts of an embracing *ecclesia*, drawing secular functions within an elaborate sacerdotal hierarchy.[228] Heiric's pronouncement admonished monks to prayer, on the basis of 'hard conditions' suffered by those at war and work. The latter shows the shaping context of West Frankish military service from ecclesiastical resources, extending the need for self-definition.[229] Reciprocity gave further force to the church's just contribution, otherwise expressed through prayer.[230] Heiric's own text celebrated St-Germain's special relationship with its royal patron, once memorably aiding Charles's defence.[231]

Alfredian usage was quite different. Detached from the church, the terms described royal instruments; lacking explicit reciprocity, their

---

[222] J. Le Goff, 'A Note on Tripartite Society, Monarchical Ideology, and Economic Renewal in Ninth- to Twelfth-Century Christendom', in his *Time, Work and Culture in the Middle Ages*, trans. A. Goldhammer (Chicago, IL, 1980), pp. 53–7; G. Duby, *The Three Orders: Feudal Society Imagined*, trans. A. Goldhammer (London, 1980), pp. 99–109; G. Constable, *Three Studies in Medieval Religious and Social Thought* (Cambridge, 1995), pp. 249–88.

[223] D. Iogna-Prat, 'La "baptême" du schéma des trois ordres fonctionnels', *Annales. Économies. Sociétés. Civilisations* 41 (1986), 101–26; E. Ortigues, 'L'elaboration de la Théorie des Trois Ordres chez Haymon d'Auxerre', *Francia* 14 (1988), 27–43; Nelson, 'Political Ideas', pp. 141–3; T. E. Powell, 'The "Three Orders" of Society in Anglo-Saxon England', *ASE* 23 (1994), 103–32, at 105–9.

[224] Haimo of Auxerre, *Expositio in Apocalypsin*, PL 117: 953A–B; Ortigues, 'L'elaboration', pp. 38–42.

[225] *De miraculis Sancti Germani*, ed. Duru, II.128, pp. 182–3; Iogna-Prat, 'La "baptême"'.

[226] Manitius, *Geschichte* I, 499–504, cf. Iogna-Prat, 'La "baptême"', p. 102 and note 3.

[227] *Miracula Sancti Bertini*, ed. Holder-Egger, c. 7, pp. 512–13; Nelson, 'Political Ideas', p. 143.

[228] Ortigues, 'L'elaboration', pp. 41–2.   [229] Above, pp. 69 and 162–3, cf. 25–7 and 278–9.

[230] Cf. Powell, 'The Three Orders', pp. 110–29, for later deployment by Ælfric and Wulfstan; Coupland, 'God's Wrath', pp. 547–53.

[231] Above, pp. 243–5.

functions were united by kingly need. All combined to express the distinctive force of West Saxon royal lordship, intensively projected by courtly mechanisms. Comparable divisions loomed large in the royal household: Asser reports the apportioning of secular revenues between (landless) 'fighting-men', craftsmen and foreigners in royal service. Threefold rotation in thegnly attendance receives some support from charter witness-lists.[232] The term *geferscipe* ('fellowship') referred else-where to a retinue of thegns; the array of 'provisions' answered aspects of royal entertainment.[233] The prominence of *gebedmen* among such *geferscipas* matched the distinctive status of bishops in the West Saxon order, aided by the service of royal priests. Yet royal 'tools' were not confined to these principal agents.[234] All three groups enabled a land 'fully manned' (*fullmonnad*): the priority reflected wider pressures of manpower and productivity. Æthelwulf's gift to *pauperes* from his her-editary land had been contingent on its occupation by men and live-stock, not being left to waste.[235] The *Chronicle* for the 890s, supported by the *Domboc*, indicates an effective shortage of peasant labour.[236] *Fyrdmen* and *weorcmen*: the distinction was implicit in Alfredian defensive reform, supplying vital manpower for burghal construction while leaving one half of the *fyrd* available 'at home'.[237] The active half was no less reliant on 'mete', edible 'provisions'.

Yet royal action extended far beyond bodily needs. 'Whatever else that the three orders need': just such a blank cheque had been amply filled with royal projects of construction. West Saxon deployment matched the scope of the common burdens, similarly applying to all types of land, now exploited with intensity under pressures of viking attack. The power of *Mod*'s 'king' lay precisely in its rhetorical status, as exclusive model for rightful need. Far from an instruction of fulfilment, the image appealed to royal duties, already being fulfilled, as guide to all other instances of rightful possession. All the Solomonic trappings of power and wealth hinged on such full acceptance of need. Royal projects were far from incompatible with legitimate prosperity. On the contrary, the latter could only be achieved through the needs of burghal construction; the connection was explicitly tied to wisdom, essential for every *cræft*.[238] Articulated by gifts of lordship, duty and need combined to express collective self-interest; Boethian Neo-Platonism now

---

[232] *VA* 100–1; above, pp. 34–6.   [233] *Bo* XXXVII, p. 111, line 15; XXXVIII, p. 116, line 21.
[234] Cf. Nelson, 'Political Ideas', pp. 150–2; J. L. Nelson, 'The Church and a Revaluation of Work in the Ninth Century?', in *The Use and Abuse of Time in Christian History*, ed. R. N. Swanson (Woodbridge, 2002), pp. 35–43, at 42–3.
[235] *VA* 6, lines 18–26.   [236] Above, pp. 95, 97–8 and 172–5.
[237] *ASC* s.a. 893; K&L, *Alfred*, pp. 285–6, note 4.   [238] *Bo* XVII, p. 40, line 28, to p. 41, line 1.

enhanced these concerns, subtly adapted to shared Solomonic rule. The entire framework added worldly benefits to wise restraint, playfully guided by royal example.

WYRD AND DIVINE JUSTICE

As indicated, the handling of Book III offers less equivocal fidelity. Boethian argument directed desire away from worldly advantages, towards the highest good; such mechanisms found full mediation in this prior framework. Each of *ða woruldsælða* is shown to be deceitful, tempting its possessor away from their counterparts, *ða soðan gesælða*.[239] The point was reinforced by a brief return for 'Boetius' as the first-person identity, enhancing appeal to wretchedness and evil rulership.[240] Desire for *wela* ('wealth') can never be satisfied.[241] 'Clothing and food and drink' are again cited, but 'no man is so wealthy that he does not need more':[242] 'sio gitsung ne con gemet, ne næfre ne bið gehealden on ðære neððearfe, ac wilnað symle maran þonne he þurfe'.[243] The same applies to *se weorðscipe and se anweald*, or *se wela and se anweald* (both rendering *dignitates*): though sometimes possessed by good men, they can never make their holders more worthy of power, but frequently encourage vices.[244] Theoderic's own kingship reinforces the 'unweorðscipe' brought by power in evil hands.[245] Nor can *se wela and se anweald* make any man truly wealthy or powerful.[246] Here rendering the *potentia* of kings, such terminology shows the fundamental unity of all forms of power.[247] Royal dependence on friends and attendants receives force from thegnly service: 'What is more pleasant in this present life ... than to follow the king and his presence, and then wealth and power?'.[248] Roman examples show the limited benefit of both to 'dear ones' (*deorlingas*), slain by 'unrighteous' rulers.[249] Limited

---

[239] *Bo* XXII.i–XXXII.iii, pp. 50–74. Cf. *Cons. phil.* IIIp1–m8, pp. 37–49.

[240] *Bo* XXVI.i–XXVII.ii, pp. 58–62; cf. also X, p. 21, line 10.

[241] *Bo* XXVI.i–iii, pp. 58–60. Cf. *Cons. phil.* IIIp3–m3, pp. 41–2.

[242] *Bo* XXVI.ii, p. 60, lines 16–19, cf. XXX.ii, p. 77, lines 7–11 (both unparalleled additions). Cf. *Cons. phil.* IIIp3.18, p. 42; IIIp9.19–20, p. 50.

[243] 'The avarice knows no moderation, nor is it ever satisfied in its need, but always desires more than he needs': *Bo* XXVI.ii, p. 60, lines 20–2. Cf. *Cons. phil.* IIIp3.19, p. 42.

[244] *Bo* XXVII.i–XXVIII, pp. 61–4. Cf. *Cons. phil.* IIIp4–m4, pp. 42–4.

[245] *Bo* XXVII.ii, pp. 62–3. Cf. *Cons. phil* IIIp4.4–10, p. 43. For the added reference to Theoderic cf. DELATORIS[QUE] (IIIp4.4, p. 43): 'i. accusatoris delator dicitur qui detegit quod latuit. oblique theoderichum designat': E1 (p. 135b).

[246] *Bo* XXIX.i–iii, pp. 65–8. Cf. *Cons. phil.* IIIp5–m5, pp. 44–5.

[247] Cf. Godden, 'Money, Power', pp. 45–6.

[248] *Bo* XXIX.i, p. 65, lines 5–7. Cf. *Cons. phil.* IIIp5.1–2, p. 44.

[249] *Bo* XXIX.ii, p. 66, line 23, to p. 67, line 24. Cf. *Cons. phil.* IIIp5.10–14, p. 45.

in geographical recognition, *þæt wuldor* and *se gielp* ('glory') frequently depend on qualities alien to their subject, through parental lineage.[250] 'Bodily pleasures' (*uoluptates corporis*) receive outright condemnation as *þa flæslican unþeawas* ('fleshly vices') and *þa woruldlustas*, enhancing association with greed and excess.[251]

Such was the basis for ascent to *þæt hehste good*, both aided and shaped by royal terminology.[252] 'Advantages' offered many lexical possibilities, including *god*, as well as *speda*, *æhta* and *gestreon*. *Gesælða* were unique in signifying both beneficial goods and the more general state of happiness or prosperity, a quality shared by the adjective *gesælig*.[253] The wider range enabled -*sælð*- formulations to extend beyond Latin 'bona' to include 'beatitudo' and the 'summum bonum'. The effect only strengthened the unity of 'þæt hehste good' with true benefit and happiness.[254] This is the context for Book IV, dominated by the first-person objection that evils exist and seemingly go unpunished.[255] Boethian arguments are conveyed quite faithfully, resting on the good that all men desire by nature, achieved only by good men: an ability to perform evil cannot be power at all.[256] Good men receive the reward of deification, becoming as 'gods'. Evil men so pervert nature that their existence is merely bestial, mirroring the descent of unrighteous rulers in the *Hierdeboc*.[257] The evil are always 'ungesæligran' (rendering *infeliciores*) when they achieve their desires; and conversely 'gesæligran' when receiving just punishment in this world.[258]

Only at this point does the text depart significantly from the emerging schema. Where Latin Prisoner had returned to 'popular' *fortuna*, the *Froferboc* appeals to *þisses andweardan lifes gesælða* ('the blessings of this present life'): at stake in both cases was the justice of respective suffering.[259] As in its source-text, the royal framework hinged on a relationship between 'foresceawung', 'foreþonc' or 'foretiohhung' (rendering *prouidentia*) and 'wyrd' (for *fatum*); even here usage differed in that 'wyrd' had occasionally earlier translated *fortuna*. The meaning and status of this problematic term

[250] *Bo* XXX.i–ii, pp. 68–9. Cf. *Cons. phil.* IIIp6–m6, pp. 45–6.

[251] *Bo* XXXI.i–ii, pp. 70–1. Cf. *Cons. phil.* IIIp7–m7, p. 47; Pratt, 'Illnesses', pp. 79–80.

[252] *Bo* XXXII.i–XXXV.vii, pp. 71–103. Cf. *Cons. phil.* IIIp8–m12, pp. 47–64.

[253] Payne, *Boethius*, pp. 69 and 89; Frakes, *Fate*, pp. 116–17.

[254] *Bo* XXXIV.ii–iii, p. 84, lines 1–10; XXIV.i, p. 52, line 14, to p. 53, line 14; and XXXIII.iii, p. 77, line 13, to p. 78, line 2. Cf. *Cons. phil.* IIIp10.10–11, p. 53; IIIp2.1–4, p. 38; and IIIp9.21–3, pp. 50–1.

[255] *Bo* XXXVI.i–ii, pp. 103–5. Cf. *Cons. phil.* IVp1, pp. 64–5.

[256] *Bo* XXXVI.iv–viii, pp. 105–11. Cf. *Cons. phil.* IVp2, pp. 66–70.

[257] *Bo* XXXVII.ii–iv, pp. 112–15. Cf. *Cons. phil.* IVp3, pp. 70–2; examples of Nebuchadnezzar and Saul discussed above, pp. 201–2.

[258] *Bo* XXXVIII.ii–vii, pp. 117–24. Cf. *Cons. phil.* IVp4, pp. 73–7.

[259] *Bo* XXXIX.ii, p. 124, lines 19–23. Cf. *Cons. phil.* IVp5.1–2, pp. 77–8.

have long aroused controversy, often identified as a relic of paganism.[260] Yet *wyrd* is only known from its use within Christian poetry, often in gnomic or elegaic contexts. Some at least of this verse has been judged 'Boethian', either by analogy or inspiration, and with reference to the translation as well as Latin *Consolatio*.[261] The context is notable given royal poetic interests, though hindered by problems of dating. The range of usage tells against any straightforward notion of 'fatalism', with varied responses of coping and control. In *Beowulf*, *wyrd* is rarely far from God, as a source of judgement or guiding restraint; though it seizes many warriors, it can also be enticed by the martial virtue of *ellen* ('courage').[262] Neither feature is pertinent in *The Wanderer* and *The Seafarer*, unconcerned with providential rule. *Wyrd* here expresses the mysterious transience of all worldly existence, only tolerable by pursuit of divine 'glory' (*ar*), the only source of true stability.[263]

Though used for *fortuna* as well as *fatum*, Alfredian *wyrd* expresses a single concept, with usage anticipating deeper Boethian explanation. In its early appearances *wyrd* is qualified as an aspect of *Mod*'s misunderstanding. His error has been to claim that 'þios sliðne wyrd ðas woruld wende buton Godes geþeahte';[264] he has abandoned *Wisdom*'s teachings in supposing that 'seo weord þas woruld wende heore agenes ðonces buton Godes geþeahte and his þafunge and monna gewyrhtum'.[265] As Frakes observes, the misperception relates to the Latin Prisoner's error in thinking Fortuna to fluctuate 'without a ruler'.[266] Yet the meaning is transformed by *wyrd*'s subsequent use for *fatum*, faithfully subordinated to 'Godes foreðonc and his foresceawung'. *Se foreðonc* is 'divine reason', 'fixed in the high creator who knows in advance how all will happen

[260] Frakes, *Fate*, pp. 83–91; E. G. Stanley, *The Search for Anglo-Saxon Paganism* (Cambridge and Totowa, NJ, 1975); G. Weber, *Wyrd: Studien zum Schicksalsbegriff der altenglischen und altnordischen Literatur* (Bad Homburg, Berlin and Zurich, 1969); J. C. Kasik, 'The Use of the Term *Wyrd* in *Beowulf* and the Conversion of the Anglo-Saxons', *Neophilologus* 63 (1979), 128–35; J. B. Trahern jr., 'Fatalism and the Millennium', in *Cambridge Companion*, ed. Godden and Lapidge, pp. 160–71.
[261] G. V. Smithers, 'The Meaning of The Seafarer and The Wanderer', *Medium Ævum* 26 (1957), 137–53; L. Whitbread, 'The Pattern of Misfortune in Deor and Other Old English Poems', *Neophilologus* 54 (1970), 167–83; Kiernan, '*Deor*'; A. D. Horgan, 'The Wanderer – A Boethian Poem?', *Review of English Studies* 39 (1988), 349–64; A. L. Klinck, *The Old English Elegies* (Montreal, 1992), pp. 18–21, 30–40 and 43–6.
[262] *Beowulf* 572–3, cf. esp. 441–2, 455, 1053–62, 2524–27 and 2813–16.
[263] *Wanderer* 114–15; *Seafarer* 107–8.
[264] '... this cruel fate guides the world, without God's direction': *Bo* V.iii, p. 13, lines 24–5. Cf. *Cons. phil.* Ip6.19, p. 15.
[265] '... fate ruled the world according to its own will, without the direction or permission of God, nor with any consideration for the merits of men': *Bo* V.i, p. 11, lines 6–7. Cf. *Cons. phil.* Ip5.2, p. 13.
[266] Frakes, *Fate*, pp. 83–100, esp. 90–4; Otten, *Boethius*, pp. 60–70.

before it happens'.[267] *Wyrd* emerges as the outcome of such 'forethought': 'that which we call *wyrd* is God's work, which he performs each day, both what we see and what is invisible to us'.[268]

This is the context for an addition, correcting the error of 'sume uðwiotan' ('some philosophers'), who suppose that 'sio wyrd wealde ægþer ge gesælða ge ungesælða ælces monnes': all is in fact ruled by divine predestination.[269] Far from contemporary defenders of *wyrd*, the target was probably classical.[270] Boethian *fatum* posed problems for commentators with its pagan origins. The 'Anonymous of St Gallen' saw the term as incompatible with divine control, accusing Boethius of speaking 'magis philosophice quam catholice'.[271] Yet *fatum* is defended by Remigius: despite the claims of Gregory and Augustine that 'fatum nihil esse', its use here merely denotes 'God's work, which descends from providence'.[272] The royal addition mounts comparable reconciliation with anti-classical criticism.[273] This is the more significant given Remigian treatment of *fortuna*, explicitly rejected as 'nothing'.[274] Alfredian *wyrd* came suggestively close to this Remigian view, both endorsing and anticipating Boethian *fatum*.

Yet *wyrd*'s operation was different, bearing special hope for rulership. The very scope of enquiry was transformed by its Alfredian setting. Renewed appeal to philosopher-rulership highlighted the just cause of 'wise men': 'For they say that they could more easily carry out and uphold their wisdom, if their power were fully over the people who are under them; and also to some extent over those who are in the nearest

---

[267] 'Se foreþonc is sio godcunde gesceadwisnes; sio is fæst on þæm hean sceppende þe eall fore wat hu hit geweorðan sceall ær ær hit geweorðe': *Bo* XXXIX.ii, p. 128, lines 15–18. Cf. *Cons. phil.* IVp6.9, p. 80.

[268] 'Ac þæt þæt we wyrd hatað, þæt bið Godes weorc þæt he ælce dæg wyrcð, ægþer ge þæs ðe we gesioð ge þæs þe us ungesewenlic bið': *Bo* XXXIX.v, p. 128, lines 18–20. Cf. *Cons. phil.* IVp6.9, p. 80.

[269] '... fate rules both the blessings and unblessings of each man': *Bo* XXXIX.viii, p. 131, lines 8–12. Cf. *Cons. phil.* IVp6.18–19, p. 81.

[270] Otten, *Boethius*, pp. 64–8; Frakes, *Fate*, pp. 96–7. Cf. Payne, *Boethius*, p. 89; W. F. Bolton, 'How Boethian is Alfred's Boethius?', in *Studies*, ed. Szarmach, pp. 153–68, at 157.

[271] FATO ... AMMINISTRAT (IVp6.12, p. 80): 'Fatum vero nihil est. sed omnia per dei nutum fiunt. uel permittuntur fieri': E1 (p. 167a), G (p. 143), N (fol. 70r). SEU CAELESTIBUS SIDERUM MOTIBUS (IVp6.13, p. 80): 'Hic magis philosophice quam catholice loquitur': E1 (p. 167a), G (p. 133), N (fol. 70r). EA SERIES (IVp6.18, p. 81): 'Hic mentitur de fato quia dei ordinatio temperat cuncta': E1 (p. 167b), G (p. 144), N (fol. 71v).

[272] DE PROUIDENTIAE SIMPLICITATE, DE FATI SERIE (IVp6.4, p. 79): 'beatus Gregorius dicit nihil esse fatum. Sed si fatum aliquid est dicendum, fatum est naturalis ordo rerum ex prouidentia dei uenientium ... Fatum igitur est opus dei quod ex prouidentia descendit': Stewart, 'Remigius', pp. 36–7. FATUM UERO (IVp6.9, p. 80): 'Nota fatum nihil esse, ut beatus Augustinus aliique dicunt, sed quod prouidentia dei disponente foris agitur fatum uocatur': *ibid.*, p. 37; Courcelle, *La Consolation*, pp. 261–2, 277–8 and 287–8.

[273] Cf. Frakes, *Fate*, pp. 96–7.   [274] Above, pp. 276–7.

regions round about, because they could chastise the evil and promote the good'.[275] The rendering made much of 'in contingentes populos'; the problem no longer corresponded with *Mod*'s own plight. The place of rulers was further isolated in the handling of divine *foreþonc*, only loosely related to Boethian rotating spheres. As Frakes observes, the royal simile of a waggon wheel bears comparison with circular diagrams accompanying the Remigian and 'Vatican' traditions;[276] its force lay firmly in the familiarity of reference, with God himself as 'craftsman' (*cræftega*).[277] Unlike the Latin, the wheel is inhabited by men of varying quality, depicting different degrees of subjection to *wyrd*.[278] Just as the hub of the wheel turns more freely than the spokes or the rims, so men are increasingly unaffected by *wyrd*'s fluctuations, the more they direct their love to God, and away from this world.[279] Of special note is the status of 'middle men', reflecting on both earthly and divine matters, 'as if ... with one eye to heaven, the other to earth'.[280] Earlier *Mod* himself had been depicted with eyes so divided.[281] Corresponding with the wheel's spokes, such men are more 'troubled and afflicted both in mind and body, the more they are separated from God'; only the 'best men' can entirely escape 'the hardships of this present life' by wholly fixing themselves to God.[282] The framework is Gregorian: a comparable distinction was drawn at the opening of the *Dialogues* between the troubles of worldly office and the greater virtue of saints, whom God 'refused to occupy ... with the toils of this world'.[283]

The distinction continues in the operation of divine *foreþonc*, the ultimate source of consolation. The Boethian solution had placed God in 'the high watch-tower of providence', arranging 'what he knows to be fitting for each person'.[284] Latin Prisoner corresponded with the fate of good men 'undefeated by punishments', offering 'an example to

[275] 'Forðæm hi secgað þæt hi mægen þe yð hiora wisdome fulgan and hine gehealdan, gif hiora anwald bið fullice ofer þæt folc þe him under bið; and eac be sumum dæle ofer ða þe him on neaweste bioð ymbutan, forðæm þæt hi mægen henan ða yflan and fyrðran ða goodan': *Bo* XXXIX.ii, p. 124, line 27, to p. 125, line 3. *Cons. phil.* IVp5.3, p. 78: 'Sic enim clarius testatiusque sapientiae tractatur officium, cum in contingentes populos regentium quodam modo beatitudo transfunditur, cum praesertim carcer, nex ceteraque legalium tormenta poenarum perniciosis potius ciuibus, propter quos etiam constitutae sunt, debeantur'.
[276] Frakes, *Fate*, pp. 163–4.
[277] *Bo* XXXIX.vi, p. 128, lines 27–30. Cf. *Cons. phil.* IVp6.12, p. 80 (*artifex*); D. Hill, 'Anglo-Saxon Mechanics: 1. The Oxcart; 2. The Anglo-Saxon Vine Dresser's Knife', *Medieval Life* 10 (1998), 13–20.
[278] *Bo* XXXIX.vii, p. 129, line 19, to p. 130, line 27. Cf. *Cons. phil.* IVp6.15–16, p. 81.
[279] *Bo* XXXIX.vii, p. 130, lines 8–18.   [280] *Bo* XXXIX.vii, p. 129, lines 27–30.
[281] *Bo* XXXVIII.v, p. 121, lines 25–31 (a significant expansion). Cf. *Cons. phil.* IVp4.29, p. 76.
[282] *Bo* XXXIX.vii, p. 130, lines 21–7.
[283] *GD* I, 6. Cf. *Grégoire le Grand: Dialogues*, ed. de Vogüé I, 14, lines 46–53.
[284] *Cons. phil.* IVp6.30, p. 82.

others that virtue was unconquered by evils'.[285] Not only suffering but all fate promoted *uirtus* alone. In the *Froferboc* God is pictured assigning 'ælcum be his gewyrhtum' ('to each according to his works');[286] the image supported a flexible picture of *wyrd*, dynamically responding to human actions.[287] Otten has highlighted the wider occurrence of retributive imagery, also paralleled in Gregorian writings.[288] Royal deployment clearly took account of punishments manifest in evil action, yet the usage supported an alternative divine agenda.[289] Virtue was no longer the sole criterion; *cræft* appears only infrequently, softening Boethian rhetoric.[290] The extreme case remains of men unconquerable through *cræft*, supplemented by an addition describing those who choose 'manigfeald earfoðu' for greater glory with God.[291] Yet neither can apply to the royal Prisoner: 'even if yet more harm came to me,' *Mod* had confessed, 'I would never again say that it was not deserved'.[292] His position corresponds with those men whom God gives good and evil mixed together, 'because they deserve both': some he 'very soon deprives of their wealth ... lest they raise themselves up through their too extended blessings, and consequently become proud'; some he 'punishes with hard affliction, so that they learn *cræft* patiently in long hardship'.[293]

Implications of testing are here avoided; the point is counter-balanced by further weight on wise reward. 'Power in this world often comes to very good men, so that the power of evil men is destroyed'.[294] The prosperity of evil men is cited as a 'very clear sign' to the wise man 'þæt he ne sceal lufian to ungemetlice ðas woruldgesælða'. A further addition addresses 'the present wealth that often comes to the good man': 'what else is it except a sign of the future wealth, and a beginning of the reward that God has intended for his good will?'.[295] 'Manegum men bioð eac forgifene forðæm þas weoruldgesælða þæt he scile þæm

---

[285] *Cons. phil.* IVp6.42, p. 83.
[286] *Bo* XXXIX.ix, p. 132, lines 16–19. Cf. *Cons. phil.* IVp6.30, p. 82.
[287] *Bo* XLI.iii, p. 144, lines 11–32; cf. M. S. Griffith, ' "Does *wyrd bið ful aræd* mean "Fate is wholly inexorable" ' ', in *'Doubt Wisely'*, ed. Toswell and Tyler, pp. 133–56, at 148–50.
[288] Otten, *Boethius*, pp. 35–41, esp. 39–40.
[289] *Bo* XXXVII.ii, p. 112, to XXXVII.iii, p. 113 line 32; cf. *Cons. phil.* IVp3.1–13, pp. 70–1.
[290] *Bo* XXXIX.x, p. 133, line 7; XXXIX.xi, p. 133, line 26, and p. 134, line 3; XL.iii, p. 138, line 23. Cf. *Cons. phil.* IVp6.37, p. 82; IVp6.40 and 42, p. 83; IVp7.19, p. 87 (line 40); *uirtus* frequently left untranslated (IVp6.51, p. 84; IVp7.10, p. 87 (lines 19 and 20); IVp7.15 and 19, p. 87; IVp7.19, p. 87 (line 39)).
[291] *Bo* XXXIX.xi, p. 133, line 31, to p. 134, line 4; and p. 133, lines 14–18 (an unparalleled addition). Cf. *Cons. phil.* IVp6.42, p. 83; IVp6.38, p. 83. 'Holy martyrs' at XI.ii, p. 26, lines 17–21 (cf. IIp4.29, p. 25), cf. Stewart, 'Remigius', p. 29.
[292] *Bo* XXII.i, p. 50, lines 18–19 (an unparalleled addition). Cf. *Cons. phil.* IIIp1.2, p. 37.
[293] *Bo* XXXIX.xi, p. 133, lines 21–7. Cf. *Cons. phil.* IVp6.40, p. 83.
[294] *Bo* XXXIX.xi, p. 133, lines 19–21. Cf. *Cons. phil.* IVp6.39, p. 83.
[295] *Bo* XXXIX.xi, p. 134, lines 7–13. Cf. *Cons. phil.* IVp6.44, p. 83.

goodum leanian hiora good, and þæm yflum hiora yfel': in the latter case, the Latin had concerned power in evil hands.[296] The overall effect was a more positive picture of divine agency in the world, focused on earthly rulership. Testing was left for the unconquerable and 'best men', closest to God; those in power received a mixture of good and evil according to their merits; to the wise ruler, resisting all worldly temptations, came obligatory gifts of power and wealth.

The picture completed with summary advice on *wyrd*, only loosely related to Boethian rhetoric. Philosophia's speech returned to *fortuna*, exposing its true susceptibility to human control.[297] The fashioning of *fortuna* lay in man's own hands: his *uirtus* supplied the basis for providential rule.[298] In the vernacular the speech is adapted to *wyrd*; *Wisdom*'s words offered a different irony, focused on earthly consequences. The striving of the wise man is equally directed 'ge wið þa reðan wyrde ge wið þa wynsuman' ('both against harsh fate and against pleasant fate').[299] Neither can be endured when accepted to 'excess' (*ungemet*): wisdom lies in finding 'þone midmestan weg' between the two, 'þæt he ne wilnige wynsumran wyrde and maran orsorgnesse ðonne hit gemetlic sie, ne eft to reðre, forðæm he ne mæg nauþres ungemet adriogan'.[300] What lies in human hands is not virtue or vice, but an active fashioning of this 'middle way', through the moderation of prosperity: 'Gif hi þonne þone midmestan weg aredian willað, þonne sculon hi selfe him selfum gemetgian þa wynsuman wyrde and þa orsorgan'.[301] Far from punishment or correction, such pursuit will postively alleviate 'harsh *wyrd*', through God's own 'moderation': 'þonne gemetgað him God þa reðan wyrde ge on þisse weorulde ge on þære toweardan, swa swa hi eaðe adreogan magan'.[302]

---

[296] 'Worldly blessings are also granted to many a man so that he may reward the good for their good, and the evil for their evil'; *Bo* XXXIX.xii, p. 134, lines 24–6. Cf. *Cons. phil.* IVp6.47, p. 84: 'quibusdam permissum puniendi ius ut exercitii bonis et malis esset causa supplicii'.

[297] *Cons. phil.* IVp7, pp. 86–7.   [298] *Cons. phil.* IVp7.17–22, esp. 21–2, p. 87.

[299] *Bo* XL.iii, p. 138, lines 24–7. Cf. *Cons. phil.* IVp7.20, p. 87.

[300] '. . . so that he does not desire more pleasant fate and more secure fate than is moderate, nor desire harsher fate, for he cannot endure an excess of either': *Bo* XL.iii, p. 138, lines 29–31. Cf. *Cons. phil.* IVp7.21, p. 87: 'Firmis medium uiribus occupate; quicquid aut infra subsistit aut ultra progreditur habet contemptum felicitatis, non habet praemium laboris' ('Seize the middle with firm powers; whatever either is positioned beneath or passes above has contempt for happiness, not reward for labour').

[301] 'If they want to find the middle way, then they ought to moderate for themselves the pleasant and secure fate': *Bo* XL.iii, p. 138, line 32, to p. 139, line 2.

[302] 'Then God will moderate the harsh fate for them both in this world and in the world to come, just as they can easily endure': *Bo* XL.iii, p. 139, lines 2–4. Cf. *Cons. phil.* IVp7.22, p. 87: 'In uestra enim situm manu qualem uobis fortunam formare malitis; omnis enim quae uidetur aspera, nisi aut exercet aut corrigit, punit' ('For what type of fortune you prefer to fashion for yourselves is placed in your own hands; for all fortune that seems harsh, if it does not either exercise or correct, punishes').

The entire framework offered earthly response to the flucuations of *wyrd*, maximizing the scope for wise intervention. There was little room for testing in such beneficial 'moderation', nor for Hercules' example, omitted from the subsequent section.[303] Alfredian silence must be judged against the metre's implications of tortuous struggle, accorded such prominence in West Frankish royal imagery.[304] Rewards of Herculean labour were surpassed by more general lessons of success, taught by 'the famous examples of good heroes and honour-desiring men who were before you'.[305] '[F]orðæm hi wunnon æfter weorðscipe on þisse worulde, and tiolodon goodes hlisan mid goodum weorcum, and worhton goode bisne þæm þe æfter him wæron': the addition endorses *Mod*'s own profession of intent, within wise Solomonic example.[306] 'Moderation' was itself Solomonic: 'harsh *wyrd*' required neither combat nor endurance, but could be wisely protected against through tempering of prosperity. There could be no question of Sedulian forbearance, trusting only in the Lord and his faithful servants, still less *The Wanderer*'s gnomic contemplation of divine *ar*.[307] Alfredian wisdom assigned determining force to collective mental priorities, actively responsible for fluctuating *wyrd*, through mechanisms of divine punishment. Such was the scope of royal consolation: far from Boethian suffering, the operation of *wyrd* matched the principles of Alfred's Prose Preface, in the urgent context of viking attack. Implicit in its kingly example, the translation itself offered much of value to collective defence.

THE *FROFERBOC* AND ALFREDIAN THEATRE

The *Froferboc*'s content strengthens the case for its central role in 're-education'. Dominated by *Wisdom*, the text's significance otherwise proceeds from the centrality of 'liberal arts' in Alfredian instruction. This was the curriculum claimed for the court *schola*, involving both Latin and English; the agenda extended to wider contexts for reading, involving multiple English books.[308] Alfred's intransigent 'judges' could

---

[303] *Bo* XL.iv, p. 139. Cf. *Cons. phil.* IVm7, pp. 87–9.

[304] Above, pp. 278–80, cf. 243–5; Regino, *Chronicon*, ed. Kurze, s.a. 888, p. 129, for parallel testing of Charles the Fat. Cf. S. Irvine, 'Wrestling with Hercules: King Alfred and the Classical Past', in *Court Culture*, ed. Cubitt, pp. 171–88.

[305] *Bo* XL.iv, p. 139, lines 5–7. Cf. *Cons. phil.* IVm7.32–5, pp. 88–9; Ecclesiasticus XXXIX. 1–13.

[306] 'For they strove after honour in this world, and obtained good fame with good works, and made a good example for those who were after them': *Bo* XL.iv, p. 139, lines 13–15; cf. XVII, p. 41, lines 3–6.

[307] Cf. Smithers, 'The Meaning'; Horgan, '*The Wanderer*'; Klinck, *Elegies*, esp. pp. 18–21, 30–40 and 43–6; Booth, 'Alfred versus Beowulf', pp. 63–5.

[308] *VA* 75, lines 15–21; c. 106, lines 39–54; *CP*, p. 6, lines 10–15.

be pictured tardily benefiting from such 'liberal' education.[309] As an expansive textbook the *Consolatio* now offered vernacular wisdom; Continental parallels suggest more 'advanced' deployment, beyond the elementary Psalter, though such status need not have been preserved. The ambiguity of translation was openly emphasized in the surviving prose preface, modestly apologizing if any 'understands it more accurately (*rihtlicor*) than he was able', suggesting certain readers familiar with Boethius' Latin.[310] Yet concern extended to 'each of those whom it pleases to read this book': the 'book' in question was the *Froferboc*, as vernacular text detached from Latin understanding.[311] Didactic purposes were only enhanced by the text's added signposting, aiding the clarity of wise exposition. Logic, rhetoric, astronomy, music: every discipline could be experienced on its own terms, within the ordered structures of *Wisdom*'s consolation.

Textual transmission is consistent with the wide and early reception of the *Froferboc*. The work is best attested of all royal texts after the *Hierdeboc* and *Domboc*. Two manuscripts preserve the text in its contrasting recensions: an early twelfth-century copy containing the text in prose, and a mid-tenth-century manuscript incorporating versified sections for many of Boethius' metres.[312] A single leaf once survived from an earlier West Saxon manuscript, from the first half of the tenth century, perhaps transmitting the prose version.[313] Behind all these witnesses lay earlier phases of copying, probably of some complexity. A further lost copy of 'Boeties boc on Englisc' was given to the cathedral library of Exeter by bishop Leofric (*c.* 1072); copies of the *Consolatio* in English are known to have been possessed by Christ Church and St Augustine's, Canterbury, in the later middle ages.[314] The work was singled out in later memory by the learned ealdorman Æthelweard, writing in the late tenth century. His Latin encomium saluted royal skill in translating 'unknown numbers of books from rhetorical Latin speech into his own language – so variously and so richly, that the book of Boethius would arouse tearful emotions not only in those well familiar

---

[309] *VA* 106, lines 54–61.

[310] *Bo*, p. 1, lines 12–15.

[311] '... and nu bit and for Godes naman he halsað ælcne þara þe þas boc rædan lyste, þæt he for hine gebidde': *Bo*, p. 1, lines 10–12.

[312] Oxford, Bodleian Library, Bodley 180 (2079) (medieval provenance unknown, s. xii^{in}); London, British Library, Cotton Otho A. vi (fire damaged; medieval provenance unknown, s. x^{med}); Ker, *Catalogue*, nos. 167 and 305.

[313] Ker, *Catalogue*, no. 337.

[314] M. Lapidge, 'Surviving Booklists from Anglo-Saxon England', in *Learning and Literature*, ed. Lapidge and Gneuss, pp. 33–89, at 65; James, *Ancient Libraries of Canterbury and Dover*, p. 51, no. 307, and p. 302, no. 991.

with it but even in those hearing it'.[315] The text's high status in later learning receives support from its availability to Ælfric and the translator of the Old English *Disticha Catonis*.[316] William of Malmesbury included Boethius in his account of Alfred's translations; the text would be used by Nicholas Trevet in the late thirteenth century.[317]

For Æthelweard, the book's reputation lay in its emotional impact, in immediate contexts of reading and recitation. The theatrical qualities of translated dialogue, subtly enhanced in many inventive passages, acquired heightened force in Alfredian mechanisms of delivery. The very act of reading replicated *Mod*'s sapiential interaction; recitation brought still deeper effects, in outward oral gesture. Once evoked, such personae could not be lost from collective awareness, joining voices and characters principally communicated in vernacular poetry. The extent of departure may well have been heightened by the various 'Gothic' components imagined in early Germanic ancestry, here shared with Danes, and notably prominent in Alfred's claimed descent.[318] Inventive translation suggested the still deeper relevance of 'Roman' philosophy and memory. 'Where are now the bones of the renowned and wise goldsmith Weland?': as Booth observes, such loss was the only role for 'Germanic' glory.[319] Theoderic now ranked with Nero in outright infamy. *Wyrd* itself found distinctive treatment, neither susceptible to martial courage, nor mysteriously symbolic of earthly transience. What gave this dialogue such power was neither Boethian nor primarily historical, but its continuous expression of royal discourse. Fundamental departures matched Solomonic and Gregorian priorities, harnessing contemporary practices of royal lordship; Neo-Platonism was reoriented towards active rule. At the heart of all changes was *Mod*'s own ambiguous status: the outcome was not only an insistent philosophy of earthly responsibility, but a recognizable drama of sapiential rule.

Reading was itself but one part of Alfredian theatre, centred on the king. Every aspect of the *Froferboc* supported Alfred's own role as Solomon, newly realized through his late acquisition of wisdom; the

---

[315] *Chronicle of Æthelweard*, ed. Campbell, Book IV, ch. 3, p. 51 (trans. in K&L, *Alfred*, p. 191).

[316] *Ælfric's Lives of Saints*, ed. Skeat I, ch. i, 10–25 (cf. Godden, 'Mind', pp. 278 and 296–8), and ch. xvii, 381–3; R. S. Cox, 'The Old English Dicts of Cato', *Anglia* 90 (1972), 1–42, nos. 77 and 80, pp. 55 and 27–8.

[317] *GR* I, 190–1, cf. 192–3; B. S. Donaghey, 'Nicholas Trevet's Use of King Alfred's Translation of Boethius, and the Dating of his Commentary', in *The Medieval Boethius*, ed. A. J. Minnis (Woodbridge, 1987), pp. 1–31.

[318] See esp. J. L. Nelson, 'Vikings and Others', *TRHS* 6th series 13 (2003), 1–28, at 27–8, with references; cf. S. J. Harris, 'The Alfredian *World History* and Anglo-Saxon Identity', *Journal of English and Germanic Philology* 100 (2001), 482–510, at 485–91.

[319] *Bo* XIX, p. 46, lines 16–21. Cf. *Cons. phil.* IIm7.15, p. 34; Booth, 'Alfred versus Beowulf', pp. 41–4 and 59–65.

identification extended to every member of his aristocratic audiences.[320] *Mod*'s own downfall, pointedly attributed to greed and loss of wisdom, matched the king's own indictment of office-holders in the Prose Preface. In the case of 'judges', the message incorporated direct threat of dismissal: in both cases the only remedy was assiduous pursuit of wisdom.[321] The correspondence was as strong with younger audiences, newly benefiting from advantages denied to Alfred in his youth.[322] 'Wela and weorðscipe' had been *Wisdom*'s gifts; wisdom actively promised power to those not desiring it. Uniting all perspectives was *Mod*'s career, detached from Boethius' prizes under *Wisdom*'s guiding nourishment: 'For I ... took you as a child, and trained you according to my instruction'.[323] '[Y]ou were dear to me before you were familiar with me, and before then you knew my instruction and my ways, and I taught you when you were young such wisdom as is withheld from many other older minds, and I promoted you with my teachings so that you were chosen as a judge'.[324] The relationship with *Wisdom* dramatized every aspect of Solomonic restraint. Corrupting effects of *ða woruldsælða*, the wise basis of good rule, *þæt hehste good* as sole true object of desire: all reinforced central gestures of Alfredian rulership, focused against pride and greed.

All this behaviour acquired force amid the complex dynamics of defensive reform. The context was openly acknowledged, not only in *Mod*'s kingly appeal. A former age of simplicity acquired deeper resonance, when 'no one had yet heard of any ship-army (*sciphere*)'; *Mod*'s tribulations proceeded from 'foreigners' (*ælðeodegum*) as well as his men and kinsmen; parallels have often been noted between viking and Gothic invasions.[325] Restrained desires supported dispute settlement as well as judgement in accordance with God's law.[326] Behind the latter lay the full force of *hlafordsearu*, supplemented by enlightened support for *pauperes*.[327] All were in turn subsumed by the most intensive congruity, with the logistical dilemmas of defensive warfare. How much was

---

[320] Above, pp. 170–6.   [321] *VA* 106, lines 28–39.   [322] *Ibid.* 106, lines 54–60, cf. c. 25.

[323] '... forþam ic ðe ... me to bearne genom, and to minum tyhtum getyde': *Bo* VIII, p. 20, lines 6–7 (an unparalleled addition). Cf. *Cons. phil.* IIp3.470, pp. 21–2.

[324] '... þu me wære ær leof þonne cuþ, and ær þon þa ðu cuðe mine tyht and mine þeawas, and ic þe giongne gelærde swylce snytro swelc manegum oðrum eldran gewittum oftogen is, and ic þe gefyrðede mid minum larum to ðon þæt þe mon to domere geceas': *Bo* VIII, p. 20, lines 9–13. Cf. *Cons. phil.* IIp3.4–10, pp. 21–2, esp. 'sumptas in adulescentia negatas senibus dignitates' ('honours enjoyed in youth denied to older men'), and the 'curule chairs' of Boethius' two sons.

[325] *Bo* XV, p. 34, lines 1–3; XXXII.i, p. 71, lines 25–7 (the latter entirely unparalleled). Cf. *Cons. phil.* IIm5.13–15, p. 29; IIIp8.4, p. 47; K&L, *Alfred*, p. 30; Booth, 'Alfred versus Beowulf', pp. 51–2; S. Irvine, 'The Anglo-Saxon Chronicle and the Idea of Rome', in *Alfred*, ed. Reuter, pp. 63–77, at 67–73.

[326] Above, pp. 153, 156–7 and 172–5.   [327] Above, pp. 174–5 and 232–41, cf. 98 and 157.

'enough'? The question assumed potent force amid the heavy burdens of mobilization and burghal construction, universally extracted through the common burdens. The effect was a double squeeze on landlords, exacerbating all problems of labour.[328] The *Froferboc*'s answer was generously open-ended, while demonstrated by appeal to the king's own universal needs. Praying-men, fighting-men, workmen; land, gifts and other 'provisions': such necessities were far from exclusive, replicated in the structures of every aristocratic estate, yet similarly subject to *cræft* and wisdom. Beyond royal needs lay those of every household: all might be more than satisfied through collective Solomonic restraint.

Needs 'at home' mirrored those of the 'king's home': the implications extended to all local behaviour, united by the *Froferboc*'s courtly script. Heightened above all were the conditional gifts of wise practice, wealth and more general prosperity, corresponding with Alfred's own gifts to landlords from the resources of nascent burhs. Distribution was itself pictured by Asser in the royal household, entirely at Alfred's hand.[329] The example of London shows land with trading privileges and rights to royal toll; at Worcester arrangements extended to a full carve-up of dues and fines, with half conceded to the episcopal church.[330] The former was especially notable as an arena of Roman memory. Winchester, Chichester, Exeter, Bath: even in such ancient locations, street plans were distinct from their Roman predecessors.[331] Another beneficiary was ealdorman Æthelred; Brooks not unreasonably posits a ninth-century origin for the 'third penny' of burghal receipts later owed to ealdormen.[332] The *Chronicle* casually refers to 'king's thegns then at home at the fortifications (*æt þæm geweorcum*)'.[333] A vital precondition for all interests was Alfred's reformed coinage, similarly shared with thegnly moneyers.[334] Here too was Roman re-use in several of its early designs (*c*. 875–80), unusually dependent on late imperial example.[335] From *c*. 880 minting expanded westwards to several new burhs.[336] In all cases such benefits could only be realized through successful construction. The *Froferboc* actively aided this connection, in its insistent promise of earthly rewards; tied to wisdom, such gifts demanded continuous

---

[328] Above, pp. 97–105.   [329] *VA* 100–2.

[330] S 346 (BCS 561); S 1628 (BCS 577 and 578); S 223 (BCS 579; *SEHD*, no. 13; trans. in *EHD*, no. 99).

[331] Biddle and Hill, 'Late Saxon Planned Towns', pp. 78–83; *VA* 91, lines 53–4 ('contradictores imperalium diffinitionum'); cf. ambivalent Alfredian treatment of Roman history observed by M. Godden, 'The Anglo-Saxons and the Goths: Rewriting the Sack of Rome', *ASE* 31 (2002), 47–68, at 55–68.

[332] Brooks, 'Administrative Background', p. 144.   [333] *ASC* s.a. 893.   [334] Above, pp. 103–4.

[335] Blackburn, 'London Mint', pp. 113–14.

[336] Keynes, 'Mercians', pp. 29–31; Blackburn, 'Alfred's Coinage Reforms', pp. 207–8.

aversion. Asser's picture reinforces the power of conspicuously 'just' division.[337] The message was embedded in further gifts, portable *ædificia*; Roman rock crystal received the full force of royal craftsmanship.[338] 'Wela and anweald': the construction reflected the wider scope of Alfredian responsibility, as shared objects of intensive restraint.

Other role-playing hinged on royal suffering; here too the *Froferboc* added another dimension, in the precise rationalization of earthly fate. This was a further aspect of Alfredian office-holding: both king and the entire political order corresponded with *Mod* among *Wisdom*'s 'middle men', looking upon both earthly and divine, and accordingly afflicted 'both in mind and body, the more they are separated from God'.[339] To such men God gave both good and evil, 'because they deserve both'.[340] The *Froferboc* strengthened retributive aspects of Alfredian suffering, prominent in the Prose Preface and Psalms, while adding much in the providential flexibility of human *wyrd*. There was no room for wise resilience: the Alfredian 'middle way' lay in actively moderating prosperous *wyrd*, with resulting alleviation of harsh *wyrd* at God's hand.[341] The advice again corresponded with Alfredian defensive co-operation, tempering much through the disruptive redeployment of land and labour, while yielding long-term safeguards against viking attack.[342] The *Froferboc*'s entire philosophy matched the effectiveness of West Saxon logistics; wisdom directly contributed to these outcomes, through Solomonic restraint. The effect was highly distinctive, in the room created for human control, very far from the divine and ecclesiastical sources of West Frankish earthly *stabilitas*. Alfredian discourse reinforced the collective experience of economic forces, channelled and guided by earthly construction. West Saxon structures were here of double significance, as effective mechanisms underpinned by shared mental priorities, subject to complex textual appeal. Uniting all was the household itself, theatrically projected in every act of local service; on this heightened stage lay Alfred's own performance, moderating *wyrd* to his own wise control.

---

[337] *VA* 100–2.
[338] Above, pp. 189–92; G. A. Kornbluth, 'The Alfred Jewel: Reuse of Roman Spolia', *Medieval Archaeology* 33 (1989), 32–7.
[339] *Bo* XXXIX.vii, p. 129, line 27, to p. 130, line 27.   [340] *Bo* XXXIX.xi, p. 133, lines 21–7.
[341] *Bo* XL.iii, p. 138, line 27, to p. 139, line 4.   [342] Above, pp. 93–105, cf. 172–8.

Chapter 14

SEEING GOD AS HE IS

Justly compared with the *Froferboc*, the remaining text in the royal corpus offers no less an expression of learned ambition. The version of Augustine's *Soliloquia* confirms the scope of royal learned resources, raising many questions of their deployment. The source-text held a distinctive place, as a product of Augustine's early Neo-Platonism; royal handling extended far beyond translation, to imaginative re-composition. Only Book I was rendered in anything approaching its entirety. Book II followed the substance of Augustinian claims, but with much independent argument; whereas the Latin text was unfinished, the vernacular version added a third section effectively 'completing' Augustine's text. There can be no single explanation for these complex manoeuvres; as with the *Consolatio*, much hinged on esoteric aspects of Latin philosophy. The *Soliloquia* offered a further instance of Christian Neo-Platonic dialogue. The nature of divine knowledge, the status of truth, the immortality of the soul: all found extensive treatment in soothing steps of wise comprehension. Surpassing even Boethius in intensity of dialectic, Augustine's philosophy maximized man's capacity for understanding while restricting its practical attainment. Not only was the dialogue incomplete; Augustine had soon abandoned Neo-Platonism, offering revised, scriptural positions in later writings.

The royal version took full account of the text's problematic status, while reorienting its implications towards contemporary priorities. The translation assigned limits to all earthly understanding, in accordance with later Augustinian pronouncement; the 'completed' text left enlightenment to the afterlife alone. Royal argumentation matched this framework with arguments appropriate to earthly need. Whole passages found alternative explanation in examples appealing to aristocratic familiarity; Solomonic example was repeatedly evoked in contexts of court life. Worldly goods found further equivocation, amid dangers of desire; their relevance extended to wisdom as the sole object of love.

Words and messages of lordship; daily experience of the 'king's home': both found prominent reference as the very basis for sapiential pursuit. The overall effect was the deepest justification of royal learning, an entire metaphysics uniquely adapted to Alfredian behaviour. Royal wisdom now answered every aspect of human potential; its implications encompassed the nature of man's soul and its earthly reception of truth.

THE *SOLILOQUIA* IN CONTEXT

The Latin *Soliloquia* epitomize Augustine's Neo-Platonism; royal handling shows clear sensitivity to his later career.[1] The text had been the most intensive product of Augustine's period at Cassiciacum, prior to his baptism by Ambrose at Easter 387.[2] Augustine had reached from Plotinus to St Paul; his early writings followed late Roman trends on the compatibility of Neo-Platonic philosophy with Christian redemption, prefiguring many aspects of the natural theology later constructed by Boethius.[3] Both writers owed much to common sources, combining Plotinus with Cicero's blend of Stoical and Neo-Platonic thought.[4] In the *Soliloquia* such parallels were heightened by the text's sophisticated harnessing of intimate dialogue, involving the author's own alter ego and the mysterious faculty of 'Reason' (*Ratio*). The book's title invited a 'speaking to oneself'; possibly internal or external to *Augustinus*, Reason's counselling anticipated the substance of Boethian therapy.[5]

Looking back on the *Soliloquia* in his *Retractationes*, Augustine characterized Book I as an attempt to explain 'what kind of man he ought to be who wishes to comprehend wisdom'.[6] The answer lay within as well as without: *Augustinus* soon summarizes his object in desiring 'to know God and the soul'.[7] A similar quest would be followed by Boethius' Prisoner, having forgotten his own self and by what government the world was ruled.[8] Philosophia's answer depended on 'faculties' of comprehension; Reason drew similar distinction between the intellect and senses, in identifying satisfactory conditions for higher knowledge.[9]

---

[1] Below, pp. 321–32.

[2] P. Brown, *Augustine of Hippo* (London, 1967), pp. 79–127; G. Bonner, *St Augustine of Hippo: Life and Controversies*, 2nd edn (Norwich, 1986), pp. 36–95; H. Chadwick, *Augustine* (Oxford, 1986), pp. 11–37; G. Watson, *Saint Augustine: Soliloquies and Immortality of the Soul* (Warminster, 1990), pp. 1–19.

[3] J.J. O'Meara, 'The Historicity of Augustine's Early Dialogues', in his *Studies in Augustine and Eriugena*, ed. T. Halton (Washington, DC, 1992), pp. 11–23; Silk, 'Boethius's Consolatio Philosophiae'; Crabbe, 'Literary Design', pp. 251–63; Chadwick, *Boethius*, pp. 249–52, cf. 220.

[4] Watson, *Soliloquies*, pp. 165–97; Bieler in *Cons. phil.*, pp. 112 and 116.

[5] Watson, *Soliloquies*, p. v.   [6] *Retractationes*, ed. Mutzenbecher, I.4, p. 14, lines 1–11.

[7] *Soliloquia* I.i.1–I.ii.7, pp. 3–11.   [8] *Cons. phil.* Ip6.18–19, pp. 15–16.

[9] *Ibid.* Vp4 and Vp5, pp. 96–9 and 100–1.

309

The entire text hinged on the unique abilities of intellectual perception. Only thus could *Augustinus* know the friendship of his friend Alypius, by perceiving his soul. 'God and the soul' were things perceived by the intellect, quite unlike the moon and one's dinner, perceived by sense.[10] Knowing God bore comparison with various geometrical truths, also perceived by the intellect.[11] Though as objects they differ greatly, both were known in the same way.[12]

This is the basis for Reason's ambitious promise: to reveal God as clearly to the mind of *Augustinus* as the sun appears to his eyes.[13] The analogy invoked divine illumination of Platonic forms, similarly exploited by Boethius.[14] Just as earthly things could only be seen in the sun's light, so the certain truths of disciplines such as geometry were illuminated by God. Both God and truths were intelligible, yet only God illuminates himself.[15] Such sense-perception required three things: a 'sense' (*sensus, oculi*), a 'looking' (*aspicere, aspectus*), and a 'seeing' (*uidere, uisio*). For the soul of *Augustinus* also, the *mens* must operate as its 'sense' or 'eye', with *ratio* as its 'looking', and *intellectus* as its 'seeing'.[16] Yet 'healthy eyes' require a mind cleansed of mortal desire, only attainable through faith, hope and love. Only love would be necessary in the perfection of virtue, yet in this life the soul will need faith and hope, to avoid deception by the senses and bodily temptation.[17]

Augustinus still fears pain, death and loss of loved ones; his 'eyes' remain diseased, though not without signs of progress.[18] Fourteen years earlier Cicero's *Hortensius* had taught him to reject desire for 'riches' (*diuitiae*); just recently he has come to abandon *honores*.[19] 'Nothing is to be fled more than copulation'; in the case of food, drink and other bodily pleasures he has sought only enough for health.[20] Yet questions remain of their relationship to wisdom. In the case of riches and honours *Augustinus* admits that he would continue to desire both, if they enabled others to engage in wise pursuit.[21] Yet this should not be called cupidity: Reason encourages the conclusion that he would abandon his friends, or even his life, if either were to hinder his goal.[22] Even pain, death and bereavement are only feared for threats to understanding: a positive sign of sapiential love.[23] Only through such unconditional commitment can

---

[10] *Soliloquia* I.iii.8, pp. 13–14.   [11] I.iv.9–10, pp. 15–18.   [12] I.v.11, pp. 18–19.
[13] I.vi.12–13, pp. 19–22.   [14] Silk, 'Boethius's Consolatio Philosophiae', p. 38, note 71.
[15] *Soliloquia* I.viii.15, pp. 23–4.
[16] 'Nam mentes quasi sui sunt sensus animis': *Soliloquia* I.vi.12, p. 19, lines 20–1; this variant supported by J. J. O'Meara, 'Augustine's View of Authority and Reason in A.D. 386', in his *Studies*, ed. Halton, pp. 140–5.
[17] *Soliloquia* I.vii.14, pp. 22–3.   [18] I.ix.16–I.x.17, pp. 24–8.   [19] I.x.17, p. 26, lines 6–14.
[20] I.x.7, p. 27, lines 5–7, and p. 28, lines 4–12.   [21] I.xi.18–19, pp. 28–30.
[22] I.xii.20, pp. 31–2.   [23] I.xii.20–1, pp. 31–3.

wisdom be enticed to reveal herself, as if a beautiful woman, naked and unveiled.[24] Yet her favours are withheld from all but the most devoted lovers. For each man embraces wisdom, as 'truest good' and 'light of minds', according to his health.[25] Some have eyes so healthy that they can turn to the sun; others have eyes which must be trained through objects of increasing brightness, until they may finally look towards the sun.[26] *Augustinus* begs to be trained in this way: Reason advises the abandonment of all sensible things as the only act lying within his power. Even then the beautiful doctor, wisdom, will only reveal herself to those whom she knows to be healthy.[27]

Book I ends with further treatment of truth, persisting even when true things pass away.[28] Because truth must exist somewhere, it can only exist in things which are immortal. 'Nothing is true in which truth does not exist'; if a thing is true it is necessarily immortal.[29] The connection between truth and immortality is central to Book II, in which Reason addresses the immortality of the soul, fundamental to self-knowledge. The investigation is both complex and tortuous, initially relying on the definition of a true thing as 'that which is as it appears to be'.[30] Because truth can never perish – for it would then be true that truth had perished – and because the perpetuity of truth necessitates the perpetuity of falsity, the soul too must live forever, in order to perceive things as true or false.[31] Yet these conditions would be satisfied by a continuous succession of mortal souls; the definition would also imply that objects lost both truth and existence when not perceived.[32] An analysis of deception, from reflections in a mirror to the refraction of an oar through water and identical twins, leads to two contradictory definitions of falsity, as product of either similitude or dissimilitude to the truth.[33] Not unreasonably, *Augustinus* insists on examining something which is clearly true.[34]

In claiming that every 'art' (*disciplina*) is necessarily true, Reason lays foundations for the proof that will shortly emerge.[35] In the art of grammar, even fables are true because they faithfully convey fictitious events as false.[36] Every art is true because all involve processes of definition, division and reasoning, by which each thing is accurately represented. As the study of such definition and reasoning, the art of dialectic (*disciplina disputationis*) is the art by which all the other arts are true; it may thus be regarded as 'true truth'.[37] Yet every art exists

---

[24] I.xiii.22, p. 34.   [25] I.xiii.23, pp. 35–6.   [26] I.xiv.24, pp. 36–7.   [27] I.xiv.25, pp. 37–8.
[28] I.xv.27–9, pp. 40–4.   [29] I.xv.29, p. 43, lines 7–13.   [30] Cf. II.v.8, pp. 55–6.
[31] II.ii.2, pp. 47–8; II.iii.4, pp. 51–2; II.iv.5, pp. 52–3.
[32] II.iv.5, pp. 52–3; II.v.7, pp. 54–5; II.v.8–II.vii.13, pp. 55–63.   [33] II.viii.15, pp. 63–5.
[34] II.ix.16–II.x.18, pp. 65–70.   [35] II.xi.19, pp. 70–1.   [36] II.xi.20, pp. 71–3.
[37] II.xi.21, pp. 73–4.

inseparably in its subject, the soul.[38] If a perpetual thing exists inseparably in a subject, it is necessary that the subject too lasts forever. Because
the art of dialectic is truth, and truth can never pass away, it follows that
the soul must be immortal. Numerous clarifications ensue, leading
Reason to substitute the forms of geometry as the inner source of
perpetual truth; but this remains the substance of Augustine's rational
demonstration.[39]

In his *Retractationes*, Augustine describes the *Soliloquia* as unfinished; the
text raises two issues which might have been resolved in a third book.
The first was a problem of ignorant souls, whose possession of the arts
would be less apparent.[40] Late in Book II Reason hints at a solution in
the Platonic notion of reminiscence; the same argument was pursued at
greater length in Augustine's *De inmortalitate animae*, written shortly
afterwards to record points which would have been included in Book
III.[41] A second problem was the fear that an immortal soul might still lose
its knowledge after death.[42] At the very end of Book II Reason promises
to remove this fear before addressing the problem of ignorant souls, yet
the former was not in fact considered in *De inmortalitate animae*.[43] The
same question was left unanswered in a further early work, *De quantitate
animae*.[44]

ROYAL TRANSLATION AND CAROLINGIAN EXPERTISE

Parallels with the *Consolatio* continue in the *Soliloquia*'s early medieval
reception. Though more equivocal, the evidence falls short of establishing full Insular access to Augustine's text in the pre-viking period.
The only manuscripts of Anglo-Saxon ownership date from the tenth
century; one, a Continental import, can firmly be dissociated from
Alfred's Latin exemplar.[45] As with Boethius' text, royal translation is the
earliest secure evidence for English availability. What remains are signs
of earlier familiarity with Augustine's work, possibly at one remove
from the text. Bede's versification of Psalm LI had invoked an interior
dialogue between the Psalmist and his mind. The text circulated as the

---

[38] II.xiii.24, pp. 78–9.   [39] II.xix.33, pp. 92–3.
[40] II.xiv.25, pp. 79–80; II.xiv.26, pp. 80–1; II.xix.33, pp. 92–3.
[41] II.xx.35, pp. 95–7. Cf. *Cons. phil.* IIIm 1 and IIIp12.1, p. 60; Watson, *Soliloquies*, p. 202.
De inmortalitate animae, ed. Hörmann, CSEL 89, 101–28.
[42] *Soliloquia* II.i.1, pp. 45–7.   [43] *Ibid.* II.xx.36, pp. 97–8.
[44] *De quantitate animae*, ed. Hörmann, CSEL 89, 131–231, at XXXVI.81, 230–1.
[45] Salisbury, Cathedral Library, MS 173 (written on the Continent, s. x²ᐟ², imported into England
shortly afterwards), with Gatch, 'Alfred's Version', p. 21 and note 21, pp. 40–1; cf. Brussels,
Bibliothèque Royale, MS 8558-63 (2498), fols. 1–79 (Gneuss, *Handlist*, no. 808; ?Southern
England or Mercia, s. x¹ᐟ²); I have study of the latter in hand.

Soliloquium Venerabilis Bedae Presbyteri; though original to Augustine, the term could also have been known from his *Retractationes*.[46] Certainly known in this period was Augustine's opening prayer.[47] An abbreviated version appears in the 'Royal' prayerbook, London, British Library, Royal 2. A. xx (Mercia, s. viii–ix), identified as a prayer of St Augustine.[48] A separate abbreviation, labelled 'Augustinus De Soliloquia' (*sic*), occurs in *De laude Dei*, a devotional florilegium attributed to Alcuin.[49] This compilation contains much of demonstrably Insular origin; Constantinescu has argued for its assembly by Alcuin while at York, perhaps in 790.[50] A Northumbrian origin is also suspected for material in the 'Royal' prayerbook, under strong Italian influence.[51] The two versions show few points of overlap, but need only imply a fuller version of the original prayer.

The context was not exclusive: Augustine's prayer exemplifies the high degree of Insular influence on Frankish devotional texts.[52] Alcuin himself quotes from the prayer to conclude his *De fide sanctae trinitatis et de incarnatione Christi libri tres* (802);[53] the first half of the 'Royal' version occurs almost verbatim in an early ninth-century prayerbook written in the vicinity of Salzburg.[54] Yet other examples suggest full access to Augustine's text. The complete prayer recurs in the *Officia per ferias*, once attributed to Alcuin, and a mid-ninth-century miscellany written in north-eastern Francia.[55] This rich tradition offers a possible context for royal interest, in the eclectic scope of private prayer. Fully attested in a single manuscript, the royal translation is only otherwise known from an abbreviated vernacular version of the opening prayer, in Cotton Tiberius A. iii, a compilation of the mid-eleventh century from Christ Church, Canterbury.[56] The text appears in a collection of confessional prayers, including a vernacular version of Alcuin's *Confessio*; the possibility of further Alfredian connections is a question worth posing.[57]

---

[46] Ed. Fraipont, CSEL 122, 447–8; *Soliloquia* II.vii.14, p. 63.   [47] *Soliloquia* I.i.2–6, pp. 4–11.

[48] Fols. 23r–24r, ptd in Kuypers, *The Prayer Book of Ædeluald the Bishop*, pp. 210–11.

[49] Bamberg, Staatsbibliothek, msc. Patr. 17/B. II. 10 (Mainz, s. xi^in), fol. 148r–v; cf. El Escorial, Real Biblioteca, MS B. IV. 17 (southern France, s. ix^3/4), transmitting *De laude Dei* on fols. 93–108.

[50] R. Constantinescu, 'Alcuin et les "Libelli Precum" de l'époque carolingienne', *Revue d'Histoire de la Spiritualité* 50 (1974), 17–56; D. A. Bullough, 'Alcuin and the Kingdom of Heaven: Liturgy, Theology, and the Carolingian Age', in his *Carolingian Renewal*, pp. 161–241, at 164–71; D. Ganz, 'Le *De Laude Dei* d'Alcuin', *Annales de Bretagne et des Pays de l'Ouest* 111 (2004), 387–91.

[51] T. H. Bestul, 'Continental Sources of Anglo-Saxon Devotional Writing', in *Sources of Anglo-Saxon Culture*, ed. P. E. Szarmach (Kalamazoo, MI, 1986), pp. 104–26, at 109–10.

[52] *Ibid.*, pp. 107–13.

[53] PL 101: 55C–56B; Bullough, 'Kingdom of Heaven', pp. 202–3.

[54] Orléans, Bibliothèque Municipale, MS 184 (161), ptd in PL 101: 1397D–1398A.

[55] *Officia per ferias*, PL 101: 580B–582D (cf. cols. 599D–600D); Laon, Bibliothèque Municipale, MS 113 (Hörmann in CSEL 89, xx).

[56] Ker, *Catalogue*, no. 186, item 9 (g).   [57] Esp. the confessional items 9(a)–(f), and (h)–(i).

The limited Insular evidence stands in contrast to the *Soliloquia*'s Continental circulation, richly attested in Carolingian witnesses. Hörmann's edition records thirteen manuscripts written before *c.* 900, with survivals from Spain and Italy, though the majority are Frankish.[58] The figure compares favourably with seventeen survivals for the *Consolatio*; wide dissemination receives support from Hörmann's inability to uncover clear lines of transmission.[59] This also restricts the possibility of identifying a precise origin for Alfred's exemplar. Royal readings do not seem especially close to O, an early tenth-century manuscript from St-Bertin.[60] The reversal of interlocutors' parts at the beginning of Book II matches manuscript J; but 'þe ic sece, þe yc folgige' follows a reading only in E.[61] 'Auge in me spem, auge caritatem' was shared with all manuscripts apart from H, Q and G; 'læd me þider þu wylle' followed 'Duc ... quo vis' only present in the main text of D, with correction also in Q, G and E.[62] Freedom of translation obscures any closer relationship to the tangled Latin tradition.

Though widely known, Augustine's text seems to have supplied only specialized uses in Carolingian learning. The *Soliloquia* matched many aspects of educational theory, but offered limited potential for practical instruction. Unlike the *Consolatio*, the dialogue never acquired status as a textbook, and received only occasional glossing in the manuscript record. Contemporary annotations to London, British Library, Add. 43460 (Northern Italy, s. viii[ex]) merely denote particular passages of interest with brief words of summary. Contemporary Old Irish and Latin glosses to Karlsruhe, Landesbibliothek, Aug. perg. CXCV (Soissons or Laon?, s.ix[med]) record the brief clarifications of an Irish reader willing to grapple with Book II.[63]

Ninth-century manuscripts are otherwise bare; citations indicate the text's principal value as a philosophical *tour de force*, in esoteric aspects of enquiry. Logic and Greek thought lay at the cutting edge of Carolingian theology; intensively focused in court arenas, the field defined the basis of Christian orthodoxy.[64] The *Soliloquia* found notable deployment in the 'Munich passages', a collection of philosophical material associated

---

[58] Hörmann in CSEL 89, xii–xxi.   [59] CSEL 89, xv–xvi and xxx–xxxi.
[60] St-Omer, Bibliothèque Municipale 267.
[61] *Solil* p. 83, lines 15–22; p. 54, lines 15–16. Cf. *Soliloquia* II.ii.1, p. 45, lines 2–8; I.i.5, p. 9, line 8.
[62] *Solil* p. 55, lines 10–11 (Jost's addition unnecessary); p. 81, lines 1–2. Cf. *Soliloquia* I.i.5, p. 10, lines 8–9; I.xv.27, p. 40, line 12.
[63] Ptd in Stokes and Strachan, *Thesaurus Palaeohibernicus* II, 1–7.
[64] J. Marenbon, *From the Circle of Alcuin to the School of Auxerre: Logic, Theology and Philosophy in the Early Middle Ages* (Cambridge, 1981); B. M. Kaczynski, *Greek in the Carolingian Age: the St Gall Manuscripts* (Cambridge, 1988); D. Ganz, 'Theology and the Organisation of Thought', in *NCMH* II, 758–85, showing the wider context of east–west debate.

with Alcuin and his circle at Charlemagne's court.[65] Such use followed a trend in the philosophical reading of Augustine.[66] The quest for knowledge of self and God also unites the 'Munich passages' as the reason for man's creation.[67] The *Soliloquia*'s value lay in the complex reasoning of Book II, supplying the argument that truth can never perish.[68] The entire passage addressed the question 'Can anything be true without truth?', inspired by Augustine's later arguments.[69] Reason had suggested in passing that, in accepting nothing to be true which was not made by truth, *Augustinus* was positing truth as a body.[70] The implication is detached by Augustinian logic; the passage's counter-argument hinges on the final claim of Book I, that true things must be immortal, which a body is not.[71]

Neo-Platonic theology intensified under 'ministerial' rulers, in heightened interaction with divine knowledge. Centre stage was the mystical theology of Pseudo-Dionysius, newly channelled to the west through courtly reception.[72] Initially translated into Latin by arch-chaplain Hilduin at the request of Louis the Pious, Pseudo-Dionysius received still greater focus at the court of Charles the Bald.[73] As vital mediator, Eriugena lay under direct royal patronage, addressing his improved translations to Charles himself.[74] The heights of Neo-Platonic speculative theology matched many aspects of Augustine's own, in the goal of ascent towards God through perfection of intelligence, a form of contemplative perception reliant on the action of spiritual vision.[75] To Neo-Platonic immateriality Pseudo-Dionysius added the Gnostic mystery of God's essential unknowability, the comprehension of which amounted to the supreme height of spiritual ecstasy.[76] The *Soliloquia* received direct attention, cited by Eriugena on a number of occasions, and at greatest length in one of his courtly texts on predestination, the *De divina praedestinatione liber* of 851.[77] Augustinian handling of truth is harnessed to counter Gottschalk's double predestination. Reliant on divine foreknowledge, only true things can be predestined; but true

---

[65] Edited by Marenbon, *Circle*, pp. 151–66, at 164–5 (item XI), cf. 3–55; authorship discussed by Bullough, 'Kingdom of Heaven', pp. 175–81.

[66] Marenbon, *Circle*, pp. 12–29, 50–5 and 140.

[67] Item IX ('PROPTER QUID HOMO FACTVS EST'): *ibid.*, pp. 163–4.

[68] *Soliloquia* II.ii.2, p. 48, lines 1–22. [69] Marenbon, *Circle*, p. 164, cf. 53.

[70] *Soliloquia* II.xviii.31, p. 89, lines 1–8. [71] *Ibid.* I.xv.29, p. 43, lines 10–13.

[72] J. J. O'Meara, *Eriugena* (Oxford, 1988), pp. 51–69; Marenbon, *Circle*, pp. 70–87.

[73] O'Meara, *Eriugena*, pp. 52–6; Wallace-Hadrill, *Frankish Church*, pp. 246–7 and 370–7; P. Godman, *Poets and Emperors* (Oxford, 1987), pp. 169–74.

[74] Staubach, *Rex Christianus*, pp. 41–104, esp. 86–90. [75] O'Meara, *Eriugena*, pp. 60–9.

[76] *Ibid.*, pp. 66–8; Marenbon, *Circle*, pp. 72–5.

[77] G. Madec, *Jean Scot et ses Auteurs* (Paris, 1988), p. 187.

things are made true by truth. There can be no predestination of sins, for as contraventions of nature, they do not exist through truth.[78]

Further texts pressed actively on spiritual vision. Eriugena's court poetry repeatedly pictured the king in special receipt of divine illumination.[79] An anonymous Rheimsian treatise addressed the soul and its substance as issues raised by Charles himself; its final chapter revealed the manner of spiritual sight after the general resurrection.[80] Hincmar too answered the needs of Charles's soul, offering hope through penitence of future divine vision.[81] Light itself was now a tool of sacerdotal admonition, decisively refracted by Eriugena's own depiction of the royal *ministerium*. Charles alone had been illuminated with wisdom's inner light, enabling divine contemplation in the midst of earthly affairs, as 'rex atque theologus' in a single self.[82] The same agenda has been detected by Staubach in key aspects of artistic production. The structure of the 'Cathedra Petri' reflected the ruler's ascent towards God; astronomical symbols on the throne's gable captured the visionary experience of divine revelation.[83] The near-contemporary Codex Aureus of 870 depicted Charles in just such ascent, wisely beholding the Lamb of God; poetic *tituli* emphasized the intensity of the royal gaze.[84]

Paramount in each case was Charles's just fulfilment of royal 'ministry', dominated by aspects of ecclesiastical duty. Pseudo-Dionysian thought situated man's ascent within an all-encompassing ecclesiastical hierarchy; its invocation drew force from Charles's special relationship with St-Denis, where he had been installed as lay abbot in 867.[85] As throne of wisdom, the 'Cathedra Petri' marked the extension of Charles's Solomonic rule; the Codex Aureus further enhanced claims of just protection for Charlemagne's church.[86] The Lamb of God may well

---

[78] *Iohannis Scotti De Divina Praedestinatione Liber*, ed. Madec, CCCM 50, c. 15, pp. 89–90, lines 103–14; c. 3, p. 19, lines 33–46. Cf. *Soliloquia* II.xvii.31, p. 89, lines 1–3; II.iv.5, p. 53, lines 5–6; II. vi.10, p. 57, lines 21–2; II.vi.12, p. 60, line 12; II.vi.11, p. 59, lines 18–21; II.viii.15, p. 63, line 21, to p. 64, line 6; II.xi.20, p. 71, line 18, to p. 72, line 10.

[79] Staubach, *Rex Christianus*, pp. 41–104.

[80] *De diversa et multiplici animae ratione*, c. 8 (PL 125: 943–8), once attributed to Hincmar (Staubach, *Rex Christianus*, p. 34 and note 62; Devisse, *Hincmar* I, 20–1).

[81] *De cavendis vitiis et virtutibus exercendis*, presented to Charles in 869, esp. cc. 4 and 7 (PL 125: 892D–895D and 911C–912B).

[82] *Iohannis Scotti Eriugenae Carmina*, ed. Herren, no. 10, pp. 96–7; Staubach, *Rex Christianus*, pp. 86–90, cf. 91–7.

[83] *Ibid.*, pp. 261–81, with plates 4–5 (fols. 5v–6r), cf. Apocalypse V. 12–14; *tituli* in MGH Poet. III, 252–3, no. IV (1) and (2); P. E. Dutton and E. Jeauneau, 'The Verses of the *Codex Aureus* of Saint-Emmeram', *Studi Medievali* 24 (1983), 75–120.

[84] Wallace-Hadrill, *Frankish Church*, pp. 246–7; Staubach, *Rex Christianus*, pp. 86–90; Nelson, *Charles the Bald*, pp. 113, 222, 235 and 253.

[86] Staubach, *Rex Christianus*, esp. pp. 261–7 and 303–7.

have recalled the interior of the dome at Aachen, briefly captured by Charles in 869.[87] The entire schema fitted royal ambitions at Compiègne, where Charles would soon build a royal chapel, as the next best location for 'imperial' prayer.[88] Both here and at St-Denis, devotion focused duties owed to the church at large, further projected by representations of the king in de luxe manuscripts and ceremonial artifacts.[89] At its heart was the power of Charles's own intensive gaze, in endless ascent towards spiritual enlightenment; the entire ecclesiastical order were effective participants in ineffable royal mystery.

ALFREDIAN ADAPTATION: WISDOM AND THE SIGHT OF GOD

The royal translation gains much from such parallel imagery. The soul and its knowledge, the centrality of inner vision and its place in broader questions of eschatology: all found intensive treatment as central aspects of wise kingship. Though dominated by Pseudo-Dionysius, Augustinian texts featured prominently for their philosophical content, including the *Soliloquia*. The ecstasy of Neo-Platonic vision combined with God's essential unknowability, only accessible through mystical contemplation of scripture and symbol. All these concerns offer a suggestive context for Alfredian treatment, extending to some fundamental aspects of departure. Though ostensibly 'completing' Augustine's text, 'Book III' greatly enhanced the significance of Last Things. As will be seen, the royal version restricted the extent of God's accessibility, tempering Augustine's heady vision. Any channels of communication remain problematic, with dangers in inferring direct influence from features of general similarity. The question is not aided by William of Malmesbury's story that Eriugena had migrated to England in Alfred's time; the claim applied wishful thinking to a certain 'Iohannes sophista', possibly John the Old Saxon.[90] Yet at least one study of Alfred's text has drawn plausible connections with Eriugenan theory, positing Grimbald or John as possible intermediary.[91]

Any correspondence was again selective: the presence of both scholars highlights the extent of departure from Augustine's dialectical reasoning, prominent in Carolingian theological expertise. As several commentators have observed, many passages of syllogistical argument are either curtailed

---

[87] *Ibid.*, p. 268.   [88] *Ibid.*, pp. 267–81; Nelson, *Charles the Bald*, pp. 235, 247–8 and 257.
[89] Staubach, *Rex Christianus*, pp. 75–86, 97–104 and 158–68.
[90] *GR* I, 190–3, with Thomson's commentary (II, 100–1).
[91] M. Treschow, 'Echoes of the Periphyseon in the Third Book of Alfred's Soliloquies', *Notes and Queries* 238 (1993), 281–6; cf. J. Ritzke-Rutherford, 'Anglo-Saxon Antecedents of the Middle English Mystics', in *The Medieval Mystical Tradition in England*, ed. M. Glasscoe (Exeter, 1980), pp. 216–33, at 216–26, less satisfactory on points of detail.

or omitted.[92] Goals to be demonstrated remained substantially the same, but supported by appeals to earthly analogy. Quite apart from the text's 'completion', only half of the *Soliloquia* is effectively translated; all in all, more than one third of the vernacular version bears no relationship at all to its Latin 'source'. Difficulties of comprehension cannot account for such radical revision.[93] The *Froferboc* suggests dialectical competence, fully rendering the highest good, and only departing substantially from Boethian logic when confronted with Book V.[94] Reason's appeal to geometry might conceivably have been problematic, but there is no reason to suspect inadequate understanding of the principal arguments in Book II.[95] More pressing are the mundane analogies that take their place, dominated by bonds and obligations of earthly lordship.[96] All were of aristocratic familiarity: telling details relate these images to Alfred's own role as lord, united by the household as the locus of personal experience.

Such argumentation must be seen against the relevance of Augustine's didactic goals, supremely focused on Neo-Platonic desire. The entire dialogue sought rational basis for sapiential pursuit; Book I was direct in identifying necessary conditions for exclusive love. Worldly goods supplied rival objects, entirely to be fled from; true desire lay only in wisdom, as a beautiful woman, uncontaminated by sensible love. The dichotomy was extended in translation, regularly dominating interlocutory exchange. The speakers themselves, *Gesceadwisnes* ('Reason') and *ic*, preserved the framework of Augustine's setting; their handling consistently replaced confrontational aspects of dialogue with gestures of friendly intimacy.[97] The desire for knowledge remained central throughout this relationship, reaching its climax in 'Book III', despite the *Soliloquia*'s abandonment. Wisdom itself received playful regulation: initially warned against desiring 'ofer gemet', the human speaker is later commended for exhibiting 'swiðe good gytsung'.[98] Such control ironically mirrored that of 'worldly desires' (*þisse worlde lustas*), as impediments to wise perception. Likening the 'mind's eyes' to anchors, fastened on God, *Gesceadwisnes* equates their acquisition with desires abandoned in the world.[99]

---

[92] Gatch, 'Alfred's Version', pp. 26–37; R. Waterhouse, 'Tone in Alfred's Version of Augustine's Soliloquies', in *Studies*, ed. Szarmach, pp. 47–85; Frantzen, *Alfred*, pp. 67–88; S.J. Hitch, 'Alfred's Cræft: Imagery in Alfred's Version of Augustine's Soliloquies', *Journal of the Department of English (Calcutta University)* 22 (1–2) (1986–7), 130–47; S.J. Hitch, 'Alfred's Reading of Augustine's Soliloquies', in *Sentences for Alan Ward*, ed. D.M. Reeks (Southampton, 1988), pp. 21–9.

[93] Cf. Gatch, 'Alfred's Version', esp. pp. 19–20, 30–1, 33–4 and 37.   [94] Cf. above, pp. 296–302.

[95] Cf. Gatch, 'Alfred's Version', pp. 33–4.

[96] Hitch, 'Alfred's Cræft'; Waterhouse, 'Tone', pp. 63–80.   [97] Waterhouse, 'Tone', pp. 47–63.

[98] *Solil* p. 56, line 23, to p. 57, line 5; p. 58, lines 13–14; p. 84, line 16. Cf. *Soliloquia* I.ii.7, p. 11, line 18, to p. 12, line 3; I.iii.8, p. 13, lines 6–9; II.i.1, p. 46, line 15 (cf. *VA* 78, lines 27–8).

[99] *Solil* p. 62, lines 14–17, perhaps loosely reflecting *Soliloquia* I.v.11, p. 18, line 21, to p. 19, line 4.

This wisdom was itself Solomonic, not incompatible with rightful possession; exposition extended to show the earthly necessity of exclusive love. To pursue God had become the 'creft ealra crefta', the highest gift of the human soul; now such inner needs received the force of royal analogy.[100] Man's understanding of God, the immortality of the soul, the nature of truth: all found courtly explanation in enquiry enacting many central principles of Alfredian discourse. The wisdom in question was again inclusive, distant from West Frankish theological elevation. Both setting and content solicited wider participation in wise perception, exemplified by the scope of experience attributed to its first-person speaker. Initially labelled 'Augustinus', his identity remains playfully ambiguous.[101] Though he rejects marriage as a priest, even this detail qualified the original Latin, implying celibacy for all wise men.[102] In appeal as in application, the soul's needs answered those of West Saxon royal lordship.[103]

These effects received pointed application for material advantages, far from rejected in wise restraint. *Augustinus* had upheld riches and honours, though only if necessary for wider sapiential pursuit; royal handling circumvented the qualification in appeal to earthly need.[104] For 'wela', the speaker's resolve was only against loving it 'too greatly' (*to swiðe*): 'Even if enough (*genoh*) came to me, I would not rejoice very greatly at this, nor enjoy it very immoderately, nor also would I gain more to keep than I could make moderate use of, and support and maintain the men whom I must assist; and the remainder I would strive to divide in as orderly manner as I could'.[105] The explanation expanded greatly on 'divitias ... sapientissime atque cautissime administrandas'; language and framework matched that of the *Froferboc*'s imagined king.[106] The priority returned in summation of advantages now restrained. Food, drink, baths, wealth, honour, or any 'worldly lusts': the speaker had desired

[100] *Solil* p. 69, lines 8–11. Cf. *Soliloquia* I.viii.15, p. 23, line 13, to p. 24, line 2; also I.vi.13, p. 21, lines 18–22 (*visio dei* as *perfecta virtus*). Cf. *CP* I, p. 24, lines 15–18: 'se cræft þæs lareowdomes bið cræft ealra cræfta'.
[101] Waterhouse, 'Tone', pp. 63–80. Cf. Godden, 'Player King', pp. 147–9, esp. 149.
[102] *Solil* p. 72, line 28. Cf. *Soliloquia* I.x.17, p. 27.
[103] Pratt, 'Authorship'; cf. Godden, 'Player King', pp. 146–9; Godden, *Misappropriation*, pp. 16–26.
[104] *Soliloquia* I.xi.18, p. 28, line 17, to p. 29, line 8.
[105] '[Þ]eah me genoh cume, ne fagnige ic hys na ful swiðe, ne hys ful ungemetlice ne bruce, ne æac maran getilige to haldænne þonne ic gemetlice bi beon mage, and þa men on gehabban and gehealdan þe ic forðian scel; and þæt þæt þær ofer byð ic hohgie swa ændebyrdlice gedelan swa ic ændebyrðlicost mæg': *Solil* p. 72, lines 14–18. Cf. *Soliloquia* I.x.17, p. 26: 'Nec aliud quicquam in his, si quo casu offerentur, praeter necessarium victum liberalemque usum cogitavi. Prorsus unus mihi Ciceronis liber facillime persuasit nullo modo adpetendas esse divitias, sed si provenerint, sapientissime atque cautissime administrandas'.
[106] Above, pp. 290–5.

none beyond bodily need, yet 'Ic beþearf ... micle maren to ðara manna þearfa ðe ic bewitan sceal – þæs æac ic wilnige and nede sceal'.[107] *Gesceadwisnes* declares *ic* to be 'in the right'; the only doubt concerns full eradication of 'your former avarice' (*seo þin ealde gytsung*).[108] As in the *Froferboc*, dangers are restricted solely to excess: 'too much wealth and too much honour, and immoderately sumptuous and luxurious living'.[109] Rather than wisdom, the suggested priority remains earthly friendship: the speaker admits he would accept such excesses 'if I cannot otherwise have their companionship (*heora geferædena*), though it would not please me very much to do so'.[110]

Only at this stage does exchange turn to the priority of wisdom, delicately posed against earthly friendship.[111] 'Geferræden', 'geferan': the bond bore implications of thegnly service. The dilemma was only heightened by earlier departures, where *Gesceadwisnes* had proposed need for 'a few learned and skilful men ... who would not hinder you in any way, but be supportive to your *cræft*'.[112] With suggestive irony, the speaker had claimed neither solitude nor help of other men, adding force to his initial insistence on retaining his friends, for the highest understanding of 'reason and wisdom'.[113] His final response is uncertain, coinciding with a lacuna in the text. As Frantzen notes, there are grounds for suspecting a reluctant dismissal of friends, if absolutely necessary for wise enquiry.[114] Yet such circumstances were now extreme, already dispelled by lordly necessity. Just a few pages later the speaker declares his love for 'all the world, each thing to the extent that I understand to be useful', before 'especially' (*huru*) things conducive to wisdom.[115] Again, for wisdom *Gesceadwisnes* advises despising 'worldly honours (*weorlde ara*) as much as you can', and 'especially immoderate and unlawful ones' (*huru ungemetlice and unalifedlice*): 'For I know that just as you are freer from the things of this world, so you will more clearly

---

[107] 'I need much more for the needs of those men that I must care for – this also I desire and must need': *Solil* p. 73, lines 15–16 (an unparalleled addition). Cf. *Soliloquia* I.x.17, p. 28, lines 9–12.

[108] *Solil* p. 73, lines 17–19. Cf. *Soliloquia* I.xi.18, p. 28, lines 13–17.

[109] ' ... ofermetta wela, and ofermytta wyrdscipe, and ungemetlice riclic and seftlic lyf': *Solil* p. 73, lines 23–4. Cf. *Soliloquia* I.xi.18, p. 28, line 17, to p. 29, line 7.

[110] *Solil* p. 74, lines 4–5. Cf. *Soliloquia* I.xi.19, p. 30, lines 9–17.

[111] *Solil* p. 74, lines 11–26. Cf. *Soliloquia* I.xii.20, p. 31, line 3, to p. 32, line 15.

[112] *Solil* p. 49, lines 17–21. Cf. *Soliloquia* I.i.1, p. 3, lines 11–13: 'Nec ista dictari debent; nam solitudinem meram desiderant'.

[113] ' ... ic nebbe nan þara, ne þone æmenne, ne oðera manna fultum, ne swa dygela stowe þæt me to swilcum weorce onhagie' ('I have none of these, neither the solitude, nor help of other men, nor so hidden a place as would be fitting to me for such work'): *Solil* p. 50, lines 1–3 (an unparalleled addition); p. 74, lines 24–5. Cf. *Soliloquia* I.i.1, p. 3, line 14; I.xii.20, p. 31, line 13; Lerer, *Literacy*, p. 83.

[114] Frantzen, *Alfred*, pp. 77–8; Carnicelli in *Solil*, pp. 74–5.

[115] *Solil* p. 76, lines 14–17. Cf. *Soliloquia* I.xiii.22, p. 34, lines 11–14.

understand about the wisdom that you desire'.[116] Even then the speaker
doubts whether he could reach sufficient understanding that 'þisse
weirulde ara' would cease to please him entirely.[117]

The position recalls that of 'middle men' in the *Froferboc*'s cartwheel,
specially vulnerable through worldly responsibility.[118] In dispelling such
doubt, *Gesceadwisnes* ironically protests to have been answered unreasonably; her solution provides a context for further adaptation. Though
the sun's light remains only partially visible, there is no reason for despair:

Þæt ne mæg furðum þam æallra halestum æagum gebyrrian þæt hy heonon of
þisse weurlde magen þa sunnan sylfe geseon. Be ðam þu miht geþencan þæt þu
ne scalt nanwiht seofian þeaht þu ne mage þone wisdom myd þines modes
eagum nacodne geseon swiclne swilce he ys. forðam þu næfre þæt ne myhð ða
hwile þu byst on ðam þeosðrum þinra sinna.[119]

Wisdom can never be seen entirely by any worldly observer; qualifying
Reason's outlook, the position was upheld throughout the royal version, with profound effects on its internal rhetoric. The intervention
mirrored Augustine's own dissatisfaction with the *Soliloquia*, later dis-
tancing himself from any notion that, in this life, the soul might be
blessed with the understanding of God.[120] This is likely to have been
known: the relevant section of the *Retractationes* regularly served as a
preface in Latin manuscripts.[121] A phrase in Asser's *Life* suggests the
additional availability of *De quantitate animae*, frequently transmitted
with the *Soliloquia*.[122] Conventionally, beatific vision could never be
attained on earth, but only after resurrection and final judgement. Neo-
Platonic confidence threatened Christian revelation; similar tensions had
been reconciled in Pseudo-Dionysian vision.

Limits of knowledge, with ascent through contemplation: royal
revision suggests contact with West Frankish mysticism. The immediate
source can be securely identified as Augustine's *De uidendo Deo*, twice

---

[116] 'Forðam ic wat, swa swa ðu freora byst þissa weorlde þinga, swa ðu sweotolor ongyst be ðam
wisdome þe ðu wilnast': *Solil* p. 78, line 29, to p. 79, line 8, esp. lines 3–4 (an unparalleled
addition). Cf. *Soliloquia* I.xiv.24, p. 37, lines 4–6: 'penitus esse ista sensibilia fugienda
cavendumque magnopere, dum hoc corpus agimus'.
[117] *Solil* p. 79, lines 9–12. Cf. *Soliloquia* I.xiv.24, p. 37, lines 14–16.   [118] Above, pp. 299–301.
[119] 'It cannot happen, even to the most sound eyes of all, that they can see the sun itself from here
in this world. From this you can learn that you must not sigh, although you cannot see wisdom
naked, just as he is, with the eyes of your mind, for you can never do that while you are in the
darkness of your sins': *Solil* p. 79, lines 17–22 (an unparalleled addition). Cf. *Soliloquia* I.xiv.25,
p. 37, line 17, to p. 38, line 3.
[120] *Retractationes*, ed. Mutzenbecher, I.5, p. 14, lines 29–30. Cf. *Soliloquia* I.vii.14, p. 22, lines 5–6
and 13–14; p. 22, line 18, to p. 23, line 3.
[121] Hörmann in CSEL 89, xii–xx; manuscripts T and D add 'hoc reprehendit' at I.vii.14, p. 23, line 1.
[122] Lapidge, 'Asser's Reading', p. 37 and note 48.

mentioned by *Gesceadwisnes* towards the end of Book II.[123] Known and used in early Northumbria, the text is unattested in manuscripts of early English provenance.[124] Though it was not cited by Eriugena, several of its key references appear in the Rheimsian treatise addressed to Charles the Bald, preceding recourse to still later Augustinian discussion in the final book of *De civitate Dei*.[125] Written in 413, *De uidendo Deo* was Augustine's fullest statement on man's sight of God.[126] Rigorously dependent on scriptural authority, his approach drew a vital distinction between 'seeing' for oneself and 'believing' secondary testimony; his argument extended the implications of I Corinthians XIII. 12, 'we see now through a glass darkly (*per speculum in enigmate*), then face to face'.[127] 'Deum nemo vidit umquam' (John I. 18 and I John IV. 12): no human had ever seen God in his fullness, whether by bodily or mental eyes; even the Patriarchs, Prophets and Apostles saw only aspects of God.[128] Yet according to Matthew V. 8, 'beati mundo corde quoniam ipsi videbunt Deum', and I John III. 2, 'scimus quoniam cum apparuerit similes ei erimus quoniam videbimus sicuti est'.[129] Full vision was reserved for the 'clean of heart' after final judgement; God would then be seen 'as he is', either by the mind itself or by physical eyes of the resurrected spiritual body.[130]

Usually considered only in relation to 'Book III', *De uidendo Deo* informed the text in its entirety, regularly shaping wisdom in Books I and II; its impact extended to concluding chapters of the *Froferboc*, sharpening the gap between reason and divine intelligence.[131] Finely observed in an unpublished dissertation by Richard Evert, the point has frequently been missed; from the outset, wisdom's full accessibility on earth had been denied.[132] As in the source-text, *Gesceadwisnes* promised

[123] *Solil* p. 92, lines 3–12.
[124] Bede, *In Epistolas VII Catholicas*, ed. Hurst, CCSL 121, 301–2, on I John III. 2; prefatory letter by Acca to Bede's *In Lucae evangelium expositio*, ed. Hurst, CCSL 120, 5–6. Cf. Goldbacher in CSEL 44, 274.
[125] Madec, *Jean Scot*, p. 185; *De diversa et multiplici animae ratione*, c. 8 (PL 125: 943–4), citing Exodus XXXIII. 20, Matthew V. 8, John XIV. 21 and 23, I Corinthians XIII. 12, cf. esp. col. 944A: 'Sed haec visio ... multu quaesitu investigatum est, et a sanctis Patribus res tanta, eo quod sit obscurissima, maxima disputatione pulsata'.
[126] Ed. Goldbacher, CSEL 44, no. CXLVII, 274–331.
[127] *De uidendo Deo*, ed. Goldbacher, cc. 1–12, pp. 274–85, esp. c. 12, p. 285.
[128] *Ibid.*, cc. 13–21, pp. 285–95; cc. 18–20 and 29–36, pp. 289–94 and 303–10.
[129] 'Blessed are the clean of heart, for they shall see God'. 'We know that, when he shall appear, we shall be like him, because we shall see him as he is'.
[130] *De uidendo Deo*, cc. 22–8, pp. 295–303; c. 37, pp. 310–12; cc. 46–54, pp. 320–31.
[131] *Bo* XLI.iv, p. 145, line 5, to XLII, p. 147, line 17; XLI.iv, p. 145, lines 10–13. Cf. *Cons. phil.* Vp4.24, p. 97, to Vp6.1, p. 102; Vp4.24, p. 97.
[132] R. L. Evert, 'The Limits of Human Knowledge: King Alfred and Old English Poetry' (unpubl. PhD dissertation, State University of Oregon, 1976), pp. 95–153, cf. 154–220. Cf. Carnicelli

an ability to see God 'with the eyes of your mind as clearly as you now see the sun with the eyes of the body'; but discussion was qualified.[133] He who looks towards the sun cannot see it 'entirely as it is'; so also in the case of God 'me þincð swiðe dysi man þe wilnat þæt we hine eallunga ongytan swilcene swilc he is, þa hwile þe we on þysse worlde beoð'.[134] Desire must be tempered towards the 'eternal and almighty sun': 'he acts very foolishly if he wishes to comprehend it entirely while he is in this world'.[135]

The tension is encapsulated by imagined physical love, formerly assigned to *sapientia*. Playfully implementing the masculine gender of *wisdom*, the vernacular briefly evokes his stroking and kissing at the hands of another man. Far from sexual love, as Frantzen has observed, the imagery exploits the chasteness of this intimate contact.[136] Latin *sapientia* had been willing to reveal herself, if only to her 'most few and favoured lovers'.[137] Though men may desire to see *wisdom* 'fully naked', 'he will very seldom show himself so openly to any man'.[138] Only a 'limb' may now be bared, 'to very few men'.[139] As *Gesceadwisnes* confirms, the speaker can never see wisdom so bare in this present life, 'though I may teach it to you, and though you may desire it'.[140]

This was the context for royal 'completion'.[141] At the end of Book II, the speaker raises the problem of knowledge after death, replicating the Latin text's final exchanges.[142] *Gesceadwisnes* twice recommends recourse to 'the book that we call *De uidendo Deo*', but the speaker is unable to pursue this; prior to a further lacuna, he appears to request some form of summary.[143] The suggestion is neither ill-informed nor misleading: future knowledge receives much attention in the latter part

---

in *Solil*, pp. 28, 100–1 and 103–7; Whitelock, 'Prose', pp. 87–8; Gatch, 'Alfred's Version', pp. 35–7; Frantzen, *Alfred*, pp. 70–1; Godden, *Misappropriation*, pp. 19–26.

[133] *Solil* p. 64, lines 6–8. Cf. *Soliloquia* I.vi.12, p. 19, lines 18–21.

[134] '[H]e seems to me to be a very foolish man who desires that we understand him entirely as he is while we are in this world': *Solil* p. 69, lines 26–8 (an unparalleled addition). Cf. *Soliloquia* I.viii.15, p. 24, lines 3–6.

[135] *Solil* p. 70, lines 3–5.

[136] *Ibid.* p. 75, lines 20–2; A. J. Frantzen, *Before the Closet* (Chicago, IL, 1998), pp. 99–104; Waterhouse, 'Tone', pp. 68–71.

[137] *Soliloquia* I.xiii.22, p. 34, lines 1–5. [138] *Solil* p. 75, line 22, to p. 76, line 1.

[139] 'On ðam timum þe he ænig lim swa bær eowian wile, þonne eowað he hyt swiðe feawum mannum' ('At those times when he wishes to show any limb so bare, he shows it to very few men'): *ibid.* p. 76, lines 1–2.

[140] *Ibid.* p. 76, lines 26–30 (a further addition). Cf. *Soliloquia* I.xiii.23, p. 35, lines 1–3.

[141] Evert, 'Limits of Knowledge', esp. pp. 142–4.

[142] *Solil* p. 91, line 24, to p. 92, line 2. Cf. *Soliloquia* II.xx.36, p. 98, lines 4–12.

[143] *Solil* p. 92, lines 3–12 and 14–21; for this exchange, cf. Alcuin, *De animae ratione*, c. 13 (PL 101: 645C, listing other Augustinian texts not to hand; (cf. above, p. 188, note 49).

of *De uidendo Deo*, as the culmination of biblical prophecy.[144] God's sons will see their father 'as he is': such vision is consistently assigned to God's future 'kingdom', postdating final judgement.[145] A single quotation in 'Book III' belies the text's deeper impact on royal reasoning, in tandem with other reading.[146] Earthly limits are recapitulated: a mind burdened by the body cannot see anything in this world 'eallunga swa swa hyt is'; both sun and moon suffer visible distortion.[147] Yet 'from the part which we see of it, we ought to believe the part which we cannot see'.[148] When the soul leaves the body, 'we will know everything that we now desire to know', ironically exceeding even that of 'those ancient men (*þa ealdan men*), the wisest of all in this world'.[149] The claim is implicitly scriptural, harnessing central references from *De uidendo Deo*: 'and efter domes dæge us ys gehaten þæt we moten god geseon openlice, ealne geseo swylce swylce he ys (cf. I John III. 2), and hyne a syððan cunnan swa georne swa he nu us can (cf. I Corinthians XIII. 12)'.[150]

Denied to the soul on earth, only then would wisdom be fully revealed: the effect of 'completion' was twofold, adding quite different, structural unity. All would one day be known, 'all that we now wish to know, and also that which we do not now wish to know'.[151] The scope of such knowledge had special relevance in an apocalyptic vision of God's future kingdom. The section has largely defied secure identification of 'sources': strong suggestions include Gregory's *Dialogues*, his homily on Luke XVI. 19–31, and the *Prognosticum futuri sæculi* of Julian of Toledo, yet each remains distant from royal deployment.[152] Departure is marked in the case of evil men, also accorded sight of God; as

---

[144] *De uidendo Deo*, ed. Goldbacher, cc. 22–8, 37, 46, 48–54, pp. 295–303, 310–12, 320–2 and 323–31. Cf. Gatch, 'Alfred's Version', pp. 35–7; Godden, *Misappropriation*, pp. 20–6; and esp. M. Godden, 'Text and Eschatology in Book III of the Old English *Soliloquies*', *Anglia* 121 (2003), 177–209, at 179–81 and 187–8 (cf. 201–2), whose proposed reordering of the dislocated sections of 'Book III' is thus unconvincing (see below, p. 328, note 185).

[145] *De uidendo Deo*, ed. Goldbacher, c. 26, p. 299, lines 20–1, c. 28, p. 302, line 16 ('tunc'), cf. c. 23, p. 297, lines 23–4; Gatch, 'Alfred's Version', p. 36, for this distinction in 'Book III'.

[146] *Solil* p. 97, lines 3–13; *De uidendo Deo*, ed. Goldbacher, c. 5, pp. 278–9.

[147] *Solil* p. 92, line 22, to p. 93, line 13.

[148] *Ibid.* p. 93, lines 13–14. Cf. *De uidendo Deo*, ed. Goldbacher, cc. 6–11, pp. 280–5.

[149] *Solil* p. 93, lines 14–18.

[150] 'And after judgement day it is promised to us that we may see God openly, to see him entirely, just as he is, and know him ever afterwards as fully as he now knows us': *Solil* p. 93, lines 18–21. I John III. 2 quoted throughout *De uidendo Deo*; I Corinthians XIII. 12 in c. 51, p. 327, lines 8–14, and p. 328, lines 9–10. Cf. Evert, 'Limits of Knowledge', pp. 146–8.

[151] 'Ac we witon ðonne eall þæt we nu wilniað to witanne, ge æac þæt þæt we nu na ne wilniað to witanne': *Solil* p. 93, lines 21–3.

[152] Carnicelli's notes (pp. 104–6) to *Solil* p. 93, line 18, to p. 95, line 1, unsatisfactory in some respects; Gatch, 'Alfred's Version', pp. 35–7; for Julian's work, cf. Godden, 'Eschatology', pp. 192–204.

Treschow has suggested, the claim may betray knowledge of Eriugena's apocalyptical schema, permitting vision of God's glory to the evil as inverted punishment.[153] Yet Eriugena had invoked the temple of Jerusalem. In royal hands the image was that of a 'guilty man ... condemned before some king': 'when he sees him and his dear ones (*deorlingas*), then his torment seems greater to him'.[154] Alfredian afterlife mirrored that of an earthly royal community, ordered on merit with full visibility.[155] The analogy continued with the example of 'men who are here brought into the prison (*carcern*) of some king, and can see their friends each day, and ask of them what they wish, and the friends can nonetheless be of no use to them'.[156] The predicament was that of evil men before final judgement, able to recall and observe their friends living in the world, but lacking potential aid.[157] The issue in question was now postmortem recollection, raised in the *Soliloquia* and unanswered in *De uidendo Deo*.[158] Its solution coincided with the final departure of *Gesceadwisnes*, in favour of the human speaker alone, answering 'his own thoughts', fully monopolizing internal dialogue.[159]

Full wisdom awaited God's kingdom: its restriction only enhanced the value of wise engagement. Augustine's wisdom had lain open to her 'most few and favoured lovers'; *Gesceadwisnes* conversely offered hope to all seeking wisdom, regardless of limits in perception. 'Look now, I think that no man is so foolish that he therefore becomes sad, though he cannot see and perceive the sun ... entirely as it is; but each man rejoices in whatever he can in the least understand, according to the measure of his

---

[153] Treschow, 'Echoes', responding to D. P. Wallace, 'King Alfred's Version of St Augustine's Soliloquies, III.23–6, The Vision of the Damned', *Notes and Queries* 235 (1990), 141–3 (cf. Godden, 'Eschatology', pp. 202–4); Eriugena, *Periphyseon* V.36, PL 122: 960B–984B, at 963D–964A and 967C–D (cf. 961D–962C, heavily dependent on the *Soliloquia*). As Treschow acknowledges, Eriugena himself was careful to distinguish God's glory or light from his nature, by definition unknowable.

[154] 'Ealle we geseoð god, ge þa þe her wyrste beoð, ge þa þe her beste beoð ... Ða yfelan geseoð god swa swa se scyldiga man þe byð wið sumne king forweorht; and he gesyhð hine and hys deorlingas, þonne þincð hym hys wite þe mare': *Solil* p. 93, line 23, to p. 94, line 4. Cf. *De uidendo Deo*, ed. Goldbacher, cc. 23–5 and 28, pp. 297–9 and 302–3, preserving vision for the 'clean of heart' alone.

[155] Treschow, 'Echoes', pp. 284–5. Cf. Alfred's will in *SEHD*, no. 11, p. 18, lines 21–3, and p. 19, lines 26–7, implying intercession for departed 'friends'.

[156] 'Ac hym byð þonne swa swa þam mannum þe her beoð on sumes kincges carcerne gebrohte, and magon geseon ælc dæge heora freond and geahsian be heom þæt þæt hy willað, and ne magon heom þeah na nane gode ne beon': *Solil* p. 96, lines 8–11.

[157] Corresponding with the implications of *Af* 1.1–1.6, cf. *II Æthelstan* 1.3–1.4 and 7.

[158] *Soliloquia* II.xx.36, pp. 97–8; cf. above, p. 312.

[159] *Solil* p. 95, line 4, to p. 97, line 16. This shift well observed by Waterhouse, 'Tone', pp. 48 and 81, note 5 (cf. K&L, *Alfred*, p. 150, assigning the speech to 'Reason'). Cf. Godden's questionable emendation of this passage ('Eschatology', pp. 185–7, cf. 201–2), otherwise an obstacle to his proposed revisions (cf. below, p. 328, note 185).

understanding'.[160] The same point emerged from wisdom's earthly clothing: even those with the sharpest eyes cannot see the sun 'as it is', yet no man has eyes so weak that he cannot still 'live by the sun, and make use of it', unless he be totally blind.[161] The view returned at the highest moment of doubt, in the speaker's reasoned attachment to 'þisse weirulde ara'.[162] Wisdom's veil offered hope, not despair; the speaker should rejoice in this earthly viewpoint. '[N]ota þæs wisdomes þe þu habbæ, and fagene ðæs dæles þe þu ongitan magæ, and higa georne æfter maran': wisdom alone will judge the manner and extent of his revelation.[163]

The solution was itself anticipated in courtly example. 'Sed non ad eam una via pervenitur': in royal hands, access to wisdom mirrored that to an earthly king, sought by many routes at many locations.[164] Similar effects had accompanied Solomon's own wise reputation; the court itself now fused with wisdom's biblical dwelling.[165] 'The king's "home" wherever he is in residence (*on tune*), or his assembly (*gemot*), or his army (*fird*)': every detail matched the scope of West Saxon itinerancy.[166] Despite journeys long and short, easy or difficult, all came to the same lord; wisdom himself shared this framework of pervasive love.[167] In his household also, hierarchies of honour and familiarity are respected, just as at every king's 'home' men are divided between the royal chamber (*bur*) and main hall, the threshing-floor and prison (*carcern*); 'yet all live by the favour of one lord (*be anes hlafordes are*), just as all men live under one sun and by its light see what they see'.[168] Such were the limits of wisdom's disclosure: whether near or far from intimate royal contact, all can recognize the benefits of his nourishing lordship. The message returned in the text's final words, from the mouth of its solitary speaker, attributing folly and wretchedness to the man 'who will not increase his understanding while he is in this world, and will not always wish and desire that he may come to the eternal life, where nothing shall be

---

[160] '[H]wæt, ic wene þæt nan man ne si to þam dysig þæt he forði unrotsige þeah he ne mage þas sunnan … eallunga geseon and ongytan swilce swilce heo is. Ac ælc fagnað þæs þe læste he ongytan mæg by hys andgytes mæðe': *Solil* p. 69, line 28, to p. 70, line 3 (an unparalleled addition). Cf. *Soliloquia* I.viii.15, p. 24, lines 3–6. 'By hys andgytes mæðe' relating to *Bo* XLI.iv, p. 145, lines 5–10. Cf. *Cons. phil.* Vp4.24, p. 97.

[161] *Solil* p. 76, line 30, to p. 77, line 4 (an unparalleled addition). Cf. *Soliloquia* I.xiii.23, p. 35, lines 1–3.

[162] Above, pp. 320–1; *Solil* p. 79, lines 9–12. Cf. *Soliloquia* I.xiv.24, p. 37, lines 14–16.

[163] '[E]njoy the wisdom that you have, and rejoice in the part that you can understand, and strive eagerly after more': *Solil* p. 79, lines 22–4 (an unparalleled addition). Cf. *Soliloquia* I.xiv.25, p. 37, line 17, to p. 38, line 3.

[164] *Soliloquia* I.xiii.22, p. 35, line 3; Waterhouse, 'Tone', pp. 73–4.

[165] III Kings IV. 34 and X. 34. Proverbs IX. 1, cf. Alcuin, *Disputatio de vera philosophia*, PL 101: 853B–D; Prudentius, *Psychomachia*, ed. Thomson I, 340–1, lines 868–87.

[166] *Solil* p. 77, lines 5–7; cf. above, pp. 34–8.   [167] *Ibid.* p. 77, lines 7–15.

[168] *Ibid.* p. 77, line 15, to p. 78, line 2, esp. p. 77, line 19, to p. 78, line 2.

hidden from us'.[169] Its tone echoed final lines of vindication in the *Froferboc*; the entire text showed facility of pursuit to men in full possession of 'worldly honours', enhanced by courtly appeal.[170]

In argumentation also, *De uidendo Deo* supplied the central force of royal rhetoric.[171] From the outset, extremities of dialectic were avoided; in each of the three books, goals found support from alternative appeals to authoritative testimony, related to Augustine's mature distinction between 'seeing' and 'believing'.[172] Recourse to scripture in *De uidendo Deo* was the necessary consequence of God's limited accessibility; that men would ultimately see God was a matter which could not be 'seen', but rightly 'believed'.[173] The distinction obtained between seeing an object through the body, or mental awareness of one's will or memory, and belief in matters open to neither sensation, such as Adam's creation or Christ's birth.[174] Other examples were Rome's foundation and parental descent: even beyond scripture, man willingly accepts many facts known only from testimony.[175] When we see, we are our own witnesses, but when we believe, 'we are led to our assent (*ad fidem*) by other witnesses ... when signs are given by voices or by written words or by whatever proofs, so that, when these are seen, unseen things are believed'.[176]

In royal hands, the distinction supplied positive support for faith in divine authority. The one direct quotation from *De uidendo Deo* summarized the truthfulness of testimonies accepted throughout discussion. The speaker's choice was stark: 'Must I not necessarily do one of two things: either believe some men, or none at all?'.[177] He had not seen the construction of Rome for himself, nor did he know the identity of his father and mother, except *be gesegenum* ('by report').[178] 'Yet not so truthful men told it to me as there were who related those things which we have sought for so long, and yet I believe it'.[179] The effect was not far from I John V. 9, 'si testimonium hominum accipimus, testimonium Dei maius est'; Augustine's examples here fused with Gregorian

---

[169] *Ibid.* p. 97, lines 14–16.   [170] *Bo* XLII, p. 149, lines 7–9. Cf. *Cons. phil.* Vp6.48, p. 106.
[171] Briefly implied by Carnicelli in *Solil*, pp. 103, 105 and 107, the connection has also generally been missed.
[172] *De uidendo Deo*, ed. Goldbacher, cc. 3–11, pp. 267–85.   [173] *Ibid.*, c. 3, pp. 276–7.
[174] *Ibid.*, c. 6, p. 280, lines 4–13; cf. c. 4, p. 278.   [175] *Ibid.*, c. 5, pp. 278–9.
[176] *Ibid.*, c. 8, p. 281, line 27, to p. 282, line 3.   [177] *Solil* p. 97, lines 4–5.
[178] *Ibid.* p. 97, lines 5–11. Cf. *De uidendo Deo*, c. 5, p. 278, line 21, to p. 279, line 11; example of Rome also used by Alcuin, *De animae ratione*, cc. 7–8 (PL 101: 642).
[179] *Solil* p. 97, pp. 11–13.

argument from the *Dialogues*, encountered in a similar context at the start of Book IV.[180] Some men doubt the existence of unseen things, because they do not know them *þurh cunnunge and afandunge* ('trial and experience'), yet a boy born in prison would doubt the existence of the sun, moon and stars: there can be no choice but to place *geleafa and treowa* ('faith and trust') in the teachings of wiser men.[181] Not even an *ungeleafful man* lives *butan geleafan*: though witnessing neither his conception nor birth, he can still identify his father and mother.[182] Impact again extended to the *Froferboc*, in *Wisdom*'s final picture of human transience: 'we know very little of what was before us except from memory and enquiries (*be gemynde and be geæscum*), and still less of what will be after us'.[183]

Each example hinged on facts known only indirectly, yet accepted as incontrovertible; Augustine's quotation was but the climax of rhapsodic royal argument. Earlier in 'Book III', the speaker had applauded *Gesceadwisnes* for showing 'such true testimony (*swa ungelygena gewittnesse*) that I can do nothing else but believe it: for, if I do not believe weaker testimony (*nanre wacran gewitnesse*), then I know very little or nothing at all'.[184] Testimony in question included I John III. 2 and I Corinthians XIII. 12, echoed a few lines before, and 'holy books' which the speaker himself had consulted; the gesture concerned still earlier passages of authoritative demonstration.[185]

The first replaced Reason's comparison with geometrical truth, on the status of divine knowledge; royal setting added explicit preconditions of worldly restraint.[186] 'How can I abandon that which I know and am familiar with and have been accustomed to from childhood, and love that which is unfamiliar to me except *be gesegenum*?'.[187] Gregorian echo now gave heightened grounds for Solomonic dilemma; its resolution harnessed the full intensity of projected analogy. 'Ðines hlafordes ærendgewrit and hys insegel', 'se wela þe he ðe er forgeaf toeacan hys freondscype': familiar tools of royal lordship, their deployment matched Alfred's own in courtly communication.[188] The former implied message

---

[180] 'If we receive the testimony of men, the testimony of God is greater'. Cf. frequent royal allusion to I John III. 2 ('seeing God as he is'); and *Solil* p. 63, lines 25–9 (cf. I John II. 3).
[181] GD IV.1, I, 260, line 21, to p. 261, line 2, and p. 261, line 9, to p. 262, line 9. Cf. *Grégoire le Grand: Dialogues*, ed. de Vogüé, IV.1, lines 18–21 and 22–45, III, 18–20 and 20–2.
[182] GD IV.2, I, p. 262, lines 14–24. Cf. *Dialogi* IV.2, lines 1–10, III, 22.
[183] *Bo* XLII, p. 148, lines 8–10. Cf. *Cons. phil.* Vp6.1–14, pp. 102–3, esp. Vp6.5.
[184] 'Forðam, gyf ic nanre wacran gewitnesse ne gelyfe, þonne wat ic swiðe lytel, oððe nanwiht': *Solil* p. 94, lines 24–5.
[185] *Ibid.* p. 94, lines 18–24; p. 93, lines 18–23. Cf. Carnicelli's confusion (pp. 105–6), missing these allusions; now continued by Godden, 'Eschatology', pp. 179–80, whose proposed reordering of passages in 'Book III' accordingly lacks support.
[186] *Solil* p. 62, line 14, to p. 64, line 3, esp. p. 62, lines 14–17. Cf. *Soliloquia* I.iv.9–I.v.11, pp. 15–19.
[187] *Solil* p. 62, lines 18–19.   [188] *Ibid.* p. 62, lines 22–7.

by written letter, repeatedly attested in Alfredian contexts; later usage suggests reference to a sealed document.[189] Received at a distance, the contact was indirect, yet *Gesceadwisnes* asks in astonishment 'whether you could not understand him by that, nor could know his will by it'.[190] As heightened demonstration of accepted testimony, the passage exemplifies Alfred's own presence in texts of royal authorship.[191] Resolution hinged on such projected loyalty. The speaker's choice between his lord's 'will' and 'wealth' mirrored Solomon's own; his answers showed the full value of distant recognition.[192] In abandoning the gift and following the giver, he traced his lord's courtly presence as 'steward (*stiward*) both of the wealth and of his friendship – unless I can have both'.[193] That outcome was not unlikely, as later discussion would reveal; yet even these gifts were ultimately 'lent', soliciting still greater love for the 'eternal lord' as grantor of all: 'ge ðas worldhlafordes freondscype ge his agene, and æce lyf æfter þise worulde'.[194]

The argument returned in Book II, on the soul's immortality. Where Reason pursued the perpetuity of truth, *Gesceadwisnes* urged faith in 'holy books', 'very nearly full' with this pressing subject.[195] Though no man can know for certain 'in the prison of this present life', many have earned the ability to understand it more clearly, including 'the holy fathers'; the analogous communication was now oral, not written, heightening the centrality of reliable detail.[196] The lordship itself was explicitly twofold, beyond the speaker's own service, incorporating parallel bonds between lord and *esne*, 'slave' or 'bonded labourer'.[197] The projected testimony matched that of Rome and parenthood as a 'message' (*spel*) which the speaker had never heard before, or report of something he had not himself seen. The speaker's response shows exemplary 'good faith' (*gooda treowa*): 'There is no message so unbelievable

[189] Cf. above, pp. 55, 122 and 212. *VA* 79, lines 36–9; cf. two written lists, presented to Asser with the monasteries of Congresbury and Banwell, described as 'epistolae' (*ibid.* 81, lines 15–27); Keynes, 'Fonthill Letter', pp. 88–9. Harmer, *Writs*, pp. 10–13, cf. 1–10; Keynes, 'Royal Government', pp. 244–8; Lerer, *Literacy*, pp. 84–7, noting the context of distant communication.
[190] '[G]eþenc ny gyf ðines hlafordes ærendgewrit and hys insegel to ðe cymð, hwæðer þu mæge cweðan þæt ðu hine ðe ðam ongytan ne mæge, ne hys willan þæron gecnawan ne mæge': *Solil* p. 62, lines 22–5. For the appeal to writing, cf. *De uidendo Deo*, c. 3, p. 276, line 18, to p. 277, line 3; c. 8, p. 281, line 27, to p. 282, line 3; this regal context remarkably paralleled in Paulinus of Aquileia, *Liber exhortationis*, c. 9 (PL 99: 205–6), quite possibly known in Alfred's circle.
[191] Pratt, 'Authorship', cf. Godden, 'Player King'; Godden, *Misappropriation*.
[192] II Chronicles I. 7–12; above, pp. 151–66.
[193] '[M]e þincð betere þæt ic forlete þa gyfe and folgyge þam gyfan, ðe me egðer ys stiward ge ðas welan ge eac hys freondscypes, buton ic egðer habban mage': *Solil* p. 62, lines 30–2.
[194] 'Both the friendship of the worldly lord and his own friendship, and eternal life after this world': *Solil* p. 63, lines 16–18.
[195] *Ibid.* p. 86, line 19, to p. 89, line 25.   [196] *Ibid.* p. 86, line 24, to p. 87, line 16.
[197] *Ibid.* p. 87, line 18, to p. 88, line 4. Pelteret, *Slavery*, pp. 271–4.

329

that, if he said it, I would not believe him'.[198] The quality extends to many 'companions' (*geþoftan*), trusted as well as himself, though less than his lord.[199] Truthfulness was a specifically royal virtue in 'ministerial' thinking, essential for justice; the treatment matched Alfred's own reputation as *ueredicus dominus*, pointedly connected with story-telling and rightful judgement.[200] Yet even worldly lords could not be 'wiser or more truthful' than God and Christ. 'Render unto Caesar the things that are Caesar's' (Matthew XXII. 21; Romans XIII. 7): rather than divided allegiance, the allusion here supported a single hierarchy, the speaker asserting honour for the former 'as one should a worldly lord', but for God and Christ 'as *their* lords' and 'just as one should the king, who is king of all kings, both creator and ruler of all creation'.[201] Both are rightly loved, but the 'higher lords' to a greater extent.[202] The same applies to their 'thegns', incorporating the full range of Apostles, Patriarchs, Prophets and Holy Fathers as human intermediaries; in all the speaker invests still greater trust than himself or thegnly 'companions' (*geferan*).[203]

Yet the context was seemingly historical, in the names attached to worldly lordship: the western emperor Honorius (395–423) and his father Theodosius the Great (379–95).[204] The identifications are doubly arresting: lacking inspiration in the source-text, they locate the present in Honorius' rulership, after 395, postdating the *Soliloquia*'s actual composition in 386–7.[205] The shift would be an unlikely misunderstanding: it gains compelling force in the broader context of royal 'revision', acquiring even the setting of *De uidendo Deo* (413), nearly three decades later.[206] The effect was an elaborate project of imagined rewriting. As Godden observes, arguments from testimony have interesting effects amid such sustained departure, some quite possibly registered by more learned readers.[207] Yet the appeal itself lost none of its conviction, underpinned by trust in everyday practice; as such, it only strengthens the case for Alfred's own recognition in texts of his authorship.[208]

---

[198] 'Ða cwæð ic: nese, la nese, nis nan to ðam ungelyfedlic spel, gyf he hyt segð, þæt ic hym ne gelife': *Solil.* p. 88, lines 5–6.

[199] *Solil.* p. 87, line 20, to p. 88, line 1; p. 88, lines 6–8.

[200] *VA* 13, lines 31–5, cf. cc. 14–15, lines 12–22; c. 105, lines 5–6, cf. 106; above, pp. 154, 170 and 176, cf. 141–2. Cf. Pseudo-Cyprian, *De XII Abusiuis Saeculi*, p. 51, quoted in *DIR* 3, pp. 188–92, and by Hincmar, *De regis persona*, c. 2 (PL 125: 835–6); also Simpson, ' "Proverbia Grecorum" ', p. 17 (iv.2), quoted in Cathwulf's letter to Charlemagne, in MGH Epist. II, p. 503, and in *RC* 10, p. 49.

[201] '[H]i ic will wyrðian swa swa man worldhlaford sceal, and þe oðre ðe þu er embe sprece, swa swa heora hlafordes, and swa man þone kyng sceal, þe byð kyng ealra kcynga and ealra gesceafta scypend and wealdend': *Solil.* p. 88, lines 17–20.

[202] *Ibid.*, p. 88, lines 21–5.   [203] *Ibid.* p. 88, line 26, to p. 89, line 5.

[204] *Ibid.* p. 88, lines 11–13.   [205] Carnicelli in *Solil.*, p. 103; Gatch, 'Alfred's Version', pp. 34–5.

[206] Pratt, 'Authorship'.   [207] Godden, *Misappropriation*, pp. 19–24.   [208] Pratt, 'Authorship'.

The references cannot be read straightforwardly: as historical markers, their force was compromised by so late a position, deep in Book II, long after such setting had been repeatedly undermined.[209] The game extended further: both rulers acquire pointed relevance against contemporary West Saxon posturing, selectively enacting Roman memory.[210] Æthelwulf's reign had seen the reservation of military service and bridge-building in West Saxon charters, evoking the *munera sordida* of Theodosius I; the enactments were present in the Code of his grandson.[211] A solidus of Honorius supplied the model for Alfred's own image on his first reformed coinage, the *Cross-and-Lozenge* type of *c.* 875–80.[212] Honorius had been in power for the Goths' sack of Rome (410), albeit in the tempered form described by Orosius (417) and the West Saxon translation. In the latter his role was partly recast, as the steadfast recipient of freely offered peace; his selection shows the boldness of Alfredian re-use.[213] Well indeed might comparisons have evoked difficulty: 'Honorius is swiðe god, þeah his feder betere were; he wes swiðe æfest and swiðe rædfast and swiðe rihte mines hlafordes kynnes, and swa is se þe þær gyt l(y)fa ð'.[214] Lacking an obvious source, the sentiments have defied interpretation: every detail pushed the double meaning of Honorius' lordship, modestly affecting 'kin' to so great a 'Roman' father.[215] Rome and parenthood returned again in appropriated royal example.[216] The drama was only heightened by such ironic self-reference, reinforcing the 'thegnship' of its human speaker. Projected throughout, the relationship gave all basis for earthly belief, artfully recapitulated in the text's closing lines.[217] Behind this delicate conjunction lay bonds of Alfredian royal lordship, intensively replicated

[209] *Ibid.* cf. esp. Godden, 'Player King', pp. 146–8.
[210] Cf. Theodosius' alternative significance in West Frankish imagery as exemplary penitent (*RC* 13, pp. 58–60). Both rulers were also revered as Christian law-givers (above, pp. 162 and 226): Anton, *Fürstenspiegel*, pp. 436–46; Nelson, 'Translating Images of Authority', esp. pp. 91–3.
[211] Nelson, 'Political Ideas', pp. 128–9; Brooks, 'Military Obligations', pp. 40–1 and notes 45–6; Brooks, 'Rochester Bridge, AD 43–1381', in his *Communities and Warfare*, pp. 219–65, at p. 227, note 16, and 229–30, with note 25.
[212] Blackburn, 'London Mint', pp. 113–14, with plate 11, coin K.
[213] *Or* VI.xxxvii–xxxviii, pp. 155–6; p. 31, lines 10–21, with Harris, '*World History*', pp. 501–3 and 505–6, comparing *CP*, p. 6, lines 8–9; cf. Godden, 'Goths', pp. 66–7. The connection has uncertain implications for Honorius' expanded treatment in the metrical version of the *Froferboc* (*ibid.*, p. 66).
[214] 'Honorius is very good, yet his father was better; the latter was very devout and very prudent and very rightly of my lord's kin, and so is he who still lives there': *Solil* p. 88, lines 15–17 (suggesting a context *after* 410: cf. *Or* VI.xxxvii, p. 155: 'feng ... Onorius to þæm wæstdæle and nugiet hæfð').
[215] Cf. Godden, 'Player King', p. 147; Gatch, 'Alfred's Version', p. 147; Bately, 'Evidence for Knowledge', p. 45 and notes 51–2.
[216] *Solil* p. 97, lines 5–11.   [217] *Ibid.* p. 97, lines 3–16.

in courtly reach. Uniting all was Alfred's own wise communication, harnessing his own testimony to delineate belief.

ALFRED'S *SOLILOQUIES* AND ALFREDIAN THEATRE

The royal version of the *Soliloquia* isolated central mechanisms of 're-education'; the intensity commands attention in assessing their role. Viewed in isolation, the text has often seemed enigmatic: attested in a single late manuscript, it somehow escaped mention by William of Malmesbury.[218] The source-text was an unlikely schoolbook, while its novel treatment all but evaded Augustinian dialectic. The whole enterprise acquires clearer rationale in the context of royal priorities. Latin *Soliloquia* offered intimate effects of Neo-Platonic reorientation; their extreme handling brought enhanced expression of Alfredian discourse. The entire drama showed wise pursuit by one placed in 'worldly honours'; rightly possessed, such gifts could readily accompany wisdom's sole desire. Far from isolated as insistent strategies, 'revision' and 'completion' were central to these Alfredian gestures. Wisdom's earthly restriction gave hope to all lovers of wisdom, regardless of ability; 'Book III' added the scope of another kingdom, one day transparent, when desire would be more than satisfied. The effect was a distinctive metaphysics, ultimately privileging neither Augustinian source, pursued with coherence in free-standing dialogue. Such qualities in themselves suggest wider reception, beyond the king's immediate circle; they gain substance from further connections with texts and display.

The evidence of transmission is not incompatible with multiple distribution. The full text has survived very narrowly, in London, British Library, Cotton Vitellius A. xv, a mid-twelfth-century manuscript from the Augustinian priory at Southwick in Hampshire.[219] Many textual problems point to a faulty exemplar, distant from Alfred's text; such problems are striking given Winchester's proximity.[220] Comparable only to the Psalm translation in the royal corpus, slender attestation would not be unexpected for a text so extraordinarily dominated by contingent references and concerns. Yet even in this case there are signs of wider availability: British Library, Cotton Tiberius A. iii, the mid-eleventh-century compilation from Christ Church, Canterbury, preserves an extract closer to the text's original state.[221] This in turn

---

[218] *GR* I, 192; above, p. 127.

[219] Ker, *Catalogue*, no. 215; K. S. Kiernan, *Beowulf and the Beowulf Manuscript* (New Brunswick, NJ, 1981), pp. 65–119; Gatch, 'Alfred's Version', p. 22 and note 27, pp. 41–2.

[220] Cf. Meaney, 'Secretariat', p. 19.

[221] Ker, *Catalogue*, no. 186, item 9(g); Gatch, 'Alfred's Version', p. 42, note 29.

strengthens evidence for a full Canterbury exemplar: the Christ Church catalogue of *c.* 1170 includes a 'Liber sermonum beati Augustini a.'. Lacking correspondence with any known vernacular text, the reference was not to Tiberius A. iii.[222]

Royal imagery openly exploited courtly arenas. At its heart was the 'king's home', now benefiting from Alfred's *schola*, yet in the lord's 'written message' appeal extended to distant communication. The scenario was precisely that of thegnly reception, matching Asser's account of local aristocratic practice; all audiences were served by the king's allusive preface.[223] Translation itself now found force as physical construction: every action matched those of textual craftsmanship.[224] 'Staves and post-shafts and tie-shafts, and handles for each of the tools that I knew how to work with': from such materials had the text been fashioned, selectively cut from a larger 'wood'.[225] 'Timbers' (*treowu*) had been Augustine's own, within the broader library of Christian Latinity; the proximity is suggestive with feminine *treow*, 'faith' or 'trust'. Yet the image blurred all distinctions of language: being built was nothing less than the royal craftsman's own courtly environment. Such structures were recognizably those of wisdom himself, only strengthened by the *Froferboc*'s 'house of wisdom', enjoined on each man against pride and avarice.[226]

Royal modesty was twofold, urging each who is able to complete for himself a 'fine residence' (*tun*), wherein to dwell 'both in winter and summer – as I have not yet done'.[227] Only possible at a single estate-centre, the latter pressed ironically on royal itinerancy.[228] Though necessarily led by those able to translate, many more might embrace this wise environment. For the craftsman's part, he must now remain in his 'lent dwelling-place' (*læne stoclif*), awaiting the eternal 'home' promised by 'Augustine, Gregory, Jerome and many other holy fathers'.[229] The list was not of 'sources', but anticipated a central prop of royal argument.[230] The entire metaphor culminated in another, insistent on active earthly practice. Harnessing terms and conditions of temporal 'loan', appeal now hinged on the consequences of royal lordship. Beyond

---

[222] R. M. Wilson, *The Lost Literature of Medieval England*, 2nd edn (London, 1970), pp. 78–9; James, *Ancient Libraries of Canterbury and Dover*, p. 51, no. 310 (Tiberius A. iii is clearly no. 296 in the same catalogue); cf. Whitelock, 'Prose', p. 73.

[223] *VA* 106, lines 46–61.

[224] Not the assembling of a *florilegium*, as noted by Gatch, 'Alfred's Version', pp. 23–5; imagery of construction observed by Lerer, *Literacy*, p. 92.

[225] *Solil* p. 47, lines 1–6; Irvine, *Textual Culture*, for probable resonances of Latin *silva*.

[226] *Solil* p. 77, line 5, to p. 78, line 2; *Bo* XII, pp. 26–7. Cf. *Cons. phil.* IIm4, pp. 25–6; Deshman, 'Galba Psalter', pp. 130–2.

[227] *Solil* p. 47, lines 6–12.   [228] Cf. above, pp. 34–8.   [229] *Solil* p. 47, line 12, to p. 48, line 3.

[230] Cf. K&L, *Alfred*, p. 299, note 4; cf. above, pp. 327–30.

construction lay benefits of possession, enjoyed conditionally as land held on lease, with the goal of bookland and perpetual inheritance.[231] Such rewards were only possible under secular lordship: prime bene-ficiaries in the ninth century were royal thegns.[232] An exchange of this kind is explicitly attested in a charter of 858; similar processes are implied by Æthelwulf's decimation, and by Alfred's own defensive land man-agement.[233] At least some of these estates are likely to have been previously held on loan; 'booking' could only have sweetened strategic exchange.[234] '[S]wa gedo se weliga gifola, se ðe egðer wilt ge þissa lænena stoclife ge þara ecena hama': the royal 'lord' was now God himself, ruling all with his conditional gifts.[235] He alone can make his craftsman fit 'for both'. '[G]e her nytwyrde to beonne, ge huru þider to cumane': 'usefulness' here encapsulated all earthly obligation.[236]

For the text as a whole, performance enacted such construction. Reading upheld Alfred's heightened presence, knowingly conveyed in personal dialogue. Such effects drew directly on translation, as imagined reading, its recording now 'staged' by the speaker's own recourse to writing.[237] The effect returned with his concluding speech, 'answering his own thoughts, alone'.[238] Within, the king retained his presence in projected didactic analogy, transferring to the speaker the imagined role as thegn of his lordship. These and many other props required no knowledge of either Latin source, openly proffered in courtly dialogue. Such reading enacted Alfred himself, as guider of speech; 'at home', as in the royal chamber, exchange was far from solitary. Activated by reading, the effect would only be heightened for hearers of recitation. Voice now replicated the scripted speaker: his persona joined *Gesceadwisnes* in collective mental awareness, sharing the contemporary familiarity of court experience. Even in performance, the text brought an enhanced projection of Alfredian royal theatre, replicated at the heart of local households; its message pertained as deeply to this environment.

Reading acted in a wider mental framework. As a route to wisdom, its effects hinged on Solomonic reorientation. Composition showed Alfred's

---

[231] *Solil* p. 48, lines 3–9.
[232] For loanland and bookland, see esp. Keynes, *Diplomas*, pp. 31–3, cf. John, *Land Tenure*, pp. 51–3.
[233] S 328 (BCS 496; *Charters*, ed. Robertson; trans. in *EHD*, no. 93); S 315 (BCS 486; *Rochester*, ed. Campbell, no. 23; trans. in *EHD*, no. 89); cf. above, pp. 66–8 and 99–102.
[234] See esp. S 347 (BCS 564; *Glastonbury*, ed. Watkin, no. 1165); S 355 (BCS 581; *Abingdon*, ed. Kelly, no. 18); cf. S 345, S 348, S 356, S 350.
[235] 'May the wealthy giver so grant, who rules both the site of these loans and of those eternal homes': *Solil* p. 48, lines 9–10.
[236] 'Both to be useful here, and likewise to arrive there': *ibid.* p. 48, lines 10–12.
[237] *Ibid.* p. 49, line 17, to p. 50, line 3, invoking *bocstafas* ('letters'); above, p. 320.
[238] *Ibid.* p. 95, line 4, to p. 97, line 16.

own desire, in the midst of royal office; his text staged a similar pursuit, positively adapted to earthly advantages. Wise celibacy was restricted to priesthood, wisdom's path opened to all in 'worldly honours', regardless of office or order. Working inwards, the *Froferboc* exposed the folly of worldly temptation; speaking alone, the text showed such striving as the full purpose of man's immortal soul, rationally guided through self-discovery. Knowledge of the soul and God: such objects were central to earthly action, under God's own craftsmanship. 'He works with us as with certain insignificant tools, just as it is written that with each man striving after good, God is a co-worker' (cf. I Corinthians III. 9): perception solicited divine assistance.[239] The soul alone now held an eternal stage, looking towards its maker with 'eyes of the mind'; every scene gave hope of universal love. The potential remained in all souls, through Platonic reminiscence; earthly obstacles were shared with the wisest of men.[240] Even ignorant souls could trust in their proven immortality, one day attaining God's eternal vision.[241] In this life, the soul could only ever gain glimpses of wisdom, clothed not bare; all could yet rejoice in their measure of insight. Remembrance was but the start of perpetual looking; the Lord would assist man's internal *cræft*. Not just here, but in every gesture of Alfredian theatre, such limits enhanced the ceaselessness of earthly pursuit.

Looking, apprehending, seeing: vision dominated this eternal stage, only heightened by future prophecy. Similar fulfilment was foretold in a Latin acrostic poem, with the legend AELFRED, plausibly attributed to John the Old Saxon. Addressing Christ, the poet pictured his future saving of the 'wise man', seizing him from flames, 'just as You Yourself destroyed death, that he may enjoy the Divine Visage beyond the stars forever'.[242] The image had a vernacular counterpart in Wulfsige's preface to the translated *Dialogues*. The book itself urged study for easier ascent to 'the heavenly home', promising 'bliss in those dwellings for those who may see the Son of God himself with their own eyes'.[243] The framework extended to *ædificia*, dominated by mechanisms of light and vision.[244] Performed by 'mind's eyes', the act of looking was in practice hidden from view. Royal technology harnessed physical sight, intensifying such gestures in daily action. The Fuller brooch showed sight's

---

[239] ' ... he wyrcð myd us swa swa myd sumum gewealdnum tolum, swa swa hyt awriten ys þæt ælcum welwyrcendum god myd beo mydwyrhta': *ibid.* p. 68, line 15, to p. 69, line 2.

[240] *Ibid.* p. 89, lines 25–8; p. 90, line 19, to p. 91, line 8. Cf. *Soliloquia* II.xx.35, pp. 95–6; *Bo* XXXV.i, pp. 94–5.

[241] Cf. the repeated failure to address ignorant souls in *Soliloquia* II.xiv.25–6 and II.xix.33, pp. 79–81 and 92–3.

[242] Lapidge, 'Some Latin Poems', pp. 69–71; K&L, *Alfred*, pp. 192 and 338.

[243] Yerkes, 'Metrical Preface', p. 512; K&L, *Alfred*, p. 187.

[244] Above, pp. 185–92; Pratt, 'Persuasion'.

special significance in royal wisdom, shared with the 'mind's eyes'.[245] The
entire scheme enabled broader comparison with physical sensation. The
Alfred Jewel offered further insight: holding a similar gaze, its sapiential
figure was no less 'clothed', physically beheld through crystal.[246]

Æstels directed eyes to the written page; royal speech developed
similar connections, in the recurring value of written testimony. The
effect was highly distinctive, in the role accorded to secular knowledge,
very distant from West Frankish mysticism; wisdom turned reason
earthwards in courtly self-reflection. God himself might be traced by a
sealed document; even the soul's fate hinged on the authority of divine
'thegns'. Behind both lay court experience of distant communication,
increasingly recorded in writing; uniting all was Alfred's own behaviour
as 'truthful lord'.[247] Projected in texts, the role was novel: to suffering
and late beginning it adds one final aspect of Alfred's unique person,
openly exploiting its intimate recognition. The gesture extended to all
sources of authority, no less familiar to contemporary experience. 'Holy
books' had been abundantly rendered on royal initiative.[248] The
Hierdeboc was itself a 'written message'; both the *Froferboc* and *Dialogues*
conveyed much on the immortal soul.[249] Apostles, Patriarchs, Prophets
and Holy Fathers: in the royal corpus, all voices bore witness to the
king's own pervasive testimony.[250] The connection was directly
exploited in royal argument: guided by scripture, their very words were
now bound to the truthfulness of Alfred's lordship. The implications
extended to every act of reading, heightened by wisdom's limited
access. The soul's needs strengthened every aspect of textual control: in
tandem with other translations they intensified an effective monopoly of
royal truth.

The text's extraordinary qualities were thus twofold, reinforcing
priorities from within, while heightening the effect of all other royal
texts. Such action was indeed the framework for an entire environment,
shaping behaviour far beyond each replicating household. Royal speech
offered wisdom directly compatible with worldly advantages; its role
complemented the *Froferboc*, showing the effects of wise restraint.
Uniting both was 'wealth' as Solomonic possession, reinforcing in every

---

[245] Above, pp. 187–9.   [246] Cf. I Corinthians XIII. 12; above, p. 191.

[247] Above, pp. 41 and 132, for cosmopolitan contact in the royal household, extending to Jerusalem
and the Arctic. Such distance could be temporal as well as spatial (*Solil* p. 97, lines 5–11; cf.
Foot, 'Remembering, Forgetting', pp. 185–7); both were intensively bridged by vernacular
prose.

[248] *Solil* p. 89, line 21; p. 94, lines 1–2.

[249] *Verse Preface to CP*, ed. Dobbie, ASPR VI, 110; *Bo* esp. XL.v–XLII, pp. 139–49; *GD* IV, I,
260–350.

[250] *Solil* p. 88, line 27, to p. 89, line 25.

detail the needs and benefits of burghal reform. The context was implicit in the text's 'Roman' allusions, ironically evoking Theodosius' legacy and Honorius' 'wealth'; the speaker might well recall his knowledge of Rome's construction.[251] Wisdom's restriction was central to this message, forestalling avarice with ceaseless pursuit. The soul's needs required only 'good greed', outwardly projected from its eternal stage, and continuously realized by access to further translations. Enveloping all souls was this transitory royal environment, uniquely communicated in textual performance; at its heart lay the testimony of Alfred's own crafted person, wisely familiar in scripted truth.

---

[251] *Ibid.* p. 97, lines 5–11. Nelson, 'Franks and the English', pp. 147–8, for the 'Leonine City', completed in 852; Hill, 'Urban Policies', extends its significance among models for burghal defence.

Chapter 15

CONCLUSION

Placed in context, Alfred's texts emerge as highly effective props of kingship, intensively vested with his agency and power. Their force drew in all directions on Alfred's own position at the heart of his household; the roots of his learning can be traced to this immediate, West Saxon environment. As ubiquitous lord his role epitomized the distinctive strengths of West Saxon kingship, consolidated under this single dynasty by his father and grandfather. Its operation tapped still deeper structures, in the West Saxon shire system, with ealdormen under royal authority, and the position of West Saxon thegns, as landed royal agents. Its basis in the ninth century was an expanding array of royal monopolies, conspicuously shared with thegnly beneficiaries. Many exploited forms of income, in tolls, renders and fines, enhanced by the acquisition of south-eastern mints; all complemented effective jurisdiction in the loaning and 'booking' of land. Such processes were critically aided by abrupt changes in the Southumbrian church, effecting the abandonment of synods and synodal culture towards structures similarly dominated by West Saxon lordship. Disputes over bookland received royal settlement, in a single hierarchy of justice. Royal mechanisms brought bishops as effective local agents, intensified by the use of royal priests as episcopal personnel.

All these structures accorded centrality to the royal household, as a constant arena of power. Patterns of attendance accentuated this status, enabling lengthy and intimate royal contact with all thegns of the king. Already in this context were practices of wise and learned kingship, united by rituals of court devotion. Especially prominent was royal gift-giving, with thegns as recipients; iconographic metalwork combined with pious emancipation of land. Collectively, such activities expressed shared principles of worldly conduct, in responsibilities of office-holding, borne before God and extending to all participants in service to the king. These principles were enshrined at local level by the liturgical

338

provisions of Æthelwulf's decimation; they found further expression in royal anointing, in the secular 'gift' of justice. The entire ritual cast the king as Solomon, in unusually extreme re-enactment. In bookland, poetry and prayer such practices harnessed written texts; Alfred's oral experiences almost certainly embodied wider court instruction.

To these prior structures Alfredian developments harnessed the medium of vernacular prose to courtly literate education. Together, these priorities created a new mental technology, extended to all participants in power, with differing yet standardizing effects. Instruction at court now included future ecclesiastics, while vernacular elements of this training were extended to young laymen. Crucially, communication also acted at a distance, enveloping bishops and thegnly residences, the latter aided if necessary by oral recitation. Underpinning all script was a new discourse of power, restricted to royal texts. Its linguistic connections were Gregorian and Solomonic, but distinctively Alfredian in formulation and deployment. Together, these languages supplied a universal framework of office-holding, extended to all bishops, ealdormen and thegns; their primary characteristic was the very need for divine knowledge, predicated on access to texts. Beyond this lay Gregorian insistence on the temptations of power, only counteracted by self-control and continuous restraint. Solomonic language reinforced these gestures, in the desire for wisdom above all other divine gifts. To humility and service, Solomon's dream added rewards of undesired wealth; wise judgement was exemplified in the king's law-book.

This was the context for Alfred's learned centrality, monopolizing authorship in acts of inventive translation. The role was a textual extension of royal lordship, already dominant in gift-giving and courtly intimacy. Its intensity gave unique force to royal texts, as conduits of wisdom endowed with the king's presence. Such qualities were heightened in all textual performance; beyond reading they provided wider enhancement of courtly behaviour, as theatre now shaped and informed by written texts. At its heart was interaction in the royal household, now projected at a distance through reading and recitation; comprehension hinged on familiarity with the king. Such theatre drew force from just three aspects of Alfred's person, intensively deployed against this textual backdrop. The king's late acquisition of wisdom, his mysterious suffering, his truthfulness in lordship: in each case the role bore deeper valency, united by gestures of persuasion and encouragement. All were heightened in textual deployment; royal texts depended on their intimate recognition. Coupled with all features of language and style, such structures only strengthen the case for Alfred's extensive input, over and above the role of imported helpers, actively exploiting his presence while continuously filtering the reception of non-West Saxon expertise.

Translation was shaped by this context. As imagined reading, the genre was inherently theatrical; such qualities fused with West Saxon courtly intimacy. Royal texts supplied Alfred as imagined reader within his *bur* or chamber, heightening all aspects of self-reference: performance recreated this restricted environment. The overall approach pushed at the limits of non-literal translation, boldly extended to biblical texts; such freedom answered royal needs, in textual enhancement of personal performance. All source-texts were refashioned within these structures, while mediating much of immediate force within royal priorities: not only departures but aspects of fidelity bore the imprint of such discourse and its courtly encouragement. The *Hierdeboc* privileged Gregorian language in its relative faithfulness, while the Psalm translation gave heightened expression of royal 'Gregorian' concerns. Both the *Froferboc* and *Soliloquies* were directly Solomonic: their freer treatment adapted Neo-Platonism to royal needs, retaining yet reorienting dangers of worldly desire. Both appealed intensively to royal lordship in gift-giving, sustenance and communication; the *Soliloquies* were especially extreme, combining re-composition with highly complex gestures of self-involvement. In the learning applied to Latin sources, such effects presuppose extensive philosophical engagement; the overall framework supports 'ritualized' aspects of royal commitment, inventively sustained across diverse source-texts through insistent harnessing of court behaviour.

Both thought and structures offer a revised view of Frankish influence, within wider use of imported expertise. The *Hierdeboc* tapped Southumbrian episcopal memory, while the Psalms and law-book suggest Irish assistance: royal discourse followed the shape of West Saxon collective office-holding. The ear for Frankish wisdom matched these existing practices, in the selective deployment of 'ministerial' language and imagery, and aristocratic extension of Gregorian duties and concerns; both gained much from Alfredian realignment. Many transformations reflected the institutional coherence of Frankish ecclesiastical reform, articulated in advice-literature yet underpinned by features of landholding and episcopal power. In its resource-base and patterns of service the West Saxon order came closer to West Frankish political structures, but to eastern practices in centralized social bonding. Gregorian language now described the universality of West Saxon office-holding, under exclusive royal correction; its deployment shaped power as service, unencumbered by lay reform. Solomon found still deeper treatment: once at the heart of West Frankish ecclesiastical distinction, his dream was now extended to all West Saxon office-holders, articulating quite different objectives of literacy and shared restraint. Such patterns continued in the law-book, actively defending English practices from West Frankish criticism; they intensified in the versions of Boethius and Augustine, refashioning many aspects of Carolingian learned contact. Wisdom's benefits applied insistently to thegns; the three orders were now West Saxon royal needs; secular service held the key to mystical perception. In each case West Frankish thinking had asserted bonds between king and church; all now felt the guiding force of Alfred's royal lordship.

Theorizing answered immediate needs; its power lay not in 'new men', but the commitment of existing aristocratic families, under material pressures. In devotional inducement the interplay was distinctively 'West Saxon'; its force matched the cost of defensive success in all burdens on income and land. Both were already threatened by the decline of 'wics' and peasant flight; burghal construction combined with the demands of strategic leasing and land exchange. Texts were central to royal 'persuasion', united by their co-ordinating languages of power. The manipulation of concepts strengthened material gift-giving; both were dominant in Alfred's personal theatre, now projected at a distance. The sharing of revenues, 'justice' in peace-keeping and landed dispute settlement, the benefits of reformed coinage: all related pointedly to textual statement. Royal texts joined symbolic to material function, in an active shaping of behavioural priorities. In West Francia similar measures had brought 'imperial' edict; West Saxon structures found power in continuous principle. Such behaviour was united by the action of desire, both Gregorian and Solomonic; its mechanisms were directly articulated by 'wealth' and 'wisdom'. Both were mental constructs under extreme monopolization and control: future revenues and prosperity were far from guaranteed. Yet 'wisdom' was contingent on restraint towards 'wealth': as paired gifts, both were heightened in this scripted framework.

Each text had its own role in royal gesture, compounded in concert. The *Hierdeboc* perceived service in West Saxon secular responsibility, articulated for thegnly bishops: its message was intensified by Alfred's conspicuous suffering. The *Domboc* asserted law as a Solomonic written mechanism, guided against treachery. Its divine principles supported peace-keeping and protection of property, with enhanced participation by local lords; this legal 'strengthening' defended *pauperes* and judicial restraint. The Psalms gave collective devotion a written Davidic focus. Tribulation combined warfare with instructive royal suffering, incurred through fleshly excess: the effects of both could be read within Alfred's symbolic body. The drama intensified with Roman re-use. Abandoning

Boethian Fortuna, the *Froferboc* showed wealth and honour as *Wisdom*'s gifts, rightly possessed with wise restraint. 'Tools and resources' offered limits of use, directly measured against the king's courtly needs, spanning his kingdom in defensive construction. *Mod*'s fall exposed the dangers of greed, while wise rule received support in God's providential order. In royal wisdom the *Soliloquies* showed the path to all human fulfilment, directly contingent on worldly restraint. Wisdom's earthly limits offered hope to all in his lordship: only judgement day would end this continuous pursuit.

Royal discourse framed wise action: its effects were as deep in rhetorical success. The impact of royal learning has generally been detected in its literate technology, correlating with many changes in documentary communication: the *Domboc* formed a starting-point for all later legislation. Yet even in these uses literacy was performative, in its ability to shape meaning and gesture; both were central to Alfredian usage in theatrical communication. In the event, there seems to have been abundant wise behaviour, beyond more general cognizance of royal writings. Enough of the burghal network was completed, and in sufficient time, to enable the successful defence of Alfred's kingdom after 893. Enough landholders were ultimately willing to accept all sacrifices of production and labour, for 'wealth' whose potential could finally be revealed. Excavations at London have confirmed the early value of Alfredian urban interests, matched by the success of many other burhs as urban centres; but not all sites went on to be fully fledged towns, with 'failures' notable among smaller forts.[1] In coinage also the absolute volume of Alfred's reformed issues was probably reduced, and minting expanded slowly outside the south-east.[2] Royal gesture smoothed all unevenness of development, just as it softened the force of royal demand. Even at the margins, bishop Denewulf's appeal was to the benificence of royal lordship, not limits of kingly need: there was no room in writing for thegnly 'advice'.[3] Yet the estate was ultimately returned, as in other such transactions; while in treachery also, 'justice' seems to have carried force.[4] In every area, effects were decisive in a concerted reorientation of resources and rule, secured for the future within received royal thought.

Uniting all behaviour were complex gestures of thegnly identity: the point is important given the weight so frequently attached to shared ethnicity, vested in history. For all Alfred's prominence in the *Chronicle*,

[1] Anon., 'Bull Wharf: Queenhithe'; Ayre and Wroe-Brown, 'Æthelred's Hythe'; D. Hill, 'Athelstan's Urban Reforms', *ASSAH* 11 (2000), 173–86, esp. 181–3.
[2] Metcalf, 'Monetary Economy', pp. 172–4.   [3] Above, pp. 212–13.   [4] Above, pp. 238–41.

its narrative actually did little to explain or contextualize his wider power. While upholding his uniting leadership, the portrayal pressed largely on warfare, in an account relatively restrained in 'persuasive' urgency. Alfred's legal legacy offered much of strength to his 'English' successors, yet its role needs integrating with all other structures of tenth-century rule. Wormald's 'structures' attribute priority to 'allegiance': in isolating ethnicity, his case takes no account of many other distinguishing features of West Saxon kingship.[5] One was certainly communicational, in the ready availability of a shared tongue: even here royal rhetoric fell short of politicizing persuasion. Translation was seen to elevate this gentile vernacular, yet *Angelcynn* retained its force within wider 'ecclesiastical' unity. Alfred's fusion was more qualified, in his kingship of 'Anglo-Saxons', no less 'chosen' than preceding 'Mercian' or 'West Saxon' peoples; its genesis masked the latest extension of West Saxon lordship and office-holding. As much was implicit in the *Domboc*, enhancing 'royal' justice, already understood in biblical terms. *Hlafordsearu* hinged on the king himself, as the object of widened offence; his projection in local peace-keeping was a structural source of unity, primarily reliant on elite enactment. Ambiguously embracing all 'Anglo-Saxon' subjects, royal theory pushed the benefits for every just man. At the heart of its biblicism lay merciful limits of impact; such features were central to the *Domboc*'s uniting script.

More potent for Alfred were 'wise' mentalities, framing intersections of mind and rule. Such theatre matched the position of Alfredian power, as mental object; its role heightened what was shared among thegnly participants, as a source of temptation demanding restraint. This was the strength of *cræft*, as the means of continuous control: combining divine gift with wise improvement, such skill united all purposes of learned engagement. The mind itself was effectively mechanized by royal construction, through books and æstels; its application lay firmly in the world, regulated at court by the rhythms of Alfred's candle-lantern.[6] Combining earthly with divine, holders of power bore burdens as 'middle men' on the royal cartwheel of fate, receiving both good and evil according to their qualified merits. Yet this role was essential for the needs of men; wise action assisted God's work on earth as the supreme architect and uniting source of all *cræft*. This was the basis for all material possession: 'tools and resources' fulfilled the royal needs of Alfred's own wise craftsmanship. The effect was an entire technology of rulership,

---

[5] Wormald, '*Engla Lond*', pp. 362–71, esp. 370–1.
[6] Cf. Elias, *Civilizing Process*, pp. 322–3, for the court as a finely balanced machine, magnifying the effects of its 'cautious manipulation'.

harnessing creation at every level of Alfred's kingdom, with burghal building as its earthly product. In the toil of 'workmen' among royal 'tools' was God's own wise work.[7]

With power lay 'wealth' as a further gift of wisdom, similarly regulated by continuous restraint. This too was essential for service, plentifully given by good lords; upheld in coinage, its force encompassed wider material distribution. The court itself was an exemplum for wise apportionment, realized locally in revenue; recitation re-enacted this royal environment.[8] With wealth was prosperity and more general 'worldly blessings': all depended directly on wisdom, as the object of sole desire. All such blessings were wisdom's gifts, jeopardized by greed; the relationship was replicated in God's providential architecture, flexibly responding to earthly endeavour. In wisdom lay scope for human intervention, through active 'moderation' of prosperous fate; God himself would temper all future harshness. Such effects were implicit in every contribution to burghal building and defence, sacrificing short-term agrarian production; as such, they show not only the deep impact of economic forces on courtly interplay, but the dynamic position of royal thought in all aspects of elite exchange.[9] Royal wisdom was quite literally 'economic', embracing each household and its consumption. Behind wealth and prosperity lay the broader exchange-based potential of protected urban markets.[10] Though expressed as gifts, wider benefits were implicit in their divine source, collectively secured through earthly 'moderation'. In wisdom lay shared means of prosperous entrenchment; tying rural to urban, its role was formative in wider 'commercializing' control.

Such were the uses of royal knowledge, tapping the potential of each thegnly soul. Both wisdom and *cræftas* were divine gifts, central to the soul's immortality; striving was heightened within God's created forms. Learning could be seen as internal reminiscence, while wisdom's limits, on earth, enhanced all ceaseless pursuit. Full vision was reserved for God's own eternal kingdom; Alfred's wisdom probed this edge of all earthly understanding, in habitual 'investigation of things unknown'.[11] The king's candle-lantern supplied temporal balance; both brooch and Jewel showed the earthly scope of mental vision. All guidance led back to the written royal page; this too bore the imprint of courtly self-enquiry.

---

[7] Cf. Nelson, 'Revaluation of Work', pp. 39–43; Le Goff, *Time, Work*, pp. 43–57.

[8] Cf. Elias, *Court Society*, pp. 41–65, for the structural identity of aristocratic and other residences.

[9] Cf. the general observations of Maddicott, 'Debate: Trade, Industry', pp. 164–75.

[10] See esp. Jones, 'Transaction Costs'; cf. J. Campbell, 'Was it Infancy in England? Some Questions of Comparison', in his *Anglo-Saxon State*, pp. 179–99, esp. 188–92; Hodges, *The Anglo-Saxon Achievement*, pp. 155–66 and 196–200; Dyer, *Making a Living*, pp, 58–70.

[11] *VA* 76, line 20.

Apostles, Patriarchs, Prophets and Holy Fathers: texts alone invoked these wisest of witnesses, their message embedded within royal 'truth'. 'Must I not ... believe some men, or none at all?': such theorizing exploited secular knowledge within court communication, no less enhanced by writing.[12] Distant contact had gained written record; while across the spectrum of vernacular prose, past witnesses now jostled with oral memory. Yet in royal texts alone all voices bore witness to Alfred's own uniting presence, refashioning much as 'truthful lord'. In letter and spoken message, this testimony solicited wise understanding; this again led back to 'holy books'. All were aspects of contemporary royal communication: behind such gestures lay the unique status of translated text, as the performance of lordship in sapiential disclosure. Tracing wisdom by every means of earthly witness, Alfred's theatre gave exclusive voice to this crafted truth.

It remains to observe the lasting impact of royal construction. The inherent strengths of Alfred's political legacy have been much observed in tenth-century expansion and stability. Burghal defence became a tool of conquest, retaining and intensifying its commercial stimulus; where burhs began, shiring would follow in a concerted extension of West Saxon structures. All was aided by a marked intensity of documentary communication, now effecting a two-way dialogue between centre and locality; its legal focus was Alfredian peace.[13] 'Centre' remained the royal household: though no source approaches Asser in detail, a strong case remains for the continuing force of royal education. Ælfric in the late tenth century reserved special praise for those books which King Alfred had 'wisely' translated, and were still to be found; among Ælfric's own lay patrons was ealdorman Æthelweard, equally respectful of Alfred's Boethius.[14] Yet neither memory is surprising. Many Alfredian agents had long outlived their king, Plegmund, for example, until 923; early tenth-century bishops included Æthelstan and Frithestan as former royal priests. Such practices of service continued throughout the later Anglo-Saxon period, aiding a continuing context for court-based learning.[15] Crucially, this extended to lay recipients, documented well beyond Alfred's reign. To the king's children must be added his grandson Æthelstan, of immense learning according to later memory, and reportedly educated in the Mercian household of Æthelred and Æthelflæd.[16]

---

[12] Above, pp. 327–32.

[13] Keynes, 'Royal Government', pp. 235–41; Wormald, *MEL* I, 310–12 and 446–9.

[14] *Ælfric's Catholic Homilies: the First Series*, ed. Clemoes, pp. 173–4.

[15] Keynes, *Diplomas*, pp. 145–53.

[16] *GR* I, 210–1; S. Keynes, 'King Athelstan's Books', in *Learning and Literature*, ed. Lapidge and Gneuss, pp. 143–201, at 144.

Æthelstan's own household is illuminated by the upbringing of bishop Æthelwold, only known from Wulfstan's later *Life*. Brought to court in the 'flower of youth', Æthelwold spent much time there 'in inseparable companionship, learning much from the king's wise men that was useful and profitable to him'.[17] Only at a later stage was he tonsured: the case preserves a wider pattern of secular career. A similar route was accorded to Dunstan by one of his biographers, though the account is less secure.[18] Among Æthelstan's 'wise men' were a new group of cosmopolitan scholars, encompassing Irish, Frankish and Breton learning; activities seem to have focused on Latin court poetry and hermeneutic Latin prose.[19] There is a more general restriction in evidence for fresh vernacular composition before Æthelwold's own later efforts.[20] The *Chronicle* received additions, poetry was evidently in circulation, but no substantial prose output can be securely dated to this period. Such silence seems explicable given extensive further copying of Alfredian prose texts, now bearing the regularized imprint of Square Minuscule script.[21] The *Hierdeboc, Domboc* and *Froferboc* are all known from such witnesses, supplying a context for still later transmission of royal texts, in the eleventh and twelfth centuries. Ælfric saw his own writings as in some sense complementing Alfred's work. Coupled with Wulfstan's precious testimony, all evidence points to the essential survival of Alfred's court curriculum, far from forgotten amid all later composition for lay audiences.

There is an exciting prospect of Alfred's own 'memorialization' in texts, now shorn of an intimate association with the ruling king. Literate inducement need no longer have been pressing; royal discourse would have supported many familiar features of later rule. The Solomonic Second *Ordo*, possibly constructed under Alfred, remained in use throughout the tenth century, with only minor revision. Gregorian duties gain substance from the styling *rex et rector*, frequently deployed in charters of the 930s and 940s.[22] Secular office-holding was upheld in the framework of ealdormen, reeves and king's thegns, fully participant in peace and the profits of power; only from Æthelred's time would this

---

[17] *Wulfstan of Winchester: the Life of St Æthelwold*, ed. Lapidge and Winterbottom, c. 7, p. 11.

[18] N. P. Brooks, 'The Career of St Dunstan', in *St Dunstan: his Life, Times and Cult*, ed. N. Ramsay, M. Sparks and T. Tatton-Brown (Woodbridge, 1992), pp. 1–23, at 4, cf. 4–11.

[19] M. Lapidge, 'Schools, Learning and Literature in Tenth-Century England', in his *ALL* II, 1–49, at 18–23; Lapidge, 'Some Latin Poems', pp. 71–85; M. Lapidge, 'Israel the Grammarian in Anglo-Saxon England', in his *ALL* II, 87–104.

[20] D. N. Dumville, 'Between Alfred the Great and Edgar the Peaceable: Æthelstan, First King of England', in his *Wessex and England*, pp. 141–71, at 162; for Æthelwold's texts, see M. Gretsch, *The Intellectual Foundations of the English Benedictine Reform* (Cambridge, 1999).

[21] Dumville, 'Tenth-Century Reform', p. 202. [22] Keynes, 'King Athelstan's Books', pp. 156–7.

Conclusion

order face disturbance.[23] Throughout the tenth century there are suggestive contexts of gift and fiscal benefit. 'Reconquest' was nothing of
the kind, accompanied by considerable aristocratic displacement; the gap
in Edwardian charters suggests concerted use of folkland and land on
loan.[24] Meanwhile in Edward's laws trading was restricted to 'port'
environs.[25] Under Æthelstan minting expanded rapidly across midland
burhs and as far as York; its authorization accompanied a loosening of
the terms for witnessed trade.[26] Other measures saw further deployment
of psalmody.[27] Edgar's momentous reform established new mechanisms
of regular recoinage; his laws describe an ordered web of shire justice,
overseen by bishop as well as ealdorman.[28]

These and many other interests tapped deeper economic forces in the
intensifying exploitation of land and commercial exchange. Social
consequences have been well observed in signs of 'conspicuous consumption' down an increasingly stratified thegnly hierarchy.[29] Closely
linked was a semantic widening of the adjective *rice*, 'powerful', to
convey attributes of wealth.[30] Now implying abundance as a 'marker' of
power, the connection was perhaps still more direct, in the fiscal and
material benefits of royal service. The shift coincides with seemingly
concerted efforts on Ælfric's part to highlight dangers arising from
wealthy possession, while defending its use for just purposes: his
understanding extended to *publicani*, 'tax-collectors', twice translated as
gerefan, 'reeves'.[31] In Ælfric's hands this morality extended to merchants
as well as landholders; his concerns lay especially in salvation and
endowment. Yet much of this message was far from new: condemning
greed, his rhetoric upheld generous distribution to those in need. As the

[23] See esp. S. Keynes, 'Cnut's Earls', in *The Reign of Cnut*, ed. A. R. Rumble (Leicester, 1994),
pp. 43–88, at 78–81 and 87–8. Cf. Innes, *State and Society*, pp. 237–9, 245–7 and 260–1;
J. L. Nelson, 'Rulers and Government', pp. 99–100 and 119–22, and J. Dunbabin, 'West Francia:
the Kingdom', esp. pp. 375–6, 384–7 and 392–7, both in *NCMH* III, 95–129 and 372–97, for the
respective fates of comital office-holding in East and West Francia.
[24] S. Keynes, 'England, c. 900–1016', in *NCMH* III, 456–84, at 465–6; cf. *I Edward* 2–2.1.
[25] *I Edward* 1–1.5.
[26] C. E. Blunt, B. H. I. H. Stewart and C. S. S. Lyon, *Coinage in Tenth-Century England from Edward
the Elder to Edgar's Reform* (Oxford, 1989), pp. 264–8, cf. 255–7; *II Æthelstan* 12 and 13.1, cf. *IV
Æthelstan* 2.
[27] *V Æthelstan* 3.
[28] R. H. M. Dolley and D. M. Metcalf, 'The Reform of the English Coinage under Eadgar', in
Anglo-Saxon Coins: Studies presented to F. M. Stenton, ed. R. H. M. Dolley (London, 1961),
pp. 136–68; *III Edgar* 5–5.2.
[29] R. Fleming, 'The New Wealth, the New Rich and the New Political Style in Late Anglo-Saxon
England', *Anglo-Norman Studies* 23 (2001), 1–22; cf. also C. Senecal, 'Keeping up with the
Godwinesons: in Pursuit of Aristocratic Status in late Anglo-Saxon England', *Anglo-Norman
Studies* 23 (2000), 251–66.
[30] Godden, 'Money, Power', pp. 48–55; cf. Clemoes, *Interactions*, pp. 334–62.
[31] Godden, 'Money, Power', pp. 55–64, esp. 63–4; cf. Newhauser, *Greed*, pp. 125–6.

ultimate source of goods, God again had the role of 'lending' for wise enjoyment.[32] Far from an unprecedented view of wealthy responsibilities, such statements only strengthen the case for much continuity of royal teaching, its arguments now appropriated to Ælfric's agenda.

Much else had changed to distinguish Ælfric's world from that of Alfredian memory. In the ecclesiastical sphere, the West Saxon order had been effectively transformed by the cumulative impact of tenth-century reforms. In royally promoted Benedictinism these reforms opened quite separate vistas of Carolingian inspiration, now thought to have been first pertinent in Æthelstan's household; collectively, they took ecclesiastics far from Alfredian relationships.[33] The new context was 'English' rule, congruent with Pope Gregory's church; now this structure could bear a special relationship with Æthelstan and his successors. Reform reasserted the distinctiveness of monastic endowment; royal protection combined with a wider canonical framework of ecclesiastical unity.[34] Such interplay saw new forms of royal gesture, now reserved for this emerging relationship and intensively expressed in manuscripts of court association.[35] Its obverse was ecclesiastical 'advice', proffered by Ælfric and archbishop Wulfstan in heightened expression of such duties: their writings conveyed wider goals of 'corrected' social order.[36] No less significant were social effects in the multiplication of learned centres. The young Edgar was educated not at court, but by Æthelwold, possibly at Abingdon: such routes may well have been common among offspring of lay benefactors.[37] Ælfric's patronage shows the strength of such local relationships.

The court's own position had been qualified by the effects of expansion. The household retained patterns of attendance and itinerancy, yet remained restricted to vills south of the Thames and in western Mercia.[38] Intense contact with the court may well have been reserved

---

[32] Godden, 'Money, Power', p. 61.

[33] D. A. Bullough, 'The Continental Background of the Reform', in *Tenth-Century Studies*, ed. D. Parsons (London, 1975), pp. 20–36; Gretsch, *Intellectual Foundations*; Blair, *Church*, pp. 346–54; cf. Dumville, 'Tenth-Century Reform'.

[34] Seminally represented in *I* and *II Edmund*, and the *Constitutiones* of archbishop Oda (Dumville, *ibid.*, p. 202); N. Banton, 'Monastic Reform and the Unification of Tenth-Century England', in *Religion and National Identity*, ed. S. Mews (Oxford, 1982), pp. 71–85.

[35] Keynes, 'King Athelstan's Books', pp. 173–4 and 180; R. Deshman, 'Anglo-Saxon Art after Alfred', *Art Bulletin* 56 (1974), 176–200, at 195 and 197–9; Karkov, *Ruler Portraits*, pp. 55–63 and 85–99.

[36] Powell, 'The "Three Orders"', pp. 110–29; D. Bethurum Loomis, '*Regnum* and *sacerdotium* in the Early Eleventh Century', in *England before the Conquest: Studies in Primary Sources presented to Dorothy Whitelock*, ed. P. Clemoes and K. Hughes (Cambridge, 1971), pp. 129–45; P. Wormald, 'Archbishop Wulfstan and the Holiness of Society', in his *Legal Culture*, pp. 225–51.

[37] Lapidge, 'Schools, Learning', p. 31, cf. 34–6.   [38] Campbell, 'United Kingdom', pp. 47–9.

for southern, and especially West Saxon, king's thegns. Territorial enlargement gave new significance to royal assemblies, more regularly attested in charter evidence as the principal arena of wider contact.[39] Associated with religious festivals, these too were largely restricted to sites within Alfred's former kingdom. Only in special circumstances did kings travel further afield; visits north of the Humber were generally conducted by military expedition. Tenth-century stability suggests the relative success of assemblies as the locus of consensus, regulating the participation of families who had often gained much from West Saxon conquest. Outside the heartlands, much rested on inter-aristocratic contact beyond these arenas, in local assemblies, towns and 'at home'. The tenth-century household was in some ways even more critical, as a source of authority and dynastic power, yet direct participation seems likely to have been territorially limited. Such tensions were probably decisive in upholding the Thames as a natural fault-line in division or dispute.[40] In general both the centre and its unity held, aided by all aspects of shared monopoly; yet collectively these features suggest a balance of power behind royal performance, less exclusively court-centred and uneven in personal intimacy.

The legacy only sharpens all junctures of the Alfredian moment, combining multiple processes of intense and pervasive transition. Dynamic and responsive, the political and cultural forces of Alfred's reign drew strength from their engagement with wider aspects of ninth-century social, economic and religious change. Alfred's rule held many advantages in its integral uniformity, the convenient conjunction of size, structures and logistics; in the latter it gained from a singular revolution in royal communication. What remains extraordinary is the manner in which all opportunities were actually taken, in this supremely material realization of learned kingship. Royal thinking did not merely describe power but addressed contemporary needs and pressures; its force hinged on Alfred's wider activities in gift-giving and judgement. The effect was a co-ordinated reordering of his assembled kingdom, played out against the king's own philosophical script. Dominant within as without his written theatre, royal role-playing was united by persuasive direction. Connecting David, Solomon and all other *exempla* was Alfred's own royal lordship, heightened in the performance of his intimate person. In its textual legacy, this wisdom moulded all aspects of kingship to the

---

[39] Keynes, *Diplomas*, pp. 269–73; Wormald, *MEL* I, 431–8.
[40] Keynes, 'England, *c.* 900–1016', pp. 467–8 and 477–9, cf. division between Cnut and Edmund in 1016.

distinctive needs of Alfredian rule. Guided by its royal craftsman, text and behaviour had combined to reshape an entire landscape and economy, harnessing the minds and resources of its ruling agents. Scripting this connection, projecting household to kingdom, was the learned power of Alfred's enacted thought.

Appendix

Appendix

WEST FRANKISH DEPLOYMENT OF SOLOMON'S DREAM

The following passages document West Frankish use of Solomon's dream by ecclesiastical writers under Charles the Bald (see above, pp. 159–63, cf. 278–9); generally addressed to the ruler himself, deployment shows consistent sensitivity to his political circumstances.

1. Letter of Lupus of Ferrières to Charles the Bald, written shortly after the quashing of a rumour that Charles had been killed in battle against the Bretons on 22 November 845:

'Praeterea mementote, quod Salomon ad regendum populum Israel, cui diu in maxima pace praesedit, sapientiam potissimum postulavit' ('Moreover, remember that Solomon asked, in preference to all else, for wisdom in order to rule the people of Israel, over whom he presided for a long time in the greatest peace'): *Epistolae*, ed. Marshall, no. 33, p. 45.

2. Dedicatory verse by Audradus Modicus to Charles's First Bible, made at Tours and presented by the canons in 845:

'Ante tamen reserat clare primordia cosmi / Et per quam illius esse fuit sophiam ... Quoque modo quisquis caveat munitus ab armis / Hostis perversi tela inimica nimis. ... Quisquis es instructus mundanis usibus hisce, / Quis Salomone opibus ditior emicuit? / Hoc concessa cui dives sapientia fecit, / Regibus ac cunctis hunc ea proposuit. / Tu quoque, qui es humilis, prudens – intentio sancta – / Se propter sophiam dilige, posce, cape' ('Yet earlier [the bible as divine law] reveals clearly the beginnings of the universe, and through [the bible's] wisdom it came into existence ... Let anyone who is only defended by arms fear the greatly hostile weapons of the wicked enemy. ... Those of you equipped with worldly benefits, gape: who shone forth richer in riches than Solomon? Rich wisdom, when granted to him, did this, and placed him ahead of all kings. You also, who are humble and prudent – a holy intention – love, seek, grasp wisdom on its own account'): Dutton and Kessler, *First Bible of Charles the Bald*, pp. 110–13, lines 157–8, 163–4 and 179–84 (my translation differs slightly).

3. Letter of Hincmar of Rheims and certain other bishops to Louis the German, in the context of his invasion of West Francia of November 858:

'Propterea oportet, ut, qui rex estis, et dominus appellamini, in illum semper suspenso corde suspiciatis, a quo, videlicet, rege regum et domino dominorum, nomen regis et domini mutuatis; et, sicut ille disponit orbem terrae in aequitate et ad hoc, sicut in libro Sapientiae dicitur, constituit hominem, ut ipse similiter faciat, imitamini illum, si vultis regnare cum illo ... Propterea ita oportet vos vivere, iudicare et agere etiam in occulto, quasi sitis semper in publico ... Sic autem, ut dicimus, adiuvante domino vivere, iudicare et agere prevalebitis, si vos non stimulaverit amor privatus; si non vos inflammaverit cupiditas gloriae, divitiarum, possessionum et potentatus; si non plus credideritis alienae linguae quam propriae conscientiae ... si vos non vexaverit neglectus animae et amor carnis' ('Therefore it is fitting that you who are king, and are addressed as lord, always look with lifted heart on him, namely the King of kings and Lord of lords, from whom you obtain the name of king and lord; and, just as he orders the orb of the earth in equity and to this end, as it is said in the Book of Wisdom, he created man, that he should do likewise, it is beholden on you to imitate him, if you wish to reign with him ... Therefore it is fitting that you live, judge and act, even in secret, as if you were always in public ... But thus, as we say, with the Lord's aid, will you be able to live, judge and act, if you are not goaded by self-love; if you are not kindled by the desire for glory, riches, possessions and power; if you do not believe the tongues of others more than your own conscience ... if you are not agitated by neglect of the soul and by love of the flesh'): MGH Conc. III, no. 41, c. 11, pp. 419–20.

4. Sedulius Scottus, *Liber de rectoribus christianis*, written for Charles the Bald in 869:

'Omnis autem regia potestas ... non tam caducis opibus ac terrestri fortitudine, quam sapientia cultuque divino est exornanda, quoniam procul dubio tunc populus providi arte consilii gubernabitur, adversarii Domino propitiante profligabuntur, provinciae regnumque conservabitur, si regia sublimitas reli-gione et sapientia perornetur ... Est autem religiosa sapientia saluberrimum decus ... haec Salemon prae cunctis terrarum regibus sublimavit ... Unde regibus terrae egregium datur exemplum, quatinus spiritualia dona plus quam carnalia pio desiderio ab Omnipotenti exposcant, si diu et feliciter in hoc saeculo regnare desiderant' ('But all regal power ... should be adorned not so much with fleeting riches and earthly might, as with wisdom and divine veneration, because, if the regal dignity is adorned with religion and wisdom, then without doubt the people will be governed with the art of prudent counsel, enemies will be cast down with the Lord's help, and provinces and the realm will be preserved ... Indeed, religious wisdom is the most beneficial virtue ... this raised Solomon above all the kings of the earth [III Kings III. 11–14] Wherefore an excellent example is given to kings of the earth, that they should with a holy desire seek spiritual gifts rather than carnal gifts from God, if they wish to reign long and prosperously in this world'): *RC* 4, pp. 30–2.

5. Dedicatory verse to Charles's Second Bible, made for the king at St-Amand in the early 870s:

'Rex Salomon, quoniam potius tua dona petivit / Ut sapiens posset fieri, praecelsior ullis / Regibus existens opibus pollebat opimis ... Ergone tute tuum Karolum non diligis ultro? ... Est modus, ut nec habens habeat nec habere cupiscat, / Est et habens sicut nec habens, sed et erogat ultro: / Ista virum virtus condigno nomine comit. / Ecce patet, Salomon quoniam, o sapientia temet / Non plus dilexit Karolo sine fine beando ... Ergo nec hunc David nec Iob magis esse probatos / Apparet plane, pro te nec plura tulisse, / Quanta tuus Karolus mitis, pius atque benignus' ('[addressed to Wisdom] King Solomon, because he preferred to seek your gifts (so that he could become wise), being more splendid than other kings, he was strong with the best riches ... Do you not therefore love your Charles willingly? ... There is a way, so that not having, one has and does not desire to have, and, having, one is just as not having, and even willingly dispenses things: this virtue adorns the man with a worthy name. Behold it is clear, o wisdom, that Solomon did not love you more than Charles, blessed forever ... Therefore it is clear that neither David nor Job was tested more, nor bore more things for you, as much as your Charles, gentle, tender and kind'): MGH Poet. III, pp. 255–7, lines 41–3, 49, 82–6 and 95–7.

6. Verse preface by Hucbald of St-Amand (875×877) to a poem on sobriety written for Charles by the poet Milo:

'Quin etiam tanti congaudens principis omen / Orbis Roma caput subdidit ipsa caput ... Praeterea, quoniam commissi iura decenter / Disponis regni tu quoque lege dei, / Interius dum praefulget sapientia sensus / Exteriusque domus praenitet ex opibus, / Cum Salomone potens, prudenti pectore pollens / Terram laude reples, mente superna tenes' ('But also, rejoicing at the sign of so great a prince, even Rome, the head of the world, submits its head ... Moreover, because you also order fittingly the laws of the realm committed to you according to the law of God, while internally your understanding shines with wisdom and externally your house shines forth through wealth, powerful with Solomon, strong with a prudent chest, you fill the earth with praise and hold the earth with a supernal mind'): MGH Poet. III, p. 611, lines 11–12 and 15–20.

BIBLIOGRAPHY

For metalwork, 'æstels' and time-measurement, see Pratt, 'Persuasion', in *Court Culture*, ed. Cubitt, pp. 189–221. For ninth-century vernacular texts, cf. G. Waite, *Annotated Bibliographies of Old and Middle English Literature VI: Old English Prose Translations of King Alfred's Reign* (Cambridge, 2000). For Psalter commentaries, cf. texts listed by O'Neill in *Ps(P)*, pp. 352–3. For Boethius and his medieval reception, see also Chadwick, *Boethius*, pp. 261–84, and N. H. Kaylor jnr, *The Medieval Consolation of Philosophy: an Annotated Bibliography* (New York and London, 1992).

MANUSCRIPT SOURCES

(★ denotes manuscript consulted via microfilm)

★Bamberg, Staatsbibliothek, msc. Patr. 17/B. II. 10 (Alcuin, *De laude Dei*, etc: Mainz, s. xi^{in})

Cambridge, Corpus Christi College, MS 279 (*Liber ex lege Moysi*, etc: written at Tours or under Turonian influence, later at Worcester, s. ix$^{2/2}$)

Cambridge, University Library, MS Ii. 2. 4. (*Hierdeboc*: Exeter, s. xi$^{3/4}$)

Cambridge, University Library, MS Kk. 4. 6. (*Liber pontificalis*, marginal *Dicta* of Alfred: Worcester, s. xii)

Einsiedeln, Stiftsbibiothek, 179 (continuous commentary to *Cons. phil.*: St Gallen, s. x^{med}), in transcription supplied by Petrus Tax

★Krakow, Biblioteka Jagiellonska, Berl. Lat. Q. 939, formerly Maihingen, Bibliothek Wallerstein, I. 2. IV. ms. 3 (glossed *Cons. phil.* plus continuous commentary: Cologne and Tegernsee, s. x$^{4/4}$)

London, British Library, Add. 43470 (*Soliloquia*: Northern Italy, s. viii^{ex})

London, British Library, Cotton Otho E. xiii (*Liber ex lege Moysi*, etc, fire damaged: probably written in NW Francia, later at St Augustine's, Canterbury, s. x^{in})

Naples, Biblioteca Nazionale, IV. G. 68 (glossed *Cons. phil.*: Tours?, s. ix, glosses added s. x at St Gallen), in transcription supplied by Petrus Tax

★Paris, Bibliothèque Nationale de France, lat. 15090 (glossed *Cons. phil.*: St-Evre, Toul, s. x)

★Paris, Bibliothèque Nationale de France, nouv. acqu. lat. 1478 (glossed *Cons. phil.*: Cluny provenance, s. x–xi)

Bibliography

St Gallen, Stiftsbibliothek, 844 (glossed *Cons. phil.*: St Gallen, s. ix, glosses added s. x^med), in transcription supplied by Petrus Tax

★Trier, Stadtbibliothek, 1093/1694 (glossed *Cons. phil.*: Echternach, s. x$^{4/4}$)

PRINTED SOURCES

Ælfric, *Lives of the Saints*, ed. W. W. Skeat, EETS, os 76, 82, 94 and 114 (London, 1881–1900)

    First Series of Catholic Homilies, ed. P. Clemoes, EETS, ss 17 (1997)

Æthelweard, *Chronicle*, ed. A. Campbell, *The Chronicle of Æthelweard* (London, 1962)

Alcuin, *Epistolae*, ed. E. Duemmler, MGH Epist. IV (Berlin, 1895), 1–493

    Carmina, ed. E. Duemmler, MGH Poet. I (Berlin, 1881), 160–351

    De animae ratione, PL 101: 641–50

    De virtutibus et vitiis, PL 101: 613–38

    Disputatio de vera philosophia, PL 101: 919–50

Aldhelm, *Aenigmata*, ed. F. Glorie, CCSL 133 (Turnhout, 1968)

Alfred, *Domboc*, ed. F. Liebermann, *Die Gesetze der Angelsachsen*, 3 vols. (Halle, 1903–16) I, 16–123

    ed. M. H. Turk, *The Legal Code of Alfred the Great* (Halle, 1893)

Alfred, *Froferboc*, ed. W. J. Sedgefield, *King Alfred's Old English Version of Boethius: De Consolatione Philosophiae* (Oxford, 1899)

    trans. W. J. Sedgefield, *King Alfred's Old English Version of the Consolations of Boethius. Done into Modern English, with an Introduction* (Oxford, 1900)

    Alfred's Metres of Boethius, ed. B. Griffiths (Pinner, 1991)

Alfred, *Hierdeboc*, ed. and trans. H. Sweet, *King Alfred's West Saxon Version of Gregory's Pastoral Care*, EETS, os 45 and 50 (London, 1871)

    ed. I. Carlson (completed by L-G. Hallander *et al.*), *The Pastoral Care, edited from British Library MS. Cotton Otho B. ii.*, Stockholm Studies in English 34 and 48 (Stockholm, 1975–8)

    ed. C. Schreiber, *King Alfred's Old English Translation of Pope Gregory the Great's Regula Pastoralis and its Cultural Context: a Study and Partial Edition* (Munich, 2002)

Alfred, *First Fifty Psalms*, ed. P. P. O'Neill, *King Alfred's Old English Prose Translation of the First Fifty Psalms* (Cambridge, MA, 2001)

Alfred, *Soliloquies*, ed. T. A. Carnicelli, *King Alfred's Version of St. Augustine's Soliloquies* (Cambridge, MA, 1969)

    trans. H. L. Hargrove, *King Alfred's Old English Version of St. Augustine's Soliloquies Turned into Modern English* (Albany, NY, 1904)

Anglo-Saxon Chronicle, ed. C. Plummer, *Two of the Saxon Chronicles Parallel*, 2 vols. (Oxford, 1892–9)

    trans. D. Whitelock, D. C. Douglas and S. I. Tucker, *The Anglo-Saxon Chronicle: a Revised Translation* (London, 1961)

Ansegisus, *Capitularium Collectio*, ed. G. Schmitz, MGH Capit. nova series I (Hanover, 1996)

Asser, *Life of King Alfred*, ed. W. H. Stevenson, *Asser's Life of King Alfred, together with the Annals of St Neots, erroneously ascribed to Asser*, new imp. (Oxford, 1959)

Bibliography

trans. S. Keynes and M. Lapidge, *Alfred the Great: Asser's Life of King Alfred and other Contemporary Sources* (Harmondsworth, 1983)

Astronomer, *Gesta Hludowici imperatoris*, ed. E. Tremp, MGH Scriptores rerum Germanicarum in usum scholarum separatim editi 64 (Hanover, 1995)

Attenborough, F. L. (ed.), *The Laws of the Earliest English Kings* (Cambridge, 1922)

Augustine, *De ciuitate Dei*, ed. and trans. G. E. McCracken, *et al.*, *Saint Augustine: the City of God against the Pagans*, 7 vols. (Cambridge, MA, 1963–72)

De inmortalitate animae, ed. W. Hörmann, CSEL 89 (Vienna, 1986), 101–28

De quantitate animae, W. Hörmann, CSEL 89 (Vienna, 1986), 131–231

De uidendo Deo, ed. A. Goldbacher, CSEL 44 (Vienna and Leipzig, 1904), 274–331

Enarrationes in Psalmos, ed. E. Dekkers and J. Fraipont, CCSL 38–40 (Turnhout, 1956)

Retractationes, ed. A. Mutzenbecher, CCSL 57 (Turnhout, 1984)

Sermones de Vetere Testamento, ed. C. Lambot, CCSL 41 (Turnhout, 1961)

Soliloquiorum libri duo, ed. W. Hörmann, CSEL 89 (Vienna, 1986), 3–98

trans. G. Watson, *Saint Augustine: Soliloquies and Immortality of the Soul* (Warminster, 1990)

Bately, J., *The Tanner Bede*, EEMF 24 (Copenhagen, 1992)

Bede, *Historia ecclesiastica gentis Anglorum*, ed. C. Plummer, *Venerabilis Baedae Opera Historica*, 2 vols. (Oxford, 1896)

The Old English Version of Bede's Ecclesiastical History of the English People, ed. T. Miller, EETS, os 95–6 and 110–11 (London, 1890–8)

Bede, *Hymni et Preces*, ed. J. Fraipont, CCSL 122 (Turnhout, 1955), 406–70

In Epistolas VII Catholicas, ed. D. Hurst, CCSL 121 (Turnhout, 1983), 179–342

In Lucae evangelium expositio, ed. D. Hurst, CCSL 120 (Turnhout, 1960)

Martyrologium, ed. J. Dubois and G. Renaud, *Edition pratique des martyrologes de Bede, de l'anonyme lyonnais et de Florus* (Paris, 1976)

Birch, W. de G. (ed.), *Cartularium Saxonicum*, 3 vols. (London, 1885–93)

Boese, H., *Die alte Glosa Psalmorum ex traditione seniorum: Untersuchungen, Materialen, Texte*, Vetus Latina 9 (Freiburg, 1982)

Boese, H. (ed.), *Anonymi Glosa Psalmorum ex traditione seniorum*, Vetus Latina 22 and 25 (Freiburg, 1992)

Boethius, *Consolatio philosophiae*, ed. L. Bieler, CCSL 94, 2nd edn (Turnhout, 1984)

ed. R. Peiper, *Philosophiae Consolationis Libri Quinque* (Leipzig, 1871)

trans. V. E. Watts, *Boethius: the Consolation of Philosophy* (London, 1969)

Boniface, *Epistolae*, ed. M. Tangl, *Die Briefe der heiligen Bonifatius und Lullus*, MGH Epistolae Selectae 1 (Berlin, 1916)

Campbell, A. (ed.), *Charters of Rochester* (London, 1973)

Capitularia Regum Francorum, ed. A. Boretius and V. Krause, MGH Legum sectio II, 2 vols. (Hanover, 1883–97)

Cassiodorus, *Expositio Psalmorum*, ed. M. Adriaen, CCSL 97–8 (Turnhout, 1958)

Institutiones, ed. R. A. B. Mynors (Oxford, 1937)

Charles the Bald (patron), *Bibliothecarum et Psalteriorum Versus*, ed. L. Traube, MGH Poet. III (Berlin, 1896), 241–64

Cockayne, O., *Leechdoms, Wortcunning, and Starcraft of Early England*, 3 vols. (London, 1864–6)

Colgrave, B. (ed.), *The Earliest Life of Gregory the Great* (Lawrence, KA, 1968)

Bibliography

Colgrave, B., *et al.*, *The Paris Psalter*, EEMF 8 (Copenhagen, 1958)

Concilia Aevi Karolini, MGH Legum sectio III, Concilia II.i–ii, ed. A. Werminghoff (Hanover, 1906–8); III–IV, ed. W. Hartmann (Hanover, 1984–98)

Cox, R. S., 'The Old English Dicts of Cato', *Anglia* 90 (1972), 1–42

Cross, J. E., and Hamer, A. (eds.), *Wulfstan's Canon Law Collection* (Cambridge, 1999)

Deshusses, J., *Sacramentaire grégorien*, Spicilegium Friburgense 16, 24 and 28 (Freiburg, 1971–82)

Dhuoda, *Liber manualis*, ed. M. Thiebaux (Cambridge, 1998)

Dumas, A., and Deshusses, J. (eds.), *Liber sacramentorum Gellonensis*, CCSL 159 and 159A (Turnhout, 1981)

Dutton, P. E., *Carolingian Civilization: a Reader* (Ontario, 1993)

Einhard, *Vita Karoli*, ed. O. Holder-Egger, MGH Scriptores rerum Germanicarum in usum scholarum separatim editi 25 (Hanover, 1911)

trans. P. E. Dutton, *Charlemagne's Courtier: the Complete Einhard* (Ontario, 1998)

Eriugena, *Carmina*, ed. and trans. M. W. Herren, Scriptores Latini Hiberniae 12 (Dublin, 1993)

De divina praedestinatione liber, ed. G. Madec, CCCM 50 (Turnhout, 1978)

Expositiones in ierarchiam coelestem, ed. J. Barbet, CCCM 31 (Turnhout, 1975)

Periphyseon, ed. and trans. I. P. Sheldon-Williams, L. Bieler, E. Jeauneau and J. J. O'Meara, Scriptores Latini Hiberniae 7, 9, 11 and 13 (Dublin, 1968–); Book V in PL 122: 859–1022

Versio operum S. Dionysii Areopagitae, PL 122: 1023–94

Flodoard, *Historia Remensis ecclesiae*, ed. M. Stratmann, MGH SS XXXVI (Hanover, 1998)

Gesta episcoporum Autissiodorensium, ed. G. Waitz, MGH SS XIII (Hanover, 1881), 393–400

Gibbs, M. (ed.), *Early Charters of the Cathedral Church of St Paul, London* (London, 1939)

Godman, P., *Poetry of the Carolingian Renaissance* (London, 1985)

Grat, F., *et al.* (eds.), *Annales de Saint-Bertin* (Paris, 1964)

Gregory the Great, *Dialogi*, ed. A. de Vogüé, with P. Antin, *Grégoire le Grand: Dialogues*, SC 251, 260 and 265 (Paris, 1978–80)

Homilia in Evangelia, PL 76: 1075–1312

Moralia in Iob, ed. M. Adriaen, CCSL 143, 143A and 143B (Turnhout, 1979–85)

Regula pastoralis, ed. F. Rommel, with B. Judic and C. Morel, *Grégoire le Grand: Règle Pastorale*, SC 381–2 (Paris, 1992)

trans. H. Davis, *St Gregory the Great: Pastoral Care*, Ancient Christian Writers 11 (Westminster, MD, and London, 1950)

Haddan, A. W., and Stubbs, W. (eds.), *Councils and Ecclesiastical Documents relating to Great Britain and Ireland*, 3 vols. (Oxford, 1869–79)

Haimo of Auxerre, *Expositio in Apocalypsin*, PL 117: 937–1220

Harmer, F. E. (ed.), *Select English Historical Documents of the Ninth and Tenth Centuries* (Cambridge, 1914)

Heiric of Auxerre, *De miraculis Sancti Germani episcopi Autissiodorensis libri II*, ed. M. L.-M. Duru, *Bibliothèque historique de l'Yonne*, 2 vols. (Paris, 1850–63), I

Herren, M. W., 'The De imagine Tetrici of Walahfrid Strabo: Edition and Translation', *Journal of Medieval Latin* 1 (1991), 118–39

Bibliography

Hincmar of Rheims, *Epistolae*, ed. E. Perels, MGH Epist. VIII.1 (Berlin, 1939)
   Ad episcopos regni, PL 125: 1007–18
   De cavendis vitiis et virtutibus exercendis, PL 125: 857–930
   De divortio Lotharii regis et Tetbergae reginae, PL 125: 619–772
   De ecclesiis et capellis, ed. M. Stratmann, MGH Fontes iuris Germanici antiqui in usum scholarum separatim editi 14 (Hanover, 1990)
   De ordine palatii, ed. T. Gross and R. Schieffer, MGH Fontes iuris Germanici antiqui in usum scholarum separatim editi 3 (Hanover, 1980)
   De regis persona et regio ministerio, PL 125: 833–56
   Opusculum, PL 126: 282–494
   Quaterniones, PL 125: 1035–60
Hrabanus Maurus, *Epistolae*, ed. E. Dümmler, MGH Epist. V (Berlin, 1899), 381–515
Hucbald of St-Amand, *Carmina*, ed. L. Traube, MGH Poet. III (Berlin, 1896), 610–12; ed. P. De Winterfeld, MGH Poet. IV.1 (Berlin, 1899), 261–75
   Vita sancti Lebuini, PL 132: 875–94
Isidore of Seville, *Etymologiae*, ed. W. M. Lindsay, 2 vols. (Oxford, 1911)
   Sententiae, PL 83: 537–738
Jackson, R. A. (ed.), *Ordines Coronationis Franciae: Texts and Ordines for the Coronation of Frankish and French Kings and Queens in the Middle Ages*, 2 vols. (Philadelphia, 1995 and 2000)
Jerome, *Commentarius in Esaiam*, ed. M. Adriaen, CCSL 73 and 73A (Turnhout, 1963)
   Commentarius in Ecclesiasten, ed. P. de Lagarde, CCSL 72 (Turnhout, 1959)
   Commentarius in Sophoniam, ed. M. Adriaen, CCSL 76 and 76A (Turnhout, 1970)
John of Worcester, *Chronicle*, ed. R. R. Darlington and P. McGurk, with J. Bray, 3 vols. (Oxford, 1995–)
   ed. B. Thorpe, *Florentii Wigorniensis monachi Chronicon ex Chronicis*, 2 vols. (London, 1848–9)
Jonas of Orléans, *De institutione laicali*, PL 106: 121–278
   De institutione regia, ed. A. Dubreucq, *Jonas d'Orléans: Le Métier de Roi (De institutione regia)*, SC 407 (Paris, 1995)
   trans. R. W. Dyson, *A Ninth-Century Political Tract: the De Institutione Regia of Jonas of Orleans* (Smithtown, NY, 1983)
Kelly, S. (ed.), *The Charters of Shaftesbury Abbey* (Oxford, 1996)
Kelly, S. (ed.), *The Charters of St Augustine's Abbey, Canterbury, and Minster-in-Thanet* (Oxford, 1996)
Kelly, S. (ed.), *The Charters of Abingdon Abbey* (Oxford, 2000)
Ker, N. R., *The Pastoral Care*, EEMF 6 (Copenhagen, 1956)
Keynes, S., *The Liber Vitae of the New Minster and Hyde Abbey Winchester*, EEMF 26 (Copenhagen, 1996)
Klinck, A. L., *The Old English Elegies* (Montreal, 1992)
Kotzor, G. (ed.), *Das altenglische Martyrologium*, 2 vols. (Munich, 1981)
Kuhn, S. M., *The Vespasian Psalter* (Ann Arbor, MI, 1965)
Kurze, F. (ed.), *Annales Fuldenses*, MGH Scriptores rerum Germanicarum in usum scholarum separatim editi 7 (Hanover, 1891)
Kurze, F. (ed.), *Reginonis abbatis Prumiensis Chronicon*, MGH Scriptores rerum Germanicarum in usum scholarum 50 (Hanover, 1890)

Bibliography

Kuypers, A. B., *The Prayer Book of Ædeluald the Bishop, Commonly Called the Book of Cerne* (Cambridge, 1902)

Lactantius, *Divinae institutiones*, PL 6: 111–822

Leges Nationum Germanicarum, MGH Legum sectio I, ed. K. Zeumer, K. A. Eckhardt, *et al.*, 6 vols. (Hanover, 1892–1969)

Liebermann, F., *Die Gesetze der Angelsachsen*, 3 vols. (Halle, 1903–16)

Lupus of Ferrières, *Epistolae*, ed. P. K. Marshall (Leipzig, 1984)

Lutz, C. A. (ed.), *Remigii Autissiodorensis Commentum in Martianum Capellam*, 2 vols. (Leiden, 1962–5)

Malone, K., *Deor*, rev. edn (London, 1977)

Malone, K., *Widsith* (London, 1936)

McNamara, M. (ed.), *Glossa in Psalmos: the Hiberno-Latin Gloss on the Psalms of Codex Palatinus Latinus 68 (Psalms 39:11–151:7)*, Studi e testi 310 (Vatican City, 1986)

Migne, J.-P. (ed.), *Patrologiae Cursus Completus. Series (Latina) Prima*, 221 vols. (Paris, 1844–64)

Miracula Sancti Bertini, ed. O. Holder Egger, MGH SS XV.1 (Hanover, 1887), 509–16

Mohlberg, R. C., Eisenhöfer, L., and Siffrin, P. (eds.), *Liber Sacramentorum Romanae aecclesiae ordinis anni circuli (Sacramentarium Gelasianum)*, Rerum Ecclesiasticarum Documenta, series maior 4 (Rome, 1960)

Norman, F., *Waldere* (London, 1933)

Notker the Stammerer, *Gesta Karoli Magni Imperatoris*, ed. H. F. Haefele, MGH Scriptores rerum Germanicarum, nova series 12 (Berlin, 1959)

O'Donovan, M. A. (ed.), *The Charters of Sherborne* (Oxford, 1988)

Orosius, *Historiae aduersum paganos*, ed. C. F. W. Zangemeister, CSEL 5 (Vienna, 1882)

The Old English Orosius, ed. J. M. Bately, EETS, ss 6 (London, New York and Toronto, 1980)

Paschasius Radbertus, *Expositio in Matthaeum*, PL 120: 31–994

Vita sancti Adalhardi, PL 120: 1507–56

Epitaphium Arsenii seu Vita venerabilis Walae, PL 120: 1559–650

trans. A. Cabaniss, *Charlemagne's Cousins* (Syracuse, NY, 1967)

Paulinus of Aquileia, *Liber exhortationis*, PL 99: 197–292

Prudentius, *Psychomachia*, ed. H. J. Thomson (Cambridge, MA, and London, 1949–53)

pseudo-Bede, *In psalmorum librum exegesis*, PL 93: 477–1098

pseudo-Cyprian, *De XII Abusivis Saeculi*, ed. S. Hellmann, Texte und Untersuchungen zur geschichte der Altchristlichen Literatur 34 (1) (Leipzig, 1910)

pseudo-Hincmar, *De diversa et multiplici animae ratione*, PL 125: 929–48

Richter, M. (ed.), *Canterbury Professions* (Torquay, 1973)

Robertson, A. J., *The Laws of the Kings of England from Edmund to Henry I* (Cambridge, 1925)

Robertson, A. J. (ed.), *Anglo-Saxon Charters*, 2nd edn (Cambridge, 1956)

Sabatier, P. (ed.), *Bibliorum Sacrorum latinae uersiones antiquae seu uetus Italica*, 3 vols. (Rheims, 1743–9)

Salmon, P. (ed.), *Les Tituli Psalmorum des manuscrits latins*, Collectanea Biblica Latina 12 (Vatican City, 1959)

Sedulius Scottus, *Liber de rectoribus christianis*, ed. S. Hellmann, *Sedulius Scottus*, Quellen und Untersuchungen zur lateinischen Philologie des Mittelalters 1(1) (Munich, 1906)

Bibliography

Carmina, ed. L. Traube, MGH Poet. III (Berlin, 1896), 151–240

trans. E. G. Doyle, *Sedulius Scottus: On Christian Rulers and the Poems* (Binghamton, NY, 1983)

Shippey, T. A., *Poems of Wisdom and Learning in Old English* (Cambridge, 1976)

Silk, E. T., *Saeculi Noni Auctoris in Boetii Consolationem Philosophiae Commentarius*, Papers and Monographs of the American Academy in Rome 9 (Rome, 1935)

Simpson, D., 'The "Proverbia Grecorum"', *Traditio* 43 (1987), 1–22

Smaragdus, *Via regia*, PL 102: 931–70

Stephanus, *Vita Wilfridi*, ed. B. Colgrave, *The Life of Bishop Wilfrid* (Cambridge, 1927)

Stevenson, J. (ed.), *Chronicon Monasterii de Abingdon*, 2 vols. (London, 1858)

Stewart, H. F., 'A Commentary by Remigius Autissiodorensis on the De Consolatione Philosophiae of Boethius', *JTS* 17 (1915), 22–42

Stokes, W., and Strachan, J. (eds.), *Thesaurus Palaeohibernicus*, 2 vols. (Cambridge, 1901–3)

Symeon of Durham, *Historia regum*, ed. T. Arnold, *Symeonis Monachi Opera Omnia*, 2 vols. (London, 1885)

The Anglo-Saxon Poetic Records, ed. G. P. Krapp and E. van K. Dobbie, 6 vols. (New York, 1931–42)

Thegan, *Gesta Hludowici imperatoris*, ed. E. Tremp, MGH Scriptores rerum Germanicarum in usum scholarum separatim editi 64 (Hanover, 1995)

Theodore of Mopsuestia, *Expositio in Psalmos* (fragmentary), ed. L. de Coninck, *Theodori Mopsuesteni Expositionis in Psalmos Iuliano Aeclanensi Interprete in Latinum Uersae Quae Supersunt*, CCSL 88A (Turnhout, 1977)

Theodulf of Orléans, *Ad iudices*, ed. E. Duemmler, MGH Poet. I (Berlin, 1881), 493–517

Vita Alcuini, ed. W. Arndt, MGH SS XV.1 (Hanover, 1887), 182–97

Vleeskruyer, R., *The Life of St Chad: an Old English Homily* (Amsterdam, 1953)

Wærferth, *Dialogues*, ed. H. Hecht, *Bischof Wærferths von Worcester Übersetzung der Dialoge Gregors des Grossen*, 2 vols. (Leipzig, 1900–7)

Warren, F. E. (ed.), *The Leofric Missal* (Oxford, 1883)

Wasserschleben, H. (ed.), *Die irische Kanonensammlung*, 2nd edn (Leipzig, 1885)

Watkin, A. (ed.), *The Great Cartulary of Glastonbury*, 3 vols. (Frome, 1947–56)

Weber, R. (ed.), *Le Psautier romain et les autres anciens psautiers latins*, Collectanea Biblica Latina 10 (Vatican, 1953)

Weber, R., et al. (eds.), *Biblia Sacra Iuxta Vulgatam Versionem*, 4th edn (Stuttgart, 1994)

Whitelock, D. (ed.), *Sweet's Anglo-Saxon Reader*, 15th edn (Oxford, 1970)

Whitelock, D. (ed.), *English Historical Documents, c. 500–1042*, English Historical Documents I, 2nd edn (London, 1979)

Whitelock, D., Brett, M., and Brooke, C. N. L. (eds.), *Councils and Synods with other Documents relating to the English Church I*, 2 vols. (Oxford, 1981)

Wickham Legg, L. G., *English Coronation Records* (London, 1901)

William of Malmesbury, *Gesta Regum Anglorum*, ed. R. A. B. Mynors, R. M. Thomson and M. Winterbottom, 2 vols. (Oxford, 1998–9)

De Gestis Pontificum Anglorum, ed. N. E. S. A. Hamilton (London, 1870)

Williams, ab Ithel, J. (ed.), *Annales Cambriae* (London, 1860)

Bibliography

Wordsworth, J., and White, H. J. (eds.), *Nouum Testamentum Domini Nostri Iesu Christi Latinae secundum editionem Sancti Hieronymi*, 3 vols. (Oxford, 1889–1954)

Wright, C. E., *Bald's Leechbook. British Museum Royal Manuscript 12. D. xvii*, EEMF 5 (Copenhagen, 1955)

Wright, D. H., *The Vespasian Psalter*, EEMF 14 (Copenhagen, 1967)

Wulfstan of Winchester, *Life of St Æthelwold*, ed. M. Lapidge and M. Winterbottom (Oxford, 1991)

Zupitza, J., 'Drei alte Excerpte aus Alfreds Beda', *Zeitschrift für deutsches Altertum* 30 (1886), 185–6

PRINTED SECONDARY WORKS

Abels, R. P., *Lordship and Military Obligation in Anglo-Saxon England* (Berkeley and Los Angeles, CA, 1988)

Alfred the Great (Harlow, 1998)

Ackroyd, P. R., and Evans, C. F. (eds.), *The Cambridge History of the Bible I* (Cambridge, 1970)

Airlie, S., 'The Aristocracy', in *NCMH* II, 431–50

'The Anxiety of Sanctity: St Gerald of Aurillac and his Maker', *JEH* 43 (1992), 372–95

'Private Bodies and the Body Politic in the Divorce Case of Lothar II', *P&P* 161 (November 1998), 3–38

'The Palace of Memory: the Carolingian Court as Political Centre', in *Courts and Regions in Medieval Europe*, ed. S. R. Jones, R. Marks and A. J. Minnis (York, 2000), pp. 1–20

'True Teachers and Pious Kings: Salzburg, Louis the German, and Christian Order', in *Belief and Culture*, ed. Gameson and Leyser, pp. 89–105

Alberi, M., '"The Better Paths of Wisdom": Alcuin's Monastic "True Philosophy" and the Worldly Court', *Speculum* 76 (2001), 896–910

Althoff, G., *Spielregeln der Politik im Mittelalter* (Darmstadt, 1997)

'Friendship and Political Order', in *Friends and Friendship*, ed. Haseldine, pp. 91–105

Otto III, trans. P. G. Jestice (Pennsylvania, PA, 2003)

Family, Friends and Followers, trans. C. Carroll (Cambridge, 2004)

Amory, P., 'The Meaning and Purpose of Ethnic Terminology in the Burgundian Laws', *EME* 2 (1993), 1–28

Anderton, M. (ed.), *Anglo-Saxon Trading Centres: Beyond the Emporia* (Glasgow, 1999)

Andrieu, M., 'Le sacre épiscopal d'après Hincmar de Reims', *Revue d'Histoire ecclésiastique* 48.1 (1953), 22–73

Anlezark, D., 'Three Notes on the Old English Meters of Boethius', *Notes and Queries* 51:1 (2004), 10–15

Anon., 'Bull Wharf: Queenhithe', *Current Archaeology* 14.2 (no. 158) (July 1998), 75–7

Anton, H. H., *Fürstenspiegel und Herrscherethos in der Karolingerzeit*, Bonner Historische Forschungen 32 (Bonn, 1968)

'Synoden, Teilreichsepiskopat und die Herausbildung Lotharingiens', in *Herrschaft, Kirche, Kultur: Beiträge zur Geschichte des Mittelalters*, ed. G. Jenal and S. Haarlander (Stuttgart, 1993), pp. 83–124

Bibliography

Arquillière, H.-X., *L'Augustinisme politique*, 2nd edn (Paris, 1955)

Ayre, J. and Wroe-Brown, R., 'Æthelred's Hythe to Queenhithe: the Origin of a London Dock', *Medieval Life* 5 (1996), 14–25

Backhouse, J., Turner, D. H., and Webster, L. E. (eds.), *The Golden Age of Anglo-Saxon Art 966–1066* (London, 1984)

Bakka, E., 'The Alfred Jewel and Sight', *Antiquaries Journal* 46 (1966), 277–82

Balzaretti, R., Nelson, J. L., and Maddicott, J., 'Debate: Trade, Industry and the Wealth of King Alfred', *P&P* 135 (1992), 142–88

Banniard, M., 'Language and Communication in Carolingian Europe', in *NCMH* II, 695–708

Banton, N., 'Monastic Reform and the Unification of Tenth-Century England', in *Religion and National Identity*, ed. S. Mews (Oxford, 1982), pp. 71–85

Barrow, J., 'Friends and Friendship in Anglo-Saxon Charters', in *Friends and Friendship*, ed. Haseldine, pp. 106–23

  'Survival and Mutation: Ecclesiastical Institutions in the Danelaw in the Ninth and Tenth Centuries', in *Cultures in Contact*, ed. Hadley and Richards, pp. 155–76

Bassett, S. (ed.), *The Origins of Anglo-Saxon Kingdoms* (Leicester, 1989)

Batany, J., 'Le vocabulaire des fonctions sociales et ecclésiastiques chez Grégoire le Grand', in *Grégoire le Grand*, ed. Fontaine, Gillet and Pellistrandi, pp. 171–80

Bately, J. M., 'Grimbald of St. Bertin's', *Medium Ævum* 35 (1966), 1–10

  'King Alfred and the Old English Translation of Orosius', *Anglia* 88 (1970), 433–60

  'The Compilation of the Anglo-Saxon Chronicle, 60 BC to AD 890: Vocabulary as Evidence', *PBA* 64 (1978), 93–129

  'World History in the Anglo-Saxon Chronicle: its Sources and its Separateness from the Old English Orosius', *ASE* 8 (1979), 177–94

  The Literary Prose of King Alfred's Reign: Translation or Transformation? (London, 1980)

  'Lexical Evidence for the Authorship of the Prose Psalms in the Paris Psalter', *ASE* 10 (1982), 69–95

  'Evidence for Knowledge of Latin Literature in Old English', in *Sources of Anglo-Saxon Culture*, ed. Szarmach, pp. 35–51

  'Old English Prose before and during the Reign of Alfred', *ASE* 17 (1989), 93–138

  ' "Those Books that are Most Necessary for All Men to Know": the Classics and Late Ninth-Century England, a Reappraisal', in *The Classics and the Middle Ages*, ed. A. S. Bernardo and S. Levin (Binghampton, NY, 1990), pp. 45–78

  The Anglo-Saxon Chronicle: Texts and Textual Relationships (Reading, 1991)

  'An Alfredian Legacy? On the Fortunes and Fate of some Items of Boethian Vocabulary in Old English', in *From Anglo-Saxon to Early Middle English: Studies presented to E. G. Stanley*, ed. M. Godden, D. Gray and T. Hoad (Oxford, 1994), pp. 8–32

  'Boethius and King Alfred', in *Platonism and the English Imagination*, ed. A. Baldwin and S. Hutton (Cambridge, 1994), pp. 38–44

  'The Alfredian Canon Revisited: One Hundred Years On', in *Alfred*, ed. Reuter, pp. 107–20

Beaumont, J., 'The Latin Tradition of the De Consolatione Philosophiae', in *Boethius*, ed. Gibson, pp. 278–305

Bibliography

Becher, M., *Eid und Herrschaft: Untersuchungen zum Herrscherethos Karls des Grossen* (Sigmaringen, 1993)

Beck, H. G., 'Canonical Election to Suffragan Bishops according to Hincmar of Rheims', *Catholic Historical Review* 43 (1957), 137–69

'The Selection of Bishops Suffragan to Hincmar of Rheims 845–882', *Catholic Historical Review* 45 (1959), 273–308

Beer, J. (ed.), *Translation Theory and Practice in the Middle Ages* (Kalamazoo, MI, 1997)

Bentley, M. (ed.), *Companion to Historiography* (London and New York, 1997)

Bestul, T. H., 'Continental Sources of Anglo-Saxon Devotional Writing', in *Sources of Anglo-Saxon Culture*, ed. Szarmach, pp. 104–26

Bethurum Loomis, D., '*Regnum* and *sacerdotium* in the Early Eleventh Century', in *England before the Conquest: Studies presented to Dorothy Whitelock*, ed. P. Clemoes and K. Hughes (Cambridge, 1971), pp. 129–45

Biddle, M., 'Late Saxon Planned Towns', *Antiquaries Journal* 51 (1971), 70–85

'The Evolution of Towns: Planned Towns before 1066', in *The Plans and Topography of Medieval Towns in England and Wales*, ed. M. W. Barley, CBA Research Report 14 (London, 1976), 19–32

'The Study of Winchester: Archaeology and History in a British Town, 1961–1983', *PBA* 69 (1983), 93–135

Biddle, M. (ed.), *Winchester Studies I: Winchester in the Early Middle Ages* (Oxford, 1976)

Bijsterveld, A. J., 'The Medieval Gift as Agent of Social Bonding and Political Power: a Comparative Approach', in *Medieval Transformations: Texts, Power, and Gifts in Context*, ed. E. Cohen and M. de Jong (Leiden, 2001), pp. 123–56

Binchy, D. A., 'The Pseudo-Historical Prologue to the *Senchas Már*', *Studia Celtica* 10–11 (1975–6), 15–28

Bischoff, B., *Mittelalterliche Studien*, 3 vols. (Stuttgart, 1966–81)

Bischoff, B., and Lapidge, M., *Biblical Commentaries from the Canterbury School of Theodore and Hadrian* (Cambridge, 1994)

Bjork, R. E., and Niles, J. D. (eds.), *A Beowulf Handbook* (Exeter, 1997)

Bjork, R. E., and Obermeier, A., 'Date, Provenance, Author, Audiences', in *A Beowulf Handbook*, ed. Bjork and Niles, pp. 13–34

Blackburn, M., 'Mints, Burhs, and the Grately Code, cap. 14.2', in *Defence*, ed. Hill and Rumble, pp. 160–7

'The London Mint in the Reign of Alfred', in *Kings, Currency and Alliances*, ed. Blackburn and Dumville, pp. 105–23

'Alfred's Coinage Reforms in Context', in *Alfred*, ed. Reuter, pp. 199–215

'"Productive" Sites and the Pattern of Coin Loss in England, 600–1180', in *Markets in Early Medieval Europe: Trading and 'Productive' Sites, 650–850*, ed. T. Pestell and K. Ulmschneider (Macclesfield, 2003), pp. 20–36

Blackburn, M., and Dumville, D. N. (eds.), *Kings, Currency and Alliances: History and Coinage of Southern England in the Ninth Century* (Woodbridge, 1998)

Blair, J., *The Church in Anglo-Saxon Society* (Oxford, 2005)

Blair, J., and Sharpe, R. (eds.), *Pastoral Care before the Parish* (Leicester, 1992)

Bloch, M., *Ritual, History and Power* (London, 1989)

Blunt, C. E., Stewart, B. H. I. H., and Lyon, C. S. S., *Coinage in Tenth-Century England from Edward the Elder to Edgar's Reform* (Oxford, 1989)

Bibliography

Bolton, D. K., 'Remigian Commentaries on the Consolation of Philosophy and their Sources', *Traditio* 19 (1977), 381–94

'The Study of the Consolation of Philosophy in Anglo-Saxon England', *Archives d'histoire doctrinale et litteraire du Moyen Age* 44 (1977), 33–78

Bolton, W. F., 'How Boethian is Alfred's Boethius?', in *Studies*, ed. Szarmach, pp. 153–68

Bonner, G., *St Augustine of Hippo: Life and Controversies*, 2nd edn (Norwich, 1986)

Booth, P. A., 'King Alfred versus Beowulf: the Re-education of the Anglo-Saxon Aristocracy', *Bulletin of the John Rylands University Library of Manchester* 79.3 (Autumn 1997), 41–66

Bostock, J. K., *A Handbook on Old High German Literature*, 2nd edn, revised by K. C. King and D. R. McLintock (Oxford, 1976)

Bourdieu, P., *The Field of Cultural Production*, ed. R. Johnson (Cambridge, 1993)

Boynton, M., and Reynolds, S., 'The Author of the Fonthill Letter', *ASE* 25 (1996), 91–5

Bremmer, R. H., Dekker, K., and Johnson, D. F. (eds.), *Rome and the North: the Early Reception of Gregory the Great in Germanic Europe* (Leuven, 2001)

Bright, J. W., and Ramsay, R. L., 'Notes on the Introductions of the West-Saxon Psalms', *JTS* 13 (1912), 520–58

Brook, C. N. L., 'Alfred the Great', *History Today* 13 (1963), 143–51

Brooks, N. P., *The Early History of the Church of Canterbury* (Leicester, 1984)

'The Career of St Dunstan', in *St Dunstan: his Life, Times and Cult*, ed. N. Ramsay, M. Sparks and T. Tatton-Brown (Woodbridge, 1992), pp. 1–23

'The Administrative Background to the Burghal Hidage', in *Defence*, ed. Hill and Rumble, pp. 128–50

Communities and Warfare 700–1400 (London, 2000)

Anglo-Saxon Myths: State and Church (London, 2000)

'Alfredian Government: the West Saxon Inheritance', in *Alfred*, ed. Reuter, pp. 153–73

Brown, G. H., 'Latin Writing and the Old English Vernacular', in *Schriftlichkeit im frühen Mittelalter*, ed. U Schaefer, ScriptOralia 53 (Tübingen, 1993), 36–57

'The Dynamics of Literacy in Anglo-Saxon England', *Bulletin of the John Rylands University Library of Manchester* 77.1 (1995), 109–42.

Brown, G., 'Introduction: the Carolingian Renaissance', in *Carolingian Culture*, ed. McKitterick, pp. 1–51

Brown, M., *The Book of Cerne: Prayer, Patronage and Power in Ninth-Century England* (London, 1996)

Brown, M., and Farr, C. (eds.), *Mercia: an Anglo-Saxon Kingdom in Europe* (London, 2001)

Brown, P., *Augustine of Hippo* (London, 1967)

Brown, V., 'Lupus of Ferrières on the Meters of Boethius', in *Latin Script and Letters AD 400–900: Festschrift presented to L. Bieler*, ed. J. J. O'Meara and B. Naumann (Leiden, 1976), pp. 63–79

Brown, W. H., 'Method and Style in the Old English Pastoral Care', *Journal of English and Germanic Philology* 68 (1969), 666–84

Brunhölzl, F., 'Der Bildungsauftrag der Hofschule', in *Karl der Grosse. Lebenswerk und Nachleben*, ed. W. Braunfels, 5 vols. (Düsseldorf, 1965–8) II, 28–41

Bibliography

Bullough, D. A., 'Anglo-Saxon Institutions and Early English Society', *Annali della fondazione italiana per la storia amministrativa* 2 (1965), 647–59

The Age of Charlemagne (London, 1973)

'The Continental Background of the Reform', in *Tenth-Century Studies*, ed. D. Parsons (London, 1975), pp. 20–36

'*Albuinus deliciosus Karoli regis*: Alcuin of York and the Shaping of the Early Carolingian Court', in *Institutionen, Kultur und Gesellschaft im Mittelalter: Festschrift für Josef Fleckenstein zu seinem 65. Geburtstag*, ed. L. Fenske, W. Rösener and T. Zotz (Sigmaringen, 1984), pp. 73–92

Carolingian Renewal: Sources and Heritage (Manchester and New York, 1991)

Bullough, D., and Corrêa, A. L. H., 'Texts, Chant, and the Chapel of Louis the Pious', in *Charlemagne's Heir*, ed. Godman and Collins, pp. 489–508

Burke, P., *The Fabrication of Louis XIV* (New Haven, CT, 1992)

Burns, J. H. (ed.), *The Cambridge History of Medieval Political Thought c.350–c.1450* (Cambridge, 1988)

Cam, H. M., *Local Government in Francia and England* (London, 1912)

Campbell, J., *Essays in Anglo-Saxon History* (London, 1986)

The Anglo-Saxon State (London, 2000)

'Anglo-Saxon Courts', in *Court Culture*, ed. Cubitt, pp. 155–69

'Placing King Alfred', in *Alfred*, ed. Reuter, pp. 3–23

Campbell, J. (ed.), *The Anglo-Saxons* (Oxford, 1982)

Carlyle, A. J. and R. W., *A History of Medieval Political Theory in the West*, 6 vols. (Edinburgh, 1903–36)

Chadwick, H. M., *Studies in Anglo-Saxon Institutions* (Cambridge, 1905)

The Heroic Age (Cambridge, 1912)

Chadwick, H., 'Introduction', in *Boethius*, ed. Gibson, pp. 1–12

Boethius: the Consolations of Music, Logic, Theology, and Philosophy (Oxford, 1981)

Augustine (Oxford, 1986)

Chaney, W. A., *The Cult of Kingship in Anglo-Saxon England* (Manchester, 1970)

Chaplais, P., 'The Origin and Authenticity of the Royal Anglo-Saxon Diploma', *Journal of the Society of Archivists* 3.2 (1965), 48–61

Charles-Edwards, T. M., *Early Christian Ireland* (Cambridge, 2000)

'Wales and Mercia, 613–918', in *Mercia*, ed. Brown and Farr, pp. 89–105

Chase, C. (ed.), *The Dating of Beowulf* (Toronto, 1981)

Clanchy, M., *From Memory to Written Record: England 1066–1307*, 2nd edn (London, 1993)

Clement, R. W., 'A Handlist of Manuscripts Containing Gregory's *Regula Pastoralis*', *Manuscripta* 28 (1984), 33–44

'Two Contemporary Gregorian Editions of Pope Gregory the Great's *Regula Pastoralis* in Troyes MS. 504', *Scriptorium* 39 (1985), 89–97

'King Alfred and the Latin Manuscripts of Gregory's *Regula Pastoralis*', *Journal of the Rocky Mountain Medieval and Renaissance Association* 6 (1985), 1–13

'The Production of the Pastoral Care: King Alfred and his Helpers', in *Studies*, ed. Szarmach, pp. 129–52

Clemoes, P., 'King Alfred's Debt to Vernacular Poetry: the Evidence of *ellen* and *cræft*', in *Words, Texts and Manuscripts*, ed. Korhammer, Reichl and Sauer, pp. 213–38

Bibliography

Interactions of Thought and Language in Old English Poetry (Cambridge, 1995)

Clunies Ross, M., 'Concubinage in Anglo-Saxon England', *P&P* 108 (August 1985), 3–34

Collins, R., *Early Medieval Spain: Unity in Diversity, 400–1000*, 2nd edn (Basingstoke, 1995)

Conner, P. W., 'Religious Poetry', in *Anglo-Saxon Literature*, ed. Pulsiano and Treharne, pp. 251–67

Constable, G., '*Nona et decima:* an Aspect of Carolingian Economy', *Speculum* 35 (1960), 224–50

Three Studies in Medieval Religious and Social Thought (Cambridge, 1995)

Constantinescu, R., 'Alcuin et les "Libelli Precum" de l'epoque carolingienne', *Revue d'Histoire de la Spiritualité* 50 (1974), 17–56

Contreni, J., 'The Pursuit of Knowledge in Carolingian Europe', in *'The Gentle Voices of Teachers'*, ed. Sullivan, pp. 106–41

Cook, A. S., 'Alfred's "Word for Word" Translation', *The Academy* 30 (1886), 108

Copeland, R., *Rhetoric, Hermeneutics and Translation in the Middle Ages* (Cambridge, 1991)

Corrain, D. O., Breatnach, L., and Breen, A., 'The Laws of the Irish', *Peritia* 3 (1984), 382–438

Coupland, S., 'The Rod of God's Wrath or the People of God's Wrath? The Carolingian Theology of the Viking Invasions', *JEH* 4 (1991), 535–54

'The Fortified Bridges of Charles the Bald', *Journal of Medieval History* 17 (1991), 1–12

'From Poachers to Gamekeepers: Scandinavian Warlords and Carolingian Kings', *EME* 7 (1998), 85–114

Courcelle, P., 'Étude critique sur les commentaires de la consolation de Boèce', *Archives d'histoire doctrinale et littéraire du moyen âge* 12 (1939), 5–140

'La culture antique de Remi d'Auxerre', *Latomus* 7 (1948), 247–54

'Les sources antiques du prologue d'Alcuin sur les disciplines', *Philologus* 110 (1966), 293–305

La Consolation de Philosophie dans la tradition littéraire: Antécédents et postérité de Boèce (Paris, 1967)

Crabbe, A., 'Literary Design in the De Consolatione Philosophiae', in *Boethius*, ed. Gibson, pp. 237–74

Craig, G., 'Alfred the Great: a Diagnosis', *Journal of the Royal Society of Medicine* 84 (1991), 303–5

Crenshaw, J. L., *Old Testament Wisdom: an Introduction* (Atlanta, GA, 1981)

Crépin, A., 'Bede and the Vernacular', in *Famulus Christi*, ed. G. Bonner (London, 1976), pp. 170–92

'L'importance de la pensée de Grégoire le Grand dans la politique culturelle d'Alfred, roi de Wessex (871–899)', in *Grégoire le Grand*, ed. Fontaine, Gillet and Pellistrandi, pp. 579–87

Crick, J., 'Church, Land and Local Nobility in Early Ninth-Century Kent: the Case of Ealdorman Oswulf', *Historical Research* 61 (1988), 251–69

Cubitt, C., *Anglo-Saxon Church Councils c.650–c.850* (Leicester, 1995)

'Pastoral Care and Conciliar Canons: the Provisions of the 747 Council of *Clofesho*', in *Pastoral Care*, ed. Blair and Sharpe, pp. 193–211

'Rape, Pillage and Exaggeration', in *Not Angels, but Anglicans: a History of Christianity in the British Isles*, ed. H. Chadwick and A. Ward (Norwich, 2000), pp. 32–9

'Introduction', in *Court Culture*, ed. Cubitt, pp. 1–15

Cubitt, C. (ed.), *Court Culture in the Early Middle Ages: the Proceedings of the First Alcuin Conference* (Turnhout, 2002)

Curley, T. F., (III), 'How to Read the Consolation of Philosophy', *Interpretation* 14 (1986), 211–63

'The Consolation of Philosophy as a Work of Literature', *American Journal of Philology* 108 (1987), 343–67

d'Alverny, M.-Th., 'La Sagesse et ses sept filles. Recherches sure les allégories de la philosophie et des arts liberaux du IXe au XIIe siècle', in *Mélanges dédiés à la mémoire du Felix Grat*, 2 vols. (Paris, 1946) I, 245–78

'Le symbolisme de la Sagesse et le Christ de saint Dunstan', *Bodleian Library Record* 5 (1956), 232–44

Daly, E. J., 'An Early Ninth-Century Manuscript of Boethius', *Scriptorium* 4 (1950), 205–19

Danaher, G., Schirato, T., and Webb, J., *Understanding Foucault* (St Leonards, 2000)

Davies, R., 'The Medieval State: the Tyranny of a Concept?', *Journal of Historical Sociology* 16 (2003), 280–300

Davies, W., *An Early Welsh Microcosm: Studies in the Llandaff Charters* (London, 1978)

'Land and Power in Early Medieval Wales', *P&P* 81 (November 1978), 3–23

'Celtic Kingships in the Early Middle Ages', in *Kings and Kingship in Medieval Europe*, ed. A. J. Duggan (London, 1993), pp. 101–24

Davies, W., and Fouracre, P. (eds.), *The Settlement of Disputes in Early Medieval Europe* (Cambridge, 1986)

Property and Power in the Early Middle Ages (Cambridge, 1995)

Davis, K., 'The Performance of Translation Theory in King Alfred's National Literary Program', in *Manuscript, Narrative, Lexicon: Essays in honour of Whitney F. Bolton*, ed. R. Boenig and K. Davis (Lewisburg, PA, 2000), pp. 149–70

Davis, R. H. C., 'Alfred the Great: Propaganda and Truth', *History* 56 (1971), 169–82

'Alfred and Guthrum's Frontier', *EHR* 97 (1982), 803–10

DeGregorio, S., 'Texts, *topoi* and the Self: a Reading of Alfredian Spirituality', *EME* 13 (2005), 79–96

de Jong, M., 'Power and Humility in Carolingian Society: the Public Penance of Louis the Pious', *EME* 1 (1992), 29–52

de Jong, M., and Theuws, F. (eds.), *Topographies of Power in the Early Middle Ages* (Leiden, 2001)

Dekker, K., 'King Alfred's Translation of Gregory's *Dialogi*: Tales for the Unlearned?', in *Rome and the North*, ed. Bremmer *et al.*, pp. 27–50

Delisle, L., 'Registre des professions et des associations de l'abbaye de Saint-Rémi (IXe et Xe siècles)', in his *Littérature latine et histoire du Moyen Age* (Paris, 1890)

de Lubac, H., *Medieval Exegesis I: the Four Senses of Scripture*, trans. M. Sebac (Grand Rapids, MI, 1998)

Dempsey, G. T., 'Aldhelm of Malmesbury and the Paris Psalter: a Note on the Survival of Antiochene Exegesis', *JTS* 38 (1987), 368–86

Bibliography

Deshman, R., 'Anglo-Saxon Art after Alfred', *Art Bulletin* 56 (1974), 176–200

'The Exalted Servant: the Ruler Theology of the Prayerbook of Charles the Bald', *Viator* 11 (1980), 385–417

'The Galba Psalter: Pictures, Texts and Context in an Early Medieval Prayerbook', *ASE* 26 (1997), 109–38

Devisse, J., *Hincmar et la Loi* (Dakar, 1962)

'"Pauperes" et "paupertas" dans le monde carolingien: ce qu'en dit Hincmar de Reims', *Revue du Nord* 48 (1966), 273–87

Hincmar Archevêque de Reims 845–882, 3 vols. (Geneva, 1975–6)

Discenza, N. G., 'Power, Skill and Virtue in the Old English Boethius', *ASE* 26 (1997), 81–108

'"Wise wealhstodas": the Prologue to Sirach as a Model for Alfred's Preface to the Pastoral Care', *Journal of English and Germanic Philology* 97 (1998), 488–99

'The Influence of Gregory the Great on the Alfredian Social Imaginary', in *Rome and the North*, ed. Bremmer *et al.*, pp. 67–81

'Alfred's Verse Preface to the *Pastoral Care* and the Chain of Authority', *Neophilologus* 85 (2001), 625–33

'Symbolic Capital and the Ruler in the Translation Program of Alfred the Great', *Exemplaria* 23 (2001), 433–67

'The Old English Bede and the Construction of Anglo-Saxon Authority', *ASE* 31 (2002), 69–80

The King's English: Strategies of Translation in the Old English Boethius (Albany, NY, 2005)

Dolley, R. H. M., and Metcalf, D. M., 'The Reform of the English Coinage under Eadgar', in *Anglo-Saxon Coins: Studies presented to F. M. Stenton*, ed. R. H. M. Dolley (London, 1961), pp. 136–68

Donaghey, B. S., 'The Sources of King Alfred's Translation of Boethius' Consolation of Philosophy', *Anglia* 82 (1964), 23–57

'Nicholas Trevet's Use of King Alfred's Translation of Boethius, and the Dating of his Commentary', in *The Medieval Boethius*, ed. A. J. Minnis (Woodbridge, 1987), pp. 1–31

d'Onofrio, G., 'Giovanni Scoto e Remigio di Auxerre: a proposito di alcuni commenti altomedievali a Boezio', *Studi Medievali* 22 (1981), 587–693

Doren, A., 'Fortuna im Mittelalter und in der Renaissance', *Vorträge der Bibliothek Warburg* 2 (1922–3), 71–115

Dubuisson, D., 'L'Irlande et la théorie médiévale des "trois ordres"', *Revue de l'histoire des religions* 188 (1975), 35–63

Duby, G., *The Three Orders: Feudal Society Imagined*, trans. A. Goldhammer (London, 1980)

Duggan, A. J. (ed.), *Nobles and Nobility in Medieval Europe* (Woodbridge, 2000)

Dumville, D. N., 'The Anglian Collection of Royal Genealogies and Regnal Lists', *ASE* 5 (1976), 23–50

'Kingship, Genealogies and Regnal Lists', in *Early Medieval Kingship*, ed. Sawyer and Wood, pp. 72–104

'The Ætheling: a Study in Anglo-Saxon Constitutional History', *ASE* 8 (1979), 1–33

'The "Six" Sons of Rhodri Mawr: a Problem in Asser's Life of King Alfred', *Cambridge Medieval Celtic Studies* 4 (Winter, 1983), 5–18

'The West Saxon Genealogical Regnal List and the Chronology of Early Wessex', *Peritia* 4 (1985), 21–66

'English Square Minuscule Script: the Background and Earliest Phases', *ASE* 16 (1987), 147–79

Wessex and England from Alfred to Edgar (Woodbridge, 1992)

Liturgy and the Ecclesiastical History of Late Anglo-Saxon England: Four Studies (Woodbridge, 1992)

English Caroline Script and Monastic History: Studies in Benedictinism, A.D. 950–1030 (Woodbridge, 1993)

'The Terminology of Overkingship in Early Anglo-Saxon England', in *The Anglo-Saxons*, ed. Hines, pp. 345–65

A Palaeographer's Review: the Insular System of Scripts in the Middle Ages I (Osaka, 1999)

Dunbabin, J., 'West Francia: the Kingdom', in *NCMH* III, 372–97

Durkheim, E., *The Elementary Forms of Religious Life*, ed. and trans. K. Fields (New York, 1995 [1912])

Dutton, P. E., *The Politics of Dreaming in the Carolingian Empire* (Lincoln, NE, and London, 1994)

Dutton, P. E., and Jeauneau, E., 'The Verses of the *Codex Aureus* of Saint-Emmeram', *Studi Medievali* 24 (1983), 75–120

Dutton, P. E., and Kessler, H. L., *The Poetry and Paintings of the First Bible of Charles the Bald* (Ann Arbor, MI, 1998)

Dyer, C., *Lords and Peasants in a Changing Society: the Estates of the Bishopric of Worcester, 680–1540* (Cambridge, 1980)

'Recent Developments in Early Medieval Urban History and Archaeology in England', in *Urban Historical Geography: Recent Progress in Britain and Germany*, ed. D. Denecke and S. Shaw (Cambridge, 1988), pp. 69–80

Making a Living in the Middle Ages: the People of Britain 850–1520 (London, 2002)

Dyson, T., 'King Alfred and the Restoration of London', *London Journal* 15.2 (1990), 99–110

Eagleton, T., *Literary Theory: an Introduction*, 2nd edn (Oxford, 1996)

Eberhardt, O., *Via Regia: Der Fürstenspiegel Smaragds von St. Mihiel und seine Litterarische Gattung* (Munich, 1977)

Edwards, C., 'German Vernacular Literature: a Survey', in *Carolingian Culture*, ed. McKitterick, pp. 141–70

Edwards, H., *The Charters of the Early West Saxon Kingdom* (Oxford, 1988)

Elias, N., *The Civilizing Process*, trans. E. Jephcott, rev. edn (Oxford, 1994 [1939])

The Court Society, trans. E. Jephcott (Oxford, 1983 [1969])

Evans, G. R., *The Thought of Gregory the Great* (Cambridge, 1986)

Faith, R., *The English Peasantry and the Growth of Lordship* (Leicester, 1997)

Finberg, H. P. R., *The Early Charters of Wessex* (Leicester, 1964)

'The Churls of Hurstbourne', in his *Lucerna* (London, 1964), pp. 131–43

Fischer, B., 'Bedae de titulis psalmorum liber', in *Festschrift Bernhard Bischoff zu seinem 65. Geburtstag*, ed. J. Autenrieth and F. Brünholzl (Stuttgart, 1971), pp. 90–110

Bibliography

Fleckenstein, J., *Die Bildungsreform Karls des Grossen als Verwicklung die norma rectitutidinis* (Bigge-Ruhr, 1953)

Die Hofkapelle der deutschen Könige, I: Grundlegung: Die karolingische Hofkapelle, Schriften der MGH 16.1 (Stuttgart, 1959)

Fleming, R., 'Monastic Lands and England's Defence in the Viking Age', *EHR* 100 (1985), 247–65

'The New Wealth, the New Rich and the New Political Style in Late Anglo-Saxon England', *Anglo-Norman Studies* 23 (2001), 1–22

Fontaine, J., Gillet, R., and Pellistrandi, S. (eds.), *Grégoire le Grand* (Paris, 1986)

Foot, S., 'The Making of *Angelcynn*: English Identity before the Norman Conquest', *TRHS* 6th series 6 (1996), 25–49

'Remembering, Forgetting and Inventing: Attitudes to the Past in England at the End of the First Viking Age', *TRHS* 6th series 9 (1999), 185–200

'The Historiography of the Anglo-Saxon "Nation-State"', in *Power and the Nation in European History*, ed. L. Scales and O. Zimmer (Cambridge, 2005), pp. 125–42

Foucault, M., *Les mots et les choses: une archéologie des sciences humaines* (Paris, 1966); Eng. edn *The Order of Things: an Archaeology of the Human Sciences* (New York, 1970)

Surveiller et punir: naissance de la prison (Paris, 1975); Eng. edn *Discipline and Punish: the Birth of the Prison*, trans. A. Sheridan (London, 1991)

The Foucault Reader, ed. P. Rabinow (Harmondsworth, 1991)

Fouracre, P., 'Carolingian Justice: the Rhetoric of Improvement and Contexts of Abuse', *Settimane* 42 (1995), 771–803

Fournier, P., 'Le Liber ex lege Moysi et les tendances bibliques du droit canonique irlandais', *Revue Celtique* 30 (1909), 221–34

Frakes, J. C., *The Fate of Fortune in the Early Middle Ages* (Leiden, New York, Copenhagen and Cologne, 1988)

Frantzen, A. J., 'The Tradition of Penitentials in Anglo-Saxon England', *ASE* 11 (1983), 23–56

The Literature of Penance in Anglo-Saxon England (New Brunswick, NJ, 1983)

King Alfred (Boston, MA, 1986)

Before the Closet (Chicago, IL, 1998)

'The Form and Function of the Preface in the Poetry and Prose of Alfred's Reign', in *Alfred*, ed. Reuter, pp. 121–36

Fried, J., 'Der karolingische Herrschaftsverband im 9 Jhdt. zwischen "Kirche" und "Königshaus"', *Historische Zeitschrift* 235 (1982), 1–43

Gaehde, J. E., 'The Bible of S. Paolo fuori le Mura in Rome: its Date and its Relation to Charles the Bald', *Gesta* 5 (1966), 9–21

Gameson, R., 'Alfred the Great and the Destruction and Production of Christian Books', *Scriptorium* 49 (1995), 180–210

Gameson, R. (ed.), *The Early Medieval Bible, its Production, Decoration and Use* (Cambridge, 1994)

Gameson, R., and Leyser, H. (eds.), *Belief and Culture in the Middle Ages: Studies presented to Henry Mayr-Harting* (Oxford, 2001)

Gannon, A., 'The Five Senses and Anglo-Saxon Coinage', *ASSAH* 13 (2005), 97–104

Ganshof, F. L., 'Recherches sur les capitulaires', *Revue historique des droits français et étranger* 4th series 35 (1957), 33–87 and 196–246

Bibliography

The Carolingians and the Frankish Monarchy, trans. J. Sondheimer (London, 1971)
Ganz, D., 'The Preface to Einhard's "Vita Karoli"', in *Einhard: Studien zu Leben und Werk*, ed. H. Schefers (Darmstadt, 1997), pp. 299–310
    'Theology and the Organization of Thought', in *NCMH* II, 758–85
    'Le *De Laude Dei* d'Alcuin', *Annales de Bretagne et des Pays de l'Ouest* III (2004), 387–91
Gatch, M. McC., 'King Alfred's Version of Augustine's Soliloquia: Some Suggestions on its Rationale and Unity', in *Studies*, ed. Szarmach, pp. 17–46
    'Perceptions of Eternity', in *Cambridge Companion*, ed. Godden and Lapidge, pp. 190–205
Geary, P. J., *The Myth of Nations: the Medieval Origins of Europe* (Princeton, NJ, 2002)
Geertz, C., *The Interpretation of Cultures: Selected Essays* (London, 1973)
    Negara: the Theatre State in Nineteenth-Century Bali (Princeton, NJ, 1980)
Gibson, M., 'Boethius in the Carolingian Schools', *TRHS* 5th series 32 (1982), 43–56
    'Illustrating Boethius: Carolingian and Romanesque Manuscripts', in *Medieval Manuscripts of the Latin Classics*, ed. C. A. Chavannes-Mazel and M. M. Smith (London, 1996), pp. 118–29
    'Carolingian Glossed Psalters', in *The Early Medieval Bible*, ed. Gameson, pp. 78–100
Gibson, M. (ed.), *Boethius: his Life, Thought and Influence* (Oxford, 1981)
Gibson, M., and Nelson, J. L. (eds.), *Charles the Bald: Court and Kingdom*, 2nd edn (Aldershot, 1990)
Gibson, M., and Smith, L. (eds.), *Codices Boethiani: A Conspectus of Manuscripts of the Works of Boethius. I. Great Britain and the Republic of Ireland* (London, 1995)
Gifford, E. and J., 'Alfred's New Long Ships', in *Alfred*, ed. Reuter, pp. 281–9
Gneuss, H., 'King Alfred and the History of Anglo-Saxon Libraries', in *Modes of Interpretation in Old English*, ed. P. Rugg Brown (Toronto, 1986), pp. 29–49
    Handlist of Anglo-Saxon Manuscripts: a List of Manuscripts and Manuscript Fragments Written or Owned in England up to 1100 (Tempe, AZ, 2001)
Godden, M., 'Ælfric and the Vernacular Prose Tradition', in *The Old English Homily and its Backgrounds*, ed. P. E. Szarmach and B. F. Huppé (Albany, NY, 1978), pp. 99–117
    'King Alfred's Boethius', in *Boethius*, ed. Gibson, pp. 419–24
    'Anglo-Saxons on the Mind', in *Learning and Literature*, ed. Lapidge and Gneuss, pp. 271–98
    'Money, Power and Morality in Late Anglo-Saxon England', *ASE* 19 (1990), 41–65
    'Wærferth and King Alfred: the Fate of the Old English Dialogues', in *Alfred the Wise*, ed. Roberts and Nelson, pp. 35–51
    'Editing Old English and the Problem of Alfred's Boethius', in *The Editing of Old English*, ed. D. G. Scragg and P. E. Szarmach (Cambridge, 1994), pp. 163–76
    'The Player King: Identification and Self-Representation in King Alfred's Writings', in *Alfred*, ed. Reuter, pp. 137–50
    'The Anglo-Saxons and the Goths: Rewriting the Sack of Rome', *ASE* 31 (2002), 47–68

Bibliography

'King Alfred's Preface and the Teaching of Latin in Anglo-Saxon England', *EHR* 117 (2002), 596–604

'Text and Eschatology in Book III of the Old English *Soliloquies*', *Anglia* 121 (2003), 177–209

The Translations of Alfred and his Circle, and the Misappropriation of the Past, H. M. Chadwick Memorial Lecture 14 (Cambridge, 2004)

Godden, M., and Lapidge, M. (eds.), *The Cambridge Companion to Old English Literature* (Cambridge, 1991)

Godman, P., *Poets and Emperors* (Oxford, 1987)

Godman, P., and Collins, R. (eds.), *Charlemagne's Heir* (Oxford, 1990)

Goebel, J., *Felony and Misdemeanor: a Study in the History of Criminal Law* (New York, 1937)

Goffman, E., *The Presentation of Self in Everyday Life* (Edinburgh, 1956)

Goldberg, E. J., '"More Devoted to the Equipment of Battle than the Splendor of Banquets": Frontier Kingship, Martial Ritual, and Early Knighthood at the Court of Louis the German', *Viator* 30 (1999), 41–78

Struggle for Empire: Kingship and Conflict under Louis the German, 817–76 (Ithaca, NY, 2006)

Goody, J., and Watt, I., 'The Consequences of Literacy', in *Literacy in Traditional Societies*, ed. J. Goody (Cambridge, 1968), pp. 27–68

Gottlob, T., *Der kirchliche Amtseid der Bischöfe* (Amsterdam, 1963)

Green, D. H., *The Carolingian Lord* (Cambridge, 1965)

Grégoire, R., 'Le interpretazioni altomedievali dei testi veterotestamentari sulla giustizia', *Settimane* 42 (1995), 423–41

Gretsch, M., *The Intellectual Foundations of the English Benedictine Reform* (Cambridge, 1999)

'The Junius Psalter Gloss: its Historical and Cultural Context', *ASE* 29 (2000), 85–121

Grierson, P., 'Grimbald of St. Bertin's', *EHR* 55 (1940), 529–61

'The Volume of Anglo-Saxon Coinage', *EcHR* 2nd series 20 (1967), 153–60

Grierson, P., and Blackburn, M., *Medieval European Coinage I. The Early Middle Ages* (Cambridge, 1986)

Griffith, M. S., 'Does *wyrd bið ful aræd* mean "Fate is wholly inexorable"?', in *'Doubt wisely'*, ed. Toswell and Tyler, pp. 133–56

Grinda, K., 'The Myth of Circe in King Alfred's Boethius', in *Old English Prose: Basic Readings*, ed. P. E. Szarmach (New York, 2000), pp. 237–65

Grundmann, H., '*Litteratus – illiteratus*: der Wandel einer Bildungsnorm vom Altertum zum Mittelalter', *Archiv für Kulturgeschichte* 40 (1958), 1–66

Guillot, O., 'Une ordinatio méconnue: le Capitulaire de 823–825', in *Charlemagne's Heir*, ed. Godman and Collins, pp. 455–86

Guilman, J., 'The Illuminations of the Second Bible of Charles the Bald', *Speculum* 41 (1966), 246–56

Hadley, D. M., and Richards, J. D. (eds.), *Cultures in Contact: Scandinavian Settlement in England in the Ninth and Tenth Centuries* (Turnhout, 2000)

Halsall, G., 'Review Article: Movers and Shakers: the Barbarians and the Fall of Rome', *EME* 8 (1999), 131–45

Halsall, G. (ed.), *Violence and Society in the Early Medieval West* (Woodbridge, 1998)

Hamilton, S., 'Review Article: Early Medieval Rulers and their Modern Biographers', *EME* 9 (2000), 247–60

Hannig, J., *Consensus Fidelium*, Monographien zur Geschichte des Mittelalters 27 (Stuttgart, 1982)

Hansen, E. T., *The Solomon Complex* (Toronto, 1988)

Harmer, F. E., *Anglo-Saxon Writs* (Manchester, 1952)

Harries, J. and Wood, I. (eds.), *The Theodosian Code* (London, 1993)

Harris, S. J. 'The Alfredian *World History* and Anglo-Saxon Identity', *Journal of English and Germanic Philology* 100 (2001), 482–510

Hartmann, W., *Die Synoden der Karolingerzeit im Frankenreich und in Italien* (Paderborn, 1989)

Haseldine, J. (ed.), *Friends and Friendship in Medieval Europe* (Stroud, 1999)

Haslam, J., 'King Alfred and the Vikings – Strategies and Tactics 876–888 AD', *ASSAH* 13 (2005), 122–54

Hassall, J. M., and Hill, D., 'Pont de l'Arche: Frankish Influence on the West Saxon *burh*?', *Archaeological Journal* 127 (1970), 188–95

Hastings, A., *The Construction of Nationhood: Ethnicity, Religion and Nationalism* (Cambridge, 1997)

Hen, Y., and Innes, M. (eds.), *The Uses of the Past in the Early Middle Ages* (Cambridge, 2000)

Herlihy, D., 'Church Property on the European Continent, 701–1200', *Speculum* 36 (1961), 81–105

Herren, M. W., 'Walahfrid Strabo's De Imagine Tetrici: an Interpretation', in *Latin Culture and Medieval Germanic Europe*, ed. R. North and T. Hofstra (Groningen, 1992)

Higham, N. J., and Hill, D. H. (eds.), *Edward the Elder 899–924* (London, 2001)

Hill, D., *An Atlas of Anglo-Saxon England* (Oxford, 1981)

'Anglo-Saxon Mechanics: 1. The Oxcart; 2. The Anglo-Saxon Vine Dresser's Knife', *Medieval Life* 10 (1998), 13–20

'Athelstan's Urban Reforms', *ASSAH* 11 (2000), 173–86

'The Origin of King Alfred's Urban Policies', in *Alfred*, ed. Reuter, pp. 19–33

Hill, D., and Rumble, A. R. (eds.), *The Defence of Wessex: the Burghal Hidage and Anglo-Saxon Fortifications* (Manchester, 1996)

Hill, T. D., 'The Crowning of Alfred and the Topos of *sapientia et fortitudo* in Asser's *Life of Alfred*', *Neophilologus* 86 (2002), 471–6

Hines, J. (ed.), *The Anglo-Saxons from the Migration Period to the Eighth Century: an Ethnographic Perspective* (Woodbridge, 1997)

Hitch, S. J., 'Alfred's Cræft: Imagery in Alfred's Version of Augustine's Solilquies', *Journal of the Department of English (Calcutta University)*, 22 (1–2), (1986–7), 130–47

'Alfred's Reading of Augustine's Soliloquies', in *Sentences for Alan Ward*, ed. D. M. Reeks (Southampton, 1988), pp. 21–9

Hobley, B., 'Saxon London: *Lundenwic* and *Lundenburh*: Two Cities Rediscovered', in *The Rebirth of Towns in the West AD 700–1050*, ed. R. Hodges and B. Hobley (London, 1988), pp. 69–82

Hodges, R., *The Anglo-Saxon Achievement* (London, 1989)

'Trade and Market Origins in the Ninth Century: Relations between England and the Continent', in *Charles the Bald*, ed. Gibson and Nelson, pp. 203–23

Bibliography

Hollister, C. W., *Anglo-Saxon Military Institutions on the Eve of the Norman Conquest* (Oxford, 1962)

Horgan, A. D., '*The Wanderer* – A Boethian Poem?', *Review of English Studies* 39 (1988), 349–64

Horgan, D. M., 'The Relationship between the Old English Manuscripts of King Alfred's Translation of Gregory's Pastoral Care', *Anglia* 91 (1973), 153–69

'The Old English Pastoral Care: the Scribal Contribution', in *Studies*, ed. Szarmach, pp. 109–28

Howe, N., *Migration and Mythmaking in Anglo-Saxon England* (New Haven, CT, 1989)

'The Cultural Construction of Reading in Anglo-Saxon England', in *The Ethnography of Reading*, ed. J. Boyarin (Berkeley and Los Angeles, CA, 1992), pp. 58–79

Howlett, D. R., 'The Iconography of the Alfred Jewel', *Oxoniensia* 39 (1974), 44–52

British Books in Biblical Style (Dublin, 1997)

Hughes, A., *Medieval Manuscripts for Mass and Office: a Guide to their Organisation and Terminology* (Toronto, 1982)

Hunt, L. (ed.), *The New Cultural History* (Berkeley and Los Angeles, CA, 1989)

Huppé, B. F., 'Alfred and Ælfric: a Study of Two Prefaces', in *The Old English Homily and its Backgrounds*, ed. P. E. Szarmach and B. F. Huppé (Albany, NY, 1978), pp. 119–37

Hyams, P., 'Feud and the State in Late Anglo-Saxon England', *Journal of British Studies* 40 (2001), 1–43

Innes, M., 'Memory, Orality and Literacy in an Early Medieval Society', *P&P* 158 (February 1998), 3–36

State and Society in the Early Middle Ages: the Middle Rhine Valley, 400–1000 (Cambridge, 2000)

' "A Place of Discipline": Aristocratic Youth and Carolingian Courts', in *Court Culture*, ed. Cubitt, pp. 59–76

Innes, M., and McKitterick, R., 'The Writing of History', in *Carolingian Culture*, ed. McKitterick, pp. 193–220

Iogna-Prat, D., 'Le "baptême" du schéma des trois ordres fonctionnels', *Annales. Économies. Sociétés. Civilisations* 41 (1986), 101–26

Iogna-Prat, D., Jeudy, C., and Lobrichon, G. (eds.), *L'école carolingienne d'Auxerre de Murethach à Remi 830–908* (Paris, 1991)

Irvine, M., *The Making of Textual Culture: 'Grammatica' and Literary Theory, 350–1100* (Cambridge, 1994)

Irvine, S., 'Ulysses and Circe in King Alfred's Boethius: a Classical Myth Transformed', in *'Doubt Wisely'*, ed. Toswell and Tyler, pp. 387–401

'Religious Context: Pre-Benedictine Reform Period', in *Anglo-Saxon Literature*, ed. Pulsiano and Treharne, pp. 135–50

'Wrestling with Hercules: King Alfred and the Classical Past', in *Court Culture*, ed. Cubitt, pp. 171–88

'The Anglo-Saxon Chronicle and the Idea of Rome', in *Alfred*, ed. Reuter, pp. 63–77

Jaeger, C. S., *The Origins of Courtliness: Civilizing Trends and the Formation of Courtly Ideals 939–1210* (Philadelphia, PA, 1985)

Bibliography

The Envy of Angels: Cathedral Schools and Social Ideals in Medieval Europe, 950–1200 (Philadelphia, PA, 1994)

James, M. R., *The Ancient Libraries of Canterbury and Dover* (Cambridge, 1903)

Janson, T., *Latin Prose Prefaces: Studies in Literary Conventions* (Stockholm, 1964)

Jaski, B., 'Early Medieval Irish Kingship and the Old Testament', *EME* 7 (1998), 329–44

Jeudy, C., 'L'œuvre de Remi d'Auxerre: État de la question', in *L'École Carolingienne d'Auxerre*, ed. Iogna-Prat *et al.*, pp. 373–96

'Remigii autissiodorensis opera (Clavis)', *L'École Carolingienne d'Auxerre*, ed. Iogna-Prat *et al.*, pp. 457–500

John, E., *Land Tenure in Early England* (Leicester, 1960)

Orbis Britanniae (Leicester, 1966)

Jones, S. R. H., 'Transaction Costs, Institutional Change, and the Emergence of a Market Economy in Later Anglo-Saxon England', *EcHR* 2nd series 46 (1993), 658–78

Judic, B., 'Structure et fonction de la Regula pastoralis', in *Grégoire le Grand*, ed. Fontaine, Gillet and Pellistrandi, pp. 409–17

Judin, H., and Dolan, J. (eds.), *The Church in the Age of Feudalism*, trans. A. Briggs, Handbook of Church History 3 (New York and London, 1969)

Kaczynski, B. M., *Greek in the Carolingian Age: the St Gall Manuscripts* (Cambridge, 1988)

Kantorowicz, E. H., *The King's Two Bodies* (Princeton, NJ, 1957)

Laudes Regiae (Berkeley and Los Angeles, CA, 1958)

Karkov, C., *The Ruler Portraits of Anglo-Saxon England* (Woodbridge, 2004)

Kasik, J. C., 'The Use of the Term *Wyrd* in Beowulf and the Conversion of the Anglo-Saxons', *Neophilologus* 63 (1979), 128–35

Kaske, R. E., '*Sapientia et fortitudo* as the Controlling Theme of Beowulf', *Studies in Philology* 55 (1958), 423–56

Keene, D., 'Alfred and London', in *Alfred*, ed. Reuter, pp. 235–49

Kelly, S., 'Anglo-Saxon Lay Society and the Written Word', in *The Uses of Literacy*, ed. McKitterick, pp. 36–62

'Trading Privileges from Eighth-Century England', *EME* 1 (1992), 3–28

Kemble, J. M., *The Saxons in England*, 2 vols. (London, 1849)

Kempshall, M., 'No Bishop, No King: the Ministerial Ideology of Kingship and Asser's *Res Gestae Aelfredi*', in *Belief and Culture*, ed. Gameson and Leyser, pp. 106–27

Kennedy, A. G., 'Disputes about *bocland*: the Forum for their Adjudication', *ASE* 14 (1995), 175–95

Ker, N. R., *Catalogue of Manuscripts Containing Anglo-Saxon*, Reissue with Supplement (Oxford, 1990)

Kershaw, P., 'Illness, Power and Prayer in Asser's *Life of King Alfred*', *EME* 10 (2001), 201–24

'The Alfred-Guthrum Treaty: Scripting Accommodation and Interaction in Viking Age England', in *Cultures in Contact*, ed. Hadley and Richards, pp. 43–64

Kessler, H. L., *The Illustrated Bibles from Tours* (Princeton, NJ, 1977)

Spiritual Seeing: Picturing God's Invisibility in Medieval Art (Philadelphia, PA, 2001)

Keynes, S., *The Diplomas of King Æthelred 'the Unready' 978–1016* (Cambridge, 1980)

'King Athelstan's Books', in *Learning and Literature*, ed. Lapidge and Gneuss, pp. 143–201

'Anglo-Saxon Church Councils', in *Handbook of British Chronology*, 3rd edn, ed. E. B. Fryde, D. E. Greenway, S. Porter and I. Roy (London, 1986), pp. 583–9

'A Tale of Two Kings: Alfred the Great and Æthelred the Unready', *TRHS* 5th series 36 (1986), 195–217

'Royal Government and the Written Word in Late Anglo-Saxon England', in *The Uses of Literacy*, ed. McKitterick, pp. 226–57

'The Fonthill Letter', in *Words, Texts and Manuscripts*, ed. Korhammer, Reichl and Sauer, pp. 53–97

'Rædwald the Bretwalda', in *Voyage to the Other World*, ed. C. B. Kendall and P. S. Wells (Minneapolis, MN, 1992), pp. 103–23

'The Control of Kent in the Ninth Century', *EME* 2 (1993), 111–31

'The West Saxon Charters of King Æthelwulf and his Sons', *EHR* 109 (1994), 1109–49

'Cnut's Earls', in *The Reign of Cnut*, ed. A. R. Rumble (Leicester, 1994), pp. 43–88

The Councils of Clofesho, Brixworth Lecture 1993, University of Leicester Vaughan Paper 38 (Leicester, 1994)

'England, 700–900', in *NCMH* II, 18–42

'England, c. 900–1016', in *NCMH* III, 456–84

'On the Authenticity of Asser's Life of King Alfred', *JEH* 47 (1996), 529–51

'The Reconstruction of a Burnt Cottonian Manuscript: the Case of Cotton MS Otho A. I', *British Library Journal* 22.2 (1996), 113–60

'Anglo-Saxon Entries in the "Liber Vitae" of Brescia', in *Alfred the Wise*, ed. Roberts and Nelson, pp. 99–119

'The Vikings in England, c. 790–1016', in *The Oxford Illustrated History*, ed. Sawyer, pp. 48–82

'King Alfred and the Mercians', in *Kings, Currency and Alliances*, ed. Blackburn and Dumville, pp. 1–45

'The Cult of King Alfred the Great', *ASE* 28 (1999), 225–356

'King Alfred the Great and Shaftesbury Abbey', in *Studies in the Early History of Shaftesbury Abbey*, ed. L. Keen (Dorchester, 1999), pp. 17–72

'Mercia and Wessex in the Ninth Century', in *Mercia*, ed. Brown and Farr, pp. 310–28

An Atlas of Attestations in Anglo-Saxon Charters, c. 670–1066 (Cambridge, 2002)

'The Power of the Written Word: Alfredian England 871–99', in *Alfred*, ed. Reuter, pp. 175–97

Anglo-Saxon History: a Bibliographical Handbook (Cambridge, 2005)

'The Kingdom of the Mercians in the Eighth Century', in *Æthelbald and Offa: Two Eighth-Century Mercian Kings*, ed. D. H. Hill and M. Worthington (Oxford, 2005), pp. 1–26

Keynes, S., and Lapidge, M., *Alfred the Great: Asser's Life of King Alfred and other Contemporary Sources* (Harmondsworth, 1983)

Bibliography

Kiernan, K. S., 'Deor: the Consolations of an Anglo-Saxon Boethius', *Neuphilologische Mitteilungen* 79 (1978), 333–40

Beowulf and the Beowulf Manuscript (New Brunswick, NJ, 1981)

King, M. H., and Stevens, W. M. (eds.), *Saints, Scholars and Heroes. Studies in Medieval Culture in honour of Charles W. Jones*, 2 vols. (Collegeville, MN, 1979)

Kirby, D. P., 'Northumbria in the Reign of Alfred the Great', *Transactions of the Architectural and Archaeological Society of Durham and Northumberland* 11 (1958–65), 335–46

'Asser and his Life of King Alfred', *Studia Celtica* 6 (1971), 12–35

The Earliest English Kings (London, 1991)

Bede's Historia ecclesiastica gentis Anglorum: its Contemporary Setting, Jarrow Lecture 1992 (Jarrow, 1993)

Kirkby, H., 'The Scholar and his Public', in *Boethius*, ed. Gibson, pp. 44–69

Klaeber, F., 'Zu König Ælfreds Vorrede zu seiner Übersetzung der *Cura Pastoralis*', *Anglia* 47 (1923), 53–65

Kleinschmidt, H., 'The Old English Annal for 757 and West Saxon Dynastic Strife', *Journal of Medieval History* 22 (1996), 209–24

Koehler, W., and Mütherich, F., *Die karolingischen Miniaturen*, 6 vols. (Berlin, 1930–)

Korhammer, M., Reichl, K., and Sauer, H. (eds.), *Words, Texts and Manuscripts: Studies in Anglo-Saxon Culture presented to Helmut Gneuss* (Cambridge, 1992)

Kornbluth, G. A., 'The Alfred Jewel: Reuse of Roman Spolia', *Medieval Archaeology* 33 (1989), 32–7

Kortüm, H.-H., 'Weltgeschichte am Ausgang der Karolingerzeit: Regino von Prüm', in *Historiographie im frühen Mittelalter*, ed. A. Scharer and G. Scheibelreiter (Vienna, 1994), pp. 499–513

Kottje, R., *Studien zum Einfluß des alten Testamentes auf Recht und Liturgie des frühen Mittlelalters (6.–8. Jahrhundert)* (Bonn, 1970)

'Die Lex Baiuvariorum – das Recht der Baiern', in *Überlieferung und Geltung normativer Texte des frühen und hohen Mittelalters*, ed. H. Mordek (Sigmaringen, 1986), pp. 9–23

'Der Liber ex lege Moysis', in *Irland und die Christenheit*, ed. Ní Chatháin and Richter, pp. 59–69

Koziol, G., *Begging Pardon and Favour: Ritual and Political Order in Early Medieval France* (Ithaca, NY, 1992)

Kretzschmar, W. A., 'Adaptation and *anweald* in the Old English Orosius', *ASE* 16 (1987), 127–45

Lampe, G. W. H. (ed.), *The Cambridge History of the Bible II* (Cambridge, 1969)

Lapidge, M., 'Surviving Booklists from Anglo-Saxon England', in *Learning and Literature*, ed. Lapidge and Gneuss, pp. 33–89

Anglo-Latin Literature 900–1066 (London, 1993)

Anglo-Latin Literature 600–899 (London, 1996)

'The Archetype of Beowulf', *ASE* 29 (2000), 5–41

'Asser's Reading', in *Alfred*, ed. Reuter, pp. 27–43

'Acca of Hexham and the Origin of the *Old English Martyrology*', *Analecta Bollandiana* 123 (2005), 29–78

Bibliography

Lapidge, M., and Gneuss, H. (eds.), *Learning and Literature in Anglo-Saxon England: Studies presented to Peter Clemoes* (Cambridge, 1985)

Lapidge, M., Blair, J., Keynes, S., and Scragg, D. (eds.), *The Blackwell Encyclopaedia of Anglo-Saxon England* (Oxford, 1999)

Larson, L. M., *The King's Household in England before the Norman Conquest* (Madison, WI, 1904)

Lawrence, A., 'Alfred, his Heirs and the Traditions of Manuscript Production in Tenth Century England', *Reading Medieval Studies* 13 (1988), 35–56

Lear, F. S., *Treason in Roman and Germanic Law* (Austin, TX, 1965)

Lees, B. A., *Alfred the Great: the Truth Teller: Maker of England 848–899* (New York, 1915)

Le Goff, J., *Time, Work and Culture in the Middle Ages*, trans. A. Goldhammer (Chicago, IL, 1980)

Le Jan, R., 'Justice royale et pratiques sociales dans le royaume franc au IXe siècle', *Settimane* 44 (1997), 47–90

Lerer, S., *Literacy and Power in Anglo-Saxon Literature* (Lincoln, NE, 1991)

Leroquais, C. V., *Les psautiers manuscrits latins des bibliothèques publiques de France*, 3 vols. (Mâcon, 1940–1)

Levison, W. H., *England and the Continent in the Eighth Century* (Oxford, 1946)
'Aus Englischen Bibliotheken II', *Neues Archiv* 35 (1910), 333–431

Leyser, K., *Rule and Conflict in an Early Medieval Society: Ottonian Saxony* (Oxford, 1979)
Medieval Germany and its Neighbours 900–1250 (London, 1982)
Communications and Power in Medieval Europe: the Carolingian and Ottonian Centuries, ed. T. Reuter (London, 1994)

Liebermann, F., 'King Alfred and Mosaic Law', *Transactions of the Jewish Historical Society of England* 6 (1908–10), 21–31

Liggins, E. M., 'The Authorship of the Old English Orosius', *Anglia* 88 (1970), 289–322

Liuzza, R. M., 'On the Dating of *Beowulf*', in *Beowulf: Basic Readings*, ed. P. S. Baker (New York, 1995), pp. 281–302

Lloyd, J. E., *A History of Wales from the Earliest Times to the Edwardian Conquest*, 2 vols., 3rd edn (London, 1939)

Lowe, K. A., 'Lay Literacy in Anglo-Saxon England and the Development of the Chirograph', in *Anglo-Saxon Manuscripts and their Heritage*, ed. P. Pulsiano and E. M. Treharne (Aldershot, 1998), pp. 161–204
'The Nature and Effect of the Anglo-Saxon Vernacular Will', *Journal of Legal History* 19 (1998), 23–61
'The Development of the Anglo-Saxon Boundary Clause', *Nomina* 21 (1998), 63–100

Loyn, H. R., 'The Term Ealdorman in the Translations Prepared at the Time of King Alfred', *EHR* 68 (1953), 513–25
'Gesiths and Thegns in Anglo-Saxon England from the Seventh to Tenth Century', *EHR* 70 (1955), 529–49
'Wales and England in the Tenth Century: the Context of the Athelstan Charters', *Welsh History Review* 10 (1980–1), 283–301
The Governance of Anglo-Saxon England, 500–1087 (London, 1984)

Bibliography

Lund, N., 'Allies of God or Man? The Viking Expansion in European Perspective', *Viator* 20 (1989), 45–59

Lund, N. (ed.), *Two Voyagers at the Court of King Alfred* (York, 1984)

Lutz, C. E., 'Remigius' Ideas on the Classification of the Seven Liberal Arts', *Traditio* 12 (1956), 65–86

MacLean, S., *Kingship and Politics in the Late Ninth Century: Charles the Fat and the End of the Carolingian Empire* (Cambridge, 2003)

Maddicott, J. R., 'Trade, Industry and the Wealth of King Alfred', *P&P* 123 (1989), 3–51

    'Two Frontier States: Northumbria and Wessex, c. 650–750', in *The Medieval State: Essays presented to James Campbell*, ed. J. R. Maddicott and D. M. Palliser (London, 2000), pp. 25–46

    'Prosperity and Power in the Age of Bede and Beowulf', *PBA* 117 (2002), 49–72

Madec, G., *Jean Scot et ses Auteurs* (Paris, 1988)

Magoun, F. P., and Smyser, H. M., *Walter of Aquitaine: Materials for the Study of his Legend* (New London, CT, 1950)

Mahl, S. *Quadriga Virtutum* (Cologne and Vienna, 1967)

Maitland, F. W., *Domesday Book and Beyond* (Cambridge, 1897)

Maitland, F. W., and Pollock, F., *The History of English Law before the Time of Edward I*, 2 vols., 2nd edn (Cambridge, 1898)

Manitius, M., *Geschichte der lateinischen Literatur des Mittelalters*, 3 vols. (Munich, 1911–31)

Marenbon, J., *From the Circle of Alcuin to the School of Auxerre: Logic, Theology and Philosophy in the Early Middle Ages* (Cambridge, 1981)

    Early Medieval Philosophy (480–1150): an Introduction (London, 1983)

    'Carolingian Thought', in *Carolingian Culture*, ed. McKitterick, pp. 171–92

    Boethius (Oxford, 2003)

Markus, R. A., *Saeculum: History and Society in the Theology of St Augustine* (Cambridge, 1970)

    'Gregory the Great's *rector* and his Genesis', in *Grégoire le Grand*, ed. Fontaine, Gillet and Pellistrandi, pp. 137–46

    'The Latin Fathers', in *Medieval Political Thought*, ed. Burns, pp. 92–122

    The End of Ancient Christianity (Cambridge, 1990)

    Gregory the Great and his World (Cambridge, 1997)

Marsden, R., *The Text of the Old Testament in Anglo-Saxon England* (Cambridge, 1995)

Martin, L. H., Gutman, H., and Hutton, P. H. (eds.), *Technologies of the Self* (Amherst, MA, 1988)

Matthews, J., 'Anicius Manlius Severinus Boethius', in *Boethius*, ed. Gibson, pp. 15–43

Maund, K., *The Welsh Kings: the Welsh Rulers of Wales* (Stroud, 2000)

Mauss, M., *The Gift: the Form and Reason for Exchange in Archaic Societies*, trans. W. D. Halls (London, 1990 [1925])

McKeon, P. R., *Hincmar of Laon and Carolingian Politics* (Chicago, IL, 1978)

McKitterick, R., *The Frankish Church and the Carolingian Reforms 789–895* (London, 1977)

    The Frankish Kingdoms under the Carolingians, 751–987 (London, 1983)

    The Carolingians and the Written Word (Cambridge, 1989)

Bibliography

'Perceptions of Justice in Western Europe in the Ninth and Tenth Centuries', *Settimane* 39 (1992), 1075–104

Books, Scribes and Learning in the Frankish Kingdoms, 6th–9th Centuries (Aldershot, 1994)

The Frankish Kings and Culture in the Early Middle Ages (Aldershot, 1995)

'The Illusion of Royal Power in the Carolingian Annals', *EHR* 115 (2000), 1–20

History and Memory in the Carolingian World (Cambridge, 2004)

McKitterick, R. (ed.), *The Uses of Literacy in Early Medieval Europe* (Cambridge, 1990)

Carolingian Culture: Emulation and Innovation (Cambridge, 1994)

The New Cambridge Medieval History II c.700–c.900 (Cambridge, 1995)

Short Oxford History of Europe: the Early Middle Ages (Oxford, 2001)

McNamara, M., 'Psalter Text and Psalter Study in the Early Irish Church (AD 600–1200)', *Proceedings of the Royal Irish Academy* 73, section C, no. 7 (1973), 201–98

'Tradition and Creativity in Early Irish Psalter Study', in *Irland und Europa: Die Kirche im Frühmittelalter*, ed. P. Ní Chatháin and M. Richter (Stuttgart, 1984), pp. 338–89

'The Psalms in the Irish Church: the Most Recent Research on Text, Commentary, and Decoration – with Emphasis on the So-Called Psalter of Charlemagne', in *The Bible as Book: the Manuscript Tradition*, ed. J. L. Sharpe III and K. van Kampen (London, 1998), 89–103

Meaney, A., 'King Alfred and his Secretariat', *Parergon* 11 (1975), 16–24

Meens, R., 'Politics, Mirrors of Princes and the Bible: Sins, Kings and the Well-being of the Realm', *EME* 7 (1998), 345–57

Mennell, S., *Norbert Elias: an Introduction*, 2nd edn (Oxford, 1992)

Metcalf, D. M., 'The Prosperity of North-Western Europe in the Eighth and Ninth Centuries', *EcHR* 2nd series 20 (1967), 344–57

'The Monetary Economy of Ninth-Century England South of the Humber: a Topographical Analysis', in *Kings, Currency and Alliances*, ed. Blackburn and Dumville, pp. 167–97

Metcalf, D. M., and Northover, J. P., 'Debasement of the Coinage in Southern England in the Age of King Alfred', *Numismatic Chronicle* 145 (1985), 150–76

Moorhead, J., *Theoderic in Italy* (Oxford, 1992)

Mordek, H., 'Frühmittelalterliche Gesetzgeber und iustitia in Miniaturen Weltlicher Rechtshandschriften', *Settimane* 42 (1995), 997–1052

Studien zur fränkischen Herrschergesetzgebung (Frankfurt, 2000)

Morrish, J., 'King Alfred's Letter as a Source on Learning in England in the Ninth Century', in *Studies*, ed. Szarmach, pp. 87–108

'Dated and Datable Manuscripts Copied in England during the Ninth Century: a Preliminary List', *Mediaeval Studies* 50 (1988), 512–38

Morrison, K. F., *The Two Kingdoms: Ecclesiology in Carolingian Political Thought* (Princeton, NJ, 1964)

Nash, R. H., *The Light of the Mind: St. Augustine's Theory of Knowledge* (Lexington, KY, 1969)

Nees, L., 'Charles the Bald and the Cathedra Petri', in *Charles the Bald*, ed. Nelson and Gibson, pp. 340–7

Bibliography

A Tainted Mantle (Philadelphia, PA, 1991)

Nehlsen, H., 'Zur Aktualität und Effektivität germanischer Rechtsaufzeichnungen', in *Recht und Schrift im Mittelalter*, ed. P. Classen (Sigmaringen, 1977), pp. 449–502

Nelson, J. L., *Politics and Ritual in Early Medieval Europe* (London, 1986)

    'Kingship and Empire', in *Medieval Political Thought*, ed. Burns, pp. 211–51

    Charles the Bald (Harlow, 1992)

    'Kingship and Empire in the Carolingian World', in *Carolingian Culture*, ed. McKitterick, pp. 52–87

    'Kingship and Royal Government', in *NCMH* II, 383–430

    The Frankish World 750–900 (London, 1996)

    'The Frankish Empire', in *The Oxford Illustrated History*, ed. Sawyer, pp. 19–47

    'Review Article: Waiting for Alfred', *EME* 7 (1998), 115–24

    Rulers and Ruling Families in Early Medieval Europe: Alfred, Charles the Bald and Others (Aldershot, 1999)

    'Monks, Secular Men and Masculinity, *c.* 900', in *Masculinity in Medieval Europe*, ed. D. M. Hadley (Harlow, 1999), pp. 121–42

    'Rulers and Government', in *NCMH* III, 95–129

    'Power and Authority at the Court of Alfred', in *Essays on Anglo-Saxon and Related Themes in memory of Lynne Grundy*, ed. J. Roberts and J. Nelson (London, 2000), pp. 311–37

    'The Voice of Charlemagne', in *Belief and Culture*, ed. Gameson and Leyser, pp. 76–88

    'Aachen as Place of Power', in *Topographies*, ed. de Jong and Theuws, pp. 217–41

    'Alfred's Carolingian Contemporaries', in *Alfred*, ed. Reuter, pp. 293–310

    'The Church and a Revaluation of Work in the Ninth Century?', in *The Use and Abuse of Time in Christian History*, ed. R. N. Swanson (Woodbridge, 2002), pp. 35–43

    'Was Charlemagne's Court a Courtly Society?', in *Court Culture*, ed. Cubitt, pp. 39–57

    'Vikings and Others', *TRHS* 6th series 13 (2003), 1–28

    'Rights and Rituals', *TRHS* 6th series 14 (2004), 1–24

    'Dhuoda', in *Learned Laity*, ed. Wormald (forthcoming)

    'The First Use of the Second Anglo-Saxon Ordo' (forthcoming)

Newhauser, R., 'Towards *modus in habendo*: Transformations in the Idea of Avarice', *Zeitschrift der Savigny-Stiftung für Rechtsgeschichte (Kanonistische Abteilung)* 106 (1989), 1–22

    The Early History of Greed (Cambridge, 2000)

Nichols, S. G., 'Philology in a Manuscript Culture', *Speculum* 65 (1990), 1–10

Ní Chatháin, P., and Richter, M. (eds.), *Irland und die Christenheit: Bibelstudien und Mission* (Stuttgart, 1987)

O'Brien O'Keeffe, K., *Visible Song: Transitional Literacy in Old English Verse* (Cambridge, 1990)

O'Brien O'Keeffe, K. (ed.), *Reading Old English Texts* (Cambridge, 1997)

Ó Corráin, D., 'Nationality and Kingship in pre-Norman Ireland', in *Nationality and the Pursuit of National Independence*, ed. T. W. Moody (Belfast, 1978), pp. 1–35

    'Irish Vernacular Law and the Old Testament', in *Irland und die Christenheit*, ed. Ní Chatháin and Richter, pp. 284–307

Ó Corráin, D., Breatnach, L., and Breen, A., 'The Laws of the Irish', *Peritia* 3 (1984), 382–438

O'Daly, G., *The Poetry of Boethius* (London, 1991)

Odegaard, C. E., 'Carolingian Oaths of Fidelity', *Speculum* 16 (1941), 284–96
    'The Concept of Royal Power in Carolingian Oaths of Fidelity', *Speculum* 20 (1945), 279–89

O'Donnell, J. J., *Cassiodorus* (Berkeley, LA, 1979)
    Boethius: Consolatio Philosophiae, Bryn Mawr Latin Commentaries (Bryn Mawr, PA, 1984)

O'Meara, J. J., *Eriugena* (Oxford, 1988)
    Studies in Augustine and Eriugena, ed. T. Halton (Washington, DC, 1992)

O'Neill, P. P., 'The Old English Introductions to the Prose Psalms of the Paris Psalter: Sources, Structure, and Composition', in *Eight Anglo-Saxon Studies*, ed. J. S. Wittig (Chapel Hill, NC, 1981), pp. 20–38
    'On the Date, Provenance and Relationship of the "Solomon and Saturn" Dialogues', *ASE* 26 (1997), 139–68

Orchard, A., *The Poetic Art of Aldhelm* (Cambridge, 1994)
    'Oral Tradition', in *Reading Old English Texts*, ed. O'Brien O'Keeffe, pp. 101–23

Ortigues, E., 'L'elaboration de la Théorie des Trois Ordres chez Haymon d'Auxerre', *Francia* 14 (1988), 27–43

Orton, P. R., 'King Alfred's Prose Preface to the Old English Pastoral Care, ll. 30–41', *Peritia* 2 (1983), 140–8

Otten, K., *König Alfreds Boethius*, Studien zur englischen Philologie n.f. 3 (Tübingen, 1964)

Palgrave, F., *The Rise and Progress of the English Commonwealth*, 2 vols. (London, 1832)

Parkes, M. B., 'The Paleography of the Parker Manuscript of the Chronicle, Laws and Sedulius, and Historiography at Winchester in the Late Ninth and Tenth Centuries', *ASE* 5 (1976), 149–71
    'A Note on MS Vatican, Bibl. Apost., lat. 3363', in *Boethius*, ed. Gibson, pp. 425–7

Patch, H. R., 'The Tradition of the Goddess Fortuna in Roman Literature and in the Transitional Period', *Smith College Studies in Modern Languages* 3 (1922), 131–77
    The Goddess Fortuna in Early Medieval Literature (Cambridge, MA, 1927)
    The Tradition of Boethius: a Study of his Importance in Medieval Culture (New York, 1935)

Patterson, L., *Negotiating the Past: the Historical Understanding of Medieval Literature* (Madison, WI, 1987)

Payne, F. A., *King Alfred and Boethius* (Madison, WI, and London, 1968)

Pelteret, D. A. E., *Slavery in Early Mediaeval England* (Woodbridge, 1995)

Pfaff, R. W. (ed.), *The Liturgical Books of Anglo-Saxon England*, OEN Subsidia 23 (Kalamazoo, MI, 1995)

Philp, M., 'Michel Foucault', in *The Return of Grand Theory in the Human Sciences*, ed. Q. Skinner (Cambridge, 1985), pp. 67–81

Pitkin, H. F., *Fortune is a Woman: Gender and Politics in the Thought of Niccolò Machiavelli* (Berkeley and Los Angeles, CA, 1984)

Bibliography

Plummer, C., *The Life and Times of Alfred the Great* (Oxford, 1902)

Pocock, J. G. A., 'Introduction: the State of the Art', in his *Virtue, Commerce and History* (Cambridge, 1985), pp. 1–34

Pohl, W., 'Conceptions of Ethnicity in Early Medieval Studies', in *Debating the Middle Ages: Issues and Readings*, ed. L. K. Little and B. H. Rosenwein (Oxford, 1998), pp. 15–25

Pohl, W., with Reimitz, H. (eds.), *Strategies of Distinction: the Construction of Ethnic Communities, 300–800* (Leiden, 1998)

Potter, S., 'The Old English Pastoral Care', *Transactions of the Philological Society* (1947), 114–25

Powell, K., 'Orientalist Fantasy in the Poetic Dialogues of *Solomon and Saturn*', *ASE* 34 (2005), 117–43

Powell, T. E., 'The "Three Orders" of Society in Anglo-Saxon England', *ASE* 23 (1994), 103–32

Pratt, D., 'The Illnesses of King Alfred the Great', *ASE* 30 (2001), 39–90

'Persuasion and Invention at the Court of King Alfred the Great', in *Court Culture*, ed. Cubitt, pp. 189–221

'Problems of Authorship and Audience in the Writings of King Alfred the Great', in *Learned Laity*, ed. Wormald (forthcoming)

English Coronation Ordines in the Ninth and Early Tenth Centuries, ASNC Guides, Texts and Studies (forthcoming)

'King Alfred's *Handbook*' (forthcoming)

'Asser's *Life of King Alfred* in the Context of Anglo-Welsh Relations' (forthcoming)

Prinz, F. E., 'King, Clergy and War at the Time of the Carolingians', in *Saints, Scholars*, ed. King and Stevens II, 301–29

Klerus und Krieg im frühen Mittelalter (Stuttgart, 1971)

Proppe, K., 'King Alfred's Consolation of Philosophy', *Neuphilologische Mitteilungen* 74 (1973), 635–48

Pulsiano, P., and Treharne, E. (eds.), *A Companion to Anglo-Saxon Literature* (Oxford, 2001)

Rabinow, P. (ed.), *The Foucault Reader* (Harmondsworth, 1991)

Ralegh Radford, C. A., 'The Pre-Conquest Boroughs of England, Ninth to Eleventh Centuries', *PBA* 64 (1980 for 1978), 131–53

Ramsay, R. L., 'Theodore of Mopsuestia and St Columban on the Psalms', *Zeitschrift für Celtische Philologie* 8 (1912), 421–51

'Theodore of Mopsuestia in England and Ireland', *Zeitschrift für Celtische Philologie* 8 (1912), 452–97

Rauer, C., 'The Sources of the *Old English Martyrology*', *ASE* 32 (2003), 89–109

Raw, B., 'The Probable Derivation of most of the Illustrations in Junius II from an Illustrated Old Saxon *Genesis*', *ASE* 5 (1976), 133–48

Readman, P., 'The Place of the Past in English Culture, c.1890–1914', *P&P* 186 (February 2005), 147–99

Reiss, E., *Boethius* (Boston, MA, 1982)

Remley, P. G., 'Aldhelm as Old English Poet: *Exodus*, Asser and the *Dicta Alfredi*', in *Latin Learning and English Lore: Studies in Anglo-Saxon Literature for Michael Lapidge*, ed. K. O'Brien O'Keeffe and A. Orchard, 2 vols. (Toronto, 2005) I, 90–108

Bibliography

Reuter, T., 'Plunder and Tribute in the Carolingian Empire', *TRHS* 5th series 35 (1985), 75–94

Germany in the Early Middle Ages c. 800–1056 (London, 1991)

'Pre-Gregorian Mentalities', *JEH* 45 (1994), 465–74

'The Medieval Nobility in Twentieth-Century Historiography', in *Companion to Historiography*, ed. Bentley, pp. 177–202

'The Making of England and Germany 850–1050: Points of Comparison and Difference', in *Medieval Europeans*, ed. A. P. Smyth (Basingstoke, 1998), pp. 53–70

'Nobles and Others: the Social and Cultural Expression of Power Relations in the Middle Ages', in *Nobles and Nobility*, ed. Duggan, pp. 85–98

Reuter, T. (ed.), *The New Cambridge Medieval History III c.900–c.1024* (Cambridge, 1999)

Alfred the Great: Papers from the Eleventh-Centenary Conferences (Aldershot, 2003)

Reynolds, S., *Kingdoms and Communities in Western Europe 900–1300* (Oxford, 1984)

Fiefs and Vassals (Oxford, 1994)

'The Historiography of the Medieval State', in *Companion to Historiography*, ed. Bentley, pp. 117–38

Richards, M. P., 'The Manuscript Contexts of the Old English Laws: Tradition and Innovation', in *Studies*, ed. Szarmach, pp. 171–92

Richardson, H. G., and Sayles, G. O., *Law and Legislation from Æthelberht to Magna Carta* (Edinburgh, 1966)

Riché, P., 'Le Psautier, livre de lecture élémentaire d'après les vies des saints mérovingiens', in *Etudes Mérovingiennes. Actes des Journées de Poitiers 1952* (Paris, 1953), pp. 253–6

Education and Culture in the Barbarian West: Sixth through Eighth Centuries, trans. J. J. Contreni (Columbia, SC, 1976)

Écoles et enseignement dans le Haut Moyen Age: fin du Ve siècle – milieu du XIe siècle, 2nd edn (Paris, 1989)

Ritzke-Rutherford, J., *Light and Darkness in Anglo-Saxon Thought and Writing* (Frankfurt, 1979)

'Anglo-Saxon Antecedents of the Middle English Mystics', in *The Medieval Mystical Tradition in England*, ed. M. Glasscoe (Exeter, 1980), pp. 216–33

Roberts, J., '*Fela martyra* "many martyrs": a Different View of Orosius's City', in *Alfred the Wise*, ed. Roberts and Nelson, pp. 155–78

Roberts, J., and Nelson, J. L., with Godden, M. (eds.), *Alfred the Wise: Studies in honour of Janet Bately* (Cambridge, 1997)

Robinson, F. C., 'Secular Poetry', in *Anglo-Saxon Literature*, ed. Pulsiano and Treharne, pp. 281–95

Rondeau, M.-J., *Les Commentaires patristiques du Psautier (IIIe–Ve siècles)*, Orientalia Christiana Analecta 219–20 (Rome, 1982–5)

Salmon, P., *L'office divin au moyen âge*, Lex orandi 43 (Paris, 1967)

Sawyer, P. H., *Anglo-Saxon Charters: an Annotated List and Bibliography* (London, 1968)

The Age of the Vikings, 2nd edn (London, 1971)

'Kings and Merchants', in *Early Medieval Kingship*, ed. Sawyer and Wood, pp. 139–58

Bibliography

Sawyer, P. H. (ed.), *The Oxford Illustrated History of the Vikings* (Oxford, 1997)

Sawyer, P. H., and Wood, I. N. (eds.), *Early Medieval Kingship* (Leeds, 1977)

Scharer, A., 'The Writing of History at King Alfred's Court', *EME* 5 (1996), 177–206

    'The Gregorian Tradition in Early England', in *St Augustine and the Conversion of Early England*, ed. R. Gameson (Stroud, 1999), pp. 187–201

    Herrschaft und Repräsentation: Studien zur Hofkultur König Alfreds des Großen (Vienna, 2000)

Schepss, G., 'Zu König Alfreds Boethius', *Archiv* 94 (1895), 149–60

Schipper, W., 'Style and Layout of Anglo-Saxon Manuscripts', in *Anglo-Saxon Styles*, ed. C. Karkov and G. H. Brown (Albany, NY, 2003), pp. 151–68

Schmitt, J.-C., 'The Rationale of Gestures in the West: Third to Thirteenth Centuries', in *A Cultural History of Gesture*, ed. H. Bremmer and J. Roodenburg (Cambridge, 1991), pp. 59–70

Schneider, G., *Erzbischof Fulco von Reims (883–900) und das Frankenreich* (Munich, 1973)

Schott, C., 'Zur Geltung der Lex Alamannorum', in *Die historische Landschaft zwischen Lech und Vogesen*, ed. P. Fried and W.-D. Sick (Augsburg, 1988), pp. 75–105

Schreiber, C., *King Alfred's Old English Translation of Pope Gregory the Great's Regula Pastoralis and its Cultural Context: a Study and Partial Edition* (Munich, 2002)

    'Dialects in Contact in Ninth-Century England', in *Bookmarks from the Past: Studies in honour of Helmut Gneuss*, ed. L. Kornexl and U. Lenker (Frankfurt-am-Main, 2003), pp. 1–31

Schütt, M., 'The Literary Form of Asser's *Vita Alfredi*', *EHR* 62 (1957), 209–20

Scragg, D. G., 'The Nature of Old English Verse', in *Cambridge Companion*, ed. Godden and Lapidge, pp. 55–70

Scull, C., 'Urban Centres in Pre-Viking England?', in *The Anglo-Saxons*, ed. Hines, pp. 269–310

Sellert, W., 'Aufzeichnung des Rechts und Gesetz', in *Das Gesetz in Spätantike und frühem Mittelalter 4. Symposion der Kommission 'Die Funktion des Gesetzes in Geschichte und Gegenwart'*, ed. W. Sellert (Göttingen, 1992), 67–102

Senecal, C., 'Keeping up with the Godwinesons: in Pursuit of Aristocratic Status in late Anglo-Saxon England', *Anglo-Norman Studies* 23 (2000), 251–66

Shepard, J., 'The Ruler as Instructor, Pastor and Wise: Leo VI of Byzantium and Symeon of Bulgaria', in *Alfred*, ed. Reuter, pp. 339–58

Sheppard, A., 'The King's Family: Securing the Kingdom in Asser's *Vita Alfredi*', *Philological Quarterly* 80 (2001), 409–39

    Families of the King: Writing Identity in the Anglo-Saxon Chronicle (Toronto, 2004)

Shippey, T. A., 'Wealth and Wisdom in King Alfred's Preface to the Old English Pastoral Care', *EHR* 94 (1979), 346–55

Siems, H., 'Zu Problemen der Bewertung frühmittelalterlicher Rechtstexte', *Zeitschrift der Savigny-Stiftung für Rechtsgeschichte (Germanistische Abteilung)* 106 (1989), 291–305

Silk, E. T., 'Boethius's Consolatio Philosophiae as a Sequel to Augustine's Dialogues and Soliloquia', *Harvard Theological Review* 32 (1939), 19–39

Sims-Williams, P., *Religion and Literature in Western England 600–800* (Cambridge, 1990)

Bibliography

Sisam, K., *Studies in the History of Old English Literature* (Oxford, 1953)

'Anglo-Saxon Royal Genealogies', *PBA* 39 (1953), 287–348

Skinner, Q., *The Foundations of Modern Political Thought*, 2 vols. (Cambridge, 1978)

Machiavelli (Oxford, 1981)

Visions of Politics, 3 vols. (Cambridge, 2002)

Smalley, B. (ed.), *Trends in Medieval Political Thought* (Oxford, 1965)

Smith, A. D., *The Ethnic Origins of Nations* (Oxford, 1986)

Smith, J. M. H., 'Gender and Ideology in the Early Middle Ages', in *Gender and Christian Religion*, ed. R. N. Swanson (Woodbridge, 1998), pp. 51–73

Smithers, G. V., 'The Meaning of The Seafarer and The Wanderer', *Medium Ævum* 26 (1957), 137–53

Smyth, A. P., *Scandinavian York and Dublin. The History and Archaeology of Two Related Viking Kingdoms*, 2 vols. (Dublin, 1975–9)

Scandinavian Kings in the British Isles 850–880 (Oxford and New York, 1977)

King Alfred the Great (Oxford, 1995)

Spiegel, G. M., 'History, Historicism, and the Social Logic of the Text in the Middle Ages', *Speculum* 65 (1990), 59–86

Stafford, P., 'The King's Wife in Wessex 800–1066', *P&P* 91 (May 1981), 3–27

'Charles the Bald, Judith and England', in *Charles the Bald*, ed. Gibson and Nelson, pp. 139–53

Stancliffe, C., 'Kings who Opted Out', in *Ideal and Reality*, ed. Wormald, pp. 154–76

Stanley, E. G., *The Search for Anglo-Saxon Paganism* (Cambridge and Totowa, NJ, 1975)

'King Alfred's Prefaces', *Review of English Studies* 39 (1988), 349–64

'On the Laws of King Alfred: the End of the Preface and the Beginning of the Laws', in *Alfred the Wise*, ed. Roberts and Nelson, pp. 211–21

Stanton, R., *The Culture of Translation in Anglo-Saxon England* (Cambridge, 2002)

Staubach, N., *Rex Christianus: Hofkultur und Herrschaftspropaganda im Reich Karls des Kahlen – Teil II: Grundlegung der 'religion royale'*, Pictura et Poesis II/2 (Cologne, Weimar and Vienna, 1993)

'Herkules in der Karolingerzeit', in *Gli umanesimi medievali*, ed. C. Leonardi (Florence, 1998), pp. 676–90

Steger, H., *David Rex et Propheta*, Erlanger Beiträge zur Sprach- und Kunstwissenschaft 6 (Nuremburg, 1961)

Stenton, F. M., *Preparatory to Anglo-Saxon England*, ed. D. M. Stenton (Oxford, 1970)

Anglo-Saxon England, 3rd edn (Oxford, 1971)

Stewartby, Lord, 'Moneyers in the Written Records', in *Kings, Currency and Alliances*, ed. Blackburn and Dumville, pp. 151–3

Stock, B., *The Implications of Literacy: Written Language and Models of Interpretation in the Eleventh and Twelfth Centuries* (Princeton, NJ, 1983)

Listening for the Text: On the Uses of the Past (Baltimore, MD, 1990)

Stoneman, W. P., ' "Writ in Ancient Character and of No Further Use": Anglo-Saxon Manuscripts in American Collections', in *The Preservation and Transmission of Anglo-Saxon Culture*, ed. P. E. Szarmach and J. T. Rosenthal (Kalamazoo, MI, 1997), pp. 99–138

Bibliography

Story, J., *Carolingian Connections: Anglo-Saxon England and Carolingian Francia, c. 750–870* (Aldershot, 2003)

Straw, C., *Gregory the Great: Perfection in Imperfection* (Berkeley, CA, 1988)

Street, B., *Literacy in Theory and Practice* (Cambridge, 1984)

Social Literacies: Critical Approaches to Literacy in Development, Ethnography and Education (London, 1995)

Stubbs, W., *The Constitutional History of England*, 3 vols., 5th edn (Oxford, 1891–8)

Sullivan, R. E., 'Introduction: Factors Shaping Carolingian Studies', in *'The Gentle Voices of Teachers'*, ed. Sullivan, pp. 1–50

'The Context of Cultural Activity in the Carolingian Age', in *'The Gentle Voices of Teachers'*, ed. Sullivan, pp. 51–105

Sullivan, R. E. (ed.), *'The Gentle Voices of Teachers': Aspects of Learning in the Carolingian Age* (Columbus, OH, 1995)

Swan, M., 'Authorship and Anonymity', in *Anglo-Saxon Literature*, ed. Pulsiano and Treharne, pp. 71–83

Swanton, M. J., 'King Alfred's Ships: Text and Context', *ASE* 28 (1999), 1–22

Szarmach, P. E., 'The Meaning of Alfred's Preface to the Pastoral Care', *Mediaevalia* 6 (1980), 57–86

'Alfred's Boethius and the Four Cardinal Virtues', in *Alfred the Wise*, ed. Roberts and Nelson, pp. 223–35

Szarmach, P. E. (ed.), *Studies in Earlier Old English Prose* (Albany, NY, 1986)

Sources of Anglo-Saxon Culture (Kalamazoo, MI, 1986)

Tax, P. W., 'Remigius of Auxerre's Psalm Commentary and the Matthew Commentary Attributed to Him: Questions of Authenticity', in *L'École Carolingienne d'Auxerre*, ed. Iogna-Prat *et al.*, pp. 413–24

Temple, E., *Anglo-Saxon Manuscripts 900–1066* (London, 1976)

Thacker, A., 'Some Terms for Noblemen in Anglo-Saxon England, c. 650–900', *ASSAH* 2 (1981), 201–36

'Bede's Ideal of Reform', in *Ideal and Reality*, ed. Wormald, pp. 130–53

'Monks, Preaching and Pastoral Care in Early Anglo-Saxon England', in *Pastoral Care*, ed. Blair and Sharpe, pp. 137–70

'Memorializing Gregory the Great: the Origin and Transmission of a Papal Cult in the Seventh and Early Eighth Centuries', *EME* 7 (1998), 59–84

Theuws, F., and Nelson, J. L. (eds.), *Rituals of Power from Late Antiquity to the Early Middle Ages* (Leiden, 2000)

Thomas, H. M., *The English and the Normans* (Oxford, 2003)

Thomas, K., 'Politics: Looking for Liberty', *New York Review of Books* (26 May 2005), pp. 47–53

Thomas, R., 'The Binding Force of Friendship in King Alfred's *Consolation* and *Soliloquies*', *Ball State University Forum* 29.1 (1988), 5–20

Toswell, M. J., and Tyler, E. M. (eds.), *Studies in English Language and Literature: 'Doubt Wisely' – Papers in honour of E. G. Stanley* (London and New York, 1996)

Trahern jr., J. B., 'Fatalism and the Millennium', in *The Cambridge Companion*, ed. Godden and Lapidge, pp. 160–71

Treschow, M., 'Echoes of the Periphyseon in the Third Book of Alfred's *Soliloquies*', *Notes and Queries* 238 (1993), 281–6

Bibliography

'The Prologue to Alfred's Law Code: Instruction in the Spirit of Mercy', *Florilegium* 13 (1994), 79–110

Troncarelli, F., 'Per una ricerca sui commenti altomedievali al De Consolatione di Boezio', in *Miscellanea in memoria di Giorgio Cencetti* (Turin, 1973), 363–80

Tradizioni perdute: La Consolatio Philosophiae nell'alto medioevo, Medioevo e Umanesimo 42 (Padua, 1981)

Boethiana Aetas: Modelli grafici e fortuna manoscritta della Consolatio Philosophiae tra IX e XII secolo, Biblioteca di scrittura e civiltà 2 (Alessandria, 1987)

'Boezio nel circolo d'Alcuino: le più antiche glosse carolinge alla Consolatio Philosophiae', *Recherches Augustiniennes* 22 (1987), 223–41

Tully, J. (ed.), *Meaning and Context: Quentin Skinner and his Critics* (Princeton, NJ, 1988)

Ullmann, W., *The Carolingian Renaissance and the Idea of Kingship: the Birkbeck Lectures 1968–9* (London, 1969)

The Growth of Papal Government in the Middle Ages, 3rd edn (London, 1970)

Law and Politics in the Middle Ages: an Introduction to the Sources of Medieval Political Ideas (Cambridge, 1975)

Ulmschneider, K., 'Settlement, Economy and the "Productive" Site: Middle Anglo-Saxon Lincolnshire A.D. 650–780', *Medieval Archaeology* 44 (2000), 53–72

van der Horst, K., 'The Utrecht Psalter: Picturing the Psalms of David', in *The Utrecht Psalter in Medieval Art*, ed. K. van der Horst, W. Noel and W. C. M. Wüstefeld (Utrecht, 1996), pp. 23–84

van Deusen, N. (ed.), *The Place of the Psalms in the Intellectual Culture of the Middle Ages* (Albany, NY, 1999)

van Dijk, S. J. P., 'The Bible in Liturgical Use', in *The Cambridge History of the Bible II*, ed. Lampe, pp. 220–52

Venuti, L., *The Translator's Invisibility: a History of Translation* (London, 1995)

Vince, A., *Saxon London: an Archaeological Investigation* (London, 1990)

Vollrath-Reichelt, H., *Königsgedanke und Königtum bei den Angelsachsen* (Cologne and Vienna, 1971)

Wainwright, F. T., *Scandinavian England*, ed. H. P. R. Finberg (Chichester, 1975)

Wallace, D. P., 'King Alfred's Version of St Augustine's Soliloquies, III.23–26, The Vision of the Damned', *Notes and Queries* 235 (1990), 141–3.

Wallace-Hadrill, J. M., 'The Franks and the English in the Ninth Century: Some Common Historical Interests', *History* 35 (1950), 202–18

The Long-Haired Kings (London, 1962)

'The Via Regia of the Carolingian Age', in *Trends*, ed. Smalley, pp. 22–41

Early Germanic Kingship in England and on the Continent (Oxford, 1971)

Early Medieval History (Oxford, 1975)

'A Carolingian Renaissance Prince: the Emperor Charles the Bald', *PBA* 64 (1978), 155–84

The Frankish Church (Oxford, 1983)

Wallach, L., *Alcuin and Charlemagne*, Cornell Studies in Classical Philology 32 (Ithaca, NY, 1959)

Waterhouse, R., 'Tone in Alfred's Version of Augustine's Soliloquies', in *Studies*, ed. Szarmach, pp. 47–85

Bibliography

Weber, G., *Wyrd: Studien zum Schicksalsbegriff der altenglischen und altnordischen Literatur* (Bad Homburg, Berlin and Zurich, 1969)

Webster, L., '*Ædificia nova*: Treasures of Alfred's Reign', in *Alfred*, ed. Reuter, pp. 79–103

'Two New Parallels to the Alfred and Minster Lovell Jewels: the Bowleaze and Warminster Jewels', in *'Through a Glass Brightly': Studies presented to David Buckton*, ed. C. Entwhistle (Oxford, forthcoming)

Webster, L., and Backhouse, J. (eds.), *The Making of England: Anglo-Saxon Art and Culture A.D. 600–900* (London, 1991)

Weeks, J., 'Foucault for Historians', *History Workshop Journal* 14 (1982), 106–19

Wehlen, W., *Geschichtsschreibung und Staatsauffassung im Zeitalter Ludwigs des Frommen*, Historische Studien 418 (Lübeck, 1970)

Werner, K.-F., '*Missus-marchio-comes.* Entre l'administration centrale et l'administration locale de l'empire carolingien', in *Histoire comparée de l'administration IVe–XVIIIe siècles*, ed. W. Paravicini and K.-F. Werner, Beihefte der Francia 9 (Munich, 1980), 191–239

Whitbread, L., 'The Pattern of Misfortune in Deor and Other Old English Poems', *Neophilologus* 54 (1970), 167–83

White, S. D., 'Kinship and Lordship in Early Medieval England: the Story of Sigeberht, Cynewulf and Cyneheard', *Viator* 20 (1989), 1–18

Whitelock, D., 'Some Charters in the Name of King Alfred', in *Saints, Scholars*, ed. King and Stevens I, 77–98

From Bede to Alfred: Studies in Early Anglo-Saxon Literature and History (London, 1980)

Williams, A., *Kingship and Government in Pre-Conquest England, c.500–1066* (Basingstoke, 1999)

Wilson, R. M., *The Lost Literature of Medieval England*, 2nd edn (London, 1970)

Wittig, J. S., 'King Alfred's Boethius and its Latin sources: a Reconsideration', *ASE* 11 (1983), 157–98

Wood, I. N., 'Ethnicity and the Ethnogenesis of the Burgundians', in *Typen der Ethnogenese unter besonderer Berücksichtigung der Bayern I*, ed. H. Wolfram (Vienna, 1990), 53–70

The Merovingian Kingdoms 450–751 (London, 1994)

Wood, J., *Wisdom Literature: an Introduction* (London, 1967)

Wormald, P., 'The Uses of Literacy in Anglo-Saxon England and its Neighbours', *TRHS* 5th series 27 (1977), 95–114

'Bede, *Beowulf* and the Conversion of the Anglo-Saxon Aristocracy', in *Bede and Anglo-Saxon England*, ed. R. T. Farrell, BAR, British series 46 (Oxford, 1978), 32–95

'Bede, the *Bretwaldas* and the Origins of the *gens Anglorum*', in *Ideal and Reality*, ed. Wormald, pp. 99–129

Bede and the Conversion of England: the Charter Evidence, Jarrow Lecture 1984 (Jarrow, 1985)

'Anglo-Saxon Society and its Literature', in *Cambridge Companion*, ed. Godden and Lapidge, pp. 1–22

'The Venerable Bede and the "Church of the English"', in *The English Religious Tradition and the Genius of Anglicanism*, ed. G. Rowell (Oxford, 1992), pp. 13–32

Bibliography

'The Emergence of the *Regnum Scottorum*: a Carolingian Hegemony?', in *Scotland in Dark Age Britain*, ed. B. E. Crawford (St Andrews, 1996), pp. 131–60

'Sir Geoffrey Elton's *English*: a View from the Early Middle Ages', *TRHS* 6th series 7 (1997), 318–25

Legal Culture in the Early Medieval West: Law as Text, Image and Experience (London, 1999)

The Making of English Law: King Alfred to the Twelfth Century. I: Legislation and its Limits (Oxford, 1999)

Wormald, P. (ed.), *Learned Laity in the Carolingian Era* (Cambridge, forthcoming)

Wormald, P., with Bullough, D., and Collins, R. (eds.), *Ideal and Reality in Frankish and Anglo-Saxon Society* (Oxford, 1983)

Yerkes, D., 'The Full Text of the Metrical Preface to Waerferth's Old English Translation of Gregory's Dialogues', *Speculum* 55 (1979), 505–13

Yorke, B., *Kings and Kingdoms of Early Anglo-Saxon England* (London, 1990)

Wessex in the Early Middle Ages (Leicester, 1995)

'Alfredism: the Use and Abuse of King Alfred's Reputation in Later Centuries', in *Alfred*, ed. Reuter, pp. 361–80

Zotz, T., 'In Amt und Würden. Zur Eigenart "offizieller" Positionen im früheren Mittelalter', *Tel Aviver Jahrbuch für deutsche Geschichte* 22 (1993), 1–23

UNPUBLISHED PAPERS

Dumville, D. N., 'Manuscripts and Literate Culture in Ninth-Century England', at the Southampton Eleventh-Centenary Conference, September 1999

Pratt, D., 'Desire and its Restraint at the Court of King Alfred the Great', at the 347th meeting of the Cambridge Historical Society, January 2002

Stone, R., 'Power Corrupts? Carolingian Moralists on Noble Power and Wealth', at the Leeds International Medieval Congress, July 2001

Wormald, P., '*Anglicanum legum conditor*: King Alfred as Law-maker', at the Southampton Eleventh-Centenary Conference, September 1999

UNPUBLISHED PHD DISSERTATIONS

Brinnegar, J. H., ' "Books Most Necessary": the Literary and Cultural Contexts of Alfred's Boethius' (University of North Carolina, 2000)

Carroll, C. J., 'The Archbishops and Church Provinces of Mainz and Cologne during the Carolingian Period, 751–911' (Cambridge University, 1998)

Dammery, R. J. E., 'The Law-Code of King Alfred the Great', 2 vols. (Cambridge University, 1990)

Discenza, N. G., 'Alfred's Cræft of Translation: the Old English Boethius' (The Medieval Institute, Notre Dame, Indiana, 1996)

Evert, R. L., 'The Limits of Human Knowledge: King Alfred and Old English Poetry' (State University of Oregon, 1976)

Foot, S., 'Anglo-Saxon Minsters A.D. 597–ca.900: the Religious Life in England before the Benedictine Reform' (Cambridge University, 1989)

Bibliography

Garrison, M. D., 'Alcuin's World through his Letters and Verse' (Cambridge University, 1995)

Goldberg, E. J., 'Creating a Medieval Kingdom: Carolingian Kingship, Court Culture, and Aristocratic Society under Louis of East Francia (840–76)' (University of Virginia, 1998)

Kershaw, P. J. E., '*Rex Pacificus*: Studies in Royal Peacemaking and the Image of the Peacemaking King in the Early Medieval West' (King's College, University of London, 1998)

O'Neill, P. P., 'The Old-English Prose Psalms of the Paris Psalter' (University of Pennsylvania, 1980)

Pössel, C., 'Symbolic Communication and the Negotiation of Power at Carolingian Regnal Assemblies, 814–840' (Cambridge University, 2003)

Wertz, D. M., 'The Influence of the Regula Pastoralis to the Year 900' (Cornell University, Ithaca, 1936)

INDEX OF MANUSCRIPTS

Index of manuscripts

GENERAL INDEX

Aachen 65, 317; council of (836) 144
Aaron, brother of Moses 191
Abba, reeve 21
Abels, Richard 4, 23, 32, 95
Abingdon: sword found at 65, 262; monastery
    of 99, 346
Acca, bishop of Hexham 118, 322
access to the king 34, 36–8, 39–42, 55, 168,
    325–7, 340
action / contemplation 135, 136–7, 187, 204–9,
    299–301, 307, 321, 343
Adalard of Corbie 42
Adalbert, bishop of Thérouanne 145
Adam, first man 327
advice, see 'Mirrors for Princes'; rhetoric
ædificia 185–92, 307, 335–6, 343–5
ærendgewrit 55, 122, 141, 142, 183, 328–9, 333,
    336, 345
æstels 189–92, 336, 343; see also Alfred Jewel
Ælfred, ealdorman of Surrey 33, 86, 172
Ælfric, King Alfred's hrægldegn 30
Ælfric, abbot of Eynsham 293, 304, 345, 346,
    347–8
Ælfthryth, daughter of King Alfred 167
Æthelbald, king of the Mercians (716–57)
    140–1
Æthelbald, West Saxon king (855–60) 23, 33,
    100
Æthelberht, king of Kent (d. 616), laws of 218,
    220
Æthelflæd, daughter of King Alfred 99, 106,
    111, 244, 345
Æthelheard, archbishop of Canterbury 46
Æthelhelm, ealdorman of Wiltshire 239
Æthelhelm Higa, Wiltshire layman 101
Æthelmod, King Æthelwulf's discðegn and
    ealdorman of Kent 33, 86
Æthelred, archbishop of Canterbury 50, 51,
    100, 210

Æthelred, ealdorman of the Mercians 39, 54,
    99, 105–6, 108–9, 110, 175, 244, 306,
    345
Æthelred, West Saxon king (865–71) 38, 63–4,
    262
Æthelred the Unready, king of the English
    (978–1016) 235, 346; laws of 217, 233, 236
Æthelric, son of Æthelmund 85–6
Æthelstan, king of the English (924–39) 1, 106,
    111, 222, 240, 344, 346; laws of 217,
    233, 234–5, 236, 239–40, 241, 244, 325,
    345–6
Æthelstan, priest 57, 345
Æthelswith, daughter of King Æthelwulf
    39, 105
Æthelwald, son of ealdorman Ælfred 33
Æthelweard, son of King Alfred 121, 167
Æthelweard, ealdorman and chronicler 303–4,
    345
Æthelwold, abbot of Abingdon and bishop of
    Winchester 346, 348
Æthelwulf, West Saxon king (839–58) 17, 30,
    33, 35, 37, 39, 40–1, 46–7, 47–8, 55, 56,
    64–72, 74, 87, 88, 105, 107, 183, 185, 289,
    294, 331–2; decimation of land by 66–72,
    77, 78, 88, 235, 244, 246, 334, 338; see also
    rings, royal
Agobard, archbishop of Lyon 159
Airlie, Stuart 62, 147, 177, 263
Alaric, Gothic king 118, 282
Alcuin 69, 75, 124–5, 139, 144, 146, 159, 270,
    277; Confessio 313; De animae ratione 188,
    323, 327; De fide sanctae trinitatis et de
    incarnatione Christi libri tres 313; De laude
    Dei 313; De virtutibus et vitiis 150–1, 165;
    Disputatio de vera philosophia 123, 270–1,
    275, 276, 288, 326; and the 'Munich
    passages' 314–15
Aldhelm 81, 83, 91, 270, 277

397

General index

General index

166–8, 170–6, 289; relationship to *Anglo-Saxon Chronicle* 109, 166–8; relationship to *Hierdeboc* 135–9

Assyrians 251

Athanasius, St 251

Athelney, Somerset 57, 189, 192

Attenborough, Frederick 215

Audradus Modicus 160, 353

Augustine, St (of Canterbury) 141, 142–3, 212

Augustine, St (of Hippo): early writings of 265–6, 308, 309, 312; mature thinking of 308, 309, 321–2, 327; *De inmortalitate animae* 312; *De quantitate animae* 312, 321; *De civitate Dei* 197, 267, 298, 322; *De uidendo Deo* 188, 321–32; *Enarrationes in Psalmos* 246–7, 254, 255; *Retractationes* 267, 309, 313, 321–2

Soliloquia 283, 309–12, 321; manuscripts of 314, 321; and earlier Insular learning 312–13; Carolingian study of 314–16; and West Frankish discourse 315–17; Alfred's translation of 34, 36–7, 129, 132, 157, 170, 177, 186, 187–9, 264, 308–37, 340, 341, 342; Latin source-text for 128, 314; dating of 166–8; textual transmission of 127, 313, 332–3; Preface to 126, 130, 333–4; relationship to Alfred's *Handbook* 127

Auxerre (Yonne) 125, 161–2, 245, 293

Babylon 201–2, 251

Bald, *Leechbook* of 118, 176

Balzaretti, Ross 4, 17

Banwell, Somerset 87, 329

Barrow, Julia 37, 210, 211

Bately, Janet 50, 116–17, 118, 131–2, 195, 219, 272

Bath, Somerset 104, 306–7

Bathsheba, wife of Uriah 256

Beddington, Surrey 210, 212–13

Bede 45, 82, 83, 139, 249–50, 270, 282, 312, 322; *Historia ecclesiastica* 74, 81–2, 90, 106, 110, 138, 143, 154, 155, 228; translation of 50, 51, 85, 116, 118, 126, 128, 131, 143, 195, 199, 211–12, 226

bellatores 24, 25, 35, 292–5

benefices held on ecclesiastical land 26–7, 58, 69, 101, 147–8, 162–3, 226, 278–80, 293, 340

Beocca, ealdorman 172

Beorhtwulf, ealdorman of Essex 32

Beorhtwulf, ealdorman 172

Beornthryth, wife of ealdorman Oswulf 244

Beowulf 29, 81, 91–2, 157–8, 297

Berhtwulf, king of the Mercians (840–52) 51

Biddle, Martin 97

bisceop 195–6

bishops: Southumbrian 44–52, 139–41, 145; appointment of 56–8, 171–2, 173, 175, 210–12, 345; professions of 49, 53, 56, 145; ideal practices of 48–9, 69–70, 77, 139–41; criticism of 50–2, 211–12; and secular service 26–7, 52–4, 54, 68–9, 96, 173–4, 210–11, 212–13, 219, 244, 294, 347; and viking activity 26–7, 46–8, 49–50, 52, 54, 96, 97, 99–101, 104, 153–6, 173–4, 209–13; and the royal household 52–4, 338; and Alfredian learning 56–8, 120, 122, 138–9, 139–41, 142–3, 153–6, 168, 171–2, 173–4, 189–90, 193, 195–6, 198, 207, 209–13, 261–3, 304–7, 332–7, 338–45, 349–50; Frankish 58–62, 71–2, 124–5, 143–8, 162–3, 244, 278–80, 340–1, 354–5; *see also* ecclesiastical structures; synods

Blair, John 44, 49, 210, 348

Boethius, Anicius Manlius Severinus 195, 264–6, 282; Latin *Vitae* of 272, 282; *Consolatio philosophiae* 264–70; and Augustinian thought 265–6, 308, 309–10; manuscripts of 185, 270–7, 314; and earlier Insular learning 270, 312; Carolingian study of 270–7; and Carolingian political discourse 277–80; and later medieval thought 265, 276–7

Alfred's translation of the *Consolatio* 90, 129, 132, 157, 170, 175, 177, 184, 186, 259, 264–5, 280–307, 308, 318, 319–20, 321, 322, 327, 328, 333, 335–6, 340–2, 345; two recensions of 281; and Latin commentary material 264, 271–7, 287–9, 292, 295, 298, 299; Latin source-text for 128, 271–2; dating of 166–8; textual transmission of 127, 303–4, 346; Prose Preface to 130, 281, 303

Boniface, archbishop of Mainz 75, 140–1

bookland 20, 23–4, 26–7, 38–9, 47–8, 54, 67–8, 77, 85–6, 100, 123, 175, 238, 338, 339, 347; as image 333–4; *see also* charters

books: as gifts 43, 62, 86, 90, 123; production of 49–50, 59, 160–3, 179–85, 238–9; 'most necessary' 120, 127–9, 133–4, 148–9, 156–7; poetic voice attributed to 126; texts as 184, 241, 261, 303; depiction in Alfred's *Soliloquies* of 328, 329, 336–7, 345; use of *ædificia* with 187, 189–92, 335–6, 343, 344–5

Booth, Paul 89, 115, 122, 120, 304

bot 174, 227–30, 231, 232–3; 'botleas' offences 234, 237

Bourdieu, Pierre 9, 40

General index

folkland 20, 23–4, 38, 67–8, 79, 86, 347
Fonthill, Wiltshire, dispute over 37–8, 101–2, 218, 239–40
'Fonthill letter' 37–8, 101–2, 172, 212, 239–40
foreknowledge, divine 269–70, 278, 315; Alfredian handling of 296, 297–8, 299–301, 341–2, 344
forfeiture 98, 174, 233, 235, 237–8, 239–41
Formosus, Pope 210, 211–12
fortifications, *see* bridges; burhs
fortuna: Boethian role of 266–9; Carolingian interpretations of 276–7, 278–9, 298; Alfredian handling of 280–1, 281–2, 283–7, 296–302, 342; *see also wyrd*
Foucault, Michel 9, 130
Frakes, Jerold 267, 276, 281, 285, 288, 292, 297, 298, 299
Frantzen, Allen 320, 323
friendship 13, 53, 86; king's 37–38, 53, 71, 126; role in Alfred's translations of 292, 295, 318–21, 325, 328–9
Frisians, in King Alfred's service 109
Frithestan, priest 57, 345
Fulk, archbishop of Rheims 25, 41, 51–2, 57–8, 148, 160–2, 167, 211, 219, 223, 226–8, 273
Fuller brooch 187–9, 190–2, 335, 344
fyrd, see military service

Ganshof, François 102, 234
Gauzlin, bishop of Paris 162
geæmettian 187, 207
Geertz, Clifford 8, 12, 13
geferræden 201, 320
geferscipe 35, 291, 293–5
Gelasius I, Pope 147
gemet, as limit of earthly need 287–9, 290–5, 295; *ungemet* 301; *ofer gemet* 318
gemetgian 301–2
gemetgung 290
gemetlic, ungemetlic 199, 291, 320
gemetlice, ungemetlice 207, 291, 319; *to ungemetlice* 207, 300; *ful ungemetlice* 319
genealogy, royal 28, 183, 304
Genesis B 90
geometry, discipline of 310, 318, 328
Gerald of Aurillac 149, 150–1
Gerald of Wales 110
Germanus, St (of Auxerre) 245
gesælig 143, 296
Gesceadwisnes, Alfredian interlocutor 318–21, 322–7, 328–32, 334
gesið 20, 29, 35
gestures: and elite communication 12–14; interpretation of 8–11, 12; West Frankish

27, 60, 61–2, 64, 66, 69, 73, 133, 160–3, 177, 203, 225, 243–5, 262, 278–80, 302, 315–17, 353–5; East Frankish 64–5, 66, 71, 128, 133–4, 160, 164, 244, 245; Alfredian 96, 168–72, 176–8, 187, 188–9, 190–2, 201, 208–9, 212–13, 218, 240–1, 245, 261–3, 304–7, 333–7, 339–50; dramatization of 283–7, 290–5, 298–302, 304–7, 318–27, 328–32, 332, 333–7, 339–42, 343–5, 349–50; *see also* theatricality
gewyrhta 297, 300
gifts, gift-giving 26, 43, 63, 82–3, 86, 91, 158, 286–7, 293–5, 304–7, 338–47; annual 26, 43, 58; West Saxon 38–41, 65, 68–9, 118, 134, 338; Alfredian 41, 53, 99, 104, 118, 134, 178, 188, 191, 210, 339–50; depiction in Alfred's translations of 175, 199–200, 208, 283–7, 290–5, 304–7, 328–9, 332, 333–4, 339–42, 343–5, 349–50; *see also* loan, land on
Gifts of Men, The 199
glory: role in Alfredian discourse of 152–3, 156, 158, 290–5, 296, 300, 304; Boethian treatment of 268–70, 277, 278
glosses: vernacular 84; 'Leiden family' of 128; Latin 271–2, 314
Godden, Malcolm 116, 121, 169, 188, 283, 289, 291, 306, 319, 330, 324, 325, 328, 329, 331, 347
Goebel, Julius 234, 236, 237
Goffman, Erving 13
Goldberg, Eric 4, 10, 42, 65, 66, 90, 160, 164, 244, 245
'Golden Rule' 229–30, 241
Goliath, Philistine warrior 262
goods, goodness: false goods, seemingly distributed by Fortuna 268, 271, 276, 277, 280, 287; Alfredian handling of 287–96; highest good, as Platonic form 266, 268–70, 271, 278, 311; Alfredian handling of 292, 295–6, 305; *see also sælða*
Goths, Gothic identity 282, 304, 305, 331
Gottschalk of Orbais 315
Grately, Hampshire 236
greed 135, 156–7, 157–8, 163–6, 170–6, 264–5, 280–1, 284–7, 287–96, 301–2, 304–7, 318–21, 333, 336–7, 342, 343–5, 347–8; *see also* desire
Greek learning 155, 265–6, 276, 314–17
Gregory the Great, Pope 194–5, 265; saintly status of 139–43; pastoral ideals of 48–9, 135, 139–41, 194–5, 196–8, 205; and *De civitate Dei* 197; *Homiliae in Evangelia* 298, 324; *Libellus responsionum* 25, 51, 226;

General index

Hucbald of St-Amand 160, 276, 355; career at St-Bertin and Rheims of 161–2, 273

humility, as expectation of rule 69–72, 77, 135, 137–9, 165–6, 170–1, 176–8, 198–204, 205–9, 242, 256–63, 280–1, 283–7, 290–5, 339–44; within the Frankish world 59–62, 148–51, 177, 203, 243–5, 278–80, 331; *see also ministerium*

hunting 34, 53, 121, 207; imagery of 155, 157, 189–90, 206

Hurstbourne, Hampshire 22

Hyfaidd, king of Dyfed (d. 893) 108–9, 110

Hywel ap Rhys, king of Glywysing 108

immunities, debate over 31, 235

Ine, West Saxon king (688–726) 18, 31; laws of 30, 88, 98, 154, 215, 216, 218, 219–20, 221–2, 228, 229, 237

Innes, Matthew 6, 10, 11, 42, 149, 347

Ipswich 18

Ireland 11, 41; Irish learning 82, 84, 129, 132, 216, 230–1, 248–51, 275, 314, 340, 346; Irish law 223, 230–1

Irvine, Susan 272, 302

Isaiah, Old Testament prophet 205

Isidore of Seville 84, 140, 147, 156–7, 164, 203, 285, 293

Jacob, son of Isaac 206

Jehosaphat, Old Testament king 164

Jeremiah, Old Testament prophet 205

Jerome, St 141, 146, 195, 230, 267, 270, 333; and the Psalter 245–6, 250

Jerusalem 41, 118, 176, 255, 262, 263, 325, 336; council of (*c.* AD 49) 222, 225, 226–8, 229–30

Job 177, 243, 262, 281, 355

John I, Pope 282

John VIII, Pope 50, 51, 100

John of Worcester 141

John the Old Saxon 41, 57–8, 131, 160–1, 317–18, 335

Jonas, bishop of Orléans: *De institutione regia* 146–8, 150, 163–4, 330; *De institutione laicali* 150–1, 164–5, 243

Jones, S. R. H. 21, 105, 344

Josiah, Old Testament king 59, 223

Judas Iscariot 233, 237

'judges' 101–2, 121–2, 153, 156–7, 157, 163–6, 170–1, 171–2, 175, 217–18, 302, 305; role in Alfred's translations of 254, 257, 283, 305; *see also* just judgement; dispute settlement

Judith, wife of Louis the Pious 61

Judith, daughter of Charles the Bald 40, 64, 72

Julian of Æclanum 249

Julian of Toledo 324

Junius, Francis 181, 182

just judgement: as expectation of rule 27, 31, 59–60, 75–8, 101–2, 148–9, 152–3, 155–6, 156–7, 157, 159, 161–6, 175–6, 238–41, 304–7, 338, 339–44, 349–50; and written law 59–60, 71, 133, 148–9, 149–50, 153, 157, 159, 216, 217–23, 225–6, 228, 231–3, 240–1, 341; and truthfulness 330: *see also* desire; dispute settlement; law

Juvenal 288

Kelly, Susan 67, 85

Kent: under Mercian rule 18, 28, 44–6, 96; under West Saxon rule 18–19, 35, 46–8, 52, 53, 67, 75, 86, 97, 105, 222, 239, 338, 342

Ker, Neil 181–2, 182, 183

Keynes, Simon 30, 41–2, 49, 66, 86, 119, 140, 172, 347

kingship: interpretation of 5–7, 9–14; learned aspects of 2–5, 7–13, 72–8, 82, 86–92, 115–29, 130–78, 179–92, 201, 203–4, 206–9, 209–13, 240–1, 261–3, 304–7, 332–7, 338–50; and dynasticism 28, 33–4, 61–2, 73, 229, 232, 349; and economic resources 17–27, 66, 93–105, 172–6, 238, 293–5, 301–2, 305–7, 336–7, 341–4, 346–8, 349–50; role in Alfred's texts of 34, 36–7, 198, 200–4, 228–9, 231–3, 250–63, 282, 286–95, 295, 298–302, 304–7, 319–21, 325–7, 328–32, 333–4, 336–7, 339–42, 343–5, 349–50; *see also* Mercia; Wessex; eastern Francia; western Francia

Kingston, Surrey: council of (838) 18–19, 45–8, 53, 76, 77, 78, 87; royal anointings at 74, 74–5

Kirby, David 109

Klaeber, Friedrich 153

knowledge: organization and conception of 41, 115–16, 127–9, 133–4, 187–9, 205–9, 265–6, 269–70, 308–9, 309–12, 315–18, 321–32, 333–7, 339–50; limits of earthly 188, 315, 317, 321–7, 332, 335–7, 342, 344–5; *see also* wisdom

Königsnähe 37–8, 53–4; *see also* favour, royal

labour, organization of 19–25, 97–8, 172–4, 174–5, 238, 294–5, 305–7, 341–4, 349–50

Lactantius 267, 279

General index

land: as basis for aristocratic power 19–21,
38–9, 231, 338; public liability of 23–7,
96–8; ecclesiastical 23–7, 53–4, 99–101,
209–10, 210–11, 278–80; royal 19, 67;
held on lease 26, 85, 100–2, 173, 175,
212–13, 237, 334, 341; sale of 19, 38, 98;
strategic negotiation of 66–8, 99–102,
172–3, 175, 210–11, 212–13, 307, 334,
341; and written law 175, 217; depiction in
Alfred's translations of 291, 294–5, 306,
333–4; *see also* benefices; bookland;
charters; folkland; loan, land on
Laon (Aisne) 161
Lapidge, Michael 49, 50, 118, 119, 274, 346
lar 154, 155, 254
lareow 196, 198, 200, 203–4, 205, 206
last judgement 164; and God's future kingdom
316, 317, 321–5, 332, 342, 344
Latin ability of laymen 83–4, 87, 89–90, 171
Latin learning 83–4; ninth-century decline of
49–50, 55, 85, 154–5; role under Alfred of
108–11, 119–20, 120–1, 122, 123, 124,
128–9, 131, 131–2, 155, 169–70, 171, 184,
195–7, 228–33, 246–51, 264–5, 270–7,
280–1, 303, 317–18, 321–4, 327–8, 333,
335, 340; tenth-century 346
law: preservation of 60, 73, 218, 221–2, 225–6;
amendation of 218, 229–30; royal giving of
73, 153, 160–2, 163–4, 217–23, 227–41,
331; written 84, 88, 157, 214–18, 230–2,
237–41, 341; oral transmission of 88,
217–18, 237–8; as 'book' 184, 241; and
wisdom 75–6, 77–8, 156–7, 158–66, 167,
174, 225–6, 228–9, 252–3, 262, 278–80,
304–5, 305, 330, 341; divine 136, 159,
163–4, 209, 215–16, 222–3, 223–32,
252–61, 262, 275, 278, 305; of nature 225;
tenth-century 'English' 172, 222, 228, 235,
241, 343; Bavarian 223; Irish 223, 230–1;
Continental Saxon 238; *see also* canons
Lebuin, St 276
Le Goff, Jacques 293, 344
Leicester 210
Leo I, Pope 224
Leo III, Pope 46
Leo IV, Pope 51, 94
Leo VI, Emperor 133
Leofric, bishop of Crediton and Cornwall 303
letters: royal 55, 87, 122, 153–6, 328–9, 336;
ecclesiastical 50–2, 57–8, 75, 100, 140–1,
159, 160, 161, 210, 211–12, 212–13; lay
37–8, 101–2, 172, 212
Lex Salica 73, 163, 216
Leyser, Karl 12
Liber ex lege Moysi 230–1

Liber Pontificalis 282
liberal arts 123, 124–5, 128, 167, 246, 261,
270–1, 274, 275, 302–3, 311–12
Lichfield 45
Liebermann, Felix 221, 234, 236
Lindsey, see of 210, 211
literacy 13, 78–92; of ecclesiastics 49–50, 55,
83–4, 120–1, 122; lay 82–4, 86–92, 120–2,
122–3, 124–6, 170–1, 171–2, 345;
Alfredian implications of 166, 168–72,
179, 218, 229–30, 232, 237–41, 261–3,
302–7, 332–7, 338–47; within the Frankish
world 82, 83–4, 87, 124–6; in Ireland 82,
83–4
litteratus / illiteratus 123
liturgy 68–70, 83, 242–51, 313; liturgical
commemoration 68–70, 82, 86, 244, 246,
325, 339, 347; *see also* anointing, royal;
prayer, private
loan, land on 38, 67, 333–4, 338, 347; as image
286–7, 333–4
London 18, 21, 22, 24, 45, 47, 52, 56, 97, 103,
212, 236, 262; 'restoration' of 99, 104–5,
105–6, 106, 107, 176, 239, 306, 342
lordship: over land 20, 97–9; over men 20–1, 47,
97–8, 174–5, 233–8, 329, 341; and
vernacular poetry 29, 157–8; of monasteries
45–7; archiepiscopal 53, 145; royal 20,
29–43, 47, 53, 69, 122, 134, 168–9, 170,
174–5, 212–13, 304–7, 333–7, 339–50; and
loyalty 33–4, 37, 56, 232–8, 239–41; role in
Alfred's texts of 34, 36–7, 200–1, 202, 204,
214, 232–8, 253, 282, 283–7, 290–1, 293–5,
295, 318–21, 325–7, 328–32, 333–7,
339–42, 343–5, 349–50; *see also hlafordseau*
Lothar II, king of Lotharingia 61–2, 147, 165,
177, 224, 225–6, 263
Lotharingia 59, 61–2, 160, 162, 279
Louis the German, East Frankish king 59, 61,
65, 66, 88, 90, 126, 133–4, 150, 160, 161,
164, 185, 244, 245, 354
Louis the Pious, Frankish king and emperor 27,
43, 58, 59–60, 61, 64, 102, 159, 163–4,
225, 277, 315; *Admonitio* of (823×825)
71–2, 73, 149–50, 163, 225
love, as social bond 37–8, 53; depiction in
Alfred's translations of 319–21, 323,
325–7; *see also* Christ
Lupus, abbot of Ferrières 55, 64, 160, 353

Machiavelli, Niccolò 267
MacLean, Simon 6, 11, 110, 244, 276
Maddicott, John 4, 17, 39, 103, 344
Mainz, council of (813) 144
Malmesbury, Wiltshire 101, 104

General index

Cambridge Studies in Medieval Life and Thought
Fourth Series

Also published as a paperback